ROBERT ALTMAN

JUMPING OFF THE CLIFF

ROBERT ALTMAN

JUMPING OFF THE CLIFF

A BIOGRAPHY OF THE GREAT AMERICAN DIRECTOR

PATRICK McGILLIGAN

ST. MARTIN'S PRESS ■ NEW YORK

ROBERT ALTMAN: JUMPING OFF THE CLIFF. Copyright © 1989 by Patrick McGilligan. All rights reserved. Printed in the United States of America. No part of this book may be used or reproduced in any manner whatsoever without written permission except in the case of brief quotations embodied in critical articles or reviews. For information, address St. Martin's Press, 175 Fifth Avenue, New York, N.Y. 10010.

Design by Glen M. Edelstein

Library of Congress Cataloging-in-Publication Data

McGilligan, Patrick.
    Robert Altman.

    1. Altman, Robert, 1925–   . 2. Motion picture
producers and directors—United States—Biography.
I. Title.
PN1998.3.A48M44 1989   791.43'0233'0924 [B] 88-29807
ISBN 0-312-02636-6

First Edition

10 9 8 7 6 5 4 3 2 1

The book is dedicated to Robert Taylor, good friend, great editor, and nonpareil tap-dancer of words.

CONTENTS

ACKNOWLEDGMENTS

This book was blessed with many benefactors. Chief among them were Robert Blees and Reza Badiyi, who opened their hearts and their homes to me, and who, apart from helpful interviews, also facilitated contacts, unearthed photographs and rare footage, and provided significant guiding insights. Without them, the task would have been greater and the finished form less satisfactory.

The screenwriters who were interviewed were especially tolerant: Stewart Stern, Joseph Walsh, Joan Tewkesbury, Patricia Resnick, John Considine, Allan Nicholls, Donald Freed, Robert Harders, and particularly Brian McKay. Gillian Freeman wrote me a series of illuminating letters, and Ring Lardner Jr. answered questions by correspondence and by telephone.

Family members who cooperated with interviews and selected queries include Pauline Altman Walsh, Virginia Altman Woolcott, Susan (Kiger) Davis, LaVonne (Elmer) Cubbison, and Richard Sarafian. Carolyn Whitney of Hawaii not only supplied information and perspective but took the time to read and comment on the early chapters.

In Kansas City, Missouri, Gwen Brooks of St. Peter's selflessly dug through parish records to provide material on Altman's grade-school years. Norma Maring squired me around Wentworth, Altman's military academy in Lexington, Missouri, and introduced me to schoolmates and Lexington historians. Frank Barhydt Sr. and Robert Woodburn crucially filled in the Calvin Company years. Sol Margolin of the Jewish Community Center organized a gathering of Kansas City radio, television, and theatre people, which expedited my understanding of one early phase of Altman's growth as a director. Harvey and SuEllen Fried hosted this evening of reminiscences and then stayed in touch.

Other Kansas City people who made contributions to my recounting of the Calvin Company years include Charley Paddock, Arthur Goodell, Sanford White, Stanley Mack, Bill Cohen, Jack Shefrin, Arthur Ellison, Dan Rose, Dory D'Angelo, Mrs. Elmer C. Rhoden, and Carl Rhoden Jr. My gratitude to Colonel J. M. Sellers Jr. and Colonel James M. Sellers Sr., Richard McDuff, Larry Belger, Rolf Dickson, Marshall "Bucky" Hatfield, Roger Sellers, Richard W. McDuff, and Dawson "Slick" Heathman, all connected with Lexington and/or the Wentworth Military Academy.

Singer/songwriter Jerry Wallace reminisced about the filming of *Corn's-A-Poppin'*. Evan Connell, Eileen Ford, and Keith Painton answered my letters.

The director's formative World War II experience was recalled, anecdotally, pictorially, and with copies of military records by John Horoschak of Altman's bomb squadron. Other flying mates who shared their recollections of Altman—and who labored mightily to make sure I understood the context of the specific theater of battle in a war that was over before I was born—include John Lister and C. W. McKay Jr., Bob McGuire of the Liberator Club, Amos Golisch, S. S. Britt Jr., Keith Hinsman of the Wisconsin Veterans of Foreign Wars, Thomas C. Fetter of the 90th Bomb Group, and Irwin Equitz. James M. Kendall, the historian of the 307th bomb group, was a mentor in this regard and circulated copies of the World War II chapter to knowledgeable veterans, collated their criticism, and added notes of his own.

There is an underground of television fandom, scholars, and buffs without whom Altman's television years would have been impossible to reconstruct. Larry James Gianakos volunteered Altman's credits from his several books (*Television Drama Series Programming*, etc., Scarecrow Press), which are a starting point for all television enthusiasts. Howard Prouty came forward with items from his private collection of video classics and with his own astute observations about individual episodes. Rick Prelinger offered his expertise on the history of industrial and sales films, and also went into the Calvin Company storage with me to see what might be worthwhile to retrieve. Professor Fred MacDonald made it his business that I diligently view as many of the Altman television episodes as could be hunted down.

The director's pre-*M*A*S*H* years of struggle in Hollywood were brought to life from conversations with Robert Ecton, Warren Driver, Robert Longenecker, Lou Stoumen, Dann Cahn, Mort Briskin, Don Fedderson, John T. Stephens, Allen Rivkin, Harold Green, William T. Orr, Richard Bluell, Hugh Benson, Ray Danton, Herbert B. Leonard, Roy Huggins, Barry Elliott, Lili St. Cyr, Dan Fitzgerald, Fabian, David Dortort, Gene Levitt, Rick Jason, Richard Peabody, Pierre Jalbert, Muriel Seligman, Gene Milford, James Lydon, and Bobby Troupe. Crissy Rickard was instrumental in clarifying details about her father, James Rickard. Letters from Gordon Hessler, Norman Lloyd, Joan Harrison (writing through Eric Ambler), Jo Napoleon, Robert Pirosh, and Richard Maibaum cleared up some matters.

Altman's post-*M*A*S*H* undertakings have been documented extensively in countless newspaper and magazine articles. I have tried to peruse whatever references exist or can be located, but rather than assemble a long list here, I would direct the interested reader to the indispensable *Robert Altman: A Guide to References and Resources* (Virginia Wright Waxman and Gretchen Bisplinghoft, G. K. Hall, Boston, 1984), a purely bibliographical work. Otherwise, this principal period of Altman's career, as well as more private aspects of his character and working habits, have been traced in interviews with Ingo Preminger, Elliott Gould, Joseph Walsh, Graeme Clifford, Danford B. Greene, Louis Lombardo, Tommy Thompson, and Peter Newman. Letters and a tape-recorded self-interview (responding to my questions) came from Susannah York.

Alan Rudolph was interviewed by the author (but not expressly for this book) for the alternative newspaper *TakeOver* in 1976. Likewise, Robert Evans, Harry Nilsson, Jules Feiffer, Shelley Duvall, Robin Williams, and Paul Dooley were interviewed on the island of Malta for *American Film* magazine. The Paul Newman material derives from a press conference in New York City in 1976. Although Altman himself has been interviewed several times by the author, including one long, hazy evening in Malta about which I recall practically nothing, little from those sessions was used in this book, whose genesis came afterward. This biography is entirely unauthorized. Altman cooperated only to the extent of releasing certain photographs and telling intimates that he did not care one way or another if they chose to talk.

Of course, many people did refuse to see me. The more prominent holdouts include Joan Altman and Barbara Altman, George W. George, Barbara Turner, and Robert Eggenweiler. Many others spoke off the record or for background only.

People who read chapter drafts and commented for accuracy's sake include Robert Blees, Reza Badiyi, James Lydon, Ring Lardner Jr., Ingo Preminger, Brian McKay, Joseph Walsh, Joan Tewkesbury, and Frank Barhydt Sr. The present commandant of Wentworth Military Academy, Colonel J. M. Sellers Jr., corrected my impressions of Altman's high-school alma mater. In all cases the observations and conclusions belong to the author, and no one but he is to blame for error or misinterpretation.

Thanks also to John Altman, Cori Wells Braun, Wendy Daniell, Barbara J. Humphreys of the Library of Congress, Alvin H. Marill, Ivan Goff, Ray Delman of Campbell-Ewald, Kristie Blees, Booker McClay, Ben Maddow, Oscar Arslanian, Leonard Kech, Dave Belzer of the Jewish Community Center in Kansas City, Ray Taylor Jr., Mrs. Darvin L. Stover of the Society of Mayflower Descendants, Harry Essex, Sister Mary Joan and Sister Mary Adrian of Glennon Convent, Kansas City, and Simone Burn of the Wentworth Library and Kaylenne Howard of the Lexington Public Library.

Among librarians and archivists, in general, I found friends and assistance. Leith Adams of the Special Collections at the University of Southern California relentlessly combed his resources and kept me busy with leads from the Warner's files. Tise Vahimagi of the British Film Institute supplemented his terrific book (co-authored with Christopher Wicking) *The American Vein* (E. P. Dutton, 1979) with research and suggestions. Maxine Fleckner of the University of Wisconsin Center for Film and Theater Research provided Altman's production files from the early 1970s and arranged screenings of segments of *The Troubleshooters* series. The Museum of Broadcasting in Chicago, in league with the Kraft film archives, facilitated research into the *Kraft* series. Marge Kinney and Gloria Maxwell of the Missouri Valley Room of the Kansas City Library helped with city and state lore. The departments of the Milwaukee Public Library, and the resourceful reference librarians, expedited every phase of the work.

For making possible the screenings of rare Altman industrials, television episodes, and films, I am indebted to Kingsley of Morcraft Films, Steve Newmark of Image Works, Inc. (Madison, Wisconsin), David Dortort and the Republic Pictures Corporation of Delaware, UCLA Film Archives, University of Wisconsin Center for Film and Theater Research, Kent Coscarelly, David Miller (M & M Enterprises), Dr. Stanley Yates of the American Archives of Factual Films at

Iowa State University, Ira Deutchman of Cinecom, Wayne E. Welk of Patten Industries, Inc., Fritz McGinnis and Rice Durban of the National Federation of State High School Associations, Stewart Shokus and Shokus Video, Rick Prelinger, Robert Walsdorff, and Fred MacDonald.

The photographs are courtesy of Tommy Thompson, Joan Tewkesbury, Floyd and Pat Klang, Norma Maring and Wentworth Military Academy, Donald Hoffman, Leith Adams, Douglas Finn, Gillian Freeman, Dan Fitzgerald, Mark S. Willoughby and Collectors Bookstore, Maxine Fleckner and the University of Wisconsin Center for Film and Theatre Research, John Horoschak, Arthur Goodell, Critt Davis, Mary Corliss and the Museum of Modern Art, Abigail Shelton Kelley, Reza Badiyi, Lili St. Cyr, Robert Blees, Tise Vahimagi and the British Film Institute, Carolyn Whitney, James M. Kendall, Ned Comstock and the University of Southern California, Warner Brothers, Larry Edmunds Bookshop, Eddie Brandt's Saturday Matinee, Backlot Books, Academy of Motion Picture Arts and Sciences, Gavin Smith and *Film Comment*, *The Milwaukee Journal*, Ron Pennington at Metro-Goldwyn-Mayer, Los Angeles Actors' Ensemble, the Kraft television archives, Universal Pictures, and Robert Altman.

The title (and prefatory Altman quotation) of this book is expropriated, gratefully, from the headline of an unbylined article in the December 1978 *Monthly Film Bulletin*. Portions of Chapter 33, about *Popeye*, originally appeared in the December 1980 issue of *American Film* magazine, as written by the author.

Thoughtful colleagues who came forth with advice, memoranda, and their own (published or unpublished) interviews relating to Altman include Joseph McBride, David Thomson, Nat Segaloff, Allen Eyles, Danny Peary, and Gerald Peary. Robert W. Butler of *The Kansas City Star* extended some professional favors. Jordan Elgrably kept track of Altman's print appearances in Paris. Henry Schipper aided, again and again, with the penetration of *Variety*. *TakeOver* former comrades Ken Mate, Michael Fellner, Candace Cooper, and Michael Wilmington all pulled strings for research requests.

Howard Gelman was generous in thought and deed. Respite and hospitality in New York City was provided by Regula Ehrlich; and in Los Angeles by Robert Smoodin, and by Mark Rowland and Rosemary Aguayo.

Finally, I am grateful to my editor, Toni Lopopolo, who gave me her faith and the opportunity, and to Bowie, Clancy, and Tina, especially, for living with the consequences.

INTRODUCTION

The seeds for this biography were planted in the spring of 1974 with the realization after seeing *California Split* that several of my favorite moviegoing experiences of the early 1970s were orchestrated by the same man, someone I knew very little about—Robert Altman. At the time I was working on the arts staff of *The Boston Globe* and in a position to flaunt my press credentials. It happened that Altman came to the Boston area to deliver a lecture to students at Tufts University. I attended the event, and later that evening telephoned Altman's motel in Cambridge and arranged to meet the film director the next day. We had an early breakfast, and I wrote a Sunday column about Altman, who at the time was expounding about a movie he was working on whose title meant absolutely nothing to me—*Nashville*. Then as now, something about the man, quite apart from his films, nagged at me.

Over the years there were several other close encounters—
in New York City, in Altman's Westwood offices in Los Angeles, and on one prolonged stay on the island of Malta for
the filming of *Popeye*, the only time I observed the director
in action on the set. The ups and downs of his career were
reflected in his attitude toward me, a representative of the
fickle media. His wariness at one moment and his courtship
of publicity the next were positively Nixonian, even though I
never wrote anything but friendly words about him and his
work in the *Globe*, *American Film* magazine, and other venues. As the nature of the films grew more disparate, and the
career more endangered and improbable, I found myself wondering more and more about the relationship between Altman's life and his work. I wondered how his life infused his
films, and vice versa.

Though an extremely personal director in terms of his
ideas and conceits, and an unmistakable one in terms of his
filmmaking style, Altman was not in some ways, it occurred
to me, a particularly autobiographical director. Although he
has made of this a strength as much as a weakness in his
career, it is something of a paradox for a modernist, and
something of an evasion for a self-promoter. When Altman
does choose to unmask himself in his films, it is typically
through riddles and prisms, mirrors and twin images, mind
games, numerical allusions, and cloaked parables. Auteurist
film critics, it seems to me, too often stop at deciphering the
meaning and message of heavily encrypted films, when they
ought to go further and inquire about the behind-the-scenes
process and, in the case of Altman, about the life that has
coded the work.

Pauline Kael's provocative remark that so many of the best
contemporary U.S. directors operate from a Catholic psychology intrigued me. So did the fact that Altman, unlike so
many of the younger generation of directors, is from the Midwest, not New York or Los Angeles, and springs from a
rather ordinary middle-class upbringing. His long apprenticeship in Kansas City at the Calvin Company filming industrials, and in Hollywood working in relative anonymity

in television, interested me. So did the relationship between his recurrent themes and their real-life corollaries—the free-flight metaphor and the antimilitary stance, the family bond and female neuroses, the Catholicism and the questioning of leadership, and so on. In tracing Altman's life, in interviews, clippings, archives, and in viewing the rare as well as better-known films, I discovered much that confirmed my instincts and much—particularly in the trail of broken friendships and dreams—that surprised me; there is much in this director's life that is a continuum with his films, as there is of course much that is tangential.

Altman's gypsy-caravan style of filmmaking intrigued me. I was curious about its derivation and its evolving method. I felt that Altman's problematical relationship with writers and his own difficulty in writing was a central subtext of his career. What I found beneath the gloss of critical praise was more fascinating than any simplistic auteurist mystique. Only Altman is artist (and determined) enough to create a film—against all odds sometimes—that is unarguably an Altman film. But he has been dependent on others crucial to that process, and understanding their role helps explain some of the successes and failures as well as some of the subtleties of his career.

When I started this project, I believed that Altman was the most important post-Sixties English-language filmmaker on several counts: the sheer bulk of his work with its handful of truly important films, his stylistic breakthroughs and domi-nation of the medium, and—something more intangible—his example as a productive independent working outside the mainstream of Hollywood commerciality. And I believed (and still believe) that, at the least, he would in time be seen as a kind of Preston Sturges of his era, a brilliant comet that had shot through the firmament, briefly, lighting up the mo-tion-picture industry with his peculiar genius.

This biographer crosses the finish line with a sigh of relief. Much has been found out—and much remains a mystery. I am happy to say that Altman, like any challenging subject, remains an elusive figure in part, but that in the process of investigating his life my enthusiasm has not been dulled for his work. No matter how many times I see the best films, they remain a joy and a revelation. No matter the ungainly, sometimes unattractive strands of his life, his stature as a serious and influential filmmaker—not to say, sometimes, an extremely entertaining one as well—has not been diminished in my eyes. Indeed, Woody Allen seems to be the only other film artist who could give him a run for his money as the great American director of our time.

PART
1

"Admire me, not for how I succeed, and not for how 'good' the films are, but for the fact that I keep going back and jumping off the cliff."

—*Robert Altman*

PROLOGUE

In August 1956, *The Floating Opera* by John Barth was published. At one of the periodic low points in his career, the estimable Orson Welles, between movies, was ensconced at Desilu Studios in Hollywood developing a television series of adaptations of classic stories (eventually rejected by the networks as being too sophisticated for the "average viewer"). Deaths in the news included the "Action painter" Jackson Pollack.

Pollack, drunk on gin and driving recklessly, wrapped his car around a telephone pole in Springs, East Hampton, New York, killing himself and one of two female companions. A leading Abstract Expressionist, Pollack's drips and spatters, his "poured" and black paintings, his wallpaper and necktie designs, had outraged and captivated the art world. At times his personal flamboyance overshadowed his creativity. His critical reception in the popular press, to quote one monograph, "tended toward a baffled skepticism and a derisive emphasis on the apparent unconventionality of his working methods."

And in the last week of August, after a weekend of farewell binges and bashes, Robert Altman left Kansas City, Missouri, to seek fulfillment as a motion-picture director in Los Angeles, California. He had been there before, once, twice—his family and his friends had lost count. He had always come back broke and drained, disillusioned, yet resilient. His name had appeared on a couple of Forties screenplays. He could be glimpsed in the crowd scenes of at least one Danny Kaye vehicle. He had made the party scene, and he had met a lot of the right people; but he could never score the house on the hill. Maybe his gambling debts ran too high and people with mob connections pressured him out of town. That is what Altman claimed when he got back to Kansas City. In any case, it made for good Altman folklore.

Altman had been back in the dull home territory for going on six years then, excluding brief escapes, and he had learned everything a guy like him thought he could ever learn about making movies while working for the Calvin Company. He could cut and splice, operate the camera, write or improvise, coax the performers, direct and produce; he could do it all day and all night, and then he could do it some more the next day without any sleep. At thirty-one, he could do all these things exceedingly well.

He had raised eyebrows and won instructional category awards from making at least sixty Calvin films, not counting one full-length feature restricted to the prairie circuit, the advertisements and short films he hustled on his own, and the syndicated television programs that never quite got off the ground. Now he was "shaking the dust of this crummy little town" off his feet, like the James Stewart character, George Bailey, had hoped to do in director Frank Capra's sentimental Christmas perennial *It's a Wonderful Life*.

Altman was going in style. He had purchased a Thunderbird '56 convertible. Because it had minor scratches left over from the filming of *The Delinquents*, a low-budget juvenile delinquent flick that Altman had just finished directing, it had been sent out to be painted red. By mistake it came back a lustrous black. Altman was disappointed beyond belief, but he would not delay his departure.

Piled in the back of the two-seater was a jumble of suitcases. Altman was cutting the umbilical cord of his Calvin job, leaving behind two marriages and three children, his father, B.C., and mother, Helen, his sisters Joan and Barbara, plus a conglomeration of Altman relatives and a vast network of acquaintances from the days of his youth.

A mile outside city limits, Altman became drowsy. On top of the weekend exertions, he had been drinking steadily from a big bottle. He turned to his passenger, Reza Badiyi, and asked him to take over at the wheel. Altman slid over to the right and promptly fell asleep. Badiyi took the wheel of the beautiful car, pulled into a gas station, filled up the gas tank, and just drove until dawn, clear across the map into Colorado.

In Badiyi, a native Iranian who had been resident in the United States for less than a year, a film acolyte who could scarcely speak English much less drive a sports car, Altman had found yet one more in a never-ending line of adoring friends. He and Badiyi had been brought together purely by chance, but in life Altman had come to treasure nothing if not chance. Chance was already providing all the fundamental connections in his life.

All of eighteen, Badiyi had led a relatively sheltered middle-class existence in Iran before becoming an audiovisual student in a program sponsored by a branch of Syracuse University at the University of Teheran. Long before he became a top-notch television director, Badiyi was an accomplished photographer, and as a teenager he happened to be on hand to record *The Flood in Khousestan*, which won him an international film award, which in turn brought him on scholarship to the Calvin Company as an observer.

When he deplaned in Kansas City in 1955, who should he meet at the Calvin Company but the local legend, Robert Altman, who was seething to return to Hollywood after so many turndowns, and whose love of film enveloped a host of his friends and colleagues.

Altman took Badiyi everywhere and instructed him in matters great and small. For example, Altman gifted Badiyi with a fishing rod and taught him how to be patient with a trout. From this point in time, it's hard to imagine Robert Altman being patient with a trout—but he could be, especially back then, says Badiyi. Sometimes Altman would keep the catch of the day, sometimes he would throw it back. Always, he would politely explain to Badiyi what he was doing and why.

The world of Kansas City and America unfolded for Badiyi through Altman's point of view, and not only through Altman, but through the Altman family.

Altman's father, B.C., a demon insurance salesman, immediately sold Badiyi a policy. Altman's mother, Helen, invited Badiyi over for his first Thanksgiving dinner in 1955. Badiyi was entranced by Altman's two younger sisters, the budding poet Joan and the ladylike Barbara. Badiyi became the first of many surrogate brothers for Altman, and like many of the men in Altman's circle, he would admit to a lingering attraction to Joan, whose fair looks resembled her mother's and whose artistic temperament echoed her brother's.

Bernard, or B.C. (the "C" was for Clement), Badiyi recalls, was bigger than life—a colossus, a Paul Bunyan among insurance salesmen, chopping down indemnity policies like so much towering timber. The stories people told about him! B.C. was always up to something—holed up at the club, gambling downtown in a rented suite, roistering in the duck blinds.

Helen Altman was on another planet, an astral sphere. She was like an angel. Badiyi says there is little of her in Altman. Altman is more like his father, Badiyi says; a killer. B.C. was a *dear* man, but a killer. As for Helen, she had her own personal agenda—becoming intensely involved in whatever it was that had for the moment caught her attention—a golf or bridge match, a charity benefit, her nutritional theories. A family disaster might be imminent, yet she would be plan-

A wedding: (from above) The familial Altmans, assembled at Aunt Pauline's ceremony, 1928. B.C. is the third man from the left; his brother, Frank Altman, is the third man from the right. The darling aunts are Annette Altman Kiger (second lady from left), Virginia Altman Wolcott (fifth lady from left), Marie Altman Keshlear. Helen M. Altman is standing next to Marie. Pauline Altman Walsh is in her matrimonial gown at center, next to the groom, John Walsh. Young, white-suited Robert, of course, is the ringbearer. (Carolyn Whitney)

ning a fashion show for the benefit of charity, for the House of Good Shepherd, and it was, "Would you please come and take the pictures, Reza?"

It was a family, Badiyi remembers, not unlike the family of lovable eccentrics in George S. Kaufman and Moss Hart's play *You Can't Take It With You*, full of whimsical emotion and divine afflatus, each family member off on their own tangent, sometimes never truly intersecting.

So this, thought Badiyi, was the American family: their

outlook toward life, toward each other, toward sex and incidentals. . . .

Altman had known Badiyi for only two months, but he was already sending him to his home at night—with Badiyi knowing full well that Altman was at a hotel shacked up with a mistress—to inform Altman's second wife, Lotus, that Altman was detained at the office. In fact, Altman was jumping from one woman to another, getting wild and crazy drunk, and getting chased by the husband of a woman he was fucking a certain specified number of times a week. Such were the priorities of this offspring of the delightful Altmans. It was quite an education in the American family, Badiyi recalls.

The winter before they left Kansas City, B.C., Joan, her husband, the artist and designer Chet Allen, and Charley Paddock, the Calvin photographer, had visited Palm Beach to film the American League's spring training for the area-based Holsum Bread company. The short film that resulted, called *Grand Stand Rookie*, composed of spring-training shots and interviews with notable baseball personalities, would inaugurate the first season of the Kansas City Athletics, recently relocated from Philadelphia.

B.C. did not care much for movies, but he always put a little bit of money in, and besides, he loved baseball, the sun, and the betting down South, so he was along for the fun of it. Chet Allen drew the words "A Bob Altman Production" on the sides of the station wagon before they left. They stayed in a wonderful place down there with a circular driveway. Every day they went to the set, either Paddock or B.C. did the driving.

One day, just as they came out of the place they were staying in, before anyone could occupy the driver's seat, Altman announced, "Reza, you drive!" Just like that. Then he calmly opened up a newspaper and started to read. Badiyi, of course, had never driven an automobile in his life. Charley, Chet, and B.C. sat in the back. Badiyi put the car in reverse and backed over some steps—boom, boom, boom—heading the wrong way down a one-way thoroughfare. Altman never put the newspaper down, just kept reading, seemingly oblivious.

Somehow, Badiyi made it to the stadium. Charley Pad-dock, always a very nervous man, broke into a rash and did not work at all that day. Chet Allen went absolutely white. B.C. got out of the car and said to his son dryly, "Well, you're lucky to be alive." But Altman never flinched. It was that way with Altman. When you were his ally, he went all the way with you. He let you do the driving, even if you didn't have the slightest notion how.

Now, as he and Badiyi crossed Colorado, Altman stirred and woke up. They put the top down. Altman was very dili-gent in explaining everything about America, answering Badiyi's questions about politics and culture. When they en-tered mountainous terrain, Altman took the wheel; he didn't trust Badiyi on the sharp curves. It began to flurry—snow in August!—and Badiyi perched up on the back of the car seat with his 16mm Bell and Howell on his shoulder and they drove slowly, taking motion pictures of that crisp, luminous scene. Badiyi still has that footage somewhere in the closet of his house. It was all very memorable.

Over the car radio came the strains of "California, Here I Come!" at the Republican Convention in San Francisco. Alt-man insisted on listening to the convention, though the only real drama of the affair was whether Richard Nixon, slippery, controversial Nixon, would again be selected as Eisenhower's running mate. Altman was all for Stevenson, nominated by the Democrats the week before in Chicago. To Badiyi, Altman painstakingly explained the differences between the Demo-crats and the Republicans. For years, all Altmans had been Republicans. Altman was very proud to be unlike them, a Democrat. Harry Truman was his kind of Democrat, a hard-scrabble maverick and independent, from Missouri besides. Truman had been in some Calvin films, and, quite amazingly, Altman, as part of one of his fly-by-night business ventures, had once managed to tattoo Truman's dog in the White House.

"The enslavement of any people in the world is a threat to peace . . ." Nixon's voice crackled over the radio. *"The tri-*

umph of aggression in any part of the globe is a cloud of war over the entire world. And when freedom loses anywhere it is threatened everywhere."

Altman and Badiyi arrived in Las Vegas in a kind of ecstasy. Badiyi had never dreamed of such neon splendor, and Altman was in a gambler's paradise. Altman had an idea worthy of Altman. When he couldn't arrange a last-minute reservation, he pulled over to the side of the road and made a call from a pay phone to one of the best hotels in the casino city, announcing the imminent arrival of a State Department official charged with showing the red carpet treatment to a Persian press attaché. Altman always had ideas like that, scenes he would improvise at the drop of a hat from the non-stop movie in his mind.

And it worked. They were assigned a luxury suite. Judy Garland was performing the supper show, and Altman and Badiyi sat up front as guests of management, and had their pictures taken with her afterward. Badiyi was not permitted to utter a word of English. Altman acted the role of interpreter. When they ran out of money, they called up some of Altman's old friends in Hollywood, who telegraphed cash. Others came up to join the ongoing charade, until four or five days later when Altman and Badiyi hit rock bottom again.

Pooling their pocket change for a tank of gas, cigarettes, coffee, and a bite to eat, they set off across the miles of desert and highway that lead to Los Angeles.

They arrived with empty pockets, past schedule, giddy and excited, at the General Film editing room reserved for the cutting of *The Delinquents*, their bargain basement, teenage hoodlum picture. Altman had managed to get a clause in his contract that required the editing, and the postproduction touches, to be executed under professional conditions in Hollywood. It was his Kansas City "escape clause." *The Delinquents* was going to be his entree into Hollywood, where so many other Altman schemes and assaults had faltered.

This would be the first full-length feature film to be "directed by Robert Altman," the director who was destined to become the most prodigal and visionary of American film directors to emerge from the ashes of post-Sixties Hollywood.

It is now August of 1987, some thirty years hence. Reza Badiyi is remembering all this as the clock rotates toward midnight in a spacious hilltop home on the east side of the Hollywood Freeway overlooking the dense city sparkle of Los Angeles. His residence is cluttered with precious Iranian art objects and mementos that show the refined private nature of a mass-medium director who has never lost his appreciation for the more elegant things in life.

Badiyi swirls his brandy, lost in thought. A beautiful young woman appears in the archway and reminds Badiyi that he is due on location tomorrow to film a rigorous and demanding episode of television's award-winning series *Cagney and Lacey*. He ought to get a good night's sleep.

Nowadays Reza Badiyi is one of the in-demand directors of episodic television, with credits dating from the late 1960s that include multiple episodes of *Get Smart, Mission Impossible, Hawaii Five-O, Six Million Dollar Man, The Rockford Files*, and *Baretta*. In an exhaustive and definitive survey of American television credits called *The American Vein* (Christopher Wicking and Tise Vahimagi, E. P. Dutton, 1979), which rates the quality of directors who have toiled with relative anonymity in television, Badiyi is placed in the uppermost category as one of the "Kings of the Stardust Ballroom." Badiyi is one of many who learned at the knee of Altman and then moved on to forge their own distinctive careers.

A short, dignified man with crinkly hair and a wistful smile, he says to his visitor, stay a little longer, let me show you something else. He bounds out of the room and returns with a photograph album of loving, carefully composed portrait photographs dating back to those happy days over thirty years ago. Photographs of Altman and his sister Joan and Badiyi together, of Altman and various members of the Altman family, of B.C. and Helen, of Altman, working on various projects that never came to fruition, of Altman filming in Kansas City.

Badiyi's voice is filled with a mixture of longing, nostalgia, bitterness, and regret—and yet, in spite of everything, with manifest affection. "I saw America through Bob's point of view," says Badiyi, choosing his words carefully. "In those days, you have to understand . . . something wonderful was waiting for us, beyond that rise. We wanted it badly, and we were so full of hope."

PART

2

"The childhood shows the man,
As morning shows the day."

—*John Milton, quoted on a
Wentworth Military Academy calendar*

Portrait of the young Altman as an artist, in this formal sitting, displaying hoped-for talent as a writer. (Carolyn Whitney)

Chapter

1

THE
FAMILY
TREE

The Altman family tree is like a gnarled old juniper, as twisty-turny as the background conversation in one of Altman's movies, seemingly every bit as fragmented and curlicued as the interrelationships in his film *A Wedding*. Fact has been handed down from generation to generation liberally sugar-and-spiced. The newspaper clippings are yellowed, and the grave markers of the doyens of the bloodline have vanished. The younger generations of Altmans have abandoned the home soil of Kansas City and are spread far and wide.

In the mid-1800s German immigrants came to the Midwest by the hundreds of thousands.

The black earth, the rivers, and the bountiful hunting in the wilderness reminded them of home country. Besides farming, there was ready work in the vineyards and breweries, sausage factories and foundries, the new schools and the new industries, the small shops, of the German-language meccas. Books such as *Report* by Gottfried Duden (1829), a German scholar who resided in St. Charles and Warren counties, described life in Missouri in majestic terms, alerting Germans to the atavisitic thrall of this region of the Midwest. The popular translations of James Fenimore Cooper's *Leather-Stocking Tales* and the heroic "westerns" of German novelist Karl May also idealized the New Eden.

Many German immigrants came to America under a political cloud. The German intellectuals and libertarians who could not abide the priest-ridden regency, the leaders of the *Burschenschaften* movement, and later, the "Forty-eighters" (the failed revolutionaries who fled the fatherland), formed the municipal (often socialistic) backbone of such Midwestern cities as Milwaukee, Chicago, Cincinnati, and St. Louis. Many others were simply escaping the ravages of the potato famine.

Yet there is no hint in the family scrapbook of any early Altman with political views. The family line was relatively apolitical. And as far as anyone can say, what beckoned a petit bourgeois by the name of Clement Altmann to America, sometime in the late 1840s, was simply the dream of a fresh start in a virgin land.

The family name was originally Altmann with two *n*'s. Altman's great-grandfather, Clement Altmann, was born in Schleswig-Holstein, Germany, of part-Dutch ancestry. Clement and his brothers were respectable linen manufacturers until their factory happened to burn to the ground. After Clement was rejected by the army because of a hearing impairment, he and his two brothers sailed for the greener pastures of America. The two brothers were stricken with cholera and buried at sea, while Clement landed at New Orleans, sailed up the Mississippi, and settled in Quincy, Illinois. Initially he found employment making bricks by hand for a brick manufacturer. Soon, he became a contractor.

In 1852 or 1853, nobody know precisely when, Clement married Altman's great-grandmother, Wilhelmina Rolling, who had been born in Hanover, Germany. They had nine children, of whom one, the fourth, was Frank Sr., Americanized from Franz Gerhardt to Frank G. Of the brood, this forebear of Altman became the most prominent of the Altmann brothers and sisters, which is indicated by the fact that wherever he went, the brothers and sisters followed, and ultimately the parents too. Most of the family ended up, after moving about a bit, in Kansas City, Missouri.

Frank Sr., Altman's grandfather, was quite the entrepreneur, a strain that runs deep in the family. He learned the watch repair trade from a large jewelry store owner in Quincy, and at eighteen, left town with a "thousand dollars represented in his own savings and with a loan of some capital from his father, which he soon paid back with interest," according to the American Historical Society, which documented the early Altmanns for a Missouri report.

Frank Sr. settled temporarily in Edina, Missouri, northwest of Hannibal, where he opened the first Altmann jewelry store. It was so profitable that, in 1882, at the age of twenty-one, Frank Sr. was compelled to relocate to the broader horizons of Kansas City, with its *gemütlich* community. Frank Sr. opened the next Altmann jewelry store at 725 Main in a building owned by the Scarritt estate. That's when, according to family lore, Frank G. Altmann Sr. dropped the second *n* in his last name. He was painting the outdoor shingle for the store when he just ran out of room.

In 1857, a New York *Tribune* reporter had declared Kansas City to be "*the* City of the Future." The city had survived the antislavery/proslavery schism of the Civil War (Altman liked to point out that Missouri had supplied both sides in the conflict); and by 1865, the first railroad into the city— the Missouri Pacific, which followed the natural water-level grades that converged at the mouth of the Kaw—was in operation.

Indeed, Frank Sr. had arrived in Kansas City just in time

for its boom days. According to the biographical sketch of Frank Sr. in *Missouri: Mother of the West, Volume IV*, published in 1930 by the American Historical Society, his Altman jewelry store quickly gained a following among the wealthier denizens of the city: "He was a master of the art of merchandising, understood the appeals made by quality and by good taste in the selection of goods, and his store immediately gained an extensive patronage and became known not only to local shoppers but throughout the territory served by Kansas City." In fact, Frank Sr. did so well in precious gems that he branched out, dabbling in "Real Painless Dental Parlors" and other ventures, before plunging into real estate, where there was not only higher risk but potentially unlimited gain.

Literally as well as figuratively, then, the Altman family was part of the early foundations of modern Kansas City. As a youth, Robert Altman could walk around the downtown area and savor standing monuments to his own family name, including a locally famous "Altman Building." It is not everyone who basks in the shadow of a city landmark, and not everyone who must live up—or down—to that sort of legacy.

Frank Sr. was farsighted. A fish market at the corner of Eleventh and Walnut, the old Central Market House, became transformed into the Ben Bolt Building. In 1895, the "Altman building" (which was what everyone called it) was some distance from the heart of the business district. Frank Sr. adorned the interior with hand-carved ceilings, intricate wrought-iron railings, and Turkish baths in the basement where, in the 1920s, many a Kansas City businessman soaked and relaxed. When the Emery Bird & Thayer Dry Goods Company erected the main building of their department store on the opposite corner, that intersection shortly became the center of the commercial district of Kansas City, an integral part of the "quality" stretch of Walnut Street, where "quality merchandise for deep pocketbooks," everything from jewelry to furs, was sold. The siting of the Ben Bolt building, "which marked the highest degree of his [Frank Sr.'s] faith in the future and business of foresight," according to one local history source, is credited as being crucial to the directional sprawl of downtown Kansas City.

That was only the beginning. Frank Sr. also erected the American Hotel Building, revitalized the Locust Street Garage Building and constructed a seven-story fireproof New Center building at the intersection of Troost Avenue and Fifteenth that became, with the symmetry of time, the headquarters for the Calvin Company, where the grandson he never met, Robert Altman, got his start directing motion pictures.

By 1894, Frank Sr.'s net worth was estimated in contemporary newspaper accounts at $200,000 (which would make Frank Sr. a millionaire several times over in today's terms), and he was looking for a bride. He found one in Annetta Matilda Bolt of Peoria, Illinois, known to friends and loved ones affectionately as Nettie Bolt. The local papers mourned her betrothal to a delegate from another city. "As charming as she is handsome," reported one. "One of Peoria's fairest and most charming daughters," noted another. Her father, Benjamin Bolt from Bavaria, was described as "one of the oldest traveling men in the city and [he] slings a grip for the Wilson Grocery Company."

The wedding ceremony, a Catholic one, took place in Peoria at the astonishing hour of 6:30 A.M., so that, after an elaborate breakfast and reception, the couple could catch an early honeymoon train East. The bride was attired in a broadcloth traveling suit and carried a spray of lilies of the valley. The music chosen for the occasion was from the old country, Mendelssohn's "Wedding March," a passage from Wagner's *Lohengrin*, and that old standby, Schubert's "Ave Maria."

If one is looking for the seeds of artistic expression in the Altman family, it is here, in the person of Nettie. From an affluent family background (one relative was a burgomaster in Switzerland, another was a cardinal), she was reared in a convent, and in Peoria had developed a reputation as a talented concert keyboardist. She was still of the generation of Germans obsessed with *Kultur* which, writes Richard O'Connor in his book *The German-Americans*, "died out, of necessity, but the second generation replaced it with a fixation on hard work and success." Her grandson the movie director would have one foot in both fixations.

After coming to Kansas City and taking up residence with Frank Sr. (their wedding was reported in all the Kansas City papers), Nettie continued to give occasional recitals. To her children, especially her daughters, she would impart an undying appreciation for music and the classical arts; and to her sons, who turned out, like Frank Sr., to be businessmen, she bequeathed, if not a love of, at least a tolerance for, things aesthetic.

In all there were six children, four girls and two boys. The oldest was Marie (b. 1895), the youngest was Virginia (b. 1908). In between there were Annette (b. 1896), Frank Jr. (b. 1900), Bernard (b. 1901), and Pauline (b. 1902).

Annette became an accomplished harpist, and also performed publicly, while Marie, quite the pianist and singer, graced various civic recitals, benefit theatricals, and church choir events, "the pleasing, natural quality of her voice having been trained by noted masters in Washington, New York and in Europe," according to one printed source. Both married staid Kansas City businessmen, Annette a wholesale jeweler by the name of Kiger, Marie a tire and rubber dealer. Virginia, meanwhile, took after her mother by specializing in piano, though after studying two years at the Conservatory of Music in Paris and winning prizes, she could not resist the stability of Kansas City, where she too married and settled down.

The only Altman-Bolt female to endure in show business, after a fashion, was Pauline, who cultivated the study of violin and opera at the Kansas City Conservatory of Music, at the Wilson Green School of Music in Washington, D.C., and for periods in France. She sang in the opera at Cannes. In the mid-twenties, during her yearlong study in France, Pauline was tutored by Jean de Reszke, a celebrated tenor of the day. In New Jersey, she had her own radio show. In Los Angeles, she performed with the Philharmonic Orchestra. An occasional songwriter (she introduced "Little Sir Echo" on Rudy Vallee's radio program in the 1930s), she gravitated to Los Angeles, where she wrote popular tunes for motion pictures, the best-known of which was "Christmas Story," recorded by Doris Day and used in the movie *On Moonlight Bay.* Alone among Frank Sr. and Nettie's children to forsake Kansas City, she proved a kind of beacon to Altman.

Robert Altman's four aunts are remembered by all who knew them as showstoppers, unique for Kansas City, but extraordinary in any setting. Socialites in the Kansas City orbit, adorable and ultra-feminine, they had an artistic, eccentric flair that endeared them to everyone they met. Though their playing of a variety of instruments and their singing and reciting poetry were definitely part of their charm, their reputation seems to have been based less on any special artistic stature than on something ineffable that the Altmans were convinced reposed in the genes.

In any case, Frank Sr. did not live to see the blossoming of his family. He was a retiring man, humble and generous, who seems to have given much to charity, community, and friends, a selfless Altman trait that manifests itself through the years. His chief hobby and sole passion was horses and horse racing. He once owned a stable of thoroughbreds, of which he especially prized three pet steeds, named Charles D., Mein Herr, and Bonanza (an interesting coincidence in light of his grandson's subsequent involvement with the television show of that name). "He enjoyed driving his own horses, particularly the spirited team of blacks," relates the biographical sketch of him in the American Historical Society papers.

He died suddenly on June 21, 1917, at fifty-seven. After driving his car home from work, Frank Sr. complained of feeling weak and nauseous. A physician diagnosed acute indigestion, adding that the condition was not serious. Frank Sr. retired and appeared to rest easy. At one-thirty in the morning, the family became concerned, and a priest was summoned. Father Fowler lived directly across the street and reached Frank G. Altman's bedside in time to administer the last rites. The patriarch of the Altman family died at 1:50 A.M.

His moral and charitable habits were eulogized in a leading Catholic newspaper of the day. The thronged funeral had a forty-voice choir made up of volunteers from all the city parishes. His generosity to the Catholic Church was praised—all his children had been or were being educated in the Catholic school system—but the full extent of his benefactions was only partly known. "He [Frank Sr.] was a regular financial contributor to almost every charitable institution in the city," the Catholic press reported, "and he is receiving his reward a hundred fold now in the prayers and Masses being offered up for him by the inmates of these institutions. Not long ago, the House of Good Shepherd needed some coats and the need came to Mr. Altman's ears. Within a short time, a hundred and fifty coats from his own stock were sent out. . . ."

Upon his death, the mantle of family leadership passed to Frank Jr., who at twenty-one, was the eldest son. Yet Bernard ("B.C."), who had also gone the approved family route of education at De LaSalle Academy and at St. Thomas College in Minnesota, was decidedly the more charismatic and engaging personality. Frank Jr. could be counted on to keep family affairs on an even keel. B.C. was magnetic, restless, full of zest. Though Frank Jr. always had the seniority, it was B.C. who became the informal paterfamilias. You could count on B.C.. He was very giving, very forgiving, always hospitable, and involved with any crisis. Whereas you had to "contact Frank," B.C. kept in touch with everyone, even at great distances, by phone or by mail.

Together Frank and B.C. had a brief professional fling as partners with Charles M. Singleton in the Altman-Singleton Insurance Company downtown in the Lee Building. But B.C. was too independent and mercurial for his brother, and there was a relatively amicable split-up. B.C. went into business for himself, operating a large garage in the Locust Street Building, which had been acquired by the Altman estate. For a while he represented the area dealership for Peerless Motor Cars.

But selling insurance exerted a powerful spell on these Altman brothers, and ultimately, sometime in the early 1930s, B.C. moved over to Kansas City Life, where he began to fill his niche as a supersalesman.

Frank and B.C.'s business acumen was not always as sharp as Altman père's, and particularly in the case of B.C.—a gambler and a risk-taker on investments—there would be periods of distress. But there was always the family trust, such as it was, to fall back on. Even if the Altmans liked to say there was not really all that much family money, in fact, there was. The second generation Altmans were not upper-upper, but they were definitely upper-middle class. This psychological parachute—the illusion of subsistence and the reality of a cushion of wealth—Robert Altman inherited from boyhood, and he made a chronic strategy of it in his personal life and film career.

Frank Sr.'s original fortune took care of Nettie Bolt Altman and helped nurture the siblings for half a century, even as it dwindled. It was a loving, devoted, long-lived (all of Frank Sr.'s sons and daughters lived into their eighties or nineties) family. They never kept tallies or ledgers, partly at B.C.'s insistence, partly because Nettie argued that Frank Sr. would not have done it that way. The family was run like an ideal Altman filmmaking experience—"virtually as a communistic society," remembers Annette's daughter, Carolyn Whitney. "Whoever needed, got."

In turn, Frank Sr.'s grandchildren were instructed by their parents never to interfere with their uncles' or aunts' magnanimous disbursement of the fund. The inheritance lasted, for funerals or for family emergencies, at least until 1975, almost sixty years after Frank Sr.'s death.

The gravy years were the Twenties, when the original six Altmans had servants and a stable of horses and plenty of fancy everything. The four daughters and their mother all sojourned in Europe during Pauline's year of musical study, attending the opera and the annual fashion parade and the museums in Paris. (The Altman aunts all spoke French fluently.) It was a very glamorous escapade for those who went—and the trip came up in family conversation again and again over the years.

B.C. was the only family member to stay in Kansas City. He was marrying Helen Mathews, from Nebraska, and settling down to family life. His bride traced her lineage to ancestors who came over on the *Mayflower,* and she was as sensible and low-key as B.C. was wanton and irresistible. It was not an obstacle that she was not Catholic. She was willing to convert and did, and in time became one of the devout.

Into this heritage one Robert Bernard Altman was born on July 20, 1925, the first grandchild—the first male heir—of the Altman dynasty. To see the world through his eyes you must first enter it as he did, with the world seeming to be his oyster. He was the oldest boy in an extended family that valued a male heir. He lived in a provincial city where the name of Altman was honored. He was the grandson of the fabled Frank Sr. and the son of the storied B.C.

The four aunts doted on him from the first. They brought back a gorgeous christening gown from Paris, which became a family heirloom handed down from generation to generation for baptisms. Family snapshots show a handsomely garbed boy with a tuft of hair, beaming, at the center of many family occasions. "That guru-looking boy was a ring-bearer at my wedding," Pauline Walsh proudly exclaims.

By the beginning of the 1930s, the flush years were already past. The reality of the Depression was setting in, and there was middle-class belt-tightening. The fair-haired boy of the Altman family was forced to grow up hearing secondhand about faraway, exotic metropolises like Paris, in the company of those beautiful, quirky aunts who never ceased to pamper him. His imagination was fired up by this Paris, which came to symbolize the unobtainable. His own parents never traveled abroad when he was growing up and rarely took a special vacation, unless it was a day at the races.

It is remarkable how little of this specific family background is in Altman's movies. In later years, after working himself into a certain mood, Robert Altman would recall that the original spelling of his surname was Altmann, commenting to friends that he was a forced into being a "closet German" by trivial circumstance. But unlike, say, directors Francis Coppola or Michael Cimino, Altman, in his filmmaking, has shown a singular lack of interest in his own or America's immigrant past, except to comment on the melting pot obliquely with characters whose ethnic identity is all but swallowed up by their immersion in the rat race.

It is next to impossible to find Helen or B.C. explicitly evoked by a character in one of his movies. Altman could never bring himself to portray B.C. Indeed, you can search his movies in vain for a credible, complex, or significant "father figure," unless you think of McCabe as a romanticized B.C. (Some people think he is a romanticized Altman.)

For that matter, unless being white-skinned and privileged is the point, there is very little at all of the Kansas City Altmans in the barren and screwed-up families of the bride and the groom as fictionalized in *A Wedding*, a movie that, more than most, Altman insists in interviews is in part autobiographical.

"People kept asking me which one were you?" says Pauline Walsh of *A Wedding*. "Those crazy, nutty women. I don't think any of them were me. But if it made for a better movie . . ."

Sixty years later, the Kansas City phone book is still full of Altmans, though the name-bearers are no longer the civic movers and shakers; and Altman himself does not often journey back to his hometown. "If I went there now, I wouldn't know who to call," he told a Kansas City journalist in 1982, forgetting the fact that he probably knows quite a few of his many relatives, both direct and by marriage.

When the Altman building fell victim to a wrecking ball in 1978, the Altman family could do nothing about it, for Frank Sr. had neglected to purchase the land more than a half century earlier and the owner finally sold the property out from under them. The five-story Roman brick facade was battered into dust, and construction was begun on a Mercantile Bank Tower. An Altman first cousin and great-grandson of Frank Sr., named John, was on hand (with his cofilmmaker Mary A. Nelson) to photograph the demolition for a thirteen-minute documentary short they entitled *Coming Down*, silent except for a baroque-type music sound track.

Later, John Altman and another great-grandson of Frank Sr., Frank G. Altmann III (who has reclaimed the second *n* in the family name), and Carolyn Whitney, the daughter of Annette Altman, tramped the oldest city graveyards searching for traces of a stone identifying the graves of Wilhelmina and Clement Altmann, parents of Frank Sr., great-grandparents of Robert Altman. The family believed their bodies lay in either Union or St. Mary's cemeteries, but they could find no marker. They are still looking.

Chapter

2

KANSAS CITY

In the Twenties, Kansas City was still very much under the sway of the late William Rockhill Nelson, the editor of *The Kansas City Star*, who had labored mightily to convince the local titans of bromidic greeting cards, real-estate development, hogs and cattle, agricultural implements, and grain processing that Kansas City could be an ideal city, a Midwestern almost-utopia.

Through the medium of the *Star* and the influence of a group of civic heavyweights, Nelson was instrumental in promoting an elaborate boulevard system in the city, complete with sculptures brought from Europe; pergolas and sunken gardens; vast, picturesque

The Altman building (note the shop sign), a landmark of downtown Kansas City.

parks; modern, planned neighborhoods and housing projects; imposing public buildings; plazas, city centers, a proper museum, and other civic ornaments.

Though Nelson died in 1915, Altman grew up in the aftermath of his rah-rahmanship, and this burst of metropolitan boosterism, in a city that has always been as defensive about its limitations as it has been proud of its attributes.

Kansas Citians are not the only Midwesterners to believe their city to be an oasis of the flatlands; and Kansas City is not the only city to have a lopsided home-state city rivalry— a San Francisco vs. Los Angeles type of rivalry—with the perhaps more glittering city of St. Louis nearby to overshadow its distinctions. But when Altman was growing up, the ostentation of the sculpted boulevards must have seemed especially vulgar and smug, when the backdrop happened to be the stockyards and auto assembly plants, widespread unemployment and poverty, and the 10 percent nonwhite neighborhoods that most of the Kansas Citians never took notice of—"its closely-packed, happy-go-lucky Negro sections, exulting in Joe Louis, and proud of Marian Anderson and Paul Robeson and swing band leaders," according to a guide to the "Show Me" state underwritten by President Franklin Delano Roosevelt's Works Progress Administration in the 1930s.

Not that Altman had much personal contact with the underclass of Kansas City. All the Altmans, all of Frank Sr.'s sons and daughters and all of their families, in time, lived south of Forty-seventh Street and west of Rockhill Road, an area that contained the city's finest homes and that had the added distinction of being its first platted residential district.

It was at the urging of William Rockhill Nelson, in 1908, that developer J. C. Nichols had begun moving out Negro shanties and trash dumps, transforming the rock quarries, and carving out the landscaped stretch of broad, winding streets that followed the natural contours of the land and constituted the Country Club district. As with the Paseo downtown, the park intersections boasted statuary and other objets d'art imported from Europe. Nearby, at Forty-seventh Street and Mill Creek Parkway, Nichols conceived the Country Club Plaza, an upscale complex of Spanish-style buildings of cream-colored brick and stucco regarded by many students of urban planning as the first shopping center in the U.S.

When Robert Altman was born, the Altmans lived at 200 East Sixty-seventh Street. And by 1936, when he was eleven, the address was comfortable, tree-lined 127 West Sixty-eighth Street, within a few blocks of the Catholic church and parish school, and within walking distance of the elm-lined parkway and the streetcar line leading to the Country Club Plaza.

B.C. did not seek or enjoy a lofty social status, and the Altmans say B.C.'s house was a relatively "modest" Tudor, always smaller and less tidy, more informal, than any of the other Altmans' homes. Partly, this was because B.C. was extraordinarily carefree with money. In those days if he had money, he lost it gambling, or he *gave* it away. It always seemed to be feast or famine with B.C. That was the attitude toward money that became deeply ingrained with Altman. He never forgot the wild pendulum swings and the insecurity. His cousin, Susan Davis, says the insecurity fostered in Altman a preoccupation with the downside. On the other hand, there always seemed to be lots more money somewhere just around the corner.

To everyone who met B.C. even once, then, or forty years later, when Altman was an important director and introducing his father around Hollywood, B.C. was a kind of swashbuckling Babbitt, mild-mannered and Midwestern on the one hand, but bluff and colorful all the same. B.C. was not a particularly prepossessing guy. He was very ordinary-looking (in fact, his son came eventually to look a lot like him, only B.C. did not have the goatee or the flickering edge in the gemlike eyes). Yet when he spoke, B.C. came alive. He would be standing quietly in the room, unnoticed, and then suddenly explode with magnetism, clever conversation, roguishness. He never failed to make an impression. People remember him as vividly as yesterday.

"No matter what you think of Bob," says Pauline Walsh, "he doesn't have half the charm of Bernard. He was an outstanding personality."

"B.C. had the charm of the world," says LaVonne Cubbison, Altman's first wife. "He was adored by everybody, a great gentleman and *kind.*"

B.C. was always elsewhere—putting the lock on some deal, or drinking whiskey and playing poker at the Indian Hills Country Club, or just nesting somewhere. He was a die-hard gambler and would rent a hotel room with friends (a habit he passed on to his son) and stay up all night upping the ante. Then he would start in again, playing a new round, in the morning. Even in St. Peter's newsletter he was referred to by his nickname, a nod to his horse-racing fever, "Nag."

Like Frank Sr., B.C. was a soft touch and donated a lot of

time and money to the Catholic Church, whether it was on the small scale of taking a priest down to Union Station or on the larger scale of contributing substantially to parochial education. Though not as zealous a Catholic as Helen, he was nonetheless a devoted one, a churchgoer, a relied-upon donor, and an active participant in diocesan affairs. When someone was needed to spearhead fundraising for Bishop Hogan High School, B.C. was the man. When someone was needed to chair a reduction of the parish debt, B.C. was the man.

No one can remember any marital tension between Helen and B.C. Yet Altman's father is described by many as having a roving eye for women, which, if it did not legitimize this particular aspect of human relations for his son, certainly opened the mind up to possibilities. One of Altman's high-school girlfriends remembers hearing from her mother that B.C. was one of the world's worst rounders. Another Kansas City acquaintance says that, in the 1940s, when Altman and his father were both out in California, there was a rumor going around Kansas City that both of them were competing for the same woman. At the least, nobody thought it out of the question.

B.C. had only a passing interest in movies. He would invest in his son's movies—or in his son's lifestyle, which amounted to the same thing—again and again. Screenwriter Brian (*McCabe and Mrs. Miller*) McKay remembers they were always arguing good-naturedly about money and debts.

But that did not mean, necessarily, that B.C. *liked* his son's movies. Later on, B.C., not to mention *all* the Altman aunts and uncles, were amazed at this proclaimed genius arising in their midst, and a bit bewildered by his work. Their generation still preferred the Fred Astaire or Doris Day type of old-fashioned fare. Once, after Altman had become a famous director, B.C. confessed privately that there was not a single one of his son's movies that he enjoyed, excepting *M*A*S*H*. He was not the only Altman to voice this opinion.

Images, for example, received a special premiere at a theatre in the Country Club section of Kansas City. Altman's mother and his sister Barbara attended the first showing. Altman was certain they would be swept away by this strange suspense fable starring Susannah York. Between showings, Frank Barhydt, Altman's former boss at the Calvin Company, overheard Altman ask for their reaction. Both hemmed and hawed until Helen finally volunteered a diplomatic: "Interesting."

Another family story tells of the reaction from the pixieish Aunt Marie after the premiere of *The Long Goodbye* at the Plaza Theater in Kansas City. Altman and his third wife, Kathryn Reed, were in town for the occasion, and all the various family members proudly trotted out to see Altman's latest production. Aunt Marie always put everything in the best possible light, but she could not tell a lie. So she had a difficult time after the movie when Altman cornered her and asked, "How did you like the movie, Marie?"

"Oh, Bob," she is said to have replied, "the scenery was beautiful, and the costumes were beautiful, and the directing was wonderful . . ." Altman, impatient, persisted. "But the movie, Marie, how did you like the movie?" "The movie?" sighed Aunt Marie. "Oh, I didn't like it."

Since Altman often insisted that his friends like his work, this particular burr, the lack of enthusiasm from his own family—especially B.C.—became a subtext of aggravation. "Now, that's really *interesting*, Bob . . ." Helen would tell her son diplomatically. But B.C. would say, "I haven't understood one film that Bob has done."

It seems incredible that this bacchanalian, iconoclastic, surpassingly gifted film director should be in the shadow of someone in the realm of his own family, his somewhat absentee father.

Yet when Altman was growing up, it was B.C. who quietly bedazzled everyone he came in contact with. In time the son came to emulate his father. Like B.C., he became the outgoing con salesman and the mischievous charmer, the incessant gambler, and the scandalous womanizer. But at the same time—unhappily—Altman grew remote from his father.

Altman's mother, Helen, and his two sisters
(Joan is next to Robert) in their front yard on W.
68th Street in Kansas City, circa 1937. (Carolyn
Whitney)

*   *   *

Since B. C. and Helen had preceded everyone else in marrying and having children, there weren't many other play-
mates in the family. Joan Altman (b. 1929) was the next
oldest Altman grandchild—younger than Robert Altman by
some four years—after which came his other sister, Barbara
(b. 1931). The cousin closest to Altman in age, Frank G. III
(Frank's son), was more than six years younger. "There are
lots of pictures of me playing with Joan and Barbara," writes

Carolyn Whitney, "and I remember being at their house frequently on Saturdays, but there is no picture of Bob playing with us. Frankly I don't remember him being around much at all. He was doubtless in the neighborhood with some other boys, or at the movies. . . ."

It was that kind of family—tight-knit yet sort of loose-knit too. There were many family get-togethers and much expressed love, but at the center of the whirlwind was a boy often left to his own solitude. Altman has said he learned to "manipulate" the houseful of women. He was doted on, but set apart—at the nucleus, but floating free. It gave him a perspective from which to observe people, and time in which to feed his imagination. His upbringing fostered individuality, yet at the same time it made him hunger for and be dependent on family.

Childrearing was left to Helen, who gave endless time to the children. According to everyone who knew her, she was a sweetie pie, very pretty, very much of a mother. She served her children, and also basked in B.C.'s afterglow. To Pauline Walsh, she confided once, "I'm just drowned. It's like I am a nobody." But to the family-at-large she was viewed more as someone who could stand up to B.C. and be very insistent about her own whims.

She was not a Junior Leaguer, not at all bourgeois. She was very down-to-earth, an early fitness buff, and a nutrition nut. (Once she had all the kids on a diet of grapes, says one family member, practically nothing but grapes.) She was quite social, entertained royally, and it was always open house at the Altmans. As devoted to golf and bridge as B.C. was to hunting and gambling, she donated to charity, chaperoned a Girl Scout troop, and had a busy calendar of Catholic fashion shows and charity events.

Photographs show her as a petite blonde who looks very much like her daughters, Joan and Barbara, both of them blonde and fetching—very much, indeed, like the heroines of many Altman films, and not unlike the English actress Susannah York in *Images*. But Helen was not at all like that character, disturbed and fanciful—at least on the surface. She was a perfect, all-American heartland mom.

"Give me a child for the first seven years of his life, and I will form the man" is said to be a Jesuit credo.

No one can trace the origin of that provocative maxim, which is often twisted into an impugnment of Catholic parochial education in general; and there is some dispute as to whether or not it was ever actually uttered. But in Altman's case, it bears quoting. His upbringing was staunchly Roman Catholic for seven and more of the formative years of his youth.

In interviews, Altman has often denied the Catholic influence. He has said Catholicism "ceased to have a hold on me in fifth grade"—which seems a rather astounding leap for a fifth-grader. Altman has also said that his Catholicism was diluted, since his mother, Helen, was "not a Catholic," which would be news to a lot of people who regarded her as quite the dedicated convert.

"Catholicism was to me school," he has said. "It was restrictions; it was things you had to do. It was your parents. It was Mass on Sunday and fish on Friday. And then when I got out of that, I got into the Army. It was the same thing—you had to have a pass to get out. You had to wear this kind of clothes, and you had to address them so-and-so . . . you've got to wear a tie to get into this restaurant or you've got to have a suit if you're going to the party. Or you don't try to fuck a girl on the first date if she comes from a good family. All of those things. I was never a revolutionary. Those were just some of the things in life that you had to do."

Yet many people who know Altman feel his half-denials of Catholicism are but proof in reverse that Catholicism is embedded deeply in his life and in his films. And that the guilt, the fatalistic viewpoint, the themes of death and redemption, the ambivalent attitude toward women and family, the furtive sex and love, the questioning of command and leadership (which is a kind of Jesuitical questioning of God)—all of these, so prevalent in his films—have their roots in his early Catholicism.

That Catholicism began in the home and was furthered in parochial school.

Whereas it was more prestigious (and expensive) to attend Pembroke Country Day School (and some of the other Altmans did just that), B.C. and Helen's children were enrolled in St. Peter's right down the block at the corner of Meyer and Holmes. St. Peter's was a truly excellent parochial school in 1931 when Robert Bernard Altman formally began his primary education at the age of six.

It was a school with an unusual degree of emphasis on personal expression through the arts—owing to the influence of a young and forward-looking pastor, Monsignor McKay. Early in the 1930s, in the midst of the worst economic downturn in the history of the United States, St. Peter's could boast a school radio (for listening to American School of the Air broadcasts) and 16mm film equipment for educational screenings. It had a cafeteria with a tearoom and a daily changing menu. It had compulsory dancing, primary school plays and operas, music (waltzes and polkas as well as classical) and piano and violin lessons. Everyone, from the earliest grades on, was expected to perform in the school plays and operettas. Even if no one can recall noticing any particular theatrical aptitude in a little boy named Robert Altman, it is clear that something other than mass and doughnuts was on the agenda at St. Peter's.

Of course, the curriculum stressed the fundamentals of arithmetic, reading, writing, and spelling; but there was also room for bazaars and holiday programs, fair-weather picnics, and even a special two-reel comedy at a pre-Lenten party hosted by the pastor, with soda pop and ice cream for treats afterward. The attitude toward motion pictures was refreshing and contemporary, and when there was a particularly appealing film at the local neighborhood movie shrine, there would be a class excursion. All this, and the tuition was only one dollar a month!

Quite unlike the first generation of movie directors—in

whose rough-and-tumble life stories you discover juvenile detention, running away to join the circus, adventures with the Lafayette Escadrille or Pancho Villa, and in some cases a backstory of virtual beggardom—Altman was involved in the organized middle-class Catholic routine of Boy Scouts, junior league sports (especially basketball—for he sprouted up to a good height right away), and honor roll (he rarely failed to place). That is one of the reasons why the William Wellmans and the Raoul Walshes, the early sound-era directors, made the type of movies they did—the Foreign Legion and manly derring-do stories that Altman devoured as a boy—and alternatively, one of the reasons why Altman's films are so different from theirs.

When Altman graduated from St. Peter's at the age of thirteen in June of 1938, he would go on to Rockhurst High School, where reports of his school involvement briefly become more erratic, moving like radar blips across a screen. Rockhurst, run by the Jesuits (who, in reality, can claim to have had Robert Altman in their grasp for only a few months), was a highly structured secondary school that emphasized philosophy, the classics, and Greek and Latin.

Decorum was bred in him, at home and at St. Peter's, but his inclinations were, like B.C.'s, more mischievous. Friends remember that Altman attended Rockhurst school plays with appetite and then made sport of them with equal zest afterward. Altman grew bored in classes, and was reprimanded for putting snakes from biology experiments in lockers and writing frivolous letters in study hall. The Jesuits' idea of punishment was to make him sit in a corner and read a book, which suited Altman. It was more escape than punishment.

His personality was manifesting itself as sensitive, precocious, strong-willed. He was growing tall and lanky, with a shock of dark hair, and beautiful eyes that just danced. He was good company to his friends. One friend who often walked home from school with him remembers Altman's disarming way of telling jokes and spinning yarns. At other times, he could be very serious. Another childhood friend

In California in 1947, playing croquet with B.C. and Helen. (Carolyn Whitney)

distinctly remembers Altman trying to convince her of the correctness of Catholic doctrine, which offended him less at that point than the regimentation at Rockhurst.

There was some final straw with the Jesuits. Or maybe the teenager finally convinced Helen and B.C. to let him go to Southwest, the public school at Sixty-fifth and Wornall Road, which was then at the heart of the upper middle-class suburbs of the Kansas City nouveau riche. There, in grades ahead of him and behind him, were most of the non-Catholic kids from his neighborhood, generally from slightly more affluent families, lily-white and WASP.

The middle class of Kansas City was not that much affected by the Depression, certainly not as much as the lower strata. Cash might be less readily at hand, but the affluence was still there. At St. Peter's, Monsignor McKay had to chide his parishioners for using "the smokescreen of the Depression" to reduce their Sunday offerings.

Certainly there was no poverty in Altman's neighborhood, though his house was only half a block from the streetcar line that ran up Wornall Road, and the down-and-out people would ride the cars out to the more prosperous areas asking for work and handouts. As Helen was always very generous, it was not unusual for Altman to come home from school to discover some drifter eating a plate of supper on the back steps.

If Altman was touched at all by the mass despair, the unemployment, the protests, the riots, and the Hoovervilles of the Depression era, that vivid backdrop is absent from his movies—as are so many elements of his life story. Indeed, his movies are rarely about any class except his own middle class. Most of the characters in his movies exist in a financial unreality in which unemployment, job conditions, or the weekly paycheck are rarely at issue. Like Pinky Rose (Sissy Spacek) in *Three Women*, his characters tend to have no economic moorings; they are a tabula rasa, and if they don't have a life savings, as in *Nashville*, "It don't worry them."

In all of Altman's films, there is but a single reference to the wider world of his boyhood: the adaptation of the Depression Era novel *Thieves Like Us*. Here, drawing on a literary source, Altman dug deep into his memory bank to recapture the angst and flavor of the hard times he had lived through, unscathed.

For the middle class as well as for the lower classes, going to the movies was part of the flight from reality. (And in Kansas City, one must remember, the importance of movies was accentuated by the dearth of ballet, opera, and serious theatre.) The Altman children all rode their bikes down to the Saturday matinees at the Brookside Theatre (now a supermarket), and Altman has said he vividly remembers seeing *King Kong*, *Gunga Din*, *The Four Feathers*, and other heroic, action-filled movies quite unlike any he would ever direct. His parents had to hunt him down and drag him out of *Viva Villa!* after he had sat through the film starring Wallace Beery some four successive times. That would be in 1934, with Altman all of nine years old. Later on, in high school, he and his friends would play hookey to catch an afternoon matinee of, say, *Beau Geste*.

Apparently public school was no more congenial to Altman than Rockhurst, and his reputation at Southwest was as even more of a cutup. He participated less and less in organized peer activity, and he appears only once in the school yearbook—*The Sachem*—of 1941. The future director of *M*A*S*H* and *Nashville* is wearing an ROTC uniform in the midst of a group of other boys identified as Company A of the largest drill team in the school's history. He does not show up in the homeroom photos, the literary society, the school plays, or on any of the sports teams.

Indeed, it was at Southwest that Altman began to hone his self-image as a lone wolf and an outsider—of someone who was a maverick, a gadfly, a posturer above the fray. This was partly the result of being young and delicate-minded, and partly, perhaps, the result of being shunted from school to school; but for Altman it developed into a credo.

He once told a friend that the main thing he remembered about Southwest was that, going to school each day, he was attacked by swarms of purple grackles that roosted and nested in the corners of the great building. Altman maintained that these purple grackles took a particular dislike to him and would swoop down and dive-bomb him day after day. If the Jesuits gave him the classical grounding for his lifelong Icarus theme, Southwest gave him that sophomoric image that so startles audiences—the deadly bird droppings in *Brewster McCloud*.

Though he prided himself on his pranks, Altman showed friends a more industrious and imaginative side of himself. One friend remembers a hilarious monologue on french fries, the uses and flavors thereof. With fellow student Robert Woodburn, Altman became involved in a teenage Christmas card partnership. Woodburn was looking for someone to illustrate his gags, and Altman drew well. It was Woodburn's mother, a teacher of art at both St. Peter's and Rockhurst, who remembered Altman's sketchpad skills and brought him and her son together. This was their first collaboration, and in what was to become a pattern in Altman's career, Woodburn wrote the words while Altman supplied the visuals.

One girlfriend remembers that back in high school Altman was already intrigued by exploring the dimensions of sound. Tape recorders had just started to be sold, and everyone would gather at her home to amuse themselves with a newfangled Zenith recorder. They would spend hours recording each other's voices.

Then, after everyone else had left, Altman would return, still fascinated, and recite for hours into the microphone, dappling the sound, experimenting with the texture of his voice. "The Bells" by Edgar Allan Poe was a favorite:

> Keeping time, time, time,
> In a sort of Runic rhyme,
> To the tintinnabulation that so musically wells
> From the bells, bells, bells, bells,
> Bells, bells, bells—

He and she made a disc recording of Altman intoning Rudyard Kipling's "Gunga Din" from memory from start to finish. She still has it somewhere in a closet.

"His mind was always going, fantasizing, entertaining," recalls one friend.

"A very deep thinker," says another.

"I'd never met a more gentle, courteous, gentlemanly boy," says another girlfriend.

Chapter
3

WENTWORTH

Altman left Southwest in the middle
of his junior year, and was sent to Wentworth
Military Academy in Lexington, Missouri.
Whether he was expelled or left Southwest by
choice, or whether B.C. decided the boy was in
need of a firmer hand, there are varying opinions and no records to consult.

It may have been that his parents had been
saving up all along to send him to Wentworth.
Waiting until the junior year was one of the
ways the Depression elite bought a diploma of
note without paying for it for four entire years.
Altman seems to have been captivated by the
military, as so many young people were, especially in light of the war menace in Europe.

Then again, knowing Altman, he may have welcomed the move simply as a way to be "on location"—away from his parents, their discipline and expectations.

In the one-hour drive of some fifty miles from Kansas City to Lexington, one comes across markers for the Santa Fe Trail, the Lewis and Clark Trail, the old overland stagecoach lines, and for Indian burial mounds. And one passes over land that Daniel Boone explored and Quantrill's raiders raided, past rich farmlands and numerous sites of Western history, all of it—with the exceptions of *McCabe* and *Buffalo Bill and the Indians*—curiously ignored in Altman's films.

Lexington is an old town on the banks of the Missouri, not known for much besides the presence of Wentworth Military Academy, a military preparedness school and junior college. Wentworth has been there since 1880, a military boarding school providing a foundation for business and professional studies, 137 acres of shaded campus, banked flower beds, athletic fields, rifle ranges, laboratories, gymnasiums, barracks, and woodlands ideal for hikes or military maneuvers. Wentworth has educated over ten thousand cadets in the past hundred or so years.

The tuition was not cheap in the early 1940s—about $995 annually for room and board, education, incidental fees, free use of sports and medical facilities, and the standard garb. In 1941, the year Altman came to Wentworth, there were approximately 350 students instructed by a faculty of 29 teachers and two military advisors. The focus of study included English, Latin, Spanish, and German; algebra, geometry, and trigonometry; history and science; and business classes from law to shorthand, from banking to marketing. In addition, most of the students were obliged to fill their course lists with various social behavior options: salesmanship (between Wentworth and B.C., no wonder Altman became such an effective promoter of himself), etiquette, dress and personal habits, introductions, foreign travel, social letter-writing, and formal participation (defined in the catalogue as "social techniques as applied to formal dances, receptions, and affairs of state"). The Wentworth tradition held that knife and spoon politesse, or how to introduce one's girlfriend to one's mother, was every bit as important as calculus.

At Wentworth there was a heavy emphasis on sports of all kinds, including tennis, golf, and riding. Wentworth students also had the benefit of a private airport with a six-plane hangar. Although there is no record that Altman took lessons, certainly it was here, at Wentworth, that the future film director began to think about flying—that freedom in flight took shape as a metaphor in his mind. The yearning for the heavens that is corrupted by the values of earthbound society is a purely Altmanesque theme that crops up again and again in his work, from TV episodes to *Brewster Mc-Cloud* to *Streamers.*

In those World War II days of preparedness, at least one school hour a day was given over to rigorous military training. By the third year this included machine-gun work, combat principles, chemical warfare, tactical exercise, first aid, map reading, musketry, and drill command, which further consisted of elements of military law, company administration and supply, combat strategy, military history, and aerial photography. Each day, there were calisthenics after morning classes and an hour of drill before lunch.

Because Wentworth professed to be "Christian-oriented," there were nondenominational chapel exercises weekly on Saturday, and cadets were required to attend church services somewhere in town every Sunday. The use of cars was forbidden, except for special events. Cadets had to be in uniform at all times. These uniforms were described in the school literature as "one of the most complete and beautiful in America," consisting of a field uniform, a daily uniform, a semidress uniform similar to the Army "pinks and greens," and a blue field-dress uniform.

Altman served as platoon sergeant of his ROTC unit. He was on the honor roll and earned special academic distinction. He played reserve center on the ten-man basketball squad; he lettered in track. (For Wentworth, that was a mod-

The running team photo (Altman at center) from
the 1943 yearbook of Wentworth Military Academy. (Wentworth Military Academy)

est record in sports: Altman was never much of an athlete,
and he always had the "closet jock" ardor of one who is
physically soft and aesthetically inclined. Heavy betting has
provided one outlet for Altman's energies, the occasional
sports scenes of his movies, another; but the long football
sequence of *M*A*S*H* has the stoned gambler's point of
view—interested in the flashpoints and the outcome, oblivious to the subtleties and the rules.)

Wentworth offered forensics, music, dramatics, hobby
clubs; but Altman does not show up in any of these activities in his nearly three years there. He preferred to keep a
low profile. Colonel Sellers Sr., the commandant of Wentworth in the 1940s, says Altman was one of the hardest

kinds of boys to keep track of—he did not do well enough to excel, and he did not misbehave enough to be kicked out.

Wentworth friends recall him as jolly, outgoing, and laid-back. He was tall, thin, sallow-complected, with long and fair hands. One former Company A roommate remembers Altman as "not as military-minded as the rest. He walked with a kind of question mark, his chest out, not in, with a slouch." Others recall that he loved reading and books, especially the Harvard Classics and biography, as well as lusty historical novels like Marguerite Steen's *The Sun Is My Undoing*, about an eighteenth-century slave trader, his African mistress, and mulatto daughter.

Though Altman was not a "problem boy," there were occasional restrictions and loss of privileges for rule infractions. One girlfriend remembers Altman as always being "on report" for formal dance occasions. Yet he was irrepressible, and would sneak out to the Wentworth field and grandiosely reenact a famous Civil War battle for his "date"—the cannons here, the cavalry there, and so on.

Wentworth was very strict regarding girls in the barracks, and evening permits went only to boys entrusted with the mission of safe entertainment in town. Yet the cadets could skip barracks at will, dummy up their beds, and don civvies for a night on the prowl, a movie at the theatre downtown, or all-you-can-eat shrimp at ten cents a draw at a certain roadhouse. A little of that was expected of a cadet.

For miles around, coincidentally, Lexington was known at the time for its nightlife, for its bars and nightspots and pool halls, for a barbershop with a regular card game in the back, and above all, for something called "Block 42," one block west of the courthouse, so called because it was supposed to have forty-two bars in one block.

Actually, that just happened to be the number of the lot, although there was a high proportion of taverns. (Through a twist of post-Prohibition law, Lexington was one of just thirteen Missouri municipalities legally permitted to serve liquor by the individual drink.) And then, there was Helen's, or latterly, Betty Boop's, just across the street from the courthouse down behind Main Street, the most famous whorehouse in the territory.

It was at Helen's in Lexington, Altman confided to friends in Hollywood, that he lost his virginity.

Even today, older men in Missouri speak with great fondness of Helen's. It was well known among men and teenage boys in that part of the Midwest in the 1940s. Not only traveling salesmen, businessmen, and high-school students driving miles out of their way, but also farmers coming into town for the open market would visit Helen's. First, they would send their wives off shopping and their kids to the moving pictures; then they would settle in at Helen's until the twilight hours. Old-timers can still remember the caravan of farmers' cars parked outside, with the wife and kids patiently waiting for the man of the family to emerge, hitching up his pants.

The house of ill repute was shiny and clean, with expensive furnishings, a dance-floor, gambling room with crap tables, a large eat-in kitchen. Wentworth students were welcome—as long as they were not caught. The "day dodgers," the townies who attended the military academy, would help the barracks-dwellers by sneaking out their "civvies" and furnishing elaborate alibis.

The whorehouse in *McCabe and Mrs. Miller* was nothing like Helen's, says Dawson "Slick" Heathman, the town assessor of Lexington in 1986, and someone who remembered the atmosphere of Helen's. McCabe's was dirtier, languid and drug-ridden—very romanticized—highly entertaining; *McCabe* is one of "Slick"'s favorite Altman movies. But Helen's, "Slick" says, was clean, classy, full of goodwill, too good to be true.

In any case, Altman came of age at Wentworth Military Academy, and like most young men during World War II, he got as much education under his belt as possible before the age of eighteen, when he would either have to enlist or be drafted into the armed services. He elected to continue at

Wentworth through junior college, which emphasized pre-engineering, prelaw, prebusiness administration, pre-West Point and pre-Annapolis training.

Some of Altman's early publicity releases claim that he attended the University of Missouri in 1943 and somehow acquired a B.A. in (depending on which publicity form is consulted) journalism, architecture, or mathematical engineering. Mention of the extra stint at Wentworth is studiously avoided. This may have been a typical Altman (and typical Hollywood) attempt to touch up his resume. But it is an interesting touch-up, nonetheless.

In 1945, Altman quit Wentworth altogether and never spent another day in pursuit of higher learning. He enlisted in the Air Force and embraced the rather romantic notion of himself as a fighter pilot. He was only nineteen.

Chapter

4

WORLD
WAR II

As with so many young men coming of age during the 1940s, World War II proved a seminal experience for Altman.

In his film career, Altman has been drawn again and again to treatments of combat and military life, to examinations of soldier interaction and insubordination. He was instrumental in developing the conceptual framework and first season's episodes of *Combat*, still the grittiest war program ever shown on television. He directed *M*A*S*H*, that surreal, acid-etched comedy about the trauma of war (ostensibly about Korea but equally about World War II or Vietnam); *Streamers*, a corrosive, barracks stage drama adapted for the

Altman's B-24 crew on Morotai. Note the cavalier young officer's (Altman is second from left, front row) wristband and nonregulation slippers. (John Horoschak)

screen; and, for television, an adaptation of Herman Wouk's *The Caine Mutiny Court-Martial,* a bleak and world-weary view of high-seas exigencies.

Indeed, it may be that the director is never so powerful as when he is dealing with the subject of men in war, one of the few strands of his own somewhat untroubled early life that he has offered up to film audiences. The "cavalier" attitude Altman displayed as a young officer is carried over into the skepticism and cynicism of the film and television work that dissects the military code.

While such a "cavalier" attitude was not unknown in the army during World War II, it may have been engendered, in Altman's case, by an initial disappointment in his assignment. Ever since the white-silk-scarf days of the First World War, being a fighter pilot had been something to be—dan-

gerous and glorious. Altman, like so many fledgling pilots of
the Army Air Force, yearned to be tapped for the job. Probably because there was a greater need for bomber pilots at this
juncture of the war, the young Kansas Citian was designated
instead as MOS (Military Occupation Specialty) 1051—a
B-24 copilot, which, in that wartime atmosphere of danger
and risk, was considered, at least by some fighter pilots, to be
almost a truck-driving job of delivering the goods.

The war brought Altman for "phase training"—three in-
tensive months during which young men learn to work together as a bomber crew—to March Field, near Riverside,
California, where, as important to him as the military milieu, he was introduced to the social whirl of Hollywood. His
eyes were opened, for the first time, to a world outside of the
Altmans and Kansas City; and he was shaped by the desire to
understand and possess it.

The family—mother, father, and sisters—moved to Los
Angeles to be in close proximity to Altman. B.C. took up
duties as a meat contractor for the American Meat Company, trading on his private club associations to establish accounts for specialty cuts. Joan and Barbara, still teenagers,
transferred to high schools in the Los Angeles area.

Altman's fellow crew members recall him as being smit-
ten by Hollywood, by the electric wartime atmosphere, by
the gala previews, by the publicity in the fan magazines that
trumpeted each celebrity's call to colors, by the bond rallies,
by the endless party scene, and by the rubbernecking at the
Hollywood Canteen in a refurbished barn on Cahuenga Boulevard.

When orders came to go overseas in the winter of 1945, the
Altmans threw a memorable party at Aunt Pauline's. Pauline
Walsh was still on the ambivalent fringe of show business,
living in Beverly Hills. Her songwriting was developing, and
she had a couple of minor hits, including "My Songs Are for
You" and "Polka Dot." Although she occasionally contributed music to the sound tracks of motion pictures, basically
she was just a dabbling Altman; and though she was a mem-

ber of ASCAP and came to be listed in *Who's Who Among American Women*, she never pushed herself or her aptitude very hard.

The members of Altman's flight crew will never forget her hostessing of that splendid farewell party. To them, Altman seemed well set up in life, with a seemingly wealthy businessman for a father. The unmarried enlisted men were chauffeured about by B.C. in a Cadillac convertible. Pauline's mansion boasted a swimming pool and separate accommodations for the singles and the marrieds. All of the cigarette boxes had cigarettes in them! There was a huge sand-filled practice bomb on the piano that had been emptied out so that members of the training crew could sign their names on it with paint and a brush. There was a three-piece orchestra in the living room, servants to handle the catering, and formally dressed UCLA coeds as dance partners. (Altman insisted to the others that his date later in the weekend was to be the actress Bonita Granville, who played girl-detective Nancy Drew in the movies. "Really?" said Pauline Walsh, when apprised of this recently, "What an imagination!")

The morning after the party, Aunt Pauline dismissed the servants and made a point of serving the crew members breakfast herself. It was a very heartwarming send-off.

From Hamilton Field just north of San Francisco, in March of 1945, the crew flew a brand-new B-24 to Biak, New Guinea. From Biak they were ferried in a C-47 to Nadzab in eastern New Guinea for advanced combat training, and later to the island of Morotai in the Dutch East Indies, where they were assigned to the 307th Bomb Group.

By 1945, the entire expanse of the South China Sea and the Asian coastline was covered by Allied bombers and submarines blocking the Japanese from shipping vitally needed oil, rubber, and other military commodities from the Southeast and Southwest Pacific to the homeland. General Douglas MacArthur's U.S. Sixth Army, supported primarily by the Fifth Air Force, had been given the job of completing the sweep of Luzon, and his U.S. Eighth Army, backed primarily by the Thirteenth Air Force and the Seventh Fleet, was expected to clear the Southern Philippines and the islands farther south. The Thirteenth Air Force were using Pitoe and Wama airstrips on Morotai as crucial cogs in this strategy.

During earlier days, Morotai had earned the reputation of being the most bombed-out American base in the Pacific. But by the time Altman's crew joined the 307th, in April of 1945, the newsmaking missions were over; the Japanese fighter planes were almost gone. Only the remoteness, the dangerous flights over great distances, and the weather (heavy rain alternating with blistering tropical sunshine) remained.

The mission targets at this stage of the war were oil storage, supply dumps, gun positions and defensive positions, airfield installations, personnel, and possible staging bases of Japanese aircraft. On twenty-odd missions, Altman was second-in-command, the copilot. The bombing was very impersonal, most targets all but indistinguishable from the heights.

There were no fatalities in Altman's crew, no serious injuries.

Altman had his one close call flying over Balikpapan. Anti-aircraft flak burst in through the window, wounding an aerial photographer, hitting Altman and tearing the sleeve off his uniform. The wound was superficial. One engine and the intercom were lost, and the plane limped back to base full of holes, with a Catalina escort.

The story his crew most savor about Altman is the time Altman's plane had to be ditched in the sea when he was coming back from New Guinea, where he had gone on a whiskey run for the Officer's Club. Altman, they say, was safely out of the plane before he remembered his cigarettes. So he turned and swam back inside the slowly sinking craft to retrieve them. This may be apocryphal, but it illustrates what his buddies all remember about Altman in his World War II days: He was someone who managed to have a good time and look out for himself no matter what the peril.

Though Altman started as a flight officer and ended as a

lieutenant, crew members remember he was always more individualistic than most officers and at odds with his senior pilot. Like "Hawkeye" and "Trapper John" in *M*A*S*H*, he saw himself as dedicated to, and highly skilled at, his assigned Army task, but unwilling to play by the rules. He preferred to fraternize with the enlisted men. He would remove his insignia in order to visit the island's NCO facility, which had the added attraction of Aussie enlisted women. He used to throw his cigarette butts on the ground and say with comic fierceness, "I'm not going to pick up my butts just because the Army says pick up your butts!"

Certainly he had more than one scam going. Altman and another crew member skimmed off supplies for night-long beach parties with the nurses from the Australian hospital unit. These were all-island affairs, and Altman and his pal seemed to have a monopoly on the nurses, who obviously furnished some inspiration for scenes in *M*A*S*H*.

"If we ever got on an island somewhere, if there were only five women, he'd get familiar with one of the women in just a couple of days," says John Horoschak, a crew member. "He was very personable and just loaded with sex appeal. Bob ran on very, very extensive social activity, and he was only bored if nothing was happening. But he seemed always able to find it, to dig it out."

Morotai, by June of 1945, was definitely more *M*A*S*H* than *Combat*. There were few Sgt. Saunders on the island, but there were a plethora of Hawkeyes, Dukes, and Trapper Johns. There was even a guy on their ground crew they had nicknamed "Radar" (hardly uncommon). There was plenty of booze and cigarettes and socializing. Come payday there were awesome poker games with chips, Australian pounds, Dutch guilders, Filipino pesos, and whiskey in the pot.

There were also occasional USO shows, GI-produced shows, and regular movies as well as newsreels. What with swapping films with the Australian field hospital, the Seabees, and the Navy boys, the Morotai flyers had a different film practically every night at dusk. It relieved the monotony and stoked the home fires. Crowds of servicemen gathered

The outdoor movie screen on Morotai. (James M. Kendall)

on the ground and bunched on boards set on sections of co-
conut logs erected in concentric 90-degree areas in front of a
huge outdoor movie screen hanging from the top of a covered
stage. It was a good idea to grab your poncho, as it rained
several nights a week.

There were daily athletic activities (softball games between the pilots/co-pilots and the bombardiers/navigators
were always a big attraction), a good library (one could take
correspondence courses), and plenty of fishing and swimming. Even so, Altman has said that he grew bored on Morotai and began to write short stories and blackout sketches
and long rambling letters.

"I started writing letters to people I didn't know well.
When I wrote to my parents and to close friends, I was nearly
inarticulate," he once told *The New York Times.* "But I
found that I could fantasize to near strangers."

Altman's old school friend, Robert Woodburn, was living
in New York just before entering the Navy. Woodburn was
acting a small role on Broadway and stage-managing Sally
Benson's *Junior Miss,* directed by Moss Hart. Though Woodburn had known Altman since grade school, Altman was not
a close friend; and Woodburn was surprised to hear from

him. When Altman expressed a desire to come to New York and write plays and work in the theatre, it was the first time Woodburn became aware that his boyhood acquaintance was so inclined.

"He wrote good letters," says Woodburn.

Some Hollywood people were transformed by World War II—particularly those sensitive Hollywood people who saw their world of fantasy and idealism turned upside down by the horror and devastation. People like George Stevens (director of such farces as *Woman of the Year*), who led military cameramen into the Dachau death camp and later said that because of the experience he could never quite *believe* in filming another frivolous comedy. Or like James Stewart, a gangly, rib-tickling male ingenue who found himself flying combat missions in Europe. Stewart's real-life experience transformed him, credibly, into a mature leading man-who-knew-too-much, for Alfred Hitchcock; sundry neurotic gunslingers, for director Anthony Mann; and a guy who tries to commit suicide on Christmas Eve, for Frank Capra.

Altman seems to have come through World War II without much psychological scarring. His own experience was low-key. When he first sought a form to convey his World War II adventures, he tried to option James Michener's novel *Tales of the South Pacific*, which takes place in the earlier critical days of war in the Pacific. In the end, the partylike *M*A*S*H* may be the most autobiographical of his combat zone depictions.

Although embellished by Altman's imagination, *M*A*S*H* and the other films were also highly dependent on the writers. It is hard to say how much of the re-creation of war and of wartime dynamics springs directly from Altman's own experiences. With Altman, a compulsive self-dramatist, even his close friends have never been sure where the facts left off and the fiction began.

"He regretted one thing [about World War II]," says Brian McKay. "He told me if the mission was aborted, or if they had bombs left over, they'd drop them on farmhouses on the way back. His moments of complete ingenuousness were rare and I paid attention to him. That was something he was really sorry about. But that could have been bullshit too, because he is a spellbinder, the rarest of storytellers."

Before going overseas, Altman had met another Midwesterner, LaVonne Elmer, whom he described uncharitably in one interview as "the last person I met before World War II" and consequently the first person he married afterward.

An ethereal blonde, LaVonne was working for Pacific Telephone and Telegraph in northern California when she met Altman, then stationed in Salinas, on his last furlough before going overseas. She recalls him as a "party boy," aggressive and friendly, with a ton of personality. She is one of the people he wrote letters to from Morotai, very amusing letters, with poetry and anecdotes about the pilots, illustrated with funny little Walt Disney-type cartoon characters. The letters were always about other people, not about himself, with observations of island life but not much indication of his own feelings or concerns. Altman kept a photo of LaVonne in the clear-plastic Plexiglas handle of his .45.

LaVonne was home, in Fremont, Nebraska, visiting her mother and father, when Altman returned from the war. He besieged her with phone calls, and B.C. and Helen sent her the Christmas gift of a vacation trip to California. She stayed with the family in Westwood Village, across from what was then the public golf course. She and Altman made the party rounds—including one especially extravagant party, she remembers, celebrating the crowning of California beauty queen Marilyn Buferd as Miss America of 1946. Altman always seemed to have a fistful of party invitations.

LaVonne had returned to Nebraska, to think things over, when Altman called from the Omaha airport and materialized to meet her family. He was on his way to attend a Wentworth reunion in Kansas City. She was inveigled to go along with him, and to stay with his grandmother Nettie Bolt Altman at the Sophien Plaza. The night of the reunion, they picked up two other couples and went to the festivities across the state line in Kansas. Afterward, coming back, the young man who was driving hit a Greyhound bus. Altman was the only one in the car able to walk away from the dreadful accident.

LaVonne suffered broken jaws and cheekbones besides trauma and shock. She had to stay in a Kansas City hospital for three weeks and have her jaws wired, beyond which was scheduled at least three months of reconstructive dental surgery. Family lore has it that, in the meantime, B.C. talked Altman into marrying the sweet-natured LaVonne. But LaVonne says that when they realized how long she was going to have to stay in Kansas City, Altman offered a proposition: "Either we're going to live in sin, or we're going to get married. . . ."

They were married the day she was released from the hospital, a small Catholic ceremony, with B.C. and all the aunts and uncles in attendance. LaVonne had her jaw wired together during the exchange of vows, a scene not unlike the one in *A Wedding* where the bride (Amy Stryker) wears those god-awful braces. The one thing people remember about LaVonne at the wedding is that sugary smile through clenched teeth. That was in June 1946, and Altman was already representing himself on the marriage certificate as being a resident of Los Angeles.

After LaVonne's recovery, she and Altman returned from Kansas City to California, where the immediate family still resided, and where lay the excitement and come-on of Los Angeles.

At first, Altman was in the mood to try anything. He tried selling insurance for Kansas City Life. He tried working under B.C. at American Meat Company. He had a spot with Southern California Edison as their representative in Mexico trying to persuade the government to invest in a big power plant there. LaVonne could not keep up with what he was trying next. "He was searching," says LaVonne. "Inwardly, he knew he was going to be more creative. He needed lots of experiences. Maybe it was for stories for the future."

He was still roving, basking in the prospects, enjoying the postwar glow of Hollywood, and doing his best to avoid a retreat to Kansas City and what he increasingly perceived as its vapid Babbittism. He had a tireless personality and a loose zipper, and he was good at circulating. He had a gift for talking his way into mixers and gambling sessions and star-studded events. Gradually, Altman decided he wanted to do something in movies. He was not quite sure what, but *something.*

Altman says himself, in interviews, that he had begun to view motion pictures differently. It was not until Altman saw such postwar films as British director David Lean's *Brief Encounter* and Italian director Vittorio de Sica's neorealist masterpiece *The Bicycle Thief* that he first became aware of an intelligence behind the camera. "I never imagined they were directed," he has said. "I just thought they happened."

The ex-flyer was young, tall, and good-looking, and people who encountered him on Hollywood Boulevard mistook him for the actor Robert Hutton. Altman flirted with the idea of being an actor. He met an agent who wangled him a short-term contract at Fox, mostly based on his looks. Shortly, Altman appeared, on loan-out, among the extras in the background of at least one Danny Kaye movie. He was a big Danny Kaye fan; Kaye's shtick was exactly Altman's idea of funny. And there, in the background of a nightclub scene in *The Secret Life of Walter Mitty,* is Altman, grinning and smoking a cigarette and looking dead-on into the camera.

He could not get anywhere as an actor. His voice was too high-pitched, too twangy. But it was an ambition that nagged. Much later, when Altman returned to Kansas City, he had the notion he might become a special-events announcer at KNBC, the local network radio affiliate. When he auditioned for the position, they laughed him out of the building because of his voice.

Perhaps under the influence of Aunt Pauline, Altman began to think of himself as a budding songwriter. He was introduced to a struggling nightclub performer, pianist, composer, and vocal coach by the name of Robert Ecton, who played around town and on albums, including some that featured Pauline Walsh's material. Through Aunt Pauline, Altman also met James Rickard, a knockabout writer ten years older than Altman, who had won an MGM talent contest fresh out of UCLA law school in the early 1930s. Their relationship was cemented on the golf course, where the Altmans spent a considerable amount of time.

A witty, likable, self-effacing writer, Rickard had worked as a story analyst, script doctor, and story editor in the studio system. He had done some minor screenwriting prior to World War II. He had also worked on radio shows for his brother-in-law, song-and-dance-man Ray Bolger, who played the scarecrow in *The Wizard of Oz*. After a fling in the publicity mill, Rickard was stalled in his career and ripe for a collaborator.

Altman proved congenial. He wanted to do anything Rickard wanted to do—radio plays, Broadway plays, publicity, whatever. So they began to write together, with Rickard doing most of the actual writing. How much they wrote is unclear—in interviews Altman claims unpublished novels, magazine pieces, one-act plays, and radio credits during this period. In any event, they did make headway on a musical comedy intended for Broadway, called *The Rumors Are Flying*.

It was supposed to be a frothy Broadway musical satirizing the life of inventor and philanthropist Atwater Kent, a fabulous partygoer of the era, who delighted in seeing his name in print; and it showed an early, lightweight fixation on pop celebrityhood that Altman brought to fruition in films ranging from *The James Dean Story* and *Come Back to the Five and Dime, Jimmy Dean, Jimmy Dean* to *Nashville* and *Health*. Rickard wrote the book, Ecton the score, Altman the lyrics. Among the tunes was a rhymey one poking fun at Louella Parsons's column, called "Lolly Hasn't Mentioned Me in Weeks."

Ecton remembers no one had any illusions about actually selling the thing; the experience of writing it was sheer fun. The songs eventually went into Ecton's lockbox. Some thirty years later, Ecton was surprised to be telephoned by Altman to see if the songs still existed for consideration for use in *Nashville*. They did, but Altman opted to hold off until *Health*, where he resuscitated a song he cowrote in his salad days in Hollywood, called "Let's Begin Again." (Ecton was invited to the usual V.I.P. screening of *Health* at Lion's Gate, and afterward was pained by the cruel twist in Altman's remark to him, "I hope you're satisfied, at least you got a song in the picture.")

At intervals, Rickard and Altman would embark for New York City and live there for several months, where their Broadway musical made the rounds, puttered, and stalled, and where they pursued other pipedreams. Ray Bolger was in a radio series, and Rickard could find work; it is unclear whether Altman did much, if any, credited radio writing. He has said he wrote continuity for a recipe program. "I'd look up a recipe and write out a script for, uh, Dick Smith and Mary Marbles, somebody. 'What have you got for the folks today, Mary?' 'Well, Dick, I was thinking about meatloaf.' 'Oh, that's my favorite because I love meatloaf sandwiches.'"

During one of Altman's absences LaVonne returned to Fremont with their daughter, Christine, who had been born in 1947. Not that Altman was a negligent father. "He bathed her, he diapered her, I don't think there was a bar in Los Angeles she wasn't sitting on top of and probably wetting," LaVonne says. "He was so proud of her."

But they were always living "between stories," she felt. They never had a place of their own. They always resided with B.C. and Helen. Their marriage was strained by Altman's lifestyle and by his frequent prolonged absences. "It was a lifestyle I didn't feel I was capable of supporting," she says. "It was a survival system for him—it helped make him what he is—either you lived it or you got out."

By now, Altman was beginning to see a future for himself as a writer. At one point, Altman's mother and father took up residence in Malibu, where they had a tenant in another part of the house by the name of George W. George. That is how Altman met his first important show business contact, strictly by chance, and how, after he returned to Los Angeles from one of his many New York excursions, he achieved his first Hollywood screen credit.

George was a fellow with an inside track. The son of the famous *New Yorker* cartoonist Rube Goldberg, he was also the nephew of contract director Edward L. Marin, for whom he was presently working as an assistant director. In George, Altman found his legitimate entree into film circles. In Altman, George found an indefatigable junior partner eager to avail himself of George's expertise and connections. They collaborated on at least one screen story that was purchased and filmed, while George provided the stepping-stone to Altman's involvement on another.

Bodyguard (1947) was based on an "unpublished story" ascribed to George and Altman (with George billed first). It is a typical-of-the-period *film noir* about a tough, honest cop (Lawrence Tierney), suspended from the force, who is hired as a bodyguard for a corporation executive. Though it is relatively undistinguished as filmed by director Richard Fleischer, you can detect Altman's touches in the high society milieu, the family tensions that trigger the action, and the subplot about a crooked meat-packing skim-off that draws on the Altman family's Kansas City slaughterhouse know-how.

Altman also managed to finagle an off-screen story credit for *Christmas Eve* in 1948. He told pals that he caught wind of the fact that independent producer Benedict Bogeaus wanted his latest film to have a Yuletide theme. An army of studio writers had failed to satisfy Bogeaus in this regard. After talking his way past the boss's secretary, Altman pitched a vague storyline in which the first shot would linger on the ornament of a Christmas tree before pulling back to begin the narrative, which otherwise had very little to do with the holiday season. Thus, Bogeaus was appeased, and Altman's contribution secured. (It may have helped that the director was George W. George's uncle, Edward L. Marin.)

Though Altman offered to help develop the actual screenplay for free, his involvement ceased. *Christmas Eve*—a crime melodrama—turned out to be standard fare, albeit intriguing for its family-centered plot, another of so many Altman movies to be preoccupied with simmering blood tensions.

Two screenplay credits. You would think Altman had it made. But in the late Forties, Hollywood was coming apart at the seams, and for the first time in twenty years there was a surfeit of writers for a dearth of films. As Otto Friedrich observes in *City of Nets* (Harper & Row, 1986), a sociopolitical history of Hollywood in the 1940s that draws on some five hundred other books for its amalgamated narrative, the film studios had begun the decade as "conquering heroes," but by the end of the Forties Hollywood was "in a shambles, its biggest studios losing money, its celebrities embroiled in charges of Communist influence, its audiences turning to television." It was the worst possible time for newcomers.

"He's about to buy the house on the hill," says Robert Woodburn, "but he can't get any kind of work. He's playing gin with everybody, he knows everybody, but he can't get any work."

B.C. had money to invest, and the Altmans always seemed to have plenty of by-the-by ideas. At one point Pauline Walsh conceived the idea of a "Play-a-Tune" organ, which Altman took up with a passion. They had plans to market it together (with B.C.'s investment), and they actually demonstrated it on the local television variety program, *The Betty White Show*. But another organ company came along and beat them to the patent.

For another unlikely enterprise, Altman again turned to Rickard, this time teaming up for the momentary brainstorm of dog tattooing. It seems Altman had made the acquaintance, probably on the golf course, of a person by the name of H. Graham Connar, or Captain Connar. Captain Connar had an idea for making money with a dog-tattooing process that stamped state and county license numbers inside the upper

Altman, as an extra, in the background of a
scene from *The Secret Life of Walter Mitty* with
Danny Kaye, whom he admired, at right. (Frame
enlargement)

right front leg of dogs. All Captain Connar needed was additional financing and press agentry. B.C. was persuaded to
come up with some money, and Altman seemed capable of
generating steam for practically anything.

Between B.C. and Captain Connar, a lot of money was invested in this Identi-Code numbering system. Altman and
Rickard began to travel around the country, publicizing their
stopovers in New York and Washington, D.C., where Altman called in his Missouri contacts. Of all things, he tat-
tooed President Truman's dog while Truman was still in the
White House. He and Rickard were applying for a patent and
lobbying for publicity and "on the verge of being bought out
by National Dog Week—which is a corporation owned by
four major dog-food companies," according to Altman's recollection in one interview, "when we went broke."

For some time, Altman had been moving freely between
Kansas City, Los Angeles, and New York City. But now he
was broke again, and he must have realized he was going

nowhere fast. In California, he had a backlog of debts. In Fremont, Nebraska, he had, dependent on his support, a wife who had separated from him, and an infant daughter.

Movies had rejected him, yet Altman was sanguine, neither disillusioned nor crushed. He told himself it was only a temporary setback. Hollywood could be put on the back burner.

In the meantime the Altman family had returned to Kansas City and the siren call (for B.C.) of the insurance field. So now Altman went back to Kansas City too, with a sheaf of stories and scripts under his arm. He went back, pretending to be flush. Maybe the dog-tattooing future would somehow work out. Otherwise, he had no idea what he was going to do next.

PART
3

"It is not just the life that we know. It is not just the life that has been successfully hidden. It is not just the lies about the life, some of which cannot now be disbelieved. It is also the life that was not led."

—*Julian Barnes,*
Flaubert's Parrot

Chapter
5

THE CALVIN COMPANY

"It was the greatest training ground in the world for a motion picture director," says Frank Barhydt, head of production at the Calvin Company for twenty-five years. "After this Calvin course of training, if you will, there's not much you don't know about making motion pictures. It's a huge advantage. Bob has said everything he ever learned he learned at Calvin—or I taught him. He was undoubtedly drunk at the time, but there's a lot of truth in that. I've never seen anything he's done—*anything*—that you can't find the seeds at Calvin."

In 1986, Frank Barhydt was seventy years old and still residing in Kansas City proper.

The Calvin building, Fifteenth and Troost, built
by Altman's grandfather, Frank G. Altman Sr.

Unlike Robert Altman, he had never left. Barhydt had
worked at the Calvin Company for nearly thirty years, had
been head of production there for twenty-five of those thirty
years, before retiring in 1972. The Calvin organization had
come under new management in the mid-1950s, and business had begun to decline thereafter.

By the late Sixties, the production staff had been cut drastically. Studios in Louisville, Pittsburgh, and Detroit were
sold. Longtime accounts drifted away. Finally, there was
only the Calvin operations in Kansas City, where it had all
begun, and in the 1980s the company formally dissolved.
The seven-story building built by Robert Altman's grandfather at the corner of Truman and Troost stood empty and
shimmering. There were newspapers and empty paper cups

next to the editing machines, as if people had gotten up and left for a cigarette break.

Barhydt was phlegmatic. Back in 1942, he had given up a promising career in broadcasting and journalism to devote himself to work at Calvin. There he was seduced by the steady income for twenty-nine years. He was beguiled by a business "where, for the first time, you could see what you'd done and keep looking at it." He must have supervised the making of several hundred nuts-and-bolts films. He had two or three in his closet left over from being loaned for screening to his daughter's high-school classes. Nothing else. Not a still photo of a Calvin production or one of those national awards, framed, anywhere in the house. Didn't even know where all those thousands of films were stored, nowadays.

"Don't know why anybody would be interested in those films anyway," says Barhydt. "They are dull enough to halt a herd of charging rhinos."

At Calvin, Robert Altman met Frank Barhydt and learned from him and others, including a guy by the name of Larry Sherwood, who was one of the knowledgeable Calvin elders, the language, the fundamentals, the psychology of making movies.

What's the camera doing? Watching the action. Long shot, medium shot, close-up. How to advance the story. How to point the camera from A to B.

Simple logic. Yet it had to be learned before it could be discarded and improved upon. There were no film schools after World War II, as there are such a glut of in the present day. Or, if there were, they did not have the same cachet as USC or UCLA or NYU today. And the folks at Calvin had precisely zero cachet on Hollywood's terms, for they were making industrial movies strictly for the money. Strictly for information purposes. What entertainment value they contained served to sugar-coat the message.

Still and all, they were good little movies.

"Those were good days," even Barhydt has to admit. The Calvin filmmakers were young, enthusiastic. There was es-

Calvin production head Frank Baryhdt, who helped teach Altman the ABCs of filmmaking, circa 1953. (Frank Baryhydt)

prit d'corps. They were all violent liberals. "Bob [Altman] hasn't changed that much," says Barhydt. "He's still a violent liberal. I've changed, though. I've gone completely in the opposite direction.

"Do you know my son? He wrote a couple of films with Bob. *Quintet* was one. Did you see it? One of the damndest things I ever saw—didn't make any sense to me."

Barhydt's son Frank, a co-screenwriter of *Health* as well as *Quintet*, and an actor in *Tanner '88*, is one of many young people who found in Altman their cinema grandee as Altman's mystique grew in the latter half of the 1970s. More than once young Barhydt quoted to his father Altman's maxim that a filmmaker should be making films for himself first, and audiences second. "Stupidest thing I ever heard of," says Barhydt, this gentleman who spent his life in service to movies with corporate sponsors and utterly functional messages.

Is it not strange how Frank Barhydt and Robert Altman, two old Calvin hands, physically resemble each other?

Until you visit Kansas City you might think that no one in the world could possibly look much like Robert Altman, a man whose imposing visage has been compared to everyone from "a frenetic latter-day Papa Hemingway" (Frank Rich in *The Guardian*) to a "prairie Buddha" *(The Los Angeles Times)* to a "benevolent Captain Bligh" *(Playboy)* to "a cross between Santa Claus and Mephistopheles" *(Newsweek)* to "an overweight Toscanini" *(Rolling Stone)* to "Burl Ives" (a Kansas City waitress).

Until you meet Frank Barhydt. Barhydt, who, in his seventies, had grown a very familiar, silvery Vandyke beard. Barhydt, whose face, though leaner, bonier, was yet uncannily evocative of Altman's. Barhydt, whose voice was pure Missouri inflection, just like Altman's. Had Barhydt grown to resemble his old friend?

"Maybe vice versa," says Barhydt, after a pause, unflattered.

"I think when two people work together for a long time they might grow to look alike," he muses.

Along with Jam-Handy, Wilding, and others, Calvin was one of the major industrial film companies in the United States. For nearly half a century it dominated the field in terms of quantity as well as quality. Calvin handled many accounts of the Fortune 500—such companies as Du Pont, Goodyear, Caterpillar, and General Mills. It pioneered the use of 16mm sound technology, of new Kodak processing methods, and of 8mm film. It won more than its share of accolades at trade festivals. It held nationwide sales and training seminars that attracted a who's who of business. Whatever paid, it made—government films, commercials, educationals, industrials, documentaries, and every variety of short subject. It was as good a hothouse for a green tomato of a film director as you could hope for in the middle of the Midwest.

It happened to be headquartered in Kansas City because a married couple with energy and enterprise, F. O. Calvin and Betty Calvin, were residents there, and operating an advertising agency during the time America was mucking its way through the Depression and American movies were just beginning to talk.

Betty Calvin managed the business side; F. O. Calvin was the salesman. Together they had the idea of investing in the future of 16mm films as an in-house advertising and promotional tool. The third member of the Calvin leadership was Lloyd Thompson, F. O. Calvin's onetime University of Kansas City fraternity brother, and a graduate, as so many of the Calvin higher-ups were, in journalism. Thompson and the Calvins raised the capital and in 1931 began production on a modest scale, taking advantage of Kansas City's proximity to locations, industry, and commerce. They were good at selling the Calvin concept, and they signed up accounts that would stay with the company for three decades.

They took other people's bad, amateurish films and fixed them up so they were serviceable. They made their own movies from scratch—short, inexpensive ones in the studio as well as long, big-budget ones on location in other time zones. They went further: They held entrepreneurial conferences and gave advice on how to use the 16mm medium. They also began to manufacture some equipment and boasted an excellent processing laboratory.

World War II proved a gold mine for the Calvin company. F. O. Calvin was a dollar-a-year man for the Navy in Washington, D.C., where he advised on the running of a filmmaking system similar to the Calvin Company's. The Navy wanted Calvin to move his operations to D.C., but F.O. resisted, and the Calvin personnel remained in Kansas City. In effect, Calvin became a military subcontractor, turning out Navy training films, such as informational ones about boiler-

Altman (halfway up crane) directing, on-location in the Southwest, one of the *Better Football* training films for the nation's high-school teams. (Arthur Goodell)

room operations on battleships, maintenance of submarine engines, or the handling of PT boats. This proved extremely lucrative for the company at the same time as it built up contacts, prestige, and goodwill for business after the armistice.

By the time Altman came to the company, the Calvin firm was a fixture in Kansas City and known as a brand name of merit across the country. And the business of making films for businesses was booming. "Calvin turns out 18 million feet of film a year, or enough to make one 16-millimeter strip stretching from Key West to Seattle and part way back," reported one contemporary local newspaper.

The Calvin building was an impressive one. The old New Center Building at Fifteenth and Troost, just east of downtown, had been erected by Frank G. Altman Sr. back in 1907. Frank Sr. had made the mistake of presuming the downtown would spread eastward, which it never did. Consequently, it was one of the few high-rises in the area with plenty of space for a regular staff of two hundred. Altman, after floundering in Los Angeles, could feel right at home on premises annointed by the family name.

The first floor held a magnificent sound stage, 80 by 120 feet with a 30-foot ceiling, converted from the former New Center theatre. The second floor held offices for directors and writers, plus a recording studio. The third and fourth floors were given over to the craft departments—the laboratory, processing, which accounted for at least half of Calvins' income, and printing. The fifth floor held the executive offices. Sixth floor was animation. Seventh floor was the Movie-Mite Corp, a subsidiary that manufactured motion-picture projectors and other equipment.

Robert Woodburn was already working on the premises. He was back in Kansas City, visiting, when someone told him about the Calvin Company. Woodburn had been thinking about concentrating on movies instead of Broadway, so the timing was right. He faked a resume, so the folks at Calvin would think he was almost thirty (he was only twenty-two) and that he had had experience writing advertising scripts for the J. Walter Thompson Agency in New York City. When he was hired, he immediately went to the how-to books. The next thing Woodburn knew, the phone rang, and it was Altman, who was also back in town.

Altman was "nothing if not a con man" back then, as ever, says Woodburn. Altman called Woodburn over to an office where he was fronting the dog-tattooing business with some broad as his supposed secretary. When it got right down to it,

Altman did not have a job, but he had heard about the Calvin setup. Would Woodburn help him get a foot in the door?

Sometimes, whatever fate deals you makes all the sense in the world. That is the moral of many an Altman film, and the basis of much that has happened in his own life. Here fate was dealing Calvin—the perfect outfit for someone hungering to make movies but locked out of Hollywood—a guy who had ideas and capabilities but no credentials. Calvin offered training, obscurity, freedom, a paycheck, and the sort of bargain-basement alternative to established ways and means that Altman, in his career, has wisely looked on the bright side of and adopted as an ethic.

Industrials already had a rich and vital history. Caravel Films of New York was in business with a feature-length sales and training film on the Hoover vacuum cleaner way back in 1921. The association of industrial filmmakers had its own awards, film festivals, merit organizations, magazines, judges, and critics. Occasionally, featured Hollywood players picked up a little extra money doing narration or "billed" character spots. At the national conventions, the little "Oscars" were handed out by such guests of honor as Gloria Swanson and Myrna Loy.

On Woodburn's recommendation, Altman was brought in for an interview, and he pestered Barhydt enough to be hired. "He knew nothing," says Barhydt. "He said so. You could tell."

He was hired, *not* as a director—Altman was just an ordinary, good-looking, youthful vet as far as the Calvin Company was concerned—and he started out on the service end, driving the generator truck and handling new accounts. But like his father, he was full of demon energy and wisecracks. He did not go home at night, he hung around the camera and story departments, ingratiating himself and making a nuisance of himself. Within six months, he was elevated to a director's slot.

Even at that, it was no big deal. Directors occupied only a slightly superior position in the Calvin universe. Their field was industrials, after all—selling a higher grade motor oil, touting a new model refrigerator—films that would be shown by a manufacturer to his sales crews, and by salesmen to retailers.

At any given time, there were four or five directors at Calvin, usually operating with the same number of rotating camera crews. The subjects were doled out largely according to who was available, or who had handled the account previously. Several titles would be in the process of being filmed simultaneously—on the studio sound stage or outdoors. And sometimes, even while a director was working on his own project, he would be doing inserts or narration for someone else's film.

Whenever a director was working on a film to be developed entirely by Calvin, he was usually writing the script too. That way, figured Barhydt, who organized the system, a director would not write something he could not film, and in the long run there would have to be adherence to the dollars and cents.

Budget was always a primary concern. In those days, in the 1950s, it cost Calvin about twelve hundred dollars to produce each finished minute of film. The films were usually twenty to twenty-five minutes in length, and production could take anywhere from six weeks to six months. A large firm might order as many as three or four hundred prints for distribution.

According to Barhydt, a director might be involved in ten or twelve separate films in a year—adding up, perhaps, to some sixty productions Altman worked on during the roughly five to six years he was associated with Calvin, or roughly the equivalent of ten feature films. There is no precise accounting. The records are in dusty vaults, and because credits take up time and money on the screen, and the clients did not always want to pay for them, credits were not always formalized on the screen.

It was quite a place, Calvin. The longtime Calvin hands— and there were many who worked there from the beginning straight through to the bitter end—remember it as a happy place. Hours, especially for the creative people, were flexible, as long as deadlines were met. There were company picnics and annual Christmas parties at the Calvins' house. On payday the employees would flock to the Cork 'n' Bottle pub and bet their paychecks on shuffleboard bowling.

It was like a surrogate family. There was camaraderie, profit sharing, access to top management, promotion from within, encouragement of initiative. Unlike other companies that made industrial films, at Calvin a union was voted out several times because people were fundamentally satisfied. People were well paid, and by annual salary rather than piecework, which made a difference. There was always plenty of work, and while the Calvins were around, goodwill.

Some were there just for the salary. Others, like Barhydt, reared in journalism or an allied profession, found themselves intrigued by documentaries. Never for a moment did they consider leaving Kansas City and the Calvin Company. Still others, like Altman, worked with one eye cocked on Hollywood. And even those who never escaped Kansas City watched the new Hollywood movies and in their own way tried to ape the latest tricks and techniques. They regarded themselves as professional filmmakers and thought of themselves as being involved in a minor-league Golden Age.

"It was as exciting as the days of D. W. Griffith and Billy Bitzer," says Charley Paddock, one of Altman's regular Kansas City cameramen. "I went to the movies and would see what had been done and then, because I would have access to the Calvin facilities, I would go and recreate the lighting and techniques and camera movement and front projection and rear projection and all that. I can't imagine any other industry would be more interesting than what we were doing."

In Kansas City, these industrial films of Calvin added an aura of make-believe to peoples' ordinary lives. It was not really glamorous work—but it was part of the local cultural hub of people who did their best, being stuck in the Midwest, to live and breathe the performing arts.

For them as for Altman, it was not just the money. It was

the performing and the show-business feeling, and the small-pond filmmaking that might lead to something bigger and better.

All the local theatre people performed in the Calvin films again and again; the same faces appeared in thousands of Calvin reels shipped to corporate offices all over the world. These same people also dominated Kansas City's radio waves, television channels, and civic theatre presentations. Every U.S. city has its Arthur Ellisons, its Jim Lantzs, its Leonard Beloves, who are clasped to the bosom of local theatregoers. But people in Kansas City believe the group of that generation was really something special. This group was given flashes of immortality not only by the occasional theatrical motion-picture unit passing through Missouri for verisimilitude—hey, that's Art Ellison in *Paper Moon!*—but by their presence in these Calvin films. In a sense, these Kansas Citians were Altman's first stock company, though of course they were more than that; broadly speaking, they were Calvin's.*

The Calvin company could also call on local notables or public figures with Missouri ties. Harry Truman, President of the United States from 1945 to 1952, is glimpsed in more than one Calvin production, and since he was accessible at least part of the time in nearby Independence, most of the crews filmed him at least once. He was spoken of as if he were an affable next-door neighbor. Truman made the idea of the Presidency human and foibled, and spurred Altman's fascination with the top job in films as disparate as *Nashville*, *Health*, *Secret Honor*, and *Tanner '88*.

Barhydt's old-school ties included former Kansas City radio and newspaper colleagues Walter Cronkite, John Cameron Swayze, Howard K. Smith, and Chet Huntley—all of

---

*Many of the Kansas Citians followed or preceded Altman to Hollywood, and they crop up over and over in bit parts in Altman's television episodes and films. They are not particularly well known to the public, but for many years they were part of Altman's extended "family": radio broadcaster turned actor Richard Peabody, ingenue Diane Brewster, Susan (Kiger) Davis (who has made a specialty of playing suburban moms), Owen Bush (the laconic character actor), Al Christy (an ex–Kansas City insurance man), among others.

these big network news names did occasional Calvin moon-
lighting. Bob Considine, the World War II broadcaster who
was an uncle of actor John Considine, was another journalist
who appeared as on-camera narrator in more than one Calvin
production directed by Altman.

The Hollywood actors and actresses brought to Kansas
City for a week of character chores were not the illustrious
stars of the profession, but they were well paid and much
appreciated. William Frawley was one, used more than once,
and he became Altman's contact, later on, with Desilu television. John Carradine, lean, lantern-jawed father of the Carradine clan, including actor Keith Carradine, was another.
Altman's generational link with the Considines and the Car-
radines origated, thusly, miles and years away from Hollywood.

One suspects that the director has searched all of his life
for a substitute for the idealized family of his boyhood. At
Calvin, Altman found in a small circle of friends and associates the first professional expression of this deep-seated need.

A Calvin crew filming President Harry Truman
in nearby Independence, Missouri. (Arthur
Goodell)

*   *   *

Two or three times Altman was fired by Barhydt and/or quit after demanding more money and/or quarreling about the way to film something and/or alienating a client and/or screwing up. Altman would curse the dullness of industrial films, stalk out, then slink back sheepishly the next day to reclaim his job. He was considered a "wild man," a "problem child," a "swinger" before the term was coined. But he certainly did get the job done.

"Bob was a character unto himself, and I've never known anybody quite like him," says Barhydt. "But at the same time he wasn't a madman. He was an average, ordinary, young Air Force guy out of the service trying to make a living and screw all the girls he could find—and he was fairly successful at it. But his love was pictures and trying to succeed.

"If you were his boss, you put up with an awful lot, because, well, you *liked* the guy, and he did have enormous talent," says Barhydt.

Twice Altman left to knock on doors in Hollywood. He would vanish overnight from Calvin, then return months later, broke and deflated, to resume his former responsibilities with barely a whimper.

Once, Altman left with the idea of selling his treatment for a prescient comedy about UFOs that he had conceived with James Stewart in mind for the lead role. Nothing came of it. When Altman came back to Calvin, Barhydt stole the title of his James Stewart script and stuck it on one of the more innocuous industrials in production. Then Barhydt let the title drop in a staff meeting. "God, he just turned red," recalls Woodburn. "Bob was amazed, just furious. Then he started to laugh."

The second time Altman went out to Hollywood, Louis Lombardo and his family went along with Altman and Lotus Corelli, by then Altman's second wife. Lombardo was a young Calvin gaffer and gofer from the Italian neighborhood, who was several years Altman's junior. Altman told Lombardo he had some big television deal worked up as a sure thing. Instead he ended up doing some spots for The National Catholic Bishop's Fund. But there was some problem about getting paid, and Altman's money ran out. When Altman left, Lombardo stayed on—going to work at a Los Angeles blueprint shop as a Photostat operator.

This time, when Altman came back, he made the vow to a Calvin staff meeting they all remember: "If I come back one more time, you get to keep me."

"Directing" was sometimes the least of his obligations. Like the other Calvin directors, Altman was doing everything hands-on—scripting, sound, editing, camerawork, production design, budget details. Very few of today's feature film directors understand the intricacies of laboratory processing; Altman does. One reason why his visual standards

William Frawley in *The Dirty Look*.

are so high is that he knows every step and opportunity available in the lab. At Calvin, Altman learned the film business alphabet from *A* to *Z*, and he was moving in directions at Calvin that he became famous for later on in Hollywood.

The habit of experimentation for the sake of experimentation, always within the confines of the budget, began at Calvin. Calvin filmmakers would often try out new things—in part because they were continually learning, and in part because it was a means of dressing up otherwise prosaic subjects. "Altman was always trying something different," says Barhydt. "In fact, he'd choose difference over quality or meaning. He can't stand to be derivative, or to be thought of as copying something that has already been done."

Altman's most creative efforts did not always pay off in terms of the sponsors' appreciation, because sponsors were primarily interested in the pitch. The Calvin crew might have found a way to simulate back projection or some other complicated process shot, easily accomplished in Hollywood but a matter of some ingenuity on a low budget in Kansas City. Or the script might be flavored with some clever puns or one-liners. So what?

Once, Barhydt remembers, Altman executed a perfect 180-degree turn with the camera. It was not easily done. Altman combined six or seven scenes, cut-ins and close-ups, and worked until 3 A.M. when the camera moved around in a circle smoothly and perfectly. It was beautiful. Everybody was proud of the scene. Right in the middle of a sales film.

"Absolutely a waste of time for the picture," says Barhydt, "but at least Altman got a chance to try it and do it and he got the crew all excited, and put it in the picture. Great scene. The client never noticed it. Altman was just trying to see if he could do it."

The young director was overlapping sound back then—which used to drive Barhydt crazy. "Altman tried that several times, and several times we had to rerecord because you're not getting the essential words the client wants you to get," recalls Barhydt.

They used multiple cameras for the first time for *The Dirty Look*, one of everyone's favorites, a gas station short that featured William Frawley in a comic spin. Using simultaneous cameras was Charley Paddock's idea, and Altman went for it whole-hog. It may have come up in conversation with Frawley, who had just hit the stratosphere, after a lifetime of character vignettes, as the upstairs neighbor, Fred Mertz, in TV's *I Love Lucy*, a program that was pioneering the use of three simultaneous "live" cameras in prime-time episodic television.

Altman was known at Calvin for his angles, overheads, intense close-ups. His camerawork (and editing) was definitely agitated. It was not so much a style as it was a reaction against the subject matter.

Says Paddock: "That's the reason we got along together. I had the knack of using a lot of camera movement. He encouraged me, and I always thought it was good to move the camera. To my way of thinking, it made the movie more interesting than just static shots. It gives a third dimension. The minute you move the camera, it brings a scene to life. . . ."

Says Barhydt: "Camera movement, he's crazy about. Always has been. He can't stand to have the camera standing still. That's probably a reflection of his own nervous personality. [If he was a camera] . . . he wouldn't want to be standing around looking at you, he'd want to be rambling."

The Calvin actors and actresses (which is stretching the point, as many of them were other things in private life, from disc jockeys to socialites) remember Altman fondly as someone who always gave them positive feedback, and urged them on to a higher level—as someone who always made the work titillating and worthwhile. His intuition for their potential was extraordinary.

Says Paddock: "The minute they met him, why, people would love to talk to him and be around him. He had the knack of getting people to do what they do best—naturally. He'd sit back and watch and see what he liked about what they did. That was his long suit, and that has been his trademark in all of his movies, to get people to do their own thing."

His trademark at Calvin was a relaxed and jokey atmosphere. On the set there was unflagging good humor, and Altman would alleviate the tension after the filming of a particularly complicated scene by crying out exasperatedly: "What do you mean there's no film in the camera?" It never failed to break them up. He made the work seem important and unimportant at the same time.

There were postmidnight bull sessions and rounds of parties and protracted socializing. Barhydt remembers the expense accounts and the bar tabs. For *The Dirty Look* with William Frawley, Barhydt says, the wining and dining bill was probably bigger than the total talent budget. On his Calvin allowance, Altman was perfecting the family sales techniques and spending habits: plying the actors and actresses, chasing out-of-town mistresses and paying off bookies, wooing account reps and Hollywood feature players alike.

"The truth is," says Woodburn, in Altman's defense, "he'd spend twice as much [as he put in for] and make up the difference out of his pocket—taking clients to dinners, the gin mills, gambling—showing them the town."

"This guy's great talent is his enthusiasm for a project," says Barhydt. "Doesn't last—but when he goes into it, this is the biggest thing he's ever done. He would transmit this to actors and get actors so damned enthusiastic and fired up about a job, a part, that they'd kill themselves for him. He'd keep them on a set until three o'clock in the morning, until they were dropping—but they loved him."

All of this, it must be emphasized, was in the service of some of the most deadly, routinized film subjects imaginable. Like the sort of auto safety films most American high school students suffer through at one time or another in Driver's Ed. Or the one-note sales monologues with which corporations brainwash new apostles. Truly horrid, un-

No, not a scene from *Combat*—a tableaux from the the improvised opening sequence of *The Magic Bond*, the Calvin documentary sponsored by the VFW and directed by Altman. (Floyd and Patricia Klang)

watchable stuff—"dull enough to halt a herd of charging rhinos."

Yet there were touches. That is what distinguished Altman at Calvin—his touches, his moments of lightness, his imaginative digressions. These touches might manifest themselves as a provocative camera movement or an elaborate gag setup or an in-joke, the derivation of which is all but forgotten forty years later. There would be occasional gemstones within the context of salesmanship.

It is not that Altman is unable to tell a conventional story. It is more than he *will* not—in part because he has had a bellyful of linearity. Two-thirds of his career before

M*A*S*H was spent at Calvin and in television, and the entire remainder of his career has been not only an extension in some ways of Calvin methods and ideas but also a violent rebellion against stultifying restrictions. The Calvin years contained the seeds of everything the director would do in the future, according to Barhydt; they also contained the seeds of everything he would refuse to do.

Chapter
6

FRIENDS
AND
LOVERS

Not only did the Calvin years yield professional fortification, but they saw the beginnings of relationships that were to span the decades ahead.

At first, in the early 1950s, LaVonne moved to Kansas City, with Christine, to give her marriage to Altman another try. The Calvin people loved her—she was always so pleasant. But Altman did not stay at home in Kansas City any more than in Los Angeles, and eventually LaVonne returned to Fremont, Nebraska, to arrange for a divorce.

Altman seems to have been going through an endless succession of one-night stands, mistresses and call girls, all-night gambling jags, booze-outs and drinkathons, and impromptu and/or lavishly coordinated parties that everyone recalls as being wonderful fun and a social highpoint of their lives.

One of Altman's fellow revelers was Richard Peabody, who had been working as a writer-director with a company that created local advertisements for Kansas City area movie theatres. Peabody employed Joan Altman—who, as a model, had blossomed into quite the winsome blonde. He was also dating her. Altman introduced himself to Peabody after seeing one of Peabody's trailers for a Ford dealer's association at an uptown theatre. He wondered if Peabody would be interested in working for Calvin.

Peabody vividly remembers going up to a hotel room in downtown Kansas City with Altman, and watching B.C. play long card sessions in a suite rented for the weekend. He remembers the leather jacket Altman wore and used to be so proud of. Altman had purchased it in Los Angeles, and he would not trust anyone in Kansas City to clean it. Altman sent it to Hollywood for cleaning. Altman was very enamored of Los Angeles, says Peabody, and always reminding people that he had been there and was going back.

Peabody recalls Altman's office at Calvin, lined with the collected bound volumes of two improbable literary gods. One was Norman Corwin, the broadcaster and social commentator noted for his radio adaptations of literature and verse, latterly in Hollywood as a writer-producer. The other was Tennessee Williams, the flowery and eloquent dramatist of the South. Altman always talked about the way they strung words together," says Peabody. ("If one had an effect," says producer and writer Robert Blees, with a laugh, when informed of this, "the other most assuredly canceled it out.")

Peabody and Altman became carousing buddies, at work and during their off-hours. This period of Altman's life might make an interesting movie—a guy who makes prosaic tractor-and-tire films by day, and philanders and binges at night, responsible at work, irresponsible at play; his tremendous appetites for food, drink, and women—and how the two worlds

Altman's first wife, LaVonne, and F. O. Calvin,
owner of the Calvin Company, at one of the annual company Christmas parties. (Floyd and Patricia Klang)

overlap and impinge. But that is the type of first-person film
that Altman has shied away from.

They were amorous rivals, Peabody and Altman; and according to Peabody, there was always a Hollywood take to
Altman's sexual conquests, even in Kansas City. Always it
was—how many films can he make? how many girls can he
screw? His debauchery was a searching for love and rein-

forcement, says Peabody. Altman was always acting a role, playing the director, conscious of manipulating an image. He seemed fueled by the need to prove himself, over and over. And the irony is, says Peabody, Altman had little to prove: As with making movies, he was very, very good at "making" women.

"He was the best I've ever seen," says Peabody, "in that he was like a magnet to women."

"He's always had tremendous energy, both creative and sexual, or any way you want to look at it," adds Peabody. "Huge appetites, food, drink, women, marathon work sessions."

Once, while stranded in Arizona on location, Peabody and Altman competed at picking up women in bars. One night, Peabody was successful and Altman was left outside Peabody's adjoining room, pounding on the door and drunkenly demanding to have "seconds."

The next night, Altman got even in Altman fashion. Peabody was asleep alone, at about two or three in the morning, when the apparition of a beautiful lady appeared beside his bed. Waking him up, she began to slide her arms sinuously around his neck. Suddenly a voice rang out: "Okay, that's enough, cut!"

It was Altman, playing director games, hovering inside the adjoining doorway. Before Peabody could react, the sexy apparition had slipped away and Altman had slammed the door in Peabody's face.

Another time, during a lunch hour at Calvin, Altman surprised Peabody by asking, "If you're not particularly hungry, instead of going to lunch why don't I take you up the street to this lady I know?" She turned out to be a professional, a couple of blocks from the Calvin building, who performed fellatio over the lunch hour for the munificent sum of two dollars. Altman went first and then Peabody, who remembers that the lady in question was rather chatty while conducting her transaction. Afterward, Altman bragged about his ability to make such arrangements in the nowheresville of Kansas City.

"Altman had this idea that that was a very Hollywood thing to do," says Peabody, "to get your cock sucked on your lunch hour."

One of Peabody's problems was that he was also friends with LaVonne. Altman's friends were always being drawn into the conspiracy of lying to his wife. It always troubled them, even as they went along with it.

LaVonne, says Peabody, was a dream wife—sweet, even-tempered, always vexed at Altman for running around. Or, if he wasn't running around, he would show up at the apartment at 2 A.M. with six pilots and six stewardesses in tow, ready to party.

Altman, says Peabody, was thoroughly preoccupied with his vow to screw all the TWA stews who lived communally between flights in a rented mansion on the other side of town. He was on number eight, working his way up through number twelve. Meanwhile, LaVonne would be home at their apartment in the Country Club Plaza, stranded with Christine and without groceries, and she would end up calling mutual Calvin friends for a lift to the grocery store.

One night, when Altman could not be located, Joan Altman and Chet Allen volunteered to baby-sit for the toddler Christine while Peabody and LaVonne went out for a drink. They hit a bunch of after-hours roadhouses off the highway, closed the last one, and got back around 6 A.M. The door opened, and Altman grabbed LaVonne, pulled her inside, and slammed the door.

The next day, everything on Peabody's desk at the Calvin offices had been swept onto the floor. Altman was fuming. The two of them came pretty close to exchanging blows in The Blue Room, a favorite gathering place near the Plaza. Barhydt heard about it, called Peabody in, and noting that his and Altman's "intense love/hate relationship" was getting out of hand and was becoming a threat to company morale, he fired the lowlier employee, Peabody.

The Altman family was putting its bets on Joan Altman—at least in the sense that everyone felt she would ultimately

Altman in his Kansas City party-animal regalia.
(Floyd and Patricia Klang)

achieve a brilliant marriage. An attractive blonde like her
mother, she was considered very bright, a kind of a lioness,
with a tawny, expectant look about her. She did some posing
for advertisements, and she did some parts at Calvin; and it
seems that anybody who came into contact with her during
the decade of the 1950s, when she was often at Altman's
side, struggling alongside him and helping him with projects,
fell in love with her.

The men in Altman's circle were bewitched by her: not
only Richard Peabody and the Iranian film pupil Reza Badiyi,
but also the sensitive artist Chet Allen and the wild-child
Richard Sarafian. Altman was closer to his oldest sister than
to anyone, it seemed: He was flattered if one of his friends
had a crush on her, and defensive and wary if it developed
into more than that. Sometimes Altman felt he was "too
fond" of his sister, he confided to friends.

Sometime in the early 1950s, Joan Altman married Chet Allen. One of Altman's close friends, Allen stuck by the director throughout the Calvin years; worked as an artist and actor in the independent Kansas City films, in the Calvin industrials, and in television; and followed him to Hollywood. An aesthete whose Tyrone Power-like looks made him catnip to women, Allen was the first and one of the longest-lasting of Altman's art directors.

Also during the Calvin period, Altman and his sister met Richard Sarafian. Sarafian was a naïf, innocent and unworldly, devilishly handsome and impetuous (especially when drunk). Altman and Sarafian became inseparable.

Again, it was chance. They happened to be neighbors out at Lake Lotawana, east of the city, one of hundreds of lakes in that part of Missouri, where Altman had taken up housekeeping with Lotus. Altman came by one day when Sarafian and some Army buddies were grilling Greek shish kebab. Altman took an instant liking to the chubby American serviceman. To Sarafian, Altman described himself as a "gourmand." Sarafian thought Altman was more of a "Kansas City gourmand," but in a way it was their mutual appetites that brought them together and sustained their passionate love of food and drink, women, filmmaking, and backgammon.

A native of Brooklyn, Sarafian had already undergone his own personal odyssey before ending up in Kansas City by way of the military. He had briefly attended the University of Tennessee and New York University, and as a studio publicity release once noted: "He was a biologist before he became a filmmaker, and even then he was so successfully experimental he once crossed a cricket, butterfly and grasshopper, and got a long-beetled, white mutation he named a Crickerhop."

Sarafian had escaped being sent overseas because he was overweight and had a bad back. While a bartender in an officer's club, he had begun to do some writing for an Army magazine. When Altman realized Sarafian had writing ambitions and other native intelligence, and that he became quite the riveting joke-teller and ham actor when inebriated, Altman adopted Sarafian—into the bosom of the Altman family—into industrials, plays, and films. They began to drive into Kansas City to work every day. Sarafian began to think of himself, like Altman, as a filmmaker. And when, in time, Chet Allen and Joan Altman separated, Altman's sister began spending all her time with Richard Sarafian.

Apart from those who resent never having been invited along to Hollywood, few people who knew Altman in those Kansas City days remember him with other than affection and gratitude for the pleasure of his company. At this stage of his career, before his perceived rejection, betrayal, and disillusionment in Hollywood, and with youth as his armor, Altman was at the center of an admiring "second" family. If

The fourth of July, 1953: (from left) Altman's sister, Joan, his second wife, Lotus, his daughter, Christine, and Patricia Klang. Seated: Chet Allen (Joan's first husband) and Richard Sarafian (her second husband). (Floyd and Patricia Klang)

there was a dark streak in his nature, or any indication of the director who was to become such a cutting observer and driven soul in Hollywood, it is simply not in people's memories.

Still, not everyone could fathom the way he behaved. F. O. Calvin worried about him as if he were a wayward son. Barhydt would get angry when Altman would occasionally neglect to show up for filming, or materialize at a sales meeting with a hangover, or be diverted by a pretty female on location.

Everyone has a story about loaning him money that was never repaid, but these stories are usually followed by laughter at having been conned and buffaloed. Following in his father's footsteps, Altman always lived beyond his means and threw lavish parties no matter what the household balance. He was as generous with out-of-pocket loans and picking up the check as he was irresponsible about debts.

Debt was no more shameful than affluence. At least once, in Kansas City, in 1952, Altman filed for bankruptcy. Apart from small debts to Los Angeles collaborator Robert Ecton and to Calvin performer James Lantz, the outstanding sums were $7,200 owed to his father and $1,700 owed to the producer of one of his sundry film projects. Altman listed his total worth, in savings and cash, as $241. It is revealing when a son files bankruptcy against his own father, even if Altman withdrew the bankruptcy application within a matter of weeks.

Altman had a sense of humor about his debts. Woodburn remembers him borrowing three hundred dollars three weeks before a bankruptcy filing. Some time passed and Woodburn encountered Altman at a party. Altman asked Woodburn for a C-spot. Woodburn began to reach into his wallet, then thought a minute and asked Altman if he could trust him for the payment in light of recent circumstances. Altman laughed and said of course, especially as he could not file bankruptcy legally for another seven years.

Flush or flat-broke, Altman continued to gamble on the next roll of the dice—figuratively and literally. Everyone seems to think this was a highly entertaining facet of his character, not in the least desperate or disturbing. Everyone has their favorite "Altman anecdote" in this regard.

One time, Altman and Woodburn and some other Calvin friends were sitting in a bar in Kansas City.

"We used to go to a lot of the mob's hangouts," recalls Woodburn, "because they always had the best booze and a lot of attractive women. The guy sitting in the bar was watching Wednesday-night boxing on television.

"They used to have a lot of boxers come through Kansas City, and nobody but real aficionados knew much about them. Bob said, 'I like the guy in black trunks.' The guy at the bar says, 'How much do you like him?' The guy's wearing pinstripes, he's got powder over black jowels—a vacationing hit man, if I ever saw one. Altman said, 'Whatever you prefer.' We all looked at each other because we had just run a survey of our pockets and Altman had about two dollars. The guys says, 'Well, let's say a C-note.' Altman says, 'You got it.'

"I'm sitting there thinking, 'If he loses this bet, this guy is going to kill him. This guy is not going to take an I.O.U.' The one Bob picked took a beating, a real beating, until somehow or other, in the third round, he picked himself up off the floor, shook his head, and knocked the other guy cold. Don't ask me how.

"The guy takes out a roll of bills that thick, peels one off, hands it to Bob, and says, 'You win some, you lose some.'"

Chapter

7

CORN'S-
A-POPPIN'

Altman does not own up to much of his career before *M*A*S*H*, and he is very unspecific about most of it before his coming to Hollywood in 1956. He has said that everything he did before he began to direct motion pictures in earnest is "garbage."

But during this period in Kansas City he was as busy as he ever was in Hollywood, full of crackpot schemes and whirling-dervish energy, churning out an amazing amount of film independent of his Calvin work. A full account of what he did, exclusive of Calvin, would no doubt astonish even Altman. There was at least one independent feature before *The Delinquents*, several TV series and pilots, local commercials, and a formative crack at directing small theatre. Aside from sheer volume, this work is notable because it heralds a number of the stories and themes that will recur time and again in Altman's career.

In interviews, Altman does not own up to the single feature film he made during this period, perhaps with good reason. A quarter of a century before *Nashville*, there was *Corn's-A-Poppin'*, Altman's first film with a country-and-western score and a show business milieu. Few cineastes have ever heard of it, perhaps because it was produced in Kansas City, distributed spottily in the Midwest, and then withdrawn from circulation; perhaps because it has not been seen publicly since 1950 (the ownership rights are in dispute); and perhaps because it is (Altman would agree) one of the worst movies ever made.

Although Altman did not belong to the old-boy network in Hollywood, he could at least claim membership in the Kansas City one. At Southwest, briefly, he went to school with Elmer Rhoden Jr., whose father, Elmer Rhoden Sr., was one of the owners of Commonwealth Theatres, a chain of some 102 regional theatres. Elmer Jr. wanted to get into producing movies; he had the distributing apparatus at hand, and he had the necessary capital to invest.

Altman's old greeting card collaborator (and latterly, Calvin associate) Robert Woodburn had been tapped as director of *Corn's-A-Poppin'*, and Altman was brought in almost as an afterthought to help on the script.

It may have been Elmer Jr. who insisted on the film's premise—certainly no one else is bragging about having thought of it. The idea and title (a variation on *Hellzapoppin'*) was a facile spoof of backstage musicals, and the plot revolves around a double-dealing press agent for the Pinwhistle Popcorn Company, who pushes the sponsorship of a corny TV hour in order to discourage sales and boost competitors. Only, the scheme backfires with the discovery of a new high-quality popcorn and the sensational debut of an amateur country-and-western performer.

Jerry Wallace (with guitar) and Little Cora Weiss in the bargain-basement forerunner to *Nashville*, *Corn's-A-Poppin'*, co-written by Altman and produced in Kansas City. (Eddie Brandt's Saturday Matinee)

Woodburn and Altman casted for the lead in Hollywood, a place both of them believed in for luck and magic. A singer by the name of Jerry Wallace was just then starting out in Los Angeles, doing club dates with a solo act consisting of impressions of country, pop, and blue artists—everyone from Gene Autry and Tex Ritter to Nat King Cole and Billy Eckstine. Wallace had a colorful style. For a while he was emcee at a club at Florence and Western avenues, where he was the only white performer in an all-black ensemble. When Woodburn and Altman found out in the interview that

Wallace had been born and raised in Kansas City, why, they liked that fact about him too.

This is an early instance of Altman's developing someone from obscurity or another field—a favorite stratagem—and proving himself years ahead of the public. Young, gawky Jerry Wallace would go on almost a decade later to record the Top Ten pop hit "Primrose Lane" and to have a substantial career as a country-and-western artist as well as a writer for themes of television shows such as *Flipper*.

Wallace was brought to Kansas City for about a week, where, with breakneck speed, most of the scenes for *Corn's-A-Poppin'* were filmed on two or three threadbare sets erected on the stage of the old Lyceum Theatre. Two stalwart Calvin regulars, Jim Lantz and Keith Painton, are in the cast along with a legitimate country-and-western unit, Hobie and the Hep Cats. Chet Allen is credited as art director for what appear to be painted flats. Woodburn is culpable for the stodgy camerawork. And Altman was on hand, scribbling lines and walking around nervously with a notepad trying to keep up with the pace of filming. He shares the writing credit with Woodburn.

The musical numbers are the film's only high points—for Wallace, youthful with lacquered hair and a laminated grin, had a raw flair. But overall, the movie is slumberous, hammy, amateurish and clichéd, ultra-boring. Folks who rate *Quintet* the nadir of Altman's career have not seen *Corn's-A-Poppin'*.

"It was all so humdrum and thrown together," says Wallace.

Elmer Jr.'s father was acquainted with film editor Carl Pierson, a man who helped cut the first Oscar-winning picture, *Wings*, so Pierson agreed to edit *Corn's-A-Poppin'* in Hollywood (uncredited). It did not help.

Back in the Midwest, *Corn's-A-Poppin'* opened with appropriate Podunk hoopla and died a quick death with audiences and exhibitors. It never got beyond the local circuit. Woodburn, who never directed another theatrical feature, winces with embarrassment when it is mentioned, and says some of the old guys at Ryder Sound Services in Hollywood still roar with laughter at the memory of having worked on that ludicrous early "Altman film."

Also in Kansas City, Altman directed some television commercials for Nellie Don, one of the most famous medium-priced garment companies in the United States. Then, through his social connections, Altman formed a partnership with a woman who operated a fashion show agency, booking upper-class models for special presentations. With her financial backing, Altman wrote and directed a thirty-minute fashion parade called "Fashion Faire," which he tried to sell to the NBC network as a one-shot or series. He spent some "rec" time in New York hawking the series.

On one of these trips to New York, he wangled an introduction to the beautiful brunette running the most prestigious modeling agency in the nation, Eileen Ford. He convinced her to come to Kansas City, of all places, to make a television pilot featuring glamour tips from the Ford Agency.

When Eileen Ford arrived in town with Dorian Leigh, one of her top models, that was the excuse for Altman to rent a hotel suite for one of his famous round-the-clock blowouts that went on for three or four days. Eileen Ford's husband, Gerald Ford, who was scheduled to appear on camera as co-host with Eileen Ford, delayed his own arrival and became aggravated by the obvious fact that Altman was chasing after his wife.

A nip of further tension was added to a project that may have already been foredoomed by the fact that Gerald Ford insisted on writing his own very monotonic script.

At the least, the thirty-minute pilot, called *The Model's Handbook*, was ahead of its time by three decades in anticipating future feel-good fitness trends. There were strenuous Jane Fonda-type physical exercises in front of a cheap scrim, with diet and posture tips promised for future episodes. Pretty Dorian Leigh did the preening and demonstrating, while the Fords hosted and provided commentary.

In any case, few people ever saw it. The networks were not yet revolutionary enough to buy a program featuring a sexy model bending and stretching. For a while, Altman took calls from potential network buyers between drinks at The Blue Room, but despite feelers, the show never sold.

While still in Kansas City, Altman turned to television as a new and more wide-open market.

The television microseries called *Pulse of the City* was a kind of poor man's *Dragnet*. It was an anthology series about ambulance-chasing and crime incidents in the big city. Some episodes were takeoffs, others were sharply dramatic. Episodes were fifteen minutes long (the fifteen-minute program was not so unusual in those days) and were shot in 16mm color. Television reference books (without mentioning Altman's involvement) indicate that *Pulse* ran from September of 1953 to March of 1954 on the independent Dumont network. Altman and steadfast pal Woodburn were cocreators and alternating directors.

Before going off to live in Detroit to handle the Chevrolet account for Campbell-Ewald and to launch a career as an independent producer of commercials, industrials, and educationals in this country and abroad, Robert Woodburn recalls that he and Altman cranked out yet another syndicated microseries. This companion series, another dramatic anthology, was called (Woodburn is not quite sure of the title) *The City*. But Woodburn sold his interest to Altman after the syndication was picked up in New York; and the financing did not congeal; nor was there enough interest from stations. Though Woodburn and Altman filmed something like thirteen scripts back-to-back in eyeblink time, nobody can remember much about the series—whether it was good, what it was about, or whether, in fact, it truly did exist. It is part of the jumbled activity of a period in which Altman shot more film than can be traced or remembered.

Practically everybody who was anybody in Kansas City checked in at the Resident Theatre of the Jewish Community Center for a spell, and it was only a matter of time before Robert Altman did. Though there was regular traffic between Calvin films and Resident productions, it was Altman's second wife, Lotus Corelli, who encouraged his participation in the Resident program.

When they met in the early 1950s, Lotus and Altman were both in the process of getting "unmarried" from first spouses. A leggy and statuesque blonde, gregarious and fun-loving, Lotus was a model, originally from California, who had ended up stranded in Kansas City. She and Altman were wed in 1954 and, despite only a three-year marriage, they had two children, both boys, Michael and Stephen.

The people of the Resident Theatre remember Lotus vividly as a leading actress in several of their better productions. The consensus is that she was "absolutely brilliant" as an actress. At the Resident Theatre, she played the female leads in productions of Arthur Miller's *The Crucible* and Garson Kanin's *Born Yesterday.*

At the time, comments one member of the Resident Theatre, people who knew Lotus and Altman as a couple thought Lotus to be the superior talent. Altman had not yet found himself as a film director. He was considered a kind of floundering half-genius.

Altman joined the Resident Theatre toward the tail end of his Calvin tenure, in January of 1954, and for a brief time, with his customary fervor, he plunged into volunteer activity. After a full day at Calvin he would go to the Jewish Community Center at night to work on plays and production planning. For learning about acting, it was "one of the wisest things he'd ever done," he told Richard Peabody.

Much of his work at the Resident had little to do with acting. For *The Crucible,* he sketched a poster. After joining the executive committee (not for him, ordinary membership), Altman headed up a subscription drive, beginning with his own circle of friends and relatives. Mr. and Mrs. Chet Allen and Richard Sarafian dutifully began showing up at Resident Theatre meetings.

At Altman's initiative, an unusual Sunday entertainment

and activity program was launched. The "art form" of movies was featured, an indication of Altman's growing seriousness of purpose. For these "Sundays at Three" film programs, Altman arranged a seminar on the effects of sound on films (described in the newsletter as "a light and space show" with running commentary by Altman) and a program of Norman MacLaren's short films. He also organized and stage-managed readings of T. S. Eliot's and Edna St. Vincent Millay's poetry, as well as a recitation (by Lotus) of "More Complex Mother Goose Rhymes" with analysis by an eminent local psychologist.

The Resident Theatre lifers still remember the infusion of Altman's drive and energy, his bottomless idea-hatching, and of course his parties at Lake Lotawana with Lotus, Sarafian, Chet, and Joan. A group of Resident veterans gathered in a living room in Kansas City thirty years later could muster nothing but fondness in their recollections of him. They *liked* Altman. He was *fun*. At the time, they said, Altman was just about the most interesting person you could ever hope to meet. Funny, charismatic, refreshingly intelligent, gracious when sober. A hit with the ladies; palsy with the husbands.

They did not necessarily feel they understood him.

Altman was "ethereal," opines Bill Cohen, the Resident Theatre publicist for many years, "remote."

"He was searching," says SuEllen Fried, a Resident Theatre participant, "never satisfied with what he did. His mind was always elsewhere."

"One thing about Bob," she adds, "when he did talk to you, I think of the reason why they say everyone fell in love with Aristotle Onassis. Because when he talked to you, he gave you his absolute full attention. Somehow or other, I remember that when Bob would have a discussion with you, there would be this kind of intensity. You felt he was really, really listening to you and really talking to you."

Bill Cohen and some of the other executive committee members badgered Altman to direct one of their regular season three-act plays, but Altman wouldn't. Maybe because he couldn't be paid enough; maybe because he didn't like the warmed-over Broadway material. Altman had an alternative proposal. Something grandiose—experimental theatre, an outdoors happening. Saturday-night performances for the general public at Center Roff gardens, Sunday nights at Goodman Park for center membership only, preceded by a picnic supper. An evening of one-act plays to build subscriptions for the next season's playbill.

The board debated the proposal at length, finally deeming it too daring and expensive. Instead, Altman's scenario was toned down to three one-act plays on one weekend in mid-August of 1954. Altman was given the go-ahead to direct, the budget was set at a hundred dollars per play, and the program would take place on the roof of the center.

Two of the one-acters were written by Tennessee Williams—*Hope Is a Thing With Feathers* and *Portrait of a Madonna*. The third one may or may not have been written by Altman. Some people remember him giving that impression.

Portrait of a Madonna, with Altman directing his wife Lotus, was a particularly indicative selection, as it presaged (and no doubt influenced) all of the fractured, glassy-eyed women who proliferate in his dream-movies, *That Cold Day in the Park*, *Images*, *Three Women*, and *Come Back to the Five and Dime, Jimmy Dean, Jimmy Dean*.

Madonna is basically a one-character monologue in which a childless woman breaks down emotionally while reflecting on the failures of her love life. With such material Altman could indulge a lifelong empathy with repressed women and mental fragility.

On opening night, there was a terrific windstorm. People held onto their hats, flats fell down, one actor left the stage never to return, and according to Altman "the whole thing disintegrated." The actor who deserted was Richard Sarafian, who—wrought with insecurity and panicked by the weather conditions—walked off to have a drink in a bar. Afterward,

Joan Altman told him, "Dick, you were . . . adequate!" At that moment Sarafian felt certain he had fallen in love with her.

Even though fewer than a hundred people attended this unusual event, the program was deemed meritorious as an experiment. Yet when Altman moved to incorporate these unconventional programs into the regular schedule, the motion was denied.

By early 1955, Altman had come to the conclusion that Kansas City held nothing further for him, and that it was time to concentrate on feature films. He resigned from the Resident Theatre board and moved on. They would miss him. He and his retinue were always so stimulating.

Chapter
8

THE DELINQUENTS

By 1955, Elmer Rhoden Jr. had shaken off the disaster of *Corn's-A-Poppin'* and was ready to bankroll another movie. This time the son of the Midwest moviehouse magnate had an oracular notion. He would produce exploitation pictures targeted for burgeoning teen audiences, and budget them cheaply enough so that if he peddled them to his own Commonwealth Theatres chain in Missouri, Kansas, Arkansas, Iowa, Nebraska, and South Dakota, he would be guaranteed a tidy profit. Though the major studios were constrained from booking their own chains by an antitrust ruling, the Commonwealth circuit, by virtue of not having previously existed as a film producer, was

Happy days in Kansas City: Altman, associate
Reza Badiyi, and Joan Altman planning scenes
for *The Delinquents*. (Reza Badiyi)

exempt from the "consent decree" of 1953. Rhoden Jr. seems
to have been one of the first of the independent exhibitors to
have perceived this loophole, and he was photographed and
lionized in *Time* magazine as one of the "new wave" of producers. There, he expounded on his theory of can't-miss
teen-flick genres, namely "rock 'n' roll, drag races, horror
stories, that sort of thing."

Not really much for details, Rhoden Jr. usually began with
thinking up a title and nothing else (which is how they do it
in Hollywood sometimes too). The first title he thought up
was *The Delinquents*, and he hired Robert Altman to write
and direct.

It took Altman all of one week to write the script, he says—which may have been a leisurely amount of time from a Calvin perspective. Apart from any intrinsic literary value, the screenplay for *The Delinquents* has the distinction of being one of only two feature scripts of Altman's career for which there is no evidence, yet, of an acknowledged or closet collaborator.

In the 1950s there was a vogue for teenage hoodlum pictures, and Altman, who thought of himself as an intellectual delinquent, was not immune to vogue. He admired *The Blackboard Jungle*, the 1955 adaptation of Evan Hunter's hard-hitting "problem youth" novel (with a young Vic Morrow in the cast). Casting in Hollywood, Altman and Rhoden Jr. came up with Peter Brown, straight from *The Blackboard Jungle*; Richard Bakalayan, who had made a slight name for himself playing punks; and the future Billy Jack, Tom Laughlin, here making his motion-picture debut.

It was not a marriage made in heaven: the square, freewheeling Altman and the bohemian, mercurial Laughlin, both of them future counterculture heroes. Altman has described Laughlin during the filming as "an unbelievable pain in the ass," totally egomaniacal, guilty that he had not become a priest, with a "big Catholic hang-up" and a James Dean complex.

For one thing, remembers cameraman Charley Paddock, Altman and Laughlin had conflicting theories of acting. Altman would be ready to shoot a scene in which Laughlin was supposed to appear physically drained, and Laughlin would excuse himself with, "I've got to get in the mood now." Then Laughlin would insist on running around the block a couple of times while cast and crew cooled their heels.

Altman was not the only one to dislike Laughlin's "living-the-part" pretensions. The crew gave him a wide berth. Laughlin wanted to quit the film halfway through the filming, before Altman worked out a compromise for communication whereby Altman would tell him exactly what he wanted in any given scene. "And he was as good at doing that as when he was really working in the first part of the

The newspaper advertising for the "gala world
premiere," in hometown Kansas City, of *The
Delinquents*, Altman's first-directed feature.
(Dan Fitzgerald)

picture," Altman has said. Laughlin, adds Altman, performed
"the last half of the picture under protest."

Altman filmed the story in two weeks at a budget of
around forty-five thousand dollars—using the locations of
Swope Park, Luce Park, and The Jewel Box nightclub. Most
of the cast were Calvin and Jewish Community Center recruits, including reliable James Lantz, Leonard Belove, and
Kermit Echols. Altman family members in the cast included
his second wife, Lotus, and eight-year-old Christine Altman,
his daughter from his marriage to LaVonne. Louis Lombardo
played the leader of a rival gang in an outdoor drive-in scene.
Lombardo, who was in town visiting from Los Angeles, also
contributed uncredited camerawork. Reza Badiyi was the as-

sociate producer of title. Joan Altman served in a production executive capacity, and Chet Allen is credited with the art direction.

Except for Laughlin, the filming was full of spontaneity, good humor, and happy incident. It was like a party, cast members say—and indeed, in the movie was Altman's first life-is-a-party sequence, an otherwise minor scene that, for Altman, was a kind of signature. Parties, often filmed at Altman's own house, have found their way into virtually every other Altman production over the years. Indeed, it can be said that parties for this director are a metaphor for life, a Barthian "floating opera" of ebb and flow, of conversation and happenstance, of intermingling chance and fate.

SuEllen Fried, then a dancer associated with the Resident Theater, was playing a small part.

"He rented an old house off Walworth Boulevard," she recalls, "and told us to pretend we were having the wildest party of our lives, while he moved the camera from room to room and just filmed whatever was going on. We didn't know when the camera was going. We were just having a wild party."

The finished movie was picked up by United Artists and released in March 1957 with a crisp running time of seventy-one minutes, and with Altman credited as producer, director, and screenwriter. It has not been shown theatrically for some thirty years, nor is it available in video. But Altman himself, while disparaging the film on occasion, has enough of a soft spot for it to have kept a copy for his personal library, and to have shown it to Todd McCarthy (nowadays the senior film reviewer and reporter for *Daily Variety*) when McCarthy wrote about the film for his anthology *Kings of the B* (E. P. Dutton, 1975).

In his book, McCarthy, a discerning critic, comments on the "sanctimonious narration" (claimed by Altman to have been added by United Artists), the "overblown melodramatic moments," and the "extremely mannered" acting of Laughlin ("He couldn't keep his eyes fixed in one place for more than two seconds").

The quality of the black-and-white photography is "brilliantly sharp and rich," notes McCarthy.* This "passable but hardly distinguished film" has "two notable features," continues McCarthy, "its technical excellence and its paradoxical relationship with the director's subsequent work."

In McCarthy's view, this relationship is intriguing because here Altman is playing the genre straight—as opposed to much of his subsequent work, which is "genre inversion." If anything, McCarthy notes, this is one more indication that Altman was still trying to achieve acceptance by working within the tradition, and had not yet progressed to the "anti-Hollywood" stage of his filmmaking.

In his contract with Elmer Rhoden Jr., Altman had a clause stipulating that *The Delinquents* would be edited in Los Angeles. But Rhoden Jr. would not approve the air fare to Los Angeles—which is why Altman and Reza Badiyi were traveling across the country by automobile in August 1956.

The second Elmer Rhoden Jr. production in the new indie "teen wave" was yet another delinquency film, *The Cool and the Crazy*, whose scriptwriting chores were bequeathed in Altman's absence to his future brother-in-law, the budding and blooming Richard Sarafian. *The Cool and the Crazy* was made. But despite the laurels of *Time*, Rhoden Jr.'s minimogul reign was short-lived. A hard-living man, he died of a heart attack before the age of forty.

---

*Paddock says Altman advised him to watch John Huston's version of W. R. Burnett's *The Asphalt Jungle* and to imitate that style of lighting.

Chapter
9

THE
JAMES
DEAN
STORY

Altman was already six years older than Orson Welles had been when Welles dazzled the film world by directing his enduring screen masterpiece, *Citizen Kane*, in 1941. In Hollywood for the first time just a couple of years later, Altman was profoundly mesmerized by the example of the wunderkind Welles. Altman admired the director's texturing of sound; he appreciated the experimental lighting and optics of Welles's director of photography, Gregg Toland. Altman was acutely aware of

A scene from *The James Dean Story*, which eulogized the anti-heroic Dean, whose troubled
and creative nature Altman could not help but
identify with. (Wisconsin Center for Film and
Theatre Research)

having grown older in Kansas City, of somehow being in
Welles's shadow, even though for all intents and purposes
they did not exist in the same universe of comparison.

To his only passenger and companion on that long cross-
country drive in 1956, to Reza Badiyi, Altman rhapsodized
about Welles and his genius. He talked about how he, Altman, was going to break into Hollywood, and how, like
Welles, he was going to break the Hollywood rules. "He always had that feeling the world was against him," says
Badiyi. "That they weren't letting him do his thing. That he
was a martyr."

     *   *   *

A year elapsed.

Though details of the divorce were still to be ironed out, Altman had left Lotus. His sister Joan had separated from Chet Allen. Altman and Joan and Badiyi lived in a big rented house in the Hollywood hills. Sarafian came out from Kansas City, halfway through the postproduction work on *The Delinquents*, and they all used to romp together.

Badiyi was not quite certain he was not romantically attracted to Joan, and they spent a lot of time in each other's company before Sarafian arrived. Like Altman, Joan was in quest of some kind of exotic passion. Badiyi was writing Persian poetry, and she was writing her own poetry as well as beautiful, keep-the-chin-up short stories. Like her brother, she seemed to have infinite patience and a great interest in all phenomena. While Altman was off socializing and "making contacts," she and Badiyi shared gay times together. They would go walking on the beach at night and try to catch the little fishes that came in with the tide, scooping them up in a bucket, getting their best clothes wet because they had come straight from dinner at a nice restaurant.

Altman had "big eyes" from the beginning, remembers Badiyi. Jim Bloodworth, a writer from Kansas City and Calvin days who had preceded Altman to Hollywood, now advised him on social and professional etiquette. Altman took tennis classes several times a week, trying to look fit and trim and very Californian. Altman knew that parties were very important for making contacts in Hollywood—perfect!—and he tried to penetrate the correct circles. The household had very little income—Joan was trying to manage groceries, while Badiyi would contribute his exchange-student check. But that did not stop them from throwing extravaganzas like the one that featured Badiyi's home-cooked Iranian dinner with sit-down invitations for fifty.

One night, toward the end of this period, Joan and Badiyi went out and got drunk and spent a platonic night on the beach together. Morning came, and when they returned to the house in the hills, Altman was waiting, truly angry.

"I got very hurt that Bob felt that way," says Badiyi. "I said to him, 'You know I would never do anything to your sister.'"

Altman taunted Badiyi: "I want the telephone number of your sister in Iran." Says Badiyi: "I realized he never slept that night, waiting for us."

The incident was never mentioned again, and Badiyi was shortly to leave the country, to renew his visa in Iran. But he had a feeling he had violated his friendship with Altman.

Altman had some job interviews, but the tide of teenage delinquent pictures had ebbed, and nobody was interested in the Midwestern director of a cheapie starring a bunch of unknowns.

Altman rediscovered what he already knew: that being an Altman in Hollywood, unlike Kansas City, was no big deal. The prestigious television programs of the "Golden Age of Television" were being doled out to the bright and conscientious youth movement from the East Coast. College ties, family connections, acting classes, directing for the New York stage—these were the criteria that counted. Altman found himself, despite all of his bluster, essentially without portfolio.

The initial euphoria of being in Los Angeles passed. Altman had to figure child support in with his spendthrift lifestyle.

On one of his trips back to Kansas City—Altman lectured at the Calvin seminars and kept up family obligations—he mentioned to someone he was thinking of working on a documentary about James Dean, capitalizing on the automobile crash that killed the young film idol on September 30, 1955. "'James Dean Lives!'" he exclaimed, wide-eyed, pointing to the headline of a newspaper feature story. "Can you believe this? People believe he survived the crash! I think there's a film in James Dean. . . ." He mentioned his idea to Louis Lombardo, who could contribute much more than just photography, and who never said no to Altman.

Because he always functioned better with a collaborator, Altman went back to his early writing partner George W.

Writer-producer George W. George and Altman
at the editing table, a publicity still from *The
James Dean Story*. Their collaboration was intermittent for forty years. (British Film Institute)

George, who could raise money on the East Coast. They
started to film, according to their own publicity, with only
twenty thousand dollars raised by George—"no script, no
budget, no completion bond, and no idea what studio would
release the picture."

Altman and Lombardo had done quite a bit, if not most, of
the interviews and transition footage by the time they
sought the services of screenwriter Stewart Stern. Stern was
already a well-known scriptwriter in Hollywood. His first
script was *Teresa*, for director Fred Zinnemann in 1950, and
he was one of the writers of credit on Dean's most impactful
picture, *Rebel Without a Cause*. It may have helped that
George and Stern had a long family acquaintanceship. In any

case, the well-known screenwriter said yes. (Stern, coincidentally, had his own boost up the ladder of success by being related to two Hollywood ruling-class families, the Zukors and the Loews.)

At first, the project was, for Altman, a meal ticket and an early, halfhearted stab at dismantling the myth of Hollywood stardom. Likewise, Stern felt Dean's tough-guy mystique had mushroomed after the actor's death. Besides being the scriptwriter of his most famous vehicle, Stern had also been close friends with Dean and with *Rebel* composer Leonard Rosenman. Stern felt that the vulnerable and socially positive sides of Dean's personality and life had been gainsayed by the Hollywood publicity machine. For Stern, it was an opportunity to humanize the memory of Dean.

Stern recalls that when he came into the project, there was no script per se. He began by reviewing the interviews and footage that was already compiled. He believed George to be the "chief creative force" of the filmmaking effort, and he describes a muted, apparently unhappy Altman who did not contribute much to the script sessions. (Much later, in fact, when Stern saw *That Cold Day in the Park* and was floored by it, he was at a loss to make the connection between the piercing direction of that film and the low-key personality he had first come to know as Robert Altman.) "My memory is that Bob, literally, had no contact with me while I was doing the script, except for a few meetings which to my recollection were pretty social. I really don't know what he did [on the film]."

Yet Stern does remember liking Altman and feeling drawn to him. "At that point in his life," says Stern, "as many of us were, he was in search of himself." Stern recalls Altman as admitting to marital troubles and mid-life crises, as being (like himself) immersed in therapy.

"My impression was that he was under stress, and that he perspired [heavily] when we talked about our quest," says Stern. "You were instantly comfortable with him. He had wonderful humor. I felt trust for him, and I liked him. We shared a lot of personal stuff that we were going through and very quickly—which was unusual. I have enormous respect for him as a director. What he's done is phenomenal, and it's still in process."

The part about undergoing therapy may or may not be consistent—Badiyi says he never saw Altman so happy in his life as during that first anonymous year in Hollywood. And no other friend or associate recalls Altman, not the most introspective character in the world, as ever having been in therapy. (Judging by the superficial, derisive comedy of *Beyond Therapy*, his only film to linger on the subject, Altman, in any case, has nothing very cosmic to say about the "rational religion.")

It may have been Altman's protective coloration, his way of presenting himself as simpatico with Stern, as when Altman told writer-producer Robert Blees, more than once, that he was "half-Jewish." Altman may have meant that metaphorically, but he led Blees to believe it literally. There is nothing in the family genealogy to confirm it.

From Stern's point of view, Altman kept a respectful distance from the writing and honored the script.

It is true enough that scripts are not always sacred with Altman—a credo learned, early on, in industrials, where perforce, scenes had to be improvised and Altman himself was often the sole writer of indifferent matter; a belief reinforced in television, where things ought not to be improvised perhaps, but where the situation often invited it; and a subtext embedded in his own psychology and in his own defenses against revealing himself.

Yet Altman has often been faithful to a script he respects (even where credits or publicity indicate otherwise), especially in the early stages of his career. He has worked with some of the best writers, from Ring Lardner Jr. to Leigh Brackett to Jules Feiffer to Garry Trudeau, and more. Stern's experience is a good example of Altman's willingness to defer to a script. The script for *The James Dean Story* is pure Stern—imbued with his turns of phrase, his insights, his sensitivity toward human frailties, and his love for Dean.

*   *   *

Altman was more drawn to the other principal collaborator—an artistic "street photographer" named Lou Stoumen. Billed in those days as Louis Clyde Stoumen, Stoumen had studied with montage theorist Slavko Vorkapich and had developed a reputation in Hollywood as a troubleshooter in mise-en-scène. His career as a filmmaker includes the direction of two widely acclaimed documentaries, *The Naked Eye*, Oscar-nominated in 1957, and *The True Story of the Civil War*, Oscar-awarded for Best Documentary Short Subject in 1956.

Primarily a noted still photographer whose collections record the street life of Times Square and New York City environs, Stoumen was supporting his habit of photography and personal documentaries by churning out television commercials for 7-Up and Helene Curtis hair spray, and by directing informationals for Encyclopaedia Britannica. In other words, Stoumen was a real Altman prototype. He took up the *Dean* film because of the salary and also because it meant a more direct involvement in the film industry.

Stoumen, too, remembers Altman as an affable go-getting guy who was going through a "psychologically unhappy period," drinking a little much and "on his ass" professionally. "Bob seemed a little sad to me, and he wasn't riding high," says Stoumen. "He was having money troubles, and he had to do this thing. But I did admire the way he approached this, the way he worked on it, the way he attended to detail, and the way he worked with people."

Altman, Louis Lombardo (who is credited as an assistant to the producers), and Stoumen did pick-up filming in Indiana (at the cemetery, the train station, and the Dean farm); New York City (in Rube Goldberg's apartment and at Georgie's restaurant); and in California (at Schwab's drugstore and other Hollywood hangouts). Near Paso Robles, California, with a special low-slung camera, they restaged Dean's fatal high-speed car crash, and interviewed the highway patrolman who sped to the scene of the actual accident. They devised atmospheric (and somewhat silly) scenes of a

Dean "double" as transition material between interviews and as filler.

"Bob was very ingenious in devising means and things to shoot," says Stoumen.

"He [Altman] had a great temperament back then," says Louis Lombardo. "Once I drove down to the beach in the station wagon for one of those symbolic scenes with dead sea gulls, and the car just sank into the sand. Bob just laughed and laughed."

"When he talked to the people in Indiana," recalls Stoumen, "he was very gentle and yet directed the talk and the information at getting the locations and toward their deeper understanding about what was happening to Dean."

It was tricky to flesh out the material. There were rehearsed interviews with Dean's first dramatic coach from high school, with his fraternity brothers, with an actress he dated, with Fairmount, Indiana, relatives, with a bartender and restaurant maitre d'. But that was not enough. Interspersed between the interview clips were charcoal sketches, recitation of bits of poetry and letters, "secret recordings" of Dean's musings, and the manipulation of many, many still photographs. Still, the film ran only eighty-eight minutes, and was "put together with stick-um," in Stoumen's words.

The resourceful Stoumen developed a system he called "photo motion" to lend the illusion of variety and movement to the use of dozens of still photos—a process of scanning photos and creeping into a close-up of considerable detail in order to give some energy to film foredoomed as static. Though he was no stranger to such camera mobility, Altman learned from Stoumen and incorporated this stylistic device into his visual language. It was, in fact, his education in the zoom lens, which was in the process of being widely introduced into the motion-picture industry.

The zoom lens permitted a cameraman to alter the size of any sharply focused image as the camera was continuing to film. For a half-century of filmmaking, the zoom effect had been achieved through the use of expensive, moving dollies or cranes. Now, there were to be new sensations of depth and dimension, and a new freedom and flexibility in framing. To a great extent, the zoom lens came to replace cutting between long, medium, and close shots. The slow zoom close-up was to become characteristic of Altman's films—his most characteristic visual trademark—one that helped the director articulate emblematically what was not explained in the script.

Both Altman and Stern admit that the film ended up with an attitude of profound ambivalence toward James Dean. Ultimately, it is more of an *hommage* than a demystification. "We weren't as tough on him as we originally had intended to be," Altman has said.

"Partly it was the interviews," says Stern. "They [the interview subjects] were all people who were fond of Jimmy. Those qualities in him which fed into those roles and made him seem that way were the energy of a very intensely creative, imaginative, searching artist, and that in the core of him he was somebody who believed in the human connection, and in the gentleness of peace. That was the core that so many kids responded to in him, even though they may not have known it themselves.

"In selecting certain of the things we elected to dramatize, by emphasizing those to the exclusion of any qualities which today one might talk about a lot more freely, the emphasis of the film was on a kind of sentimental deification, and in that sense it was a kind of reinstitution of the legend that we were trying to avoid."

In his career Altman has made a sideline out of debunking Presidents, astronauts, detective heroes, western frontiersmen, and other pompous celebrities, an attitude that is in part derived from the psychology of someone who, away from Kansas City, always has been on the outside looking in, and who has never felt properly lionized. But he was stymied by Dean, who was, like Altman, a Midwesterner, a "searching artist," and someone who had transformed himself into a sympathetic public figure.

It is clear, as the film unspools, that the director is seeing himself in Dean—in the shy, gawky, mercurial farm boy who sought the answer to life's questions in films and performance art. It might seem absurd on the face of it—Altman and Dean would seem to have very little in common—but Altman has mined himself over and over again through other people, actors, and characters. Indeed, he has found his voice more than once in the symbol of James Dean. If one is looking for an explanation of their subliminal bond, one does not have to look further than Stern's stirring passage from the film's narration, in which he quotes a "writer friend" (actually Stern himself) who analyzed Dean at some point shortly before the actor's death.

Over dinner in the film, the "writer friend" has sketched a symbolic picture of Dean on a napkin, a little circle with dots in the center, and labeled it Dean's "secret self."

"Most of us put a wall around it, mirrors like this. . . ." says the "writer friend" as he continues to sketch.

"If we don't trust people, you use them to keep them out so they can't hurt us. But you . . . mirrors aren't enough for you . . . you've got to have this too, a second wall, and it's covered with thorns and spangles and

shockers to dazzle people, so they say, 'Boy he's really a hot apple, look how interesting he is . . .'"

Then the "writer friend" draws a second, jagged circle.

"You never give anyone a chance to really like you or not . . . because you never let them in to see the first wall . . . You never say, 'Step right this way, and see the real Jimmy Dean.'

"So, what's in the middle, Jimmy? Why do you shut people out? Why don't you think you deserve anything?

"You think you're so dull that if they get inside they won't find anything and they'll walk out on you. Is that why you run out on them before they get too close?

"Do you think you're empty, Jimmy? Is that why you're scared?"

Owing in large measure to George's salesmanship, the film was picked up for distribution by Warner Brothers and released in 1957. The Warner's contract gave George and Altman $35,000 in negative costs and the first $200,000 after prints, advertising, and distribution, and fifty-fifty thereafter after deduction of expenses.

As part of the arrangement, Warner's contributed clips from the Hollywood premiere of *Giant* and the unseen screen test of Dean for *East of Eden*. Also, the studio was instrumental in coaxing teen idol Tommy Sands to croon a theme song, "Let Me Be Loved," penned by two-time Oscar winners Jay Livingston and Ray Evans, and in securing ex-Shakespearean actor Martin Gabel to intone the narration.

Seen today, the movie looks rather desperately meager. Yet one also has to admire its "fantastical feeling of reality" (Altman's own description from the publicity notes). The imaginative presentation, the camera expertise, the juxtaposition of sound, and the feverish kaleidoscope of images—the *film* choices keep it absorbing. The photography is highly theatrical, the interviews (with their quaint, staged quality) oddly affecting, and the script has lost none of its mesmerizing force. With hindsight, one can see clues in the script to Dean's bisexuality and masochism; and the ambivalence of the filmmakers comes across as a strong point of complexity. In the end, it is a superior and unusually styled documentary.

Warner's, which had a natural vested interest in the deification of Dean, pulled out all the stops to promote the movie—approving publicity stunts not always in the best of taste. A Capitol Records LP, with a score by Leith Stevens, was sent to six thousand disc jockeys. The racing car in which Dean was killed was exhibited (in conjunction with a traffic accident prevention program) at a downtown theatre in Los Angeles. A friend of Dean's who was also typed as a restless young lead—Nick Adams from the *Rebel* cast—was dispatched to Fairmount to preside over the preview festivities there. In Los Angeles, the exploitation nature of the film was emphasized when the movie was released on the lower half of a double bill with a movie about an army of giant, man-eating insects called *Black Scorpions.*

After decidedly mixed reviews, the movie disappeared from circulation and became one of the more obscure items in the Altman catalogue of pre-*M*A*S*H* trinkets. Nearly thirty years later, the rights to *Dean* reverted to George W. George, by then a successful Broadway producer, and it was released on video with a more auspicious billing: "A film by Robert Altman." Indeed, in spite of all, it truly bears his mark.

Chapter

10

GUERRILLA WARFARE

Altman was meeting a lot of people—agents and producers and writers. Jim Bloodworth knew a big-name lady writer with a mansion who kept her fireplace roaring in July, and that's where Altman, by prearrangement, met director Alfred Hitchcock.

Hitchcock, in his mid-fifties, was halfway through one of the cinema's greatest careers, a career that managed to combine box-office appeal and production values with the highest aesthetic standards. Besides Catholicism (Hitchcock was more of a practitioner than Altman), Hitchcock had in common with the struggling director a passion for technical innovation and camera experimentation. More

importantly, in 1955, Hitchcock had begun to host and su-
pervise a television program called *Alfred Hitchcock Presents*, and though the extent of his involvement waxed and
waned over the seven-year history of the program, he was
alert to recruiting younger writers and directors.

According to some reports, Hitchcock was enamored with
the low-budget *The Delinquents* when it was screened for
him. To series producer Joan Harrison he recommended that
Altman be given a directing slot on *Alfred Hitchcock Presents*, a considerable opportunity for a novice, since Hitchcock's program was already prospectively one of the most
prestigious shows on television. Indeed, it was to prove a
springboard for such ascendant stars as Burt Reynolds,
Charles Bronson, Robert Redford, Steve McQueen, Gena
Rowlands, and many others. Notable writers like Ray Brad-
bury, Roald Dahl, Garson Kanin, John Cheever, Robert
Bloch, and Evan Hunter contributed scenarios. The lineup of
contemporary directors who cut their teeth on Hitchcock
material would include William Friedkin, Sydney Pollack,
Arthur Hiller, and Stuart Rosenberg—not to mention certain
veterans, who, like Hitchcock himself, occasionally took a
turn behind the lens.

Hitchcock had "enormous respect" for Altman, remembers Louis Lombardo; and the great established director
graced the set of the tyro's first episode with his presence,
formally addressing him as "Mr. Altman" in front of the cast
and crew. At this point, Lombardo had serendipitously taken
a job with the Revue camera department, so Altman's lieutenant was on the lot when the Hitchcock segments were
being filmed.

That first episode was "The Young One," broadcast in
1957, the third season of the series. No wonder Hitchcock
thought of Altman. This was juvenile delinquent territory
once again, with a "Hitchcock twist." A half-hour thriller, it
brought Carol Lynley, Vince Edwards, and Jeanette Nolan together in the story of a nubile teenager (Lynley) who picks up
a rootless drifter (Edwards) at a roadhouse and frames him for
the murder of her guardian (Nolan).

This was almost a dry run of the later Fabian episode of *Bus Stop*, and it is chock-full of Altman signposts: drifters and j.d.s, after-hours joints, an ice-cool, deranged blonde. It is surprisingly stark for Hitchcock material, and deftly handled by Altman, especially the trio of performances.

For Altman's next episode, broadcast early in 1958, Hitchcock entrusted Joseph Cotten to the director for "Together." This nasty ditty posited Cotten, a womanizer, as accidentally locked in an office with the body of his mistress (Christine White) whom he has murdered after a wild Christmas party. There is not much suspense, only a gruesome crime and the killer revealed by chance. And Altman manages it all on a single interior set—which over time would become more and more characteristic of his approach to certain films.

It would be wrong to argue that these early TV pieces represent Altman at his best, or even the Hitchcock program at its best. But Hitchcock buffs agree that Altman's two episodes are in the solid middle range of quality so far as the series is concerned, and show Altman as very assured and capable in his network prime-time debut.

Also for Hitchcock, Altman was employed behind the scenes on the short-lived *Suspicion* television series, doing location work as a production manager for director Robert Stevens. In retrospect, this is a rather baffling assignment. One of Hitchcock's most frequent television directors, Stevens would seem to require little backup. Yet Altman was clearly on the job for more than just routine production manager chores. One reason may be that this particular episode, "Heartbeat," broadcast in 1958, called for unaccustomed practical location filming. And Altman was already known, on the basis of *The Delinquents* and *The James Dean Story*, for a vérité style, not to mention the chutzpah to solve any problems arising from the elements.

Hitchcock asked Altman to assist with location details. Altman agreed, on the proviso that he not be credited in any subordinate capacity.

Kansas Citians Lombardo and Chet Allen were drafted by

Altman to go along to New York City and to help out on the second-unit chores. Here, during his first important stint in television, is where Altman met Warren Beatty (who was playing a bit part), the future star of *McCabe and Mrs. Miller*, and more pivotally, actress Barbara Turner, who was Vic Morrow's wife. Both were in the cast of the Ernest Kinoy teleplay about a man with a serious heart condition who is mistakenly given a clean bill of health by his doctor, indulges in a hedonistic weekend spree, collapses, and dies.

With Lombardo as his "personal cameraman" and Allen as his "visual consultant," Altman toured and arranged locations, and filmed second-unit scenes. At Coney Island, Lombardo remembers, Altman wanted to try all the amusements, and Altman held the Aeraflex and Lombardo held the batteries while they filmed the parachute jump, the roller coaster, and the other thrill rides. Lombardo remembers Altman, strapped into the centrifugal force ride, holding the camera on actor David Wayne (who played the unwitting heart-attack victim) and Barbara Turner (playing his companion), as the ride spun round and round. The rubber grip on the lens became stuck in his eye, and afterward Altman proudly displayed a black-and-blue mark.

According to Altman, he was supposed to direct a third Hitchcock program—until he made the mistake of criticizing the inadequacies of the teleplay. The sponsor of that teleplay, he has enjoyed telling interviewers, was none other than the producer of the series, Joan Harrison, Hitchcock's former secretary from England, who had risen up in the world to become a proficient screenwriter and a producer of suspense films in her own right. "Which," Altman has said, "left me only one way to go—out!"

At best, this is apocryphal, an early example of Altman's self-acutalization at the expense of writers. Joan Harrison was not the author of a single script for *Suspicion* or *Alfred Hitchcock Presents* that season. She does not remember any such contretemps. Though she hired all directors and supervised all scripts in her capacity as producer, she recalls Altman (writing from England through her husband, novelist

Eric Ambler) as a technically efficient, highly disciplined second-unit man who probably dressed up his ill-advised comments during a script conference for grandstanding purposes.

It may be more pertinent that, upon returning from New
York City, Altman gave a simply astonishing interview to
Variety, the so-called show business bible, denouncing the
strong-arm tactics of the Teamsters Union while filming in
New York. Considering the political climate of the 1950s
and the power of unions in Hollywood, what he said was
either courageous or foolhardy—depending on your point of
view. In any case, it marked the beginning of Altman's long
conflict with the film industry unions and their hostility to
him.

This singular front-page news item was trumpeted by an
editor's note: "Although there have been widespread charges
of payola in many branches of show biz for many years, this
is the first open contention that the practice has invaded, or
interfered with, filmmaking. . . ."

Altman charged that the budget on the *Suspicion* episode
was boosted almost 100 percent in New York City by "hold-
ups by landlords, city officials and police." Licenses and permits were easy to obtain, he reported, but afterward "the
payoffs are so bad that I'm scared to talk about them." Altman said Teamsters forced his filmmaking unit to use extra
trucks for transporting furniture, even though "three empties
with two Teamsters apiece drawing overtime sat around
while we had to hire two extra trucks to move furniture."
Then he added "angrily," according to the article, the movers
neglected to bring cushion-pads, damaging expensive rented
furniture beyond repair.

"We had to shoot in Steeplechase Park and their electricians said if we drew power from them we'd have to use
their men. We said we'd furnish our own power and our own
men, which we did. When we got set up, they shut the job
down and said that regardless we had to put ten electricians
on standby. We finally negotiated it down to three—and we
never saw the three men."

Altman concluded: "The electrical inspectors will let you

get away with anything you want—even if it's illegal as hell—if the payola is high enough."

These remarks would have hobbled him in Hollywood, if upbraiding Joan Harrison did not. In the event, Altman was dismissed, and from riding high on one of the quality shows on television, he moved to catchpenny production at Desilu.

Altman certainly had a way of transcending adversity. He found his niche at Desilu, where the welcome mat was out because of his relationship with William Frawley and because of the Hitchcock episodes. There, Lucille Ball and Desi Arnaz, unraveling domestically, were booming professionally, and Desilu was beginning to crank out a highly profitable syndication lineup. It was the kind of low-key setup where Altman, accustomed to Calvin, was likely to thrive.

The Whirlybirds may have been bottom-of-the-barrel by industry standards, but at Desilu Altman was given license to freewheel without being under the magisterial gaze of a Hitchcock. "A Western with helicopters," in the words of *TV Guide*, this half-hour series featured two California egg-beater pilots who captured escaped gorillas and criminals on the lam, rescued the jeopardized, and whatnot, as part of their weekly escapades. The two pilots were played by Kenneth Tobey and Craig Hill. Altman became a mainstay director of the series for two years.

In those days they completed two and a half episodes a week, filming a five-day week. It was a grueling pace, and one of the criteria that recommended a director was his ability to stay the course. Mort Briskin, a resident Desilu writer and producer of *The Whirlybirds*, credits Altman as arriving full-blown, very tough and knowledgeable. He could manage the budget and the day-to-day juggling of many locations, which was one of the things that made the show unusual.

"We worked rain or shine," remembers Dann Cahn, a Desilu editor who cut *The Whirlybirds* as well as many other Desilu series. "If it was raining, we changed it [the script] to rain." Altman flourished outside the studio, never minding

The Whirlybirds, the low-budget series that was Altman's proving-ground as a television director, with series stars Kenneth Tobey (left) and Craig Hill. (Wisconsin Center for Film and Theatre Research)

the day's forecast. Stamped in Cahn's memory is the image of Altman in Griffith Park, beaming, up to his knees in mud, shouting as he directed a scene during a rainstorm.

"He was very sure of himself, very exciting to work with, not just doing it by the numbers, 1-2-3, but trying to be clever. He didn't know all the answers, but he sure thought he did, and he was moving. It was improv time, he worked fast, and no one bothered him."

The Whirlybirds had a modest reputation in the 1950s. The series had an immediacy about it that was in part a function of the low budget. The naturalistic photography made use of the weather and reflections: the locations perked up the weak scripts. Moreover, Altman could indulge his ceaseless brooding on men and machines airborne. (Anyone who has ever seen *The Whirlybirds* and *M*A*S*H* will notice the striking similarity in the opening credit sequences.) The flying footage and flashy visuals compensated for stories that were for the most part retreads.

Altman offers many colorful anecdotes to interviewers about directing the *Whirlybirds* episodes: Each was a "mimic-movie" copycatting some classic film; each was Altman's attempt to avoid being bored by the strictures of television; he tossed out the script and wrote his own improvements on the way to locations; and so on—maybe true, maybe not. There was not an intelligent director in television who was not trying to do all of this all of the time anyway.

The assistant director, Tommy Thompson, would pick Altman up every weekday morning at 5:30 A.M. "I never read the scripts," Altman once told a French journal, "so he [Thompson] would tell me about them in the car. One was always worse than the others."

On the set Altman was introduced to the actors, who had been cast by the Desilu producers. On Wednesday at noon they would finish one episode. After lunch, they would begin the second.

Altman has called *The Whirlybirds* and the other low-budget shows of the television period his "underground work," because of the inferences and subtleties that he dashed off under the noses of Desilu producers.

"In the end," Altman told a French interviewer, "I got so fast that I could do them in two days flat. I used to take terrible chances just to challenge the boredom of it all. I remember one scene where we had two guys walking through a thick wood. It was a static scene. Anyway, I remembered seeing a mock telephone booth in the back of the prop truck, so I said, 'Get that booth and put it among those trees.'

"So we did the scene—along come the two guys, they come to the booth, one says, 'You got a dime?', the other says 'No!' The two guys walk on. There was no line of dialogue about what was a phone doing in the middle of a forest? We never explained a thing. And when the producer saw the rushes—nothing. I doubt if he noticed anything out of the ordinary.

"I learned guerrilla warfare while I was doing television. I was actually doing what the French critics praise the early American directors for. I was making films under a system and trying to sneak my own personal messages through all that veneer. [Later on] I set out to make one of the *Millionaire* segments really erotic, but so that the top brass would miss every nuance. And I did it. I got it by all of them because those people can't see. In television, I learned to say things without saying them."

An admirable ethos—very much in the Calvin tradition. Even if Tommy Thompson, the assistant director on *The Whirlybirds* and one of Altman's best friends for many years thereafter, laughs at some of this.

"We carried that phone booth with us all the time," says Thompson. "Nowadays it's called rewriting. In those days, it was called 'finishing the show on time.' If you start running long, and you need some exposition—put him in the phone booth and have him call the office. 'What, he's out of prison?' Out of the phone booth you go. Back on schedule. That was true of most of the shows at that time."

When the The *Whirlybirds* tapered off after two years, Altman stayed on at Desilu to direct numerous episodes of *U.S. Marshall* (a.k.a. *Sheriff of Cochise*), a series created by Mort Briskin and produced by John Auer, a Budapest-born Hollywood old-timer whose specialty was low-budget programmers.

But *U.S. Marshall*—about a Western federal marshal of Arizona territory—lacked the pizzazz of *The Whirlybirds*. Altman was not averse to the cops-and-robbers genre at this point in his career (some of his pilots and failed television proposals of the 1960s had a police angle), but the budget was plainly minimal, and stiff-jointed star John Bromfield was not exactly putty in Altman's hands.

Yet Altman's Desilu output did serve to promote his name around town, and the director was meeting many of the people who would serve as his support network throughout the 1960s, right up to *M*A*S*H*. Besides Barbara Turner and Vic Morrow, there were actors Charles Aidman, Philip Abbott, Albert Salmi, Dianne Foster, Robert Ridgeley—anything-goes performers whom Altman relied upon heavily during his television years. And there was Altman's third wife-to-be, Kathryn Reed, and there was Tommy Thompson.

So many people claim credit for introducing Altman to Kathryn Reed, a former Earl Carroll beauty toiling as a screen and television extra. Tommy Thompson remembers the call sheet that stipulated the future Mrs. Altman had to own the right kind of stockings for the day's filming on *The Whirlybirds*. On the set, both Altman and she were independently hung over, says Thompson. Altman was looking over the extras when he spotted her.

"How are your morals?" Altman asked. "Not good," she replied. "How's yours?" "Not good either," Altman countered. "Can we meet later?"

It is an anecdote relished and retold, in various versions, by many people who know them both.

At Desilu, Altman also cemented his relationship with Tommy Thompson. Thompson was a Los Angeles native who—Orson Welles-like—had helped perpetrate a hoax on the U.S. military establishment when, as director of an armed forces radio show in Tokyo in late 1945, he reported the invasion of Japan by sea monsters. After the war, he had done stints as floor manager and director of daytime television shows and remotes in Los Angeles, and as a second assistant director on *The Mickey Mouse Club*, before winding up as an assistant director at Desilu.

A bright, personable young man with a magnetic smile, Thompson was good with budget, good at expediting detail, good at getting the below-the-line together, and moving the production. He was sweetness personified, and always brought charm and equipoise to his authority. Nobody stayed in Altman's so-called inner circle longer—roughly twenty-five years—and he was one of the few who could regard the director, one-on-one, as a friend.

"We hit it off right from the start," says Thompson. "Bob always said that making movies was so difficult, so hard, that if you weren't having a good time, it wasn't worth doing. I think that too. And for a long, long time, we tried to do just that, keep it a good time, and make it a good movie."

Chapter

11

THE MILLIONAIRE

By 1958, Altman was feeling his oats as a television director (it was not so very different from Calvin, after all), his second divorce was clear, and he had a steady income. But he was still unable to break through to network status and remained essentially a beggar at the banquet.

By chance, he ended up directing for that squarest of American TV shows, *The Millionaire.* His one-year stint with this popular program—his eight or nine sum-total hours of film—provide a capsule illustration of how he managed to prosper in television while playing fast and loose with the rules.

The Millionaire was one of a string of syndicated shows produced by Don Fedderson, whose cornball delights included *My Three Sons, The Lawrence Welk Show,* and *Family Affair.* First broadcast in 1954, *The Millionaire* had a healthy seven-year run. Altman came on in the fifth season, on the heels of his Desilu experience, when the show was already established as a hit and as a formula.

"We were really middle America," says John Stephens, the associate producer of the series. "Every show had to have a moral, it had to have a happy ending, and Fedderson was a fanatic for telling a story. He always wanted to tell a story."

Each story began, typically, with the reclusive, super-rich John Beresford Tipton, who was never glimpsed face-on, offering a million-dollar cashier's check to some deserving (or perhaps undeserving) soul. It was a great "weinie," or gimmick, as they say in Hollywood—borrowed from a celebrity-studded 1932 movie called *If I Had a Million.* The weekly format allowed for individual episodes with revolving guest stars, shifts in tone from tragic melodrama to featherweight comedy, and endless variations on the American Dream theme that psyched up the entire Eisenhower era. Each story, of course, followed the fate of that week's fortunate millionaire.

Of all Fedderson's many series, *The Millionaire* was considered his lucky ace, the linchpin of his syndicated empire. The name of the generous John Beresford Tipton was a composite of Fedderson's hometown, his wife's hometown, and his lawyer's first name. His wife was in every weekly cast as an extra. When Tido Fedderson did not appear in the flesh, she was represented in a portrait or wall calendar. Nurse, maid, salesgirl, bar hostess—that would be Tido, never uttering a word, and picking up a check for her duty as an extra.

Altman had come to the attention of Stephens early in 1959 when Altman's agent invited industry producers to a screening of *The James Dean Story.* Stephens, in effect, the line producer of *The Millionaire,* was suitably impressed. At a cocktail reception afterward, he and the director met, and Altman's agent followed up by arranging another meeting.

In conversation, Stephens discovered they had a lot in

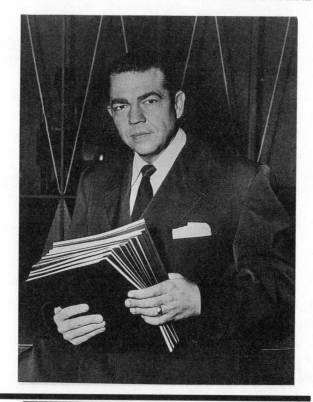

Marvin Miller, who played the reclusive Millionaire's errandboy. (Collectors Bookstore)

common. For one thing, they were both fanatical football fans (Altman was diehard for the "Big Eight," Stephens remembers). Most important, they both felt they wanted to do something "different" in television.

It did not hurt that Fedderson was himself originally from Kansas City. Altman was an unknown quantity to Fedderson. But when Stephens told Fedderson Altman was from Kansas City, Fedderson okayed hiring him with the comment that "Anyone from Kansas City can't be all bad."

Stephens became Altman's ally within the Fedderson organization. This was Altman's M.O. in television: to seek out an older or more experienced producer, to nurture a relationship with him, and to use that individual as leverage against the higher-ups. This was a pattern he repeated with other creative writer-producers in television. Perhaps, at this stage of his career, Altman truly needed the producer's input as much as he led Stephens to believe. But his producer friendships also allowed him to be something of a pet and to circumvent much of the company red tape.

"He did not like to work within the confines of a company," says Stephens. "He'd find one person and he'd align himself with that person, and in the case of Fedderson it was really me, so we would just make the shows. He didn't want to bother with the rest of the company. . . ."

Whenever Altman was assigned to a show, initially he and Stephens would discuss the script. Altman would outline the changes he envisioned. His changes might not be radical changes—deviations in dialogue, locale shifts, a new ending. ("Altman loved to change endings," remembers Stephens.) Yet Fedderson was riled by script tinkering, so Stephens would caution Altman against the more flagrant changes. Over drinks or dinner, they'd argue about the script some more.

"You know, this material really is just cut-and-dried. Just pat. We're going to make it good. . . ." Altman would say.

Altman, Stephens remembers, had a way of getting his way. Altman would sweet-talk you into something, says Stephens, or coax you, or attempt to steamroll you, or ultimately, just go ahead and wing it on the set when you weren't looking, relying upon the friendship to patch over any "misunderstanding."

"He was really the first improvisational TV director I'd run into," says Stephens. "But when Fedderson looked at it, he would freak, saying, 'What is this? Why did he do this? This wasn't in the script.'" Stephens continues: "I'd say, 'Look how funny it is, how different.' But he'd say, 'John, we're telling a *story* here, you can't ever do that to me anymore.' I'd say, 'Let me give him another chance.' He'd say, 'Just one more.' The same thing would happen. He'd say, 'Get rid of him. Fire him.' I'd call Bob and say, 'You know, you shouldn't have done this . . . we discussed this.' He'd say, 'I know, but it's much better, isn't it?' I'd say, 'I'm not saying it's better or worse, but it's not what Don wants.' Bob would say, 'Well, alright, okay. . . .'"

After which, Fedderson and Fred Henry, another company executive, might go off to New York or Europe or somewhere, leaving Stephens in charge of daily production. Stephens would immediately hire Altman back. They had become chums, dining out and double-dating frequently. It was more than just a work thing. Stephens admired Altman—his wit and his ambition and his intellect.

"Most of the people I had to deal with were very dull," he recollects. "I was young at the time and I found it fun. At least he was someone I could work with that I could also have fun with. Also, I felt we were doing something different. I was aware of the fact that we were called corny. He was an up guy, really refreshing, rather than dealing with these dolts [all the time]."

One time, in Fedderson's absence, they went to Las Vegas to shoot a segment. Nothing whets Altman's appetite more than filming in Las Vegas. They groggily awakened to responsibilities one morning in which they were scheduled to film in downtown Las Vegas. They were on their way through the hotel lobby to meet the crew at the bus when Altman was struck by the tableaux of two attractive women in bathing suits drinking cocktails with an elderly gentleman.

He turned to Stephens and said, "This is sensational, get the cameras in here." Stephens weakly protested that the scene was not accounted for in the script. But the producer let himself be convinced. "Well," says Stephens, "we got the cameras and shot the scene. It was hysterical, absolutely never written, and it had nothing to do with anything, but it was a very, very funny scene."

When Stephens returned from Las Vegas, Fedderson summoned him again. "What are you doing!?" Fedderson demanded angrily. "I told you about Altman. We are making a show called *The Millionaire*. It goes right to middle America . . . and what is *this scene*? You explain *this scene* to me." Stephens did his best to explain how funny the scene was.

Fedderson countered: "But it isn't the story." That's the way it went. "I would keep bringing him back and he would keep giving me static." Then Altman would be fired anew.

One time, Stephens went out on a limb and gave Altman his own pilot, a would-be Fedderson Western called *The Quiet Man* (no relation to the John Ford film), starring Jack Lord. They filmed it. It was never aired. Altman had turned the concept upside down and had broken rules with the camerawork. Once again Fedderson said: "Out!"

The hardest part about *The Millionaire* was those different openings—always the same really, so very narrowly conceived. But they had to *seem* different from each other, and the stunt was how to do the same thing all over again—with the shadowy John Beresford Tipton slouched in a chair as he delivers his opening discourse—without actually appearing to do the same thing all over again.

One time, with Altman in the doghouse, Stephens asked him to do five or six openers for Fedderson, just to make amends. Altman needed the money, he liked Stephens, and "he would shoot a fire hydrant if asked," says Stephens.

Altman did the handful of openings. They were "improv-type" scenes that did not, as yet, even have a script as basis. "You could put Bob in the middle of the Gobi desert and say, 'Bob, imagine this is the Coliseum, there are eight thousand people here,' and he'd say, 'Okay, uh-huh,' he'd walk around, and five minutes later he'd come up with something unbelievable that was brilliant.

"I remember one—out in the garden, behind some weird statues. There was a line about how beautiful the statue was, then the hand [of John Beresford Tipton] protruded, and there was some pronouncement about the statue and the ideal of perfect beauty. 'And speaking of beauty . . . our next millionaire . . .'"

Visually, they were above the norm. Even the performance of the customarily stodgy Marvin Miller (who was in every opening scene as the executive secretary to the reclusive billionaire) seemed to improve. When Fedderson saw them, he sat up in his chair. "Who shot these?" he asked. "Bob Altman," came the reply. "Well," he said reluctantly, "give him another chance."

Television actors and crews always liked Altman, remembers Stephens, even if the producers didn't. "Especially in TV, back in the Fifties and early Sixties, actors were told to come in and hit the marks and don't ask any questions," he notes. "Bob worked with them. There was a rapport, a balance, a give-and-take."

The technical people—except maybe the editors—appreciated the director's derring-do. "The biggest rule you used to have in episodic TV is never have people walking and talking. Because if you do that, you can't cut in and you are in a time frame. If you're running long, especially, the editor has to know when to cut. An editor can also punch up a scene by stealing looks. You had old-time rules [back then] like if the people moved, the camera didn't, or vice versa. Altman had people walking and talking, he had the camera moving and the people moving, he'd be doing dolly shots without coverage. It was unheard of to do a walk-and-talk two-shot, two and a half pages, and not cover it—but he did it, and it worked.

"It was always Bob's show," explains Stephens. "Even in the early days, when he first came out here, it was always *his* show. Nobody else in episodic TV was doing that. Even the young guys that came out from New York, as much as they put on airs, they were still organized to the system. They worked within the system. Bob was a filmmaker, even in episodic TV. He was going to make his own film, and that was that."

Stephens and Altman grew very close. Their mutual loneliness had something to do with it—both, early on in their friendship, were looking for love. Stephens, for one, thinks Altman's reputation as a womanizer may be something the director himself exaggerates to live up to a certain image of himself. Although he admits that Altman liked to walk on the wild side.

One time, Stephens recalls, he introduced him to "one of

the best-looking lady agents in Hollywood." It was a torrid, short-lived affair that had no long-term potential. It ended with the lady chasing Altman down the middle of a Los Angeles street, screaming obscenities. "He liked that kind of stuff," says Stephens. "It was like living on the fringe."

Kathryn Reed was working on *The Millionaire*—no doubt simultaneously with *The Whirlybirds*—and Stephens believes he helped bring Reed and Altman together. Stephens remembers Kathryn because she was one of the regulars who, in return for steady employment, would occasionally agree to do sub rosa bits without being bumped up on the pay scale.

Later on, the four of them—Stephens and his wife, an actress, and Altman and Kathryn—would go out regularly to a Chinese restaurant on Pico Boulevard. Sometimes Altman would drink his drink, Stephen's drink, Stephen's wife's drink, and then reorder before dinner was served.

"He'd drink very, very heavily in the evenings," says Stephens. "He would never, ever drink at work in those days. I'm death on that."

Stephens says he and Altman used to have long philosophical discussions about things like religion and drinking. Stephens believed Altman to be very conflicted about his Catholic upbringing, and guilty, still, for having torn himself away from it. "He was fighting against it. That was probably another factor in his drinking. Anyone with a strong Catholic upbringing who breaks away from it will always have those guilt feelings as to whether or not you're really doing the right thing. Once you're exposed, once you're taught, you can say anything you want to say about what you don't believe—but what *is* it you don't believe?"

Stephens says Altman explained his heavy drinking to him one time.

" 'I don't really know why I'm here. I don't know why I'm doing this. My whole dream as a little child was to do this, but I never thought I'd do it. And it so scares me that I have to drink. It then brings me to grips with myself and I can

Writer John T. Kelley, one of Altman's early and influential writing partners. He wrote many television episodes for the director, beginning with *The Millionaire*. (Abigail Shelton Kelley)

really say, 'Okay, Bob, you can do it. This isn't really a fantasy. You've got it. You can do it.'"

Steven believes: "As each new success came, it was like, 'Can I really handle this? Should I really be here?'"

In all, Altman directed eight or nine *Millionaire* segments. They are not the high-water mark of his work in television, nor the dregs. The best of them show Altman exercising his options within claustrophobic settings, with a range of lighting and noise. They were being directed much like Calvin industrials, with moments that, for the director, justified the overwhelming clichés. But these were, by and large, just moments—at best subtleties, at worst clichés of a different variety; they hardly stand out like raisins in rice.

If there was ever a *Millionaire* of Altman's that was "erotic" (as he often claimed in interviews), it escaped Stephens and evidently audiences too.

At least one significant relationship for Altman evolved out of *The Millionaire*, and that was his friendship and involvement with writer John T. Kelley.

A Catholic, Kelley had been a writer-director of the *Family Theatre* radio series on the Mutual Broadcasting System. Altman had picked up and read a screenplay of Kelley's called *The Enemy*, about a World War II regiment befriended by a spy. Altman was very enthusiastic about the script and gave Kelley an idea. The central character, Altman suggested, ought to be a black man. Much later, Kelley's script, which never sold to movies, was produced on *The Danny Thomas Hour* with Sammy Davis Jr. in the lead.

At the time Altman met him, Kelley was a relative nonentity, in Hollywood's terms. He liked and needed Altman as much as Altman liked and needed him—needed a writer to latch on to. Kelley's scripts for *The Millionaire* were his entree into serial television, after which he followed Altman into *The Troubleshooters, Bonanza*, the *Kraft* anthology series, and more.

But independent of Altman, Kelley came into his own—as a writer of television episodes (he wrote a celebrated segment of *Dr. Kildare* called "Shining Image," which earned for its star, Suzanne Pleshette, an Emmy nomination) and as an often anonymous "script doctor" brought in to revise or patch motion pictures already in production. He is credited on *The Sand Pebbles*, and uncredited on rewrites of *Planet of the Apes* (coming after Rod Serling and before Michael Wilson in the procession of writers), *A Man Called Horse, Le Mans*, and *Zig Zag*.

A witty leprechaun of a man, with tremendous force of character, Kelley is one of those individuals about whom people still get misty-eyed when reminiscing. In those early days in television, Altman was wont to describe him as "the greatest influence of my life." That was before Kelley's death, and before they had a strained parting of the ways.

The last straw, as far as Fedderson was concerned, was a *Millionaire* episode starring Jim Backus in which there was a seemingly interminable scene in a bar with Backus shooting pool. Altman encouraged Backus and the extras to improvise. A three-page scene could become a cutaway if Altman didn't like it. A two-page scene could become a seven-page scene. In this case, Altman drew in the onlookers and had Backus order a cocktail from the bartender and then ruminate on drinking with the waitress, all the while shooting pool. It was just "too far out" for Fedderson, says Stephens. This time, Altman was let go for good.

That was just fine with Altman. Already, Altman had a knack for getting kicked out just when he wanted to scram anyway. He was planning to mount his own series at Desilu called *The Troubleshooters*. It was going to be Altman's show, with Altman's imprimatur. It would star Keenan Wynn and decathlon champion Bob Mathias and a fleet of those old familiar Caterpillar trucks.

Once set up at Desilu, Altman called John Stephens every other night and implored him to join up as his producer. Altman had Stephens over to Desilu, showed him the offices, and offered to triple his salary. Stephens told Altman he would never make it in episodic TV because he would not stick to the script or take supervision. Altman said, "It'll work out, trust me." Stephens said no.

Stephens, nowadays a top television producer at Universal, says Altman never got over being turned down. Though they are "friends whenever they meet," in the parlance of Hollywood, they never worked together again.

Chapter

12

THE TROUBLE-SHOOTERS

█ t was the dying days of Old Hollywood and the boom days of television, a period every bit as volatile and anarchic as the early sound era or the video explosion of today.

Syndication was a relatively new concept—a way for the independents and entrepreneurs to bypass the networks and service the affiliates directly—and a way that passé old-timers and upclimbing no-names could toil in television and make some bucks on their way to something bigger and better. Syndicated programs were usually looked down on by the critics and networks because they were cheap and

Cast and director of the short-lived *Trouble-shooters* series, which was Hawksian melo-drama mingled with Altman precocity. Next to ex-Olympian Bob Mathias (fourth from left) is series star Keenan Wynn, followed (at right) by the redoubtable Bob Fortier, Chet Allen (Alt-man's ex–brother-in-law), and the shirt-sleeved director. A Caterpillar truck provided the back-ground for this publicity shot and many epi-sodes. (Wisconsin Center for Film and Theatre Research)

threadbare, spewed out quickly, imitative. And because they were not sold in prime-time blocks, syndicated programs were not necessarily seen by the multitudes.

The Troubleshooters is an example of a syndicated series that probably few people saw in its day and that few would ever pause to consider again if it were not for the fact that Robert Altman directed thirteen of the twenty-six episodes in its first and only season of production. The series was a veritable crossroads for directors on the way up or on the way down in their careers. German-born stage veterans such as John Brahm toiled alongside such former studio contract directors as Richard Whorf, Don

Weis, and Robert Altman, who, at thirty-five, was half Brahm's age. The producer was Frederick Ziv, a Fedderson prototype who packaged some 143 syndicated shows in his lifetime.

In lieu of Stephens, Altman was teamed up with an older Warner's screenwriter-producer by the name of Allen Rivkin, who had left New York and newspaper ink behind to migrate to Hollywood in the early 1930s, staying to write movies at Warner Brothers for James Cagney, Bette Davis, and other durable stars. Besides producing half the shows, Rivkin wrote or rewrote half of the segments, credited or otherwise. Rivkin produced every one of Altman's episodes, whereas the other thirteen *Troubleshooters* were divided up among as many as eight directors.

They were strange bedfellows: Rivkin, a short, bespectacled, graying story expert, and Altman, younger, towering, bursting with juices. Both were with *The Troubleshooters* at the behest of Keenan Wynn. Rivkin had written comedy shorts for the series star during his long career as a second banana at MGM. (Ed Wynn, Keenan's father, once described these film parts unflatteringly. "Well, in an Esther Williams picture, when she jumps into a pool, he's the fellow who gets splashed.")

Altman, too, was a friend of Wynn's. Where they met is unclear: Some people seem to think it was during the making of some long-forgotten Caterpillar opus. Wynn was the kind of gruff, comical, pants-hitching character actor Altman has always preferred: less than a star, and therefore more susceptible than one. His ilk is echoed in the Henry Gibsons and Paul Dooleys and Bert Remsens who populate Altman's movies later on.

Wynn and Altman talked about doing something ambitious together—and at one point made noises about staging, of all things, *Rasho-Mon* at the Jewish Community Center in Kansas City. Among other things they had in common was a problematic relationship with their fathers. Mostly they drank and argued together, and rode motorcycles through the the back lanes of the Hollywood hills.

Olympian Bob Mathias was the second lead—one of those people from another field that Altman swooped down on occasionally and tried to imbue with a screen persona. There was a big publicity buildup for Mathias and seemingly endless sessions with still photographers. But Mathias never hit the groove. Something in the ex-all-sports champion's sinewy limbs refused to flex before the cameras. (Altman had more success, much later, with baseball pitcher and chronicler Jim Bouton in *The Long Goodbye.* As much as Altman mocked the macho fraternity, he was always longing to be part of it.)

The Troubleshooters series was meant to be exceedingly Hawksian—the camaraderie, the action and risk-taking of a cadre of professionals. The continuing storyline had Wynn and Mathias leading a troubleshooting construction crew to points around the globe, repairing roads, bridges, dams, and dikes, while mixing in the affairs of the local folk. Through Calvin, Altman had the crucial Caterpillar connections. The Cat equipment dominated the plotting, and occasionally the show resembled Calvin outtakes, with a line of charging Cats gouging the earth to the accompaniment of triumphant musical strains.

The episodes included at least one explicit "mimic-movie" called "Gino," about an Italian urchin who steels Kodiak's (Wynn) cherished motorcycle—a nod to the postwar neorealist classic *The Bicycle Thief.* And there is a provocative episode written by John T. Kelley called "No Stone Unturned," which is an allegory about American intrusion in Southeast Asia.

During the single season production of *The Troubleshooters,* Rivkin found himself increasingly at odds with Altman, and later he described his experience on the series as one of the worst of his life. Rivkin says Altman changed dialogue and scenes and was filming straightaway without the producer's approval. The pace was so relentless—two episodes a week—and the budget so minimal that after a time Rivkin threw up his hands. No matter what he did, Altman would be out in the hills somewhere, simulating some exotic locale, and doing exactly what he liked.

Wynn, enamored of his director, would back Altman up. So would the other regulars on the series, who just happened to include Chet Allen (Altman's ex-brother-in-law, abandoning his design background and making a modest stab at an acting career) and Robert Fortier, a jack-of-all-trades player who may hold the record for appearances in Altman's television, short films, and features—invariably as a tottering drunk. An ex-MGM dancer who had hoofed it in *Singin' in the Rain* and *Show Boat*, among others, Fortier was the sort of personality who seemed to have everything necessary for stardom—range and good looks—except the relentless ambition.

Whenever Rivkin ventured onto the set, he met a united front.

No matter. The series lasted only twenty-six episodes. The budget was a factor; the premise was dubious; and the series never went for the jugular with blood-and-guts melodrama. Though interesting to followers of Altman's career for its multicharacter ensemble—the first of its type on the director's list of credits—*The Troubleshooters* failed, and Altman was back looking for work.

Chapter
13

WARNER
BROTHERS

The demise of *The Troubleshooters* was a blow. At the same time as Altman was getting serious about fitting in, he found himself starting over.

Altman had been in Hollywood almost five years. He was thinking about getting married for the third time. John F. Kennedy had been sworn in, and the Beatnik Era was seguing into the civil rights movement, antiwar rumblings, and the dawning of the Age of Aquarius. Altman was beginning to be affected by something in the air.

Indeed, the director was beginning to think of himself as an artist who was being denied his means of expression. He was writing poetry and reciting it over flickering candles with his sister Joan and his cousin-by-marriage Susan Davis. He was reading more. He took up painting (he was already an excellent still photographer) and spent long hours between job interviews daubing at the canvas.

Visitors from Kansas City during the tail end of the 1950s and the early months of the 1960s noted that he was keeping up an effervescent front in spite of the lull in his career.

"He asked us to meet him for lunch at the Brown Derby," says Harvey Fried, who with his wife, SuEllen, was vacationing in Los Angeles. "Lunch for Altman was eight martinis—and he had no money. He said, 'You get this, and I'll get dinner.' At that time he was living up above Sunset Strip with another guy. He was divorced from Lotus—although she was out there at the same time trying to get him back. They invited us up to their place for dinner, a nice place they had rented. I think the other guy was paying the rent. But when we got there, he had made no plans.

" 'C'mon,' he said, 'we're going to go out and get dinner.' So we drove down on the strip to a Safeway store where they had chickens on a rotisserie. We bought a couple and then took them back up to his house for dinner.

"I remember there was a big tennis exhibition in town. [Pancho] Gonzales was playing against Ken Rosewall at the L.A. Racket Club. He said, 'How would you like to see this?' I said, 'I'd love to.' He said, 'I'm going to take you to the tennis matches.' The Racket Club is like a small stadium. We walked all around to every gate looking for 'so-and-so.' Obviously, Altman had no money, and he was trying to find a way to get us in. After we had been to every gate, then it became apparent I was going to have to buy some tickets, or we weren't going to get in, so we went in. But I was never offended by that because he was such an entertaining guy to be with."

When, later on, Reza Badiyi passed through Los Angeles on his way to the Orient, he found that Hollywood had already tainted Altman. The director had changed enormously from the happy-go-lucky character he had once seemed, on the road from Kansas City.

"He was living with Kathryn now," says Badiyi. "His life was organized for him. All of a sudden he was tamed. The apartment above, the garage below—and Bob was painting pictures! He was an artist! Bob had never painted before.

"But he wasn't that wild, crazy, passionate man. He was a different man. Tamed a bit. But in a painful way. He didn't have as much patience as he had before. He was not so much the teacher any longer. Now, he was just a friend, and he wanted to know how long was I going to be in the Orient, and how long would I be in town. 'On the way back,' he said, 'stop and see me,' which I did. And he gave me a painting, which I still have—a couple of empty bottles of wine that he drew."

During the long writers' strike of 1960, Richard Peabody, visiting from Denver, looked Altman up. After their clash at Calvin, Peabody had landed on his feet as the news anchor of a local network affiliate. He and Altman had mended fences, and Peabody eventually ended up working as an actor in several of Altman's sales films. They had stayed in touch.

Peabody remembers that the walls of Altman's apartment in Brentwood, which he shared with Kathryn, were plastered with drawings and paintings of candles. Altman had a tremendous preoccupation with candles. Later on, during the filming of an episode of *Combat*, Altman lit an entire scene, a monastery where a German doctor was going to perform an operation without electricity, with hundreds of quivering candles. Peabody remembers thinking it was all very Catholic.

Altman was very hospitable to Peabody and invited him over to dinner. After the meal, Kathryn excused herself, and Altman grabbed a full fifth of bourbon for Peabody and a full fifth of scotch for himself and announced, "Let's do some serious drinking." Then about three in the morning, Altman jumped up and hid behind the chair and began to act real jittery and paranoid. "What are you doing here?" he demanded of Peabody. "You're my archenemy!"

"He just sort of flipped out," says Peabody, who called a cab and went back to his hotel.

During this transition stage of his career, Altman made a decision to hunker down and toil in the Hollywood trenches. Chet Allen was thinking of giving up acting and any show business aspirations, Louis Lombardo was bouncing around Hollywood camera departments, and Tommy Thompson had taken what would turn out to be a ten-year job assistant directing and producing Lucille Ball's various television series.

Alone among Altman's closest friends and family, Richard Sarafian appeared to be doing well. He was writing scripts for Vera Hruba Ralston vehicles at Republic. It was grind-work, of course—and Ralston was a hopeless case of a champion ice skater elevated to star status by her husband, chief executive Herbert Yates, who ran the studio and spent lavishly on her productions. But Sarafian was doing a lot of good writing on his own, and with Joan Altman. Altman envied Sarafian that the most—not the career progress—but the fact that Sarafian could write so easily and unselfconsciously. For Altman, writing was a difficult, very personal act of self-revelation.

Altman had written one story for a Warner Brothers television series called *The Lawman*, a one-hour Western about a fatherly, righteous Old West sheriff, and in doing so had impressed the producer of that series, Jules Schermer. Schermer knew that Altman could direct, and he lobbied on Altman's behalf with Burbank executives. Hugh Benson, the executive assistant to the president of the division, suggested a directing tryout.

Although Altman had directed a feature drama, a documentary film (distributed by Warners), hours of Calvin industrials and educationals, and some fifty-odd episodes of syndicated and serial television; though he had cowritten some of what he had directed (and had two Hollywood screenplay cocredits, apart from *Corn's-A-Poppin'* and *The Delinquents*), he was now working for one of the major Hollywood studios—on their own feudal terms—as just another new kid on the Burbank lot.

When the television division of Warner Brothers had started up in 1954, it was regarded as a loathsome necessity by studio head Jack Warner, who feared and despised television and refused on principle to watch anything on the small screen. He would not allow a television set to be shown in any of his movies. Indeed, he would not allow the word *television* to be uttered in his presence.

By 1960, however, the aging Warner had acquired a grudging respect for tube fare. For one thing, the TV division was now raking in $6 million net annually, according to Hugh Benson, who served under television president William T. Orr, a former small-time actor in Andy Hardy pictures who just happened to be Warner's son-in-law and also a capable and creative manager.

In less than a decade, Warner's had established itself as a major force in television programming, in terms of quantity as well as quality. In the early 1960s, the studio had as many as ten shows slotted on the ABC network. They were often scintillating shows like *Maverick* (which was created by Roy Huggins, and which won an Emmy for Best Western, though many people thought it was a sardonic anti-Western), *77 Sunset Strip* (based on a novel by Huggins), *Sugarfoot*, *Cheyenne*, *Bronco*, *Surfside Six*, *Hawaiian Eye*, *The Roaring Twenties*, and others. These were shows that reaped awards and notices as well as ratings.

The contract players on the lot rotated among shows, starring in one serial and guesting in another the same week. They included Clint Walker *(Cheyenne)*, Roger Moore *(Maverick)*, James Garner *(Maverick)*, Dorothy Provine *(The Roaring Twenties)*, Ray Danton *(The Alaskans)*, Richard Long *(Bourbon Street Beat)*, Anthony Eisely *(Hawaiian Eye)*, Will Hutchins *(Sugarfoot)*, Jack Kelly *(Maverick)*, Peter Brown *(The Lawman)*, Ty Hardin *(Bronco)*, and many more. Warner's was a good springboard for any director and a step up for Altman. If the shoestring and syndicated programs on his resume were ultimately considered déclassé in Hollywood, the Warner Brothers studio, steeped in movie history, had snob appeal.

Ironically, Warner's was a notoriously frugal operation. The filming for a half-hour show took place inside of three days, an hour show within six. There were roughly thirty-nine episodes of any given series a year, roughly one and a half times the number of today's series. (A one-hour episode ran forty-nine or fifty minutes before commercials, as opposed to forty-five minutes today.) Directors were paid scale; there was rarely creative participation in the profits. Offices were lucky to have a chair, a desk, a telephone, and a filing cabinet. More often than not, a director shared his desk with an assistant director. Benson and Orr considered it a coup to have persuaded Jack Warner to permit them a carpet and modest furnishings befitting their executive status.

Orr and Benson ran a very centralized system. All the television personnel—producers, front-office execs, and production department—were in the same office area, a two-story building at the rear of the lot. The producer of a series had his own office, a secretary, and perhaps an adjoining office for an assistant. The series' directors and writers were allotted makeshift quarters as assignments were made.

Everything was strictly by the numbers. Each day of filming ran from 8 A.M. to 9 P.M. There were roughly two hundred scenes in a half-hour script, twenty-five setups a day, budgeted at seventy thousand dollars an episode. All of these subtotals were supervised closely by factotums, and each day was accounted for to higher-ups in memos totting up the minutes, pages, scenes, setups, and that most ignominious of all categories, "days behind." There were memoranda and records kept of costs, story synopses, story changes, scene-by-scene breakdowns, costume and historical data, pertinent correspondence, and dictums from the studio research department regarding authenticity and legality. One wonders when anyone found time to turn on the camera in those good old days.

The television complex was centered around a courtyard with a ship's railing hung with ivy on the second floor where the executive offices were located. On the balcony outside the executive offices, at lunch or at intervals, people congregated. You might find anyone from André de Toth, a colorful, eye-patched veteran of the 1940s to young Sam Peckinpah, cutting his swath as a brilliant and sometimes sodden maverick.

The doors to the executive offices were always open, with people coming and going. The triumvirate of Orr at the top, Benson for administration, casting, and hiring, and Richard Bluell on the story and script side, prided themselves on always being accessible. It was one way they kept track of costs, maintained a positive morale, and ensured the sameness of excellence and tone that distinguished Warner's television output. At times it seemed a maelstrom, but they kept track of every script and every series; and at the end of every day for many years, Bluell, Benson, and Orr looked at every foot of dailies shot the previous day—several hours of dailies nightly, until midnight, followed by a dinner conference for discussion and resolution of problems, and some mornings not home until dawn.

The movie lot itself was a grand 104 acres. The television unit had been dubbed "The Annex" by the studio management, but the people in "The Annex" quite rightly dubbed themselves "The Studio," knowing full well that the features department was practically moribund while the tail was wagging the dog.

In 1959, the television division was manufacturing four hundred hours of entertainment a year. A *TV Guide* piece summed up the situation. The number of sound stages set up for shooting television: 23. For movies: none. Television writers on hand: 62. Movie writers: none. Television producers embroiled in preparation: 10. Movie producers: 3. Twenty TV shows presently filming; one movie shooting, at a Utah location.

"We were keeping the studio afloat," says Benson matter-of-factly.

Because of the high television production, the Warner's staff producers were obligated to go out and purchase writers and directors "in wholesale lots" (in Benson's words) at the beginning of each season so that the studio would be assured of fulfilling its guarantees to the network. Many writers and directors would be given a "six-pack," or six-segment, deal; there would be implicit trade-offs—and a more prestigious program might be guaranteed to a director in exchange for a teleplay on "spec." It was considered a definite plus if a director could also write, albeit *not* a disadvantage if he could not. (Few could.)

For his tryout ritual, Altman was ordered to observe a more experienced director at work and to learn the Warner's method—the tight scheduling, the massive equipment (the studio-bound Mitchell cameras), the short crews, the dominance of the producer in the hierarchy. The Warner's "observer-director" system had been pro forma for many years, and more eminent figures than Altman, such as actor-director Francis Lederer, who had many years of familiarity with the studio system as a contract player, had gone the route. "Altman didn't like it, of course," recalls Benson, "but we did that with a number of directors."

If Altman bristled, he also complied—and duly he became an "observer-director." At this particular low point of the many such in his career, intermittently employed, drinking too much, short of money, he needed the work as well as the status of Warner's. But it was to be a short-lived humiliation, for he was given a full directing assignment within weeks. According to Benson, Altman immediately showed himself to be professional, assertive, knowledgeable of the camera, attentive to actors, and intolerant of delay.

Altman began in the fall of 1959 on the old *Sugarfoot* series—a picaresque Western about a shy, retiring would-be lawyer (played by Will Hutchins) who is studying for the bar as he odd-jobs his way through the frontier—before being introduced into the Warner's rotation, or "doing the circuit," as it was called. Over the next two years Altman notched an

Contract player Roger Moore, filmdom's future 007, confers with Altman on the set of "Bolt Out of the Blue," the *Maverick* segment that Altman wrote and directed. (Warner Brothers)

episode each as director of *Hawaiian Eye, Lawman, Sugarfoot, Surfside Six,* and *Maverick.*

Maverick was considered top-drawer at Warner's, and Altman's one segment was a good one.

His "Bolt Out of the Blue" episode, which he wrote as well as directed, found Beau Maverick (Roger Moore, the once and future James Bond) befriending an old horse thief and being mistaken for one himself. Here at Warner's Altman was permitted to pitch his stories orally, and it was a veteran screen-writer by the name of Ardel Wray who initially wrote up the director's treatment. There was immediate enthusiasm from the story department for this Altman story as "one of the best (and most fully developed *Maverick* outlines) we've seen." (Of course, the story department objected that Altman had named the horse thief "Nixon." So did the ABC censors, arguing that Maverick must remain apolitical. The name of the character was changed.)

The acting in the episode was deft—by Moore, by Will Hutchins guest-starring as "Sugarfoot" (a lawyer who "hasn't lost a case yet . . . 'cause he hasn't had a case yet"), and by Tim Graham as the prevaricating horse thief. It was a loopy Western parody, with mock heroism and mock romance. Much of the script derived from Altman's own preoccupa-tions—the "Nixonish" (a likable scalawag, after all) horse thief fakes his heart condition—and there was an abundance of religious punning.

No doubt this is the sort of television that Altman is refer-ring to when he says he leapfrogged the mass medium by "kidding the material." It is telling, at this stage of his ca-reer, how often he would couch his storytelling in sweet-natured, almost hokey comedy—and how absent that aspect would be from his later caustic and more embittered work.

Though Altman is cocredited on other scripts at Warner's, more often than not he is uncredited, except in story and expense logs. "There wasn't a script we would give him that he wouldn't rewrite and then make it better. He would re-write everything," says Benson. This was regarded as quite the dividend of his stay at Warner's, even if it was no big deal with Altman (he would do it whether or not it was expected of him).

The "remedial writing" shows up in accounts as five hun-dred dollars extra on top of his directing fee. If Altman wrote the entire script, the writing fee would amount to $2,515. Directing a single episode, by contrast, brought $2,768, so if Altman could manage both, as he did with "Bolt Out of the Blue," he would more than double his salary. That was always one of the benefits of a writing credit, for Altman—the additional money.

Benson attests to Altman's ability to weather any script crisis. One night, for a rocky episode of *Hawaiian Eye*, they stayed up all night talking over the storyline—Altman, Benson, and two secretaries. Altman dictated changes, Benson wrote them down, and then the pages were passed on to the secretaries, who kept up with the typing. The task was finished around dawn. Altman had a hearty breakfast. Then he went out and shot the morning's pages without any sleep or grumbling, "which is an example of his perseverance and dedication," says Benson.

From all reports, Altman was very well integrated at Warner's, which means he ought to have been gravitating to steady work on the more highly regarded shows. But he preferred a more shadowy zone of endeavor, and soon positioned himself on one of the lowlier Warner's series, *The Roaring Twenties* (where Jules Schermer was a staff producer). This is a tendency he has nurtured throughout his career, a real Kansas City streak of preferring to work outside the main geography, out of the limelight, against expectations, slouching toward the low-budget, the scabrous, the offbeat, and the obscure. The better to prove himself; the better defense against failure.

There was also the rumor everyone remembered twenty-five years later: that Altman was infatuated with series star Dorothy Provine. She was a shy, talented, blue-eyed platinum blonde with a history of nervous breakdowns, a self-taught singer and dancer who choreographed her own routines, a tiger on the set, and a perfectionist. Apart from Provine, playing a Texas Guinan–like nightclub entertainer, the cast also included Donald May and Rex Reason (as two beat reporters covering the action), Gary Vinson (as an ingenuous copyboy), and Mike Road (as a police lieutenant invariably racing to the rescue).

The anthology series was based ever so loosely on the 1939 Cagney-Bogart movie of the same title, but jazzed up enough for contemporary viewers that ABC censors were kept busy

Guest star Ray Danton and series regular Dorothy Provine in a scene from the "White
Carnation" episode of *The Roaring Twenties,*
Altman's series of preference while dues-paying
at Warner's. (Warner Brothers)

complaining about the casual brutality, vulgar speech and
slang, physical intimacy, sexual overtones, and predominant
imagery of women's underclothing. It was in the graphic, sophisticated mode of *The Untouchables,* yet there was opportunity for comedy and romance. At the time, *TV Guide* rated
the show as "inaccurate, adolescent, embarassing and dull."
But former Warner's executive Hugh Benson says that, as

Warner's shows go, *The Roaring Twenties* was every bit as good as *Maverick*, if not better.

In that two-year period, Altman directed at least ten episodes of *The Roaring Twenties*. They included a striving two-parter ("Right Off the Boat") with Roger Moore as a star-crossed rumrunner; a tough, scaled-down episode about a dance marathon derivative of the Horace McCoy novel *They Shoot Horses, Don't They?*; and, most fulfilling, a sledge-hammer suspense ("The Prairie Flower") about a psychotic small-town girl (Pat Crowley) who schemes to murder and stand in for a Broadway star (Patrice Wymore). "The Prairie Flower" is yet one more link in the chain from Tennessee Williams to *That Cold Day in the Park, Images, Three Women,* and *Come Back to the Five and Dime, Jimmy Dean, Jimmy Dean.*

Ray Danton remembers those frenetic days as a Warner's contract actor.

He remembers filming three shows simultaneously and making a thousand dollars a week and being one of the highest paid persons on the lot besides—working one show in the morning with James Garner, going to work in the afternoon on another show with someone else, and acting in his own movie, *The Rise and Fall of Legs Diamond,* at night.

Nowadays, Danton is himself a television director—for episodes of a variety of series including *Cagney and Lacey.* He is now accustomed to the relative luxury of working on a Top Ten Nielsen-rated program, where he is constantly surrounded by a galaxy of assistants. At his beachside home in Malibu, he reflected recently on the difference between then and now, and on the director who had tremendous influence on him, and on his directing.

"In those days two men produced eleven shows," says Danton. "Now, eleven men can't produce one show. What's the difference? You tell me."

Years later, they meet—Roger Moore, Efrem Zimbalist Jr., Angie Dickinson, James Garner—and they still talk about how hard they were working for so little money. And how gratifying it all was. And how, as a result, the ego, the self-importance, got swept away in the busyness of just plain working.

Danton did several shows with Altman, including a subsequent *Combat* episode. In the "White Carnation" segment of *The Roaring Twenties*, Danton was playing a fatalistic gambler by the name of Dandy Jim. Very Altmanesque.

Danton remembers that, literally as well as figuratively, Altman was a man of many hats. When Danton first met him, the director was wearing an old fedora, and Danton couldn't figure out why Altman would be wearing a hat in Southern California in the middle of the summer. Was it an affectation, or was he sensitive about going bald?

Altman was very pleasant to Danton and very animated. Danton waited for him to say something about what he wanted from the character. Altman asked him if he minded improvising. Danton said no. After all, he had been trained in New York in improvisation. Altman said he did not have any idea how he was going to shoot the crap-game sequence in the upcoming episode, but he was probably just going to give Danton a lot of greenbacks and let him play the craps for real. Did Danton know how to shoot craps? Sure—Danton was in the service for three years. That's all they discussed.

Danton picks up the story, "We got on the set and we got into a crap game. He gave us all some money and we started a crap game and I had no idea where the camera was. Fortunately, I was winning. He must have shot this crap game for thirty, forty minutes. I won this guy's belt, someone else's suit, one guy's tie. I won everything. The dice were rolling well. I thought, 'The dice must be loaded.' 'No,' he said, 'good fortune is riding with us.'"

A couple of days later they were doing the last scene of the episode. Danton will never forget what happened.

They were working on a tiny set. Altman had been closeted in whispers with Harold E. ("Hal") Stine, an older cameraman who was doing the photography for the occasion.

Altman came over to Danton and told him they were two minutes short on the program.

"So what?" responded Danton.

"What can you do to make up two minutes?" asked Altman. "Why don't you think of something, and I'll be back in five minutes. Only we don't have time to light anything, so we'll put the camera here by the window. What can you do by the window that will give us about two minutes of film?"

"Alone?" Danton asked.

"Yes," said Altman.

"All right," said Danton.

That might have bothered some people, but Danton had had all the New York grounding.

"He came in and set up the camera and I looked out the window and asked Hal to put a new light out there blinking on and off," says Danton. "He said okay. Bob handed me some dice. I said, 'What are these dice for?' He said, 'At the end of whatever you're going to be doing, I want you to roll the dice and I will pan with the dice. If you play the scene properly, the dice will come up seven.' I said, 'C'mon Bob, you've loaded the dice again.' 'No,' he said, 'good fortune is riding with us.' I rolled the dice a few times and they came up five, three, two. But he said, 'Don't worry, if you play the scene right, they will come up seven.'"

When he thought about it later, Danton realized that in giving him the spiel about the dice Altman had diverted his concentration so that he would not worry about playing the scene.

"I wound up making some speech about 'the girls out there, the high heels, and the hookers at night, and so on and so forth, and now it is time for me to go out there,' and I threw these dice. Sure enough, they came up seven. He said, 'Wrap, print,' and we went home. I never forgot that. That was a magic moment for me."

Altman was now picking up work on other network shows—*Peter Gunn*, *Route 66*, and so on. But he never lasted beyond a single episode, and it may be that the discipline he evidenced within the structure of Warner's—not to mention the steady paycheck—permitted him to be more high-handed with other producers.

In the case of *Route 66*, Altman's then agent, Harold Green, showed producer Herbert B. Leonard some silent 16mm party footage that was probably a forerunner of the later short subject *The Party*. "It was terribly interesting and much better than [anything by] anybody at the time that I had seen," says *Route 66* producer Herbert B. Leonard.

When Leonard met Altman, he believed the director to be in some private distress, unhappy in his personal life, physically unfit, addicted to gambling and booze. Although this was around the same time that Altman was working productively at Warner's, Leonard was unaware of his Burbank employment. Leonard was content (and led) to believe that he was discovering Altman as if he were some fresh film-school find.

According to Leonard, the preliminary script conversations were very frank, and Altman vowed to conform to the script, called "Some of the People, Some of the Time" and written by series creator Stirling Silliphant. It was a seriocomic tale to star Altman's shadowman Keenan Wynn as a traveling bunko artist who sponsors a small-town talent contest with a trip to Hollywood as the prize. Rich, subtextual implications for Altman!

On location (in Boiling Springs, Pennsylvania), Altman and Keenan Wynn were "drunk all the fucking time, fighting all over the bar. They tore up the town," according to Leonard.

Back in Hollywood, where Leonard was receiving dispatches, the dailies indicated Altman was tearing up the script as well. "He was rewriting it sideways," says Leonard. "He didn't make a big move forward in the material. He didn't hurt it any really, but he just did it his own fucking way and changed a lot of values. In the end it didn't matter so much, but it was all just so arbitrary. I said, 'Fuck you. I'm never going to hire you again. I just didn't need the aggravation.' I really liked him, but he gave me a royal pain in the ass."

It may be inconsiderate to note that the episode itself reflects none of this behind-the-scenes Sturm und Drang. It was quite the folksy slice-of-wry, of the sort that Altman and Keenan Wynn usually arrived at, after some circumnavigation, in their television collaborations. And the director evinced more than his customary empathy for the small-town atmosphere, the diners and pool halls, and the Altmanesque yearning of a young woman to escape reality and fulfill her fantasies in movies.

Meantime, Altman's ambitions to launch a television series of his own did not end with the cancellation of *The Troubleshooters.* Shortly thereafter, and continuing throughout the 1960s, he would have frequent series brainstorms, and would invest a flurry of time and money in an effort to convince the right people that it was the next sure thing.

During this period, there was something called *Night Watch,* a title Altman liked well enough to recycle later in the decade for another project. This first *Night Watch* was a police procedural about a widowed city detective with two children. Altman wrote the story, Larry Marcus wrote the pilot script, and Collier Young, the partner of Ida Lupino and Howard Duff, was involved as producer.

A pilot episode, starring Stephen McNally, was filmed. In those days, the big advertising agencies kept memoranda of programs in development and gauged their viability, reporting on screenings and industry gossip. The agency score card for this one was "excellent," and the pilot was deemed "superior" to many television shows, "though not in the same league as *Naked City.*" But, the report concluded, since the program sacrificed suspense and action for the sake of characterization, *Night Watch* might be better for syndication than for network. The pilot was dead, and no further episodes were produced.

Chapter
14

BONANZA

During this same time span, the 1960–1961 television season, when Altman was supposedly endeavoring to carve out a foothold at Warners, he was also helping to establish the number-one show on television—*Bonanza.* Strange! Although in interviews Altman reminisces freely about shows like *The Whirlybirds* or *Combat,* he rarely expatiates on his connection with the granddaddy of all dynastic Westerns. Yet his role as one of the early directors of the series was not marginal. David Dortort, creator, writer, and producer of *Bonanza* for its fourteen-year run, says flatly: "In some respects he was my best director . . . a giant

The original four Cartwrights: (from left) Dan Blocker as Hoss, Lorne Greene as Ben, Pernell Roberts as Adam, and Michael Landon as Little Joe. The mercurial Pernell Roberts quit the popular Western series in 1965. (Republic Pictures)

among pygmies. He had a large share in the strength and the popularity of the show."

In 1959, NBC commissioned Dortort to create and produce a prime-time Western to go up against *Perry Mason* in its Saturday-night slot. Dortort proposed a quality hour-long show boasting a weekly budget of $100,000 and treatment of "important" themes. Dortort sagely convinced NBC to film the series in color and to anticipate the boom in color television sets—he thought the evergreens of Lake Tahoe, the snowcapped peaks and beautiful blue skies, would look simply great in "living color." *Bonanza* would draw its source material from the era of the Comstock Lode, the great Virginia City strike of 1859 that spawned silver barons whose only allegiance was to their own aggrandizement. The explosion of fortune hunters would be seen from the point of view of the eco-conscious, square-dealing Cartwrights, a family of three young half brothers with different mothers (all deceased), living on the spacious Ponderosa ranch with their father.

The character of noble, masculine, all-wise Ben Cartwright was a psychologically projected ideal—modeled after Dortort's own father, a failed candy store owner. Lorne Greene, once an announcer for the Canadian Broadcasting Company, was plucked from a *Wagon Train* episode for the role of patriarch Ben Cartwright. Pernell Roberts, from the New York stage, filled the network's demand for a Brando type for the part of the moody eldest son, Adam. Two-hundred-and-seventy-five-pound Dan Blocker, a bookish ex-schoolteacher from Texas, was cast as the bumbling Hoss (his name means "good luck" in Norwegian). Michael Landon, theretofore best known as the juvenile star of *I Was a Teenage Werewolf*, was set as Little Joe, the youngest son, who, it was hoped, might have some heartthrob appeal. (*TV Guide* promptly hailed him as a "Kookie in chaps.")

Altman came into the series after its troubled first year. Early episodes had wavered in tone, *Bonanza* could not crack the Nielsen Top Twenty, and Dortort's series was consistently whomped in the ratings by *Perry Mason*. Panicking, NBC drafted old-time studio screenwriter John Lee (*Red Dust, Bombshell*, etc.) Mahin to refine Dortort's concept. Dortort held firm.

Then, partly because color sets were exploding in sales (*Perry Mason* never did go to color), the show caught on—this decorous, Freudian Western with scripts of literary pretension, an inexhaustible foreground of love affairs and shootouts, and in the background, a simmering sibling rivalry among the three sons—a callow romeo, a genial giant, and a haunted soul. By the end of the second year, *Bonanza* trailed *Perry Mason* by only one position in the ratings, and by 1962—when Altman was no longer associated with the program—the series had moved to Sunday night, surpassed *Perry Mason*, and lodged itself in the Top Ten, where it remained entrenched for the next ten years.

Dortort was acquainted with George W. George. On the lookout, during the uneasy transition season of 1960–1961, for interesting directors for the *Bonanza* series, Dortort asked to see the James Dean documentary. Dortort says he was no more aware of Altman's activity at Warner's than that studio was cognizant of Altman's relationship with *Bonanza*—such was the anonymity under which most television directors toiled. It might have interested both parties to realize that *The Roaring Twenties* ran opposite *Bonanza* in the early Saturday-evening time slot, so that on at least two separate occasions, Altman was scheduled against himself (as it were), credited with the direction of episodes of competing series.

After viewing *The James Dean Story*, Dortort says he perceived Altman as a director who was mentally curious, an innovative cameraman, someone who was trying to stretch the medium to some extent. He asked around town about Altman and got the word back that the director was unreliable, crazy, sometimes falling-down drunk. That intrigued Dortort further.

So he brought Altman in for an interview, and what he vividly remembers is how pathetic Altman acted. That may have been part of Altman's endearment routine—he was as good at being adopted by sympathetic producers as he was at adopting wayward actors—but Dortort remembers Altman as being ballooned up, strapped financially, very meek, with breath that could kill a horse at twenty paces. The director was pale, trembling, and shabbily dressed in clothes that he might have slept in.

Altman told Dortort that he was being harried to death by child support and alimony demands from his ex-wives. "Sometimes on the set," says Dortort, "he'd be screaming into a telephone, 'All right, put me in jail, will that do any good?' It was embarrassing."

Dortort warmed to Altman instantly (and still warmed to the memory of him when interviewed twenty-five years later). He gave Altman an episode of *Bonanza* to direct on the proviso that Altman would promise to abstain from drinking, stay on budget and on time, and honor the script.

Indeed, throughout his *Bonanza* hitch, Dortort stresses, Altman kept his word. The director was always on time, on budget, and he followed the script (Altman never wrote a *Bonanza* episode). His story sense could be illogical, says Dortort, but there was "a quality to his work immediately," an intuitive quality and an intellectual quality that placed him above the other series directors.

"First of all his camerawork, or let's say the way he uses his cameraman, was consistently brilliant," says Dortort, "and I think that the show [under him] always had an extremely professional look. There was never anything amateurish about Altman and any of his setups. His setups were immaculate. He would take chances with the camera, as opposed to just *medium, close, long*. He would move the camera, use pan shots, take great chances. And almost always successfully. He's an extremely good cameraman. So he gave the show a wonderful look.

"Also, because of his savage wit and savage commentary, in another way he made his shows stronger than most directors. Not in terms of action, but the impact, the emotional impact, it was strong. Very strong. There were never any loose or flabby moments with Altman."

Bonanza, of course, had many first-rate directors in its time—among them, Tay Garnett, Joseph Sargent, and Gerd Oswald. Altman was not the best on pure action terms (William F. Claxton and William Witney were, says Dortort); stunts, fisticuffs and gunplay, cavalry and Indians—that was not the director's strong suit. But, says Dortort, Altman seemed to be searching for something in the scripts that would allow him to express something inchoate inside himself, "something deep down in his own psyche." Sometimes that gave his episodes an unusual and reckless, off-kilter quality.

Bonanza creator and producer David Dortort in a publicity photo from the beginning of the show's fourteen-year run. Altman directed some quality episodes. (David Dortort)

"Altman was happier in a situation where cruelty was part of the story," says Dortort, "where malicious, vengeful action was part of the story. He wasn't terribly patient with soft, gentle stories. He needed something with bite. There was always this thing in Altman's story where he would look for something . . . he would detect something that wasn't in the script . . . but it was an *extension* of something that was in the script.

"He'd take something one step beyond what was in the script or what was necessary, sometimes to the point where we would have conflicts, where he would add something I felt was extraneous and which suddenly changed the whole tenor of what we were doing. It would only confuse the audience and the actors. Always one step more. Always a very strong kind of thing, like a startling, wonderful image appearing out of nowhere. . . ."

Like John Stephens before him, Dortort became attached to Altman as a friend as well as an employer. Dortort felt Altman was an essentially lonely man, and at the end of the day of filming or editing, they'd often be left together and go off to dinner or drinks. Like Stephens, Dortort found Altman to be a kindred spirit—"a stimulating companion to talk with"—an "intellectual talent"—if sometimes too intellectual for his own good (and for television).

"He is one of the few people I've known," says Dortort, "and I've known many intellectuals—who at times can be profound."

It is tempting nowadays to deprecate the formula of *Bonanza*, as it has been much imitated and stiffly parodied. But in the early 1960s, *Bonanza* was the archetype for a kind of thinking-person's Western that theretofore did not exist. There was the usual gunplay and the black hats, but at the same time this series tried, oh how it tried, to be meaningful!

The three holstered *Bonanza* sons were forever being tortured by some ethical conflict that could only be mediated in a (Rooseveltian) fireside chat presided over by a fantasy father figure. Usually, the dilemma could be boiled down to, "Does might make right, Pa?" It was simplistic, sometimes simpleminded; but other Westerns did not often pause to ask such questions. And sometimes, in the emotional family interplay and the questing for story values, the episodes could be affecting and powerful.

To a French interviewer many years later, Altman boasted of introducing satire into the *Bonanza* quartet and their imbecilities, and he compared his approach to that of writer-director Preston Sturges, whose nutball inversions of the American Dream made for some classic film comedies of the 1940s. But this was hardly Altman's contribution. Comic inversion was par for the course on *Bonanza*, especially when the script featured Little Joe and Hoss in a comic outing.

But Altman did execute a number of memorable early episodes with unusual scripts that lifted the series above the norm. "Silent Thunder" with Stella Stevens, "The Dream Riders," (a manifest forerunner of *Brewster McCloud* and *Streamers*), and "The Rival," with Charles Aidman and Peggy Ann Garner, were all gripping segments.

If anything, Altman seemed to find solace in Hoss, who was stuttering and malapropistic when sparking women, eloquent and philosophical when speaking to his pa. When Altman was drawn to a character, he was also drawn to the actor who was playing the character. Both from middle America, Altman and Dan Blocker became good friends, though Blocker stopped short of ever being a camp follower. According to Dortort, Altman was especially attentive in episodes to the Hoss character, which became a sort of directorial alter ego.

In a relatively serious episode like "The Dream Riders," it is Hoss who reveals "adventure in his soul" and bespeaks what is also the director's passion—flying. In a decidedly more comic episode like "The Many Faces of Gideon Finch," where Hoss competes with Little Joe for the affections of a dithery ingenue, the director wears his heart on his sleeve for the klutzy older brother, and the episode becomes an Altmanesque parable about being loved for one's inner self.

Still, Altman seemed equally taken with the character of Little Joe. That was certainly one of Altman's emerging gifts, to find himself in disparate characters. Even as Hoss expressed the "inner Altman," to some extent Little Joe signified the more shiny "exterior Altman," the callow womanizer. It may be that it embarrassed the director, years later, to recall that there was as much kinship as there was "satire" in his treatment of both characters.

As Altman got back on his feet professionally, there were little things that began to bother Dortort—Altman's intol-

Hoss soars aloft in the "The Dream Riders," a *Bonanza* episode directed by Altman that rehearsed themes later developed in *Brewster McCloud.* (Republic Pictures)

erance of stupidity, his indecision about endings, his flagrant pursuit of women.

For the third season, Altman was picked by Dortort to direct an outdoor episode, a plum assignment since only a minimum of filming was done outside the standing set. On location at Lake Tahoe, Altman embarrassed Dortort by staying up all night at the tables with "a rather striking television actress with a hollow leg" who bested Altman at drinking and at playing craps. Altman, pale and wobbly, showed up the next morning to put in a full day of filming. But because Dortort knew and liked Kathryn, he felt sorely compromised.

There was also a cathartic showdown with John T. Kelley, who had been drafted to write some *Bonanza* episodes. Struggling to make their mark together (and separately), Kelley and Altman had become soulmates as well as creative collaborators, although some people feel Kelley was a passive, kindly person who did not receive his due for giving polished form to Altman's free-form ideas. Now, Kelley was heard to complain more and more, "I do all the work on these things."

Dortort had engaged Kelley to write a spin-off pilot for another series about a fantabulous, Paul Bunyanesque Western character called Sam Hill. There was more than the usual amount of disagreement about the script, and behind Altman's back Kelley felt obliged to side with Dortort. There was an ugly confrontation between Altman and Kelley in Kelley's apartment; and though Kelley ultimately tried to write a middle ground, the intended pilot never jelled. The "Sam Hill" episode became just another *Bonanza* segment, one of Altman's last. (The script is, in fact, credited to Dortort.)

It was almost as if Altman was deliberately poisoning the *Bonanza* relationship. His pride was returning, and with it his manifest contempt. Now, there was vague sloppiness in his work.

"I can't put my finger on it," says Dortort, "but suddenly we began to have conflicts. He was doing what I felt were more reckless things. I knew it wasn't his best work anymore, though it was still good. But I wondered what was bothering him. I thought it through and I came to the conclusion that he was getting bored. A little bit of burn-out, maybe. I was working him awfully hard but that was at his request, because he always needed more money. Other directors resented me because I was favoring him and everybody knew it.

"He was drinking again, even on the set at times, and I

would chew him out. I think he drank because he felt that, even though he tried, and I respected him for trying to bring that one step beyond, that extra dimension, to the show—something crazy, perhaps *bizarre* is a better word—it wasn't really there.

"I really liked him. I really respected him. But I called him in and I said, 'Something's bugging you.' He said no. I said, 'Yes there is, Bob, and I think I know what it is. I think you're tired of doing the show.' He said that it wasn't that he was tired of the show. He loved the show and everything it had done for him. He had found his self-respect again, and he really was putting money away in the bank. He was taking care of his family responsibilities. He was making his child support money. He said, 'It's something else. I want to do feature films.' So I said, 'Ah.'

"I almost felt a lack of patience. I said, 'Bob, you're like an actor walking through his part.' He said, 'I still do good work.' I said, 'Of course you do, you do great work. But you want off the show. . . .' He said, 'I don't know what I'd do about income.' I said, 'Then, I'll write you a deal for the next year right now.' He said, 'Look, it may be a mistake, but I want to do a film, and I think if I don't take that chance right now, when will I take it?'

"So he left a number one show, and we parted the best of friends. Dissolved."

But Altman and John T. Kelley did *not* part the best of friends. There had been tension between Kelley and Altman for some time. Altman wanted to control and shape Kelley's career, but Kelley would not let him. Altman tried seducing Kelley with his fast-lane lifestyle, but Kelley could not be maneuvered into the position of acolyte, and he began to stay away from the Altman bashes—the Saturday-night drinkathons and the Sunday-morning hangover parties followed by brunch. Kelley and actress Abigail Shelton were monogamous, and they were wary of the "open marriage" bit.

At one point Altman summoned Kelley to a lunch meeting at a Smokehouse restaurant in the valley. When Kelley arrived, he was greeted by Altman and a certain well-known television actress of the day, with whom Altman was having a steamy affair. Altman proceeded to have lunch with Kelley, eschewing business, and behaving matter-of-factly about the pretty female draped around his shoulders. Kelley, who was on strong terms with Kathryn, went storming home, mad, vowing to stay away from Altman.

Their formal collaboration came to an end, though Altman would sentimentally call Kelley in, or ask him for advice, now and then, for years thereafter. Abigail Shelton and Kelley would occasionally attend Altman parties as their paths drifted apart. At one such occasion, Altman sauntered up to Kelley and glared drunkenly at him.

"I don't need you anymore . . ." Altman said vehemently.

"Isn't it wonderful?" Kelley replied.

Altman could not get to John T. Kelley.

Within a few months of the success of *M*A*S*H* (on which Kelley did some uncredited spit 'n' polish), Kelley was diagnosed with cancer. In 1972, he died.

Kelley and Dortort had remained in touch. Dortort and his wife went to the funeral ceremony at a Catholic church in Beverly Hills. Everyone was waiting for Altman, the newly crowned king of Hollywood, with his dread of death and funerals, his love for and his complicated relationship with Kelley, to show up. He didn't appear.

"It was kind of indicative," is what Dortort says.

After the memorial was over and people were getting into their cars to leave, Altman pulled up with a squeal of tires, as if making a grand late entrance, slammed the door of his car, and lurched out, asking, "Am I late?" Abigail Shelton Kelley just looked at him and said nothing.

In any case, Altman, fed up with both Warner's and *Bonanza*, had decided to move on. At Warner's, in the spring of 1961, he had the chance he was looking for to escape television and direct a motion picture.

Out of Warner's story files, Altman had rescued an old treatment by a 1930s aviator-screenwriter named John Monk

Saunders, who was actress Fay Wray's first husband. Altman updated the treatment by Saunders and gave himself a credit as cowriter. *The Force*, as it was called in embryo, involved narcotics, international smuggling, and the lustre of the Royal Canadian Mounted Police. It was the first of numerous Altman projects to be planned for location filming in Vancouver, his alternative of preference to a Hollywood backlot.

The Force was announced in the trades, locations were scouted in Canada, the budget was approved . . .

Meanwhile, Altman was signed to direct a two-hour pilot for a television program called *The Gallant Men*. As a generation of World War II veterans came of middle age, there was a craze for shows about the wartime experience—everything from the ludicrous *McHale's Navy* to the drama about flying aces, *Twelve O'Clock High*. *The Gallant Men*, Warner's entry in the World War II sweepstakes, was to follow the adventures of a war correspondent marching with the Fifth Army from one theater of war to another, depicting the stress, heroism, and the human drama of ordinary Americans caught up in a foreign war.

The series was conceived jointly by executive producer Orr and story editor Bluell, who was donning producer stripes. Bluell had served in the Italian campaign, and admired director John Huston's documentary *The Battle of San Pietro*. So did Altman; they screened it together.

Altman had a luxurious eight-day schedule (one for tests and one for postproduction) and a $170,000 budget, his highest ceiling to date. The primary scenes were shot at the Bell Ranch in December of 1961 and January of 1962. But the resulting telefilm was schematic and slow-moving compared to the later *Combat*. The Warner's executives insisted on substantial use of vintage newsreel footage, thereby diminishing the impact of the personal drama. Still, *The Gallant Men* pilot sold for the 1962–1963 season.

Altman was offered a substantial contract to head up the series, but he was chafing under the close supervision of the staff producers at Warner's.

Also, Warner's had let *The Force* go by the boards, and Altman's disappointment was intense. Everything had gone as prescribed right up to filming. Warner's came within a month of the actual start date before the studio yielded to anxieties about location costs and a first-time feature director. The project was unceremoniously canceled. It would be another five years before Altman would be given another chance to direct a motion picture—also, ironically, at Warner's.

Partly as a result of *The Gallant Men*, Altman's stock was rising elsewhere around town. Two years previous, the director had been working at the low rate of approximately three thousand dollars per half-hour episode. Now, he could command at least six thousand dollars per episode, or double the salary. After considering offers, Altman departed for quarters at Twentieth Century-Fox. In the end, for a director like Altman, says Richard Bluell, directing under the factory system at Warner's was too much like "making sausage."

Chapter
15

BUS
STOP

Over at Twentieth Century-Fox, the studio was preparing a television series of William Inge's *Bus Stop*, loosely based on his Broadway play (which previously had served as the basis for the Marilyn Monroe film). Though Inge was announced as the "nominal script supervisor," the playwright declined to have anything to do with the program. In the end, his name did not appear on the program credits, though he duly received his royalty.

Bus Stop was to be an anthology program about a small town called Sunrise—an opportunity for adult material with top-flight writers and the casting of the finest New York actors and actresses. Fox had a contract with

ABC that encompassed a block of time on Sunday nights for the 1961–1962 season. It was a tough block—up against *Bonanza, The Jack Benny Show,* and *G.E. Theater,* among others. But Inge was a Pulitzer Prize–winning author, who, like Tennessee Williams, exploded psychosexual depth charges in his works, and that would be a fillip.

The executive in charge of the production was Roy Huggins, the creator of *Maverick* and *77 Sunset Strip.* Only here, Huggins was to be more in the background, while the day-to-day decisions fell to Robert Blees, another stiff-backed character from the old movie-studio days, a blunt, insightful ex-newspaperman (formerly a writer-photographer with Time, Inc.) who, before becoming a notable writer-producer for television, had written the screenplay for the quintessential 1950s film *Magnificent Obsession* and packaged *High School Confidential.* Both strong-willed mavericks, Huggins and Blees became the pivotal relationships for Altman at this stage of his career.

Huggins and Blees were already hiring fine writers like Sally Benson, the *New Yorker* magazine short story writer who had helped to write Alfred Hitchcock's *Shadow of a Doubt* and whose fiction had provided the basis for *Meet Me in St. Louis.* They were also plumbing the Fox story files, where they had access to plays and novels that were owned by the feature department.

Tuesday Weld was set for the pilot episode (directed by Don Siegel, and aired sixth though it was filmed first), and from New York acting classes or agents the producers recruited as stellar a lineup of past, present, and future stars as any series on the air—including Robert Redford, Barbara Baxley, Rod Taylor, Nina Foch, Wendell Corey, Ruth Roman, Steve Cochran, Dean Stockwell, Joan Hackett, Diane Baker, Lloyd Nolan, Buddy Ebsen, James MacArthur, Cliff Robertson, Lew Ayres, George Hamilton, and Mark Stevens, among others.

Blees cannot remember ever having seen a *Bonanza* directed by Altman—though Blees himself was to become a writer-producer of the Ponderosa series later on in the 1960s.

But Blees had seen segments of the relatively obscure *The Roaring Twenties*. He was struck by the acting and the thoughtful composition of the shots in those segments directed by someone he had never heard of before named Robert Altman. He pursued Altman and persuaded the Fox executives to okay hiring him for one segment. That was the Robert Redford–Barbara Baxley episode, "The Covering Darkness," which was a challenge for any director in that half of it was shot in a motel room and the other half was an outdoor chase. Altman performed the task admirably, and he was kept on, one show at a time, for five additional episodes.

The fictional town of Sunrise was constructed on the Pico lot, replete with Grace's Diner, the local gas station and eatery. The revolving cast included Sunrise residents Grace Sherwood (Marilyn Maxwell), waitress Elma Gahringer (Joan Freeman), Sheriff Will Mayberry (Rhodes Reason), District Attorney Glenn Wagner (Richard Anderson), and a local policeman (James Brolin). But these roles were less important than the ones assigned in each episode to a guest star, whether citizen or stranger. This was perfect Altman terrain—the "floating opera" of a small town—the type of one-set panorama he would return to in movie after movie, and which would anchor films such as *Three Women, Fool for Love*, and *Come Back to the Five and Dime, Jimmy Dean, Jimmy Dean*, each, among other things, a Western bus stop.

Bus Stop was a superior television series, and Altman had no little part in the thrust of its single season. He did some writing, characteristically in the form of story contributions, not entire scripts—including a murky segment called "Door Without a Key," about a detective double-crossed by a femme fatale, and starring longtime Altman crony Howard Duff. And he directed at least one intended spin-off that did not survive cancellation of the series, the "County General" segment, starring Frank Lovejoy and Donald May. This was scripted by David Shaw, a well-known writer for *Playhouse 90, Westinghouse, Goodyear-Philco*, and *Lux*.

But there is one Altman segment that overshadows the rest of the series—an episode that will always have a foot-

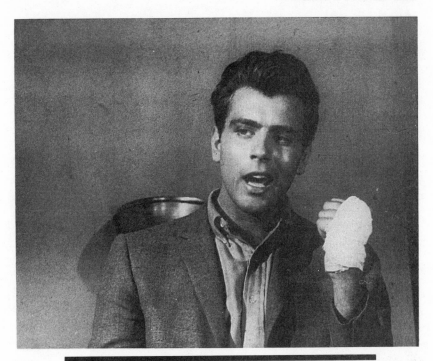

Fabian, in the notorious "A Lion Walks Among Us" episode of the single-season *Bus Stop*. (British Film Institute)

note in television history among buffs, critics, and scholars of the medium—one that was dubbed at the time and forever after as "the notorious Fabian episode."

"The notorious Fabian episode" was aired once (on December 3, 1961), and only once. Then, rejected by advertisers, shunned by affiliates, excoriated by critics, and attacked by a Congressional committee, it was tossed into the Fox vaults never to be aired legally again. To the creative executives of *Bus Stop*, what happened to the "A Lion Walks Among Us" segment is still a salty wound—one that, to Huggins, illuminates "a terrible moment in television history in that it revealed almost everything that was wrong with television, including the critics of television."

The story was adapted by Ellis Kadison (and revised by Blees) from a novel called *The Judgement* by *New York*

Times writer Tom Wicker. It had been languishing in the motion-picture story department of Fox. *The Judgement* was a Hitchcockian suspense melodrama with a moralizing premise. A charismatic drifter, so truly likable that nobody can believe he is a murderer, succeeds in beguiling (and ultimately killing) his own defense attorney. A plot not unlike *The Jagged Edge*, the 1985 box-office thriller in which wife-killer Jeff Bridges seduces defense attorney Glenn Close in order to barter her trust.

This was a heavy dose of evil for prime-time 1961. And if a double murder was not enough, there were other wrinkles in the story. To quote the disapproving synopsis published in *TV Guide*, the episode featured a "penniless itinerant of eighteen who makes obscene advances towards a woman driver who gives him a lift, then robs and murders an elderly grocer. When caught, Luke burns his hands to try to prove police brutality, destroys the reputation of the woman driver in court and kills the lawyer who successfully defended him. In the end, the woman driver, an alcoholic, lures Luke into her car and takes him with her on a suicide crash."

Gulp. The evil that lurks in Everyman—obscene murder, sexual psychosis (the female driver was an implied nymphomaniac), alcoholism, small-town provincialism—this was Altmanville. It was all given a publicity boost by the casting of Fabian, the bubble-gum idol (described in the studio notes as an "attractive Jimmy Dean type"), as the Mephistophelian lead. This was not Altman's idea (Fabian was under contract at Fox), but it was certainly not out of keeping with his practice of raiding celebrities from other fields for shock value in casting.

Fabian, a handsome Italian-American kid who had been manufactured into a teenage singing star, studied acting and had an intermittent career in motion pictures before and after *Bus Stop*. He recalls this part as meaty, an extreme and welcome departure from his all-American image.* His read-

---

*"Frankly, I thought it was going to help me a lot in my career," says Fabian. "It got me a lot of roles, but it didn't get me the meat I wanted." Why? "Because my name's Fabian"—he shrugs—"and they stick you in a pigeonhole."

through was at Altman's Mandeville Canyon home, with Altman simultaneously "very relaxed but very intense, if that makes any sense—he was really looking at me and watching how I was working."

At the point at which the director sensed Fabian was psyched for the role and secure with the physicality, they both "relaxed totally." He says Altman said very little to him about the part—maybe "a key word and then he'd let you go."

The teen heartthrob gave a cunning and cold-blooded performance, turning his croon-swoon charm (he gives a nasty twist to a musical interlude) into something slithery and vile. Others in the uniformly excellent cast included Dianne Foster (as the victimized woman), Philip Abbott (as the ingenuous liberal attorney), and Kansas Citian Owen Bush as the old codger who gets bashed to death by Fabian in the opening scene.

The Fox hierarchy knew beforehand that the episode was excessive. After early screenings, certain cuts were made in the graphic scene where Fabian tosses the old man over a store counter and proceeds to bludgeon him. But according to Blees and Huggins, plans to air the episode continued blithely on the assumption that this was a high-caliber drama with such obvious moral overtones that it would bring credit to the network and the series.

Indeed, Huggins wanted to open the season with the Fabian episode. Blees wanted to add on two weeks of filming and turn it into a feature. "For about two minutes the studio feature side seriously considered it, but by that time the *Cleopatra* debacle* was going downhill," says Blees.

The sponsors were the first to balk. After early agency previews, representatives of Brown and Williamson Tobacco Co., Johnson and Johnson, and Singer Sewing Machine withdrew their advertising pledges. One account representative

---

*Four hours long and millions of dollars over budget, *Cleopatra* laid an egg with audiences and forced an executive upheaval.

stood up at a screening and lectured the *Bus Stop* producers on the horrors of alcoholism, which in his view they had dramatized for exploitative purposes in the Dianne Foster character. The account rep said he had an alcoholic wife, and the producers had no idea of how to portray truthfully such terrible addiction to drink. (Of course, the director had a very good idea how to do just that.)

As a result, the segment was postponed and rescheduled for New Year's Eve while new sponsors were sought. But sponsors did not emerge, and Fox was threatened with an estimated $130,000 loss in advertising monies. Meanwhile, when the show was previewed to affiliates on closed circuit, some twenty-five stations, including affiliates in such big cities as Philadelphia, Atlanta, and Dallas, announced they would not carry the Fabian episode. The drumbeat of Fox publicity had begun to backfire.

Amazingly, the studio continued to demonstrate faith in the episode. This may have been because Leonard Golden-sohn, president of television programming at ABC, was not paying close attention. As he later pleaded to a Congressional Committee investigation, "I happened, I think, to be out of town at the time and I did not view it before it went on the air." In any case, at Huggins's urging, Fox moved ahead with plans for the broadcast, shifting the airdate to the first weekend of December. Warner Brothers came through with some motion-picture advertising, and Fox decided to run promos for future *Bus Stop* episodes as filler.

The title of the episode was changed, softened, made pointedly clear. It had been known as "Told by an Idiot," derived from Shakespeare's line in *Macbeth*: "[Life] is a tale told by an idiot, full of sound and fury, signifying nothing." Huggins was going hoarse insisting to all and sundry that the show was actually a parable about the true nature of evil, so he had the notion of changing the title to "A Lion Walks Among Us." This was a quotation from 1 Peter 5:8: "Be sober, be vigilant; because your adversary the Devil, as a roaring lion, walketh about, seeking whom he may devour."

That citation would precede the episode. Who could argue with the framework of the Bible?

But it was bad timing all around. The curtain had not quite rung down on the smug, self-righteous mores of the Eisenhower and McCarthy eras, and on a period of censorship and repression ironically abetted by people like Huggins himself, who as a cooperative witness before the House Committee on Un-American Activities (HUAC), investigating Communists in Hollywood in the early 1950s, had helped validate a watchdog cultural atmosphere.

This was also the time of the Swearingen Theory of Madison Avenue—a theory that was like a religion to the advertising representatives. According to this theory, television drama ought not to be too powerful because it will "wash over the commercials and diminish their impact," in the words of Huggins.

Though Fabian was a relatively innocuous Elvis imitation, the moral guardians did not differentiate between Elvis's bump-and-grind and Fabian's more tasteful gyrations. Fabian was high on the list of rock idols parents warned their sons and daughters against. The same year as his fateful *Bus Stop* appearance, Fabian had the misfortune of headlining a June beach party concert in Santa Monica where an estimated twenty-five thousand people showed up, and according to news reports, one woman was raped, others beaten, and fifty cops and highway patrolmen called out to quell the mob. The information that Fabian himself "refused to go on [stage] when it [the riot] began to get out of control" was buried in paragraph three of the wire-service story. But the incident was still fresh in the media, and, indeed, congressmen were brandishing news clippings of the concert riot when Congress got around, months later, to investigating the advancement of juvenile delinquency by network television.

As part of the general all-around bad timing, there was in Congress a Senator from Connecticut by the name of Thomas J. Dodd, who was something of a crusader in the area of media influence on juvenile delinquents, and already in the midst of subcommittee inquiries into that and related matters. Senator Dodd did not himself view the Fabian episode when it was broadcast in December of 1961, but he was incensed by reviews such as *Newsweek*'s, which described it as a "cynical, perverted, and flacked-up opus"; *TV Guide*'s blistering put-down; the column by Cecil Smith in *The Los Angeles Times* that termed it "a sleazy, nasty, sex-laden, slice-of-sensational trash remiminscent of the worst in drugstore fiction"; and the much-quoted verdict of Jack Gould in *The New York Times* that it amounted to "an hour of dark and sordid ugliness."*

Senator Dodd scheduled an inquiry into *Bus Stop* when the Committee on the Judiciary resumed hearings in January of 1963. For several months before, television writers, producers, agency representatives, and network executives had been systematically interrogated by the committee about their lack of civic responsibility in programming choices. The Federal Communications Commission was castigated for weak-kneed policy. *Bus Stop* was not the only program to invite scrutiny, and was preceded to the whipping post by defenders/detractors of *Naked City, The Untouchables, Cheyenne,* and others. In the nation's newspapers there was much editorial endorsement of FCC Chairman Newton Minow's harsh characterization of most television programming as a "vast wasteland."

In this atmosphere, *Bus Stop* was raw meat for the ravenous committee.

As no one on the subcommittee could claim to have seen the episode, portions were screened in a congressional meeting room—namely, the beginning and the end, which certainly pointed up the violent highlights while ignoring any thematic development, a point that never ceased to irritate Huggins. Quoting from newspaper accounts, Madison

---

*Senator Dodd's penchant for ethical issues that inflamed the media and the public might seem a touch curious in light of the fact that his career as a public servant effectively ended with his censure by the U.S. Senate for irregularities in his financial affairs.

Avenue personnel, and cautionary network continuity memos, Dodd painstakingly reconstructed the history of the production in order to ascertain how all of this potboiling madness had escaped the dutiful minions who normally safeguard TV.

Neither Huggins nor Blees nor Altman were subpoenaed as witnesses. Instead, the subcommittee went after Goldensohn, the programming head, who kowtowed, and Oliver Treyz, an executive of the network, who jousted with mild bravery with his inquisitors.

Congressional rituals of this kind have a protocol all their own, including a coded, superficial decorum that masks the subcurrents and hostility of the opposing sides.

The Treyz testimony verged on the ludicrous at one point when he and Dodd swapped views on the raising of their respective children during an argument over whether *Bus Stop* had damaged the moral fiber of youth. Treyz said he had two children, ages thirteen and ten, who did not watch television with regularity. Dodd said he had six (one of whom, Christopher, grew up to become a U.S. Senator also) who did so constantly.

When later in his testimony Treyz attempted to place on the record a letter from a Santa Barbara eighth-grade class that had written to the network to commend the airing of the Fabian episode because it showed "life-in-the-raw relations," Dodd parried with a question:

DODD: What is the average age, do you know, of that eighth grade?

TREYZ: I do not know. I suppose, Senator Dodd, it is a typical eighth grade. I do not know the town myself. It is just something that came to my attention and something I was interested in.

DODD: That is the only eighth grade you heard from?

TREYZ: I think there were other letters. I have an eighth-grade son myself in my own family.

DODD: I do, too, that is why I was interested.

TREYZ: The eighth graders I know, Senator Dodd, which

include my own son and his friends, are studying for their next day's school at nine o'clock on Sunday night [when the Fabian episode was broadcast].

DODD: Apparently, those youngsters out in Santa Barbara weren't.

TREYZ: Apparently not.

Score this verbal duel of wits a toss-up. The hearing moved on to Goldensohn. He was not allowed to finish his prepared remarks (Dodd had to rush to the Senate floor for a vote on cloture), but Goldensohn was permitted to insert into the record of the proceedings a statement that indicated the intentions of ABC to institute "a broader base of program balance" in the future. This, in the very next TV season, would include the futuristic cartoon *The Jetsons*, *McHale's Navy*, and the immortal *I'm Dickens, He's Fenster*.

If television was a wasteland when Newton Minow paused to contemplate it, just stay tuned. In an amusing footnote to the entire brouhaha, the Fabian episode of *Bus Stop* can be said to have helped usher in the entire *Beverly Hillbillies* period of mid-Sixties mind-paralyzing sitcoms. This trend was not just happenstance, but in part molded by a fear of government regulation.

Altman, one suspects, was chortling over these developments; but *Bus Stop* was canceled after the first season, and never offered for syndication. ("The cancellation came, as all cancellations do, from low ratings," says Huggins. "If it had high ratings, the furor would have been irrelevant.") And, ironically, the director of the episode was never mentioned; Altman's name does not appear in committee transcripts or in media accounts. "They never talked about Altman," says Huggins. "It was as if the show didn't have a director. They only talked about ABC and Fox."

But in industry circles, it was very different. For the first time, Altman basked in the recognition of his peers. No less a luminary than the esteemed motion-picture director William Wyler praised the Fabian episode magnanimously in the trade papers. Novelist James Jones was quoted as saying it was a show that "held some hope for the future of TV" in America. At least in Hollywood, Altman was no longer an "invisible man."

"It brought him to the attention of a lot of people who had never heard of Bob Altman," says Blees.

Chapter
16

COMBAT

There have been two great television series about war—*Combat* and *M*A*S*H*. The former was downbeat, stark, vérité drama; the latter was irreverent, abrasive, almost surrealistic comedy. Each, at an early stage, was to a critical degree formulated by Robert Altman. Both (like *Streamers* and *The Caine Mutiny Court-Martial*) spring out of the crucible of the director's World War II experience; and both, albeit very differently, comment on authority, camaraderie, suffering, and the futility of war.

Combat was Altman's first real opportunity to direct "mini-movies" (as opposed to "mimic-movies") for television. He was on the show from the beginning; he helped to cast and write it; he functioned as a director and producer. Unlike the ill-fated *The Troubleshooters*, where his options were limited, here Altman had a reasonable budget, an accomplished cast, first-rate technical backup, and a canvas with deep personal and social resonances. Others were instrumental creatively—but Altman gave it his stamp.

It was to be the director's most sustained, and perhaps only genuine, whack at television. He had a handful of actors with pay-or-play contracts. He had a rugged, Hemingway-esque setup in which he could indulge heroics and thematics. In Robert Blees, the director had a shrewd, confident producer who was protective of him. In series star Vic Morrow, he had an alter ego who in real life was haunted by unobtainable goals, and who was hypersensitive as an actor.

Morrow became the perfect human symbol for Altman in what was an exceedingly Catholic perspective on the fate of men in armed struggle. In episode after episode, his Sgt. Chip Saunders was filmed by Altman as well as by succeeding directors as a martyr to the vagaries of war—riddled with wounds, backlit with bursting flames, condemned to agonize over his own responsibilities while others died marching under the stupid orders from higher-ups.

Certainly, it would have been a different *Combat* without Altman. The pilot (never aired) was pejoratively dubbed "The Rover Boys in Normandy." Cute. Too cute. It had to be toughened up. Producer Blees, fresh from his *Bus Stop* imbroglio, was recommended to executive producer Selig Seligman by ABC. Blees asked for Altman as a condition of his hiring, for "a continuity of feeling" and "an honesty of look and ideas."

Robert Pirosh, the writer of the pilot, credits Altman with being the mainstay of the series as it evolved. Blees says *Combat* was Blees, Altman, Vic Morrow, and cameraman Robert Hauser, not necessarily in that order. Series costar Rick Jason says the program owed more to Altman than Blees, because "Blees is not the strongest of producers. Alt-

Vic Morrow, in one of the many "living martyr" episodes of *Combat*, the ultimate World War II series, which was crucially shaped by Altman during its first season. It was the director's first significant opportunity to direct "mini-movies" on television.

man's personality Sherman-tanked him down." Jason goes on to say, "I think Altman saw the first real opportunity he had to be in first-time, hot-time, prime-time TV, and it was the opportunity he had been looking for for a long time and he grasped at it. It was teeth and claws all the way with him."

Altman would direct thirteen of the first twenty-six episodes, and then he and Blees would vanish in their usual puff of controversy. But by that time, they—and others—had set the pattern, and *Combat* would flourish for five and a half years.

Vic Morrow and Rick Jason had already been cast for the pilot.

Morrow, Altman knew well as the husband of Barbara Turner. An intensely driven performer ("the Method actor personified," observed *TV Guide*), Morrow in person could be as brooding as the character of the knife-wielding juvenile delinquent that propelled him to stardom in *The Blackboard Jungle*. Like Altman, the Bronx-born actor was a middle-class rebel who had joined the Navy at seventeen and belatedly picked up his high-school diploma in night school. While driving a cab, he attended the Actors' Workshop in New York. He married Barbara Turner, and they collaborated on a satirical stage musical while preparing a film version of Jean Genet's *Deathwatch*, a play which Morrow had starred in Off-Broadway.

"The whole thing is, the thing I'm trying for," Morrow would say in interviews, "not only in my acting but in my life, is *to learn to paint with more colors.* Discover more colors, more dimensions. Y'see the point? . . . like you have to go through the depths before you can be a saint."

Both the "painting with colors" and the "suffering for art's sake," for a kind of aesthetic sainthood, were also core motifs of Altman's.

By contrast, Rick Jason was more of a "likable poseur who likes to play movie star," according to one contemporary profile. Jason had been brought out from New York by MGM in 1952 in time to serve as drapery in a few costume vehicles in the twilight of the studio's heyday. A Don Juan, at one point during the run of *Combat* he could count three wives within a span of nineteen months. Smoothly handsome with a cavernous voice, Jason was supposed to be the "star," Morrow the "actor."

The rest of the troupe included Jack Hogan as "Wild Man" Kirby, Pierre Jalbert as the exotic Caje, and Richard Peabody as lanky, deep-voiced Littlejohn. Jalbert (actually from exotic

Canada) was a journeyman MGM editor who had never acted professionally; and Peabody, whose previous acting experience was limited to Calvin industrials and Kansas City commercials, had renewed his intermittent acquaintance with Altman and was cast in *Combat* after a chance encounter with the director.

Peabody had decided to switch careers and make a stab at acting professionally. Newly arrived in Los Angeles, he was attending a preview screening at Desilu. Afterward, as he walked around the Desilu lot, the venetian blinds in a nearby office parted, and Altman boomed out, "Dick Peabody, of all people!" Over coffee at Nickodell's, Altman assured him that he, Richard Peabody, of all people, was least likely to make it as an actor in Hollywood. But for auld lang syne, Altman promised to give him one line, and billing, in this new infantry series he was working on. Altman recommended an agent. After that, it was up to Peabody.

Combat was never a big-budget, high-gloss production. It was the same cost-consciousness and long hours Altman had grown accustomed to at Calvin, Desilu, and Warner's. Jason says that even though *Combat* became the showpiece of ABC, the network was very economy-minded, and there would have been a "shit hemorrhage" in the executive chambers if Altman had gone over budget even once.

Not to worry. Despite some bad publicity to the contrary (especially on *Popeye*), Altman has always worked close to the bone, no matter what the budget, and probably no director of his generation has made more movies for as little money. So *Combat* was filmed on time and at cost; and that first season they did thirty-six one-hour shows, so that while they were filming one, they were preparing another, editing a third, and developing the script of yet two or three for the future.

ABC had selected MGM because of its famous Lot 2, which already had a French village, complete with lakes and bridges and patches of forest, plus the train station from *Anna Karenina*, not to mention Andy Hardy's house. MGM

Writer-producer Robert Blees (1961 photo),
whose relationship with Altman was key to the
director's best television work. (Robert Blees)

was in such a foundering state, and the French village in
such disrepair, that the scenery already looked bombed-out.
Along the road in Europe that Sgt. Saunders and company
were always trekking down could be spotted pampas grass
and California eucalyptus trees. The cast jokingly called it
"Euchy Road." All the tremendous verisimilitude of the old
MGM sound stages and backlot provided a perfect foil for
Altman's cluttered visual style and cameraman Hauser's vérité photography: Scenes were deliberately cobwebbed,
obscured by smoke or fog, sunlight-bedazzled, illumined by
candles, veiled in moonlight, glimpsed in heavy weather. As
often as not, the camera was handheld. This gritty, naturalistic camerawork announced the show as different and im-

portant from the outset (Hauser was Emmy-nominated that first season), and it was the natural corollary to material as uncompromising as any ever filmed for television.

The caliber of the ensemble was another element; in that regard, this was TV's first *Hill Street Blues*—or an early TV version of *Platoon*. Morrow and Jason were the stars, to be sure, but it was not unusual for a guest star to usurp the limelight, or for one of the other characters—Kirby or Little-john or Caje—to shoulder an entire episode. The group rapport was extraordinary for television and represented Altman's first "family-style" filmmaking outside Kansas City and Calvin.

The off-camera closeness spilled over onto the set. Blees and Altman, already friendly with each other from *Bus Stop*, grew closer. At MGM, they were near Hollywood Park, and in the summer, with an hour for lunch, they could make it to the track, catch the first race and even the second race, eat lunch, and make it back for the afternoon's filming. They talked of buying a racehorse together; and they probably would have if Altman could have ever climbed out of debt.

The cast as a whole ate, drank, practically lived together twenty-four hours around the clock. "On that show, particularly, it was a dream because it was an all-male show and that sometimes makes a difference," says Blees. "You don't have to watch your language quite as much. You can talk in a shorthand that sometimes you can't use when you're talking to women."

Instinctively, Altman gravitated to Morrow.

Both were iconoclasts, frustrated artists, malcontents. "Vic had come up the hard way, and he and Bob had the same ideas about *Combat*," says Jason. "With Vic, it was also teeth and claws."

Morrow wanted to stretch his acting. Altman wanted to stretch his directing. After hours, Altman and Morrow and sometimes Barbara Turner, and Jalbert and Peabody and Hauser and maybe Blees would unwind in Blees's office in the Producer's Building, where there was a standing bar. Seligman would not be around (he maintained a huge office at

ABC, and according to Blees, showed up on the MGM lot no more than twice a month), so they could call up the dailies and run them. They might stay up until dawn arguing about the dailies, changing the scenes, poring over the next day's pages.

"I'm not saying they were drunk," says Gene Levitt, a *Combat* writer and producer, "but the bottle was out. They'd see the film, they'd talk it over, they'd work up things. They might change the schedule for the next day or two. They *cared*, and they shot from the hip a lot. But it was not exactly the way to run a TV show."

Jason was the odd man out. He was not part of the after-hours clique; he would be long gone home, he says, to a martini and bed. According to Jason, he knew there was a kind of love affair going on between Altman and Morrow, and rather than fight it, he went willingly to a neutral corner, content in the knowledge that his contract guaranteed equal billing and equal pay, no matter what happened on the set. He says he had already grown weary of the Hollywood star trip. "Besides," he says, "I got a lot of time to go fishing and hunting."

Jason claims to have been in Altman's corner regardless. Though Morrow was in the ascendancy—people were talking about his tough-tender, affecting characterization all over town—Altman also featured Jason several times in episodes that showed the actor to advantage. And the rest of the ensemble felt treated likewise; no matter how small their parts, Altman gave them trust and freedom, and they in return gave their utmost.

"The actors would rather work with Altman than anybody," says Peabody. "For one thing, he never blocked a scene, and we would move around the way it was natural to, and he would shoot it. It was totally organic. We would do whatever felt right to us, and he would arrange to put the cameras so they would cover the action.

"Also, he was meticulous about never saying anything to an actor that could be overheard by any member of the crew or other members of the cast. It was always whispered in your ear, if he had anything to say to you. His sensitivity towards the actors' nature was pronounced. Especially in TV. People just weren't used to that. Most TV directors were little more than traffic directors."

A lot of "name" actors made a point of dropping in for a *Combat* episode or two. James Caan, Robert Redford, James Coburn, Tab Hunter, Lee Marvin, Richard Basehart, Robert Culp, Robert Duvall, Charles Bronson, Sal Mineo, John Cassavetes, Fernando Lamas, Dan Duryea, Jack Lord, James Franciscus, Ricardo Montalban, Telly Savalas, Dennis Hopper—all did at least one *Combat* episode. Sometimes more than one. If an actor became part of the *Combat* family, it did not matter if he was killed off in episode #33; he would simply appear with a new accent/identity later in the season—and be killed again.

The emerging Altman stock company dominated the first season: Donald May, Howard Duff, Albert Paulsen, Peggy Ann Garner, Michael Murphy, Ted Knight, Robert Ridgeley, John Alonzo, Richard Bakalayan, Robert Fortier—many of them TV pros who worked prolifically for many series but also often worked for Altman. Keenan Wynn, for example, did his usual turn for Altman in the first season's only comedy (directed by Altman). In "The Prisoner," Wynn played a barking, cigar-chomping general whose hapless driver, Shecky Greene, is captured by the Germans and mistaken for a ranking officer.*

Also during that first season of *Combat*, the director made the acquaintance of John Considine, his future *A Wedding* cowriter. Considine's father had been a studio film producer. Fresh out of college, studying acting while he was playing piano in bars around town, Considine had been among the last group of contract players at MGM; but his career had not

---

*Comic monologuist Greene was one of the *Combat* actors on a pay-or-play contract, so he was used regularly in first-season episodes. However, he was also appearing in Las Vegas, so when he was working in an episode, he would get in an ambulance in Vegas after the Sunday-night show and be driven to Los Angeles—sleeping on the way. Then he would act in *Combat* on Mondays and Tuesdays, and fly back to Las Vegas Tuesday night. The producers knew they had to kill him off (or film his scenes) within a day and a half of shooting.

gotten rolling, and he had acted professionally only once or twice.

Considine tested for the part of a meek-mannered dancer among the new recruits in the "Rear Echelon Commandos" segment. When push comes to shove in the plot, the character's courage rises to the fore, and he is the only one who can balletically tiptoe over the rooftops of buildings to dislodge an enemy gunner (Robert Fortier was the ever-reliable stunt double).

Considine remembers that, right before he read for the part, which they were having a hard time casting, Altman said he wanted the characterization, which has an implied homosexual subtext, to have "dignity."

"I knew Bob was something special even in those days," recalls Considine, "because [when we were filming] he had this complicated shot set up outside on the backlot with the French village ringed by water. We were supposed to dive in [the river] and swim over [to the other side] with the bullets spraying. Just before we started to shoot, he walked over and looked into the water and said, 'Wait a minute, I've got a better idea.' And everybody went, 'What?' I've never heard that repeated yet in television: 'I've got a better idea.' He changed the whole shot and made the whole sequence a reflection sequence."

Though Considine was not "killed off," neither was he a continuing character—and his *Combat* segment, and contact with Altman, temporarily ground to a halt. Later during the season, Considine was in the MGM commissary, just about to begin his first movie, and growing a beard for his part in director George Stevens's religious epic *The Greatest Story Ever Told*, when he bumped into Altman.

Altman wondered why the beard.

Considine said he had a bit role in this new movie about to start filming.

"Aw," said Altman, "when do you leave? I was thinking of using you again [on *Combat*]."

"Six days," said Considine.

"Well," said Altman. "Maybe I'll just kill you off."

Considine says: "So he put me in this part where I was blown up by a land mine early in the episode and I was dying a little bit every day in case I had to leave. So he really had to tailor that part for me."

With Blees in the background, Altman was doing wholesale rewriting and revising of scripts. He was still having trouble originating scripts. And it is true that some of the most memorable episodes from that first year were spun from scripts, not written by Altman, which had, in fact, very little dialogue.

The debut episode, "Forgotten Front," directed by Altman, was a standout. It was about a German POW captured by the *Combat* squad behind enemy lines. He has become a liability, and they must consider the moral dilemma of how to dispose of him. "Forgotten Front" prompted critic Cleveland Amory to hail *Combat* as "*the* war show," head and shoulders above the rash of others—*The Gallant Men, The Rat Patrol, Twelve O'Clock High, Garrison's Gorillas*, and so on.

"Off Limits," about a complex marital triangle, became in Altman's hands an almost searing meditation on love and guilt, while "Cat and Mouse," based on Altman's own script, trapped Sgt. Saunders and a hard-ass lifer (Albert Salmi) in a secret German command post, a windmill. As powerful emotionally as it was visually, *TV Guide* hailed this latter episode as "a kind of petit *Grand Illusion*."

"The Volunteer," about a young French boy whose idolization of the American platoon leads him to a fatal rendezvous with a German officer who befriends him, was considered so unusual that it was shown out of competition at the Venice Film Festival that year, Altman's first foreign film festival.

But the episode that many people remember best from that first season is the last one Altman directed before he was fired, or quit, depending on whose version of events you believe.

It is said that, as the series evolved, Seligman wanted more platoon-type stories, less individual heroics; he wanted battle scenes, more derring-do, not so much philosophy. "Somebody had to have a point of view," Altman was quoted in *TV Guide* at the time. "Selig wanted action. I wanted to do the war stories you couldn't do in 1946."

In interviews Altman has taken some credit for the unmistakable antiwar tone that permeated the series, supposedly counter to Seligman's wishes. But Blees shrugs this off, saying: They were all against war, not just Altman. Who wouldn't be?

Certainly the antiwar attitudinizing survived the departures of both Altman and Blees. Seligman had other reasons to feel uneasy about the cosy, thriving twosome who had such creative momentum. For one thing, they sidestepped his decision-making whenever possible. The word around town was that, without Blees and Altman, there would not be a *Combat*. Seligman was rankled by this, and he and Blees had some "terrible political fights"—in Blees's words—over creative control.

Combat had proven enormously profitable. Each episode was costing only $110–115,000, including the MGM overhead. There was talk of spin-offs.

Blees and Altman had their own grab bag of ideas for which they needed ABC's and Seligman's backing. For one thing, they wanted to use Nina Foch in a pilot episode for a new series as a Martha Gellhorn-type female war correspondent. Seligman said no, and instead shot his own pilot of *Alexander the Great* starring William Shatner for a reported $1 million budget; it was never aired and was written off as a loss. Meanwhile, Blees's and Altman's ideas were simply held up, and resentment grew all around.

Seligman was increasingly cool to the machinations of Blees and Altman, and made nervous by the late-night bull sessions and script changes. There were arguments, insults and apologies, recriminations.

Around this time Roy Huggins, *Bus Stop*'s executive producer, had managed to wind up in high office at Universal. After dreaming of a retreat from crass television and an idyllic life in academia, Huggins had found himself bored and frustrated by a stint of thesis work at UCLA—at which point Universal executive Lew Wasserman called him up and offered him supervision of *Kraft Mystery* and *Kraft Suspense Theatre*, "high-gloss anthology series" out of which Wasserman hoped Huggins would concoct a spin-off series or two.

Huggins, ever the square peg in a round hole, said yes, on the proviso that he could hire his own producer-writers, give them absolute creative freedom, and keep his own behind-the-scenes involvement unbilled. Huggins was talking to Blees about coming over to Universal, and through Blees, to Altman.

In the event, Blees left for an exclusive contract at Universal. Altman was the obvious heir apparent to his slot as producer of *Combat.* Indeed, Altman was already being listed as producer of certain individual episodes, which, according to Blees, was simply in the nature of an agreement between friends.

Seligman was temporarily undecided. He was not sure if Altman alone would be better or worse than Altman and Blees together. Seligman talked to Altman about coproducing with Gene Levitt, but Gene Levitt, thinking better of sharing power with Altman, turned Seligman down. So Altman pushed the point.

The first post-Blees program was "Survival," which many people who saw it at the time recall vividly even after everything else about *Combat* has faded from memory. It had an audacious script—by John F. D. Black—with scant dialogue or plot; only the Vic Morrow character, wandering shell-shocked, crazed, and wounded through one hour of intense reverie. Even Blees had not given the episode the go-ahead; deemed too "out there," the script was sitting on the "development" shelf, where Altman had been eyeing it hungrily. It was not supposed to be on the schedule. In the interim between Blees and his successor, when Seligman was momentarily distracted, Altman slated it for a Monday start.

Arguably, it turned out to be the most indelible show of the series. Seen today, the episode has lost none of its capac-

ity to startle. Here was the ultimate ravages-of-war man-
ifesto—a deafened army grunt wandering through blasted
rubble, fallen timber, smoke and fire, deserted battlefields,
amidst filth, stench, and fear, blathering incoherently about
his beloved dead brother (who may or may not exist outside
his imagination). The rest of the squad is glimpsed only
fleetingly in crosscutting.

Much of it was filmed, by Altman, with journalistic immediacy—in harrowing, extreme close-up, the lighting secondary to the handheld movement, so that the image is
constantly dappled by sunlight and glare, and spinning with
Morrow's perspective. One memorable scene has Morrow,
filmed from above, reaching for a glistening apple bobbing on
a branch just out of reach of his trembling, charred hands.
The usual Leonard Rosenman sound track was reduced to
the eerie chaos of a babbling brook, a howling wind, lightning and thunder, inchoate sobbing.*

The episode ends on a somber note when Morrow, carrying
the body of a dead German whom, in his hallucinatory state,
he has mistaken for his brother, stumbles into the path of an
oncoming tank brigade. There is no tidy happy ending, no
saving moral, no reunion with the rest of the squad—just the
call for "Medic!" from Michael Murphy, one of Altman's regular bit players. The End.

The episode was truly a tour de force for Morrow, who
picked up his only Emmy nomination for Best Actor for this
segment. Soaked in mud and water, the actor was encouraged to gamble with his performance, to do interesting physical things with his body movements and blackened hands
("Vic had really many schticks with his hands," says Peabody), to articulate his subconscious, to depict the agony of
Sgt. Saunders in excruciating detail.

On the set, the atmosphere was special. Cast and crew

Combat composer Leonard Rosenman, whose theme song and incidental music
were such a vivid highlight of the series, happened to be living in Rome during the
initial season of the program. Scripts were sent overseas, and cue sheets returned
by messenger. There were sometimes problems with cutting; but this is an
unusual case of memorable television music being composed eight thousand miles
away from the actual production.

knew they had something out of the ordinary. "Altman was pulling it out great," says Peabody. "By the time Seligman found out about the episode, he was furious."

It was at some industry function shortly thereafter that Altman, very plastered, with Blees and the Universal horizons on his mind, staggered up to Seligman and berated him in abusive language. Seligman himself was no small drinker—a fifth of Scotch a day, they say—but he was civil and a genial drinker, unlike Altman, whom Jason, who was at that party, remembers as always being "a very obstreperous drunk."

Altman says Seligman complained that the show was becoming too grim. "Kids watch this show," grumbled Seligman, "and there's not enough jokes for them!"

"You mean there's a danger of kids not liking war?" snapped Altman.

According to sources, the remarks Altman unloaded in Seligman's direction were more crudely personal than antiwar in nature. The precise text of that nasty exchange was the subject of industry gossip and much speculation on the *Combat* set. Whatever happened, Altman was fired; or quit—as he was in the process of being fired.

Altman was replaced for the last six shows of the first season by Gene Levitt and subsequently by a rotation of Dick Caffey and Gene Levitt. "Altman was, in a sense, in my mind, too good for the job," says Levitt today.

Jason—"because I felt we needed him," and because he regarded himself as Altman's friend—says he called Altman up and offered to quit if Altman was not brought back on the show. But Altman talked Jason out of it and said he preferred to move on.

Morrow, so magnified in stature as a result of the *Combat* episodes, did nothing, curiously. On the set, he took up the creative leadership, inherited Altman's coterie, and occasionally insisted on directing episodes himself. The affinity between Morrow and Altman was on the wane, partly because Altman had a Svengali-like relationship with budding writer

Barbara Turner, whose marriage to Morrow was undeniably rocky. The rumor that Altman was intimate with Turner was rife among the *Combat* cast. In any event, Altman did not work with Morrow again.

The mold had been set, and *Combat* was solid in the Nielsen ratings for five and a half years. Yet the series was dropped from television under somewhat unusual circumstances.

In the fifth year, the show went to color photography and began a modest decline in viewers. But the show was still immensely popular, and there was no hint the filming would cease—no hint at all until the day Seligman turned up on the set and announced the series was to be terminated after just a few more episodes.

Morrow and Jason had become increasingly querulous and activist regarding the scripts. From Altman, partly, they had learned to trim and polish dialogue, work visually if possible, and to create through characterization. Also, both had five-year contracts with "short terms" or low money. Both were planning to ask stiff terms for renewal.

In those days, a program usually aired on the network for five years before becoming eligible for syndication. ABC was worried that, with the general trend toward color, the black-and-white episodes of *Combat* would not sell if the series did not become immediately available for syndication. At that time there was a network rule that a program could not be in prime-time and syndication simultaneously. So, in order to preserve its syndication prospects, and to ensure a quick profit for ABC, *Combat* was canceled. Ironically, it has never gone out of syndication.

It might be added that Vic Morrow, so terrific in the series, and later a director and writer (usually uncredited) of memorable segments himself, never really fulfilled his promise as an actor. Generally felt to be a tormented soul whose ego could run amok, in 1966 he directed and co-produced the film of Jean Genet's *Deathwatch*, co-written with Barbara

Turner. However, Morrow never directed another film, and after *Combat,* Morrow acted sporadically, without ever reaching the same plateau.

At one point there was thought given to reuniting the *Combat* ensemble for one of those nostalgic television journeys into the past that are such a trend. That was before Morrow's life ended tragically on July 23, 1982, when a helicopter bearing a camera crew crashed after being hit by special-effects debris on the set of *The Twilight Zone* movie. Three people on the ground were killed, two underage Vietnamese children working in violation of state code, and someone who had survived countless hours of simulated combat, Vic Morrow.

Chapter
17

"AS BLAND AS ITS CHEESE"

Universal Studios, that beacon of show business in the San Fernando Valley, was always, at least until the 1970s and 1980s, the least distinguished "major" motion-picture company. Even in the Golden Age of Hollywood filmmaking, it was known primarily for horror, low-budget Abbott and Costello comedies, and the occasional fluke hit with broader artistic merit. Notorious for its "factory psychology," Universal remains the only major studio in Hollywood to have never produced or released a Robert Altman film—no small thing, when Altman has shopped practically everywhere else, from Disney to Cannon to New World. Neither is it likely to be the sponsor of an Altman film in Lew Wasserman's lifetime, nor in the lifetime of the memory of his torch-bearers.

The reasons go back to 1963.

Though Altman and Blees never again worked together on a major film project, they went to Universal at roughly the same time, in mid-1963. Both became producer-directors for Kraft, working under Roy Huggins. Though Huggins had been important behind the scenes at Twentieth Century-Fox, Altman had had little direct contact with him there. But at Universal, Huggins intended to be very much hands-on.

Huggins is indisputably in the Cooperstown of television all-stars. Son of an Oregon lumberman, he graduated Phi Beta Kappa from UCLA, wrote for the *Saturday Evening Post* and authored three novels before settling down in the film industry as a minor screenwriter and director.

In 1952, Huggins achieved notoriety when he was summoned before the House Committee on Un-American Activities, and in public testimony, the "crisp, crewcut, UCLA graduate" (to quote a contemporary newspaper account) gave a "well-worded, unfaltering" recitation of the names of twenty-two persons he knew to have once been fellow members of Communist organizations. It may or may not be coincidental that two of the later television programs associated with his name were about unfairly condemned individuals fleeing from the fickle finger of accusation.

Publicly lauded by HUAC, in the early 1950s Huggins found an enclave in television production on the West Coast. While many of his social circle were fleeing to Europe or scrounging new occupations, in part courtesy of the HUAC hearings, Huggins was beginning a remarkable career in television as the creator-writer-producer of such vaunted series as *Maverick, 77 Sunset Strip, The Fugitive, Run for Your Life*, and (as cocreator) *The Rockford Files*.

By the time Altman arrived in 1963, Huggins was ensconced as executive producer at Universal. He worked side by side with Altman on *Kraft*. Huggins was still rabid on the

The Hollywood trade papers' advertisement for the "Once Upon A Savage Night" segment of *Kraft.* Altman's television kiss-off, it was also released theatrically as a 'B' feature. (Dan Fitzgerald)

subject fifteen years later, and paced and virtually spat when mentioning the director's name.

"I thought he was one of the finest directors I ever worked with in my life—bar none," says Huggins flatly, adding with emphasis. "But I didn't like him personally. He is a strange, strange fellow."

One person's strange is another person's normal. Altman and Huggins had an insurmountable personality conflict that sprang, in part, out of professional differences. Altman was beginning to feel cocky about his career. He was no longer so compliant and crafty with producers. He was beginning to be more confrontational and to relish the confrontational aspect. The insider in Kansas City by now defined himself as the outsider in Hollywood, and a concomitant rancor had begun to seep into his work and his personality.

Because Huggins was such an exemplar of television, Altman had a "terrible neurotic hang-up" about him, says Huggins. "He'd come down to my office and say things like, 'You know I never have liked you—not from the minute we met at Fox.' Then he'd come down the next day and say, 'I read that thing you wrote in the *Reporter*. That was typical Huggins.' I'd say, 'Okay, Robert.' He'd say, 'No, I don't mean typical Huggins bad, I mean typical Huggins good. That was great.' I'd say, 'Thank you, Robert.'

"So he and I never got along and we were always throwing insults at each other. Every now and then he'd tell me he only had a little while to live and he wasn't kidding. I always thought it was because he wanted me to like him. And I didn't like him. I thought he was and is a terribly talented asshole who has fucked up his career by confusing art with an attitude."

According to Huggins, their opposition to each other was symbolic of the things festering inside Altman's brain. "I represented what he hated most in television, and that is the very commercial, highly plotted story, and he hated commercial storytelling with a vengeance."

In particular, Altman hated endings, says Huggins. Altman loved to change endings so that a script would end with a whimper instead of a bang. The bang was very Hollywoodish, and the whimper was more subtle, elliptical, artistic. That's old-fashioned stuff, Altman would say, that type of bang ending. Huggins might win the argument, but then Altman would turn around and defiantly shoot his whimper ending behind Huggins's back. Sometimes Huggins would recut the film to undo the damage; sometimes he would reshoot it himself as director; and sometimes he was stuck with the result. "And sometimes," Huggins admits ruefully, "it really didn't matter."

One *Kraft* script, Huggins remembers, was about a father-son rift, a theme that dovetailed with Altman's own sometimes awkward relationship with B.C.

In the script, the son has become a journalist who has an assignment that brings him back to his hometown. Through resolution of the subplot, he and his father arrive at a mutual understanding of each other. Finally, at the finis, which takes place at an airport, the young man is waiting for a departure flight—without there having yet been any conciliatory gesture between them. The son looks over to see his father waiting behind a chain-link fence. In the script Huggins supervised, the young man is supposed to break free, run to the fence, and clasp hands with his father through the chain-link. Fade-out.

"There wouldn't have been a dry eye in the house, as they say," says Huggins. "What does Altman do? The kid sees his father, looks at him, the father looks at the son, the son turns and gets on the airplane—so, the son never grows up. I thought 'That's okay. That's another way to go.'

"But endings that tied in with what went on before he had an emotional difficulty with . . ."

There were also positive aspects of Altman's stay at Universal; he forged professional relationships and in effect began to solidify the "talent trust" that would carry him through the next ten years of low and high points.

Louis Lombardo, who had not worked with Altman for years, happened to be at Universal learning a new craft—editing. He was an assistant to Danford B. Greene, an ex-Wichita, Kansas, native who knew the Altman family, through Joan, going back to World War II. Lombardo and Greene would become the editing team that gave embryonic form to Altman's loose-knit visual style of storytelling, as imaginative in the cutting as it was in the filming.

John Williams, the composer who went on to score Steven

Spielberg's best-known films and to act as resident conductor of the Boston Pops, was under contract at Universal, and he began affiliating himself with Altman on studio titles as well as some Altman projects that were independent of studio sanction. Producer Ray Wagner was on the lot, working in television, but willing to edge toward motion pictures with Altman. Also at Universal was a line producer by the name of Robert Eggenweiler.

Eggenweiler had the reputation of being one of the best production executives in the business, and had been with Howard Duff and Ida Lupino for years. He understood Hollywood protocol. He knew how to dress for this or that kind of situation. He would be the first one in the door of an executive office, preparing the atmosphere for an important meeting, and the last one to leave. He could negotiate contracts. On location he was able to juggle the picayune noncreative details and logistical nightmares of preproduction, and during filming he functioned with the ease and good nature that was ingrained in his personality. Eggenweiler was susceptible to Altman's charm, and somewhat in awe of this maverick who was heaping invective on one of the current gods of television, Roy Huggins.

"Egg" was being groomed for higher levels at Universal. And editor Danford B. Greene had pipe dreams of running a studio one day. Eventually both would leave salaried positions to associate with Robert Altman. "I just couldn't conform any longer," says Greene.

It was at this point in time that the Altman team began to cohere, not just as a bunch of friends scheming and drinking and reading dreamy poetry.

Cut off not only from the social circles of Kansas City but also from the family dynasties and East Coast circuits that have always dominated Hollywood, Altman began to consolidate his own "family." This had the effect of reinforcing his own paranoia and isolation at the same time as it gave him an independent base of power. That doting family structure—with Altman as its ex officio B.C.—Altman needed psychologically as much as professionally. Just as the films became the life of his imagination, the filmmaking family became a surrogate for the family of his youth.

The best of Altman's several *Kraft* episodes was "The Long, Lost Life of Edward Smalley," which unfolds like a future-tense segment of *Combat*. Richard Crenna plays a deranged Army veteran whose court-martial for the murder of a fellow soldier is revealed in flashback. Strong stuff: lovemaking in the ruins of a church, ruminations on guilt and God, and an Altmanesque absorption with drunken, teetering madness. The latter half of the telefilm is a courtroom drama with a plot twist that absolves Crenna, when, twenty years later, he seeks psychotic revenge on his defense attorney (James Whitmore). Dizzying camerawork and editing are aided by the performances of Crenna and Whitmore, with Philip Abbott (as the prosecutor) and future cinematographer John Alonzo (one of the Altman group) among the acting ensemble.

Ray Danton remembers visiting Altman in his office at Universal during this period and finding the director restless and disturbed, pacing around nervously, swinging a golf club in imitation of some swaggering image of himself. Others remember him as frankly depressed that he was under contract to Huggins and Universal, while the Arthur Hillers and Sydney Pollacks and Sidney Lumets of the world were breaking out as film directors.

The constant disagreement between Huggins and Altman erupted before the director found much of a rhythm. At one point Altman was preparing his co-story for filming, "The Hunt," a zinger of a yarn about a rural, bloodthirsty sheriff and his ritual posse murders. It was going to star Mickey Rooney, James Caan, and Bruce Dern—quite a cast—but Altman wanted to cast a black actor in the role of one of the escaped prisoners hunted down and killed by the posse packdogs. That would have given the telefilm a biting racial twist.

But for some reason, Huggins said no, and Altman stalked off the lot. William Graham stepped in as director.

His agent tried to effect a reconciliation between Altman and Huggins, but it was no go. Altman and Huggins ended up shouting at each other over lunch tables in the middle of a swank Hollywood restaurant. Then Altman gave a front-page interview to *Variety*, announcing that he had left *Kraft*—so much the better, he was quoted—a series "as bland as its cheese."

This was in September of 1963—in advance of the season premiere of *Kraft Suspense Theatre*. Altman told *Variety* that the J. Walter Thompson advertising agency representing *Kraft* had rejected ten of the scripts he had submitted for the series "without any indication of why they were turned down. In one of my stories, the lead was a Negro; in another, a slap was taken at local TV stations. However, they never specifically told me why they turned the scripts down. They didn't want the kind of material I felt was good, dramatic, provocative material. They didn't feel it was suitable for their show."

Altman elaborated. *Kraft* was little more than "show by committee," the director told *Variety*, and worst of all was that Roy Huggins "wouldn't leave me alone. . . ." Altman was further quoted as saying: "I've about had it—the agencies, the winking, the networks, the ratings. Anybody who thinks TV is an art medium is crazy—it's an advertising medium.

"I don't mean artsy-craftsy, and I don't blame what is happening on the sponsor or agency necessarily," he continued. "The exec producer [Huggins] or the producer is to blame because he presupposes that they would rather not try for better things, so they play it safe and hold back."

Not only was Altman publicly attacking one of the most powerful corporations in the industry, but he was impugning the sponsor. The height of heresy—unforgivable and unforgettable. Thirty years later, this remark ("bland as its cheese") is repeated, verbatim, by everyone around at the time. It is a statement that could hardly be believed for its brazenness, its self-destructiveness. (Never mind that it might be true.)

His own agency could hardly believe it, that's for sure. In a follow-up story in the trades, it was reported that Altman had been dropped by his "percentery," the Ashley-Steiner agency. Or, as Altman put it in the news item, he and his agency had "parted company . . . under not-so-amicable circumstances" after his agents "vanished" during negotiations in which he was trying to seek fair terms of release from his Universal contract.

"This represents the kind of power the studio has. Agents are afraid to buck it," Altman was quoted as saying.

In his own circle, Altman fostered the half-truth that he had publicly spat in (MCA president) Lew Wasserman's eye and told Universal to go screw itself. It is one of the chief bricks in the foundation of his pre-*M*A*S*H* legend.

But in less puffed-up moments, the director has admitted that he was wrong in storming off the lot. That it was all a "misunderstanding." That he had misinterpreted his contract and believed erroneously that he could refuse to direct telefilms that he himself had not produced, developed, or written. That, after some impetuous things had been said by both sides, in public and private, any basis for amity was destroyed, and by then Altman had no choice but to leave *Kraft*.

There was one last piece of unfinished business for Universal. Altman had been preparing a telefilm for *Kraft* to be shot on location in Chicago. The studio had tentatively planned to release it as a feature in Europe. According to the terms of his contract, Altman could still insist on directing the adaptation of William P. McGivern's novel *Killer on the Turnpike*, and he did.

Altman's creative unit was already in place, cast and script were set, locations scouted. It would be expensive to delay the project or replace the director. Producer Jennings Lang consulted Huggins. Huggins thought about it and decided not to bad-mouth Altman. Huggins says he was always trying hard to *like* the guy, especially because he still respected Altman as a director. Altman kept the assignment.

Greene and Lombardo were to be the editors. Reza Badiyi was the color consultant and second-unit director. Barbara Turner, who was also acting (one of her last performances before she turned to writing full-time), was around to cater to Altman's script needs. The musical score was supplied by John Williams. John Alonzo, Dan Fitzgerald, another former Calvin art director, and others were involved on the periphery. And "Egg" would mother-hen all the production arrangements on location.

Part of Altman's mystique at the time was his facility with virgin technology. He had found out about a new Kodak Ektachrome that permitted high-contrast, nighttime photography, and which was being sponsored by the government as "missile stock" for test launchings. Badiyi had the idea to "push" the film and "hot process" it for a kind of lurid sharpness in the image. Everyone thought it was a crazy thing to do except Altman, and he sold Universal on the newness of it.

Chicago was one of Altman's old stomping grounds, and a location he has returned to again and again in his career. As a born flatlander, Altman has managed to resist, for most of his career, eastern urban vistas. (No other major post-Sixties director has managed to eschew, for his entire career, shooting a motion picture on location in New York City.) Indeed, Altman might be dubbed "the poet of fly-over country" for his sweet-sour celebrations of Houston, Nashville, Reno, Las Vegas, and Chicago—places he first hit, on the road, for Calvin.

Nightmare in Chicago (as it was eventually titled) is more of a cityscape than most Altman films—more of an "exterior" film than most—as if the director was suddenly awakened to blinking neon, belching factories, nightlife, traffic, the melting blur of bodies and faces—all the congestion of a modern metropolis. In that respect, purely photographic, the film is a riot of visceral color.

The script was by Donald Moessinger, but Altman modulated it to build up the part of Barbara Turner (playing a turnpike waitress), and to organize the cross-plotting of the extended climax.

The film was set at Christmastime, which appealed to Altman's grisly sense of humor. It opened with a rural murder keyed by the disquieting image of a shrieking woman in a torn black negligee fleeing down a lonely winter-white road. The camera flits past her to linger on bare trees, an empty cornfield, a cemetery carpeted with snow. The "Georgie Porgie" serial killer (Philip Abbott) is revealed to be on the loose—and is being hunted by police through Midwestern vistas, farm country, Chicago bump-and-grind nightspots, and finally on the great turnpike.

Lady-killer "Georgie Porgie"—who prefers his victims to be diminutive blondes—has a ludicrous Achilles heel. He suffers from extreme photophobia. His disturbed psyche— his mother was rather dominant in his upbringing—is revealed by feverish, voice-over flashbacks.

In the somewhat farfetched subplot, a mysterious government convoy of explosives-bearing trucks (led by actor Ted Knight) threatens to cross paths with the "Georgie Porgie" killer, who is eluding state police in a nip and tuck high-speed chase on the O'Hare Turnpike. The denouement is a violent, all-out, multi-car pileup that has to be seen to be believed. It was legendarily expensive, and set the pattern for car crashes as the deus ex machina, or fifth business, of many an Altman film, not the least of which was the serendipitous opening of *Nashville.*

According to accounts, Universal did not know what to make of the film when Altman and friends returned from Chicago and assembled his last *Kraft* before exiting from Universal.

It was certainly splashy and unusual, and it was certainly gruesome and distasteful. But this was the era of Alfred Hitchcock's *Psycho,* also a Universal film (certainly there are more than casual similarities between the two films); so Universal decided to show it at least once on the *Kraft* television hour and then, capitalizing on the lurid sex and violence, release it as *Once Upon a Savage Night* on the bottom of double bills in the Midwest, in Canada, and overseas. In spite of this history, or perhaps because of it, film buffs, perverse in their preference for whatever studios or audiences disallow, have over the years stoked its reputation as a sinful "B" film. It is that.

Nightmare in Chicago was also a descent into Altman's own primal negativity. It has the air of a valedictory—Altman's goodbye to all that—and of a project where the mechanics of the turnpike finale were perhaps uppermost in the mind of the veteran Calvin director of car crash-ups.

Chapter

18

THE
TALENT
TRUST

Within days of the "bland as its cheese" item in the Hollywood entertainment industry papers, Universal producer Ray Wagner called up agent George Litto and made an appointment for lunch with him and Robert Altman. Litto could not figure out why an astute professional like Wagner was involved with "the community crazy" (Litto's words) who had just been quoted as saying extremely ill-advised things about *Kraft* and Universal in the trades.

"All I knew about Bob Altman was he was Peck's bad boy, a talented, maverick, crazy, hard-drinking, contrary, impossible prick to get along with," says Litto.

As agents go, Litto was a bit of a lone wolf himself. An ex-saxophone player who represented a dynamic list largely of clients just emerging from the HUAC blacklist of the 1950s, Litto was every bit as against the grain as Altman.

After a Southside upbringing in Philadelphia, Litto had spent nineteen years as a talent agent—first with the William Morris Agency, then with the William Schifrin Agency, before branching out on his own in 1962. Among Litto's clients were such people on the relative outs as expatriate Wisconsin-born filmmaker Joseph Losey, a heralded *metteur en scène* in Europe and unemployable in the U.S. because of left-wing associations; Melvin Van Peebles, who worked outside the unions and Hollywood because, being black, it was very difficult for him to channel his goals through the white-ordered universe of Hollywood; and at various points, such pick-of-the-lot blacklisted screenwriters as Dalton Trumbo, Waldo Salt, Michael Wilson, and Ring Lardner Jr.

In Altman's career, there was no more important and symbiotic catalyst than agent-producer George Litto.

Over lunch, Wagner and Altman showed Litto a number of scripts they had been nursing through early stages of development, or rewriting. One was *Petulia* (or *Me and the Archkook Petulia*, as it was then known); another was a treatment for *Death, Where Is Thy Sting-a-ling-ling?* (sometimes called *The Bells of Hell Go Sting-a-ling*).

Litto remembers Altman as not being in the least bit repentant about his bad behavior. On the contrary, Altman was still irate, righteous, adamant, vowing never to work in television again. That's just fine, responded Litto, as it is quite unlikely that anyone will ever let you.

But Litto was impressed by the number of scripts the two of them had on the back burner. And after he read *Petulia* and *Death*, he readily agreed to represent "the community crazy."

For anyone interested in Altman's career, the mid-Sixties loom as the key transition phase of his life. This was the

The agent George Litto, whose faith in Altman
helped nurture the director through the low ebb
of the Sixties.

period in which, after so many years of being enamored of
Hollywood, Altman first tried to break free of the studios
and of conventions; when he tried to redefine himself with
projects that explored his deeper self; when the first Altman
circle, the filmmaking "talent trust," matured; when professional ignominy and personal turmoil began to weigh him
down and color his psychology.

The two properties Litto remembers—which everyone remembers—as being of crucial importance to the director are
the benchmarks of these years.

Death evolved from a projected television anthology series
about World War I flying aces, with a leading man who
would be replaced after being killed off every five or six episodes, supposedly taking into account the mean amount of

time that such a pilot could survive aerial combat. It was yet another poetry-of-the-skies opus that recurs in Altman's realized or hoped-for filmography.

Originally called *Chicken and the Hawk*, it was sold by Litto, in its television manifestation, to Screen Gems, where enthusiasm for its development was demonstrated by Jackie Cooper, the child trouper turned television executive.

Me and the Arch-kook Petulia was always intended as a motion picture. Based on an unpublished book, described in publicity as a series of comic essays about the relationship between a recently divorced doctor and an unhappily married free spirit, *Petulia* was purchased from a "dentist who writes in his spare time" (in the words of *Variety*) by the name of Dr. John Haase.

Altman wanted *Petulia* to be the director's bold statement on the vicissitudes of American romance, to some extent his baring of soul on a subject on which he was normally evasive, his breakthrough as a major motion-picture director. So the transformation of *Petulia* from unpublished tome to screenplay would be closely supervised by Altman, even it if was actually written by someone else.

Among the "talent trust" were two writers who served Altman's by-now-chronic writing insecurity and his need for a collaborator to give dramatic structure and clarity to his thoughts—not to mention actually getting words on the page. The two, Brian McKay and Barbara Turner, served alternate needs.

McKay was a hard-living character who came into Altman's life in storied fashion. Briefly, in the late 1940s, a Hollywood contract player for Warner Brothers, McKay had been an extra with more than a passing friendship with Kathryn Reed before she met Altman. A believer in the adventure and romance of crime, McKay had overstepped legal bounds and been nabbed for cashing stolen postal money orders in the late 1950s. He woke up to reality when he was sentenced to a long prison term at McNeil Island, Washington.

"I was so amazed that this baby-faced little darling could

be getting any time that I actually looked over my shoulder to see who the hell the judge could be talking to," he recalls.

Eventually, he was to log almost five years behind bars. While in prison, McKay began writing prison radio shows for rehabilitative purposes, and he also wrote long, colloquial letters to his close friend Kathryn Reed—who in the meantime had become Kathryn Reed Altman. In an echo of Altman's own experience during his World War II enlistment, McKay's letters revealed a blossoming writing talent—so Kathryn passed them on to her husband. When McKay was released in 1962, he and Altman met and instantly formed a complicated and turbulent rapport.

Altman took McKay under his wing. He gave him bit parts in the odd television show and began to draw on him for closet writing and script development for both television segments and prospective motion pictures—including *Death*. McKay, as a former actor, had a knack for characterization and dialogue. By everyone else in the group, the future cowriter of *McCabe and Mrs. Miller* was regarded as Altman's blood brother as well as his principal collaborator—though their relationship always did have its sharp edges.

"They had something quite nice together when they were working together," says Litto. "I read a lot of material. All the best writers in town. Their material had something special about it, a style, a technique, a humor, a twinkle. It was original. It wasn't always good, but it was original."

The moment the *Death* material was in shape, it was going to be turned over to the well-known suspense literateur Roald Dahl, whom Altman had courted over a long and stimulating correspondence. The first McKay knew of this, however, was a phone call from Hawaii, where Jackie Cooper and Altman were meeting with Dahl. Would McKay tell Dahl what the story was going to be about? It was a rarity that Dahl would agree to work on someone else's unformed material, and McKay was too proud and complimented to wonder what his eventual credit might be.

"One of the high points of my life was when Roald Dahl called me, wanting to know some things about the story,"

The consummate writer Barbara Turner (photographed in 1965). Altman's protegé relationship
with her helped speed up the end of her marriage
to Vic Morrow. She wrote *Petulia* for Altman,
initially, and later married one of his best
friends, Reza Badiyi. (Reza Badiyi)

says McKay. "I was suitably honored but I didn't even know
enough to be impressed. I was not in the literary world yet
and I was feeling my oats and everything."

Besides, Altman had told him upfront, in one of their first
long conversations about writing and movies, that he, Altman, took "all of the credit and most of the money." At the
time, to someone newly out of prison and without any writing inroads, that seemed just fine to McKay. And admittedly,
he was in awe of the director.

While McKay worked mostly on *Death*, Barbara Turner
concentrated on *Petulia*. Less reliant than McKay, she was a
"true talent" (in the words of Litto, who rates her above any
other writer Altman ever worked with), the first in a line of
female writers Altman has employed to help himself articulate his ideas about the frigidity/instability of women.

"He was ahead of his time in thinking they [women] were
very good writers at the time when they never had a
chance," says Badiyi. "When he was telling stories to us,

he'd tell the stories from the point of view of, let's say, a member of his family. Often, he'd pick Barbara, or Joan, rarely Joan, or his mother, or another girlfriend or another woman. That person became the narrator in the story, not the man, not always, but often. . . ."

When Altman was on location in Chicago filming *Nightmare in Chicago* with Turner in the cast, word drifted back to Hollywood that the director was "amorously involved" in Rick Jason's words, with his protégée, at a convenient geographical remove from husband Vic Morrow. That may or may not have been the case, but certainly Altman was not one to discourage the gossip. The *Combat* cast members remember Vic Morrow as being in a strange funk at the time and as literally at one point butting his head in frustration through the presswood walls of a building on the MGM lot. "He was acting erratically on the set but I don't think anybody knew why," says Peabody.

When Altman's cast and crew returned from California for editing and to pursue their other projects, a frothing Morrow began to follow Altman and Turner to restaurants and bars, hoping to catch them in flagrante delicto. One night he parked outside a motel unit across from Universal Studios, and waited until after midnight before bursting in on a typical late-night Altman drink and gab session with Reza Badiyi and Louis Lombardo present besides Turner. Morrow was abusive, and for hours everyone tried to calm him down. Nothing was admitted.

When at last it was nearly dawn, and the crisis appeared past, they all filed to their respective cars and headed home. Only, Morrow followed Turner in his car, forced her over on the side of the highway, and the long night deteriorated into further abuse and violent recrimination.

Their marriage was already coming apart, and now there was this added impetus for divorce. Turner rarely acted again and devoted herself to *Petulia* and some ideas of her own for scripts. After living with Reza Badiyi for the next five years, she married him for twelve.

*   *   *

As the Altman group began to jell, the Us vs. Them dichotomy began to take hold. Long before Nixon, Altman had his "enemies" list, and it was topped by Roy Huggins and Lew Wasserman. But now Vic Morrow was on it too, and others. It was no longer enough to be from Kansas City. People began to be measured in terms of their personal and professional loyalty to Altman.

There had been some dropouts from the formative circle of the 1950s. Chet Allen had begun to design and build swimming pools. John T. Kelley and his wife Abigail Shelton Kelley kept their distance. Tommy Thompson was prospering as an assistant director and producer of Lucille Ball's network television show.

Susan Davis had been more than constant. She was related to Altman by marriage. She had appeared in his Calvin industrials and television episodes. They had composed and recited poetry together. She was particularly strong friends with Joan.

Her husband, writer Worley Thorne, had been the publicist for *The Troubleshooters*. Thorne had put out a call for chorines to pose for publicity shots with Bob Mathias. Susan Davis and Abigail Shelton were two of the leggy starlets drafted for the photo sessions, and they all became friends.

But Thorne had higher aspirations. Among other things, he was mounting a Broadway play (poet Edna St. Vincent Millay's *Conversation at Midnight*). During this period Altman asked Thorne to be his personal publicist. Thorne demurred. Thorne said he had writing of his own to do. Altman said there would be plenty of time for that, after hours. When Thorne said a more definite no, the relationship was breached.

Davis never worked for Altman again. She continued to find other steady work—she made a specialty of playing moms and daft housewives, and recently played Matthew Broderick's mother in *WarGames*. And she continued to be friendly with Altman. But he never again cast her in a film. Nor did he ever allude to the subject in conversation; she

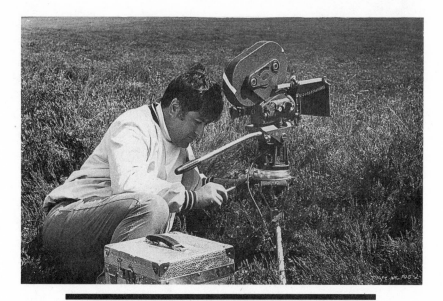

All in the family: the "wild child" director Richard Sarafian. Despite the fact that Sarafian was married to his beloved sister, Altman carried on a personal and professional feud with his ex-best friend for over twenty years.

was sure she was being punished for Worley Thorne's mistake.

Then there was Sarafian.

After coming to Hollywood in the mid-1950s, Richard Sarafian had returned to the Midwest to direct a low-budget, showcase Western, *Terror at Black Falls*. Not many people saw that film, and there were lean years in the early 1960s when he just wrote scripts on his own while hovering around the Altmans in Hollywood. He was in love with Joan Altman and, to hear him tell it, he was equally in love with Robert Altman.

Everyone thought they were best friends on the best of terms. Apart from being uncommon pranksters and two-fisted drinkers, they had a love of backgammon in common, the mutual background of Calvin years, the adoration of Joan. There were little jealousies—Sarafian was strikingly handsome and a magnetic personality, and when he entered a room, heads swiveled in his direction. He was every bit as charismatic as Altman, if not more so, and his later clippings would describe him as everything from an avant-garde enfant terrible, to a 270-pound pixie, to a "mad Bear" who resembled an Armenian Brendan Behan.

Yet nobody was happier than Altman, it seemed, when Sarafian and Joan were married, and they seemed a threesome unto dust.

When Altman was in the latter stages of his contract at Warner's, he convinced Hugh Benson to give Sarafian a stab at directing television episodes. Altman guaranteed Sarafian's job, saying he would finish any Sarafian program, for free, if there were any hitches. That was a big break for Sarafian. On Altman's say-so, Sarafian was hired, and ironically Sarafian cemented his initial reputation by directing over half of *The Gallant Men* segments for Warner's in 1962, the year of Altman's rise to prominence on the rival *Combat*.

According to Altman's version of the story, he showed up on a Warner's sound stage one day to congratulate Sarafian on his new directorial status and was ordered off the bleeping set by his newly blustering brother-in-law. Sarafian's version is different. After the day of his first full-fledged shoot, he says, he hustled over to Nickodell's, feeling very much like a son going to brag to his father about the great day of his achieved ambition.

Altman was eating a thick steak, Sarafian remembers. The veteran director listened indulgently to Sarafian's rapture and then informed him that he was going to have to extract from him a favor in kind for having arranged the Warner's opportunity.

One of the scripts Sarafian had been working on, with the assistance of Joan Altman, was a quasi-autobiographical piece culled from the memory of his street days in New York City, about a retarded Greek immigrant named Andy. It was Sarafian's most cherished script and one that everyone who was familiar with it felt to have obvious merit and personal identification.

Altman wanted the script, and he wanted the rights to *Andy*. He was, he said, planning to direct *Andy* with his friend Dan Blocker from *Bonanza* in the lead.

Sarafian was aghast. He pleaded with Altman. Anything but *Andy*.

Sarafian wasn't grateful enough, said Altman. It had to be *Andy*. This time Sarafian vehemently replied, "*Andy* is mine."

Altman said, "Then I'm going to do you a favor, Dick. I'm going to become your worst enemy in this town."

It was the last encounter they would ever have as friends. Overnight, Altman did become Sarafian's vociferous enemy. He denounced him to friends and said terrible things about him to people in the filmmaking "family." He might occasionally recommend him for jobs that he himself was turning down—after all, Sarafian was married to his sister—but more often behind his back he would bad-mouth Sarafian.

Sarafian became the embodiment of rivalry and treachery, the worst of Them. Friends of Altman—if they were also friends of Sarafian—learned not to mention Sarafian in the presence of his brother-in-law.

Once, producer David Dortort recalls, he made the mistake of praising the lilting quality of Sarafian's direction of a *Bonanza* episode, and Altman looked daggers at him, cutting him off coldly in the middle of a sentence. The imagined rivalry grew to a mania with Altman, intensified by the fact that Sarafian was succeeding, early on, where he was failing.

For Sarafian did direct *Andy* in 1964—five years before *M*A*S*H*—when Altman was still out of work. To rub it in, *Andy* was financed to the low-budget tune of $300,000 by Universal under its short-lived New Horizons program, and trumpeted with articles in *The New York Times* and *Newsweek*, where Sarafian's photograph was prominently featured. Character actor Norman Alden ended up playing the forty-year-old, mentally retarded, Greek coal shoveler, Andy, and the reviews were positive for a touching, unusual movie that ultimately shows faith in "the magnificence of all people," in Sarafian's words.

Altman was reduced to ranting and raving. Badiyi remembers being at the Mission Hills Country Club in Kansas City for some occasion when Barbara Altman's husband asked Altman eagerly: "Have you seen Richard's new film?" "I have never seen a man get so angry—ever," says Reza. "He tried desperately to calm himself, to no avail. He was in the bathroom, punching the wall."

When over the years Altman and Sarafian would meet by chance in Hollywood restaurants, they would get drunk, call each other names, and eventually end up outside taunting each other to fight, only to be separated by their wives. On special family occasions, like Christmastime, Altman would make an effort to bring them all together, both families, usually with Badiyi and Turner as the honorary neutrals. On such occasions the atmosphere would appear to be warm and familial. And it would last at least until the next morning, when Altman would stomp around his office in a pique demanding that no one ever again mention Sarafian's name in his presence.

"That was just a little moment he provided for his family, for Joan's happiness, and that was it," says Badiyi.

Badiyi was one of a number of people in the Altman filmmaking "family" who found it hard to cut off Sarafian as cold-bloodedly as Altman—who never understood how Sarafian became so loathsome to Altman all of a sudden—and who, over time, ended up on better speaking terms with Sarafian than with Altman.

"Dick never bad-mouthed Bob," says Badiyi. "Dick can curse everybody in six languages, but Dick never said anything bad about Bob. 'Altman has his own way' is the furthest Dick would go."

Attempts at peacemaking were always brushed off. "Why?" Badiyi would ask Altman. "Sarafian loves you. Why do you hate him?" Altman would reply, "Both of us have good taste."

In time Sarafian and Joan Altman had five children, but she took them over to see her brother less and less, always without Sarafian, so that in the end the Sarafian-Altman children could barely claim to know their famous uncle. This sibling relationship, a brother so close to his sister that some have described them as emotionally incestuous, became very tainted and sour. Joan Altman's life was made miserable by the hatred between her husband and her brother. She was hurt by trying to bring them together to the point where she finally gave up, her relationship with both of them was destroyed, and her own peace of mind was impaired.

Altman wrote Sarafian off to the point where his brother-in-law did not exist, and to the point where the feud between them was preserved even when the cause for its existence was decades into the past. In the early 1980s, when Altman had shifted to filming stage plays, he gave an expansive interview to *The Los Angeles Times* in which he reminisced about those days long ago in Kansas City when he had directed theatre for the Jewish Community Center. He mentioned the ill-fated night of one-act plays, the windstorm, the flats falling, and the "one actor [who] left the stage never to return. . . ."

He did not mention that the actor was Richard Sarafian, a well-known Hollywood director in his own right—his brother-in-law (actually, by this date, his *ex*-brother-in-law). There were fewer and fewer people in Hollywood who even knew they had once been related, much less close friends. Or that the director who made such a show of family—and of a filmmaking "family"—had an unfortunate history of wreaking hatred and indifference on his own without regard to the consequences.

Chapter
19

WHAT-IFFING

What people prefer to remember are the high times of the decade. The pranks, the parties, the intrigues, the what-iffing. Above all, it was always *fun* to be around Altman.

"You never had so much fun," says Louis Lombardo, "as when you were with Bob Altman."

"By the way," echoes George Litto, "before he was a busy director, we used to have a lot of fun together. We used to charter boats and go to Catalina for four days. I had a playboy friend who was a bartender. Bob Eggenweiler and myself and other people would cook. Bob would go deep-sea diving and catch the fish and clean them. We used to have wonderful, crazy ad-

A lowly tire commercial directed by Brian McKay for Altman's Westwood operations (actor unknown). (Dan Fitzgerald)

ventures, right? We'd be up on top of the hundred-foot boat with the captain, eating and drinking and carrying on. And Bob used to tell stories—he used to do impressions—with all the physical movement. He could have been an actor, he was a tremendous performer—great jokes, card tricks, a mimic! He was a real carny. . . ."

There were fabulous night-long parties. Altman would throw something on the barbecue—chicken marinated in peaches and booze—and there would be plenty to eat and drink, no matter if the checks would bounce the next day. Altman would liven up the gatherings by reciting the Klondike poems by Robert Service—or the sonnets of Shakespeare; or he would demonstrate the magic tricks that he had taught himself when he learned that Orson Welles was a consummate magician. That was the nickname his closest friends kidded him with: "Orson." (Once, when visiting *McCabe* author Edmund Naughton in Spain, Altman scrawled himself in the visitor's book as "Orson Welles," a good forgery in a few quick strokes. Altman had studied the signature and perfected the illusion.)

People always congregated at Altman's new offices in Westwood, in those days called either Red Carpet Productions or simply Westwood Productions. The Swedish director Gunnar Hellstrom might be there, and Ida Lupino and Howard Duff, who had encouraged Altman back in the 1950s, or actors like Robert Ridgeley or Michael Murphy who seemed to feed off Altman's energy.

The offices led out to a little courtyard, with two rooms downstairs, one upstairs for screenings. At various times the office had a pool table and a barbershop chair and pinball machines, strange items for a production office in those days, though nowadays de rigeur. There were always people coming and going, cheese and crackers out on the table, with screenings of Altman's television episodes, his Calvin films, and his other independent films at night. All very relaxed and informal, all very "family."

For the insiders there were many "privileged moments"— even if, later on, they were sometimes revealed to be calculated for effect.

"When you are with him, alone, and there's nobody else around, he becomes genuine," says Brian McKay, "and he says things you're almost sure he'll deny ever saying. He says things you can't prove he even said, he does things you can't prove he did, because there's nobody else there, or he wouldn't be acting like that in the first place. He'd tell me grandiose stories about fucking women that I knew were just great stories. Not a bit of truth to them, but he'd just think them up and then tell them to me."

"He used to tell the most sensitive stories," says Badiyi, "the most personal stories. And you were in awe. He would tell you for a reason—to get a reaction from you. When the story was finished, he would say, 'I made it up. It's not true.'

"I remember when we were doing *Once Upon a Savage*

A party for the children of Altman and screenwriter Gillian Freeman, where Altman and actor Robert Ridgeley (center) performed magic tricks.

Night. He came and sat next to Barbara Turner and said, 'When I was a child in Kansas City, in the morning my mother used to boil eggs. Warm, hard-boiled eggs. And we would put them in our gloves and they would keep the palms of our hands warm as we ran to school as small children. When we got to school, we'd break them and eat them.'

"We used exactly that image in *Once Upon a Savage Night.* The character of this girl keeps eggs in her gloves, and when the killer sees them, and she explains about them, suddenly, for the first time, he breaks down from what he is, and he begins to talk about his own childhood and his mother. It was the most sensitive part of the movie. We were so hooked to this image of the eggs, we drew so much out of it, that even when we finished the picture and came back to L.A., Bob ordered and had made some golden eggs, and he gave an Eggy Award to everyone that had worked on the show.

"Then, one night, he told me he had made that story up, and he me gave his reasons—and I knew that truly he had made it up. He rode that imaginary story for such a length of time. That's what Bob is: His imagination, his images, his direction, is that strong, that clear, that lifelike."

Looking around the room on any given night, one would be struck by the fact that it was predominantly a Catholic "mafia." There might be jokes about it—they might be kidding each other by quoting sections of the Mass or Latin phrases—but for the most part it was unspoken. "Maybe that was the bond we had," McKay, a former altar boy with a Jesuit education, says of his and Altman's friendship, "without ever discussing it."

This Catholicism was always an aspect of the Altman inner hub, even as the personnel mutated and revolved. It bears noting, in part because of the Catholicity of certain of the films, but also because it is another example of Altman's sometimes enforced clubbiness.

Ten years later, in the mid-1970s, Patricia Resnick, a co-screenwriter of *A Wedding* and *Quintet*, interrupted a meeting of the first echelon to muse aloud, "Bob, do you realize I am, like, the only Jew that works for you and that in Hollywood this is weird?" Altman looked around and said, "I don't want a bunch of Jews working for me. . . ."

She took it as policy as well as a good-natured joke.

Of course, this was also, god love it, the Age of Aquarius, with all that conjures up.

All around the film industry, as all around the nation, there was drug and sex experimentation, political upheaval and the shocking headlines of war and protest, the radical divisions in fashion, lifestyle, values. The excitement in Hollywood came partly from the feeling that the elderly moguls, the dinosaur unions, and the puritanical clichés of the moldy old genres were under attack and crumbling. Before, the unions had controlled things with a death grip; the guys directing and producing were over sixty; it was impossible for young people to break in. Now, everywhere you looked there was a new breed of film people coming up fast.

The Altman faction was not the squarest one in town, nor the hippest—but somewhere in the middle, roughly—which is where Altman was situated as a director: with one foot in the old traditions and in studio craftmanship, the other in the unknown future.

There were other fringe groups—for example, the Roger Corman squad (the true-blue hippies and political heavies) or the Coppola-Bogdanovich-Friedkin group (the straight faction from academia/media, determined to rise up through loop-holes in the system). But these coexisting groups were like concentric circles outside the nucleus of the motion-picture industry, not necessarily intersecting with each other.

The changes of the Sixties had a significant impact on Alt-man. "He and I embraced that period," says McKay. "The first time he and Kathryn came over to our house, he looked at me and I was wearing bell-bottoms and a flowered shirt, and he was surprised because he was wearing the same thing. He said, 'Aha, Brian, your hair is the right length—long. You're wearing the right clothes. You know all about the right things. . . .' We were a couple of peacocks."

At first, Altman would not touch marijuana. Booze was his stimulant. In script conferences, Brian McKay would roll a joint for himself (later, he or Kathryn always had to roll for Altman, who was slow to learn) and suffer Altman's offended glances. Altman used to make faces across the room. "You know, how squares do," says McKay.

"I remember how shocked he was," recalls Richard Pea-body, "when we came over to his secretary's house, her apartment, when we were still doing *Combat*. Vic [Morrow] and myself and another actor were there smoking a joint. And he walked in, and he took a toke in very amateurish way, and I don't think he'd ever seen anybody smoke a joint before, and certainly he had never smoked before. He had just dropped in unexpectedly hoping to get laid and was a little pissed that we were all there to begin with."

"As a matter of fact, he was a putter-downer," continues McKay. "He had a Nebraska mores about it. . . . I used to tell him that if anyone needs to smoke marijuana, it's you, because he could not relax, he could not lay back. He just couldn't relax. He's driven. When he sleeps, he sleeps, but when he wakes up, he is immediately awake. He's the most totally awake, for someone who's just awakened, of anybody I've ever seen."

But soon everybody was giving dope a try, it seemed—even the old Kansas City crowd.

Louis Lombardo was working as an editor over at Fox, and one day he brought a plate of marijuana cookies left over from the *Batman* set to the Westwood offices. Altman flew into a rage and told him to remove them from the premises. Lombardo said, "Aw, put them in the fridge for people who drop by," and he went off to get gas for his car. When he passed by the office later, he spied Altman and his wife sneaking out with the cookies. After that, says Lombardo, Altman was a regular fiend.

Especially in the beginning, everyone agrees, marijuana was a tonic for Altman. It calmed him down. It tempered the tensions and frustrations, and on a day-to-day basis made the director more of an agreeable human being.

"It mellowed him by one hundred percent," says McKay, "even though you wouldn't classify him as mellow. For him, it was marvelous. He was a lot more controllable, a lot more understanding, his sense of humor was gentler. Marijuana made him gentle."

Professionally, no technological breakthrough, no lens or film stock, was half as influential on the director's visual style. The gauzy atmospherics, the off-focus and the tactile lighting, the striving for an antiglamorous reality, the sifting/winnowing camerawork—these were emergent in the best of Altman's television work but were reinforced in the 1960s by the effect of marijuana on his imagination.

Marijuana shaped the storytelling. Its influence is there in the "dream" passages, the truncated narrative forms, the quirkiness and the fragmentedness, the vacillating points of view, the bent humor, the clear insights bobbing up amidst the torrent of banality. Indeed, watching some of Altman's movies is an experience akin to a stoned "high," with the characters and the storyline, the dialogue and the images, wavering in and out of focus. Movies not quite making sense, yet making profound sense.

Drugs opened the door to other experimentation. At parties, wearing his Cheshire cat grin, the director encouraged the revelers to shed their inhibitions. Always image-conscious, Altman now grew his hair long, tapered his beard, wore a turtleneck and love beads. He was attracted by the espoused philosophy of the hippies, which seemed to speak to something locked deep within him.

"I think the Sixties helped Bob," says Badiyi. "Bob used the Sixties rightly. He was nourished by the Sixties. That whole movement freed him."

Altman was not overtly political. He wanted to do a movie satirizing Lyndon Baines Johnson, and he continued to detest and denounce Nixon—but he did not march in antiwar protests, and he had little money to contribute to causes.

He was more given to symbolic gestures, as when he wore a black arm-band while Ronald Reagan was running for governor of California in 1964. But while others in the Altman clique (Reza Badiyi, Danford B. Greene, etc.) contributed time, money, and their own talents as filmmakers, first to Senator Eugene McCarthy's, and later to Robert F. Kennedy's Presidential campaign, Altman was usually too busy with his own career.*

One side effect of the Sixties, and of the marijuana usage

---

*One exception occurred after the filming of $M*A*S*H$, when Shirley Sutherland (Donald Sutherland's then wife) and writer Donald Freed were arrested in an FBI round-up and accused of fronting money and weapons for the Black Panther Party. Altman quickly donated money for their bail and defense. It was later shown, by the Senate Select Intelligence Committee report of the mid-1970s, that the FBI arrests were part of an overall COINTELPRO-like plan to break up the Hollywood coalition of left-liberal celebrities involved in antiwar and antiracist activities. "He's no quavering liberal," admiringly says Freed, who later coauthored the play basis of Altman's film, *Secret Honor*, about Richard Nixon. "He is as bold in life as he is in art. He's not politcal in the sense that some of us were and are. But he's dedicated to a kind of passionate freedom."

perhaps, was that Altman's health, which had been mysteriously precarious for years, suddenly seemed to improve.

For years Altman had been telling friends and associates that he had a "heart condition." Little beyond this was volunteered. Some people think he was inviting their sympathy; others, that Altman suffered from some sort of anxiety syndrome; and still others, that it was all some sort of elaborate prank, and that Altman delighted in shocking them.

In the middle of a conversation, he was known to drop his pants suddenly and inject himself with a coagulant. The cluster of bruises on his posterior were evidence of many such treatments. Altman claimed it was a life-preserving ritual that he absolutely had to go through some half-dozen times a day. On the other hand, he would be chagrined if he did not provoke the desired reaction. Once, he met an agent at an airport and performed his little routine swiftly and rather gratuitously in public. When the agent said nothing, Altman exclaimed, "For chrissakes, you just saw what I did. Don't you have one single comment to make?"

Especially when circumstances were bad, and there was any open conflict in the Altman "family," Altman's "heart condition" would seem to flare up—and Kathryn would hurry the director away, as he clutched his chest. Later, she would chide the offending party about having upset Altman with dissension and disloyalty. As time went on, the Sixties seemed to have an almost medicinal effect; his psychology improved, and the "heart condition" vanished without explanation.

"There was nothing wrong with Bob's heart," says Badiyi. "It made him the center of attention of everybody, so everybody would be concerned about him. In the Sixties, his health became perfect. Twenty years of heart trouble and all of a sudden his heart became perfect."

Cary Grant was very interested in *Death, Where Is Thy Sting-a-ling-ling?"* Grant had seen Altman's television episodes and films, he had written down Altman's name on a notepad he kept of up-and-comers, and now he asked to meet him. He met the director, and he liked him. Now, it remained only to arrange the financing.

The Mirisch Company and United Artists became part of the package. At his own expense, Altman filmed aerial scenes in Orange County. He strapped Badiyi to the wing of a German Fokker plane in order to photograph a dogfight with stunt flyers. Louis Lombardo edited the expensive teaser. Everyone was very enthusiastic. For a while, it looked like the film was going to be made.

But *Death* was not a cheap picture. Mirisch and UA worried that Altman was not the right person to manage the budget and direct a big star like Cary Grant. Time went on. Cary Grant was in the process of changing his mind about acting ever again. Then he dropped out of consideration. The deal went bad.

Altman likes to belabor the impression that during the mid-1960s, he was out of work and struggling, which is partly true. But during these few years, Altman shot more film than some directors do in a decade: commercials, footage for Japanese newsreel, home movies, experimental scenes, premature music videos, second-unit stuff—plus the occasional television pilot or episode stint. Often, he and the Westwood group were filming just for the heck of it—endless "test footage."

One night they sneaked into Disneyland with 35mm equipment. McKay wore some makeshift costume, Kathryn and McKay's wife smuggled in film stock and camera parts in their clothing, and Lombardo and Badiyi handled the photography. It was only stock footage to impress prospective commercial clients. Altman put up a big front when they were discovered, but of course they were thrown out of the park.

Altman was continually broke. He was being turned down around town for the more prestigious work. But he and the group at Westwood Productions were perpetually filming and editing *something*.

"He has to make film like other people need protein," says

Louis Lombardo. "When I was later cutting for him, we would stay there until all hours of the night. Just cut and run stuff. All the pictures. The ones he'd already done, the one he was doing. He used to keep me there until one in the morning, just shooting the shit and cutting.

"[Robert] Redford's like that too. I remember one time, during *All the President's Men*, he couldn't articulate what he wanted to see happen in the film. I was at a loss. So, he said to me, 'I'll act it out for you.' Here it was, one o'clock in the morning, we're the only ones on the lot, I'm slumped over the Moviola, and here's number one walking back and forth across the cutting room acting out what it is he'd like to see."

In between paying jobs, they would shoot their own "mini-movies." Altman once screened an evening's worth of them at the Institute of Contemporary Art in Boston. The program included a nine-minute salute to marijuana *(Pot au Feu)* and the eleven-minute, black-and-white *The Life of Kathryn Reed* (a jokey, mini-biopic of his wife). Other directors have "student" films and precocious short subjects in their closet, but what other Hollywood director was so much in love with filmmaking that he was directing some sort of movie, in every waking moment?

All these fine young talents—Lombardo and Badiyi, John Williams, Danford B. Greene, and so on—worked on these films as if they were top-of-the-line. They believed in the director, and they believed in the process of serving the craft. If there was not enough money to finish one of Altman's little films, the hat would be passed, or the negative would be sent back to Kansas City for developing at Calvin, where for a long time Altman had a standing account.

By and by, there was a falling-out with Roald Dahl. The British writer wanted out of *Death* because his wife, actress Patricia Neal, was semiparalyzed as the result of a series of strokes. Dahl needed money for medical expenses. Without Cary Grant, and now without Dahl, the property was, of course, much less "bankable" in Hollywood.

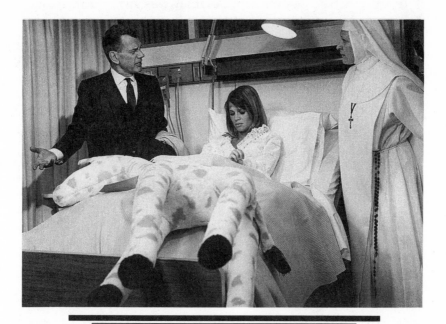

After the wife-beating: Julie Christie, in the hospital in *Petulia* (Joseph Cotten at left). Prepared as Altman's breakthrough statement as a filmmaker, *Petulia* was ceded to producer Ray Wagner and director Richard Lester, at a point of desperation. (Collectors Bookstore)

There was bitterness over the settlement, under which script rights were ceded to Mirisch and UA, with Dahl and Altman splitting the $150,000 buy-out equally.

"I remember," says Litto, "a one-sided conversation where Lazar [Hollywood agent "Swifty" Lazar] is on one side of the phone saying, 'Well, what about this need Roald Dahl has, now that he has tremendous expenses?' And Bob's reply was, 'Why don't you give up your ten percent?'"

Brian McKay received a "pittance" of the money, in his view. So the resentment was all around.

Litto had tried, but failed, to swing a deal whereby Altman would direct *Petulia*—a smaller, cheaper picture—first, if only Mirisch and UA would let Altman direct *Death*. "We wanted to get him established as a filmmaker," says Litto.

In spite of the settlement, Altman was in mounting debt. Litto lent him money. Ray Wagner lent him money. Altman was tearing his hair out over the loss of *Death*. Litto told him not to worry. The script was still "hot," and Altman was not yet out of the running for director. By the time someone got around to filming it, they would be back crawling on their knees begging for Altman to direct.

And Altman still had *Petulia*. That script was generating positive word of mouth around Hollywood. The real-life tribulations of screenwriter Barbara Turner had been channeled into the writing. One of the most excruciating scenes was the wife-beating, around which most of the narrative was structured—a piece of soul-searching, veiled autobiography such as Altman himself never dared.

The possibilities were endless. Meanwhile, there were numerous other projects, some more mercenary than others. The Westwood cadre made ends meet by picking up work elsewhere. Louis Lombardo was cutting *Felony Squad* with Howard Duff over at Fox. Danny Greene was splicing *Judd for the Defense*. Dan Fitzgerald, an art director lately arrived from Kansas City and Calvin who had taken up design responsibilities for Altman, was enmeshed at Encyclopaedia Britannica as associate producer of their educational films. But whenever Altman called with new prospects, they and others rallied, their camaraderie rekindled.

• Fleetingly, Altman wished to film Barbara Garson's *MacBird!*, an acclaimed Off-Broadway satire about LBJ and the Vietnam War. He even went so far as to journey to Greece to scout locations, but in the end, as it so often did, the money fell through.

• He also attempted to launch a one-hour television drama of Graham Greene's *Our Man in Havana*, said to be adapted from the Carol Reed feature (starring Alec Guinness), and scripted jointly by Altman and the *Petulia* dentist, Dr. John Haase, under the guidance of Screen Gems producer Jackie Cooper. Locations were scouted in Hawaii. Despite much ballyhoo in the trades, it never went beyond casting.

- Altman's vow to abandon television was short-lived (Altman was always hedging his bets). The director did a surprising amount of television directing in the mid-Sixties, especially for one "sort of blackballed" (in Reza Badiyi's words) from the business. He directed episodes of *Gunsmoke, Mr. Novak,* and *East Side, West Side.* Partly as a result of his reputation for *The Gallant Men,* he specialized in pilot episodes, and he is credited for the maiden voyage of *The Long Hot Summer* in late 1964 at Fox, directing Earl Hammer's teleplay starring Edmond O'Brien.

- A game fanatic, Altman had an idea for a television version of "Crossword." He and the Westwood group filmed a "live" pilot in a theatre up on Hollywood Boulevard with three cameras, real contestants, and a full audience. The only trouble was, in their haste they neglected coverage of the big game board; so Danford B. Greene, Dan Fitzgerald, and Brian McKay had to spend a week closeted in a room, backlighting and shooting miniatures and inserts. In the end it didn't matter because nobody went for the concept anyway.

- Depending on his mood, Altman would take anything that came along—like second-unit work. He and Lombardo flew to Florida one weekend to do location pickup scenes for *The Happening,* a 1967 caper film starring Anthony Quinn, for which he and Badiyi also filmed a car chase on Westwood Boulevard.

- He would do preproduction work, scout locations, anything, just for the opportunity to get out of town, take a break, and stay busy.

"Bob loved to travel," says Litto, "and when I couldn't get him a job, I'd send him on these preproduction services. A guy would pay him ten thousand dollars upfront. I'd get all his expenses paid. I sent him to Greece, I sent him to London, I sent him to Paris. When he wasn't working, he was traveling."

Chapter

20

RICHES
TO
RAGS

The seventy-five-thou-sand-dollar *Death* settlement and the other one-shot fees dwindled in the calendar of parties, the gambling and the high life, the upgrade of equipment, the salaries for the Westwood people.

At one low point, Altman was reduced to filming one-minute or thirty-second auto and tire commercials, not unlike the Calvin days fifteen years earlier. Ironically, they were sometimes sandwiched between scenes of Altman's former way-station, *Bonanza*.

In Los Angeles, in the mid-1960s, Barry Elliot was an agency spot producer for Campbell-Ewald, the organization behind the Chevrolet commercials for television. Elliot remembers that the "talent trust" of Altman's worked on commercials with the same ardor as if they were $M*A*S*H$ or *Nashville*. A decade later, Altman's Lion's Gate Productions would sponsor noteworthy films by directors Alan Rudolph and Robert Benton, among others, but really, these automobile commercials were the first tentative Altman branch productions, only it was Badiyi or McKay or Lombardo directing location roadwork in Santa Barbara and Long Beach.

Altman fought for his little auto-tire ideas as if they were for big films. In one instance the director argued with the sponsor's representative right up to the signing of a ten-thousand-dollar advance. Altman wanted to have a visual non sequitur of a black cat, pursued by the camera, as the cat stalks through a used car lot. The sponsor said absolutely no, no *cat.* Brian McKay was instructed to write two scripts—one with the black cat in it, one without. When the sponsor chose the one without the black cat, Altman made the sponsor's representative's life miserable by pretending he was going to shoot his preferred version. Throughout a long night the man had to keep vigil on location, with Altman and the crew, to enforce the sponsor's version.

The Westwood group were down on their luck and needed the money but Altman didn't shoot the Chevrolet commercials condescendingly. Says Elliot: "It was a film to shoot and there was a joy just in shooting film.

"At one point, we were in the editing room, and he said to me, 'Film is such a forgiving art form. Anything works. Here,' he said, 'pick out a take.' I took a strip out of the bin. He said, 'Here's the music bin, pick out a track.' He stuck them together on the Moviola and it was great."

During this particular low ebb, Robert Blees, Altman's former booster on *Bus Stop* and the *Combat* series, looked Altman up at the Westwood offices.

Now, Blees was at Paramount where he was an executive for a subsidiary manufacturing a revolutionary type of musical jukebox utilizing filmed cassettes. Tavern fans would not

"the Party"
a Colorsonics concept prepared by
the Robert altman Company

Dan Fitzgerald's sketch for the design concept of *The Party*, the ColorSonics short subject filmed during an all-out revelment at the director's Mandeville Canyon home. (Dan Fitzgerald)

only hear a song from the hit parade but they would *see* someone like Peggy Lee performing it on a small television-type screen attached to the jukebox. The people at Color-Sonics thought their idea was going to be the biggest thing since slot machines—and they were right, except they were twenty years ahead of MTV and the concept of music videos.

ColorSonics had commissioned twenty-four musical short subjects to be produced by Blees featuring such performers as Herb Alpert and the Tijuana Brass (playing their hit "Whipped Cream"), Nancy Sinatra ("These Boots Are Made for Walking"), Fran Jeffries ("Ain't Misbehaving") and Julie London ("Daddy"), among others. Lionel Newman from the venerable Fox music department was lending scoring advice, and Blees could call on salaried craftsmen from the Paramount camera department.

When Blees contacted him, Altman said he was interested

in purchasing some new camera equipment whose price-tag eluded him, and consequently he was available to direct three of the ColorSonics—$10,000 for three of them, budgeted at $3,300 apiece. "He [Altman] was struggling," says Blees. "He wasn't quite shooting Bar Mitzvahs, but almost."

ColorSonics never really got off the ground—Blees infers dubious business practices—and that is a shame, because the four (not three) musical shorts that Altman eventually did film are intoxicating fare.

The first Altman-directed ColorSonic was a jubilant throwaway, a Bobby Troup tune called "Girl Talk," lensed at the Paraphernalia boutique on Rodeo Drive. Altman had one of his brief enthusiasms for actor-musician Troup—Troup is in *M*A*S*H*, the noncom who repeatedly mutters "Goddam Army!"—and he kept telling him that under his tutelage he was going to be the biggest star that ever lived. Here, Troup chirped merrily while beautiful starlets, models, and dancers donned and doffed trendy clothes in sync-time.

The second ColorSonic is an uproarious, tour-de-force four-minute short called *The Party* with music set to Herb Albert and the Tijuana Brass's chartbuster "Whipped Cream."

All the people who usually came to one of Altman's parties are there (on camera)—and you can spot Michael Murphy, Altman's daughter Christine, Barbara Ruik (John Williams's wife), and editor Danford B. Greene, among many others, in what comes close to being a scrapbook evocation of the ultimate Altman shindig. The montage is a leering one of close-up navels, overheard party conversation, Sixties regalia (body stockings and miniskirts), martinis, and canapés. Altman's Buster Keaton for the occasion, Robert Fortier, mugs and stumbles his way through the wild goings-on until, finally, he is bumped into the swimming pool. The film ends underwater with some antic special effects of Fortier taking submerged puffs of his cigarette.

Most provocatively, there were two Altman-directed musical shorts featuring the legendary exotic dancer Lili St. Cyr.

When St. Cyr went to Altman's office at Westwood to dis-

A rare still from the Altman-directed Lili St. Cyr short during which the legendary stripper performs her tease to the accompaniment of "Speak Low." St. Cyr performed in two Altman short films, seen by few people, as ColorSonics shortly went out of business. (Dan Fitzgerald)

cuss the two ColorSonics, she was surprised at the homey atmosphere and that Altman was on a first-name basis with all the employees. The conversation was informal. Ida Lupino was there, just sitting in.

As Altman outlined his plans, they were to going to shoot her first ColorSonic in the garden of a luxurious Bel Air mansion that had belonged to producer William Goetz, the son-in-law of Louis B. Mayer. St. Cyr remembers Altman talking about the gazebo in that garden—and about his own gazebo, which he had bought in Europe and brought home yet had not had time to assemble. That made her feel at ease. The director must be a romantic personality, she thought, to have purchased a gazebo and lugged it all the way back from Europe.

St. Cyr remembers Altman told her right away that he was married to someone who had been a dancer at the spectacular Hollywood showplace of the 1940s, Earl Carroll's, at the same time she was working at the rival Florentine Gardens. "I don't know if he told me that to make me feel more at home or what," she recalls. "But I thought, 'This guy married a showgirl,' and it told me something."

The set, a baroque boudoir set in a lush Eden, was up on a hill overlooking the city of Los Angeles. Altman told St. Cyr there was to be no script or dialogue, and he would simply talk her through the movements. They would add the music in the editing room. Altman explained that, as she was a professional dancer, she could cut loose and ad-lib naturally. Just float with the camera. "It was done almost as if I was running and walking through a dream," she says. "I got the impression from him of what to do without him actually putting it into words."

This particular ColorSonic is a very dreamy, Jean Cocteauish gem. The music is "Speak Low" as recorded by a British big band. St. Cyr pulls up in a Rolls-Royce, wearing a magnificent evening cape and gown. She glides to an ornate bedroom surrealistically arranged in the middle of a voluptuous garden. Then as the camera teases, creeping in and pulling back, she proceeds from evening wear to topless and less, gyrating and supplicating as the image fades. For a director who has always been Catholic in matters of sex on the screen—coy or fumbling or cutting away—this is the closest Altman ever came to a mild pornography.

The second St. Cyr ColorSonic the exotic dancer remembers as the more enjoyable and arty of the two. This time, Altman had St. Cyr established in an Oriental tent on the beach at Malibu, changing brightly colored wigs and acting a snippet of an Arabian fantasy. Again, it was all her moves, with the camera her mistress. If Altman was unenthusiastic, he never let on. The opposite: He and his small band poured energy and ideas into the short film.

"He [Altman] acted like this was the finest work in his life and he wanted to do the best job possible," St. Cyr recalls. "You might not expect that of such a big director doing a teensy-weensy little film, but he acted like it was the best thing he could possibly be doing."

The Party and the untitled Lili St. Cyr shorts stand up as the first flowering of the free-form Altman in the flush of the Sixties attitudes that liberated him. Few people have ever seen them and few are ever likely to. There was a bunch of them marketed in Hawaii, Blees says, and in France they were called Scopitones. But the only one Blees is certain existed was installed in a video jukebox at Nickodell's near Paramount, where Altman still liked to have his steaks for dinner.

Litto was wrong. UA and the Mirisch Bros. launched *Death* right away with David Miller directing Gregory Peck in Spain. Altman was not in the least consulted. To make matters worse, after some ten days of filming, the harsh winter weather made for complications, and the production shut down. Now, *Death* was dead in Hollywood. One of Altman's nearest and dearest properties, out of his grasp, forever.

But *Petulia* was still receiving promising nibbles from the studios.

And, meanwhile, Litto had set up a Tiffany deal at CBS for Altman to do a television series called *Nightwatch* (a.k.a. *Chicago, Chicago*), based on a two-hour pilot package starring Carroll O'Connor and Andrew Duggan in a script about a fictional police unit dealing with crime throughout the Great Lakes area. The last thing Altman wanted to do was go back to television with his tail between his legs. But he was given the controls and it could be shot in Chicago away from network interference. Reza could photograph it, Brian could write it, Danny and Louis could edit it, Dan Fitzgerald could do the production design . . . it would be a Robert Altman production. The "talent trust" all agreed to sell their homes

Altman (at center) with Reza Badiyi (carrying camera) filming a nightclub scene for the ill-fated *Chicago, Chicago* television pilot. (Reza Badiyi)

and move to Chicago if the series received the green light.

Once again, part of the mystique of the pilot was the new fast film that Badiyi was using to shoot color in natural light. The pilot had everybody excited at the network, and the show was touted as a harbor *Dragnet.* The sponsor was ecstatic, and Altman was talking about *Nightwatch* as the show that would underwrite the dreams of everybody in the Westwood group.

Only trouble is, Altman and producer Ray Wagner were not getting along. Wagner disagreed with the editing of *Nightwatch* and Altman did not want him to touch the film. In addition, Wagner had been asked to vouch for Altman when he adopted his son, Matthew, through an agency, and it was said that Altman was not satisfied with Wagner's attestation.* True or not, as is often the case with Altman's film "family," the personal and professional rancor became as one, and suddenly one of Altman's biggest supporters throughout the mid-Sixties was persona non grata at Westwood.

Litto was called in to make the peace. "Though I was both their agents, in many cases people trusted me as arbitrer," remembers Litto. "I was forced to be King Solomon."

It turns out CBS would not commit to the television series unless Altman was directing it. Wagner would not waive his involvement in *Nightwatch* unless Altman surrendered *Petulia*. Broke as ever, on the verge of a triumphant TV comeback, Altman weighed his options and agreed to a deal whereby Wagner was granted ownership of *Petulia* and Altman was reduced to claiming a percentage of it.

What happened next was a debacle.

Lucille Ball had not yet signed a network contract for her new series, and she demanded the *Nightwatch* slot for one of her own sponsored pilots. The network yielded and *Nightwatch* was canceled. (Incidentally, that Lucille Ball series was *Mission Impossible*, a hit hour-long adventure series that instantly relegated *Nightwatch* to the category of what-might-have-been.)

"On the one hand, Bob was disappointed *Nightwatch* never got scheduled," says Litto. "On the other, he was relieved because he hated television. But he was disappointed because now Ray had control of *Petulia*. God! These were the two properties that were going to make him a movie director."

"Bob threw a failure party. That's the kind of guy he was," says Louis Lombardo. "He didn't give a shit."

Petulia, on the other hand, was suddenly very hot. Working with Wagner, Litto packaged a deal with director Richard Lester, fresh from the splash of the Beatles films, actress

---

*The adopted Matthew—described as "half-Negro" by *The New York Times* in 1972; as a "mulatto" by *Current Biography*—is the youngest of Altman's five children.

Julie Christie (coming off her Oscar for *Darling*), and George C. Scott. Litto negotiated a whopping $450,000 for Wagner to produce his first feature motion picture. For his part, Altman got "a lot of money" (Litto's words) just to settle the rights. But really, Altman had no choice, and he felt betrayed.

With a script that Altman had helped to forge, Lester went on to make one of the quintessential motion pictures of the late Sixties. Among other things, Lester used jump-cuts the way Altman would have used the zoom lens and sound, as a radical means of narrating and punctuating the story. "Dick Lester made it his own," says Litto. "It's a different picture. I liked it a lot better the way Bob Altman wanted to do it at that time. But Dick Lester made a helluva picture."

Now, Ray Wagner, staunch for years, joined the "enemies list." And George Litto, tired of being telephoned in the middle of the night and harangued by Altman for also representing Wagner, quit as Altman's agent. There was tremendous pressure on Barbara Turner and through her, on Reza Badiyi, to prove their primary allegiance to Altman. The entire episode went down in Altman's book as a poison barb that could never be healed.

Countdown restored some of the harmony, albeit only momentarily.

Though it was a salve to his ego, Altman's first motion picture since *The James Dean Story* ten years earlier was purely a Warner Brothers studio directing assignment, a one-picture deal, and as Altman had a tendency to look at things in reverse, it began to gnaw on him that he was merely doing Jack Warner's bidding.

Most of the Westwood group were somewhat oblivious to the filming anyway. Bob Eggenweiler was the only one Altman brought on in a production capacity, and the others knew only as much about the movie as Altman chose to reveal to them. In the end Altman stressed his supposed violent disagreement with Jack Warner, and the fact that Warners recut his version of the film. Finally, to make matters worse, for some reason Warners did not even release the film until 1968, more than a year after photography was completed.

"That [Countdown] helped to break that period of problems," says Fitzgerald. "But when the picture was taken away from him, that made him even more difficult to deal with in terms of wanting absolute control."

By now the general bad feeling around the Westwood offices was deep-rooted and nothing could break the growing sense of isolation.

"This was a tough, tough period," remembers Dan Fitzgerald. "He [Altman] was getting nostalgic, and as the sun went down, we'd put on an old *Combat* or *Chicago, Chicago,* and get the bottle of Scotch out and reminisce. It was a very painful time."

Altman would unbosom his feelings in displays of temper, acid-wit, or paranoia. At parties now, he would suddenly become annoyed at someone and announce that everyone had to leave—all the guests, instantly—and Altman would throw them out. It was disturbing, such episodes, but everyone felt for his anguish and desperation.

Altman's house went up for back taxes. There was talk of turning the Westwood offices into a restaurant. Then the Westwood headquarters had to be temporarily, some said permanently, closed. The Altmans were reduced to living off Kathryn's child support. The gambling debts did not abate and Altman schemed to stay ahead of his business manager and borrow from imaginary budgets. Anything to keep going.

Part of the downward spiral was Altman's increased unwillingness to take directing jobs that he now considered demeaning. There were offers that might bail him out, but whereas before Altman would direct tire commercials to get by, now, after *Nightwatch* and *Countdown,* his mood was more erratic.

Bonanza producer Dortort remembers running into Altman on the sands of Malibu where a tent was pitched and a small camera crew was busy capturing the immortal Lili St. Cyr. Altman seemed downcast. Dortort asked him how things were going. Altman answered, "Things are rough, man." He gave the impression of having reached his nadir. Dortort extended an offer to Altman to come back and direct a *Bonanza* or *High Chapparral*. Altman paused and said, "Let me think about it." But he never called Dortort to follow it up.

Badiyi remembers being at the Westwood office when Altman was being coaxed by his new (post-Litto) agent into reading a script that was available to him. Altman, his eyes glazed with sadness, was saying, "Whatever shit it is, I'll do it, I know I have to do it. . . ." There followed ten minutes of tense silence in the room while Altman perused the script. Suddenly, he erupted and threw it across the room. "I cannot do it!" he screamed, "I cannot do it!"

"I never saw a sadder face in my life," says Badiyi.

"He never philosophized too much about what he was doing," says Danford B. Greene, "but he would philosophize about other things in general—about people in this business, the people who ran the studios, that it was strictly money and business. And he just couldn't play that game. He couldn't go along with those kinds of people. He always had trouble with them. They were different than him.

"He would be so secure, if he had an idea or a principle, he would not budge, even if he didn't have a dime. I know that for a fact because it happened several times. Really broke! Owing the liquor stores and the camera shops . . ."

Altman's drinking was getting more out of control. It was becoming embarrassing. Fuming about the people who run Hollywood, more than once he would fall into a stupor and have to be carried out of a restaurant, "Egg" cradling him in his arms like a baby.

Ironically, Badiyi, Lombardo, McKay, and Danford B. Greene, noting how easy Altman liked to make it seem, wanted to become directors—three of the four were to reach that particular plateau. They made no secret of their goals.

But there was the feeling that your life and career had to be secondary to Altman's. When Altman summoned you for a get-together, his need was such that you'd better be there.

Altman was buoyant in the daytime, morose at night. He had to be jollied through the night, just as he sometimes had to be jollied through the final stages of filming a production.

"Everyone has to be around [constantly]," says Badiyi. "And if you weren't there, you could see he wasn't happy about it, and he'd always make a big point of it. Bob's idea was, 'If you're working with me, you're working with me—always.' There was a joy to be with Bob during work hours. After hours, either he was cranky, or too happy, or too drunk. The problem with Bob is [more] after hours."

As much as he stroked his "protégés" (which was more and more how he regarded the filmmaking "family"), he belittled their aspirations. He went so far as to tell producers inquiring about them that they were relative novices. Badiyi, for one, was already being sounded out, but Altman discouraged any feelers. "He always told people, 'Reza is my protégé,'" says Badiyi. "'He is going to be a great director—*when I say he is ready.*'"

"During that period the Scotch bottle would open up at four in the afternoon," says Fitzgerald, "and stay open until four in the morning, when everyone would go to have dinner. One night at a Mexican restaurant in Santa Monica, quite drunkenly Bob told Reza he couldn't work with him anymore. Then Bob had a couple more maragaritas. Kathryn was such a fantastic adjunct to Bob. The glaze started to appear over Bob's eyes and she moved the *Albondigas* aside and Bob passed out cold. A dozen people kept eating. Somehow, that typifies the period."

Barbara Turner was having her own hardships. A second writer, Larry Marcus, had been brought in over her head, and there were revisions made in the screenplay of *Petulia* that distressed her. She had written three or four other marvelous screenplays. Now, on the basis of *Petulia*, there was sudden interest in her other properties. And Altman was always her first choice as director.

One of these screenplays was an adaptation of a Simone de Beauvoir novel called *The Mandarins*, intended for Marlon

Brando and Anouk Aimée. Turner had spent time with Jean-Paul Sartre and de Beauvoir and had written a script that de Beauvoir paid tribute to in a letter to the screenwriter. Another was a story about an young French survivor of Auschwitz called *At Lake Lugano*, which was being developed for Columbia Pictures.

Meanwhile, Altman had received preproduction money on yet another motion picture possibility called *A Spoonful of Love*, to be produced by the publisher of *The Hollywood Reporter*, Tichi Wilkerson. It was a tale about dope and romance and it was going to star John Saxon. McKay was doctoring the script. Altman and McKay and Badiyi flew to Europe to scout locations.

It always buoyed Altman to be in Paris, the Paris of his doting aunts, the Paris of his imagination.

One night, they glimpsed Orson Welles on the boulevards. Badiyi and a drunkenly weaving Altman followed Welles down the street in the rain. Altman still revered Welles, but he was gibbering this night, and he would not go up to the great director who was, like him, "between films."

Later that night, drinking heavily, Altman proclaimed Welles to be a nobody, just lucky. "He was breaking an idol," says Badiyi, "because I think it was a hang-up [with him] for a long time."

In Seville, Spain, McKay and Altman took a hotel room and began to hash out the final details of the script. Altman got on the phone and invited Barbara Turner to come over to Spain and help out. As McKay spoke the best Spanish (Altman spoke none), he began to line up the crew and act as producer, waiting for the money to arrive from the States.

Things deteriorated. Their line of credit was rescinded, McKay came down with dysentery. When no bail-out money materialized from the U.S., the preproduction halted and they all repaired to Paris.

There, the frustrations of years boiled over. Altman and McKay were staying together at the George V Hotel—where they were drunk around the clock, gambling and recreating. There was already abundant tension between them owing to

McKay's growing sense of independence, and over the macho rivalry they sustained over money and women.

Late one night, when Altman made some remark about putting his money under the pillow so McKay would not steal it—alluding to the prison past of his best friend—McKay, not to be intimidated, drew back and cold-cocked him. The hotel management was called, and the Parisian police arrived. At Altman's insistence, McKay was ejected from the hotel, and driven by Badiyi straightaway to the airport. In the car McKay could not control his weeping.

Badiyi, Turner, and Altman stayed on in Paris to meet with Anouk Aimée to discuss *At Lake Lugano*. The French actress, who was in the midst of a stellar career and had just won an Oscar nomination for *A Man and a Woman*, had agreed to star in the film of Turner's screenplay. Altman was being promoted by Turner as the likely director and had been tentatively approved by Columbia. The very next night, they had a long, exquisite dinner. Altman was nursing a black eye and he was in a foul mood.

"Anouk needed to fall in love with her director," says Badiyi, picking up the story. "She had just come from working with Federico Fellini [in *La Dolce Vita* and 8½] and couldn't stop talking about him [Fellini]. Altman was drinking very heavily and he was nervous and he wasn't sure he wanted to do this picture, but he wanted to sell himself. He overdrank and got mean and he told Aimée off."

Back in Hollywood the word circulated that Altman had said something that Aimée, in the heat of the moment, interpreted as anti-Semitic—an echo of Altman's departure from *Combat.*

Like a hot potato, Altman was dropped by Columbia from the *At Lake Lugano* package. He wanted Badiyi and Turner to make their continued participation contingent upon his rehiring. They elected to stay in Paris and struggle with a succession of appointed directors over script revisions and cast changes for a story that was never, ultimately, to be filmed.

The damage had been done: to the friendship between Altman, Badiyi, and Turner; and as venomously, to the friendship and collaboration with McKay.

"Bob loves to have and must have a total control," says Badiyi. "If he doesn't have total control, Bob cannot function. For all that time Bob could work with Brian because Bob was in control—he was paying the bills, he was the boss, it was his company and his project. But there were things they did not do together, where they were coming together as equals, where they didn't jell together, and the chemistry didn't work.

"Always I felt that Brian understood Bob to a degree that none of the others who were around, did. Bob would think of an idea, barely start it, and Brian would be working on ending that idea. That was the kind of unique rapport they had.

"But Brian wasn't there to serve Bob, in comparison to Eggenweiler, who had such love for Bob. He'd [Eggenweiler] cook for Bob, he'd produce for Bob, he'd kill for Bob. It was total obedience. Brian wasn't like that. His [McKay's] suffering, finally, was to fall from grace, which eventually everybody did. I do not know any of his [Altman's] friends, including his sisters, his father, anybody, who stayed his friends, always. He'd discard them.

"I feel Bob reflects himself thru [sic] his friends and that he is always searching for a different image. After a little while he gets so tired of seeing himself. That helps him a great deal, that feeling of not being satisfied with what he sees. It gives him the courage to go and search for something, to try and become somebody else, to choose different kinds of friends and surroundings, and at least for a few more days, to see himself in a different image, and to at least be happy with that. Then to start to become unhappy again in a circle. And there's nothing worse than Bob becoming unhappy . . ."

When they all returned from Europe and to Westwood, passions had cooled, and they still kept company; but things were changed, utterly.

As *That Cold Day in the Park* led to *M*A*S*H* after such a long period of fits and starts, as Altman was about to crash through, the intense core of friends and associates who had sustained him through roughly a decade of Hollywood dues-paying, the "talent trust" behind the budding auteur, was already foundering at the seams.

Chapter
21

COUNTDOWN

If in episodic television Altman made some waves, it was, in 1968, with *Countdown*, his first feature produced by a Hollywood studio, that he began to emerge as a quality motion-picture director.

Not that Altman makes any grandiose claims for this behind-the-scenes glimpse of the astronaut race to conquer the moon. In interviews, in fact, Altman has made a point of renouncing the film; he says that the final form was not his; he claims the ending was reshot after studio head Jack Warner complained about the director's interpolations; and he says he was fired by the studio before the end of production.

James Caan and Robert Duvall in *Countdown*. A
Warners studio assignment, *Countdown* never
got off the ground in theaters, and became yet
one more thing of bitterness for Altman.

Altman knew the rotund character actor William Conrad
from Warners and Universal days. James Lydon, a former juvenile actor in motion pictures in the 1940s, was now coproducing the "B" motion-picture unit at Warner Brothers,
functioning alongside Conrad, familiar to later, contemporary audiences as TV's *Cannon*. Conrad and Lydon had trust
and a free hand from the aging Jack Warner as long as they
did not creep "even ten cents over one million," not counting studio overhead, the prescribed per-picture budget.

Lydon had been on the Universal payroll at the time of the
Kraft blowup, and as someone who suffered arbitrariness at
the hands of producers throughout his own career, he tended
to side with the artist and to align himself with impulse.
When Warners was seeking a *Countdown* director, Lydon

showed a piece of *Kraft* footage to Conrad and advised him to hire Altman.

When Altman came in for his obligatory interview, he was composed and forceful, and able to enthuse these two veterans of traditional Hollywood who were feeling straitjacketed by the studio system. His very unorthodoxy appealed to them as a chance to risk something out of the ordinary.

Altman agreed to abide by the "B" budget. He read and seconded the screenplay written by Loring Mandel—one of the few feature scripts by this giant of "live" drama of the Golden Age of Television. Based on a novel called *The Pilgrim Project* by Hank Searls, the story focused on the rivalry between the two leading candidates to be the first astronaut rocketed into space. Altman's decision to accent the strained love lives of the spacemen came out of his own experience, but in any event that was one of the strong points of Mandel's incisive screenplay, which managed to anticipate the moon landing of 1969, and yet balance the technological verisimilitude with humanistic insights.

The producers and Altman collaborated on the casting. Of the two leads, James Caan was in the midst of a long buildup and Robert Duvall was already known around town as an actor's actor. The fine-tuned ensemble included several Altman regulars—Charles Aidman, Joanna Moore, Steve Ihnat, Barbara Baxley, Ted Knight, and Michael Murphy, filling out the roles of space program coworkers and wives.

The National Aeronautics and Space Administration (NASA) cooperated with the filming. *Countdown* production teams visited NASA sites and conferred with scientific and technological personnel. Art director Jack Poplin did an estimable job designing mock replicates of the Apollo capsule, Mission controls, and Gemini simulators, as well as a lunar-landing module years before its actual use.

At Altman's insistence, there were to be no process shots, no miniatures. Using sound stages 14, 15, and 17 at Warner Brothers, Poplin devised a credible rendering of outer space and the moon's surface. The moon landing scene was simulated in the Mojave Desert. There is also one all-out party sequence set at Altman's then-Mandeville Canyon digs.

This fine film that launched the motion-picture phase of Altman's career in Hollywood has been overshadowed by the controversy of the filming, and by conflicting accounts as to what actually occurred behind the scenes. Along with the *Combat* and *Kraft* firings, the *Countdown* embroglio has been the keystone of Altman's pre-*M*A*S*H* "bad boy" reknown. The director himself has seen to it, telling his version of events in many interviews.

According to the producers, the filming of *Countdown* was the occasion of certain minor "excesses" on the director's part; but Lydon is of the old school, and an admirer of Altman's, so he does not elaborate except to say that he forgives and forgets. This is a gentleman who can quote Harry Cohn's credo, "I kiss the feet of talent," while adding mysteriously, "I don't mind being frightened as long as the end result is worth the pain."

Lydon and Altman did disagree about the ending—with Altman typically arguing for open-endedness rather than an emotional slam-bang catharsis.*

Altman's fascination with overlapping dialogue was another sticking point. For the first time in his career, the overlapping was pronounced (though it was yet a far cry from the multitracks and complex levels that Altman pioneered in the 1970s). Lydon says he liked the concept of overlapping, which he found natural and vital. But the producers wanted to overlap the sound in effects cutting, whereas Altman wanted to do it on the set.

Even so, says Lydon, the producers allowed the director to proceed. Their agreement with Altman was that as long as

---

*In the script Lee Stegler's (Caan) young son wears a squeaky toy mouse around his neck, which Stegler takes along with him as a memento on his trip into the unknown. Altman changed it so that when Stegler finally lands on the moon, his inner turmoil—or gambling instinct—impels him to spin the toy mouse in order to choose which direction in which to take the first moon walk. It was a departure from the screenplay that Mandel did not appreciate. Though Lydon disliked Altman's ending too, Altman wore him down. And that is the ending of the film.

the director was on time and on budget, with professional comportment, the producers would not interfere with his vision.

Characteristically, Altman has chosen to embroider his own showdown at high noon with Jack Warner, just as dime-novelist Ned Buntline performs similar puffery for Buffalo Bill Cody in one of Altman's movies. Altman likes to say that he and studio boss Jack Warner were dire antagonists during the filming of *Countdown*, which is typical of Altman's Manichean view of Hollywood, and perhaps something he truly believes.

According to Lydon, however, Altman actually met the great film mogul only once, and under quite ordinary circumstances, although in retrospect, it was quite the historic occasion on Hollywood's terms, the tottering old bull sizing up the frisky pretender.

According to Lydon, it was Warner's custom to greet new directors in the executive dining room on the lot. People were expected to be dressed in a suit or jacket and tie, and Lydon remembers having to borrow suitable attire for Altman from the wardrobe department. Lydon and Conrad escorted Altman to the table where Jack Warner was waiting. "Mr. Warner never discussed business at luncheon, *never*, or ever allowed anyone to discuss business at luncheon," says Lydon. "Mr. Warner welcomed Mr. Altman to the lot, wished him all the best to make a very good picture, and then said, 'Now have a nice lunch and enjoy yourself.' That was their only meeting."

According to Altman, when *Countdown* was finished and screened for the head of the studio, the old-fashioned Warner became agitated over the low lighting, the muted dialogue, the frank sexual conflicts. Altman says, "Jack Warner hated it with a passion."

According to Lydon, Jack Warner viewed the film only once, in his private screening room—and that was the final cut, as approved by Lydon and Conrad.

"When Warner saw a film," says Lydon, "the criteria of

how much he liked it was how often he stepped outside the screening room to relieve himself. Two, three times—you were in trouble." In this instance, Lydon recalls, Warner sat through the entire film in one continuous running and did not budge from his seat. "As I recall," says Lydon, "he was a little bit disturbed about the muddiness of the overlapping dialogue that he couldn't hear. We told him frankly that was Altman's wish and that the dialogue that was overlapping wasn't that important anyway. It was a perfectly natural thing. He said, 'Okay, it's a good picture, thanks fellas,' and he walked out of the production room."

At no time, says Lydon, did Warner suggest "firing" Altman (as Altman has claimed in interviews). That would be beside the point, says Lydon, for Altman's contract was only for one picture.

Indeed, studio records indicate that, one way or another, Lydon and Conrad were in fact reconciled to Altman's footage. Only one additional day of filming was clocked, well after Altman had finished directing, by a substitute director, Conrad himself. Duvall was the only star on the set for a day set aside for cutaways to smooth out transitions. Not all that unusual, from the studio point of view.

Any re-editing by the producers was also minimal, according to Lydon. In most areas of disagreement, says Lydon, the producers simply let Altman have his way, to the extent that even today Lydon feels certain dialogue scenes of *Countdown* are not proper and sharp.

"The final cut of *Countdown* was the taste and judgment of Bill Conrad and me—according to our contract with Altman. The changes we made were technical only—because of his wrongly shooting overlapping dialogue, which would not cut—the cut that Mr. Warner approved was ours (by contract). I believe now as I did then that it's the best film Altman ever made—except for *M*A*S*H*—and I'm still a fan."

The film *releasing* company is usually separate from the film *production* company, though they may be, and often are, corporate partners. The film releasing company, as a rule, is more market-oriented, while the film production arm is more artist-oriented. Altman has had as many problems, in his career, with the marketing, sales, and publicity executives of studios, who control the release of his films, as he has had with producers. By and large, audiences have not had an opportunity to like or dislike the majority of Altman's films. His pictures, beginning with the first one he directed in Hollywood, *Countdown*, have been barely released to theatres.

The Warners distribution arm truly blundered by releasing *Countdown* on a double bill with John Wayne's immortal-for-all-the-wrong-reasons *The Green Berets*. *The Green Berets* garnered reviews like "stupid and dull" *(Variety)*, while *Countdown* received notices like "a model example of what can be achieved on a relatively modest budget . . . far superior to cheap exploitation product" *(Variety)*. In its wisdom the Warner's distribution company quickly pulled *Countdown* from availability, and permitted *The Green Berets* to go on as a single attraction long enough to turn a profit. *Countdown* did have another cheap and wide release a year later, but in reality the studio made the film's negative cost back in airplane showings between New York and Los Angeles and in venues in small towns around the country.

No matter its dubious production history, *Countdown* is a mature film that stands among Altman's best. Its lovemaking scenes feel constrained, and it has a kind of embarrassing patriotic sincerity. But it also has a prescient script (anticipating the actual lunar landing of 1969), a top-caliber cast, a richly detailed milieu, and an overall production sheen.

If one wants to look for a movie that foreshadowed *M*A*S*H*, with its military antiheroics, male bonding, and sexual strife—and to a movie that strongly hints at Altman's destiny as a major motion-picture director—one need look no further than *Countdown*.

Chapter

22

THAT COLD DAY IN THE PARK

Somehow, amidst the perceived failure of *Countdown*, the financial morass, the used-car commercials and the ColorSonics, the impaled friendships and the incessant womanizing, the raising of children, the private and public drunkenness, anguish and pathos, Robert Altman succeeded in directing his first genuinely personal film in 1968.

It may be this quality, above all, that is monumental in his character: Altman's ability to keep going, to produce work, to create mo-

Sandy Dennis, frigid and repressed, in Altman's
first genuinely personal film, *That Cold Day in
the Park*. (Museum of Modern Art)

tion pictures; to subvert the exterior obstacles and to channel whatever the forces warring inside; to direct films that
are true to himself and even, on occasion, transcend all expectations.

The resourceful agent George Litto had reentered Altman's
life. With *Petulia*, with the packaging of Clint Eastwood's
first American box-office hit, *Hang 'Em High*, and with the
representation of the TV series *Hawaii Five-O*, Litto could
afford to be generous. Litto had sworn to give Altman one
more chance, and he called the director in for a face-to-face.
Litto arranged a partnership with Donald Factor, son of Max
Factor and a wealthy man who wanted to produce motion

pictures. Factor agreed to invest a portion of his cosmetics inheritance in a novel Altman had optioned.

That Cold Day in the Park, a Dell paperback published in 1967, was a weird story about a mute hippie "mothered" by a barren spinster who imprisons him in her apartment. It was written by Richard Miles, the brother of actress Gigi Perreau, as it happens, and set in Paris. Altman and Factor wanted to relocate the story in London, and they came to England to hire a British writer for the task. It was the heyday of British film and the "kitchen sink" school of social realism. Many in Hollywood were gravitating to London for inspiration.

The first that writer Gillian Freeman heard of the American director was a phone call one March morning in 1967 when a voice said, "You won't know me, my name is Robert Altman, and I'm here with Donald Factor looking for a writer. Are you free to have lunch with us today?" Primarily a novelist, Freeman had written only one filmed script, *The Leather Boys*, in 1965, adapted from her own novel. But she had developed a story in Los Angeles the previous year for producer James B. Harris called *Sentence for Life*. Her agency's West Coast contact, the venerable Swanson Agency, had recommended her to Altman.

With the novelist's gift for recall of details, Gillian Freeman picks up the story:

"We met at l'Escargot on Greek Street, Soho, very much the watering hole of publishers and their authors, and where in fact I'd lunched with mine the previous day! Bob and Don were already there when I arrived, and I felt there was immediate rapport.

"It was the beginning of the miniskirt era, and I remember I was wearing a very short black wool coat with a velvet collar, cut like a man's, and a black-and-white check flat cap. Don was in a turtleneck sweater and a sports jacket, Bob in a bomber jacket (he also had a flat cap), and I know I felt we epitomized the Sixties, leaving the stultifying first half of the century behind! They were full of innovative and contemporary ideas, and I very much wanted to work with them.

"Over lunch they explained they wanted to use the bare bones of the book—the older woman taking in the boy who never spoke to her, who slipped out at night even though she locked him in; who was ultimately trapped after she'd brought in a prostitute for him in the hope of keeping him. The boy's homosexuality, a club with performed sex acts, were to be dropped, as were almost all of the other relationships and details. It was the theme which appealed. If I were to be offered the job, it would mean working in Los Angeles—which is exactly what I wanted."

Within a couple of weeks, Freeman and her two daughters, then aged six and nine, were winging their way to Los Angeles. Freeman's relatives, Elsa and Morris Stoloff (the musical director of Columbia Pictures for many years) arranged for the little girls to attend a school in Beverly Hills. As she could not drive (It wasn't essential in London!"), either Altman or ("more often") Eggenweiler picked her up daily to go to the offices at 1334 Westwood Boulevard shortly after her girls had departed on their yellow school bus. ("Like them," remembers Freeman, "I waited on the sidewalk!")

Script sessions proceeded: "We talked the story through in general terms, then in detailed sections, breaking for lunch, either in a Swiss restaurant opposite, or in a place which specialized in roast beef, cut for you as you stood in line! Once we'd set a sequence, I'd go off for a couple of days and write it. Then we'd go through it, make changes, and discuss the next section. At that point the idea was still to have an older actress [in the lead part]."

Freeman remembers her Los Angeles stay with tremendous nostalgia. She was shown Altman's movies at the Westwood complex and was struck by Altman's night shots and by his use of reflections and weather. She found him an "out of the ordinary man with a very personal creative brilliance," but beyond that, he was "fun to work with," and "nothing was determined by what it might gross, only by whether it was creatively right." If there was any strain in Altman's life, it was kept from her and her family, all of whom became close with the Altmans.

There were many parties and get-togethers, including the wedding of Kathryn's daughter from a previous marriage. Konni's ceremony amounted to "an elaborate hippy wedding at the side of their swimming pool," wrote Freeman's husband, Edward Thorpe, in his book *The Other Hollywood*, "with Nehru jackets, the bride with a wreath of daisies, bell-bottoms. . . . The wedding march was a Donovan record, and everyone got high on pot."

Freeman recollects: "There was one spectacular party [on another occasion] which the children—Steve, Mike, and Bobby Altman, and Harriet and Matilda Thorpe (my daughters) have never forgotten. . . . Actor Robert Ridgeley began playing on a bongo drum and chanting nonsense, had the children chanting after him. Bob lit candles, Bob Ridgeley led the children out, Pied Piper-like, still chanting round the pool. Bob Altman leapt from the low roof and threw a substance onto the barbecued fire which changed the color of the flames and which seemed like magic to the children, who were almost in a trance."

After eight weeks of drafts and revisions, Freeman left for England, and the hard phase began—the financing, the go-aheads, the green light. Elizabeth Taylor was being talked about for the lead role, but was she bankable anymore? Was Altman bankable as a director? Who would say yes to such an unusual project? Altman and Factor came to London the following year and optimistically began to scout a location: Regent's Park, by Cambridge Gate on the Outer Circle, where there is a block of Edwardian flats.

At that point there was a depressing meeting with John Van Eyssen, a vice-president of foreign distribution of Columbia Pictures, in the studio's London offices. Freeman was suffering from influenza and got out of bed for "one of the most dispiriting professional experiences in my life," she recalls. "We all felt we were being treated as lesser people and that there was no real interest in the project. I was asked to tell the story, and such was the disinterest that Van Eyssen left the room when I was in the middle, saying as he went out of the room, 'Don't wait for me, go on with the story, X [his assistant] knows all about it.'"

Columbia was the last of the major film companies to turn the picture down. At that point, Freeman did some rewriting, adding the film's contraception clinic sequence. Then she fell out of touch. The next thing she knew, months later, a phone call came from Canada around two in the morning, and Altman's voice announced, "You know, we worked on a picture . . . well, we have just finished that picture. Five minutes ago."

In the end, Donald Factor had agreed to split fifty-fifty (putting up a half million dollars of his own money) on a $1,200,000 budget with Commonwealth-United—and that is how *That Cold Day in the Park* was bankrolled.

The filming was to be in Vancouver, Canada. This region seems to have a lucky association for Altman and certainly a congenial one. Here, away from the slings and arrows of Hollywood, he could create his own community—his own "family"—his own Kansas City ambience. Here he could stumble or soar on his own terms. It was his "alternative Hollywood," a way of being insular, with the middle-class kid in him saying, "I'll take my ball and play elsewhere."

It was a smart move for other reasons. There was less producer and writer interference. The Hollywood unions could be circumvented and costs lowered. Only some fourteen of the average fifty-man crew of *Cold Day* was imported from Hollywood; wage scales were below the Hollywood norm; and producers had to sign a contract with only one union rather than numerous locals. There was a Vancouver eagerness to show that a superior picture could be crafted at a reasonable price. And meantime, psychologically, Altman could shut out the nuisance world and dominate.

Lion's Gate, the name that lasted for his production company for a decade, is not a biblical reference, but instead refers to the bridge that leads into Vancouver, the Lion's Gate bridge, which in turn is suggested by two mountain peaks just north of the city that evoke the outlines of lions. This longest suspension bridge in the British Empire was built by the Guinness brewing family of Ireland when exploiting real estate in the dominion in 1938. The Lion's Gate company, for Altman, was his bridge away from Hollywood to a state of self-rule.

Interestingly, Altman chose to work on *That Cold Day in the Park* without his staunch army of Westwood devotees. Brian McKay, Reza Badiyi and Barbara Turner, Louis Lombardo, Dan Fitzgerald, John Alonzo, John Williams, and all the others were either unavailable or unsolicited. Altman went to Vancouver with a pared-down team—only the indispensable "Egg" and editor Danford B. Greene. It was almost as if, subconsciously, Altman was casting around for a new filmmaking "family." And indeed, this location was to serve as the magnet for a second nucleus.

The location manager, James Margellos, an integral cog in the Altman machine on location in Canada and elsewhere for the next several years, had a lot to do with it; he posted signs for cast and crew and screened local theatre professionals in interviews. Margellos found Graeme Clifford, who in the first of many such multiple credits is listed as assistant editor and second assistant director of *Cold Day.* Meantime, Laszlo Kovacs, the Hungarian-born cinematographer, and Leon Ericksen, the set designer and costumer, were recruited from Los Angeles.

Though Altman was to work with Kovacs only once, Kovacs was a stylistic link to Vilmos Zsigmond, who photographed three subsequent Altman films. Hungarian-born film students, Kovacs and Zsigmond had escaped the 1956 uprising in Budapest by bribing Russian guards with wristwatches, managing to smuggle their footage of the insurrection over the border. This footage was shown on CBS in 1966. They plied their trade at commercials and low-budget features until, eventually, both became leading cinematographers in post-1960s Hollywood.

A master of "subdued atmosphere" as well as "dazzling color effects," according to one encyclopedic source, the gifted Kovacs was the perfect choice to negotiate the cold, dreary, rainy winter of Vancouver. (Whatever one's reservations about the movie, there is no faulting the hypnotic *mise en scène* of *Cold Day*.)

Graeme Clifford was one of those exceptional utility infielders that Altman seemed to specialize in discovering—like Badiyi and Lombardo—someone who could edit, photograph, direct, produce. Originally, from Australia, where he had interrupted medical studies to work in television, by the late 1960s Clifford had worked his way to Canada, where he was presently engaged in directing and cutting short films, commercials, and documentaries. Altman offered him temporary subservience in return for safe passage to Hollywood. Clifford jumped at the chance. He shows up in disparate capacities on prime Altman films—as a general assistant on *Cold Day*, again as an assistant on Altman's personal staff for *M*A*S*H*, the editor of *Images*, casting and assistant director of *McCabe and Mrs. Miller*, and casting director of *The Long Goodbye*.

More directors have sprouted from the Altman "family" than from most film schools, and Clifford has turned out to be one of the more compleat: His *Frances*, the tragic life of actress Frances Farmer starring Jessica Lange, was sulphurous, harrowing, uncompromising. Clifford credits meeting Altman and working with him as being crucial to his interest in artistic (as opposed to strictly commercial) filmmaking.

Then there was Leon Ericksen. Altman had been essentially adrift without an art designer since Chet Allen had forsaken show business for designing swimming pools. Dan Fitzgerald filled in, but he had different strengths (for one thing, he created the company logo). Also, Fitzgerald's ties to Badiyi and Turner were suspect, and he arrived in the "family" at a period in time when it was no longer such a cachet to have been spawned by Calvin.

Chet Allen, Leon Ericksen, and in the late 1970s and early 1980s, Wolf Kroeger—for three decades these art directors advanced the "look" that Altman is famous for: the clutter of hidden meaning, the smoke, the nets, the gauze, the glass and mirrors, the symbolically charged color schemes, the hermetic interiors and the one-world exteriors. "None [of the director's creative supporting cast] has played a more sustained and imaginative role," to quote Altman's own publicity material, than Leon Ericksen.

A Wyoming native, Ericksen had studied theatre arts at Pepperdine and UCLA, but he had never been able to obtain his union card—which, at this point, put him in the good company of several others in the Altman group. So, Ericksen had turned his back on the conventional track and jobbed himself out to the independents—working ingeniously for producer Roger Corman at American International Pictures, and for directors Francis Coppola on *The Rain People* and Haskell Wexler on *Medium Cool*.

An enigmatic, frazzled, heavyset tintype of a hippie, Ericksen was described by one reporter on the set of the fabulous Western town he constructed for *McCabe* as "a well-educated free soul, who wears granny glasses, hair in a pony tail and high rubber boots."

From the very beginning, Ericksen was monomaniacal. After the set for *Cold Day* had been dressed, Ericksen would show up late at night, dirty the light switches with his filthy hands, and toss a couple of cigarette butts, hairpins, and a legging of lady's hose with a run in it under the bed. If lead actress Sandy Dennis had occasion to look under the bed— understand, there were no scripted scenes under the bed, the characters do not move the bed, the camera never even *peeks* under the bed—but if she did, Sandy Dennis would notice this subtle reinforcement of the life of her character under day-to-day circumstances, as if she had lived in that apartment for years.

Ericksen would work on one corner of the set for days before being coaxed away. He would sleep on the set. The set would become his child. He would not finish until the order was given to finish; then he was literally dragged away. But Altman could relate to him, and he was one of the primary creative people feeding into the process of filming what, from the outside, may have looked like a one-man auteurist show.

Ericksen did not work for many other filmmakers in Hollywood, and his career, apart from his association with Altman, has been erratic. But, for Altman, he organized *Cold Day*, he was behind the scenes on *M*A*S*H* and *Brewster McCloud*, he production-designed *McCabe* and *Images* and *California Split*, he worked on *Quintet* and *A Perfect Couple*—and his contribution to those films is spoken of with veneration.

The hippie character of The Boy was assigned to Michael Burns, who had played the teenage son in *Mr. Hobbs Takes a Vacation*. The other Hollywood/New York actors included stalwart Michael Murphy (who played a panderer), Luana Anders, John Garfield Jr., and newcomer Suzanne Benton as Burns's snotty and skimpily dressed sister.

After much ado in the casting, the central role of the story was set to be played by Sandy Dennis, who had just crested on Broadway with Tony Awards for her performances in *Any Wednesday* and *A Thousand Clowns*, and in films with a Best Supporting Actress Oscar for *Who's Afraid of Virginia Woolf?* Dennis had also starred in such critically acclaimed motion pictures as *Up the Down Staircase* and *The Fox*. Altman could not have snared a more prominent actress.

Honey-blond, with nervous theatrical mannerisms, she typified the women Altman preferred to depict. Indeed, she had already made a career out of playing neurotic, victimized females—from the frigid professor's wife in *Woolf*, to the harried teacher of *Staircase*, to the terrorized lesbian of *Fox*.

Though there were any number of reasons why Sandy Dennis might be attuned to Altman (from Nebraska, she had been called "anti-Hollywood" more than once herself), Altman was afraid of her at first, for he had never really dealt with a major star, an actress of stature, in industrials or in television. An Oscar-winner. Being from Kansas City, that was a hurdle for him. His egotism was always fundamentally a hedge against his insecurity.

"Those guys intimidate Bob," says Danford B. Greene. "Big stars. I sensed that when Sandy came to town. I sensed that he was very apprehensive about meeting her."

Otherwise, it was practically a Calvin job: the closely watched budget, the cast and crew living in proximity, the open rehearsals, and the malleability of the script.

The production company rented the Panorama Studios, resting on a forested bluff overlooking Burrard Inlet, several miles from downtown Vancouver. It had been largely vacant since being constructed by Canadian and British capital only six years before. The apartment set was built in its entirety on a sound stage by Leon Ericksen. Altman, "Egg," and Danford B. Greene took a grand house in the woods up a hill a mile away from the studio and were fussed over by a cook and a live-in maid. Nights, Altman and "Egg" would whip up communal meals for the cast and crew, setting a pattern for future Altman "family" filmmaking.

Litto (partially to his regret) had advised Altman to hire a publicist, so, for the first time, there was a trickle of visitors to an Altman set, writing about the Oscar prospects of the production. This trek would become de rigeur for many journalists and film critics in the 1970s; but at this time it was Sandy Dennis who was more the magnet than the "man [Altman] who is both the spirit and the master" (Vancouver Life).

Another Altman tradition, begun at Calvin and continued in television, here was evolving to sacramental status: the end-of-day mass viewing of dailies. After which, it was up to the editor to make sense of the footage. Altman rarely intervened in the editing room, says Greene. He did not have to; the fingerpoints were all there.

"He wouldn't get involved, hardly at all, up until the final cut," says Greene. "He would look at something—specifically. I remember a dinner sequence [in Cold Day]—which is always hard to cut. I put it together and he looked at it and said, 'It's screwed. Fix it.' He wouldn't sit there and be a grandstander and a showboat, like most of these directors are, saying, 'Do this, Do that.' Then you [the editor] become a mechanic, it's stifling, your mind stops.

"You have to be very secure with yourself as a director and say, 'That's screwed, too fast, or too slow. Or slant it more toward this person.' All an editor needs, if he's any good, is a one-liner. Then you're still challenged and you can go."

Everyone was so thrilled by the dailies, and by the experience of filming in Canada, that Altman immediately laid plans to shoot another picture back-to-back with *Cold Day*. It was going to be *Images*, already in one of many script drafts. James Lydon was aboard as producer, though Lydon never did agree with Altman about the perplexing ending to the script, which Lydon disliked. So, while *Cold Day* was being given the postproduction gloss, locations for *Images* were being scouted by James Margellos and "Egg." Preliminary rehearsals began with Marianne McAndrew, a Canadian thespian.

A crew was already erecting the set when word came from Lydon that the financing, promised in increments from a Texas millionaire, had fallen through. So Altman and "Egg" had to return to Los Angeles and to the Westwood offices to await the release of *Cold Day*.

There was another reason Altman ventured forth without his usual support group: *Cold Day* was the first of his quartet of motion pictures to depict and dissect frigid women, mental creativity/instability, illusions/dreams/nightmares, role reversal, and sadomasochistic relationships—ideas that have also preoccupied him in *Images, Three Women,* and *Come Back to the Five and Dime, Jimmy Dean, Jimmy Dean*. Each time Altman returns to this territory, the production baggage is stripped down, the filming becomes smaller-scale, the purpose more intense, humorless, inscrutable.

With the exception of *Jimmy Dean, Jimmy Dean*, these are the films in which Altman is more integrally involved with the screenplay. Indeed—apart from *The Delinquents—Images* and *Three Woman* are his only solo writing credits in a career of some thirty years and more than twenty-five feature films.

No one can be quite sure what Altman's female quartet of "dream movies" intend to say—they intrigue, but they never cohere. In some ways the liberating movements of the 1960s came too late for this director, who can never quite unchain his subconscious. When he gets "serious" in films like *Cold Day*, he is unable to communicate except through riddles and prisms. Each film in its way seems to be a cathartic rite of personal exorcism—but exorcism of what? Of psychosexual bondage? Of male guilt? The film professors will be debating Altman for a long, long time; one realizes, from interviews, that Altman himself does not know all of the answers.

Yet, in each of the "dream movies" Altman's bravura style has managed, at least in part, to compensate for the weaknesses of the narrative; and *Cold Day* does have that—style.

Apart from Altman's signature neurotic blonde, *Cold Day* has the added tantalizing (to put it mildly) relationship between a self-absorbed brother and sister who titillate each other sexually and in one scene end up sharing a bath together. Altman's bile is close to the surface. There are eerie forebodings throughout and a surprise slasher ending, so that ultimately *Cold Day* is either very mesmeric, or very trying, depending on one's level of patience.

There were some fairly positive reviews ("a first-rate exercise in astonishment that grows wilder and wilder, ending on an arbitrary but totally unexpected note," wrote Raymond A. Sokolov in *Newsweek*), and some negative ones ("It comes to us dolled up as an outspoken study of loneliness," wrote Penelope Gilliatt in *The New Yorker*. "That it isn't. Nothing observant, nothing strong, nothing tender toward extremity.").

But mostly, there was little notice taken of the film. It was barely released. It was barely seen. It is remembered fondly today by people in the expanding/contracting Westwood circle—who knew that, for Altman at the least, *Cold Day* marked a great leap forward into his new consciousness as a modern filmmaker.

Freeman, for one, was satisfied: "There were, of course, many changes in dialogue. The way that Bob works with actors is well known. But the changes were faithful to the original concept, and the visualization (for instance, the dinner party at the beginning where the dialogue is overlaid and which is, as I remember, true to the script) was very exciting to me. The change from London to Vancouver worked almost exactly. I thought the designer was brilliant with detail; unless my mind is playing tricks, I remember a coronation mug among the ornaments in the apartment. The old school tie episode, by the way, was suggested by my old school tie—the flame color intended to represent the flame of zeal in the hearts of British girlhood."

She adds: "The film was not a particular success. I always felt that if it had succeeded *M*A*S*H* there would have been more attention paid to it. I heard Richard Miles said if we'd stuck to his book we'd have done better."

PART
4

"Huston also hit on an unusual idea that I don't think has been repeated since. He took the entire cast [of *The Maltese Falcon*] to lunch every day at a country club near Toluca Lake, resulting in an extraordinary intimacy in the group playing. . . ."

—Hal Wallis,
Star Maker

Chapter

23

M*A*S*H

Despite having directed two solid and in some ways notable features back-to-back, Altman could not help but feel as if his career was once more in limbo. Partly for that reason, Altman was still thick with the "talent trust"—despite tensions. At this perceived low ebb, Altman still needed their reinforcement and ministrations.

Altman also kept up relationships with many of the producers he feuded with professionally. Others in the Westwood group might believe them to be on the "enemies" list, but James Lydon, who was central to the whole *Countdown* denouement, Selig Seligman, no matter what had been said to him in drunken-

Group portrait: The free-wheeling cast of the bleak-and-blue *M*A*S*H*, assembled to ogle Hot Lips in the shower.

ness at a party five years earlier, and Roy Huggins, the *Kraft* producer whom Altman had excoriated in the trades, were all talking to Altman about projects.

Huggins, who professes never to have liked Altman and to have fought with him constantly over the years, nevertheless called the director up in the late 1960s and offered him a two-hour television pilot with "complete controls" as to casting and script.

Altman gave his verbal okay and promised to get in touch with Huggins shortly thereafter to work out the details.

Three days later, Altman called Huggins and apologized. Altman said, "I know I said I'd do the picture, Roy, but you may have noticed at the time that I sounded a little doubtful. It was because I had also been reading a script for a movie. I didn't think I was going to be offered the movie. I'd like it if you would let me off the hook, because I have been offered the movie."

"Robert, for god's sake," replied Huggins, "if you've been offered a movie, I won't hold you to anything. What's it called?"

"*M*A*S*H.*"

It was synchronicity—a kind of interlocking pattern of co-incidences. Very Altmanesque—two or three things happening at the same time, seemingly unrelated, which prove to have a connection and which in fact act upon one another. Altman and *M*A*S*H* were like two strangers on a blind date who wind up falling in love and getting married. In retrospect, it was the perfect match, but at the time who could have predicted it?

M*A*S*H arrived at yet another down period in Altman's life, and also a period in which his creative juices were ripe to overflow. It brought together the no-names of the "talent trust" with Elliott Gould and Donald Sutherland, stars rising in an arc with the counterculture. It was not Altman's baby; and yet it was his type of bleak and blue humor. Its combat-zone milieu was his forte; and it was the kind of crazy-quilt, dope-and-Sixties-influenced, antiwar and antipuritanical sto-ryline that he could claim (figuratively and literally, as it turned out) as his own.

It came to pass because a pushy agent believed in Altman, because an iron-willed producer backed him to the hilt, be-cause it was the best possible script, and because the studio was not entirely cognizant of what was happening.

The synchronicity began in 1969 when Ring Lardner Jr. was asked by a New York publisher to read the galleys and write a dust-jacket blurb for a novel about U.S. surgery units operating behind battlelines during the Korean War. Lardner, the droll Oscar-winning coscreenwriter of *Woman of the Year*—who served a year in jail as one of the Hollywood Ten, and who, because he was blacklisted, went fifteen years be-tween acknowledged screen credits—was impressed by the darkly comic fiction attributed to the writer H. Richard Hornberger under the pseudonym of "Richard Hooker."

Lardner thought *M*A*S*H*, which stands for Mobile Army Surgical Hospital, would make a helluva movie, and he relayed the galleys to Ingo Preminger, director Otto Preminger's brother and Lardner's former agent, now set up with a producing deal at Fox.

After reading *M*A*S*H*, Preminger agreed to produce it as his first motion picture, with Lardner as the screenwriter. Briefly, Lardner and Preminger discussed changing the locale of the story to Vietnam in the 1960s, although ultimately they felt that would force the humor. Then they flew from New York to Los Angeles to pitch the project to Richard Zanuck and David Brown, the team in charge of Fox production. Zanuck and Brown expressed enthusiasm, suggesting that it might be an appropriate vehicle for the zany comedy duo of Walter Matthau and Jack Lemmon. Preminger and Lardner exchanged a silent glance, then Lardner said diplomatically that because of the football game at the climax, perhaps the stars ought to be virile young men.

George Litto came into the picture as Lardner's agent, to negotiate the screenwriter's terms. Because of the Litto connection, Altman knew about the Lardner screenplay early on. Litto offered it to him to read one day, saying, " 'By the way, this is a great script, read it.' No more thought than that. Never thinking that he'd [Altman] get the job." For one thing, both Litto and Preminger were certain they would get a bigger, more illustrious, established name to direct *M*A*S*H*.

"To my surprise, because everybody loved the script," says Litto, "fifteen directors turned it down, maybe more. George Roy Hill turned it down. Bud Yorkin, who was then a hot director, turned it down. Every important director in Hollywood turned the fucking project down. At first, I couldn't believe it—except that the script was unconventional at that time for this reason: Most of the time, pictures had a beginning, a middle, and an end. This was a series of vignettes."

Altman (who was not even in the running) borrowed a

copy of the script, read it, loved it, and told Litto so. It was not that different in tone and outlook from *Death, Where Is Thy Sting-a-ling-ling?*

"It was the same kind of series of vignettes as *Oh Death* was," says Litto. "The same unorthodox line, the caustic, biting, sardonic humor, outrageous humor, black comedy. I knew Bob understood this, liked this and wanted to do this, so it really wasn't out of nowhere. I knew it was a very long shot that he'd ever get the shot at it. But I do want to stress the point that when he read the script he thought it was great, contrary to some of his statements later."

After Stanley Kubrick and Sidney Lumet and still others had turned down the Lardner screenplay, Litto began to think that Altman was not such a long shot at all. Litto invited Preminger and Lardner to a viewing of *That Cold Day in the Park*—"which showed talent and art," in Litto's words—and then he also showed them *The Party*—and the *Pot au Feu* short that so well showed off Altman's "wild sense of humor." Now Preminger and Lardner were convinced that Altman could make a first-class film. Meeting the director cinched the rapport. Preminger said to Litto, "George, I can't get a director I want, so I'm going to take the director *you* want."

There was trouble convincing Fox—the only thing the people at Fox knew about Robert Altman was his masterminding of the Fabian *Bus Stop* episode. Much later, Richard Zanuck would make the point in interviews that if he had ever screened *Cold Day*, he would never have okayed hiring Altman. That does not seem like anything to brag about, especially considering that *Cold Day* is a thoroughly professional and intermittently engrossing film. In any event, it was Ingo Preminger who made the case for Altman, not Zanuck and Brown nor anyone else at the studio; and in part, what it came down to, what it always comes down to, was money.

The deal Litto had prepared for Altman called for a salary of $100,000 and 5 percent of the profits. The business manager of Fox telephoned Litto and told him the studio would not approve the deal unless it was for seventy-five thousand dollars flat—no points—take it or leave it. Litto says he screamed obscenities at the business manager. But he also said he ought to talk to his client before flatly rejecting the offer.

Altman had some obscenities of his own to scream.

"They don't want you," Litto advised him. "If you tell them you don't accept the deal, they'll be the happiest studio in town today. You really want to fuck them?"

"How?" Altman's interest was joined.

"Take the deal," said Litto.

So Altman said yes.

The forgotten man, screenwriter Lardner, also earned seventy-five thousand dollars flat.

Altman fought Preminger on the casting. In the worst way he wanted his *Bonanza* buddy, Dan Blocker, to play one of the two leads. He wanted Elaine Stritch as Hot Lips. Even after meeting Sally Kellerman, he stubbornly held out for Elaine Stritch as Hot Lips. ("There's a weakness in Altman, which is interesting," says Preminger. "He loves unattractive people. Sally Kellerman is pretty, but not so pretty. But for Altman, she was too beautiful. It's a kind of inferiority complex.")

It was Preminger who was behind the casting of Sutherland and Gould. Sutherland was already an imposing and versatile character actor (in low-budget horror pictures and *The Dirty Dozen*, among others); and Gould, besides being Barbra Streisand's husband and a veteran of Broadway (although he had just been fired, during rehearsals, from Murray Schisgal's *A Way of Life*), was under contract at Fox and had an Oscar nomination for his performance in director Paul Mazursky's *Bob and Carol and Ted and Alice*.

Tom Skerritt, the third member of the troika of hedonist surgeons, had been in Altman's television pilot for *The Long Hot Summer*. Robert Duvall, from *Countdown*, as Bible-quoting Lt. Frank Burns, Michael Murphy as Capt. "Me Lay" Marston in the Japanese interlude, and JoAnn Pflug as the sexy Lt. Dish rounded out the list of better-known principals.

Altman's primary contribution in the casting was the background people. Interviews were conducted in Chicago, New York, and San Francisco, where Altman forged an association with the American Theatre Ensemble. There, husband and wife William and Scott Bushnell, he the artistic director and she the "everything else," had a rambunctious troupe of trained, seasoned improvisers from whom Altman drew a number of his cast.

Among the lesser-knowns in *M*A*S*H* were several who went on to fruitful careers: René Auberjonois (an Altman regular who later starred in TV's *Benson*), the football player Fred Williamson (who went on to star in and direct his own films), John Schuck (subsequently, a television regular), Carl Gottlieb (later a successful comedy screenwriter), and Bud Cort (a counterculture hero in *Harold and Maude* and the lead in Altman's own *Brewster McCloud*). Publicity noted that fourteen of the twenty-eight speaking roles belonged to actors making their motion-picture debuts.

Oh yes, and Sally Kellerman. She had been knocking around Hollywood for a while, appearing without distinction in everything from the "B" quickie *Girls Reform School* to *Ozzie and Harriet*. According to Kellerman, she (who always regarded herself as "a baby-faced kind of gunky person") went to her *M*A*S*H* interview with straw-white blond hair and wearing red lipstick. Preminger was present at that casting call and (more enthusiastically than Altman) he hailed Kellerman as the character of Major Margaret "Hot Lips" Houlihan in the flesh.

When she returned to Altman's office for further discussions, she complained, "I don't want to do this one-level, cold, rotten woman standing in the background!" ("I was practically in tears," she says.) And Altman told her: "This is just an outline, and maybe a lot of stuff can happen."

Continues Kellerman: "And so for the first time I was open and honest and wanting something, rather than just settling for anything. And I did it with the right man. And it just freed me from any neurosis I had left about what I looked like . . . It was the first time I let go and said, 'I'll take chances. I'm going to be as big as it calls for in the part. It'll probably be the end of my career, but I'm going to enjoy the experience.' That's what Bob Altman inspires in you—the enjoyment."

That was also Altman's way of weeding out the complacent actors and actresses, and pinpointing the hungry and the reckless. He told everybody that they would have their moment in the film and on the set, no matter the script. When he started rehearsals, he put it another way. The nicest thing that could happen to *M*A*S*H*, he announced, would be if the entire cast was nominated as Best Supporting Actor in next year's Oscar race.

Altman already had a mystique with actors and casting. Around town, agents were advising their clients to go with him, whatever the money or the part. But not everyone followed Altman Pied Piper-like. Teen headliner Frankie Avalon, for one, was courted for the part of Radar but was chagrined to discover that it amounted to only a few lines. His agent assured him that Altman would build Radar up, but Avalon turned the part down.

Ironically, John Considine was another who could not be cajoled into the cast of *M*A*S*H*. Considine, disillusioned with acting, had dropped out to run a pottery store in Santa Monica, where Kathryn Altman ran into him one day and invited him to stop by and see her husband about a new movie he was directing. At the Westwood offices, Altman told Considine to show up on the Monday of filming, and he would find an appropriate character for him. But Considine, in a midlife crisis, could not make up his mind whether to embrace acting again, and he never turned up.

Always of equal importance to Altman was the casting of the technical personnel. As early as *Countdown*, Altman had sought his old Kansas City security blanket Louis Lombardo for the job of editor. But by now Lombardo had shown himself to be surprisingly independent of his mentor. The first of the "talent trust" to break away on his own, Lombardo had begun editing for that pent-up poet of the West, Sam Peckinpah.

After cutting the graphically violent *The Wild Bunch*, Lombardo was asked by Altman to edit *M*A*S*H*, only Lombardo had agreed to work with Peckinpah once again on *The Ballad of Cable Hogue*. So Altman settled for Danford B. Greene.

The cameraman was hired by Twentieth Century-Fox. But after only about a week of filming, Altman insisted on replacing the studio's candidate, who would not cooperate with Altman's visual strategy. It was "a very tense moment," according to Litto. "Here is Peck's bad boy, after a week of filming, acting like a star." But Preminger backed Altman, and Fox remained neutral.

Altman reached back into his past, and into the television stable of lensmen, to Harold E. "Hal" Stine, a functional old pro who had been behind the camera for Altman during his stint at Warner's. At Altman's instruction, Stine filmed most of *M*A*S*H* in an antiglamorous style that many cameramen would have balked at—with much use of zoom lens* and fog filters—aiming for a chaotic and funky look.

Because it was a Fox picture, Altman had to carry some of his Westwood people at his own expense. This was considered so unusual that there was an article about the "talent trust" in *Variety*, remarking on their involvement in the picture, though "some of them weren't even on the official Fox payroll."

These included Leon Ericksen and Graeme Clifford. Ericksen was billed as an associate producer (although he was really on the set for design purposes), and Clifford went unbilled as Altman's personal assistant (for publicity pur-

---

*"The zoom was a great help when you're dealing with actors," Altman told the press. "You can't lie to them or even fool them, that's why I let them watch the rushes. But with a zoom, no one was ever quite sure exactly what was happening. I could get a tight close-up of, say, Elliott, from a hundred feet away. If I wanted, I'd get a full figure shooting from here across the street. Everyone was confused at first, but they got used to it."

And behind-the-scenes . . . cameraman Harold E. "Hal" Stine (center, wearing white cap), a studio old-timer plucked by Altman from television and acclaimed for the unusual visual style of the film, which was largely Altman's inspiration.

poses, Clifford also directed a 16mm film about the making of *M*A*S*H*). According to *Variety*, working for Altman as a writer under "non-exclusive terms" was Brian McKay.

"Some of Altman's team have been involved with the director in making experimental or 'underground' product," commented the show business newspaper. "While a few of these films have played in special artie [sic] situations, it's always only been with pseudonyms on the credit frames. More important than any public recognition of these short experimental efforts, as Altman views it, is opportunity for the team to test new techniques and lensing styles (as well as subject matter) that might later serve as basis for a more commercially tailored celluloid enterprise."

*   *   *

The "synchronicity" was right all around. Twentieth Century-Fox was bogged down with concerns about the budget-bloated epics-in-the-making *Tora, Tora, Tora* ($20 million), *Patton* ($18 million), and *Hello, Dolly!* ($8 million). In retrospect, Zanuck and Brown may want to take unfair credit for the creation of *M*A*S*H* ($3 million); in reality, they were rarely around the set and had little input as to what was transpiring.

One early crisis involved the preliminary rating of the Motion Picture Association of America (MPAA), which categorizes U.S. film releases for so-called "moral" purposes. Fox was understandably distressed when the MPAA threatened an *X* rating because of the cumulative profanity, the parody of religion, the whorehouse interlude in Japan, the sex scenes, and the rampant nudity in the *M*A*S*H* script. At a high-level meeting, Altman deflected the prefilming controversy by saying he would film the show like a "romp," a "three-ring circus," without emphasizing all this offensive stuff, and that if the scenes did not work afterward, he would toss them out. (Think of how many industrial sponsors Altman had placated with similar rhetoric.)

Ultimately, *M*A*S*H* received the acceptable *R*.

The first weeks of filming were at the Twentieth Century-Fox ranch in the Lake Malibu area, some twenty miles from the studio complex, where a rock-bedded stream wended its way between a row of stilted Korean huts and a dozen camouflaged, worn-looking tents of various sizes that together comprised the imaginary 4077th Mobile Army Surgical Hospital unit.

Here, a visiting journalist noted the three-hundred-member cast, extras, and crew, ambulances, weapons carriers, trucks, and helicopters, and wrote that the atmosphere was surprisingly loose and democratic. "The big, sprawling outdoor set," the journalist wrote, "has the overall feeling of a summer camp. Away from the mikes and cameras, those not involved in the scene at hand play touch football, poker, one o' cat, wade in the stream, and pick wildflowers on the sunny slopes."

Yet the two nominal stars, Gould and Sutherland, were widely reported to be in a huff. For one thing, both of them were accustomed to being treated according to their paychecks and billing, and for another they were accustomed to direction, not indirection. "I told them that there were going to be no movie stars," Altman informed *Newsweek*. "I told them of my improvisational philosophy, and they got a little bugged when they saw it was happening."

Sutherland told the same magazine: "I never understood exactly what he wanted. . . ." Having "never been much of a group person," Sutherland said he could have done without the Esalenesque "camaraderie" that was already a part of the Altman experience on location (albeit, in Malibu), where at the nightly get-togethers everybody got "squiffed" and made egalitarian comments about the rushes.

Originally, Gould was supposed to play the Tom Skerritt part, but in an early discussion he informed Altman that his drawl would be a sham, whereas "this guy, Trapper John, really gives me an opportunity to come outside of myself and give you a lot of heart and spirit." But the trouble was, in early scenes, Gould was putting too much "heart and spirit" into the portrayal and pumping up a performance that was supposed to be (from Altman's point of view) low-key. Altman was fighting him to play it down.

One day at lunch, Altman rather gracelessly informed Gould that he had wasted the director's time in a certain complicated scene. "Oh, my god," said Gould, distressed. "How can you say that to me?" Altman pointed to Corey Fischer, who plays small roles in many Altman films (in *M*A*S*H*, he is Capt. Bandini), and said, "Why can't you be more like him?"

"I started to shake, and I couldn't eat my lunch," remembers Gould, "and I threw my tray up in the air, and I said, 'From here on in, you tell me what the fuck it is you want me to do. You direct me. I'm not going to stick my neck out for you.' I was conscious of just having found a relationship with the camera in *Bob and Carol and Ted and Alice*, and I said to Altman, 'You tell me what it is you fucking want, because I'm a craftsman. I make precision here. Don't tell me I'm wasting your fucking time, because it's my life. Don't tell me to be like someone else, because it's me I want to be like.' He said, 'I think I've misunderstood.'"

There was a temporary truce. Gould was still insecure, and Sutherland was stewing. In another scene, the one where Hawkeye and Trapper frolic on a golf course in Japan, again Gould overdid it, "a tendency, because of my insecurity, of wanting to give more than is necessary"; and Sutherland had a problem with not knowing what it was, *exactly*, Altman wanted. The director filmed the scene once. The stars asked him to film it again. After an exchange of words, Altman did. Still, the stars were not satisfied. There were more words.

Both Litto and Preminger had to play peacemaker as word of the rift drifted back to the Fox hierarchy. A lunchtime parley was convened, with Gould, Sutherland, and Sutherland's wife at the time, actress Shirley Jean Douglas.

Gould explains: "I said, 'I'm not on a power trip in terms of developing myself into an artist; I'm used to being told what it is you want. Now you're giving me so much freedom . . .' I always assumed the director would talk to me objectively. I don't even remember ever having an objective talk with him."

Gould says Altman was "shocked" at the meeting. "We almost blew him out of the water. It was like an infringement on something. It was like Bob had his whole family together—except for me and Donald, who were separate. He was hurt and offended, which I didn't understand. So we went back and he let us shoot it again, very quick, and I thought it was a nice expression for him, at least to give us the opportunity."

That alleviated the tension, and though Altman and Sutherland never did cozy up to each other, the rest of the cast had a joyful time of it under Altman's "beneficent monarchy." The director was certainly happy—running around clapping his hands and saying, "What a favor they're [the studio executives] doing for me!"

For a week of filming the football game, they moved over to a vast playground area in Griffith Park. Now, Altman, a sidelines football fanatic, was really having fun; and though he brought the movie in three days under the ten-week schedule, there were people who thought he spent too much time (and film stock) on the football maneuvers. He was glowing in the company of people like Minnesota Vikings quarterback Fran Tarkenton, Baltimore Colts fullback John Meyers, and a couple of Kansas City Chiefs—punt return specialist Nolan "Super-Gnat" Smith and tackle Buck Buchanan.

The "synchronicity" was still weaving its spell. Tommy Thompson had not been around Altman for years. Yet Altman was feeling he needed someone like Thompson to handle the logistics and intricacies of these major productions. Near Griffith Park for a "shoot" of his own, Thompson heard that *M*A*S*H* was filming nearby. He spotted Altman and walked up to him. Altman had a beard, and Thompson had a beard. Altman looked him over, and said, "The beard looks good." Thompson looked back at him and said, "Yours does too."

"We were right back up-to-date," says Thompson. "We were always able to be inside each other's minds to a certain degree."

The editing was taking longer than expected—three months. At one point there were two teams trying to make sense of the footage. Graeme Clifford was around, making some members of the old team nervous, and Louis Lombardo was being unofficially consulted. Danford B. Greene had to spend six weeks cutting the football game of forty-five thousand feet down to a twelve-minute sequence. Even at that, Greene wanted to take out another series of plays. But Altman did not want him to, so he didn't.

Because Altman shot so much with the zoom lens, there

was a lot that was out of focus or soft-focus. There were buckets of simulated blood and gore in the operating room. There was hitherto unacceptable coarse language (Greene surprised himself by emphasizing, in the editing, Painless's (John Schuck) improvised crack on the scrimmage line, "I'm gonna knock your fucking block off!").

For the first time, there was an Altmanesque stylization of sound. The dialogue, the background, and the sound track were "deconstructed" in the filming, and then became, in the editing, separate elements to be mixed and matched for filmic effect. Clarity became subordinate to context. The old-school notion of coordinated sound and integrated levels was thrown out the window in favor of counterpoint and warring sound.

This was Altman's genuine contribution to the poststudio age of filmmaking, to liberate sound from the perfectionists. It did not always work, but when it did, as in *M*A*S*H*, it was exhilarating—even if behind the rather Eisensteinian notion of editing sound, like images, for a certain communicative purpose, was a director who simply preferred to work that way, fast and loose.

They tried unheard-of free-associative jump cutting in the postproduction. Once they were running the part of the film where Hawkeye and Trapper are driving a jeep along the golf course, and all of a sudden Altman jumped up and said, "Stop, go back!" The projectionist backed up the reel and started over. Altman jumped out of his seat again and impulsively started spouting a Sid Caesar-type parody of Japanese. "To this day, that's in there, some dubbed Japanese," says Greene. "It was so crazy, just different."

Greene says they were never thinking big grosses, but they were sure laughing a lot when they looked at the accumulated material.

One night Altman called up Litto in the middle of the night and said, "George, I might be wrong, but I think I have a big hit."

Only, Altman did not have an ending. The original ending of the book had been adhered to by Lardner. In the book, and in the script, the ending saw Hawkeye returning to his home state of Maine and greeting his wife and kids. When Hawkeye hugs his wife, he drops his military bag on the tarmac with the word *M*A*S*H* on the side of it, prominently displayed. His child asks, "Dad, what does *M*A*S*H* mean?"

"After all this madness," says Litto, "it was thoughtful and sweet."

But Altman, untidy in his own life and endings, hated this tidy finis. Except, after he ruled against it, he had nothing left.

Altman summoned his old friend John T. Kelley to come in and ponder the assemblage. One of the distinctive things about *M*A*S*H*—and one of the devices that has recurred in many an Altman film since—is the disconnected voice-overs that created the unorthodox transitions between scenes. The loudspeaker narration was Altman's idea in postproduction, with many of the cutaways filmed by Greene, and the hilarious content taken verbatim from Twentieth Century-Fox publicity archives and Korean War–era almanacs.

Kelley seized on this idea, and suggested using a loudspeaker voice-over for a reprise of the cast. He wrote it on the spot, announcing that the night's movie had been *M*A*S*H* ("snatching laughs and love between amputations and penicillin"), with a roll call of the cast. It was the last thing Kelley ever wrote for Robert Altman, and it went uncredited.

"It was an up and great way to end the movie," says Litto. "The original was also good, but Altman's was more entertaining."

The first screening was for Zanuck and Brown, studio production manager Stanley L. Hough, executive talent head Owen McLean, and others—the upper management of Fox at the time. It was suit-and-tie time. There were about two laughs during the entire screening. Afterward, the lights went up, and the comments began slowly, while everyone tried to figure out what Zanuck was thinking. "The focus is

dim, the language is overboard, the nudity is too much"—
Altman was dealing with the objections calmly. But tension
was building.

"David Brown and Dick Zanuck thought all this blood was
excessive," says Litto. "This picture had to be completely
reedited. Which they did, all the time. It was ordinary. Except Ingo fought like a banshee. I was screaming too, in the
background, but Ingo made them agree to preview [the director's cut of] the picture in San Francisco."

In San Francisco, the top half of the bill was *Butch Cassidy
and the Sundance Kid.* Twentieth Century-Fox sprang for
limousines and hotels, and the key Altman people were
there, fretting alongside the muckamucks. Zanuck sat right
in front of Litto, Brown to his right. *M*A*S*H* came on.
Two, four, eight people got up to leave as the bloody surgery
scenes unspooled. Litto was sinking in his chair, poison in
his stomach.

"Finally something happens, and the audience laughed.
Then more laughs. Suddenly, the audience breaks into a
spontaneous ovation right in the theatre. And the fucking
picture is off like a rocket to the moon. Dick Zanuck turns
to me, twenty minutes into the movie, and says, 'We've got a
smash.' Afterward, Dick said, 'Here are some of my notes,
but just change what you want.' I think Bob changed two
frames."

The reaction cards were so overwhelmingly positive that
one Fox executive confiscated them from the Altman people,
convinced Altman had loaded the crowd with friends and
family in order to manipulate the studio's reaction.

If it is not too late to make a long story short, *M*A*S*H*,
which cost $3 million, went on to earn $40,000,000 in rental
fees for Twentieth Century-Fox, and to become one of the
ten biggest box-office successes of all time (at that time). It
was accorded many critical hosannas, was awarded the grand
prize at the Cannes Film Festival, selected as the best film of
1970 by the National Society of Film Critics in New York,
and received five nominations for Academy Awards, Best-

Picture, Best Director (Altman), Best Supporting Actress (Kellerman), Best Screenplay (Lardner), and Best Editing (Greene).

The nonlinear storytelling, the anatomized camerawork, the "tintinnabulation" of sound, the "flip" performances—on the level of technique, *M*A*S*H* was not only synchronous with the times (with *Easy Rider*, it was really the first mainstream "dope-consciousness" movie) but so avantgarde then that it is still courant now. In terms of stylistic innovation, no film comedy has had such an earthquakelike influence on post-Vietnam Era filmmakers. So many of the the director's choices were *radical*—right down to the offhand one of having his teenage son Mike compose the lyrics for the theme song (with its haunting anti-Catholic lyric, "Suicide is painless/it brings on many changes. . . ."), which is so memorable that many viewers left the theatre humming it.*

Part of the excitement of *M*A*S*H* lay in all of the taboos it assaulted and all of the ambiguities (some of them in the script, some of them in Altman's sensibility) that it flaunted. There was as much happening outside the frame as inside the plotline; and if there were rave reviews and awards, there was also much critical dissension about what it all portended—not for the first or last time in Altman's career.

Even progressive reviewers not troubled by the strong language and flagrant nudity found fault with the lack of explicit condemnation of the Korean War (and by extension, the Vietnam War); by Altman's attitude toward women (as exemplified by the shrill character of Hot Lips); and by his attitude toward homosexuality (as indicated by the quest of Painless to recoup his manhood). Some critics suspected it just did not all add up, and if it did, it added up to super-

---

*Mike Altman brought the lyric to Preminger and asked for only a new guitar as payment. Preminger took him to the studio legal department and had a contract formally drawn up, which resulted in young Altman's earning royalties from the television theme song all through the years. His father enjoyed complaining that his son made a lot more money from *M*A*S*H* than he ever did.

ficiality. But these critics had to be a bit cautious (after all, the masses were lining up to see it), so when Richard Corliss, writing in *The National Review*, weighed in on the debit side, he put it this way, "I admit it, I didn't like *M*A*S*H*."

The ambivalences in the movie are just as charged almost two decades later; just as unresolved; just as tantalizing. In part, this is because the script was never intended to be didactic and cohesive, in part because Altman takes pains to be contradictory and paradoxical.

Certainly, the Vietnam War is never directly alluded to. In interviews at the time, Altman made a stubborn point of saying the movie was "anti-war but not [specifically anti-] Vietnam." Danford B. Greene confirms there was never any discussion, on the set, in preproduction, or in the editing room, of the Vietnam War or the antiwar protest movement.

Still, Greene and others had the nagging feeling that Altman was bothered by the headlines and newscasts announcing troop buildups and mounting casualties in Vietnam.

"You know, he would come off the day by having a drink and a couple of puffs [of marijuana] on the ride back to the studio," says one of the "talent trust." "Many times the whole limo was lit up. He may not have wanted to deal with it [the Vietnam War], and that might have been his way— either to calm down from the day, or not to talk or deal with any parallels to the War that was going on. I think he was very sensitive to it."

(Ironically, according to Lardner, one of the two writers who have comprised the pseudonym "Richard Hooker" did not have any "strong antiwar intentions" and the other "was a solid reactionary and not at all opposed to the American role in Korea or Vietnam at all." Interestingly, adds Lardner, the "solid reactionary" liked the movie just fine but was said to dislike the TV program's more manifest, heart-on-the-sleeve, antiwar sentiments.*)

---

*Writer William E. Butterworth collaborated on many of the sequels to the *M*A*S*H* novel with H. Richard Hornberger, writing together as "Richard Hooker." Hornberger's politics are self-described in *Contemporary Authors* as "Republican."

If Altman did not exactly endear himself to the antiwar movement, neither, beginning with the public clamor for *M*A*S*H*, has the director scored with feminists or gay activists.

Vito Russo, the film historian who specializes in homosexual issues and themes, took Altman to task for *M*A*S*H* in *The New York Times*, a favorite arena for such pro/con debate. Russo argued that the embarrassing impotence of Painless, the dentist, indicated a value judgment on the film's part about his masculinity. The character of Painless seemed to endorse one of the classic theories of the roots of homosexuality, that it can be the flip side of Don Juanism.*

Certainly there is a lot of giggling and eye-rolling by Painless's comrades-in-arms, whose solution to the limp-dick problem is to fete him at a funereal "Last Supper" and then, while he is lying abjectly in state, to bring on the irresistible Lt. Dish. It works; and Lt. Dish wears a satisfied smile when she departs on the next helicopter—in itself quite a value judgment.

To be fair to Altman, it was Lardner (in his script) who introduced Lt. Dish as the good medicine. It was this scene, and the scene where Hot Lips is humiliated by the entire camp as she cowers, exposed in the shower, that seemed most to outrage feminists (and just plain humanists too, one might add). *Village Voice* columnist Ellen Willis wrote a letter to *The New York Times* denouncing the "blatant misogyny" of *M*A*S*H*, while Sandra Shevey wrote a Sunday piece in the same newspaper arguing that the film "obscenely degrades women."

Altman never rose with much passion to defend the antiwar perspective of *M*A*S*H* (both he and Lardner prefer to

---

*To be fair, Vito Russo, in his subsequent, groundbreaking study of homosexuality in the movies, *The Celluloid Closet* (Harper & Row, 1981), cited the "unobtrusively integrated, happy lesbian couple" of Altman's *A Perfect Couple* as one of the more humanistic portrayals of homosexuals in films of the 1970s. Even so, that instance seems an anomaly when so many of Altman's other films—*M*A*S*H*, California Split, A Wedding, Come Back to the Five and Dime, Jimmy Dean, Jimmy Dean, Streamers,* and *The Caine Mutiny Court-Martial,* among them—have scenes in which intimations of homosexuality, or sex role-reversal, occasion grief, strife, or just plain laughs.

Hot Lips (Sally Kellerman), at her moment of public humiliation in *M*A*S*H*. (Academy of Motion Pictures Arts and Sciences)

say it is "antimilitary"), but the complaints about the misogynistic treatment of women (also endemic in the "Richard Hooker" novel and the Lardner script) seemed to rankle him. "That is the way they were treated back then [during the Korean War era]," he would say.

But in Altman's cinema, Sally Kellerman as Hot Lips is not the only woman to be depicted in such a malignant fashion. In no other director's canon are you likely to find such a collection of tipsy, high-strung, fragile, screwed-up dames. They are no more a sociological mirror image of real life than anything else in Altman's films. What they are is a vital cog in the psychology of his own imagination.

It is said by more than one of Altman's friends that, paradoxically, he is ennobled by failure and oppressed by success.

Although the director's ego had been prepared for *M*A*S*H* since his birth as an Altman in Kansas City, somewhere amidst the years of struggle and disappointment he may have lost the capacity to triumph gracefully. Former friends have commented that the critical adulation and the box-office numbers of *M*A*S*H* went to his head. Success was all the more sweet because of that long period of failure, but the failure was not to be forgotten. It was to be remembered, stoked. There were accounts to be settled.

Now, at long last, Altman was a public personality—seen in photographs as bald, hatted, goateed, and described by *The Los Angeles Times* in its first profile of the *M*A*S*H* director as "a sort of squeaky clean hippie-esque fellow of bearlike proportions with a receding hairline which looks as though it flunked its hairspray wind tunnel test."

Altman could be small-minded about his success. It was still Us vs. Them, as far as he was concerned. Reza Badiyi remembers standing with Altman in the pouring rain as long lines of people formed outside a theatre showing *M*A*S*H* in New York. Altman was gleeful, chortling over a telegram from someone in California: "Congratulations to you, and fuck Dick Sarafian!"

In press interviews, Altman quickly graduated from modesty and gratitude, from thanking producer Ingo Preminger and heaping praise on Ring Lardner's "excellent" script—which opened up the hawkish book and "got the antiwar element out from under wraps"—to sniping at Fox for making so much money off of his smarts, and to claiming, eventually, that he had virtually rewritten and winged the script.

This, with *M*A*S*H*, is where the legend/reality of Altman's animus toward scriptwriters got going strong. It was always a matrix of half-truths. Even in Altman's later circle of the 1970s, people who were themselves screenwriters in

collaborations with Altman—and ought to have known better from firsthand experience—would talk about how the
great director had improvised *M*A*S*H* and created the
scenes from the tatters that was Lardner's script.

The "talent trust" of the time knew better. Says Louis
Lombardo: "His [Altman's] most successful picture. He shot
it the way it was written."

Altman's usurpation of the screenwriter's credit (whether
formally on the screen or in interviews) stems from a deeply
ingrained anxiety—his inability to express himself in writing. This persists and bothers him. His writer's block has
been explained away neatly by friends and family as "he
doesn't like to sit still for very long" or "he cannot stand to
be alone." Yet all of the explanations amount to the same
thing: Altman cannot stand to commit himself on paper.

He has had periods of good writing. He has had pages and
scenes of good writing. He has written a handful of (mostly
television) scripts by his lonesome. But he is haunted by how
difficult it is for him and by the remembered comments of
writer-producers such as Huggins and Blees, both of whom
made the point (to Altman) that he was not really a writer,
per se—no genuine "hyphenate," at least, like Orson Welles.

Louis Lombardo remembers Altman in the 1960s writing a
passage in a script about soldiers crossing a river in a jeep
and then reading it eagerly to him, aloud. "Ah," Altman exclaimed, "and they said Altman couldn't write! Listen to
that!" And Lombardo comments respectfully: "I did think it
was great." (Adds Lombardo: "He's a frustrated writer. He'd
love to be able to write like [writer-director Robert] Benton.")

Because of his block, Altman was very dependent, in the
shadow years leading up to *M*A*S*H*, on James Rickard,
George W. George, John T. Kelley, Brian McKay, and Barbara
Turner, among others. He was envious of Richard Sarafian's
writing. So, Lardner, after accepting bouquets from Altman
for his script, and after having had nothing but courteous
script sessions with the director, may have been surprised
later on to hear his work publicly disparaged. But Lardner
was only the latest in a long line to suffer that treatment.

By August of 1971, Altman was explaining to Aljean Harmetz, who was writing a Sunday magazine piece for *The New York Times*, that Lardner's script was okay but deficient in many respects. "Yet if I had done his script," Altman told Harmetz, "the picture would have been a disaster. . . . My main contribution to *M*A*S*H* was the basic concept, the philosophy, the style, the casting, and then making all those things work. Plus all the jokes, of course."

Years later, in one of the many published treatises that have decorated his career, Lardner's contribution had become reduced even further. Altman is quoted as saying he "disliked" Lardner's script because it was "awfully hawkish somehow"; thus he regarded it as only a "rough outline" from which the director had to depart. This blueprint method of filmmaking is, the treatise writer comments ingenuously, "a working habit Altman continues to follow in his filmmaking. . . ."

"As a result [of his pummeling of the *M*A*S*H* script]," Harmetz concluded in *The New York Times* profile, "most of the writers of Altman's films have ended up as his more-or-less bitter enemies. By the time one of his films is finished there is nothing left of the original script except a couple of soup bones of plot and a few expletives."

Not always true (except maybe the "bitter enemies" part); and not true, specifically, in the case of *M*A*S*H*.

Altman might have cared less, if a couple of things had not happened to raise the stakes in this ego poker game of who-wrote-the-what. *M*A*S*H* was awarded only one Oscar in the spring of 1971—and that gold-plated statuette went to Lardner for Best Screenplay. It was driving Altman crazy that the film was making so much money for Twentieth Century-Fox, and that he was not getting a percentage. The Oscar and the profits he would never pocket put him on the defensive; his remarks became offensive.

Lardner, a dignified person under even the most trying circumstances, has had varying responses. *The New York Times* (again, the Aljean Harmetz article) summed up his disposition relative to *M*A*S*H* and Altman as "publicly quite circumspect" while "his private opinions are considerably more vitriolic."

Reviewing the controversy almost twenty years later, Lardner says in a letter to the author, "I was quite favorably impressed with him [Altman] from our first meeting, and have continued to think fairly well of him ever since, even after a few assertions of ego that I found annoying, especially on the topic of his 'improvisations.' In my judgment, there were three more or less equal creators of the movie *M*A*S*H*: Richard Hooker (both of them), me, and Bob, and I would debate any contention that tried to give as much as a half a share to any one of us. I think you're right in saying the content remained pretty much the same from book to script to movie."

That seems fair (if overly modest). Any informed reading of the book and the various script drafts reveal that Altman started out pretty much where he ended up. Most of the memorable scenes are, in fact, in the book: Painless's sexual peccadilloes, "The Last Supper," the intra-Army football game, etc. The book has even less structure than the movie, and Lardner's first accomplishment was to organize the material, essentially, into three acts—Hot Lips; Painless; the Japanese excursion and the football finale. The three acts needed binding and transitions, and that was Altman's stroke: adding the loudspeaker as a sort of narrator/character.

Altman got a lot of mileage in the press out of his supposed enhancement of the character of Hot Lips. He was aided in this by Sally Kellerman, who told interviewers that, upon reading the script, she was disappointed to discover Hot Lips enjoyed a total of "one line on page seventy, three lines on page thirty-four, and one line on page forty." This became part and parcel of the general script mythology.

Of course, Kellerman was rewarded by the director, in time on the screen, for what became, in the filming, a truly winning performance. But, before Altman, it was Lardner who brought Hot Lips forth as a major character from the relatively small part she plays in only one chapter of the book. It was Lardner who conceived the cruel incident of her being exposed nude and ridiculed in the open-air shower—it is right there in the first draft.

In Lardner's final script, however, her jeering audience is comprised of only Duke, Hawkeye, and Trapper. It was Altman who invited the entire cast into the scene, making it even more humiliating and uproarious.

Altman's communal spirit embroidered more than one scene. The football climax, for example, became an exuberant whing-ding. In Lardner's final draft, there are only a "few supporters" on the sidelines. In the film, Hot Lips (who, by then, in the novel and in Lardner's draft, has departed the M*A*S*H unit in an uproar) is also at the game, somewhat inexplicably leading the cheerleaders' squad. (She has evidently become part of the gang, although there is no transition moment in the story to explain her, and their, change of heart.)

Many of Altman's best touches are in the nature of emphasis. "Moments."

The anticlericalism, for example. Altman had been brooding about Catholicism for a long time. (Ring Lardner, too, had been mulling the Catholic religion, and while blacklisted in the 1950s, he wrote a satirical novel on the subject, *The Ecstasy of Owen Muir.*) Though Altman remained a sort of Catholic (he had his children baptized), he bridled at the tenets of the Church. Here, in *M*A*S*H*, his assault on the Church was blistering.

Major Frank Burns's (Robert Duvall) self-righteous beliefs, Dago Red's (René Auberjonois) dazed cleric, the simulation of "The Last Supper," the chorale of "Onward, Christian Soldiers"—these are all in the book and in the script. But as with Hot Lips, these characters and scenes touched on some of Altman's own areas of interest, and he embellished them. Major Burns's and Hot Lips's Christianity is undercut and ridiculed via the overwrought intensity of their mealy-mouthing. In the script "The Last Supper" is a simple testimonial dinner described by Lardner as a "stag banquet." It

The Oscar for the script that Altman growingly disparaged: Ring Lardner Jr. accepting the Best Screenplay Award for *M*A*S*H* from Eva Marie Saint at the 1971 ceremonies. (Copyright © Academy of Motion Picture Arts and Sciences)

was Altman who staged it brilliantly like the da Vinci painting with sacrilegious symbolism.

And as funny as Ring Lardner is—this is a man with funnybones in his genes—Altman and the *M*A*S*H* cast did in the heat of the moment contribute some of the dialogue high points unaccounted for in the script. From book to final script draft, Hot Lips has the line that practically sums up the thesis of the film: "I wonder how a degenerate person like you could have reached a position of responsibility in the Army Medical Corps." To which Hawkeye replies, "Sister, if I knew the answer to that, I sure as hell wouldn't be here."

Not bad, but not good enough. In the movie, Hawkeye replies not at all, and Dago Red looks up from his priestly bewilderment long enough to utter the immortal: "He was drafted."

When a director lives with a movie long enough, he begins to forget what it is he has thought of and what it is the writer has thought of; that is natural, if somewhat devious.

M*A*S*H was so amazingly in synch with Altman: with its helicopters from *The Whirlybirds*, its antiwar symptoms from *Combat*, the locker-room language, voyeuristic nudity, Catholic riffs, the marijuana consciousness—even the fellow named Radar, a recall of his own World War II unit.

In an interview once, Altman claimed to have paused at one point during the shooting of one of his films and to have realized that he did not have a script on hand. He says he put out the call to locate one, but his assistant was unable to locate a copy on the set. The filming slogged on, the director undeterred.

That is certainly the wishful thought!

But it is also the distortion of a frustrated writer. At Cannes, the controversy over authorship boiled over behind the scenes, after M*A*S*H was awarded Best Film honors. (Altman was not named Best Director, incidentally; that citation was given to John Boorman for *Leo the Last*.)

According to Litto, Altman gave an interview to the press in which he "commented deprecatingly about the script." Litto flew into a rage and told the director, "Bob, for twenty years, this guy [Lardner] was denied credit by very bad people. You shouldn't do the same thing after he gave you the only important movie you've ever made."

Says Litto: "I think he was embarrassed I had called him on it. He had never thought of it on those terms."

According to Lardner, Altman's persistent claims to authorship were one of the things that really miffed producer Preminger. Preminger had always supported Altman to the hilt: He kept Zanuck and Brown at a distance during filming; he cooperated with much of Altman's casting; he soothed

Sutherland and Gould; he defended the excesses of the directorial style.

"Ingo did a magnificent job of producing," says Danford B. Greene. "Ingo told me one time: 'My job as a producer is to keep Bob's mind free and keep everyone off of him so he can just concentrate on the film, the cast, and the story without being burdened with hierarchy.' He really did that. He kept all the crap away from Bob."

Later on, Altman began to see Preminger more in terms of how much money the producer was making as against Altman's share of profits—bubkus. That boom-or-bust psychology of his childhood was still very much with him. He had to get some of that money!

At Altman's urging, Litto called Preminger and asked him to throw the director a point or two. According to Litto, Preminger, despite growing discomfort with Altman, agreed to, out of his own share. But Twentieth Century-Fox had to be consulted. And when Altman gave another interview disparaging Fox, whose big-blockbuster failures were draining the company, Fox rejected the producer's request. And by this time, Preminger no longer had any desire to go to bat for his director.

Ingo Preminger *never* produced another film: *M*A*S*H* is his solitary credit. If there is a record for profits earned for a single motion picture, totting up movie and television rights and dividends, Ingo Preminger must own that record.* Yet

---

*The Emmy-winning television series receives a footnote in this book, which is about as much as the film receives in books about the television series. Though Altman had nothing to do with the series, and he did not share in it financially, it nonetheless owed the debt of its gestation, and of its style, to him.

Television writer Larry Gelbart borrowed a subplot from the film script for the pilot—namely, what happens to the character of Ho-Jon, the Korean boy. Ho-Jon's story was actually filmed by Altman for *M*A*S*H*, and a garbled remnant of it remains in the screen version. Gelbart realized its potential and retrieved it for television.

Lardner adds an ironic postscript. The writer who recognized *M*A*S*H* as a surefire motion picture property resisted the idea that *M*A*S*H* would work, week after week, on TV. He was asked to write the pilot and to be the series's head writer. Lardner is still kicking himself for turning the opportunity down. "It could never be a success," he reckoned. "How long could they go on doing stories out of this surgical unit?"

The answer is: fourteen seasons.

even though the film made him rich, he was soured by the experience, and he dropped out of the Hollywood game. He never spoke to Robert Altman again.

Certain members of the "talent trust"—with Altman for nearly a decade—did not survive the triumph of $M*A*S*H$ either—most surprisingly, the editor, Danford B. Greene. More of a foul-weather friend, Altman has always found it advantageous to cut his supporters during a period of prosperity rather than struggle.

"When things are going badly, they're like a rock," he told one interviewer, referring to his filmmaking team. "They stay together, and they'll do anything. Success makes you more frightened."

Danford B. Greene had had a few disagreements with Altman; Graeme Clifford was still hovering around; Louis Lombardo was in the wings. The Oscar-nominated Greene had no inkling that his faithful service was over; but when the movie was over, so was his friendship and professional relationship with Robert Altman. He knew he had transgressed somehow, but how? He is still wondering.

PART

5

"It always seemed a fine idea to me to build a showboat with just one big flat open deck on it, and to keep a play going continuously. The boat wouldn't be moored, but would drift up and down the river on the tide, and the audience would sit along both banks. They could catch whatever part of the plot happened to unfold as the boat floated past, and then they'd have to wait until the tide ran back again to catch another snatch of it, if they still happened to be sitting there. To fill in the gaps, they'd have to use their imaginations, or ask more attentive neighbors, or hear the word passed along from upriver or downriver. Most times they wouldn't understand what was going on at all, or they'd think they knew, when actually they didn't. Lots of times they'd be able to see the actors, but not hear them. I needn't explain that that's how much of life works: our friends float past; we become involved with them; they float on . . ."

—*John Barth*,
The Floating Opera

Chapter

24

THE
ANTI-MOVIES

In 1972, a British journalist who had known Altman in Hollywood prior to *M*A*S*H* penned his impressions of how the director had prospered and metamorphosed since the hit movie.

"I first met Robert Altman four years ago—two years before the success of *M*A*S*H* swept him to deserved acclaim," wrote John Cutts. "I was then working with a producer Altman was hoping to interest in a project of his, and my main memory of him at that time was undistinguished. He seemed ill at ease, weary almost, with the role he was forced to play; it was a buyer's market then, Altman needing the producer far more than the vice was versa, and though I sat in on many a long meeting between them, listening to him outline various story ideas, I never got a sense of personality. At length the producer backed off, unpersuaded, and Altman went his way.

"Two years can be a lifetime in Hollywood and the next time Altman and I met . . . he had undergone quite a switch in character. Whatever held him in check before was now long gone, he was his own man now, and one felt the strength of his liberated personality (authoritative, articulate, fully aware of his success and capabilities)."

The five years following *M*A*S*H* and preceding *Nashville* were a golden era for Altman. If he did nothing else in his lifetime, he would be remembered for this streak. Six films—more than one per year—*Brewster McCloud* and *McCabe and Mrs. Miller*, both released in 1970, *Images* in 1972, *The Long Goodbye* in 1973, *Thieves Like Us* and *California Split* in 1974. Assured, arguably masterful; dissimilar; only one clinker *(Images)* among them. Except for Woody Allen, no other director since the decline of the studio production era has had such a concentrated burst of filmmaking. That Altman was able to muster such a staggering body of work in so little time shows how pent-up creatively he had been.

A major factor in this output was the "talent trust," still relatively intact and blossoming as individuals.

The auteur theory does not always take into account the subtleties of the collaborative process. As articulated by the French critics (François Truffaut was an early proponent) of *Cahiers du Cinéma* beginning in 1954, and fostered in the United States by critic Andrew Sarris, auteurism applies to directors who dominate the proceedings of their films with skill and purpose, creating a "meaningful coherence" in a lifelong oeuvre of studio product. Sarris makes the point that "author" is not an adequate translation when making the case that "a nonliterary director [i.e., not a writer] can be the author of his films." Such directors may be auteurs of stylistic or thematic consistency, or both; but in some way each of their films, good or bad, is forged by their personality.

There can be little disagreement about the occasional one-man-genius who happens along—Charlie Chaplin and Orson Welles and Woody Allen, for example. Not only do they write and direct, but they star in their own vanity productions as luminous screen presences. They are "authors" as well as auteurs! But the fun for auteurists is in endlessly debating the relative gradations of the nonliterary directors and lesser studio hacks. And in considering Altman, part of the fun is to look beyond his mystique into the extent of his writing contributions and the input of the unsung collaborators.

One of the surprising things about this director is how, for such a modernist, his films can be so guarded and "impersonal," lacking the autobiographical thread; how the subjects of his films often originate outside himself; and how paradoxically, he can find and express himself, over and over again (if sometimes only in glints and glimmers), through the go-between of other people and their involvement.

It is as if his collaborators are a bridge to the *self* for Altman, as well as to the audience. They are the missing link to an understanding of the director as well as to the meaning of the films.

One of the reasons why this period between 1969 and 1975 is so rich for Altman is that the "talent trust" that grew out of the 1960s, and survived for several years beyond *M*A*S*H*, was, of many successive Altman "circles," the most consummate. And one of the reasons these six Altman films—these "antimovies"—invert, satirize, and enrich certain Hollywood genres is that this "talent trust," which helped shape them as a body, was made up of show people on the fringe.

Five of the six films were properties developed by others that came to Altman by chance. The only one that sprang from Altman's own story bank was *Images*.

*   *   *

Airborne: Brewster (Bud Cort), the Icarus-man of
the Astrodome in *Brewster McCloud*. (Museum
of Modern Art)

Altman had *Brewster McCloud* completed and "in the
can," as they say, before *M*A*S*H* had "played out" its release. MGM had approved Altman as director, in fact, before
M*A*S*H had even opened.

Brewster had a bouillabaisse cast—many *M*A*S*H* people, including bland-faced Bud Cort as the title character—
some neophytes—and some show-business veterans. In the
latter category were William Windom (who plays a local pol-
itico, a forerunner of the unseen, blathering Presidential candidate in *Nashville*) and Margaret Hamilton (whose vitae
included playing the Wicked Witch of the West in *The Wizard of Oz*). Others, like Stacy Keach, who essayed the unctuous bigwig Abraham Wright (supposedly a relative of the
aerial Wright brothers, though the script never clarifies that
point), had a link to Altman's past as well as to the director's

future. Keach had played the Off-Broadway lead in *MacBird!*, as well as Buffalo Bill in Arthur Kopit's play *Indians*. The actress Jennifer Salt, who has a brief part as a Brewster groupie who—after watching the bikini-clad Brewster do his arm exercises—masturbates under an oscillating American flag, was flying high in such Sixties timepieces as Paul Williams's *The Revolutionary* and Brian De Palma's *Hi Mom!* Her father had an Altman connection in that he happened to be the Oscar-winning (for his *Midnight Cowboy* script) screenwriter Waldo Salt, another ex-blacklisted client of George Litto's.

The real find, at least from Altman's point of view, was Shelley Duvall, born and residing in Houston, who played Brewster's dippy romantic conquest. The story of her discovery by Altman at her engagement party to a local artist became part of the Altman folklore—especially as Duvall went on to become a central actress for the director in six films. It was also a point of further bad feeling between Altman and Brian McKay, who insists that it was he who spotted Duvall and introduced her to Altman, who thereupon took all the credit.

The original screenplay, called *Brewster McCloud's (Sexy) Flying Machine*, had been written independent of Altman back in 1967 and had a prior mystique in Hollywood as "probably the most famous unproduced script in the country," according to its author, Doran William Cannon, whose best-known previous credit was as the writer of director Otto Preminger's *Skidoo*. "Bob Dylan said he thought it was perfect," Cannon once claimed. The script was optioned many times without ever being filmed—largely because the writer refused to sell the rights without attaching himself as director.

The script eventually ended up in the hands of pop music titan Lou Adler, who, after scaling the charts as producer of the Mamas and the Papas and the like, now wanted to conquer motion pictures. At which point came the feat of *M*A*S*H*—and through George Litto, Adler came to Altman, who swiftly repaired with cast and crew to Houston, a

You can't take it with you: rich geezer Abraham Wright (Stacy Keach), dead, covered with bird droppings and dollar bills in *Brewster McCloud.*

location that always stimulated him. MGM promised no interference. Altman began to tear up and revise the script. No one consulted Cannon, who no longer controlled the rights.

Houston and the Astrodome were Altman's idea (the studio had initially approved a location in New York). There were some production wrinkles—again, Altman had cameraman problems. He dismissed up-and-coming photographer Jordan Cronenweth and supplanted him with the relatively unknown Lamar Boren, whose main credits were from Ivan Tors television shows. And at one point, Altman was hospitalized with a hernia that slowed down the hectic pace of filming.

But in general, people remember the Houston location as being the first unfettered Altman experience. There were the "family" good times and democratic dailies, the location freedom from superintending executives, the script-changing and the free-wheeling performances, the parties and lots of dope—not just marijuana, but (for some) hashish, cocaine, and opium too. There was that feeling, so endemic to the Altman experience, of having uninhibited *fun*. Perhaps the most fun ever. George Litto rates it, in fact, as "the *last* fun we had."

At this safe remove from Hollywood, Cannon's script became "simply the skeleton for Altman's creative flights," according to a piece in *Variety* on the subject, quoting producer Adler.

According to Adler, as quoted in *Variety*, the original script was "much more of a sexcapade," interestingly, with Brewster frolicking with each of the three femmes in the story. Instead, Altman bedded Brewster with the Shelley Duvall character only, devised the one-woman orgy for Jennifer Salt, and turned the Sally Kellerman character from "just an ordinary chick" into a hovering guardian angel.

The character of the deranged ornithologist was vastly expanded (his rambling lectures culled from encyclopedic sources), and the role of a vainglorious supercop created for Michael Murphy just because he happened to be one of the director's "favorite people."

"Not only was sex downgraded but violence as well, since the murders now are all offscreen," reported *Variety*. "Whole scenes were created and improvised on the spot when Altman was intrigued by a particular situation or fascinated by a portion of the Astrodome's architecture. And other scenes were often written by the director at night, to be presented to the actors the following day." (To cite an example, Michael Murphy has said the idea for the out-of-the-blue suicide of his Shaft character came up at dinner with Altman the night before.)

Brian McKay was around and did his best to comply with Altman's free-flight thinking. But it was a precarious and fantastical script structure, which only Altman had in his head, and McKay could not figure out what it was the director wanted. They began to have dangling conversations. Finally, the two old friends quarreled, and McKay angrily drove off toward Los Angeles. Altman was not concerned about finishing the screenplay—but he complained to the "talent trust" that McKay had committed the unpardonable sin of leaving an Altman set before the party was over.

Eventually, Doran William Cannon showed up for a visit. The writer was given a frosty reception. "He is very bitter because no one has suggested he look at the script," wrote C. Kirk McClelland, a young cinema student who documented the filming for a paperback called *On Making a Movie: Brewster McCloud.* As the professional animus quickly became personal, his accord (such as it was) with the director deteriorated.

In a *New York Times* article timed to coincide with the eventual release of *Brewster McCloud,* Cannon recounted the following rather surreal telephone conversation with the director who had filmed his script:

ALTMAN: Your screenplay was a piece of crap!

CANNON: My screenplay was perfect.

ALTMAN: It was crap.

CANNON: You bought it!

ALTMAN: You sold it!

"He accused me [wrote Cannon] of selling a script he had bought! Surely, I am his SOURCE and that embarrasses him; oh, Hollywood!"

ALTMAN: I will continue embarrassing you to the press.

CANNON: I'm hardly embarrassed, but you were embarrassed when I came to watch the filming in Houston. You were embarrassed to think that people might learn I exist! You felt exposed!

ALTMAN: I was embarrassed *for* you.

CANNON: Hah! You remind me of Otto Preminger. He was also embarrassed because I had written *Skidoo* as an original, and he screwed up my vision.

ALTMAN: You put me in the same class as Otto Preminger?

CANNON: Yes.

Silence.

"I suggested [wrote Cannon] that we talk the whole thing over when it has become history, perhaps in a year."

ALTMAN: See you in a year.

"We hung up [wrote Cannon]. I felt a little sorry for him. His mind, as well as mine, I knew too well, had been bent by Hollywood. I wished he had understood my good intentions. I wished his film good luck."

Cannon had an unusual clause in his contract that guaranteed his sole billing as screenwriter of *Brewster*. Ironically, Altman may have done more hands-on writing of *Brewster* than on any of his other films, but it was one script credit he could not usurp.

Brewster was even more loose-stitched than *M*A*S*H*.

The story intercut between a series of freakish murders and the activities of a young manchild living in the bowels of an enclosed baseball stadium and obsessed with building a flying machine. The murders are being investigated by a vaunted detective named Shaft (Michael Murphy), assisted by an inept policeman from the Houston force (John Schuck). The would-be Icarus (Bud Cort), who may or may not be connected to the murder spree, is abetted by an oversexed health-food addict (Salt), a mystery figure (Kellerman) who is nude under her trench coat, with scars on her back where wings would go, and an Astrodome tour guide (Duvall).

At the end—a synopsis would not do justice to the film's twists and turns—Brewster, surrounded by police, launches his flying apparatus, soars aloft in the Astrodome, from which there is no escape, and plummets to his death. The director seems to mock his own thematic pretentiousness with the Fellini-esque curtain call—which reminds audiences (like the end of *M*A*S*H* and *The Long Goodbye*) that it's only a movie. As the credits roll, there is a final, jolting cutaway to Brewster, a bag of bones crumpled beneath the flying contraption.

Seen today, *Brewster* is more sophomoric than deep-toned; more of a cartoon with an attitude than a slice of life with a point of view. It is burdened with a title character more tedious than enigmatic. It lacks warmth. And it lacks certain nexuses in the storyline. (Altman may have abandoned some of the Brewster character on the cutting-room floor, for the director had more than one skirmish on the set with the hauteur of Bud Cort.)

Yet *Brewster* is one of the Altman films that improves with time. There is simply more to behold than in anybody else's half a dozen films. Though it may have a weak center, it has a crammed periphery. *Brewster* is almost Brechtian in the sense that it is constantly winking at its audience—with an onslaught of scatalogical one-liners, sexual frankness, "in" Hollywood satire and topical put-downs, visual puns. (One that is memorable: bird-droppings on a newspaper headline about Spiro Agnew.)

If Cort's performance struck a rare hollow chord for an Altman film, there was enjoyment to be found in the acting of lesser parts—particularly G. Wood, Corey Fischer, and John Schuck (all *M*A*S*H* grads) as the hapless police, and René Auberjonois as the spaced-out ornithologist. In the intermittent lectures of Auberjonois, Altman hit on a corollary to the loudspeakers in *M*A*S*H*. In spite of the fact that the Lecturer was patently irrelevant to the main storyline, Auberjonois gave a fascinating performance, and the character sent a thread of continuity and another level to the film. (It was an old Calvin technique, the standard wraparound; and when Robert Woodburn saw the film at an MGM screening, he thought to himself, " 'My god, he's made a Calvin movie,' because that's what it was, a Calvin industrial, the whole format.")

The Icarus metaphor was Altman's great theme: man's yearning to to liberated from earthly concerns, his fate to be grounded. He had touched on it in television and in *Countdown*,* but here the director expressed great feeling

---

*Altman found a way to incorporate this motif in the most unlikely material. In an early *Kraft*, "Death of a Dream," there is thirty seconds, remarkable for having nothing to do with the episode, in which Altman's camera fixes on a pet bird, knocked loose from its cage and wildly careening around the living room in a vain effort to find an escape through the ceiling.

for a quandary that, for him, was primal. Even when the film pauses for one of those lyrical bird's-eye-view-of-the-clouds' musical interludes, the passage, as handled by Altman, is as soulful as it is corny.

Brewster is not, then or now, an easy film to like. For its part, the studio simply did not comprehend "that far-out cinema tale," reported the syndicated columnist Marilyn Beck. As Altman complained in interviews, the advance cards were twice as rhapsodic as those of *M*A*S*H*, but the studio executives could not understand why, if that were so, nobody in the audience seemed to be laughing.

Altman had never marketed a film—but he was his father's son, and he had notions about salesmanship, advertising, and promotion. According to Beck, who talked to Altman about the fate of *Brewster*, Altman wanted *Brewster McCloud* to open in New York City, "so the sophisticated big city critics, whose words have awesome influence over the opinions of movie reviewers in other cities," could spread the gospel.

Brewster's problems were compounded by the fact that it had been one of the last go-aheads of the previous studio regime. The new studio head, James Aubrey, did not like the movie, and he did not like Robert Altman (and vice versa). The studio chose to condemn the film to a quick play-off in saturation bookings in multiples around the country. Adler swore he would never produce a motion picture again (he didn't keep his vow), and was quoted publicly as saying the MGM executives were "a bunch of bag salesmen who've been put in their jobs like a bunch of pawns."

The movie grossed less than $1 million before being pulled out of theatres. The only consolation for Altman and Adler was, according to Marilyn Beck, "it has become an underground favorite on college campuses."

There was some hope that the critical reception (*Village Voice* critic Andrew Sarris, who did not particularly like *M*A*S*H*, acclaimed it as "a very subtle, perceptive comedy") would spur Academy consideration. Holding court around Lion's Gate at the time, Altman would predict: "The only serious competition against *M**A*S*H for the Academy Award is *Brewster McCloud*." But *Brewster* did not receive any Oscar nominations. Regardless, Altman has often claimed it as his favorite film.

Actually, the next movie on Altman's schedule was supposed to be that forget-me-not, *Death, Where Is Thy Sting-a-ling-ling?* The rights had reverted to Altman, and now the Mirisch company, intoxicated by the phenomenon of *M**A*S*H, was courting the director anew. But Altman could not work on *Death* without McKay, contractually or otherwise, and he was barely on speaking terms with McKay.

"We were not very friendly," remembers McKay, "but we had this thing to do together. He had signed to do it and couldn't do it without me. Or wasn't willing to do it without me, because he needed somebody to write the fucking thing. Because he won't write. He *can* write, but he won't. Which is my theory about writing, anyway. That everybody can write, but it's just [a question of] who will."

They made a stab at reconciliation. McKay flew up to Canada to meet Altman at the preproduction location of *McCabe and Mrs. Miller*, and together, on Mirisch funds, they flew to Europe, ostensibly scouting locations.

In London they were shown a spliced-together segment of the earlier, aborted version. Altman and McKay were allotted something in the neighborhood of a thousand dollars a week for preproduction costs and toward refurbishing the script. They spent a lot of their time gambling. McKay was losing badly at cribbage, and in the gaming parlors Altman was losing worse. They could make no progress on *Death*, because deep down neither of them any longer wanted to make the movie. All during this time, they were haunted by the lines of customers outside the theatres showing *M**A*S*H in London.

In a European mountain hamlet, where they were quartered while inspecting scenery, Altman used an indiscretion by McKay to get out of the deal. Since it was a Sunday, McKay announced he was flying to a city elsewhere on the

Continent to see a lady friend. Altman refused to give him the necessary twenty-four hours off. McKay said he was going anyway. Of course, the unit manager from Mirisch (who was accompanying them) sided with America's darling, the director of *M*A*S*H*. The Mirisch representative knocked on the door of McKay's hotel room, handed him a bag of money to square accounts, and Altman was on a plane back home. Once again, *Death* was dead, this time forever.

By the time it came to filming *McCabe and Mrs. Miller*, Brian McKay had more than one foot in the door of the "enemies" list. That was unfortunate, because McKay had written what everyone recalls as a very solid script, a very *exciting* script, in which McCabe was more of a cocky gunfighter than an antihero playing a shell game of life or death. Altman always said McKay's script was just a "selling tool" to wangle the production money, but in part he said that just to keep McKay under thumb.

Like *Brewster*, *McCabe* had been kicking around Hollywood for a long time, coveted, developed, never filmed. It was based on a 1959 novel by Edmund Naughton called, simpley, *McCabe*. It was a terrific, literary Western. Much of the characterization and plot occurrence of the movie is right there in the fiction—in McCabe's case, right down to his egg-and-whiskey vice and the "poetry in my soul" speech that some film critics might rush to attribute to Altman or Warren Beatty.

There had been many script drafts. At one point, poet-screenwriter Ben Maddow had contributed one. But by 1970, the rights were controlled by producer David Foster, who spoke to George Litto, who felt instinctively that it was right for Robert Altman, who assigned the writing to Brian McKay. McKay adapted it in five weeks' time, well before he and Altman came a cropper on *Brewster McCloud*.

Elliott Gould was originally considered for the part of McCabe, but the financing would not have come through if it were not for Warren Beatty. Julie Christie had already been cast, when Beatty (her lover at the time) read the script, and decided to fly with her from England to Los Angeles to sweep decisively into a meeting of Warner Brothers production executives. Beatty paused at the doorway to bestow his blessing on McKay: "Your words brought me seven thousand miles."

Yet after what had transpired in Europe, McKay was a pariah on the set. So, the filming of *McCabe* saw the director presiding over collectivist revisions, and encouraging Beatty (who had helped transform the brutal bank robber Clyde Barrow into a sexually confused outcast in *Bonnie and Clyde*) to turn the character of McCabe inside out. Partly that was the shrewd thing to do, and partly that was Altman's reaction to his final breakup with McKay.

"A little arbitrariness there, I think," says Litto. "He [Altman] and Brian had a falling-out, so he wanted to make the script irrelevant to Brian's contribution. Which is one of Bob's major weaknesses. It was better in Brian's version. In my opinion, he should have stayed closer to it."

There were several writers after McKay. Not only Altman but Beatty concocted some of the quips and snappy aphorisms. Hollywood script doctor Robert Towne, a longtime Beatty cohort (who put spit 'n' polish on *Bonnie and Clyde*) also did some work, or at least consultation by telephone. And Julie Christie wrote or rewrote much of her own dialogue.

"He [Altman] simply turned Julie's stuff over to her," says Joan Tewkesbury, the script supervisor on *McCabe*. "She had a companion with her who knew all the different kinds of dialects, and they would go off and take these scenes and redo them as a woman would do them in this position. And Warren would do the same thing. It was really wonderful to watch. They wrote very specifically because they needed lines, they needed script.

"Then what Bob would do is rehearse those things and see what would come out of the rehearsal. Then I would write all the stuff down and they would all be asked to repeat their own lines. On occasion, on Saturdays, he would dictate to me a couple of the scenes he wanted done, specific ways, and this stuff would be embellished by the actors. What I began to realize is, all Bob really needed to work was a strong spine for the story. If you could create scenes that had strong purposes—a way to get in and a way to get out, and it moved the story along—what happened in the middle would depend on the environment."

There was someone else: A professional screenwriter by the name of Joseph Calvelli (*Death of a Gunfighter*), who had left Hollywood at the end of the Sixties, and who lived down the road from the set in Vancouver. Calvelli dropped by—the Altman people knew him from Los Angeles days—and he did some spot writing, notably on the whorehouse scenes. It seems like everybody did some writing except the grip—and Joan Tewkesbury swears that there was some Altman film she worked on, maybe it was *McCabe*, where a strategic line of dialogue was, indeed, supplied extemporaneously by the grip.

By this time, Altman was sensitive about these acclaimed masterworks of his that originated elsewhere entirely, and were brought to his attention by his agent, George Litto, and were then written in the main by someone other than the director. It was already a ritual for him to claim screenplay credit. Even so, the veterans of the "talent trust" were shocked when Altman threatened to take the name of Brian McKay, his friend of ten years, off the *McCabe* script.

"He sensed what it was going to be," says McKay, "and he didn't want to share. He did everything he could to get my name off of it."

Altman did his best to bully McKay; there was talk of a Writers Guild hearing—which, had it occurred, might well have ensured the appearance of McKay's name—but not Altman's—on the screen. It was a broken McKay who compromised. He says "maybe half" of his script survived in any case. The final credit reads: "Written by Robert Altman and Brian McKay."

For the filming of *McCabe*, Leon Ericksen reached a personal zenith by designing and overseeing construction of an

Snowbound: McCabe's (Warren Beatty) dreams
are grounded in *McCabe and Mrs. Miller*. (Academy of Motion Pictures Arts and Sciences)

entire picturesque frontier town—cabins, whorehouse and
bathhouse, two saloons, a barbershop, a sawmill, general
store, and steepled church. It seemed carved out of the wilderness, and very nearly smothered under a blanket of mud,
fog, drizzle, and snow.

The cameraman was Vilmos Zsigmond, whom Altman
had tried to bring on board as early as *M*A*S*H* (Zsigmond
was booked up with commitments for penny-ante features

and advertisements). Already, Zsigmond had a reputation for being fast and for battling the elements, for the innovative use of filters and lab processes, for being "a master at evoking the intended visual mood and ambience of a given project" (Dennis Schaefer and Larry Salvato, *Masters of Light: Conversations with Contemporary Cinematographers*). He was to work on *Images* and *The Long Goodbye* for Altman, as well as *McCabe and Mrs. Miller*.

One thing everyone who has seen *McCabe* remembers is the evocative tint of the photography. That was Altman's idea—an effect obtained by "flashing and fogging" the film stock.

According to Tommy Thompson, Altman had a yellow velour sweatshirt and an inexpensive Polaroid camera. By clicking the shutter twice without advancing the film you could double-expose the roll. At one point during preproduction, Altman stuck his stomach out and took a Polaroid of the yellow velour. Then, he turned and took another Polaroid of one of the actors on the set. What he was doing, in practice, was "flashing" the film.

Thompson picks up the story: "Then he went to Vilmos and said, 'That's the look I want. I want that color.' Vilmos said, 'How'd you get that color? You're flashing the film. That's too dangerous. You can't do that. If you're shooting all day with flash film, if you're overexposed or overflashed, you will have lost the day's work.' Bob said, 'I don't care about that. That's my responsibility.'

"There was quite an argument until Bob finally won. That yellow velour [should] be framed somewhere, because if nothing else, everyone says that is one of the most beautiful pictures ever made. I love the look. It came right out of his velour. To me, if anyone else in the business wanted to do that, you would have needed the cameras, the cost of flashing film—total, you'd spend fifty thousand dollars trying to get that. He spent thirty-four dollars' worth of Polaroid film and got exactly what he wanted."

Interestingly, the layered sound quality of *McCabe* was also a result of happenstance—and a matter of some debate among the "talent trust." The weather on location was unpredictable and harsh—constant high winds, rain, and snow—and the sound people were having trouble capturing a consistent quality. There was no way around the weather—which was making Altman cranky and miserable. And not only did the director hate retakes, he hated dubbing, so he began to rationalize the imperfect sound.

Louis Lombardo was busy editing *Brewster* at Metro, and on weekends he would fly up to Vancouver and try to catch up on the filming. At one cast-and-crew bash, standing around and having drinks, Altman asked Lombardo how he liked what he was seeing at the dailies. Lombardo said he loved the visual element but the sound was "fucked." Altman complained, "Well, you haven't been up here suffering in the wind and rain and snow!" Lombardo said it didn't matter, the sound was still "fucked."

"He [Altman] stormed off into his bedroom, slammed the door, and never came out," says Lombardo. "I was trying to tell him the fucking sound is bad, and it still is bad. The sound was fucked, but he never changed it. I think he accomplished what he wanted to do with sound in *M*A*S*H*—where it was audible but it was overlapped. He did it well. But on *McCabe*, it was recorded in there—a dirty track, a muddy track. It was like trying to get an out-of-focus picture in focus. I think [it was] because he was just tired and wet and cold, a lot of things, and Bob doesn't like to do looping and dubbing."

Beatty got under Altman's skin as much as the weather. Beatty wanted to refine his characterization ad nauseum. The actor's very meticulous, very beautiful performance would emerge only from a long process of modification before and during filming—whereas Altman preferred to shoot scenes in a single take. This was a strength of Altman's, in that it had always enabled him to film swiftly and economically. But in situations such as this one, it threatened to become a weakness. It was so ingrained in Altman from Calvin days that the director could not conceive of proceeding more slowly.

Also, Altman's exploitation of younger personalities and unknowns has been touted both as a budgetary strategy and as a kind of creative courage, whereas in part it is actually a fear of big, self-confident stars like Beatty, who are always in some sense directing themselves (and the picture), and who can upstage the director. Beatty's presence in Vancouver was given an added measure of clout by his ex officio status as a producer of *McCabe*. When Beatty and Altman disagreed, it was a stalemate.*

"I think the Big Star got him a little bit," says editor Lombardo, "Wowed him, made him uptight. Usually, he was a fun fucking guy."

"Warren and Bob have totally opposed ways of filming," says Thompson. "Warren doesn't get warmed up until Take 20 or 30. Bob may like the first one. Remember the scene where Warren is alone in his room upstairs with a bottle—and he hits the bottle and it falls—and he catches it and pours himself another drink? And he's kind of talking to himself. . . . We got up to Take 20 or something, and Warren said, 'I'd like another one.' Bob said, 'I'll tell you what, Warren. I can't tell the difference anymore. I have what I like, and you obviously aren't satisfied. I'm going to take off—because I'm tired and have a full day tomorrow. I'm going to leave Tommy here, and you keep going until you're satisfied, then wrap it up.' So Bob said, 'Print seven and eleven, I'll see

---

*At one point, Beatty exercised his power by refusing to allow Altman to go to Houston for the premiere of *Brewster* in the Astrodome, with all the attendant hoopla, the press, and the parties. Beatty said he couldn't be sure Altman would be alert enough, come Monday morning, for filming. It was Beatty's way of letting Altman know who was boss.

Actually, Beatty did Altman a favor. The festive *Brewster* premiere, which was a contractual condition of the filmmakers' use of the Astrodome, was a notoriously snafu'd event. Altman has had so many of these dismal sneak previews in his career that one suspects a curse or an evil genie.

Houston's wealthy matrons bought one-hundred-dollar seats and wore bird costumes and were seated at tables on the playing field. The crowd of roughly twenty-four thousand was entertained by the not-well-known cast members blowing kisses as they emerged from limousines, and by an overlong recitation of the history of the Variety Club, which sponsored the spectacle. The world's press, flown in by MGM, viewed *Brewster* as projected on a 150-by-70-foot screen across a 500-foot playing field with the sound receding into the upper dome. This debacle, more than anything else, got *Brewster* off on the wrong foot with MGM, critics, and audiences.

you guys tomorrow,' and left. I said quiet on the set, roll 'em, action, and when Warren finished the scene, he said, 'I'd like another one, please.' We did another twenty, of which we printed two or three or four. That's kind of how it worked."

(The patient and professional Julie Christie would perform "each take over and over again," says Tewkesbury, "the same, only richer each time.")

Not only Tommy Thompson, but also Louis Lombardo (who also directed the second unit on *Brewster*), was doing some directing—filming much of the ending, the pursuit of McCabe during the blizzard, and the burning of the presbytery. Altman, meantime, was filming the hazy scene of Mrs. Miller (Christie) tripping out on opium. At one point, even Beatty took a camera crew and filmed something he fixated on—donkeys running through the snow. "It was certainly simpler than arguing with him [Beatty]," says Tewkesbury. "Why not?"*

The filming went on much too long, from Altman's point of view, from mid-October through January. The final days of photography were cold and tough, tension-filled. That is what Louis Lombardo stresses about *McCabe*, how it was so physically grinding, how the weather was depressing, and how Altman was so exhausted and wrought-up by the end.

A winter squall had given the director the idea of filming the stalking of McCabe during a snowstorm. Beatty warned Altman that the weather was fitful in Vancouver that time of year. And Beatty was right—it snowed erratically. It took forever to rig up the snow machines and finish the scenes. A lot of that snowfall is special effects in the cutting room. But even so, it is elegiac as filmed, the struggle against the forces of nature being part of the effect. There is virtually no dialogue (just shouts, groans, and muttering), and it is as if the

---

*No evidence yet as to whether a grip did any directing.

town were a miniature in a paperweight, shaken, turned upside down, filling up with whiteness and flakes.

It was while recuperating from the ordeal of Vancouver, in
Paris, that Altman had an idea for the music. Leonard Cohen
was a Montreal-born poet-novelist who turned to folksinging
in the Sixties. His debut album, *Songs of Leonard Cohen*,
had consoled Altman during the filming of *That Cold Day in
the Park*. Now, songs of romantic despair from that album
were recycled for the *McCabe* sound track.* The musical
numbers would become a connective in the storyline—like
the loudspeaker announcements in *M*A*S*H* or the or-
nithological digressions in *Brewster*.

The film is a visual banquet: If the sound, the weather, and
the script resisted him, here at least was Altman in absolute
command of the camera. One tends to remember the golden
soupiness of *McCabe* at the expense of the individual nug-
gets. Yet Altman served up many: that empty jug skittering
across a surface of ice; that sudden pull-back of Mrs. Miller
after an argument with McCabe; the recurrent floating cutaways to the town drunk (old friend Robert Fortier); the pre-
cipitous slow-mo death of Cowboy (Keith Carradine); that
final inscrutable extreme close-up of Mrs. Miller's porcelain
snuff bottle.

It helped Altman (and editor Lombardo) to have the central
character of *McCabe* as focus. Except for *Popeye* and to some
extent *Buffalo Bill and the Indians*, that was rarely the case
in Altman's "group" stories.

Indeed, there was a tremendous feeling in Altman—and in
Beatty, obviously—for the character of McCabe: in those
strange soliloquies; in that initial veiled confrontation be-

---

*At the time of the film's release, many critics excoriated the Leonard Cohen sound
track, which they considered too self-conscious and contemporary for a Western.
In its own way, Altman's choice was as courageous as having his son write the
M*A*S*H theme. One tends to forget how ingenious Altman has always been
musically, in his films—from having the cast write and perform their own songs in
Nashville, to the hauntingly repeated melody in *The Long Goodbye*, to employing
Harry Nilsson and Van Dyke Parks to score *Popeye*, and so on.

tween McCabe and Dog Butler (Hugh Millais),* the bounty hunter; in Beatty breaking down into tears ("I guess I never been this close to nobody before . . ."); in the anti-religiousness; in the love of gambling and "chippies"; in the hostility to big business and sham politics (as exemplified in the scene where Clement Samuels, the vain lawyer played by William Devane, emptily boasts of his ability to take on the zinc trust); and in the naive gambling with life.

The final prolonged stalking of McCabe through the snow is a classic in part because Altman has invested more emotion than usual in his lead character, and the audience has responded.

Here the director stuck in principle to the book. Author Naughton's luckless protagonist also cheats to win, shooting his enemies in the back one by one, only to die himself, finally. In the film, McCabe lies twitching and mounded in snow. Altman ends on this downbeat (the more personal the film for Altman, the more likely the ending will be downbeat); but it is interesting that instead of lingering on the corpse of McCabe, he cuts to Mrs. Miller, high on opium in a frontier den—a scene that is pure Altman, and not present in the novel—hypnotized, as the credits roll, by that decorative spinning snuff bottle.

McCabe, too, had a disastrous preview. The press screenings, on June 22, 1971, occurred simultaneously at Broadway's Criterion theatre in New York City and at the Academy theatre in Los Angeles. Warner's was rushing the release (Beatty's contract committed the studio to a summer date), but because the Technicolor lab in Hollywood was overbooked, it was a Canadian lab that had to hurriedly strike the first four prints. The color was off, and the sound

---

*Graeme Clifford supervised the casting, but Hugh Millais, who plays Dog Butler (and who also plays the imagined lover of Susannah York in *Images*), earned his role in most unusual fashion. The towering six-foot seven-inch Millais was spotted by *McCabe* author Edmund Naughton in Pamplona following the bulls. Naughton approached Millais and said, "Hey, you've got to be my Butler," and somehow Naughton's letter recommending his find was forwarded to Altman, who thought it was an interesting enough idea.

was virtually unintelligible. The deadline reviewers panned it fiercely (Metromedia's Rona Barrett was offended by its "obscenities"). Altman and coproducer David Foster went out and got very, very drunk.

It was one Altman film to rebound. Pauline Kael went on *The Dick Cavett Show* to urge viewers to see this "beautiful pipe dream of a movie," and the weekly critics, arriving in print, started the ground swell of acclaim. Spurred on by Kael, some reviewers—including the *Saturday Review* columnist Arthur Knight—went back to the movie a second time, to view a corrected release print, and they recanted their original negative opinions. "Half-heard," wrote Knight, "the film seemed blasphemous, and ultimately boring; with a proper sound track to illuminate Vilmos Zsigmond's rich, moody photography, it is funny, sad, touching, and curiously moral as well."

It is Altman's most poetic film. Both Beatty and Altman often seem irked by the fact that many critics consider it, respectively, far and away their best film.

Chapter

25

IMAGES

In 1972, *Images*, Altman's pet project since the mid-1960s, was finally filmed at Ardmore Studios and in and around a remote country house in County Wicklow, Ireland.*

---

*But like other Altman films that were filmed outside of the United States (think of *Beyond Therapy*, photographed in Paris), you would scarcely know it. Though the publicity emphasizes the quest for the proper setting, the Irish context is all but overlooked by the director. The cast is multinational— including a well-known British actress (Susannah York) whose character is married to René Auberjonois (American), and who is haunted by two lovers, Marcel Bozzuffi (French) and Hugh Millais (Canadian). Scenes of the landscape, while gorgeous, are transitory, and there is no Irish subtext. There are "American" phones, British cars, and vaguely European railroad stations, and so on. Critics have commented that this was Altman's attempt to dislocate the audience geographically, and force them to concentrate on the characters; but it was probably just Altman's typical disinterest in continuity.

The filmmaking group was limited to "Egg," Tommy Thompson, Vilmos Zsigmond, Leon Ericksen, John Williams, and Graeme Clifford. Altman had promised Clifford an editing slot if he ever filmed outside union (IA) dominion. (There was some rivalry between Lombardo and Clifford, and Altman played them off one other. There were some bad feelings after *McCabe*, and Lombardo had already decamped to Spain to edit *The Red Sun* for director Terence Young.)

At one time or another, nearly every studio in Hollywood had passed on this picture, which Altman had first "dreamed" several years earlier. Finally, it was Hemdale in Great Britain that came through with the $807,000 total financing.

Susannah York was an eleventh-hour inspiration to play Cathryn, "beautiful, privileged, and fragile as glass," according to the publicity notes, "who lives an affluent life in a dream cottage by a lake, who has fantasies and visions of schizophrenia, sexual guilt, and murder."

It was on an evening flight to Europe, on Aer Lingus, that Altman was struck by the presence, in an inferior film adaptation of *Jane Eyre*, of York, the blond, blue-eyed leading lady of the box-office hit *Tom Jones*, as well as *The Killing of Sister George* and *They Shoot Horses, Don't They?*

"When I read the script . . . I had never seen a film by Robert Altman," says Susannah York. "He had a sort of echo of legend about his name, but I didn't know anyone who had worked with him.

"The first time that he impinged on my consciousness, really, was on the eve of the day I was due to leave to go on a much-needed holiday with my husband to a Greek island. My agent rang up that afternoon and said, 'Robert Altman is in town, and he is interested in you playing the lead in his new film, *Images*.' I was leaving at the crack of dawn the next morning. I said, 'Look, I think I should read the script before I meet him.' But by the time the script arrived that evening, it was too late to meet with Robert Altman.

"I told my agent I would read the script on the journey

Women under the influence of the director: Cathryn (Susannah York) and Susannah (Cathryn Harrison), puzzling it out for themselves in *Images*, the first of Altman's dream-movies.

over, and I was given a telephone number to call Robert Altman in Los Angeles two or three days later.

"I vividly remember being in this noisy Greek cafe, where the only telephone in the village existed, trying to yell down the telephone in some sort of sensitive fashion that I had read his script but really didn't understand it at all. And I didn't feel that I could do it. Bob Altman said, 'I'll come over to Greece and see you for a couple of days, and we'll talk.' I was panic-struck at the idea of him coming all the way from L.A. to see me when I would surely say no. I begged him not to come. He took matters out of my hands and said, 'I'm coming.'"

With great trepidation she met Altman at the ferry in

Corfu and was confronted by this "large, generous, smiling, enormously benign, it seemed to me, man." For three days, they walked and talked together, discussing the script. Her objections included "that I simply didn't know what he was trying to get at. I felt embarrassed about saying that, because I thought that meant I was thick, but nevertheless I simply didn't. Also, the language, the vernacular, was totally American, and I didn't feel I could serve it well in any way."

The part of Cathryn was a gift for an actress in the sense that she was never off the screen. But York found the character "bloodless and undeveloped." She was not quite sure what it was she should be trying to project. "At times," she recalls, "there were emanations [in the character] of fear, or lust, or a sort of guile or wiliness, if I was reading her right. But I couldn't feel any essential heart or core. I'm just not the kind of actress who can play anything that I don't understand."

Altman was understanding.

"Look," she remembers him saying, "I don't depict my characters until I know them. I do broad outlines. I do a sketch. But until I've chosen my actors, I don't know what they're like. I don't really know what Cathryn is like, either. But I am looking for an actress who I feel the audience will not be bored by, that they can watch her, frame after frame.

"You will teach me Cathryn. You will help me find Cathryn out. She is a vacuum which you will have to totally fill."

"What about the Americanisms?" asked York.

"You will speak in your own tongue," replied Altman.

"What does she do all day? She can't just be a *wife*," persisted York.

"I don't know," said Altman. "What do you do all day, here on Corfu, while you are vacationing?"

York told the director about a children's book she was trying to write, called *In Search of the Unicorns*, a strange and magical tale of little people called UMS, who dwelled in caves and small stone houses. He asked her if he could read some of it. With reluctance, she let him read portions of an early draft.

"This is terrific!" Altman exclaimed afterward. "I want to use this. We'll have her writing a children's story, even though she herself doesn't have children. Because maybe she doesn't want to have children, or does she? That's for you to decide. . . ."

Now, in spite of herself, York began to get excited. She saw all the possibilities. She said yes.

"Of course you can't be with Bob for more than fifteen minutes without succumbing to his charm and to his geniality and to his generosity of spirit," she says. "For an actor of any kind, he's a particularly seductive director. Because he requires of them qualities, activities, and talents that they didn't know they have, or perhaps only dimly suspected. Anyway, [qualities] that aren't often tapped. That's probably the best thing you can get from a director—that he wants more of you than is normally asked. That absolutely captivated me."

Back in England, York went into London one day to drop off the manuscript of her children's book and to go in for a costume fitting for *Images*. Her doctor telephoned in the middle of the fitting to tell her that recent test results indicated she was pregnant. The reaction, because York had been trying to get pregnant for years without success, was shock— "partly pleasurable, partly terror." That evening, the actress rang Robert Altman and told him she was pregnant and would have to foresake *Images*.

"He said, 'Don't worry, that's wonderful [news],'" recalls York. " 'We'll make Cathryn pregnant. We'll use that ambivalence—about whether or not she wants children.' That's the kind of improviser Bob was. He made it all seem so simple. And that [becoming pregnant] also seemed to enter the strangeness of the film. I felt Cathryn growing in me, as the baby was."

In Ireland, the script was reworked nightly; and because York had such a demanding role, she became central to filling in the gaps of the dialogue and characterization in Altman's script.

"Usually after a day's work, we would all meet together— Hugh Millais, René Auberjonois, Marcel Bozzuffi, myself, Bob, and occasionally Cathryn Harrison," says York. "We'd meet for dinner, and we'd talk for three–four hours, and discuss, evolve, shape, and structure our scenes from bare lines. It was quite a bare script, originally. Our penny's worth was welcomed by Bob—more than penny's worth, *six-penny's worth*.

"Certainly I began to have very strong ideas about Cathryn. Cathryn and I seemed to be becoming one in many respects. But Bob drew from all of us, he wanted from us, actors love that, and we all responded. There was never any doubt that he was the master director, the master writer of the story, though he didn't necessarily put pen to paper at all during those sessions. Much more often, it would be me scribbling on a piece of paper. Or perhaps one of the others, at times."

Altman has said that, with *Images*, he wanted to make a Joseph Losey-type film. Losey was one of those few film directors, like Huston and Welles, whom Altman would admit to admiring. The Wisconsin-born director had been blacklisted, and he worked overseas, in England and France, after the early 1950s, honing his crystal-sharp dissections of bourgeois society. As it happens, Litto was still Losey's agent for U.S. matters, and when Litto flew to England to meet with Losey during the time when *Images* was being filmed, Altman screamed at him over the phone for not coming to Ireland to meet with *him*.

It was jealously of Losey, Litto thought.

Whereas Losey had the ability in his filmmaking "to digest the mores of a new environment" (David Thomson, *A Biographical Dictionary of Film*) wherever he roamed, Altman usually eschewed the social milieu and the landscape, and retreated to zones of the interior. In that respect, *Images* is the most personal and the most baffling of Altman's "dream-movies"—which one critic (Judith M. Kass, *Robert Altman: American Innovator*) has likened to "a fevered dream by someone who has been reading too much Lawrence Durrell."

Fevered dream, indeed. Strange voices taunt Cathryn on the telephone. Everywhere, amongst the mirrors, the glass and shiny objects, she encounters unsettling visions of herself. A former lover, killed in a plane crash, materializes to quarrel with her. Her mind confuses the identity of the dead lover and her husband. A surprise guest (Hugh Millais) and his teenage daughter (Cathryn Harrison) unhinge her further by their puzzling behavior. There are fantasy killings and stabbings, and in the end, a spasm of bloody business.

All of this, incidentally, filmed magnificently. Zsigmond's "black-and-white" photography, Leon Ericksen's Escher-influenced production design, the electronic noises and wind chimes of Japanese musician Stomu Yamash'ta—all contributed to the eerie, jagged mood. But if most critics appreciated the technical mastery, the consensus among them nonetheless was that *Images* was so elliptical as a story that Altman had never really answered Susannah York's original question as to what, if anything, the script did signify.*

Louis Lombardo says the key to *Images* is that the character of Cathryn is really a stand-in for Altman, more so than any other character in any other Altman film.

Graeme Clifford agrees: "That's the way Bob sees the world, sometimes, with several dimensions, or different levels of reality all at once. Sometimes it's very easy to lose track of who you are and to wake up one morning as if in a dream. Obviously, the things that occur in the movie did not happen to Bob. But I think Bob has a lot in common with the character in that the thoughts that occur, and the mixture of people and the relationships, [are] very close to the way Bob looks at things."

---

*An interesting sidelight is cast on the "subliminal sources" of *Images* by Altman's own publicity, which states that the director "has never known a woman like the one in his script." Nor, say the publicity notes, is the movie "in any sense autobiographical." But there is an intriguing mention of "a bizarre poem about mirrors" that Altman wrote when he was thirteen, "as a Jesuit school lad in Kansas City." *Hmmm.*

Susannah York says the meaning of *Images* has something to do with Altman's appreciation of women.

"He finds women fascinating and loves to work within that framework," York explains. "He understands men and can get to them much easier than he can get to a lady. It probably is frustrating. He puts all that attitude, that frustration, onto the screen, trying to find out, within that framework, what that lady is about.

"Now it's true that [in films like *Cold Day*, *Images*, *Three Women*, and *Jimmy Dean*, *Jimmy Dean*] he mostly depicts women in this manner—this difficult, suffering, searching quality. My feeling—I don't want to put words in his mouth, I'm only guessing—is that his experience of women is that they are more complex, more emotional, more demanding, and at the same time often more understanding creatures, in general, than men.

"In this very manly man, there is a strong feminine side. It's unusual in a man to have this kind of understanding and this seeking to understand. It's rare. Women, actresses, and other women, I'm sure, respond very much to this passionate curiosity, which is of course why he often draws out such extraordinary performances from women. He does that for men as well, but in women this attention is heightened.

"Because he has a passionate curiosity to understand women, he creates them on the screen, which is the medium that he knows, in order to be able to study them and also, in some way, to live in them and through them."

Even if the reception for *Images* among critics was somewhat negative, most filmgoers have never had a chance to judge it.* Hemdale pulled its advertising support, and the film was poorly distributed in the United States. Altman, in what was becoming a ritual tantrum, took to the pages of *Variety* to malign Hemdale and specifically (by name) John

---

*But not entirely negative, for every Altman film has its devotees. Judith Crist, for one, wrote that *Images* was "not only his finest film to date . . . but it is also one of the finest psychological thrillers ever made."

Daley, head of the show-business miniconglomerate. *Images* became yet another Altman film to die stillborn.

Altman could be consoled by Susannah York's prize as Best Actress at the annual Cannes Film Festival, for no one who sat through the film could fail to be impressed by her feral devotion to the riddles of the character.

Chapter
26

PURE ALTMAN

It would be pointless to defend *The Long Goodbye,* Altman's next film, from its detractors, those film noir and/or Raymond Chandler aficionados affronted by Altman's inverted contemporization of a pulp literary classic. Their point of view is fixed. Genre purists will never find consolation in an Altman film. But for the more iconoclastic, the more adventurous moviegoer, *The Long Goodbye* is a movie that will be savored through the generations.

By now it was clear what Altman was doing: reworking Hollywood motifs from the 1940s, the era in which he was banging around the film industry, on the outside looking in.

Whether it was armed forces comedies, murder mysteries, noir melodrama, or Westerns—Altman was turning a number of the eternal verities inside out. Again, synchronicity had a lot to do with it—the right properties just happened to be falling into his lap. But it was not accidental that, during the period immediately following his television indenture, Altman was reacting viscerally against conventional forms, both stylistically and in content.

The Long Goodbye came to Altman through Litto—via two producers, Jerry Bick and Elliott Kastner, who had commissioned a script from Leigh Brackett, the science-fiction writer and occasional scriptwriter who wrote the Bogart version of Raymond Chandler's *The Big Sleep*, directed by Howard Hawks, in 1946. Bick and Kastner had waved the script in front of old-timer Hawks, then in his seventies, and young-timer Peter Bogdanovich, either of whom would have taken a more classical approach. Robert Mitchum and Lee Marvin had been considered to portray cigarette-dangling tough-guy private eye Philip Marlowe. When Bogdanovich passed on it, he recommended as his successor, Altman, whom he admired.

Everyone has a different version as to how Elliott Gould came into the proposition. It may have been United Artists president David Picker's idea, partly as bait to entice Altman. It was casting against type, to put it mildly.

At the time, ironically, despite the big score of *M*A*S*H* early in his career, Gould was practically unbankable in Hollywood. After toiling for director Ingmar Bergman in the Swedish director's somber *The Touch* in 1971, Gould's career had run aground. His troubles had begun on the set of an offbeat comedy called *A Glimpse of Tiger*, where the rumors, even before the cameras rolled, had Gould bickering with co-star Kim Darby, exchanging blows with director Anthony Harvey, and freaked out on drugs, unreliable and absent. Warners pulled the plug on the film early in the production. Though Gould said he was a scapegoat for the production fiasco, everyone in the industry knew that Gould had had to pay the production forfeit—reportedly a million dollars. War-

Elliott Gould (who played Raymond Chandler's private-eye anti-hero Philip Marlowe), Altman, and director Mark Rydell (who played thug Marty Augustine) relaxing between takes on the set of *The Long Goodbye*.

ners, in fact, collected on an insurance policy that attested the actor was crazy. Thus, for *The Long Goodbye*, United Artists not only gave Gould the requisite physical before approving his contract, the studio also demanded a psychological exam to determine to its own satisfaction that the actor was mentally stable.

Gould was not the only implausible element of the casting. Rugged, gone-to-seed leading man Sterling Hayden, who rarely acted anymore, was set to play over-the-hill, boozing writer Roger Wade.* Nina van Pallandt, a European

---

*Hayden, after informing on his former political comrades to the House Committee on Un-American Activities in the early 1950s, had reneged publicly, after which he acted, in films, less and less frequently, and seemingly without enthusiasm. He lived for many years on a houseboat, guzzling alcohol and experimenting with drugs. He might be said to be playing a variation of himself in *The Long Goodbye*, even though Altman said, in interviews, the role was patterned more after Chandler himself—or after a certain empty-shelled type of writer like Irwin Shaw,

folksinger who had performed in cabarets with her second husband, a Danish baron, was cast as Wade's duplicitous wife. Baseball chronicler/New York Yankee pitcher Jim Bouton was to essay Marlowe's best friend, whose disappearance triggers the plot. *Laugh-In* comedian Henry Gibson was playing a quack doctor. And, because he said he wanted to study Altman's directorial methods, fellow director Mark Rydell came aboard as brutal gangster Marty Augustine. (When Rydell went back to directing, on the subsequent *Cinderella Liberty*, he took cinematographer Vilmos Zsigmond and production designer Leon Ericksen with him.)

Altman made some inspired technical choices as well: the score by John Williams consisted of recurrent versions of the title tune ("The Long Goodbye," by Johnny Mercer and John Williams); the cinematography was an experiment in first-person masters, the restless camera always in some kind of motion, the image diffused and sun-bleached. (Zsigmond won the National Society of Film Critics' award, for *The Long Goodbye*, as the year's best cinematographer).

Gould's Marlowe was light years from Bogey's. A man whose values are out of time, he is a social misfit. He has no one to talk to except his cat. He never changes his clothes (except for his shirt). There is deliberate time/space counterpoint in the character detail: Gould's Marlowe lives in the blissed-out California of the early 1970s (nude sunbathers loll on the balcony next door, where they dish up marijuana brownies); but his apartment is Forties-style, and he drives a 1948 Lincoln Continental.

At the end of the story, Gould's Marlowe takes a decided 1970s turn of vengeance. Altman (and adapter Leigh Brackett) surprised critics by having the detective character *kill* the friend who has been suckering him all along. (Bogey would never have done that.) It was a cold-blooded departure

---

James Jones, or Ernest Hemingway, at a time in their careers when the parade had passed them by.

"These people were all frustrated," Altman told an interviewer, "because they wondered what happened to themselves."

In any case, Hayden's is truly a magnificent performance, one that is more the anchor of the film, in a sense, than Gould's more oblique one.

from Chandler's novel, where the ending is inconclusive, but the Terry Lennox character is left alive.

In *In Manors and Alleys: A Casebook on the American Detective Film* (Greenwood Press, 1988), author Jon Tuska reports a discussion with screenwriter Brackett about the story changes from book to film, and about Altman's updating of the Chandler novel.

"The problems for me," Brackett told Tuska, "began with the plot. It broke down. You couldn't really translate it to the screen. It was hackneyed even when Chandler wrote it, riddled with clichés. The big decision we had was whether it should be done as a period piece or if we could update it. I felt we should update it. The Los Angeles Chandler wrote about was long gone; in a sense it never really existed outside of his imagination. Nor do people, even in movies, talk anymore the way they talk in a Chandler novel.

"Brian Hutton was supposed to be the director, but he got offered another picture. Bob Altman took over. Hutton had wanted Elliott Gould for the part of Marlowe. Elliott Kastner, our producer, went to United Artists and made the deal so Hutton could have Gould. Bob is a good director. But when he got on the picture, he had Elliott Gould and *The Long Goodbye*.

"I don't think they really go together," interjected Tuska.

"It's what we had though," Brackett continued. "Bob and I spent a lot of time talking over the plot, who'd done it, who lost what. I wrote one script, and then had to change the construction later. Bob wanted Marlowe to be a loser. I had to agree with him that all Chandler ever wrote had about it the feeling of a loser. . . .

"I met Chandler only once. I know he wanted Marlowe to be depicted as an honest man, and somebody who was his own man. I wanted to get that in the screenplay. But I also had to show Marlowe the way he looks to us now in the Seventies. The first script I had was too long. I shortened it, but the ending was inconclusive. I had Marlowe shooting Terry Lennox [Jim Bouton] at the end. It was the only way I could think to handle it. The alternative would be for him to just be a louse, to walk away from it. I didn't think that a moral ending. Hutton had wanted to end it this way."

"How did Bob Altman look at it?" Tuska asked.

"He wasn't so concerned about the ending as how we got there. He conceived of the film as a satire. Bob changed a lot of things. Nina van Pallandt was his idea as Mrs. Wade. So was Sterling Hayden as Wade. Bob didn't have too much choice. I wrote the part for Dan Blocker, but he died. So when Hayden was cast, the whole plot was thrown off base. The Malibu location was Bob's idea. So was Wade's suicide, walking into the ocean. I had written Blocker in as a large cowardly type who would strike his wife. A big man with nothing inside. When Bob came to do the scenes between Marlowe and Wade, he had Gould and Hayden ad-lib most of the dialogue.

"Whose idea was the scene where Mark Rydell rams the Coke bottle into his girlfriend's face?"

"Bob Altman's. That's pure Altman. So, really, is the Gould-Marlowe character. Bob built up his character from the bar and cat scenes. Gould isn't tough at all. He looks vulnerable. You have to work with what you have. Marlowe isn't what he was in *The Big Sleep*, but Elliott Gould isn't Humphrey Bogart."

"But," Tuska interposed, "when you've changed a character that much, what was the good of basing him on Marlowe at all?"

According to Tuska, Brackett sighed. "Because Marlowe, as Chandler saw him, would be unthinkable in the Seventies."

Though Altman told interviewers he was a Chandler enthusiast, he also told them he had never finished reading *The Long Goodbye*! "I read the end of the book and the beginning," he was quoted as saying, "but I didn't read it all the way through." He gave copies of *Raymond Chandler Speaking* to the cast and crew, and advised them to peruse Chandler's literary essays. As always with Altman, Chandler was not the point so much as the means to a certain end—

which was more the dead-eye satire of the genre, and of Hollywood in general.

"I think it's a goodbye to that genre—a genre that I don't think is going to be acceptable anymore," Altman told Tuska, discussing *The Long Goodbye* several years later on the set of *Three Women*. "There's also a lot of personal long goodbyes in it, making a film in Hollywood and about Hollywood, and about that kind of film. I doubt if I'll do that again."

Altman defended the savage scene in *The Long Goodbye* where the Mark Rydell character bashes a Coca-Cola bottle across the face of his pretty young mistress.*

"That was a calculating device. . . ." Altman told Tuska. "It was supposed to get the attention of the audience and remind them that, in spite of Marlowe, there is a real world out there, and it is a violent world. . . ."

Again, one feels from Altman an identification with Marlowe, a misfit in Hollywood, an underachiever, a loner betrayed by his friend. The theme of treachery aroused this director, intermittently consumed by paranoia about the constancy of his own circle. As he pointedly told Tuska: "Marlowe's biggest mistake was depending on friendships."

The Long Goodbye was previewed at the Tarrytown Conference Center in New York, where the viewing could be enhanced by food and drink and visiting celebrities. The special weekend was devoted to a retrospective of films featuring Chandler's private-eye hero, including *Murder, My Sweet*, with Dick Powell, and *The Big Sleep*. The gala was hosted by Judith Crist, then the movie critic of *New York* magazine and of NBC-TV's *Today Show*. Altman and Louis Lombardo flew in for the question-and-answer session. The screening had to be shifted to a shopping mall in Ossining to allow

---

*Pure Altman—a scene not unlike the degradation of Hot Lips, or the striptease of Sueleen Gay in *Nashville*.

room for some United Artists executives who were driving up from New York to assess the audience reaction.

In the *Saturday Review*, film critic Bruce Williamson reported that "Elliott Gould's portrayal of an inept, shuffling, unheroic Marlowe whose code of honor comes slowly unglued, surprised some people and irritated others. The characterization bore little relation to the wise-cracking private eye we had seen in five different movies within the past twenty-six hours. Among the departing patrons and noncommittal movie moguls, Mrs. Crist encountered writer-director Joseph L. Mankiewicz, who tersely summed up the film: 'Well, it's a goodbye to the Philip Marlowe legend, isn't it?'"

Ironically, the only thing the preview audience could find to be positive about was Nina van Pallandt. Many had chuckled when her name rolled up on the credits, knowing that she had been linked romantically, in press accounts, with writer Clifford Irving, who had forged a biography of reclusive billionaire Howard Hughes. But on camera van Pallandt was natural and unaffected, and even people who did not like the movie agreed she gave a credible performance. Otherwise, the mood at the discussion free-for-all was vaguely hostile. Altman, reported Williamson, admitted afterward that he was "depressed."

According to *The New York Times*, when the motion picture was released, initial receipts fell below fifteen thousand dollars at the prestigious Westwood theatres—and the take at Grauman's Chinese in Hollywood was considered "a major disappointment." The box-office receipts in Chicago, Philadelphia, and Miami were reported to be no better than Los Angeles.

The New York opening of the film was canceled at the last minute, after several advance screenings of the film had already been held for the press. Then the picture was abruptly withdrawn from release. There were rumors that *The Long Goodbye* would be reedited, drastically shortened, abandoned.

To its credit, United Artists did not waver in its support for the film and threw itself into a new release strategy. A novel ad campaign, months later, featured an illustration by *Mad* magazine artist Jack Davis showing Gould/Marlowe as a hip, slovenly detective with a pet cat, interacting on the set, in a series of cartoon panels, with Altman and other members of the cast.

The film did not receive much of a push in the smaller-city circuits, but in New York City it got a fresh lease on life. This bent detective story turned up on *The New York Time*'s year-end Ten Best list. Still, most people know it only by its notoriety, and as of this writing *The Long Good-bye* is not even available in video. (Nor are *Images, Thieves Like Us,* and *California Split*—all from this "golden period.")

Altman continued his dazzling string with *Thieves Like Us.*

This time his principal collaborator was Joan Tewkesbury. Born and raised in Southern California, Tewkesbury had been a child actress in films and at seventeen, Mary Martin's understudy in Jerome Robbins's Broadway production of *Peter Pan.* After dancing and choreographing for many years, she began directing and writing for the theatre. Hearing that Altman had enjoyed one of her plays, she phoned his secretary for an appointment, and said she was willing to do anything to learn the ropes of film production. She became the script supervisor on *McCabe,* quite a step down for such a show-business veteran, and evidence of her grit.

Soon she was writing her first screenplay, the unproduced, autobiographical *After Ever After,* about the breakup of her marriage. After Altman read it, he telephoned her during a stopover at the Kansas City airport to say that it was the best first screenplay he had ever read, adding that if he could not produce her script, perhaps she would write an adaptation of the novel that was slated as his next motion picture.

That book was Edward Anderson's 1937 novel *Thieves Like Us.* Again, the property had been channeled to Altman through Elliott Kastner and Jerry Bick, the producers of *The Long Goodbye,* who were making a specialty out of buying up and recycling Thirties and Forties story material. (Later, Kastner and Bick would produce two other Chandler adaptations, both starring Robert Mitchum—*Farewell My Lovely* in 1975 and *The Big Sleep* in 1978.) Litto was again the broker for *Thieves Like Us*, and the producer of record.

According to Tewkesbury, Altman had long had a yen for the book, and as far back as *McCabe and Mrs. Miller* he was talking about *Thieves*, and about how he was going to cast the principal roles. (At one point, Tewkesbury, who does play a cameo, was going to play Mattie.) Neither Tewkesbury nor Altman claim to be familiar with director Nicholas Ray's earlier version of the same novel, produced in 1948 and set in the 1940s, called *They Live by Night*. At least, they never discussed it. The Nicholas Ray version, with Farley Granger and Cathy O'Donnell as the doomed lovers, is more romanticized. Beginning with the casting of the two leads— "ordinary people" Keith Carradine and Shelly Duvall—Altman's approach was to be more ambient and authentic.

A draft of the script by Calder Willingham already existed, but Tewkesbury says she never read it. When she adapted the novel, she was already writing it to cast and location specificity, after which, as Altman himself has said, it was filmed as the director's "least revised script." Unlike *The Long Goodbye*, which was so bold an adaptation, the writer and director took pains to be faithful to the book. "Because," says Tewkesbury, "everything is there. The book is superb."

The tale is certainly grim. Three Southern chain-gang escapees team up for a spree of hit-and-run bank robberies. T-Dub (played by Bert Remsen), Chicamaw (John Schuck), and Bowie (Keith Carradine), objects of a manhunt, hole up with Dee Mobley (Tom Skerritt) and Keechie (Shelley Duvall), and later with Mattie (Louise Fletcher). Losers all, the trio of fugitives are betrayed by their friends and by their own foolish behavior. Ultimately, T-Dub is killed, Chicamaw is recaptured, and Bowie is fusilladed by a posse. His bloody, slow-motion death—as his sweetheart, Keechie, pregnant with his baby, gazes on in horror—climaxes the film.

Doomed lovers Bowie (Keith Carradine) and
Keechie (Shelley Duvall) in Altman's rendition
of Edward Anderson's Depression-era novel,
Thieves Like Us.

According to Tewkesbury, Altman insisted that Keechie
outlive Bowie at the end of the film, the one significant departure from the book. Producer Jerry Bick agreed with Altman that if Keechie died, the ending would be too much like
that of *Bonnie and Clyde.* And Altman, according to
Tewkesbury, "felt very strongly that if you wanted to make a
statement at all, it was that that kind of lady survived, that
the Matties survived, that the Keechies survived. Keechie

turned into Mattie. The boys got shot down, but that kind of hard, put-upon, embittered woman survived and sired a lot of us."

Another, more cinematic departure from the novel is the prevalence of Coca-Cola symbolism and the *Romeo and Juliet* radio commentary, background counterpoint to the Bowie-Keechie love story—which annoyed some film critics.

Tewkesbury was not so sure about the *Romeo and Juliet* angle either, but it was something Altman wanted. Perhaps the radio background was overused, she concedes. Altman, she says, felt strongly that the story was not just about cops and robbers. It was a psychological look at young love that starts out idealistically, as in *Romeo and Juliet*, and ends up in desperation and tragedy.

Altman's only other extrapolation, during the writing stages, was in a familiar area of concentration. The director paid an inordinate amount of attention to the family scenes of *Thieves Like Us*, says Tewkesbury, finding both "misery and joy" in their re-creation.

Tewkesbury fondly recalls the days spent driving around the state of Mississippi with Altman, Tommy Thompson, "Egg," Jerry Bick, George Litto, and the gentlemanly Thomas Hal Phillips, the representative of the state film board.

As they discovered new locales, she made "changes and transformations [in the script] in terms of what we were seeing, what would work and what wouldn't. The thing doesn't take shape until you have the sense of place. What he [Altman] taught me about any piece of material I write—a rewrite or anything—especially if I'm going to direct it—the most important thing is to get on the bus, go on the plane, in the car, go there, and feel what is going on."

Heavy rains and flooding, on location, forced occasional site changes, but in general it was one of Altman's most low-key and felicitous shoots.

Zsigmond's camera fee had soared too high (went the official explanation), so Altman conscripted the French photographer Jean Boffety for what turned out to be exquisite location work. Alan Rudolph was off working on his own screenplay ideas, and for the first time Scott Bushnell turned up, in charge of wardrobe and costumes. All of the cast members (apart from Carradine and Duvall, the others were Altman regulars: Bert Remsen and John Shuck in rare top-billed roles, and Tom Skerritt) were duly supplied with copies of the novel.

After the filming was completed, the men of the "talent trust" repaired to Missouri, where they went hunting in the country club blinds with B.C. It was one of the last gatherings of the tribe—Louis Lombardo, Bob Eggenweiler, Reza Badiyi, and others—and, as usual, they spent as much time playing cards as they did hunting quail. Altman was in an ebullient mood. He predicted Oscar nominations for Keith Carradine and Shelly Duvall.

There were no Oscar nominations. Nor were there box-office lines for such a quirky, resonant, antimelodrama. Though few people saw this perfect little jewel of a film in its limited release, film critics have kept its reputation alive with their praise.

In *Film Comment* at the time, Richard Corliss wrote:

"The film is a 'masterpiece' (to quote the first of three assertions Pauline Kael has made about the film) in the original sense of the word: the kind of work a medieval craftsman would submit to a guild for admission to the rank of master. It's textbook cinema at its best: self-contained but not confined, and full of understated, unexpected epiphanies. Precisely because *Thieves* is 'the most nearly flawless of Altman's films,' it is certainly NOT his 'most accessible.' What attracts the critics repels the spectators."

The sixth film in this productive period for Altman was a personal parable. Yet it too originated outside his company, and it had a long period of gestation under the sponsorship of Steven Spielberg.

The writer, Joseph Walsh, was an Easterner who had gone to Professional Children's School growing up as a boy in New York City (Elliott Gould was one of his classmates). Walsh had performed "live" television (*Danger, Philco Play-*

house, Studio One), and on the West Coast the boy lead in the film musical of *Hans Christian Andersen* with Danny Kaye, and in Israel the boy lead in *The Juggler* with Kirk Douglas. When Walsh returned to New York as a teenager, the stage work dried up, and he reached the awkward age of competing for more mature roles. Moving to Los Angeles, he was lucky to land two, maybe three television shows a year—including a *Combat*, though he never met Altman.

"I was really in nowhere land, and I basically didn't work for eleven years," says Walsh.

After sitting around in a bar one night getting loaded and complaining about unrealistic dialogue that actors were forced to utter, Walsh decided to write a script about his own gambling addiction. That was in 1971, and the script was the forerunner of *California Split*.

Initially, it was supposed to be directed by, of all people, Spielberg. The young director already had helmed the nerve-tingling telefilm *Duel*; still, this was before *Sugarland Express* and *Jaws*. Spielberg and Walsh were friends, and every day for nine months they would hash out the script. Spielberg was fascinated by the characters, and he had lots of hunches and suggestions. He himself would not so much write as *react* to what Walsh was writing. It was Spielberg's reactions that guided the final form.

"I don't know if Steven ever told me what to do—ever," says Walsh, "but when he didn't giggle like a little boy eating a cookie, saying 'This is great,' I knew something was wrong, and I always took that as a gauge and somehow I looked deeper into the scene."

At that time the script was called *Slide*. Spielberg and Walsh had a deal to film it at MGM under the James Aubrey regime. Walsh was attached as the producer very early on because he told his agent to tell interested parties that he would eat the script and spit it out between his teeth unless they let him produce it. His agent, Guy McElwaine, made it a condition of any deal.

MGM made some preposterous demands—the script had to come down to an exact number of pages, and Jack Haley

Bill (George Segal) and Charlie (Elliott Gould)
make their climactic roll of the dice in
California Split, a celebration/indictment of the
director's own pastime.

Jr. thought the whole story ought to be set at Circus Circus
in Las Vegas (which MGM owned); but Walsh finally extracted a go-ahead, and they were a month away from a start.

Then there was a shuffling of executives, and someone at
the top made the additional demand that it be a Mafia-re-
lated "sting" concept with Dean Martin as one of the two
main characters. Also, Walsh was out as producer. Take it or
leave it. Walsh left it.

"Well, of course, it was just too funny," says Walsh. "I
heard Hollywood stories before, but this was absolutely too
funny. I said this picture has nothing to do with the Mafia.
This story has nothing to do with outside pressure, it's all
about the pressure within themselves.

"This is a feeling for gambling. It's almost like what someone once said about having a helluva time before he realized he was an alcoholic. People have a good time as gamblers. They float. I like to gamble a little myself. You run on a high, and there's a tremendous run of excitement. You can't focus on anything—wife, family, children, anything. It's a roller-coaster ride, and you're heading up big, until you realize that if it keeps going on and on you are caught.

"I wanted the picture to be almost a celebration of the gambling, the joy of it, going along with it, and then, at the end, you could see where the trap comes in."

From MGM, Walsh and Spielberg retreated to Universal, where they had an agreement with Zanuck and Brown. Only, Spielberg chose to work on *Lucky Lady*, which he never did direct (Stanley Donen did). Walsh was disappointed. Meanwhile, Guy McElwaine got in touch with George Litto, and Altman was shown the script, which he loved. David Begelman, the new studio chief of Columbia, was a former agent who knew McElwaine. Actually, it was the first green light for Begelman ("a nice bit of trivia, his very first film decision was *California Split*—a gambling film," says Walsh).*

Walsh was still attached as producer. Being a first-time screenwriter himself, he did not know much about Altman's reputation for mauling writers. Because it took him a while to catch on, his ignorance was bliss. "All I knew was that Altman was a very big director at the time. And I liked some of his films, some I hadn't. But I always knew he had a real good feeling for that slice of life and for what was real, so I thought he would be great."

At their first meeting, at Lion's Gate, Altman warned him, "You know, I'm supposed to be your *mortal enemy. . . .*"

Walsh was thrown. "Why? What have I done?"

"Well," continued Altman, "you're a writer, and writers have a real thing against me."

Walsh asked, "For what?"

---

*Begelman eventually resigned from Columbia in disgrace, after revelations of embezzlement, juggled accounts, and forgery.

Altman said, "They seem to think I take their work and do what I want with it."

"Oh, do you?"

"I do what needs to be done."

"Okay," a puzzled Walsh responded.

At the final deal meeting at Columbia, "when the company pats you on the back and says 'go get 'em,'" (in Walsh's words), an equally bewildering conversation occurred.

"I remember the meeting specifically, because again, being very new, not knowing this history, all I knew was Begelman was saying to Bob, 'Bob, we *really* liked Joey's script. We *really* want this picture to be a very linear film.' I didn't know what that meant. Bob was saying, 'Fine, I like his script too.' I didn't realize that was the signal to him, 'Please don't go all over the place with it.' So I didn't know what the conversation was about.

"Afterward I went out to lunch with Bob and said, 'I guess they liked the script, that was nice of them.' It took me months of other people telling me, and experiencing this and that [to realize] that it could go off in certain directions."

Walsh was fiercely protective of his own material. He and Altman fought constantly over niceties in the script. To nettle him, Altman would complain about how much money Walsh was making on his contract, as opposed to Altman's. The famous director would tell the novice writer daunting anecdotes about how he had salvaged Ring Lardner Jr.'s script and improvised *M*A*S*H*. Walsh lost some ground, but hung in there.

"I would say if you are the writer and you could produce a picture with Bob, it would be a very good [situation if] you could be right there," says Walsh, "because Altman would come in and say, 'Oh, I would like for this scene, twenty-two clowns, three hookers, nine dwarfs, and whatever.' And this [scene] is supposed to be about a lonely man and one person in the bar. So I would say, 'Well, why would you do that, Bob? Because I don't see it? Why would you come up with that? That feels like off the top of your head. Let's go into it a little more because, let me tell you, it took me about two-

and-a-half months to construct this scene, it all ties together into the thing, and . . .'

"I don't know, maybe it was a plainness, a bluntness of honesty of how I would ask questions, but Bob would—*pout* would be a good word. I guess that he would pout a little bit on me. You know he actually stormed out of the room many times on me during the picture, during these conversations, but he would always come back and listen as I got to know him more. . . .

"Bob is really a guy who can't take restrictions. Restrictions of any kind. Just feels hemmed in by them. He's wonderful when he's gets enthusiastic. So if he's enthusiastic, if you question that, right away it's a damper to him. Some part of him doesn't want to listen to questions. Eventually, if you say something clearly and you're not fighting him—at any level—because I really wasn't fighting him—he *listens. . . .*"

According to Walsh, the only significant revisions before filming were in the background scenes. "I had seen Altman films before," says Walsh, "and what bothered me in Altman films was I used to see his background, and even though it was real there was always something comical about it. Sometimes it worked, sometimes it didn't. And I said that to Bob. I said, 'I want life going on in the background, especially for *California Split,* because we want this to be a slice of life, as real a feeling of this world as you're going to get, with the feeling of gambling. I have time right now, we don't start the film for a month, and I write fast. Can I write all the inner scenes that take place in the background?'

"So I wrote a full script of the inner scenes. In other words, instead of extras for the background, I wrote these wonderful three- or four-page scenes for good actors to come in and play them. Like the hooker in the bar being schnooked by someone in the background, or Elliott [Gould] and George [Segal] talking about the two guys who just punched them in the mouth, or the dialogue about Snow White and Dopey and Grumpy and the Seven Dwarfs, or the line in the paint store about 'twinkle blue.' There's a whole life going on in the background of the movie.

"We only got good actors, because they felt such a part of the film because the scene was such a great scene in an Altman film. Even though Bob would say to them, 'It's background,' he was always special with actors, and there was always a day or two given to them to film their scene by itself."

George Segal had been cast early in the discussions. Gould had been mentioned by Altman. But Walsh, though he was Gould's childhood friend, was holding back. They interviewed Peter Falk. They saw Robert De Niro. They saw other actors. They kept coming back to the idea of Gould.

Finally Gould telephoned Walsh from Germany, where he was working on a film, and told him, "Joey, you can't see me for [the character of] Charlie because you've been Charlie all your life, and I'm George to your Charlie—since we've been kids. You're the colorful one, and I'm the one who kind of went along as George. But to the outside world, *I'm Charlie*, I'm the crazy one."

Walsh recollects: "I said, 'My God, that's right,' and then when Altman said 'I want to go that way,' I said, 'I think that would be great.'"

On the set, says Walsh, it was Gould who seemed perfectly cast, full of vigor and confidence, whereas Segal was insecure and overwhelmed.

"Because Elliott *lived* his gambling," says Walsh, "he came out of the box just like in a horse race when a great horse comes out of the box. The first day of shooting, he was *there* as that character. He floated through that picture. After seven days, George Segal came to me and said, 'This guy's [Gould] unbelievable. He's an octopus. He is absolutely strangling me to death. I don't even know what to do.' The man was pleading for his life.

"I remember the one thing I said to George, which may have helped, because I had been an actor for twenty-five years before this. I said, 'George, understand one thing. Elliott has lived this life. I have lived it with him. Yes, he is coming out of the box unbelievably in this picture—I never saw a guy start faster—and if you try to keep up with him, you're going to die. Don't keep up with him—that's your character. Elliott's a vacuum, he'll sweep everything up and spit you out. That's his character. That's what he is going to do. Don't try to act with him, don't try to outdeal him. Don't try to do anything right now. Be off-base—just what you're feeling—and it's all working, George, because we have seen the first week of rushes, and it's all working."

The rest of the cast included Ann Prentiss and Gwen Welles as a couple of good-time gals, Bert Remsen as a transvestite customer, screenwriter Walsh as debt-collector Sparkie, and his brother, Edward Walsh, as Lew. In minor roles can be glimpsed Jeff Goldblum in his film debut, and John Considine, returning to the fold as a barroom Romeo. The poker players included the famous "Amarillo Slim" Preston and Thomas Hal Phillips. Barbara Ruik, John Williams's wife, played a small part as a Reno barmaid. (She died suddenly of a heart attack on location. The film is dedicated to her.)

It was the last round-up of the Sixties "talent trust." There was "Egg" and Tommy, Leon Ericksen, Louis Lombardo, Scott Bushnell moving into broader responsibilities, and Alan Rudolph, who was directing the extras and the background.* This was to be the first experimental use of the eight-track sound system, with Jim Webb, Chris Mc-Laughlin, and the rest of Altman's young sound crew aboard for the first time. The tracks are intended to be somewhat

---

*It was Altman's idea to employ members of Synanon, the rehabilitative organization of former convicts and addicts, as extras. This put him in further bad odor with the Extras Guild, which was fine with Altman. The man who had once been an extra himself, whose own wife was a former extra, hated professional extras. The Synanon organization received a flat sum payable to the organization, and they delivered as many people as necessary each day. They did not even require lunch. They played their "truth games" over the lunch hour, which would enthrall the rest of the cast and crew. "Screaming at each other, playing the 'truth game,' everybody would watch this," says Walsh. "But they were absolutely brilliant in the background."

Fools for love: George Segal and Gwen Welles in
Altman's cheerless *California Split*.

unclear, says Walsh, because "the world of gambling is a
din." Even so, sound mixer Webb nearly fainted from the
pressure on the first day of shooting. The effort to keep eight
separate channels clean and distinct drove everyone into a
state of anxiety.

Haskell Wexler had been approached to be the photogra-
pher, but Altman held out for a relative novice, Paul
Lohmann, who went on to photograph two other films for
Altman, *Nashville* and *Buffalo Bill and the Indians*.

"To me [hiring Lohmann] was a gamble," says Walsh, "because we were taking a new one, when we could have gotten

one of the real guys. When you make that first picture, you're a little protective. His [Altman's] argument was that he had an instinct. He said they could create a look together, and he might get into conflict with Haskell or other people about making it a little prettier than it should be. But with this new guy, he'd be listening to Bob a lot."

When it was all finished, Altman had one of his most impressionistic, and perversely cheerless, comedies, with a tough-tender chemistry between the two stars.

A fat, hairsprayed, throaty casino entertainer (Phyllis Shotwell) sings songs that underline the content of the scenes, and helps provide the narrative chain-link. But again, more is happening in the recesses than in the dead-center of the frame. Overheard conversations between marginal characters take place in the distance, while close-up conversations with the main characters are mumbly and indistinct. When Gwen Welles's character, a proverbial softie, clenches her eyes in anguish at a boxing match, the director cuts to a quick, poignant shot of the Mexican fighter in his corner, eyes forlorn and dull.

Screenwriter Walsh is not certain if Altman is more like the Bill (Segal) or Charlie (Elliott) character, but one suspects that the director saw himself in both men—for whom winning and losing had come to be beside the point. They are not especially nice characters (they play a nasty schoolboy joke on the transvestite "john" played by Bert Remsen); but you begin to care about them as you are swept up in their amusement ride of childishness and quick scams. Ultimately, they are addicts, and Altman's ending shows them as pathetic—for even after their big win in Reno, Bill has to admit: "Charlie, there was no special feeling. . . ."

Actually, this is one movie that made a bit of money for the studio—reportedly, over $5 million. Even so, it followed the pattern of previous Altman films and was prematurely pulled from the theatres and relegated to subrun.

And Walsh adds, "As the producer, I still have never received any money from it."

At least the film was critically lauded. *California Split* became the fifth Altman film in as many years to make *The New York Times* annual Ten Best list. Joseph Walsh received a Writers Guild nomination. And Spielberg came up to Walsh, at long last, and allowed as to how it turned out to be a truly exceptional film.

"I really saw how grudgingly he wanted to get that out," says Walsh." Remember, this was going to be Spielberg's picture, THE picture. This was a time when he wasn't making much in pictures. This is the one that really got to him. Steven said to me, 'It is good, but I would have made twenty-five, fifty million dollars with the picture.' Later on, after he had seen it three or four times, Steven said to me, 'The picture is much better than I thought it was. I had to see it again and again and again.'

"Steven would have built that last scene, that gambling scene, into one gigantic orgasm, climaxing the last forty pages of the script until you were on the edge of your seat. He would never have filmed it as loose [as Altman].

"He's a master at building it up, Steven is, whereas Altman comes from a whole different world. More of a European style. Steven could have manipulated that film into fifty million dollars at the box office, and that would have been exciting. But Steven knows it is a really special film. Yes, he might have made more money, but he didn't know if he could have made a better film."

Chapter

27

ACTION
PAINTER

Though the Academy of Motion Picture Arts and Sciences and most ordinary moviegoers remained oblivious to Altman, by 1975 the influential critics were aswarm—the European film critics (particularly the French and representatives of *Cahiers du Cinéma*, the seminal magazine of auteurism); the quotable critics from the glossy magazines; the most powerful daily newspaper reviewers; the alternative newspaper columnists; and the college critics. Even as the critics of *Time*, *The New York Times*, *The New Yorker*, and other periodicals were acclaiming Altman as the most brilliant director of his generation, his best movies were barely breaking even.

In an especially laudatory profile, a 1974 *Newsweek* article—in which "original" and "extraordinary" were the operative buzz words—compared Altman to the finest of the European directors, and hailed him as the ranking "action painter of American movies." "Action painting," according to one reference book about art, operates on the basic assumption that "the Unconscious will take over and produce a work of art." This was a view of himself ("action painter") that, if he did not prompt it himself in interviews, Altman certainly found to his liking.

There were some in the "talent trust" who felt that the director's ego was running amok as a result of all the flattering media.

"Anything, good or bad, that has to do with Bob, you can use his own quotes [to back it up]," says Tommy Thompson. "One of them is that 'The worst thing that can happen to a director in this business is to start reading your own publicity,' which a lot of that [after *M*A*S*H*] looked like."

As, in the years 1970 to 1975, Altman was moving toward the apex of *Nashville,* he was at the same time shedding the remnants of the "talent trust"—those people who had nurtured all of his best tendencies since the early 1960s. Only "Egg" and Tommy Thompson were to remain from the pre-*M*A*S*H* group, and they were the least purely creative, the most utilitarian of the "talent trust." "Egg" was profoundly loyal to Altman. Altman knew it, and consequently made him the director's whipping post on more than one occasion, because everyone knew that "Egg" would always come back. Thompson found himself outflanked by the newer and younger people, while trying to keep up the old standards in spite of the velocity of the filming.

"Most people stand in such awe of him that they would never bring up something they thought would be difficult," says Thompson. "We were shooting on *Thieves Like Us.* I went off somewhere to go to the loo. They were going to shoot in a practical location, an old general store with, of course, modern products nowadays. Set dressing and props

The nucleus of the "talent trust," fishing with Altman in Vancouver: (from left) production coordinator Robert Eggenweiler, editor and second-unit director Louis Lombardo, Altman, and producer/assistant director Tommy Thompson. Within the decade, they would no longer be on speaking terms with the director. (Tommy Thompson)

had gone in and dressed one whole side of this store for a shot. They didn't do a thing to the other side.

"While I was gone, Bob staged the whole thing on this other side, and nobody told him anything. 'That's where Bob Altman wants to do it—that's where we're going to do it.' The cameraman had put in some lighting already. He walked out with the rest of the crew behind him and the set people told me it was going to be another two and a half hours because Bob had staged it on the wrong side. I said, 'Bob, wait a minute, maybe nobody has told you, but this is the side that isn't dressed. It's got to be over here, a total reversal of what you're doing.' He said, 'Oh, why didn't someone tell me?' He staged the whole thing on [the dressed] side and we were out in an hour and a half."

Reza Badiyi and Barbara Turner were long gone, as friends and as collaborators. Altman went to their wedding, and he and Kathryn went to the occasional dinner party at their house; but the relationship was strained by Badiyi's success as a television director, and it was allowed to lapse. Turner had few other screen credits in her career as a scriptwriter, apart from that imposing one, *Petulia*.

Sarafian's name still drove Altman into a froth, and the director remained aloof from his sister and her husband. Brian McKay was another name the new-timers had never heard of, and if they had, they had better not mention it. Gone, too, were John Alonzo, Dan Fitzgerald, Danford B. Greene, John Williams, Vilmos Zsigmond, and others, each branching off into their own careers, having come to a parting of the ways with Altman.

Gone was Graeme Clifford. Gone was Leon Ericksen. Gone was Louis Lombardo, who told Altman after *California Split* that he was now ready to direct films. For twenty years, whenever Altman called, Lombardo had stopped whatever he was doing and gone to his Kansas City friend. Lombardo was crucial to everything Altman had done. Lombardo could direct the second unit; he could fix the generator if the power died; he could read Altman's mind in the editing room. But Lombardo refused to join the pre-production of *Nashville*.

Altman yelled at Lombardo and said he was not ready to be a director. Lombardo says the reviews had gone to Altman's head. It was not *fun* anymore. "He started getting cantankerous on *McCabe*," says Lombardo.

Some did not like Altman's predilection for lavish mind-tripping pranks. Some couldn't handle the drug scene and the party-down lifestyle. Not everyone could take it the way Altman could. Altman had tried opium on *Brewster* (it inspired the opiate ending of *McCabe*). He had a legendary capacity for drinking and doping and staying up all night, on his feet, talking everyone under the table. He insisted it did not affect his directing, or his behavior on the set; but it did affect those around him who did not have his stamina. At least one Hollywood "name," whose problem was reflected in the decline of his career, began his nightmarish descent into drug dalliance on an Altman set.

Gone, again and forever, was agent George Litto. It was Litto who had negotiated the two-picture deal at United Artists that was supposed to account for *Thieves Like Us* and something called *The Great Southern Amusement Company*. As for the latter, Altman, typically, loved the kernel of the idea—a country-and-western musical—but detested the script. He offered to do an original on the same theme. That hurdle was turned over to Joan Tewkesbury after *Thieves Like Us*, and she began to work on the script of *Nashville* during the filming of *California Split*. Litto was supposed to have been the producer of *Nashville* too.

Litto and Altman had quarreled when the director insisted on an assassination at the end of the film story of *Nashville*. Then, when Altman announced that the cast members would write their own songs, Litto, something of a musical purist, felt he had to get off the ship. It was just an excuse— but Litto was looking for an excuse.

"By *Brewster* he'd [Altman] read all the fantastic reviews and the press and the adulation," says Litto, "and he had gone to Paris where it was the biggest box-office picture. People made him so important. It started with $M*A*S*H$. People talk about the [television] series . . . even though the series was an enormous success, it was nothing compared to that picture. Let's face it, that picture moved mountains. It was a giant. And people made him [out to be] a genius.

"The last fun we had was *Brewster McCloud*, which I loved. It started to go sour with *McCabe*.

"Bob liked people to carry his bags, okay?" continues Litto. "And that is why, in my opinion, he never realized his true ability. When he had Brian McKay, Louis Lombardo, Leon Ericksen, the editors Danny Greene and the others, the cameramen Vilmos [Zsigmond] and Laszlo [Kovacs] and Reza

[Badiyi], the writers, the creative people—he was very open. It was a very creative period before he made it big. And that got to be less and less, because he got more isolated and more dictatorial. Eventually, he didn't want to deal with their strong personalities. Or my own strong personality, mmm?

"He just wanted people who would go into a screening room and ass-kiss him. The people who wanted to stay with him, the hangers-on, told him anything he wanted to hear. Vilmos, Louis, Brian, Danny Greene, Reza, etc.—these were all contributing guys. These were the people that helped form the period and what Bob Altman did and made. And one by one they all disappeared, didn't they? They got stifled by the overwhelming adoration of people who could contribute nothing."

The journalists reporting from an Altman set rhapsodized about the groovy and carefree atmosphere. The old guard remembered how much of a give-and-take had once preceded the actual filming. The press found magnanimity and the "beneficient monarchy" of a director with a luminous presence (Altman began to prefer that term, "beneficient monarchy," to the old collective pretense). The people who had known Altman longer found less self-deprecating humor, less grace, less trust, in the director.

"There was always that twinkle in his eye," says Litto. "He was a kid with a twinkle in his eye. One day I said to him, 'You know I'm not having fun with you anymore, and I just figured out why. Because you lost your fucking sense of humor.' And I walked out. He wasn't fun anymore. He took himself seriously. He started worrying about his subconscious instead of having fun."

That "action painter" pose was a particular burr to the old Westwood group, who view the contributions of certain individuals as crucial to any specific Altman film, and in general, to Altman's progress as a director. Almost to a person, they believe that whatever is in Altman's subconscious is buried there, deep and out of grasp; that he works very much on the surface—from available people and resources. The subconscious emerges almost *in spite of* Altman.

"Bob would like people to think he works out of his subconscious," says Litto. "No. He's clever, he's creative, he's manipulative, but he's not working out of his subconscious. He's not Truffaut, and he's not Bergman. I don't think you can dissect and disconnect a man from his work completely, but I think when we talk about a creative person working from his subconscious, we mean something very specific. And I don't think Bob Altman is doing that. I think in his conscious mind he has a feeling and a perception for what makes good ideas and interesting films, and he's going for that. But he's not, shall we say, Picasso."

The internal dynamics of the Lion's Gate group had changed. In the Sixties, though everyone in the "talent trust" was deferential to Altman, there was an implied equality. There was a sort of communalism. "It was the Three Musketeers," says Brian McKay. "All for one, one for all."

They were all aiming for the best possible result. "We were really all driving toward the same thing," says Danforth B. Greene, "to get a supreme product."

"You don't know how good it felt in the past when you brought something to Bob, and even if it was just the germ of an idea, when he recognized it and ran with it, you as the bearer of that idea to him, you felt blessed," says Reza Badiyi. "He lets you feel that way. So being with him, working with him, as a writer or in any production capacity, is good.

"And it's very hard, after all that, when he turns around and cuts the cord of friendship and the avenues of relationship that quickly. And he's not bothered by that. That again is a gift—that he can walk away. I don't think he is troubled, because no one can shoulder that much trouble and that much of a burden."

Now, there was no longer the equivalent of a "talent trust." The people surrounding Altman were more ad hoc, more transitory, more of a "coterie." He hated the word, but that was what it had become, to some extent—a "coterie."

As Altman's ego was skyrocketing, so was the paranoia factor. In her report from the *McCabe* set, Aljean Harmetz of *The New York Times* was plainly describing an Us vs. Them mentality. But with the departure of the "talent trust," it was more a matter of Me vs. Them, and are you *with* Me or *against* Me?

There was often painful, open hostility when someone associated with Altman left the circle without his blessing. There would be a screaming session, a nasty exchange of letters or phone calls, years of charged silence. Embarrassing, often pointed accusations were thrown around, with the director going for the jugular.

It was not unlike that scene in *A Wedding* where both matrimonial families believe that the bride and the groom have died in a car crash, and suddenly the exchange between them turns rotten. "He wanted people [in the scene] to say things they couldn't take back," says John Considine, the co-writer of the script. "I had experienced that with him. I'd been awestruck by it, so I understood exactly what he meant. That was a scene that he read and said, 'Yeah.' He understood perfectly."

Ironically, that same ability to "accuse" so viciously, to penetrate so thoroughly the defenses of one of his friends, also served as a positive aspect of his directorial genius—the capacity to search out the depths of a characterization.

"Bob has such great insights," says Tommy Thompson, "which is what makes him so popular with actors. He can analyze a character right down to a nub, which he does with everything he directs. But unfortunately, he does it with everyone, and sometimes that becomes a dangerous tool, because you can hit right to the quick and hurt someone. And he's very capable of doing that. You champion his friendship to such a degree that if and when he ever says anything, god, you are just crushed, crushed.

"It is such a poison barb that you can't get it out. It is almost as if he were the analyst and you had been in analysis

for fifteen years and suddenly the analyst turns on you. And
god, he just knew every point to hit."

It was petty, what he sometimes said to them, though Altman knew that it would strike deep. To Reza Badiyi he said,
"You're as bad as Ray Wagner!" To Robert Ridgeley, Altman
said, "You will never mean half of what John T. Kelley
meant to me!" Ridgeley, who had loved Altman as a brother,
knew it was ludicrous (especially considering what had happened between Kelley and Altman), but it bothered him just
the same. The ones who stayed on in the group the longest
heard the worst comments about the ones who had departed.
Altman was always undercutting them to each other.

In the old days, the circle would congregate. If the discussion was filtered through Altman, it was subtle. "He would
hear and isolate—he had the most acute hearing—and he
never lost things in a general discussion," says Tommy
Thompson. "But Bob never sat in a chair with everyone else
on the floor."

But with *M*A*S*H* and the "anti" movies, there was an
influx of students, buffs, and journalists. There were newcomers that the old-timers felt were there primarily to ride
on Altman's coattails, to feed off his prestige, and not to
strive for the "supreme product." Now, Altman *might* sit on
a chair with everyone else on the floor. Now, if his head
were to droop into the *Albondigas* soup, the party would be
over. Now, it was more of a sycophantic thing.

"We used to have rap sessions every night. . . ," says
Thompson. "The bar would open up about five o'clock. Anybody who was in town [Los Angeles] would call up or drive
up. There were great sessions going on. If there weren't a lot
of people there, there'd be just a few—you'd kick up your
feet and talk. And it was terrific.

"A lot of stuff, and I think Bob would agree, I feel, came
out of those sessions. Somebody would come in and say,
'Jesus, we just did something . . .' and that would send the
conversation off. And it always pointed toward movies."

Now, with Altman always looking over his shoulder and

looking toward his best publicity, that after-hours group was increasingly "by invitation only." It had always been a clubby atmosphere, but now the director wanted the club members to be more pliant and servile. Many of the new people *were* more pliant and servile. A number of them were ten or twenty or thirty years younger than the director, without portfolio or maturity. They fed into his "anti-Hollywood" posturing. They did not always bring out the best in him.

More and more, they were there to keep Altman buoyant, especially at night, when the director drank and extemporized and grew contrary. And they were there to keep him afloat toward the end of a particular film, when the director grew insufferably bored. The boredom is one of the reasons why the endings of his films began to seem so makeshift or illogical.

Altman had less of a perspective outside himself.* No longer did he have those six or eight or a dozen people of his peer generation to bounce off of. No wonder he "dreamed" movies, for the movies were increasingly dependent on his id, and increasingly springing out of his isolation.

He seemed to relish the isolation as part of his mystique. Altman said in one interview that, apart from filming, he nowadays rarely left the confines of his limousine, his office, or his home. He no longer knew where the best new L.A.

---

*Kathryn Reed Altman tells a story that, even if apocryphal, makes a point about her husband's isolation from the mainstream of American culture.

It seems Altman's son and Bob Dylan's son were on the same Little League baseball team in Malibu. Kathryn was a fan of Dylan's—and always on the lookout for a glimpse of the legendary singer-songwriter—though Altman seemed disinterested. One weekend, when they were at a game, Kathryn spotted Dylan, elbowed her husband, and insisted that he go over and introduce himself. Hemming and hawing, protesting, Altman shuffled over, took off his hat, and said, "Mr. Dylan, I am Robert Altman the movie director, and I am pleased to meet you." Dylan looked up without any expression of recognition. "I must apologize," continued Altman, somewhat miffed, "but I have not yet read the script that you and your wife sent me. . . ."

Back at Kathryn's side, Altman gave her a report of Dylan's unfriendly demeanor—which is when she realized that her husband had mistaken Bob Dylan, the living musical legend, for Robert Dillon the Hollywood screenwriter. Altman had not recognized Dylan, and Dylan had not recognized Altman. Two of the great cultural icons of the baby-boom generation had met and come away none the wiser.

Writer Joan Tewkesbury, on the Parthenon set of
Nashville, with Altman. Along with Alan
Rudolph, Tewkesbury was the most promising
of the "next generation," and helped shape the
transition years beginning with her adaptation of
Thieves Like Us. (Photo by Diane Michener)

restaurants were (he only knew the old haunts). No matter
where he was living, it was as if he were living strictly
within the parameters of his own psychology, of his daily
errands, of whatever film he happened to be working on.

He rarely saw other director's movies—saying he had neither the time nor the inclination. He also said, "I don't have
time to read." But he was incredible at picking things out of

the air, just from glancing through newspapers or watching TV, knowing and understanding issues as if he had researched them.

"The thing is," says Tewkesbury, "Bob may not read now, but he did as a child and in school, and he's got one of those minds that when he does read, it's like a steel trap—he's got it for the rest of his life. Also, there is a side of him that likes to say he doesn't read books even when he is reading books.

"But during the period of *McCabe, Thieves, Long Goodbye, California Split,* and *Nashville,* the years that I was with him when there was nonstop activity in the company, I don't think he had much time to read. . . . "

Yet it must also be said that by ridding himself of the baggage of the "talent trust," one way or another, Altman was challenging himself to move in new directions, to take on new collaborators, and to evolve as a filmmaker.

By 1975, the transition team was already in place: Tewkesbury, Alan Rudolph, and Scott Bushnell, whose internal power was growing; the sound people—increasingly important to Altman's approach at this stage—Jim Webb, Chris McLaughlin, and Richard Portman; and editors Dennis Hill and (Louis Lombardo's son) Tony Lombardo, both of them trained by Lombardo. Moreover, John Considine was back in the company; and with the production of *Nashville,* Altman picked up the multitalented Allan Nicholls. Patricia Resnick, Paul Dooley, and Frank Barhydt Jr. all came shortly thereafter.

Writer Joan Tewkesbury, or "Tewkes," as she was known affectionately by the men of the "talent trust," was considered one of the gang, as was assistant director Alan Rudolph. They were both from a show-business background—"Tewkes" from dance, theatre, and Broadway; and Rudolph was the son of Oscar Rudolph, a career television director. "Tewkes" had originally come to Altman through the recommendation of Michael Murphy, and Rudolph had been hired by Tommy Thompson.

Beyond that, they were sweet-natured individuals, funny, bohemian, and unpretentious, definitely on the side of the angels. Both had minds of their own as well as a love and devotion to Altman, and Tewkesbury and Rudloph would be central to the momentum of Lion's Gate for the next several years.

Chapter

28

NASHVILLE

As Louis Lombardo was concluding post-production of *California Split* in June of 1974, Altman flew to Kansas City to attend the funeral of his mother. Lombardo remembers being surprised that it affected Altman so deeply, Helen's death—much more deeply, he says, than the passing away of B.C. a few years later, in 1978. Altman's dread of hospitals and illness was now made real by events.

Altman and Sarafian crossed paths there, as they occasionally did at a family gathering. Sarafian was attending the sorrowful occasion with Joan Altman, his wife. It was, for once, a subdued, reflective Altman he encountered. The director was neither combative nor bait-ing. The three of them, Sarafian, Altman, and Joan, stayed up nearly all night before the services playing a tournament of their favorite game, backgammon.

Altman was, as ever, very quick, quite clever, and he had some very aggressive moves on the board, remembers Sarafian. The director outpaced his brother-in-law early in the evening. Joan played exceedingly well. But the night was a long one and Sarafian, by dint of patience and some cunning maneuvers of his own, began to counter Altman and to equal him in the scoring. For a brief time, there was again a conviviality between the three of them. Afterward, Altman did an unusual thing: He crawled into bed next to B.C. and fell asleep.

"That was a very personal, a very lovely gesture," remembers Sarafian.

Apart from the funeral, Altman seemed preoccupied about the next movie he was directing. United Artists, which had a hold on the script of *Nashville*, had not come forward with the financial guarantees. At the last minute, ABC had come up with the needed budget on the theory that its record company could market the sound track. From Kansas City, Altman was flying to the country-and-western capital. But the director told Sarafian that, although he had a good script, he was not yet sure what the movie was going to be about.

There is no simple explanation for the blessed zenith of *Nashville* in Altman's career. It came at a personal and career crossroads, certainly. It was highly dependent on the moment. It was, in the filming, some kind of exalted circus with Altman as ringmaster.

Being an auteur is not always a question of being the writer (the screenplay of *Nashville* is credited singly to Joan Tewkesbury), or even of having a precise, preconceived grip on how the film will eventually turn out. Sometimes it is just a question of making incremental decisions all day long, for weeks and months, during the planning, photography, and postproduction of a motion picture—the makeup and

Opal (Geraldine Chaplin), Altman's alter ego, as the interviewing journalist of *Nashville*. She helped write her own disconcerting monologues.

wardrobe choices, the design and camera selections, the dialogue and story turns, the major and the minute decisions that add up, somehow or other, to the intrinsic whole.

In one sense, *Nashville* is the least Altmanesque film, as well as the preeminent Altman film. That is to say, it differs radically from his other films, which are either more cartoonish or dream-influenced. It stands apart as the most expansive, the most organic, the most egalitarian, the most *grassroots*, of all his films—a reflection not so much of the director as of the collective filmmaking that, as a process under his aegis, here reached its peak.*

Not only did Altman have Joan Tewkesbury as his writer, he had Alan Rudolph as his assistant director. "Egg" and Tommy Thompson and Scott Bushnell were all in full throttle, Thomas Hal Phillips was coordinating the political signals, the young and unorthodox Richard Baskin was musical supervisor—and the cast was simply spectacular. Partly because of the unwieldy nature of the shoot, the top creative lieutenants had more freedom, under Altman, than before or since. And it shows.

But while they presented the filmmaking options, it was up to Altman to shoot the rapids. By 1975, the director had traveled a long road in his career, and he had achieved a temporary equilibrium, in his personality and in the working process, of the artistic and the commercial, of the narrative thread and the governing idea, of the funny bone and the dramatic impulse, of darkness and light. He was ready for the challenge he presented himself. Altman has directed other great movies, but *Nashville* is the one he will always be measured against: a once-in-a-lifetime gambler's jackpot.

The springboard was *The Great Southern Amusement Company*. But Altman has said that *Nashville* also touched on one of the many script ideas he was toying with in the Sixties: "One of [these unproduced treatments] was about four strangers, two men and two women, who were all taking a yoga class. The film would follow each of their separate lives outside the class and crosscut between them. Since the whole point of yoga is to become aware of yourself and not be aware of the people around you, none of them ever actually met. By the end of the film, you would have the feeling that if they had known each other, they could have solved each other's problems."

---

*Tewkesbury has made the interesting comment that it was always her dream "to do something buoyant as a collective, exploring something darkly," and that at the time she believed it was Altman's dream too. Long after the *Nashville* experience, she found herself wondering if that dream was not just as much a projection of everyone surrounding the director.

Altman told *New York Times* writer Tom Wicker in an interview that he was also inspired by William Price Fox's novel about the country music scene, *Ruby Red*, at least to the extent that someone told him about the novel and about one of its featured characters, a fading country music star. The person remarked that that was an inherent flaw in the novel, since country music celebrities do not really fade from the limelight. Altman thought about it and decided that that was true. Country-and-western luminaries don't fade any more than "saints in a church" (Wicker's words, quoting Altman), and the lyrics of their songs can be about as irrelevant as political speeches.*

When Joan Tewkesbury was assigned to write the screenplay, typically Altman gave her very little guidance. Tewkesbury had never spent any time in the country music capital. Her first trip to Nashville was one of those V.I.P. affairs during which she soaked up some atmosphere but felt no wiser for the experience. Then she went back as an ordinary person, a tourist, and spent a number of days getting on and off sightseeing buses, visiting the shrines, and mingling with the folk. That is when she began to develop the script in a populist direction.

In the end, she devised an ambitious dramatic screenplay about the famous somebodys crossing paths with the lowly nobodys in a city of dreams and illusions—a script that was never to change in essence, though it changed vastly in particulars. For one thing, the Watergate break-in and cover-ups had broken wide open in the headlines, and that—Nixon's scandal—dominated Altman's thinking. Altman may have ignored Vietnam when he directed *M*A*S*H*, but he was not going to ignore Nixon while filming *Nashville*. Altman insisted that Tewkesbury's sixteen characters be upped by eight—and he insisted on a political subcurrent.

According to Tewkesbury, Altman felt deeply about

---

*Not that Altman admitted to actually reading *Ruby Red*. Incidentally, his "yoga script" from the Sixties sounds suspiciously like a forerunner of *Health* and *Beyond Therapy* in its skepticism about self-help and feel-good therapy.

Nixon, and viewed *Nashville*, partly, as an opportunity to make a statement about American politics and about politicians like him. "Part of *Nashville* was because he hated what Richard Nixon was doing to the country," says Tewkesbury. "I'll never forget the image—when we were walking down the street the morning after Nixon had been elected again [in 1972]. There had been a huge windstorm the night before, and all of these umbrellas were turned inside out. And he said, 'The world is mourning. We've lost because Nixon has won.' He was really angry about that."

Altman also insisted on an assassination at the end of the storyline. The ritual killing had become a pattern in the climaxes of his films: the stabbings of *Cold Day* and *Images*, the martyrdoms of *Brewster* and *McCabe*, the gunning-down of Bowie in *Thieves Like Us*, Marlowe's shooting of his pal in *The Long Goodbye*. Some critics saw in this syndrome a kind of Catholic crucifixion of the protagonist; others, simply tried-and-true dramatics. (Tewkesbury, in one interview, said it may be that each film, for Altman, symbolized a lifetime, and that each death was for him an exorcism, a way of terminating that film's lifetime.)

Though Tewkesbury never had any appetite for the assassination—it is a bitter pill for many audience members, also—she wrote the scene. This assassination, Altman stipulated, was to be of one of the female country stars, intriguingly, a "mother figure."

"It wasn't in my first draft," she told *American Film* magazine, "but Altman felt very strongly about it, since we had just lived through those times. Bob felt that people never assassinate movie stars. They never assassinate anybody but politicians or heads of government, and the lowest thing you could do would be to assassinate this mother figure, this lady. So I redrafted the script with the assassination in mind, which gave it a harder edge and added a lot of other characters.

"I don't like it a lot," she added. "I think it's a very negative statement, but one can't deny the impact of it, the truth of it. But I love the film, and I wanted to see that film through, so you bet I wrote the assassination. I wrote it the best way I could, and the best way I could was to forget the judgment of 'assassination' and trace why someone would do that. . . ."

Like a doctor who always diagnoses his specialty, Altman always tuned in to the currents in the news that confirmed his instincts. The filming happened to coincide with the assassination of South Korean President Chung Hee Park and his wife, and the director was riveted by the on-the-scene network coverage of the spectacle.

"I know just how I'm going to shoot that final scene now," cooed Altman to a reporter on the scene. "I know just how to do it. Park was speaking at a podium when the shots went off. He ducked, and she got hit. Yeah, oh, they carried her out with her feet up, the whole thing. But the guys filming it, they zoomed in . . . and then back, and pointed here and there and all over. 'There's a shooting!' 'Where?' The whole place was in absolute pandemonium. That's just how to shoot a scene."

That is exactly how Altman did film it: very much like news bulletin footage, quick-cutting, hand-jittery, chaotic. In a first viewing of the film, the assassination seems to explode out of nowhere, the premonitions are so recessive, so few. But if you see the film more than once, you notice Altman's camera linger on the violin case carried by the walking time bomb, Kenny Fraiser (David Hayward). You realize how Kenny's presence at key moments is not in the least accidental, that he is stalking someone, that he is discomfited by his relationship with his mother and with women, that he is able to transpose his churning hatred to a female country-music idol. You see how he is Mark David Chapman personified.[*]

The characters of Kenny and the soldier, Pfc. Glenn Kelly (Scott Glenn), are almost interchangeable, and it is the soldier, an emblem of the Vietnam War, that you half-expect to

---

[*]But of course this was several years before Mark David Chapman assassinated former Beatle John Lennon—which makes *Nashville* look positively prescient.

unravel. It was Tewkesbury who decided that the assassin was going to be Kenny instead, which developed in the writing. Ironically, the seemingly quiet and respectful Kenny was originally based, says Tewkesbury, on Keith Carradine, "one of the most genuinely kind human beings I think I've ever known in my life."

When she informed Altman of her choice, he responded, "That's [Kenny] the only nice person in the script." Tewkesbury told Altman: "That's right. Let's examine that nice person. I see you're going to go for it. Let's really go for it here."

That seems to have been the strategy in general, for Tewkesbury. Believing that most actors will bring you their "best behavior" in a characterization, she chose to write the "underbelly," she says, "because I figure that between my underbelly and their best behavior we are going to come out with a human being who's real. If I write best behavior and somebody is afraid to show me any underbelly at all, I'm not going to get much except what you see on television, which is a kind of a slick cartoon. So I will usually go for the murky . . . the complex.

"I tend to go into all the dark corners or turn over rocks to find out what the underpinnings are. The actor helps me when he comes to the material and simply brings his own sunshine, which Lily Tomlin did. So that her phone call scenes, instead of being quite so desperate, became things of wonder. It seemed important, for every good or bad act of every character, to include an opposite action for balance."

The revised 176-page script (the rule of thumb is, a script films at roughly a minute a page), which went to actors in January 1974, was superabundant with detail. It reported extensive character background, provided minutiae for the art director and the cinematographer, and information about the milieu. Later, Alan Rudolph—quite the unsung hero of *Nashville*—went through and created what is known as the shooting script, stripping it down, paring the dialogue, and giving short descriptions of the action. Then Tewkesbury revised it yet again.

It was down to the 120-page shooting script by the time most of the cast arrived in Nashville in June 1975. The first thing the cast and crew did was go on a bus tour of locations, just like regular people.

As befits a movie with twenty-four billed characters, the storyline of *Nashville* is extremely interwoven and cannot be easily synopsized. It is many stories, not one—a film of high central drama as well as one of many peripheral moments—"a single story," in Tewkesbury's words, "without ever telling a single story."

By critics, who are forced by profession to encapsulate, it was dubbed "24 characters in search of a movie," "Grand Ole Soap Opry," "M*A*S*Hville," and other glib verbal takes to indicate that it is a mishmash of genres with much that is quintessentially Altmanesque thrown in. Half the personalities never encounter the other half; half have nothing to do with the primary story thread, which involves the efforts of an underhanded political advance man to persuade country-and-music Western stars to endorse his candidate by their appearance at a rally at Nashville's Parthenon replica. It is not really a plot movie—though it has plot—and not really a character study. It is more like a "group portrait" that is also a pseudo-travelogue through a richly detailed slice of Americana.

These are the key personages, around which the "assassination" storyline revolves:

● Karen Black is Connie White, a Tammy Wynette prototype. Black had read for Altman before. When she heard about *Nashville*, she brought the director several songs she had written (three are spotlighted in the film—"Memphis," "I Don't Know If I Found It in You" and "Rolling Stone"), which prompted him to add the character of the supercilious, country entertainer who stands in for the ailing Barbara Jean (Ronee Blakley) at a Grand Ole Opry gala.

When Black got off the plane in Nashville, she was informed by musical director Richard Baskin that she would be singing for five thousand people the very next day. They

The narcissistic womanizer Tom. Actor Keith Carradine's song "I'm Easy" won the film's only Oscar.

were local extras lured to the bogus Opry show for the filming and for the opportunity of glimpsing Lily Tomlin and Henry Gibson from TV's *Laugh-In*. The crowd brought their own Instamatics. Black's musical numbers and brief bitchy scenes are among the highlights of *Nashville*, though the Oscar-nominated (for *Five Easy Pieces*) actress really plays a confined cameo.

● Keith Carradine is Tom, one-third of the country-pop trio, Tom, Bill (Allan Nicholls) and Mary (Christina Raines). Tom is a narcissistic womanizer whose speed in picking up and disposing of women is practically vampirish, and very Altmanesque. By now Carradine was accepted as an Altman stock company player,* yet his throaty tenor and songwriting élan took critics and audiences by surprise. (Actually, Carradine had a long-standing musical aptitude; Altman first heard him singing on the set of *Thieves Like Us*.)

Carradine wrote or cowrote three songs in *Nashville*. One became a minor hit and won an Academy Award ("I'm Easy"), and another ("It Don't Worry Me," originally written and rejected for the score of *Emperor of the North Pole*) is the film's anthem. They are the only songs heard more than once on the sound track—since Carradine's self-absorbed character plays them over and over as background to his assignations.

● Henry Gibson is Haven Hamilton, the pure-as-the-driven Hank Snow exemplar. If Altman had not chosen Gibson, the unctuous charlatan of *The Long Goodbye*, then people might not have objected as much to the vicious satire that Gibson brings to the role. The fact is that Robert Duvall was Altman's original choice, and discussions broke down over Duvall's compensation. Duvall, who did his country-and-western humble-pie routine later in *Tender Mercies*, might have forestalled such objections. Certainly he would have played the part differently.

But Gibson proved a real linchpin of the film. Not only did he pen the lyric for the double-edged, curtain-raising Bicentennial ditty "200 Years" but he contributed the song that is probably closest to Altman's own life-strategy, "Keep a Goin'." Critics of the savagery of his characterization did not choose to note that when the assassination occurs at the climax, it is Haven Hamilton who shields Barbara Jean with his own body, calms the crowd, and keeps a-goin'.

● Geraldine Chaplin is Opal, the British broadcast journalist who muses aloud to her tape recorder with patently offensive observations about racial stereotypes and American

---

*Actually, this was Carradine's last film for Altman to date, and he was sort of "inherited" by both Joan Tewkesbury and Alan Rudolph as a leading man. As such, in recent years, he has become more identified with them (particularly Rudolph) than with Altman. His films for Alan Rudolph include *Welcome to L.A.*, *Choose Me*, *Trouble in Mind*, and *The Moderns*.

falseness, all the while breathlessly chasing some elusive celebrity interview. Chaplin, daughter of Charles Chaplin, had worked only infrequently in the United States prior to *Nashville*, though she was well known abroad, especially as the frequent leading lady of the great Spanish sociopolitical director Carlos Saura. In America, she was perhaps best known, at this point, for a supporting role in *Doctor Zhivago*.

• Lily Tomlin made her motion-picture debut as Linnea Reese, the wife of a country promoter (Ned Beatty) and mother of two deaf children, whose soul takes flight when she sings in an otherwise all-black gospel choir. At first, Tomlin says, she was uncomfortable in the part, uncertain that she was right as the rather decorous Southern housewife who is not in the least made fun of by the script. But when she realized how well everyone else was cast, she relaxed. How could Altman have been wrong only about *her*? Tomlin took gospel-singing and deaf-signing lessons; she wrote songs; the only one she performed solo was cut from the film.

• Michael Murphy is John Triplette, the political advance man, Keenan Wynn is Mr. Green, the elderly gent whose wife is dying in a hospital ward, and Barbara Baxley is Lady Pearl, Haven Hamilton's genteel companion.

These were veteran Altman players dating back to the Sixties. Murphy's character, the nexus of the storyline, might have been a two-dimensional and hissable stock villain without the actor's embroidery. Keenan Wynn got the call and flew to Nashville without knowing what he was going to be asked to do. Baxley, from *Countdown*, is secondary in the more packed scenes; but the more you watch the movie, the more you realize how respectful the camera is of her ladylike pose.

• Allan Nicholls is the cuckold of the country-pop trio. Keith Carradine and Nicholls had been in *Hair* together on Broadway, and it was Carradine who called Nicholls up about the part in *Nashville*. It is an unassuming part, the first of many unassuming parts and utility roles the multi-endowed Nicholls has executed for Altman. He wrote one song, "Rose's Cafe," very different in its bluesiness from the rest.

Nicholls's father was gravely ill the day *Nashville* began filming, and Nicholls was debating whether or not he ought to fly to his bedside. He was barely acquainted with the director, who came charging over and put his arm around him and said, "Don't worry, I will act as if it was happening to my own father." Their bond was cemented. "How could I ever forget that?" asks Nicholls.

● Allen Garfield is Barnett, Barbara Jean's nurturing–punishing husband/personal manager, and Ned Beatty is Delbert Reese, Lily Tomlin's spouse, the conduit between many of the figures in *Nashville*. Two of the premiere character actors of the Seventies, they give crucial performances in *Nashville*, though they never did quite fit into the director's "family."

Garfield argued with Altman about brandishing the American flag in the Parthenon scene. Altman resolved the dispute by including that argument in the film (in a heated exchange between Barnett and John Triplette). Beatty took "ten percent" of his usual salary to appear in *Nashville*, according to his agent, Jack Fields. He too argued with Tewkesbury and Altman about his scenes. Later, Beatty told a magazine interviewer that he could never work with the director again because Altman did not pay his actors and actresses well enough.

● Ronee Blakley is the Loretta Lynn archetype, Barbara Jean. Again, it was a role envisioned for someone else— Susan Anspach—who would not accept Altman's low-scale terms. Blakley knew Baskin, and Baskin knew she had recorded a promising early album on the Elektra label that includes two of the four songs she eventually was to sing in *Nashville*. When Anspach dropped out of the running, Altman remembered Blakley, whom he had met and whose songs he had heard. He and Baskin went to see her perform in concert in Nashville where she was appearing as a backup singer for country-folk artist Hoyt Axton.

Albuquerque (Barbara Harris), her singing debut
eclipsed by the race cars at the Nashville Speed-
way. Accompanying her is Trout, played by musical arranger-supervisor Richard Baskin.

More a political rhythm-and-blues folkie (her first album
contains a homage to slain Chicago Black Panther leader
Fred Hampton), Blakley threw herself into research for the
role—and made a point of meeting Loretta Lynn and Dolly
Parton as part of her preparation.

• Barbara Harris is Albuquerque, a typical Altmanesque
study in survival, a wayward vixen who is being pursued by
someone we presume to be her abandoned husband, Star,
played by Altman alumnus Bert Remsen.

Remsen's story is an unusual one, even in the Altman

"family." He had acted for Altman, dating back to an episode of *Sheriff of Cochise* in the 1950s. A freak accident on the set of the film *No Time for Sergeants* caused a crippling spine injury that ended the first phase of his career as an actor. Later, as a casting director at MGM, he was coaxed into playing a bit in *Brewster McCloud.* After that, he became one of Altman's most incorrigible regulars. Neither he nor Barbara Harris carry much of an on-camera burden in *Nashville*—which makes it all the more improbable, and delicious, that Albuquerque, in the final scene, becomes the newest celebrity in the Nashville cavalcade.

That's fourteen. The other ten cast members are: David Arkin, as a chauffeur with starry eyes of his own, and Timothy Brown, as a dignified Charley Pride type; Jeff Goldblum, as a spaced-out cycle-rider who meaninglessly spurts from scene to scene, and Scott Glenn, as the uniformed soldier stalking Barbara Jean; Shelley Duvall, as the self-absorbed L.A. Joan, whose pursuit of action compensates for her own narrow horizons, and country-pop singer Christina Raines (in real life, at the time, Keith Carradine's live-in lover); Gwen Welles, as the poignantly tone-deaf singer/waitress, Sueleen Gay, and Robert Doqui, as her friend, Wade, an ex-con; David Hayward, as the enigmatic assassin, Kenny; and the only actual Nashville resident of the cast, Dave Peel, playing Bud, who, in the film, is continually introduced by Haven Hamilton as his son "the Harvard Law School Graduate."*

In interviews Altman has often talked about the chaos and serendipity of filmmaking. That certainly applies to his own career as a director. Though Tewkesbury says that "very, very little that was in the script is not still in the movie," more of *Nashville* was "of the moment" than any previous Altman film. There were script contributions from many, collated by Tewkesbury, fussed over by Altman. These in-

---

*Subservient to his father, Bud's character nonetheless has an affecting moment shyly singing to Opal an a capella country composition called "The Heart of a Gentle Woman." (Dave Peel wrote it.) Opal is briefly rapt, before her attention is preempted by the walk-through of Elliott Gould.

cluded some of the prime revelations of characterization, and the many variations on the themes:

● According to the script, Barbara Jean (Ronee Blakley) has been recuperating from a burn accident at a Baltimore treatment center. Altman borrowed that idea from Blakley herself after learning that, when Blakley was six years old, her clothes caught on fire from a sparkler after a Fourth of July celebration. She suffered third-degree burns on her chest and stomach. The scars never fully healed.

The sequence of Barbara Jean's mental disintegration was originally intended to be filmed at a shopping mall as a cathartic fainting spell. The night before the filming, Blakley began to think about the scene and decided that it was not enough for Barbara Jean to just faint. That would simply repeat an earlier airport scene where the country-and-western singer collapses in public.

Instead, the first-time actress wrote a long, complicated, painful monologue, drawing on the journals she carried with her everywhere, pasting "little bits" of her own childhood together with bits of Barbara Jean's. She hoped the resulting words would be like country lyrics only without the musical accompaniment, corny but touching.

"I wanted to go deeper down the road into her [Barbara Jean], to reveal both her strengths and her weaknesses. If she collapsed again physically, it wouldn't be taking her character anywhere, or the movie anywhere. Mostly, I just wanted people to see what made her tick."

When Blakley asked to see Altman the next day, the director was already embroiled with the crowds and the logistics. He arrived in her quarters, tense and irritable.

"Ronee Blakley caught me on the worst day, emotionally, of *Nashville,*" he told *American Film.* "It was stringing out towards the end of the picture. She was in makeup. We had a motel down there and I was screaming in the telephone at somebody, and somebody else came in and said, 'Ronee wants to see you.' I thought, 'Jesus Christ, now I have to have Ronee.' So I walked over to her and I said, 'Do you want to see me?' Kind of gruffly, which would scare her. She said,

'Could I have a moment?' I said, 'I suppose you want to see me alone.' She said, 'Well, yes.' I said, 'You've got ideas for the scene, huh?' She said, 'Do you want to hear it?' and I said, 'Yeah.' So we walked outside and she took out this notebook. She said, 'Here's what I thought' and she started reading from this thing. I said, 'I don't know. Ronee, I've got too much. Let's just do what we're supposed to do.' She said, 'Okay, whatever you say.'

"We went and we got in our little camper to go out to the location and I got to feeling bad about it and finally I said, 'Go ahead. Do what you were going to do.' Well, it's just dynamite material. It's just terrific. And I sat there and I thought, 'I damn near blew this. . . .'"

It is a highlight of the film, and the scene, more than any other, that earned Blakley an Oscar nomination as Best Supporting Actress. Altman has said they filmed it in all of twenty minutes.

• The Hal Philip Walker shtick was developed by Thomas Hal Phillips, who was given a budget and carte blanche to develop the presidential campaign of *Nashville*. According to Altman, Phillips, the novelist from Mississippi who had been such a godfather during the filming of *Thieves Like Us*, had a brother who had once run for governor down South. Phillips had managed that campaign. Now, he was asked to concoct a persona for a presidential contender.

"I didn't give him any guidelines whatsoever. . . ." Altman said. "The only requirements I gave him were that he be a third-party candidate. I didn't want a Democrat or a Republican. And I told him to invent a man who he would like to see elected, and who he thought could be elected."

With production money, Thomas Hal Phillips opened up a campaign headquarters, ordered buttons and bumper stickers, recruited the marching band, the rifle twirlers, the baton girls. Sometimes, when the mobile van with the loudspeakers and the presidential banner was cruising the streets of Nashville, it was not in fact being recorded for sound. Afterward, Thomas Hal Phillips went into a recording studio and delivered his keynote speech, which became another connective (à la *M*A*S*H*) in the film. Phillip's credit, the third one up on the screen, is "campaign manager."

Howard K. Smith's television editorial, which is extremely witty and apropos, also went into *Nashville* with little or no change. Altman gave Smith the Hal Philip Walker campaign material to ponder, and asked him for a flavorful commentary, pro or con. Smith came up with exactly what he says in the film.

• Geraldine Chaplin (Opal) wrote much of her own stuff, especially the "meaningful" soliloquies. She was criticized by reviewers for these gushy interregnums, such as the one where she walks through a junkyard heaped with automobiles and buses, intoning: "I'm walking in a graveyard . . . The dead here have no crosses, nor tombstones, nor wreaths to sing of their past glory, but lie—in rotting, decaying, rusty heaps." Hers, along with L.A. Joan's, was the most absurd (and comical) characterization, deliberately out of synch with the more lifelike elements of the film.

But in the filming the director paid special attention to the Opal character, and kept telling the actress that she was Altman going through *Nashville*, making her vapid comments.

Joan Tewkesbury has defended Opal's characterization: "I was in Cannes with Geraldine in 1974, and every time she would walk down the street there'd be ten or fifteen Opals chasing her with tape recorders. Her whole life she'd been pursued by people following a famous man's daughter, trying to take a picture or ask her a question. So what she did really was show what she's been plagued with all her life. I feel it was a pretty honest interpretation."

• Barbara Baxley worked on her own scenes, particularly the long monologue in a nightclub about "the Kennedy boys" that gives the film a political heart and soul—something to be *for*, as opposed to *against*.

According to Altman: "I didn't even bother to listen to her material before we shot it. And she had rehearsed it and learned it. And we turned the camera on her till we ran out of film, and then we loaded it up again and ran another roll, so that it literally took twenty minutes. It was done once, and that was it. Because I knew that I could pull out the pieces of it that I wanted, and I could get away from it at any time. I had a song going on [in the scene] and I had all those other characters that I had to deal with."

It was not until the editing stages that the director realized he had something significant that deepened the characterization of Lady Pearl and the overall skein of *Nashville*.

● Karen Black "mostly improvised" (her words) several scenes. In one, after she has substituted for Barbara Jean in a performance, she smiles through gritted teeth as she rejects a gift proffered by the singer's husband. "Altman gave me the fact that I was in competition with her," she said, "and my refusal to take the gift just came spontaneously. In doing that, at that moment in the film, I think I discovered who the character really was."

Of course there were just as many of the cast who changed *nothing* from the pages handed to them by Tewkesbury— from relative novices Scott Glenn and Gwen Welles, to pros Lily Tomlin and Keenan Wynn.

The way it worked, the actors and actresses would have talks with Altman and Tewkesbury about the characters, and then people could choose whether or not to contribute their own dialogue or character emendations. "Keenan Wynn does what he does, for example," says Tewkesbury. "All his lines were written. He works in an old-fashioned, enclosed kind of way which worked out fine. Nobody bothered him."

Much of the "backstory" on the characters, whether written down or discussed in those conversations with Altman and Tewkesbury, never found its way into the film.

For example, there was a lot of preliminary discussion about how Haven Hamilton had had another son who was killed in a tragic hunting accident. This would certainly shed some light on his father's smothering relationship with Bud Hamilton, and would cast needed sympathy on his character as well. However, that subtext is absent from the story, as filmed.

Opal (for further example) was to be revealed as a fraud,

someone who is only pretending to be a BBC journalist. Additional scenes that rounded out Opal's character were filmed, then bypassed in the editing. It is one of the weaknesses of the film that such a seemingly emphatic character is barely in evidence in the assassination sequence.

In all of this process, Tewkesbury was, in a sense, returning to what she had done so well in the past, first as a theatre director, and subsequently, as production script girl on *McCabe*—only more so—assessing, culling, editing, rewriting, organizing, bridging the gaps. She has never been ruffled by questions about what may have been lost or cut out of the original script along the way. She insists the script was honored, even in the permutations.

"It [the original script] was simply imploded in different directions," she has said. At the same time, she admits, in broadening the characters, things became more allusive. "My tendency is to go down very far," says Tewkesbury. "Altman likes to stay up there on the surface."

Says Tewkesbury: "There were always situations that were left open for, first, Altman to fill out, and then for the actor to fill out; and lastly, because the film was structured the way it was, you the audience come to the theater as the twenty-fifth character, and you see those characters any way you want to see them, and even if you think they're wrong, you're still right."

While all this script juggling was going on, the crew was locking into rhythm.

The arranger-composer was a bold choice: a twenty-five-year-old by the name of Richard Baskin, who was in the stages of composing an orchestral suite of songs called "City of the One-Night Stands," which later became the score for *Welcome to L.A.*, the first Alan Rudolph film to be produced by Robert Altman. Baskin's sister was a friend of Gwen Welles, and after he wrote some songs for Welles, he was introduced to Altman and was enlisted. His favorite musicians were people like Béla Bartók, George Gershwin, and Erik Satie, and though he was familiar with some country-

and-western standards, that was not the kind of music
Baskin wrote or listened to.

He ended up writing the music for many of the original
songs, hiring the several backup bands that performed on and
off camera, and working with those actors and actresses who
elected to attempt their own compositions. Obviously, he
collaborated less with people like Keith Carradine and Ronee
Blakley, who were already accomplished musicians.

You can argue yourself blue in the face about the music in
Nashville—many critics did—or about Baskin's own musical élan (his portentous score for *Welcome to L.A.* also put
off many critics). It is hard to argue, however, with the
razzle-dazzle achievement of a twenty-five-year-old helping
to compose, arrange, and record some fifty or sixty songs,
mostly original tunes, within the span of eight weeks of
filming.

The cinematographer was Paul Lohmann, returning after
California Split and continuing on through *Buffalo Bill and
the Indians*. Altman and Lohmann had decided on a "post-
card" look for *Nashville*. (Lohmann was the Altman cameraman least dependent on a preordained visual design.) As
usual, Altman wanted to shoot as much in sequence as possible—the opening scene of the movie was shot first, the
closing scene was shot last—and they did not intend to
shoot "coverage"—that is, more than one version of the
same scene. With Altman it was usually three or four master
shots, each with a slight variation in angle, but with unpredictable changes in the dialogue and dramatic content. Docu-
mentary-style, Calvin-style. They decided to "push" the
reds, whites, and blues in the processing lab. They ended up
with seventy hours of dailies.

The sound people and the editing team had a daunting
task. They were using an eight-track sound system, with mi-
crophones on eight of the principals, plus an additional sixteen tracks for the musical sequences. Jim Webb and Chris
McLaughlin handled the technical challenges, while William
A. Sawyer, a longtime supervising editor for director Hal
Ashby, who was with Altman on *The Long Goodbye*,

Nashville, and *Three Women,* anchored the sound editing with his seniority.

The sound is crisper and more intricate in *Nashville* than with Altman's early multitrack experimentation in, say, *McCabe and Mrs. Miller.* Altman did much with the sound that was, to put it mildly, cinematically enterprising (at one point, Barbara Harris's character sings an entire song in long shot, her voice utterly blotted out by the roar of a drag race). Again and again the editors would discover something in the dailies—rehearsed by Rudolph or volunteered by a minor character—that was just unbelievably fitting. (Altman has commented that some of the best crowd stuff in the final assassination scene was picked up by a camera operator "down from Alabama or somewhere" for the day's shoot, completely unfamiliar with the script, weaving through the crowd on his own.)

The editors were Sidney Levin and Dennis Hill. Eggen-weiler, says Tewkesbury, was indispensable, "doing what he always did, working like elves in the night," finding and preparing locations with his immaculate visual sense. Tommy Thompson shared assistant director duties with Alan Rudolph (the latter, especially active in the performance scenes, the crowd occasions, and the Parthenon climax).

For the first time, Scott Bushnell was boosted up to equal billing with "Egg" as one of the two associate producers.

Before the movie was even released, the avalanche of controversy began thundering downhill. At first, it was a case of certain Eastern critics gnashing their teeth over the fact that Pauline Kael wrote a preview of a rough cut of the film hailing it as "an orgy for movie lovers" and "the funniest epic vision of America." She described Altman's mastery of the medium by comparing him to Norman Mailer, James Joyce, Fred Astaire, Bernardo Bertolucci, and Jean-Luc Go-dard.

It was bad timing for Kael (mentor and mother hen of many American film critics), who had rattled the profession a couple of years earlier with her perhaps-too-enthusiastic stumping for *Last Tango in Paris.* Some of what ensued concerning *Nashville* can be construed as a counterattack on her as well as the inevitable sour grapes of film critics who had not been privy to one of Altman's by-invitation-only screenings. *The New York Times*'s respected critic Vincent Canby grumbled in his column that reviews in the future might as well be based on a comma or a concept (though, to be fair, Canby enthused about the film when it was released and over time was an attentive reviewer of Altman's films). And many lesser critics took to print to spank Kael and to discount her premature evaluation of *Nashville.*

As Altman pointed out in interviews, not only had Kael seen the film, but so had quite a number of taste- and trend-makers.

Hollis Alpert wrote about the film in the *Saturday Review* after viewing an early cut; *American Film* reported on previewed portions; and Charles Michener (who, in fact, has a walk-on as a reporter in the assassination climax of *Nashville*) was permitted an advance peek for *Newsweek* for one of his periodic news magazine spreads on Altman. Many were invited down to the Nashville location, including Bruce Williamson of *Playboy* and the French representatives of *Cahiers du Cinéma.* Nor was any of this unique—every Hollywood director, in the past and to the present, favors certain critics and columnists with early screenings and on-location jaunts—for honest reaction as well as potential publicity.

It was unusual for someone of Kael's stature to go out on a limb with such a glowing review of an unfinished cut (that sort of tub-thumping is normally left to the gossip columnists) but really, the tempest was in a teapot.

In any case, this initial controversy was quickly banished from memory. When Paramount, the releasing company, sneak-previewed the film in Boston, a phalanx of executives, including company head Barry Diller, flew cross-country to collect the reaction cards. For several minutes after the final credits, the packed crowd was on its feet, booing *and* cheering. This was definitely a movie that divided audiences.

Was the movie condescending to its milieu? Was it "authentic" country-and-western music? Was it a vicious, demagogic vision of women, of the South, and of America? Was the assassination of Barbara Jean gratuitous?

Not only were there the usual Altman detractors, such as critics John Simon and Rex Reed, but there was also the *Realist* conspiratorialist Paul Krassner (he hated the one-assassin ending) and the ineffable Manny Farber—as well as certain Nashville notables who, no matter how utter their despisal of the film, usually did feel obliged to mention somewhere in the run-on paragraphs that they had not actually *seen* it.

The New York Times fed off the pro and con for weeks,* and its erstwhile popular music critic, John Rockwell, weighed in with a column that decided that the music, though "decently performed," could not be considered "nearly as good as the best country music." (Oh, really!)

The first time you see the film, you might be tempted to think the attitude toward country-and-western music is a snickering one, which it is—patently—but only in part. The second time and the time after that, you see how affectionate it is too—which is part of the brilliance of *Nashville.*† The critics did not deign to notice the premier Nashville sidemen in the background, people like Vassar Clements or the Smoky Mountain Boys. Or that the script itself, in an exchange between John Triplette (Michael Murphy) and Bill (Allan Nicholls), sides with "redneck" (or old-style) country music as opposed to new country-pop. There is certainly as much compassion as stereotyping in the portrayal of Barbara Jean. Ultimately, there is respect for Haven Hamilton.

Not one to be on the defensive, in interviews Altman expressed no love for Opryland, about which he made the

---

*Critic John Leonard commented: "Writing articles about *Nashville* and writing articles about the articles that have been written about *Nashville* is almost a light industry."

†Much later, in fact, Altman, long a dabbling songwriter, cowrote (with Danny Darst) a country chartbuster for singer John Anderson. "Black Sheep of the Family" rose to #1 in 1983.

interesting comment that "they run that place like a church"; but his indictment of the more egregious elements of the scene did not diminish his appreciation of the music and the performers. Again and again, in interviews, Altman was forced to repeat his contention that, in any case, he was not making a movie about Nashville or country music, per se. He was making a movie about Nashville as a metaphor for America. He was making a movie about America.

It was also, interestingly, a metaphor for him of Hollywood in the 1940s. (Joan Tewkesbury, too, mentions the Forties connection in interviews, perhaps because she grew up in Los Angeles during that period). Remembering Altman's own experience in Hollywood in the 1940s, *Nashville* might be seen in part as a commentary on his own illusions at the time.

"It's a place where people get off the bus, like Hollywood was many years ago," said Altman in an interview. "The money is generated, and there's a crudeness to the culture. It just seems like the proper place for me to be able to equate the analogy of our elected officials and politicians—which in many ways, I think, is a popularity contest—with the success of country-and-western music. As I say, eventually it's just a way of melding a whole view, my view, of that political climate in America today."

For anyone interested in what makes Altman tick, and in the question of how much of his essence is to be gleaned from the crevices of *Nashville,* there are at least two sides of the coin. It is his least "interior" film, his least make-believe, one of his least personal films of the 1970s. It takes in the most territory outside himself. It is one of a very few Altman films to have so much explicit topical reference (from the Kennedys and Watergate, to Vietnam and racial prejudice), and so much close real-life corollary.

On the other hand, there are the usual signposts of the director's psyche. For one thing, apart from everything else, this is a movie about the vulnerable, creative, repressed, maltreated women who form one underpinning of Altman's ca-

Gwen Welles, beginning her stripteasing for political contributions, in *Nashville*.

reer.* Three women in particular—Barbara Jean, Linnea Reese, and the most abject of the females, Sueleen Gay— whose forced striptease at a political fundraiser recalls the treatment of Hot Lips in *M*A*S*H*, and whose characterization John Malone in *The New York Times* cited when he wrote that "Altman's treatment of women often borders on celluloid rape."

---

*It may be, too, that the Keith Carradine character is a kind of Altmanesque expiation of male guilt. There is something very hard and personal in the emphasis on Tom Frank's womanizing, and there is no more uncomfortable scene in

Tewkesbury wrote that striptease scene, which is certainly degrading to the character and a red flag to feminists. She says: "It was intended not only to be a particular kind of strip scene, but in a way to signify how we've all shucked down to pursue our ambitions. We may not have literally taken our clothes off, but we may have stripped down one day to say, 'Okay, I'll do that. I'll take this job, do this thing this time to get there.' That's what that scene was about, more than anything. After writing that sequence, I felt it summed up a lot of events in my life, and somehow in everybody's lives that I knew."

Ned Beatty, playing Delbert Reese, clashed with Tewkesbury during the filming of that scene, arguing that Sueleen Gay should come *prepared* to perform a striptease, if need be. "Anyone," Tewkesbury told Beatty, "can take off their clothes. *Why* one takes off their clothes seemed important to me. The point of the scene is to show the complexity of Sueleen's self-delusion, and how she gets ensnared in her own ambition . . . how far she has to go for a chance to sing on a bill with Barbara Jean."

Altman backed Tewkesbury, even though he has admitted that the political smoker is not one of his favorite scenes. The director must have appreciated the metaphor—after all, he had "shucked down" in Hollywood for years. In any case, it is telling that that scene, less worked over than many of the others, was filmed "very intact as written," according to Tewkesbury.

Despite the occasional fuming detractor, when *Nashville* was released, it was generally written about as a landmark film, a departure from run-of-the-mill Hollywood, a work of social import as well as high entertainment. Certainly it represents a high-water mark for Altman, the film he will always be measured against. Time has not dimmed its lustre,

---

Nashville than the one in which Carradine croons, "I'm Easy" to a roomful of dewy-eyed women, each of whom is convinced he is transmitting a coded message to her. No doubt they are all wrong, and Tom Frank might as well be singing to himself in the shower.

only made more manifest its achievement, by a striving director working on a modest budget completely against the commercial grain.

Andrew Sarris in *The Village Voice* called it "Altman's best film and the most exciting dramatic musical since *The Blue Angel.*"

When Penelope Gilliatt reviewed it for *The New Yorker,* she wrote: ". . . technically and emotionally the film is a crowning work and a harbinger. This is one of the ways that films will go, and Altman will have been the first to be there."

Tom Wicker (who, one recalls, was the literary source for "A Lion Walks Among Us") wrote an appreciative piece about the social significance of *Nashville* for *The New York Times,* while Vincent Canby lauded the film as "another extraordinary chapter in the director's continuing history of America seen largely through the stories of gallant losers."

In *Newsweek,* Charles Michener described it as an "epic poem of a movie" and as "everything a work of social art ought to be but seldom is—immensely moving yet terribly funny, chastening yet ultimately exhilarating. It is also that rarest thing in contemporary movies—a work of art that promises to be hugely popular."

Because Michener was so chummy with Altman, his essay has the ring of having been dictated in Altman's self-image, and it is revealing for that.

Altman is described by the writer as resembling a cross between Santa Claus and Mephistopheles—not far off in either regard, and probably Altman's view too.

Michener also writes: "Mordant in tone and unpredictably violent, Altman's films suggest a fatalistic view of human life and mortality that may stem from his upbringing as a Roman Catholic."

Michener reveals, too, that Altman can be occasionally devastating to his favorite actors and actresses—as when he informed Keith Carradine that he had a part for him as a "faggot son" in his next movie, knowing that Carradine fancied himself more the Steve McQueenish kind of male lead.

The controversial climax at the Parthenon, with Barbara Jean (Ronee Blakley) and Haven Hamilton (Henry Gibson).

(Perhaps not-so-incidentally, they never worked together again.)

And the old myth that Altman scrapped "most" of the Ring Lardner Jr. screenplay for $M*A*S*H$ in order to improvise the movie is trotted out and rehashed.

In the course of the article, the great American director is congenially depicted as having "a stiff Scotch and soda in one hand, a joint in the other," and quoted as proclaiming, "I work a lot when I'm drunk, and I trust that all of it will eventually appear in my films."

After the controversy and excitement of the first few weeks' opening of *Nashville*, everything else was anticlimax.

For once, Altman was consulted about the advertising. When one of his extras painted a portrait of the twenty-four characters, Dan Perri (who designed Altman's film titles from *California Split* through *Three Women*) used the painting for the sales campaign and for the opening credits. Later, ABC Records used the identical concept for the cover of the *Nashville* LP. But the album failed to generate interest, and the movie stalled at the turnstiles after grossing $10 million. Overseas, despite critical hosannas, colloquialisms and overlapping dialogue made subtitling the film next to impossible for general audiences. Paramount lost steam. The studio could not figure out if the numbers had been maximized or not. The selling of *Nashville* as a work of art, and the critical brouhaha, had turned off those U.S. exhibitors whose nirvana is an "audience movie."

Though the film won Best Film, Best Director, and Best Supporting Actress (Lily Tomlin) honors from the New York Film Critics and a Best Screenplay pick by the Los Angeles Film Critics, it did not do well at the Oscars.

There were five nominations: Best Picture, Best Director, two for Best Supporting Actress (with Tomlin and Blakley canceling each other out in the tally), and Keith Carradine's "I'm Easy" for Best Song. The entire sound track was disqualified in the Best Original Score category, incredibly, because some of the songs (Ronee Blakley's, for example) had been previously recorded, a technicality. Only Carradine, among the nominees, won. In Hollywood, ironically, the longtime director of *The Millionaire, Bonanza,* and *Combat* was beginning to be perceived as the fair-haired favorite of the East Coast film critics and as an intellectual pretender who scorned the gold of the box office.

Besides, it was a year of tough competition. *One Flew Over the Cuckoo's Nest* swept the major categories, with Louise Fletcher, Altman's first choice as Linnea Reese, taking the Best Actress nod for her part as the head nurse of the insane asylum in the film adaptation of Ken Kesey's novel.

Anyone who happened to encounter Altman with his scowl and fallen face on Oscar night (he had once vowed never to attend such ceremonies) would know that this rejection was a wound that would never be healed.

For a while there was talk from ABC of expanding the film into a four-hour telefeature to be broadcast on two consecutive Sunday nights, and to include scenes deleted from the final theatrical edit of *Nashville.* But as the process of reediting the film began, the disappointment at the box office and the failure of the Oscars took its toll, and the plans were scrapped. Francis Coppola, who reedited the two *Godfather*s into one, and Steven Spielberg, who added footage to a revised theatrical version of *E.T.*, had more financial muscle. They were also more flexible and savvy when dealing with their respective film companies.

For Altman, the prospect of a new lease on life for *Nashville* ended in yet further disgruntlement. Altman did not work hard at patching up the deal. Audiences were deprived of what may have been illusory—the cinematic fullform; and the purest triumph of the director's film career became a gone and bittersweet thing.

Chapter

29

THE ACTOR'S NIRVANA

The more careerist and more genre-oriented stars of the Hollywood mainstream continued to bypass Altman (and vice versa). But, in 1976, the wide world was opening up to him. There was no English-language director more celebrated for his knack with performers.

Certainly, it was not the money. Actors in *Nashville* received only $750 or $1,000 per week. Geraldine Chaplin said she turned down a $130,000 role in London in order to fly to the Altman set for her one-of-the-crowd billing. "In Europe," she told reporters simply, "Altman is number one." Lily Tomlin told Carol Burnett she would be more fulfilled, as an

Unable to negotiate: Altman and Malibu neighbor Steve McQueen on the set of *The Long Goodbye*. Their conversations about working together led nowhere. (Wisconsin Center for Film and Theatre Research)

actress, with a walk-on in any Altman movie than with the lead role in most others.

There was the occasional legitimate box-office personality such as Warren Beatty or Paul Newman, desperate to escape their own unique straitjackets. But in general, the Altman troupe were iconoclasts or independents, unknown quantities in motion pictures, new names, stand-up improvisers and small theatre people, television people imprisoned by a boob-tube image, foreign stars whose casting would never be cheered by a U.S. film company.

Box-office luminaries like Steve McQueen (a Malibu neighbor of Altman's) usually asked for too much money; on top of which (as when McQueen was sounded out for the lead role in *The Long Goodbye*), they had a habit of asking for more writing, for motivation and detail, and worst of all, for script approval. They drove Altman crazy whenever he negotiated with them.

The Altman people would come cheap, and they would come hat in hand. Which is not to say that they might not also be among the very finest actors and actresses available.

Altman does have an almost mystical ability to coax the maximum out of his players. It is a talent not easily explained, or dissected.

It is true that the director was once a sort of frustrated actor whose debonair good looks did not suffice in the 1940s. But he does not seem to have studied acting technique formally, ever. He owes no allegiance to any particular discipline or method, though he is not above borrowing techniques, scattershot, from one or the other. He might lapse into the vocabulary of the acting profession—picked up somewhere along the way in the twenty years of dues-paying before *M*A*S*H*—and give the impression that he knows some theory behind it. But he never talked theory.

"I remember when I did *Legs Diamond*," says Ray Danton. "He came to the screening, and afterward he said, 'Where did you get that imagery from?' I said, 'What imagery?' He said, 'You were obviously playing something apart from the character.' I said, 'You're right, Bob, I was.' He was the only one who picked it up. I was playing a shadow, a man who was already dead. He said, 'My god, it was terrifying, absolutely riveting. That one thought I felt through the whole picture—but it didn't stop you from being funny.' I said, 'No, it didn't stop me from being funny; it gave me something to hold on to the whole time.' I think that was the only philosophical talk we ever had about acting.

"He was very strong in using imagery," continues Danton. "I remember he turned to another actor in a scene once—I think it was Frank De Cordova, one of our better character actors who never got the recognition he was entitled to—and said, 'Frank, this guy is not a baboon, he's a rooster. He's not

Negotiating a performance from Warren Beatty in *McCabe and Mrs. Miller.*

a gorilla, he's a cock of the walk.' It changed the actor's whole behavior. Some actors relate very well to that kind of information. Some actors would look down at you and say, 'What are you talking about?'"

'Imagery,' the 'key word,' or 'pick-a-tic'—all very "exterior" tricks of unleashing the actor. Not very "interior," to say the least.

An actor trained in the Method at the Actors Studio (Warren Beatty, for example) might feel compelled to internalize his reaction in a given scene—which could require many 'takes' while the characterization is refined from the inside out. Altman does not like to think, script- or acting-wise, from the inside out. Almost, it seems, as a formal exercise, he might insist upon taking a character in an illogical or nonsensical direction.

Once, during a script conference with the director, John Considine objected to an idea of Altman's: "I just don't think the character would do this." The director put up his hand and said: "Hold up on the drugstore psychology and let's just have this character do this anyway." Says Considine: "I really think Altman believes *anyone* is capable of doing *anything.*"

Altman has said he is "embarrassed" at rehearsals, not knowing exactly what to say to actors. The director prefers to let actors move naturally and to stalk them inconspicuously with his camera, rather than possibly to inhibit their performance by "blocking the action." This is as great a liberation to some actors as it can be a terror to others. For Altman, again, it is a strength born of a weakness.

The long Calvin and television grounding would give the director very little experience with fastidious rehearsals.

There were read-throughs, of course, at Calvin and in television. Early on, they became as important as rehearsals, for Altman, in instilling confidence in an actor. Strategically, Altman presided over such script initiations at his own home. He would befriend the actor. Adopt the actor. Says Brian McKay: "He could win you over with his hospitality and the whole ambience of his home and Kathryn and the kids. He always finds a way to get to the actor."

That was all prelude to the family atmosphere on location. The nightly movies. The requisite dailies. The communal popcorn, drinking, and dope-smoking. The parties and entertainments. All of which, even back in the television days, was evolving into an elaborate courtship ritual.

The prefilming conversations might be entirely unspecific. They might not even be *about* the film or the part. They might be about the weekend's football game, the authoritarian government of South Korea, or Watson and Crick's writings on DNA. When Altman told Lili St. Cyr that his wife, too, had been a chorus girl in her salad days, the camaraderie was implicit. Sometime in the course of the introductions and the early read-throughs, the director might begin calling the actor by the character's name. "Brewster." "McCabe." "Popeye." It was a tacit thing, a small thing, but it would worm its way into the actor's consciousness.

Altman has said that "casting is ninety percent of the creative work."

You can argue with his casting, but you cannot argue that he does not believe and subscribe to his own maxim. No other director has taken such rolls-of-the-dice on unknowns, again and again. No director has been in on the beginning of so many exceptional post-Sixties acting careers. No other director has so often trusted actors with writing, credited and not. No other director seems to rely in his motion pictures so much on improvisation, characterization, and performance.

Once an actor is cast, Altman takes pains to be deferential, to be passive, to present an atmosphere of generosity and openness. Some great film directors, such as John Ford or Fritz Lang, extracted performances through occasional tyranny and bullying; some, William Wyler for example, by arduous retake after retake until something finally clicked that had escaped the notice of everyone else.

Altman promotes an atmosphere that, if the casting is right, then the actor can do no wrong. It is this trust that is somehow magical. And somehow, the upshot is, the actor meets the expectations.

Says Paul Dooley: "Geraldine Chaplin once told an interviewer: 'Bob has a wonderful way of allowing you to contribute to something which turns out to be exactly what he wanted all along.' She says it's all in his head, he knows it's there somewhere. And it's true."

Says John Considine: "I remember a speech he gave when we were doing *Buffalo Bill and the Indians*. He assembled all the cast, really a varied cast, in his suite in Calgary. And he said he wanted to let everyone know what kind of respect he had for actors, because it was something he could never do. 'I don't know how you do it,' he said, 'because I could never do that. As of tomorrow, I just want you to know I'm looking forward to seeing what you bring to your parts. There are no wrong moves. I assume from here on in that you know ten times more about this person than I ever could. I'm just anxious to see who you are.

"Sort of like telling everybody—just go for it—you can't do anything wrong. For me, it was the actor's nirvana. He would be behind the camera, seemingly not telling anyone too much, and yet . . . I would always be conscious of him responding behind the camera, because when he's enjoying what you're doing, you see him shaking and laughing and just into it."

Says Shelley Duvall: "Bob never says much. It was the same thing on *Thieves Like Us*. I rode to work with him on the first day of shooting. I said, 'Anything you want to tell me?' He said, 'No, *you* know.' Now, *that's* direction."

Actors say that Altman, behind the camera or at dailies, is one of the best audiences a thespian could hope for. The director may say very little—maybe a solitary encouraging word—but he is extraordinarily attentive, and his enjoyment of the moment is palpable.

"I always felt I had someone to perform for," says Danton. "Bob Altman made me feel like he was a great audience. When you're working in front of a camera, especially if you're an actor used to stage work like I was, you miss that rapport. One of Bob's greatest assets was his great enthusiasm, his ability to make you feel as if he was really watching. You felt there was an active, engaged audience watching you every single moment and enjoying what you were doing. The result was, you wanted to do more. You always felt that you could do a little better and give a little more.

"As a matter of fact, that was one of Mr. Altman's key words. I'd say, 'How is that, Bob?' He'd say, 'A little more.' I'd say, 'A little more what, Bob?' He'd say, 'Just a little more.' More energy or more of whatever it was I was doing— but I never felt it was a negative criticism. I felt it was an encouragement to go further, take chances, hang out there.''

Altman has often said that the most expensive thing about making motion pictures is getting to the point of turning the camera on. After which, the actual film stock runs cheap. The director has often arranged, for actors in small parts or secondary roles, a moment in which they might shine. He has encouraged big and small parts to fiddle with the characterization. The improvisation and open-endedness can be exciting; but it can also be overwhelming to some actors. That is part of Altman's strategy—to keep the actors off-guard, and to preserve the rough edges.

Paul Dooley is emblematic of the type of actor Altman increasingly relied upon in the 1970s—a versatile character lead who, until he was spotted by Altman, was relatively unknown in Hollywood. In 1977, the Second City veteran was acting in a Jules Feiffer play in New York, called *Hold Me*. Altman went backstage one night after the show and talked to the actor. He mentioned he was looking for someone to play the father of the bride in *A Wedding*. Altman gave Dooley his card with the address of his Park Avenue apartment on it and asked him to stop up for an "open house."

When Dooley did so, it was like a scene in an Altman film. The dangled part was barely mentioned. Dooley was there for several hours of rambling conversation and conviviality, with Altman meandering in and out between phone calls, drinks, and backgammon. Constant digressions, constant diversions. Indeed, Dooley visited the apartment three times before Altman informed him in an offhand fashion, "Hey, we found your daughter," meaning the actress who would play the bride.

"He's so loose that you have to guess whether you're in the movie or not," says Dooley.

Dooley says there are many misconceptions about the way Altman directs and specifically about the way he directs actors. "I went back to New York after *A Wedding*," says Paul Dooley, "and people I knew in the business who didn't know him or know anything about him were talking in all these preconceived notions. They'd say, 'I guess he wastes a lot of film.' I'd say, 'What do you mean he wastes a lot of film?' They'd say, 'Well, you know with improvisation, you shoot a lot more than you'll ever use.' I'd say, 'No, as a matter of fact, he's more economical in shooting than you guys who do commercials. You do thirty seconds in a day and you shoot sixty-eight takes, and take seven is fine. We do takes all day because we've rented the hall for that amount of money. Bob usually gets two cameras on one angle, and that's it. Two cameras on one angle and two takes gets him four possibilities.'

"And he doesn't waste a lot of time. Even if he doesn't have everything he wants in one of those two takes, he sets up over here and over here, and then he gets what he didn't get over here and over here. Now he's got pieces in both places, and he knows how he can cut them. He knows it can be done. Whereas, some guys want the perfect master. He gets bored with the perfect master.

"People think it must be anarchy to have so much improvising. And I tell them it's really a myth that it's improvised. There's a little improvisation, because Bob leaves the door open for improvisation, and the door being open is all we have to know to just go ahead and do the parts. It's written in a way that seems free and loose and relaxed and naturalistic—that's because the door's open. We don't even have to go out. We never even have to use the door.

"If I know I'm doing a scene, if I know that five percent of it is up to me, I have that much latitude. I might not come up with something interesting in the five percent, but it informs the whole rest of it. The other ninety-five percent of it is done in kind of a joy, a kind of freedom and openness, influenced by the knowledge—and not only for the actors— that I have Bob's trust.

"Without ever having talked it over with him, this is how I worked with Bob in *A Perfect Couple*. In a scene only between myself and Marta [Heflin], I wouldn't be stepping on anybody's toes to bend the scene a little bit. So I would take his two-page scene and do it as scripted, and put my ad-libs at the top and bottom so that he would chop it off at either end and still have the scene. I would sort of improv into it. . . .

"When a scene is finished by the end of the line in the dialogue, most directors would say 'and cut!' But Bob always leaves it running a little longer. Because I think he's found that he gets things. Actors do things, they continue their behavior, and it gets trapped on camera. Something interesting and fresh will happen because it isn't all written and all planned. And it isn't costing him anything. It's just an extra ten, twenty, thirty seconds."

The slow zoom is not only a means of visual emphasis, it is Altman's way of cheating on the actor. It is eavesdropping, voyeurism, an intimacy with the actor even when the camera is at some remove. The actor is lulled into casualness.

The zoom unnerves some actors, it disarms others. Altman finds it useful as a way of creeping in on a performance without alerting the actor. It allows him to play down the energy level. This salient element of his visual style has as its basis a simultaneous fear of and admiration for the actor. The multiple sound channels are yet another way of cheating: Everyone is miked at once, so no one feels the pressure of focus.

"Always assume that everything is going to be kept [on film]," says Dooley. "I did a scene in *A Wedding*, and I was sure it wasn't the coverage of the scene. It's the scene where we're all dancing in the dance hall. There's about twenty-five of us, all couples. I'm dancing here—and over there all the way across the room are the bandstands—and the camera. All those twenty-three or twenty-five people are between me and the camera. I'm dancing with Dina Merrill. There's two cameras over there kind of up high, but it feels like they're shooting Vittorio [Gassman], the front of the crowd, or a general master, right?

"But we're all miked, the whole bunch of us. So we went through it once; Dina and I weren't even talking. Altman said, 'Let's do another one.' I said to Dina, 'Do you want to run through the lines?'—and she said okay. So while we're

dancing, he's shooting, we're just running the lines for our-
selves. And everybody's talking—everybody at once. At the
end of the day, I said to the assistant director, 'Is he going to
get a shot of Dina and me, because we have some dialogue. . . ?' He said, 'He's got that already.'

"I was really worried, because we never did do it, we just
talked it. Mainly what I thought was we didn't have any energy, though we had the right readings, more or less. Then I
found a startling thing. He played that scene [in dailies], and
it was fine. I was aware before of certain differences, but it
pointed up the differences between the stage and the screen.
Because I thought I was too far underwater, but it was fine."

The nightly gathering at dailies also cuts both ways: The
actors receive the instant gratification of seeing themselves
on film, and Altman of course can always dispense of that
footage later on at the cutting table. Much of the improvisation on Altman movies is "lost" forever—in those legendary
longer versions of *Nashville* and other Altman films that
never seem to get finished and exhibited. Much of the script
departure is remembered from the privileged moment. Yet
many of these scenes never turn up in the movie, simply
because they do not serve the larger purpose.

Altman likes to tell his casts that the real movie is at the
dailies, not in the theatres. In part, that is sincere. In part,
that soothes the savage egos that will be tossed into the cutting bins.

It is also true that Altman will sometimes scissor actors
out of a picture as much as possible when he cannot sugar
them along, one way or another.

Like Paul Smith, who played Bluto in *Popeye*. Smith aggravated Altman. In the film the director keeps cutting away
from him. To the detriment of the picture, Bluto is a half-
conceived character, and Paul Smith's performance elicits
the least time on the screen from an unsympathetic director.
Or Joann Pflug in *M*A*S*H*, about whom the director
complained cryptically to the press that they did not get
along because she sought "motivations and reasons." Vener-

able Margaret Hamilton in *Brewster McCloud* received similar treatment. It is hard to say what Hamilton's importance in the original script might have been, but friction with Altman earned her, on the screen, not much more than a half-glimpse in the opening credits.

Altman likes to say he reveres actors. But he is also terribly reliant on them—more reliant than he is on the cameraman or the editor, for in a pinch Altman can do either of those jobs. But, unlike Orson Welles and Woody Allen, he cannot act the lead in his own movies.

Brian McKay says that the director's real attitude toward actors is masked by this need. Altman has no choice but to beguile actors. The paradox is, according to McKay: His acting for *them* must be convincing, so that they will act to the hilt for *him*.

In any case, the actors know the director only superficially. Of the company, they sometimes have the least social contact with him. They are the least involved in the filmmaking process, and are thinking only of their own lines and their own screen time and the impression they must make. They *want* to be beguiled.

No matter the consequences. Tommy Thompson brings up *Quintet*, for example, which assembled Altman's most internationally distinguished cast, in Montreal, to appear in one of the unqualified stinkers of all time.

"Actors are funny," says Tommy Thompson. "Give them a costume and lines of dialogue, and they'll say it anywhere. They get so wrapped up in it that they don't look at the long picture of what is this . . . they look at their character and rightly so. They trust the producer, the director, to have the long picture in mind, and I don't think we did."

Rick Jason from *Combat* and Altman's television days believes the underside of Altman's love for actors is a secret contempt for them born of his own inadequacies. He says acting is Altman's one area of politeness. For the director cannot utter this contempt, because Altman well knows that the one category of people he cannot afford to alienate is actors.

Jason prefaces his comments by saying that he never had any trouble with Altman as a director, that he regarded Altman as a friend during the time of *Combat,* and that his relationship with Altman only declined in the years afterward, when Jason refused to become a "camp follower" paying homage to Altman at the Westwood offices.

Jason recalls Altman at a party, weaving-drunk, taunting him, "What the hell do you know? You're only an *actor.*"

Jason says: "When he drinks, it [the truth] finally comes out. I think he makes out that he loves actors. I think he loves himself too much to love anybody else. I think he considers actors puppets and uses them as such. I think Altman, down deep, feels that an actor has no animation until he gives it to them."

It is impossible to know. Not that it really matters, perhaps. In the end, the actors and actresses who began to flock to Altman, especially after *Nashville*—the famous people who throughout the 1970s and the 1980s worked for him at scale, as well as the newcomers starting out—it was enough for them that they were in the hands of a director who had proven himself one of the best in the business at showcasing talent.

Chapter
30

BUFFALOED BILL

The period immediately following *Nashville* was a heady one.

Suddenly Altman had so many projects planned, and flowering, that it was impossible to keep track of them all, except by announcements in the trades. Briefly, Altman was attractive to film companies again; in the wake of *Nashville*, the studios were wooing him for sundry projects.

● For a spell, Altman held script discussions with author Thomas McGuane pertaining to his National Book Award-nominated novel *92 in the Shade*, about rival fishing guides in Key West. Elliott Kastner was going to produce the film, until Kastner and Altman had a vehement falling-out. Altman was dropped from the film (novelist McGuane eventually directed it himself), and for many years Kastner was at the top of the "enemies" list. His name, mentioned, abbreviated many an Altman repast.

● Passingly, Altman made a bid on Eliot Asinof's engrossing reportorial history of the Black Sox scandal and the 1919 World Series, *Eight Men Out*. For years *Eight Men Out* was one of Hollywood's most coveted properties, but the deals kept falling through. Indeed, Asinof wrote another entire book, *Bleeding Between the Lines*, documenting the misadventures of the story rights. Writer-director John Sayles eventually managed to film an adaptation of the book for release in 1988. Altman told the author that one of the reasons he was interested in that tragic chapter of professional baseball history is that B.C. had lost a lot of money betting on the Sox.

● Altman worked on a film version of another sports book, Peter Gent's football best-seller, *North Dallas Forty;* but his participation fell victim to the usual preproduction disagreements, and *North Dallas Forty* was ultimately directed by Ted Kotcheff.

● High on the list of Lion's Gate priorities was *The Yigepoxy*, with a script by Altman and Alan Rudolph from Robert Grossbach's *Easy and Hard Ways Out*. The novel was a hilarious, accessible, very *M*A*S*H*-like black comedy about military-industrial-complex red tape. (Epoxy is glue; a YIG is a radar device used in aircraft for evasive action with ground-to-air missiles.)

Warner's kept insisting on rewrites and adjustments in the casting, so Lion's Gate could never quite pin down the production start date. It was a big frustration for Altman, and he and Rudolph began to look around for something more immediate to work on.

● The two best-known properties under the umbrella of Lion's Gate were Kurt Vonnegut's *Breakfast of Champions* and E. L. Doctorow's *Ragtime*. Alan Rudolph was adapting the former, while Joan Tewkesbury was writing the latter.

Breakfast of Champions was ready to go, but the producer

History (and celebrity) debunked, with Buffalo Bill
(Paul Newman) in *Buffalo Bill and the Indians,*
Altman's follow-up to the acclaimed *Nashville.*

who controlled the rights was hedging on approving
Rudolph's script. Altman even announced the tentative casting: Ruth Gordon as Elliot Rosewater, the world's richest
man ("Sure; she's an actor, why not?"), Sterling Hayden as
sci-fi novelist Kilgore Trout, Lily Tomlin as all three wives
of the lead character, Flip Wilson as all of the black servants,
plus Alice Cooper (both Alan Rudolph and Allan Nicholls
had directed Alice Cooper rock videos), Cleavon Little, Peter
Falk, and so on.

The delay of *Breakfast of Champions* left Altman with
Ragtime, Doctorow's best-selling crazy-quilt fiction about
1906 America which, with its free-associative structure, read
like an Altman film. Tewkesbury had finished a "first draft
without dialogue," and she was just beginning to go back and
layer in the dialogue, when . . .

*   *   *

Ragtime and *Buffalo Bill and the Indians* had in common the Italian film impresario Dino De Laurentiis.

At first, Altman had turned down a film based on the successful Off-Broadway play by Arthur Kopit when the project was offered to him by producer David Susskind. Later on, as other commitments stalled, Altman reconsidered. With Alan Rudolph he talked over a script about Buffalo Bill Cody and Sitting Bull. They decided the subject matter was ripe. The financing was ready, the whole production team was in place—many direct from *Nashville*—and it was perfect for filming in Calgary. Altman said yes.

It boasted the director's first king-sized budget, of $6 million, partly to cover the salaries of Paul Newman (as a wanton and florid Buffalo Bill Cody) and Burt Lancaster (as blustery dime novelist Ned Buntline, narrator of the tall tale), who head up the allspice cast that was becoming an Altman trademark.

Besides Lancaster and Newman, there was also Broadway veteran Joel Grey (as Wild West showman Nate Salsbury), Harvey Keitel (as Salsbury's flustered kin and gofer), Kevin McCarthy (as the Wild West Show's publicist), Will Sampson (as the phlegmatic interpreter), Frank Kaquitts (as Sitting Bull, who says practically nothing, and never anything in English), Geraldine Chaplin (as Annie Oakley), John Considine (milking laughs as Annie's husband and manager), a trio of divas from the opera world (Bonnie Leaders, Noelle Rogers, and Evelyn Lear), comedian Pat McCormick (as President Grover Cleveland, continuing Altman's tradition of cynical commentary on presidential timber), Allan Nicholls (playing a bit as a frontier journalist), Robert Doqui (as a wrangler), Bert Remsen (as a bartender), and Shelley Duvall (as the U.S. First Lady).

In interviews Altman insisted he had not seen Kopit's play *Indians*, nor had he ever read it in its entirety. That seems typically offensive to the writer (though Kopit good-naturedly appears in a crowd scene). Altman claims he and Rudolph boned up by reading biography and chronicles of the frontier ("the history is correct philosophically, but not actually"), before ultimately dispensing with facts in favor of the stream-of-consciousness history lesson of the film.

The screenplay shifted the emphasis of the stage play: Where Kopit focused on the plight of the Indians, Altman focused on the enigma of Buffalo Bill—which was a way, perhaps, of commenting on himself. One senses that the director feels quite at home with the character of the great Western bunko artist, and alternatively, squeamish whenever the Indians are on camera. Altman himself has made the telling comment that the epiphanic scene of Sitting Bull halting a rowdy grandstand crowd with his aura of dignity was "not one of my favorites."

It is really Bill's, not Bull's, story. "A combination of Custer, Gable, Redford, and me," said Newman at the time. "Symbolically the first star . . . someone who cannot live up to his legend."

The fabled Western hero is demonstrated to be a liar, a vain braggart, a possibly impotent womanizer (he has a penchant for opera singers who fawn over him with their arias), and a dissolute alcoholic. His charisma holds the Wild West Show together, though Buffalo Bill is haunted by the emptiness of his soul, especially as compared to the manifest spirituality of Sitting Bull. This is a consummate performance by Newman, who is alternately comical and eerie in his long golden locks, even if the movie bogs down and could use more of the other, less self-conscious characters—and more of the sidelight high jinks, the rodeo stunts.

When Bull dies, Bill falls apart altogether, and confronts his moral nemesis in his dreams. Altman, who dreams entire films, feverishly revised that thematic soliloquy himself. According to Tewkesbury and Rudolph, that scene, more than any other in *Buffalo Bill and the Indians*, is "pure Altman," expressing something inchoate about the director as filtered through the persona of Buffalo Bill Cody. The scene plays much like Barbara Jean's babbling breakdown in *Nashville*, using phrases and insights that are intriguing as emotional clues.

Altman's typical allspice cast: (from left) John
Considine, Geraldine Chaplin, Harvey Keitel,
and Joel Grey.

I got people with no lives . . . livin' through me! Proud people.
My daddy . . . died without ever seein' me as a star! Tall, profitable . . . good-looking . . . Custer was a good man. He gave
the Indians a reason to be famous! Bull, damn you! In a hundred years . . . I'm still goin' to be Buffalo Bill . . . star! You're
still gonna be The Injun! You wanna stay the same. That's
going backwards! The difference between a white man and a
Injun in all situations is that a Injun is red! But an Injun is red
for a real good reason . . . so we can tell us apart!
[Bill looks up at his picture, in which he's riding his proud
white stallion, Brigham.]
Ain't he ridin' that horse right? Well, if he ain't, how come
all of you took him for a kin? . . . Truth is whatever gets the
loudest applause.

Rudolph was not allowed to touch that speech. More's the
pity: Buffalo Bill's curious self-revelation falls within a less

incisive dramatic framework than *Nashville* and typifies the terminal murkiness of *Buffalo Bill*.

But some motion pictures rise above their flaws, and *Buffalo Bill* will never be less than a smart, flavorful, immensely appealing film, with provocative highlights. Like *Nashville*, it mused on the thin line between entertainment and politics, celebrity and illusion, private utterances and public hypocrisy; yet *Buffalo Bill* ("Robert Altman's Absolutely Unique and Heroic Enterprise of Inimitable Lustre") is the more playful film. The cast is exuberant. There is capricious incidental music by Richard Baskin, bandleading a Canadian ensemble. And the pristine photography by Paul Lohmann, the star-spangled bandstand under the clear frontier skies, as designed by Tony Masters and art-directed by Jack Maxsted, are a feast for the senses.

The involvement of Alan Rudolph, cinematographer Paul Lohmann, musical director Richard Baskin, the Lion's Gate sound team, and seemingly half of the *Nashville* cast—all seemed to ensure *Buffalo Bill*'s success as the perfect companion piece to its predecessor.

But the New York City press junket to launch the film proved disastrous.

De Laurentiis had insisted that Altman speed up the editing and preview the film at one of these publicity fetes. The assembled journalists were in a mood to be transported by Robert Altman's latest motion picture, which sounded tantalizing in publicity handouts. When it did not live up to post-*Nashville* expectations, they found themselves disappointed, somehow let down.

Newman joined the director for questions and answers after the screening. The atmosphere was set by Newman's remark, "I hope you left your grenades at the door . . ." and by Altman's acknowledgment, "I'm very nervous about this movie . . ." The ensuing queries were not particularly hostile, but there was an uncomfortable ambivalence in the room, and from Altman, a defensiveness.

One of the scribes asked Altman if he was upset about what had befallen *Nashville.*

ALTMAN: I have no bitterness about *Nashville.* I feel very, very thrilled. We got five Academy Award nominations. We won the [National Society of Film Critics Award] for the best film. And many, many other accolades. The film made money, nobody got hurt on it, everybody's career was helped by it. There's no way I could be disappointed or bitter about *Nashville.*

Another press representative asked the director whether all of the high expectations for *Buffalo Bill and the Indians* were, perhaps, unfair, considering the resounding accomplishment of *Nashville.*

ALTMAN: I think that *Nashville* will unfortunately inhibit this film more than it will help it, because they come so close together. I think there'll be comparisons made, there will be political comparisons made and extensions [made], and I would much prefer if this film were to come out of limbo, because I feel it's more important as a film. It's a film I wish I could be disassociated with—in other words, that you would not associate this as a 'quote' Altman film.

He was asked to elaborate.

ALTMAN: Everybody seems to consider *Nashville* as a kind of failure, which, I point out, it was not. It was, from our standpoint, a huge success. I think the film was made with no major studio [backing], it was made with very little money, we did very well with it. I think that a lot of critics and people that thought so much of it feel a little disappointed because it didn't do better, and I keep hearing that *Cuckoo's Nest* beat us [at the Oscars], and that's a race I really chose not to enter. I went there. We loved the award we got [Best Song]. Of all of them, if we could only receive one Academy Award, I would have opted for the one we did receive—other than Best Picture, obviously. But I am afraid that there's going to be this feeling that this is going to be another *Nashville.*

So it went. It was a Seventies watershed for Altman, this

press junket, the resulting publicity, the early reviews, and the film's sputtering release to movie theatres.

The reviews were not unkind (there were many plaudits), but the confidence of De Laurentiis, who had already been feuding behind the scenes with Altman over the editing and the length of the film, was shaken. *Buffalo Bill and the Indians* became yet one more Altman film barely available to the public for viewing.

The rumor persists that, as it is, the existing print of *Buffalo Bill* does not even represent the director's final cut. Altman (and Rudolph) insist otherwise. But there was obvious undue haste in the final postproduction stages. Louis Lombardo, for one, feels the film is sloppily patched together. He spoke with Altman about it, believing the raw material is there for one of his best films. Lombardo offered to reedit *Buffalo Bill* for free. But that became just one more argument between Lombardo and Altman.

The disappointment of *Buffalo Bill* was the first of several body blows to Altman and Lion's Gate. Somewhere in the midst of all their wrangling and sniping, De Laurentiis fired Altman from *Ragtime*, which was subsequently inherited by Czech emigré director Milos Forman.* The official explanation was that De Laurentiis disagreed with Altman's grandiose plans to adapt the novel into two separate and overlapping three-hour movies (the screenplay, at that point, was 385 pages). But the feuding had escalated with *Buffalo Bill* and spilled over into everything else.

At about this same time, Warner's dismissed Altman from *The Yigepoxy*. And even though Rudolph had written a script on good faith, Lion's Gate found itself outbid for the story rights to Kurt Vonnegut's *Breakfast of Champions*. That enviable property, too, passed from Altman's hands.

---

*Ragtime was finished and released in 1981, and despite some richly imagined scenes as directed by Milos Forman it was a disappointment—lumbering where it ought to float, narrowly focused where it ought to be far-reaching—like the book— or an Altman film.

Alan Rudolph, having seen two scripts of his abandoned in a year's interim, and having served his apprenticeship long and well, announced plans to direct his own screenplay of *Welcome to L.A.* Altman would produce. That was amicable enough; but it removed a supremely talented writer (and surpassing director, as it turned out) from Altman's midst at the same time as Joan Tewkesbury was packing her bags.

Tewkesbury left Altman's employ a third of the way through a rewrite of the *Ragtime* script. She made a decorous point of telling interviewers that her departure was by mutual agreement, so that she could meet a deadline on a paperback of the screenplay of *Nashville*. If so, that would make Tewkesbury the first writer in the history of Hollywood to surrender the assignment of dramatizing a valued literary property for the task of annotating her own previously produced script.

What actually happened is that, for some time, Scott Bushnell's power within Lion's Gate had been on the rise. She treated Tewkesbury and others previously close to Altman coolly, maneuvering for advantage. She backed up Altman's position that those who chose to thrive away from Lion's Gate were worse than ingrates; they were disloyalists.

Tewkesbury was juggling other assignments independent of Lion's Gate and was slow on calendar dates for completing stages of *Ragtime*, when Altman telephoned her one day and summarily fired her, the writer of the best film he has ever directed. Tewkesbury was shocked. She would not be the last of the inner circle to be given such an acrimonious goodbye, nor to ask herself *why*.

Chapter
31

FLICK-
OF-THE-
WRIST
MOVIES

On top of everything, in 1976, Kathryn fell grievously ill and had to be rushed to the hospital.

If there were an Oscar in Hollywood for Best Wife, the consensus among everyone who knows her is that Kathryn Reed would win it, hands down. She has been called "the glue that keeps him together." She handled the director's tantrums and low moods with equanimity. She tolerated Altman's compulsive round-the-clock activity and his attentions toward other women. (As late as 1976, Altman bragged to Sally Quinn of *The Washington Post* that he indulged himself with plenty of mistresses. "I just giggle and give in," he was quoted as saying. "Keep 'em comin.'")

Once he became a public figure, Altman was more discreet about his extracurricular love life. Few knew of his tempestuous affair with Faye Dunaway in the early 1970s. They had dodged the press and hopped in and out of limousines on their way to assignations. But in reality Altman was happy being married to Kathryn. He liked to say about her: "She is the only person who has never bored me." She liked to say the same thing about him. No matter his sexual peregrinations, Kathryn liked being Mrs. Robert Altman. After the Faye Dunaway relationship broke up, the director's wife confided to a friend that sex with her husband was twice as exciting with the knowledge that he was unfaithful at times.

Kathryn had stayed with him through the hard times. She had hostessed his parties, she had been his sounding board with estranged friends, she had balanced the family checkbook, she had raised their two children, Bobby and Matthew. Now, Kathryn lay, seemingly, at death's door. And the director was profoundly shaken. Her illness happened to coincide with the final collapse of *The Yigepoxy;* even as Altman was screaming at the top of his lungs over the phone to an executive at Warner Brothers, he realized he was terribly, terribly upset about Kathryn.

Her condition improved, but slowly. Then one night when Kathryn was still in the hospital, Altman "dreamed" *Three Women.*

Beginning with *Three Women,* the five years between *Nashville* (1975) and *Popeye* (1980) were years of highs and lows for Altman. These were the years of the "flick-of-the-wrist" movies. It had taken Altman five years to "dream," write, painstakingly rewrite, and ultimately produce *Images.* Now, he could "dream" a movie, have it scripted, cast, directed, edited, and in and out of movie theatres (if it ever got into the theatres), all within eighteen months.

Three of the five films he made during this period were barely shown to audiences before being dumped by the distributors. Yet, beginning with *Three Women*, the movie he "dreamed" when his wife was stricken, these "flick-of-the-wrist" movies are also among his most intriguing, his most effervescent, and his most original works—on balance, as full of highlights as flaws.

Patricia Resnick started work on *Buffalo Bill and the Indians* at the bottom rung of the ladder as an American Film Institute intern. She had written a college thesis on Altman, and he had liked what he read. She came aboard as an assistant to publicist Mike Kaplan, writing bios and press releases and picking people up at the airport and shuttling them to the set in Calgary. She has a tiny bit in the film as a visiting reporter sitting near the author E. L. Doctorow and Altman's agent, Sam Cohn, in one of the crowd scenes.

Resnick was surprised when, fairly early on in the production, Altman starting asking her opinion about things. Partly, she figured, it was because the production and publicity offices and the director's offices were on the same floor of the hotel in Vancouver where they were all staying, so they were in close proximity. It so happened that Patricia Resnick and Richard Baskin were the only two Lion's Gate people assigned to live on the executive floor.

After *Buffalo Bill*, her AFI grant ran out, but Altman kept Resnick on a weekly salary, still doing PR. One of her other projects was the development of a visual continuity script for *Ragtime*, using different colored pieces of paper to key the Joan Tewkesbury script-in-progress. "Like, all red was Houdini, and all blue was whatever," she says. "Bob said, 'I want to be able to look at the script and to visually identify how much of it is dealing with each of these people."

Meanwhile, Resnick was also hanging around the filming of *Welcome to L.A.* (in which she also has an acting snippet) and *The Late Show*, the two ongoing independent Lion's Gate films that Altman was producing. On the latter, Resnick became friendly with Lily Tomlin, who was playing a

flaky sidekick to aging private eye Art Carney in the Forties-
style murder mystery by writer-director Robert Benton.
Tomlin was constantly sculpting her dialogue, and Resnick
had plenty of ideas.

"Lily, who was redoing a lot of her dialogue with Benton's
blessing, had a tendency to sort of just ask the room questions about 'What can I say here?' Generally, nobody responded; so I started responding, and I was getting laughs.
Eventually, she decided to try and figure out who this voice
calling out from the back of the set was. I started working
with her on redoing her lines, and we hit it off."

Tomlin asked Resnick to write some fairly substantial
comedy pieces for her Broadway revue—one, a piece about
the Sixties, and another about a male character in a singles
bar. Though Resnick had written a dramatic screenplay that
Altman had never found time to read, Altman did see
Tomlin's show on Broadway, and afterward he remarked,
"Oh, the kid can write." With Tewkesbury gone, "the kid"
was asked if she would write up the director's "dream."

It was always a convoluted, jigsaw, atmospheric dream.*
At first, there were only "two women"—one character for
Shelley Duvall to play and one for Sissy Spacek—whom Alt-
man had been watching approvingly in dailies for Alan
Rudolph's *Welcome to L.A.* The director decided to add the
Janice Rule character later on. In the dream, the three
women would interchange personalities, one of them would
die, and in the end it would be unclear what was real and
what was imagined. The film would be sort of like Luis
Buñuel's *Belle de Jour.*

Altman and Resnick worked on a few pieces of the dream at
a time. Resnick worked upstairs at Lion's Gate, and the direc-

---

*In an interview Altman has explained the genesis of the story: "I didn't dream the
story, but I'd had this succession of dreams all in one night in which I was making
a film with Shelley Duvall and Sissy Spacek and it was called *Three Women* and I
didn't know who the other woman was. It took place in the desert, and it was
about personality-theft. And in my dream, I kept waking up and people would
come into my bedroom—production managers—and I'd say, 'Go into the desert
and find a saloon.' And when I did wake up, and realized that it was a dream, I was
very disappointed, because I was really happy with what was happening."

Millie Lamoreaux (Shelley Duvall) and Pinky Rose (Sissy Spacek), in a parable about personality-theft, in *Three Women*.

tor would yell up the circular staircase to her as she progressed. She'd come running down for a conference, and he would rattle off some spanking new idea he had while driving to the office that morning. She had to make sense of it somehow in the story, even if it did not make any real sense. Altman was insistent that it was all a godamned dream anyhow.

"Sometimes I would just say, 'Why?' And he would say, 'I don't know, I just want it that way. It's my instinct.' That was okay to say, but sometimes it was hard to get it down on paper.

"One of his visions was the ending. He said, 'Wait a minute, I see a dolly shot thru [sic] a window, and they're all there, and Janice Rule is there too—and it actually *is* 'three women.' I said, 'Why? What does it mean?' He said, 'I don't have any idea what it means, but I see it, I like it, and I'm going to do it. It's a beautiful last shot.' He couldn't articulate it, but that's what he wanted."

In the end, Resnick's fifty-page treatment provided the framework of the film. In Resnick's story, Pinky Rose (Spacek) and Millie Lammoreaux (Duvall) are both staff attendants of a Desert Springs rehabilitation center where their duties involve helping elderly people in and out of a steaming mineral bath.

A needy cipher of a personality, Pinky cultivates a friendship with Millie, who spouts a bottomless cup of consumerist clichés. They become roommates. Millie frequents Dodge City, a fake, rundown Wild West community operated by macho ex-stunt-double Edgar Hart (Robert Fortier), who also manages the Purple Sage, the singles complex where she and Pinky live. The Dodge City hangout and the spa are decorated with weird primordial frescoes that are the creation of Edgar's pregnant wife, Willie (Janice Rule).

Pinky idolizes and begins eerily to imitate Millie. But after Millie brings Edgar home for a sexual tryst, Pinky throws herself into the pool below their balcony and is seriously injured. Full of guilt, Millie devotes herself to Pinky's health. She summons Pinky's elderly parents (played by the aged film and theatre director John Cromwell and his wife, actress Ruth Nelson) from Texas, but Pinky refuses even to acknowledge their presence.

When she finally recovers, Pinky is transformed: She seems to actually *become* Millie in every peculiar detail. When Willie goes into labor, Pinky goes into shock, and Millie rushes to the occasion. The baby is stillborn. In an unsettling postscript, Millie and Pinky have taken over the proprietorship of Dodge City; the overbearing Edgar has been killed in a mysterious "accident"; and there has been some kind of personality transference among the three women.*

Altman had an open door at Twentieth Century-Fox, the studio that had cashed in on *M*A*S*H*. Alan Ladd Jr. was

---

*The ad campaign cryptically promised: "1 woman became 2/2/ women became 3/3/ women became 1."

running the production side of the studio then, and he was one of the most forward-looking executives in the industry. During his tenure, the studio produced not only the money-making *Star Wars*, but such intelligent and respected fare as *Julia* and *The Turning Point*. Ladd and his two key lieutenants, Gareth Wigan and Jay Cantor, were amenable to Altman as a director, and willing to sponsor his more ambiguous films, on the theory that the occasional money-making film would right the balance sheet.

It was enough for them when Altman brought Resnick's fifty-page treatment in for a pitch meeting. Based on that treatment, the film was financed by the studio. That is when Altman surprised Resnick by announcing that he did not want a full screenplay for this particular Altman film. He would work off the treatment. Not only would Resnick *not* write the *Three Women* script but indeed, Altman was taking Resnick off the Lion's Gate payroll. With the temporary lull in production, he could no longer afford to keep her on salary.

Resnick was dismayed; and, at first, there was talk of grievance filing and of retaining a lawyer. Ultimately, after discussing it with friends and considering the alternatives, she decided she was not an important enough personage to buck Robert Altman.

"I was disappointed because I felt that if it got financed on it [the treatment] and it went to screenplay, there was a tacit understanding I would do the screenplay with him," says Resnick, "and then that would be my entree to this world I wanted to get into. When I was laid off, I was upset, but I also had no contacts in the business outside of Bob. I didn't know what else I was going to do because Bob's world was so enclosed."

Accordingly, there was no extended script, per se, when Altman began filming *Three Women* on location in Palm Springs.

Shelley Duvall filled in the gaps, much the same way Susannah York did for *Images*. It was Duvall who wrote those quirky speeches about tuna melts and hula lessons that are

Years of highs and lows: On the set of *Three Women*, Altman talks with old-time Hollywood director John Cromwell and his wife, actress Ruth Nelson.

so revealing of the character, so painful and humorous. It was the first hint that Duvall had ambitions beyond being an actress—a potential she began to realize years later as producer of the award-winning cable television program for children, *Faerie Tale Theatre*.*

"I wrote all my own monologues [for *Three Women*]," she told The *Village Voice* in an interview. "Bob would say, 'Why don't you write a monologue just in case we can use it?' And we'd use it. I put a lot of myself in, but I'm not a consumer like Millie. I played her like a Lubitsch comedy—people taking themselves very seriously. It is great fun to watch, as long as it isn't you."

The rest of the film is certainly light-years from elegant

---

*Her *Faerie Tale Theatre* coproducer was Bridget Terry, another Lion's Gate alumna.

Lubitsch: full of disturbing images, narrative non sequiturs, edgy characterization. Altman had precise control of the mood—while Charles Rosher's hypnotic camerawork and Gerald Busby's evocative score perfectly complemented what is Altman's best film of the quartet he has directed about strange women.

If it is never quite clear what *Three Women* means, or if it means anything worth pondering, it is one of Altman's most gripping films—a human comedy flushed with the morbidity that was part of Altman's makeup. Not only the three leading women but the old marrieds, Cromwell and Nelson, are affecting in their parts—as is Robert Fortier, in the swaggering pseudo-autobiographical role that his old friend the director created with him in mind.

Sissy Spacek earned a Best Supporting Actress plaque from the New York Film Critics, and Shelley Duvall shared the Best Actress award that year at the Cannes Film Festival. In general, critics were very keen for *Three Women*, and its success with reviewers—added to the relatively positive receptions for the independent Lion's Gate productions, *Welcome to L.A.* and *The Late Show*—meant, if not high box-office numbers, at least that Lion's Gate had temporarily rebounded from the fiasco of *Buffalo Bill and the Indians*.

Patricia Resnick had to settle for a small walk-on. Feeling very alienated about a film she had helped set in motion, she was invited by Altman down to the set one day and given a number of lines as one of the Desert Springs staff.

"He felt bad because of what happened so he gave me a job as an actor and paid me SAG minimum so at least I had some money coming in," she says. But Resnick was not credited for her writing assistance on one of Altman's best-known post-*Nashville* films. The final credit reads: "Screenplay by Robert Altman."

On the set of *Three Women*, a visiting journalist asked Altman what his next film was going to be about. Partly in irritation, he snapped that he was going to photograph a wedding. Later, he surprised his associates by reflecting that that was not such a bad idea after all, to do a film about the marriage ritual. *A Wedding*, it ought to be called, he said.

In interviews, Altman has said that the Altman family photograph of Aunt Pauline's wedding was a subconscious inspiration. "*A Wedding* sprang from a picture, one of the earliest photographs I remember of myself. It was cut out of the *Kansas City Journal-Post* in the rotogravure section. I was probably five years old, I might have been three, and I was the ringbearer in a wedding. And there's my mother and my father and all my aunts and uncles, and they're all members of this wedding. And that photograph stays in my mind, and has all my life. When I went and put *A Wedding* together, it looks like that photograph. It's updated and all that, but the people who are in the wedding are my family."

His principal collaborator for the movie was selected in the same instinctual manner. John Considine had been welcome around Lion's Gate in varying capacities ever since he had returned to play a small part in *California Split*. After taking time off to appear in a television soap opera, Considine had acted in *Buffalo Bill*, and he had contributed some voice-overs and sang a song that is heard on the radio in *Three Women*. No matter how much time elapsed between his contacts with Altman, Considine had an affinity with the director, who instilled him with such confidence. And they had the same playful attitude toward life and work.

"The thing about Bob that was most attractive to me, and I have it too, is that he loved to play, his ability to play," says Considine. "He's got a kid inside of him that's so much fun that when he gives vent to it, it's just like being at a birthday party.

"I've walked down the street with him. We used to go to the theatres to check the gate of *Three Women* when we were writing *A Wedding* in New York—every performance—and sometimes on the way back, he might be in a bad mood, and I'd say something like [Russian accent], 'Well, comrade, it wasn't a good show . . .' He'd go right into a CIA character, and we'd forget about the movie. He can just play with the best of them. It's that funny mixture of someone

On the set of *A Wedding:* Altman (at left) directed the elaborate festivities (Desi Arnaz Jr. in foreground), but the script was a communal effort.

really in a position of authority who could really be this wild little kid at the same time."

Considine and his brother Tim Considine (who played Spin on Walt Disney's *Spin and Marty* and later was a regular on *My Three Sons*) had been doing some writing together, but nothing major, in the way of a feature film, had jelled. He and Altman had never discussed his writing until one day the director asked Considine to collaborate on *A Wedding* with him.

"I was very surprised," says Considine. "He said, 'If it doesn't work out, it won't work out. If you do a good job on it, we'll share the credit.'

"It was a little out of the blue, especially now when I think about it," says Considine. "Then, nothing surprised me about Bob. I think he knew we thought kind of in the same groove, or could, very easily. We had done a lot of that, sort of 'writing' in the car on the way to Lion's Gate, or walking down the street. He'd start something, and I'd go with it. I know he felt comfortable with me. I know I didn't intimidate him. I didn't really challenge him, and I really could go with his free-flow thinking."

Altman laid out "the whole basic tapestry" of the film in their early conversations.

Says Considine: "He wanted a big wedding because he wanted the story to have to do with the wedding business and what it meant in our lives. He told me a lot of key things: He outlined the two families and made them disparate in every conceivable way, religious background, educational, old money, new money, this, that. He had certain crises set up that he wanted to get to. I also remember him saying, 'And the bride and the groom should be the least important characters.'

"Suddenly," Considine continues, "I was sitting in this little room over at Lion's Gate wondering what the hell I was going to do. I read all these books about weddings, and I started making notes, and I began to put the characters on these little cards. Soon these were up all over the wall. They became the bride's family, the groom's family, the wedding personnel, the people who worked for the host family, the servants, etc. He'd come in, he'd read them, and like them, and put little ideas on them.

" 'Why don't we give her a little secret?' I found out he loves secrets. . . . So one day when he came in, every character, *every* character, had a secret, and he liked that, and we used it. It helped in the writing of it. The secrets became part of the backstories, because I kept expounding on these little cards until they became two or three pages." (As Considine had just finished two seasons of playing a character on NBC's daytime serial *Another World*, he had a plethora of soap opera-ish ideas.)

Altman wanted more characters than in *Nashville*, just to make a kind of abstract point, but he did not know how many there ought to be, precisely. Considine counted the characters in *Nashville* and came up with twenty-four. He figured he could arbitrarily double that, which is how Considine came up with the number of forty-eight featured characters in *A Wedding*. Altman loved the logic of that.

There seemed to be no pressure to write the script. It was a hoot for Considine, who was scribbling along on his little notecards, until Altman stopped up one day and said, "Oh, by the way, we've got to go over to Fox next week with some kind of treatment, so you'd better get started. . . ."

Remembers Considine: "I had six days to put something down on paper. I remember we were Xeroxing this as the limousine waited to take him to Fox, and it was really bare bones, about thirteen pages. He came back with all the money for the film and said, 'I sort of embroidered on it.' I said, 'What did you embroider?' He said, 'I don't remember some of the stuff but . . .'

"He had created all this *action*. Knowing Bob, it probably came out of someone asking, 'Yeah, but does anything happen?' 'Does anything *happen*? Oh God, there's this terrible accident . . .' And this became a movie of whispering and gossip and how lives were changed by gossip.

"I remember it was a big thing for him that there should be agony in thinking the bride and the groom had both been killed. Then when they found out it was just the other two [characters] . . . he wanted the reaction to be the most revealing thing about our central characters. It doesn't quite happen that way. It was really hard to bring off."

Considine says Altman was more of an "idea man" than someone who actually sat at the typewriter for their script sessions. In fact, when it came time to start work on the formal first draft of the screenplay, Altman made a show of coming in and sitting down, poised at the typewriter keys. Considine thought to himself, "Now, my partner is going to start writing. . . ."

"He put a piece of paper in [the typewriter] and wrote something like, 'Fade in, exterior, cathedral bells chiming, limousines lined up, a security man is directing traffic. The church door opens . . .' Then he got up and said, 'You've got the ball!' and walked out. He never wrote another word."

Considine says Altman collaborated as a writer by improvising scenes extemporaneously as if he were acting them—with Considine his rapt (and captive) audience. This may be one of the reasons why the director was so comfortable cowriting with actors and actresses, from Brian McKay

and Barbara Turner, to Considine, Paul Dooley, and Allan
Nicholls. Altman would say: "We need a wacky scene with
the Bishop here"—and he would strut back and forth spew-
ing dialogue in character that would become part of the
scene. The ideas he would rattle off had to be integrated,
credibly, into the script, by Considine.

After weeks of writing in Los Angeles and New York City,
Considine had a 134-page script ready to go. Altman planned
to shoot on locations near Chicago—in Lake Bluff on the
North Shore, with the wedding reception scenes to take
place in the palatial Armour mansion, which had been leased
for the filming.

Altman outdid himself with a smorgasbordian cast, with
representatives from world cinema, the silent-screen era,
American television, and his own personal past.

The featured players included then-octogenarian Lillian
Gish, John Cromwell and Ruth Nelson, Desi Arnaz Jr. (a nod
to *Whirlybirds* days),* Vittorio Gassman, Nina van Pallandt,
Dina Merrill, Carol Burnett, Paul Dooley, Mia Farrow,
Gerald Busby (the *Three Women* composer), Peggy Ann
Garner, Robert Fortier, Geraldine Chaplin, Viveca Lindfors,
Lauren Hutton, Howard Duff, Dennis Franz (pre-*Hill Street
Blues*), Pam Dawber, Bert Remsen, Craig Richard Nelson,
Susan Kendall Newman (Paul's daughter), and so forth.

At the Sheraton Waukegan in Waukegan, Illinois, where
the cast and crew were staying, John Considine came down
to breakfast one morning feeling blissful about his maiden
voyage as screenwriter. He found himself sitting next to Patricia Resnick and felt obliged to ask her, "Pat, what are you
doing here?" She informed him that she had been summoned
by Altman to collaborate on revisions of the script. She had
no idea that Considine had not been apprised of her arrival.
She thought: "Oh, my God!"

---

*Tommy Thompson, assistant director of *The Whirlybirds*, was working on the *I
Love Lucy* show when Desi Arnaz Jr. was born. Arnaz liked to say among the first
words he remembered hearing, as a toddler, were those of Thompson shouting
"Settle down!" on the set.

This time Altman had promised her proper payment and screen credit. It was very clear to her that this was Altman's mea culpa for *Three Women*.

As Considine was adjusting to this news, the two of them were joined by Allan Nicholls, another gifted member of the inner circle who had never written a produced screenplay before, and who had also been asked by Altman to show up in Waukegan to work on on-the-spot revisions. Altman had said nothing about any of this to Considine, whose head was spinning.

"I had a lot of ego problems with that," says Considine. "It was very hard for me for a while. I took two days off when I started realizing what the deal was going to be. I just had to think it out. What I determined was that I had the option of just saying, 'Screw it' and leaving. Or . . . what stopped me was a long friendship and thinking I definitely wanted to work as an actor for him again. So I just shined it on. It was a conscious decision. And I'm really glad I did it."

The three writers took over an entire wing of the Armour mansion. The first thing they worked on was a family tree, so that cast members could understand who they were related to in the script. Then they split up the individual characters and wrote up little booklets with bloodline histories in them, detailing the relationship of the individual characters to the overall storyline. Then they divided up the polish of the individual characters among themselves.*

Resnick took most of the young female characters. Allan Nicholls took most of the young male characters. Considine took all the Carol Burnett–Pat McCormick scenes and the John Cromwell–Lillian Gish scenes. (The scenes between Cromwell and Gish remained "very close to the page" from the beginning, says Considine, partly because those two performers were the least improvisatory. Cromwell, who was in the final months of his life, had trouble remembering his lines, but this was part of the unsteady quality that

---

*Because they were working on revisions as the filming proceeded, the writers were wired by walkie-talkie to the set; also, they were playing the small parts of wedding security personnel.

dovetailed with his character. Gish, alternatively, was letter-perfect. No matter how many times Altman said, "Call me Bob," the dignified leading lady of D. W. Griffith films insisted on calling him "Mr. Altman.")

As with *Nashville*, the actors were told they could bring their own ideas for specific scenes or dialogue changes to the writers. The writers would assist them in writing fresh material. As with *Nashville*, many stuck with their pages, while others departed freely. Once again, Geraldine Chaplin (playing matrimonial majordomo Rita Billingsley) was in the latter category: She had so thoroughly researched wedding etiquette that she knew her Emily Post better than the writers did, and *they* ended up consulting *her* on wedding protocol.

"It's really a nice thing to watch them [actors] warm to the process, because at the start they're so apologetic," recalls Resnick. " 'Oh, do you think you might have a minute tonight? I kind of have this idea, it's probably stupid, oh never mind . . .' "

One of Resnick's responsibilities, for example, was the Dina Merrill character, Antoinette Sloan Goddard, a Palm Beach socialite who keeps herself busy designing sheets for hotels like the Fountainbleau. (This was extracted from Resnick's own experience, as she was born and raised in Miami.) A relatively traditional actress, Merrill started coming to Resnick with "excellent ideas." During the scene in which she has an argument with the Ruth Nelson character, a Socialistic aunt, Merrill had the idea that her character ought to make an allusion to having once had a crush on Castro—because that sort of high-society lady would have visited Cuba during Batista's reign and may even have met Castro. "Such an attractive dictator!" the character exclaims.

"It was one of the funniest things in the movie," says Resnick, "a totally off-the-wall idea that she came up with."

As filmed, *A Wedding* can hardly be said to make any prodigious statement about American nuptials or the destructive capacity of gossip, any more than *Brewster McCloud* (as

The cast of 1977's *A Wedding*, assembled, with the director at center, a film that, as autobiography, is less than meets the eye. (Wisconsin Center for Film and Theater Research)

the director once claimed in prepublicity) is an "essay on rudeness." Those intentions, if they were ever serious on Altman's part, were lost in the surfeit of writers. Nor did Altman's claim that the families in *A Wedding* mirrored his own bear much fruit; the story and the characters can be said to hinge only superficially on Altman's life (through the "in" jokes of some character's names—the Corellis, for example).

The film is really a comedy of manners, in which the ritual of the wedding serves as a pretext for a nimble troupe to burlesque the pecadilloes of the social elite. A tad on the overlong side (124 minutes)—though at least half of the touted forty-eight characters are lost on the cutting-room floor—it is ultimately not so much a congealed story as a kind of orgasm of characterization.

The deus ex machina of the ending went down hard with some critics. The car-crash deaths of the bride and groom, which precipitates a name-calling duel between the two distraught families, after which it turns out to have been *not* the bride and groom but the film's least-loved characters who have been killed—this seemed even more arbitrary, than usual, for an Altman film. The director could never resist the Calvin touch of a car-crash, even, as here, an off-camera one.

Such off-putting elements might have ruined a lesser film, had not the three writers endowed the script with an overall sweetness and high-spiritedness. It may be that what really bothered some critics, at the time of the film's release in 1978, was not the jarring lapses of *A Wedding* so much as that here was an Altman movie that dared to be inconsequential.

While the filming of *A Wedding* was in full throttle in the Chicago suburbs, Lionel Chetwynd arrived on location to discuss the script for Altman's next film, *Quintet*. The British-born, Canadian-raised Chetwynd had written for directors Otto Preminger and Fred Zinnemann, and he had been nominated for an Oscar as cowriter of the screenplay for *The Apprenticeship of Duddy Kravitz*. He was an unlikely collaborator for Altman in two respects: Chetwynd is known to be a battler for his scripts, and he is politically more of a revisionist liberal, to the right of Altman (later on, Chetwynd would direct *The Hanoi Hilton*, an apologia for the Vietnam War).

But Sam Cohn, the latest of Altman's agents, had pursued Chetwynd on behalf of the director; and Chetwynd, an admirer of Altman's, had been talked out of his substantial set fee, even though he was still going to receive for writing *Quintet* several times what Altman was paying any other writer in his stable. It was—money always was, for Altman—an undercurrent in the relationship between them.

In preliminary discussions, Altman had spoken to Chetwynd of another dream he had had: about a fantastical game of chance that involved a quintet of people for whom the odds involved tremendous jeopardy. Altman seemed as excited about merchandising the possible game—which he believed was going to be another Monopoly—as he was about the film story. He asked Chetwynd to write a novella on which they could base a screenplay. Chetwynd was enthused. Everything seemed possible.

Chetwynd had very few conversations with Altman as protracted and as optimistic as that first one. From Waukegan, it was Scott Bushnell who telephoned and relayed messages with Altman's feedback. Chetwynd worked for the most part in isolation. He wrote a sixty-page novella involving a futuristic ice-world on the edge of Christendom. Into this society a mercenary killer comes, bearing a list of five doomed people. What the killer does not know is that the sixth victim is to be him.

Chetwynd brought the newly completed novella to Waukegan. After three days of waiting around for an audience with the busy director, he was awakened at 2 A.M. and ushered into Altman's presence. Altman informed him that he had finally read the *Quintet* draft and was ready to respond. Altman rambled on, not making much sense, criticizing the novella. Chetwynd went back to work, staying on location for over a week. This time he wrote a longer, more definitive novella, broken up into master scenes.

After finishing that draft, he returned to Los Angeles, waited in vain for some more reaction, and finally sent a bill to Lion's Gate for his work. A phone call from International Creative Management executive Jeff Berg informed him that he had been fired by Altman. Chetwynd persisted in trying to collect his fee. Altman and Scott Bushnell both phoned him in an attempt to deflect his salary demands. Altman was especially vituperative. When Altman told Chetwynd he would never work in Hollywood again, Chetwynd laughed derisively.

Enter Pat Resnick, refreshed from her chores cowriting *A Wedding*. She became the "middle writer" on *Quintet*. After Altman called her in and told her he was dissatisfied with Chetwynd's novella, she read it and decided the game, the quintet game, did not make any sense. In any case, she advised Altman, the overall concept was too much like other movies—the Italian film *The Tenth Victim*, for one. Altman said, "Never mind that. Figure out what's wrong with the damn board game. That's the key."

She never asked Altman why he wanted to do a movie,

much less a board game, that nobody seems to have been able to figure out at any point in the preproduction. The director has said that because B.C. was dying of cancer at the time, it may have pushed him in the direction of "a grim Grimm's fairy tale." But why this particular hook?

"Those discussions aren't really useful with Bob," says Resnick. "Because you don't get answers. 'I want to, I feel like it.' You never know what it is that sparks him on something. It could be such a little thing—like 'Rosebud.' He may have been looking at the ice in his glass one day—and he may have gotten this idea about cold and ice. That may have . . . intrigued him, more than any statement about a nuclear age. . . ."

With sinking heart, Resnick began to contemplate *Quintet.* "I started thinking about the fact that if [in the game] we have five people and they each have a list of five people, that's six people, unless their own name is on their own list—which sounds simple, but nobody had ever figured it out. This was basically my contribution to the movie. I went to Bob and said, 'Bob, you know, there's got to be a sixth person, and this is why you can't make this board game work. The sixth man [is] the person who runs the thing.' So Bob decided that if I was brilliant enough to figure that out, I deserved a crack at it [Chetwynd's draft]."

Back in Los Angeles, Resnick began, she says, by doing a "torch job" on Chetwynd's novella, and by starting over with only his essential ingredients. But she continued to feel inconclusive about the premise. "As I was writing, it was very grim to write, and there were things that just didn't make any sense, and I would basically say that to Bob. I gave it my best shot and handed it in."

In the meantime, Resnick was offered another professional opportunity. Altman was talking with her about coming up to *Quintet* locations in Montreal and the Arctic Circle, "which, being from Florida, didn't sound really great to me," so she decided she had the excuse she needed to get out of *Quintet.* "So I went in and told him that was the end of my

From left: Essex (Paul Newman), Deuca (Nina Van Pallandt), unidentified actor, and Ambrosia (Bibi Andersson) in the inscrutable *Quintet*. Not even Altman understood its riddles.

involvement. He wasn't very happy with me. He didn't talk to me for a long time."

In the end, Altman picked up as his "finishing writer" young Frank Barhydt Jr., son of his old Calvin boss and Kansas City friend. Montreal as a location was practically an afterthought. *Quintet* was originally supposed to be filmed in Chicago, and the first scene was going to open eerily on the El. Circumstances forced Altman to Canada, and when they were scouting brownstones in Montreal, the location manager took them to see the abandoned Expo '67 complex. They rushed into filming on that site because Altman was afraid Twentieth Century-Fox was going to pull the plug on the money.

Bar none, it is Altman's most lugubrious film—a bleak, sci-fi *California Split*—paced at a crawl, striving for pith, full of allusive dialogue, tinkling sound effects, and white-on-white imagery. It is hard, even, to praise the performances in *Quintet.* An international cast of Paul Newman, Vittorio Gassman, Fernando Rey, Bibi Andersson, Brigitte Fossey, and Nina van Pallandt added up to a big yawn.

"Everyone got caught up in it [*Quintet*]," says Tommy Thompson. "We were charmed into it by the whole magic of what was going to happen."

Quintet was the real turning point for critics and audiences. Every failure up to now could be rationalized. This one was Altman's.

No one remembers the director as being other than his usual magnetic self on the set during filming. But there was a vindictiveness, too, in pushing this film past the money people and his own cast and crew. An egomania that was also self-destructive.

In Hollywood, there was another dispute over screenplay credits. Altman wanted it to read, 'Story by Altman and Screenplay by Barhydt.' This time Resnick would not forego her cocredit; and Chetwynd, who was bloody-minded on the subject of Altman, filed grievance with the Writers Guild. When the decision came down, Altman's credit was reduced, and shared with Barhydt, Chetwynd, and Resnick.

Paul Newman is said to thunder with vulgar phrases whenever the film is mentioned. Chetwynd says: "I've never been able to sit through it all."

While *Quintet* was happening, John Considine and Allan Nicholls were brought together to brainstorm for *A Perfect Couple.* But Considine had a contract to write a television miniseries, and after thinking it over, he decided not to work on the next Altman film.

"Bob took me for a walk afterward and said, 'You're mad at me, aren't you?' I said no. He said, 'Tell me why you're mad at me.' I said, 'No, I'm not. I have this other writing project.' But it occurred to me later that he thought I had some bad feelings, which I didn't, at that time. They were all gone."

That left Nicholls—who, partly by dint of his low-keyness, was riding out the decade to become one of the director's closest friends and longest-lasting collaborators.

Independent of Lion's Gate, Nicholls had assembled the informal rock band, Keepin' 'Em Off the Streets, a six-piece band with nine singers. Band members were largely culled from friends from the casts of *Hair* and *Jesus Christ, Superstar.* The band did several Los Angeles nightclub performances before *A Wedding* had begun filming, and although the shows were meant to be a lark, they began pulling in audiences and stirring up word of mouth. At one point Altman, and Lion's Gate, sponsored some showcases, and filmed and recorded the ad hoc group.

During the filming of *A Wedding,* Altman fell in love with the performances of Paul Dooley and Marta Heflin (a *Hair* alumna, also, though she had not performed in the germinal Keepin' 'Em Off the Streets), and now he wanted to tailor a vehicle for them.

Altman had a counterpoint in mind for *A Perfect Couple.* A couple meets through a computer dating service. She is a backup singer with a communal rock-and-roll band; he comes from an uptight bourgeois family with a great love for classical music. Nicholls had been a journeyman with several rock bands—his musical background would come in handy.

While Nicholls concentrated on the rock-and-roll milieu, Altman would give time to the Theodopoulos patriarchy. The fact that they were to be a Greek family was, according to Nicholls, whimsical and without hidden meaning (or much delineation, one might add, in the script). The ailing sister was to play the cello because Altman had a fascination for cello players. The dating agency became a video service

The familial rock troupe of *A Perfect Couple*.
Left to right: Marta Heflin, Tomi-Lee Bradley,
Ted Neeley, Heather MacRae, and, kneeling,
Steven Sharp.

when they happily discovered just such an operation down
the block from Lion's Gate in Westwood.

Nicholls remembers the experience of writing the screenplay with Altman as "the most fun I've had in my life."
Once the actors were familiar with the content and the
structure of the shooting script, Altman and Nicholls continued to encourage improvisation within its parameters. There
was to be as much "flying" by the actors and actresses, dur-

ing rehearsals and in the filming, as with any Altman film since *Nashville.*

A painful romantic comedy about two ugly ducklings, *A Perfect Couple* turned out to be Altman's most personal and revelatory film of the latter half of the 1970s.

In the script the director's alter ego is Alex Theodopoulos (Paul Dooley), a middle-aged wallflower treated insufferably by his father. Theodopoulos seeks to escape his suffocating family life through a liaison with a ragamuffin rock-and-roller living with a collectivist band of musicians. His only emotional tie to his own family is to his frail sister, a dedicated cellist. Her sudden death liberates him to follow his heart in pursuit of Sheila Shea (Marta Heflin).

In part, *A Perfect Couple* is Altman's belated statement about the communalism of the Sixties, and about his own relationship with the "talent trust." As such, it is a rather harsh view of group dynamics. The leader (Ted Neeley) of the rock group is, though surpassingly talented, dictatorial and repellent. Rationalizing his petty despotism as being for the sake of art, he orders his on-stage "family" around and dumps on his real-life one. (It is not hard to see Altman writing himself into this character, as well as the Theodopoulos one.)

The Theodopoulos family, meanwhile, is decidedly more schematic. Only the sister is treated humanistically, which is part of the sister-love tradition in Altman films. In contrast, the father figure (played by Titos Vandis) is a vicious caricature. This rare father-character in Altman's cinema came, interestingly, after B.C.'s death.

The rock caravan comes across in the film with near-documentary verisimilitude—not just in the motley demographics (two of the singers are lesbians, one of whom has been impregnated by one of the male homosexual singers) but also in the concert performances, which are resounding. The score (mostly by Nicholls) is an uncategorizable blend of Sixties pop styles.* Neeley and the others are striking in their

---

*Cowriter Allan Nicholls has a bristling short scene as Heflin's other computer blind date; he and Theodopoulos (Dooley) wind up in a fistfight.

roles, while Marta Heflin's ethereal presence is breathtaking. It is a pity that she vanished from leading roles after this single starring opportunity.

The simple Boy Meets Girl, Boy Loses Girl, Boy Gets Girl story is the last thing you would expect from the director. But this is the only Altman film about love, and lovemaking, without a punchline. Here is an Altman dispatch not about celebrities or politics or Hollywood genres, but about ungainly romance, ordinary people, and (as Nate Salsbury would put it in *Buffalo Bill and the Indians*) "the show business." At the end of the film, the cast of rock-and-rollers joins hands for an exultant song of togetherness at the rim of the stage. *A Perfect Couple* is the director's paean to art and to love, which transcend mortal crises. There is not another movie like it in the Altman canon.

Few were able to see it in theatres. Many critics (coming as it did after *Quintet*) did not even deign to review it. The sales branch of Twentieth Century-Fox, bewildered as to how to promote the film, quickly abandoned *A Perfect Couple*, exacerbating the studio's increasingly prickly relationship with Altman. Yet, at a time when the director was being battered by poor reviews and receipts, *A Perfect Couple* demonstrated Altman's resilience.

Health, a comedy about "dirty tricks" at a convention of health food faddists, was the last gasp of Altman's collectivist, all-in-the-family filmmaking. Once again, Barhydt the younger was recruited to write this flick-of-the-wrist movie (along with Paul Dooley; Altman has his usual cowriting credit). Allan Nicholls contributed a blithe and trivial score, in teamwork with a New York City a cappella quartet, the Steinettes.

There had been a management exodus at Fox. Ladd was gone, and the new regime was neither as in command nor as unified on the subject of Altman as the previous one. Sherry Lansing, a pretty ex-starlet who had once acted for Howard Hawks before going the agent/producer route, was receiving

On the set of *Health:* Talk-show host Dick Cavett and the director catch up with Altman's old Kansas City acquaintance Walter Cronkite.

publicity as the first female studio boss in Hollywood's history. But in reality she had little power, and the bureaucracy of distribution/advertising/publicity—particularly a sales executive by the name of Norman Levy, who was an Altman nemesis—had the upper hand.

Altman's *Three Women* had been a succès d'estime but *A Wedding* had taken a dive at the box office, and *Quintet* was an unmitigated disaster. *A Perfect Couple* had not turned out to be, as it had been proclaimed, Altman's breakthrough rock 'n' roll movie. All of the Lion's Gate publicity about Keepin' 'Em Off the Streets had backfired when the musical group could not land a recording contract (the sound track was in fact preserved on the makeshift Lion's Gate label).

So the director rushed *Health* into production to assure the financing, decamped to the princely Don Cesar Hotel in St.

Petersburg, Florida, for safe location distance, and he and the others winged the holes in the script. There is a hurried, first-draft air to the film, but otherwise none of the tension of this background. In the best sense of the word, *Health* is a slapdash film with much to recommend it—topical innuendo, larky songs, infectious performances.

It has the requisite Altman cast of the late Seventies: the old network (Paul Dooley, Henry Gibson, Robert Fortier); the star turns (Glenda Jackson, Carol Burnett, James Garner, and Lauren Bacall); the new faces (the Steinettes, Alfre Woodard); and the walk-ons (Dick Cavett, Dinah Shore).

Its cockeyed story of a campaign for the presidency of a nutrition nuts' national organization ("Happiness, Energy, and Longevity Through Health") dished up yet another Altman lesson about American politics. With the death of his mother and father, and the siphoning off of the "talent trust," Altman, in mid-life, found an idée fixe in projects (like *Nashville*, *Health*, *Secret Honor*, *The Caine Mutiny Court-Martial*, and *Tanner '88*) revolving around questions of leadership.

Timed to coincide with the 1980 Presidential primary campaign, *Health* managed to simulate, in the representative guises of octogenarian virgin Esther Brill (Lauren Bacall) and Stevensonian antimaterialist Isabella Garnell (Glenda Jackson), the platitudes of Reagan and Carter (failing, one might add, to distinguish between them). Despite the fact that *Health* came at the fag end of a tumultous decade for Altman, the film was buoyant and chucklesome, and showed the director in surprisingly good humor still.

Sherry Lansing was said to like the film immensely when Altman screened it at Lion's Gate in the summer of 1980, but Levy, chief of distribution at Fox, most emphatically did not. *Health* sat on the shelf at the studio for over a year, when it was trickled to exactly two theatres, one in Los Angeles and one in New York. The reviews were more than favorable, but by then the propitious moment for *Health* had passed.

Chapter

32

LION'S GATE

The years between *Nashville* and *Popeye* appear to be a time of fecundity and teeming expansion for Altman. But there were personal—and professional—setbacks.

The public could detect signs of this in the gloomy *Quintet*, but in general Altman appeared to shrug off the ill effects. His sweet-tempered collaborators, particularly Messrs. Considine, Nicholls, and Dooley, ensured that the comedies of these years had more lightness than dark, and the critics, especially abroad, continued to respond favorably to the work—when they were able to view it.

Lion's Gate, the facility as well as the bulwark organization for other filmmakers, ap-

Writer-director Robert Benton and Altman, in his producer mode. Benton's dormant directing career was given a boost when Lion's Gate sponsored *The Late Show*.

peared to be flourishing, and Altman wore its success as a badge of confidence. In 1978, Altman had moved Lion's Gate from Westwood to a converted airplane-seat factory in West Los Angeles, an event that occasioned no little nostalgia from the old hands. The new postproduction facility, which included editing rooms, offices, and a dubbing stage, was turning a steady profit. Its state-of-the-art sound and editing technology attracted all the "now" people in the industry, and Altman's screenings there were the hottest ticket in town.

In 1977 and 1978, respectively, Alan Rudolph directed his

two films produced by Altman, *Welcome to L.A.* and *Remember My Name.** Rudolph has never been less than fulsome in his gratitude to Altman for taking him under his wing, and he has often acknowledged the debt to the older director in his richly stylized ensemble films. That generosity of character, on Rudolph's part, kept his relationship with Altman on an even keel.

Welcome to L.A. is a roundelay of unhappy Angeleno love lives, while *Remember My Name* is a dreamlike blues about a disturbed female parolee preying on her ex-husband's new life.

The former stars Keith Carradine, while the latter stars Geraldine Chaplin, and the players in both instances are drawn heavily from the Altman camp. In the casting, in the camera virtuosity and the fragmented narrative structures, these two Rudolph films advertise Altman's sponsorship, even if the producer himself rarely materialized on the set (and, indeed, claims to have had nothing to do with the films per se). Altman simply guaranteed the bankroll and anointed the proceedings with a no-strings-attached goodwill. Altman could not have given his blessing to a more mesmeric director than Alan Rudolph.

During this period, Altman also gave a helping hand to writer-director Robert Benton and director Robert M. Young.

Benton, a first-class talent with Texas roots, had been an *Esquire* magazine art director, and the screenwriter (with his partner, David Newman) of *Bonnie and Clyde* and other films. Benton had been stagnating since his directorial debut, the offbeat Western *Bad Company*, in 1972. Starting with *The Late Show* in 1977, producer Altman gave Benton fresh impetus—as well as the backup of Tommy Thompson, Louis Lombardo, the Lion's Gate sound brigade, and cinematographer Chuck Rosher from *Three Women*. Art Carney and Lily Tomlin headed a cast that also included the Altman

---

*Though *Welcome to L.A.* is often referred to as Alan Rudolph's directorial debut, in actuality Rudolph had helmed at least two previous horror programmers, *Premonition* in 1972, and *Barn of the Naked Dead*, a.k.a. *Terror Circus*, in 1973.

recidivists John Considine, Ruth Nelson, and Howard Duff. Benton's sly murder mystery, *The Late Show*, may not be as consummate as the writer-director's later films (including the Oscar-winning *Kramer Vs. Kramer* and *Places in the Heart*), but it is the best of his genre attempts. It has that in common with Altman, the genre kidding.

Robert M. Young's *Rich Kids*, in 1979, once again saw the familiar name of longtime Altman cohort George W. George in the credits, as producer. George's wife, Judith Ross, contributed the screenplay. The story involved the friendship of two privileged and unhappy adolescents (played by Trini Alvarado and Jeremy Levy). In the cast, Paul Dooley is the conspicuous Altman loan-out, and Allan Nicholls was in on the songs and the musical scoring.

For these productions, Altman's role was more in the line of patron. Sometimes, in fact, he seemed to resent the good karma of the other Lion's Gate productions and to begrudge his passive distance as producer. He bickered with editor Louis Lombardo over the editing of *The Late Show*, accusing his old friend of trying to undercut him by taking the side of Benton and the studio (Warner Brothers). "Whose side?" asked Lombardo in exasperation. "I'm just working on the fucking movie. That's all I'm doing." Adds Lombardo: "He was actually jealous of us fixing the movie without consulting him."

Lion's Gate's efforts at advertising and promoting these branch productions were only intermittently successful. Company publicist Mike Kaplan stumped the nation on behalf of the Rudolph-Benton-Young films, but Kaplan was only one man trying to do the work of an entire studio phalanx.

In interviews Altman boasted that his overhead at Lion's Gate could absorb the low costs of these satellite films, as well as of his own films. That was certainly true—Lion's Gate never really lost money. But in Hollywood you are expected to make a *lot* of money on a film, tens of millions of dollars. That is the philosophy. And in the end it was as if

From left: Altman's most auspicious disciple, Alan Rudolph, with Tommy Thompson and the director. (Tommy Thompson)

Lion's Gate was treading water, for Altman's own films continued to be mishandled and to decline in the marketplace.

The new inner circle were novices, Easterners, young Hollywood outsiders. They did not necessarily live in Los Angeles—Allan Nicholls lived in Vermont!—and their private ambitions were secondary. Generally they knew of the past only from hearsay or Altman's own foggy reminiscences. The two remaining loyalists from the pre-$M*A*S*H$ era, Eggenweiler and Thompson, grew more and more detached. They were feeling pressured by Scott Bushnell, and their late-night conversations were about leaving Lion's Gate.

Altman's paranoia about Hollywood was revitalized by the downward spiral of the Fox films. Hollywood was no longer fun, a splendid game, an opportunity for mischief. The filming had become a do-or-die thing, the friends and collaborators expendable, and the studio of the moment an object of hatred.

One of Altman's failings as a director, now, was his inability to thread the Hollywood needle. In the past, he had been lighthearted about such realities. George Litto remembers how Altman's sense of humor was so important as leverage in his professional confrontations. "When he got in trouble," says Litto, "he would come with a joke and he would disarm everybody. Everybody would just forget all the bullshit. I remember Perry Lafferty at CBS, the head of production during *Nightwatch*—he wanted to kill him over something. Perry said, 'We've got to have a meeting in the main executive dining room.' Altman said, 'Perry, I have a present for you.' He gave him a CBS 'eye' he had made as a tieclasp. Everybody fell on the floor. The rest of the meeting was a piece of cake."

Though the director had grown more canny about dealing with producers and financiers, over time, he also grew more rigid. He was helping to create his own problems at the box office by alienating the business people and the ad/pub people who would eventually gain control over the fate of his films.

Behind the scenes, Scott Bushnell encouraged Altman's anti-Hollywood posturing. People who could barely recall Bushnell as the low-key presence who first started working on wardrobe for *Thieves Like Us* were now astonished to realize that she alone had the director's ear about casting and story sense, about all major production decisions—and that, indeed, it sometimes seemed all messages to Altman were relayed and funneled through her. She made and returned phone calls in his name. Increasingly, she was the medium through which he spoke.

Although Bushnell had her strengths (her casting mind was encyclopedic), and many of the younger people gravitated to her, partly as an avenue to Altman, her primary ori-

entation was theatre. She believed the theatrical medium to
be innately superior to film. She did not go to films for recre-
ation or edification; she went to plays. She was "against
commerce." She was "against Hollywood," against "Hollywood casting," and against any "Hollywood turn of the
story." Only Bushnell outvinegared Altman in terms of Hollywood. Unless she warmed up to a newcomer, and she
warmed up to only a handful, she could be a dour, judgmen-
tal keeper of the flame.

"Egg" was stigmatized by his Hollywood professionalism,
and Thompson had a Mexican standoff with Bushnell. They
could not seem to get through to Altman, who was respon-
sive, more and more, only to Bushnell. Their beliefs about
planning, script, and story values were branded as old-fashioned, dumb, suspect. Their advice was throttled with:
"That's a dumb idea," or "Stop trying to be the writer."

One night "Egg" was having drinks with Thompson, talking it over, and he said to Thompson challengingly, "Why
don't you *tell* him?"

"I left the bar," says Thompson, "went to the airport, flew
to New York, went to Delmonico's, and knocked on the
door. He opened the door—and it was just like during
M*A*S*H. He wasn't in the least surprised. It was almost as
if he knew I was coming. He was playing backgammon with
Sam Cohn. He said, 'What are you doing here?' I said, 'I want
to talk to you.' I fixed a drink, sat down, they finished the
game, and Sam left.

"He said, 'What's the problem?' I told him, 'Nobody can
talk to you anymore. Nobody can get anything through to
you. Because that woman is always there. You get your
throat cut after you leave, and everyone knows it.' He agreed.
He said, 'You're right. I'm glad you pointed that out and I'll
do something about it.' I said, 'Just isolate [yourself] once in
a while so your friends can get to you—alone—without having it commented on afterward.' Then we had dinner, fooled
around for a day or so, and I came back.

"When he got back to L.A., it was fine. He had had that

talk with her, and there were daggers from the lady. But for a couple of weeks, it worked. Then she was right back in there."

"Egg" and Tommy Thompson and the old guard of the "talent trust" began to talk about Bushnell in terms of "voodoo" and "witchery."

Altman, from their point of view, was made up of "equal parts of light and dark," according to Thompson. The lighter side was that jokey little boy inside the big serious artist. The darker side was the festering ego. Thompson felt the "talent trust" of the Sixties and early Seventies always emphasized the lighter side, the balance. In a sense, they always felt they were inside the director's mind, waging a war against the darker tendencies.

They could not figure out Altman's enchantment with Bushnell. Maybe if Altman was sleeping with her, more than one of them said, they could see it. But no one could be certain of their precise relationship. No, she seemed to have cast some spell on his mind, and they believed they were truly struggling against the power of that darkness.

By the time of *Popeye*, Altman's luck had already run out in Hollywood, only it had not dawned on him.

It was not just the late-1970s flops and fizzes—it was the publicity surrounding him and his *entourage*. It was the drugs, the alcohol, the party-animal lifestyle, the script savaging, the union difficulties, the badmouthing of Hollywood studios—and the critical cheers weighed against the box-office boos.

It must be said that, in interviews, Altman was sometimes his own worst enemy. Even Pauline Kael, who had once been described by *Variety* as "chief priestess of the Altman cult," said the director spoke too much "gobbledygook" when declaiming to journalists. Yet the press relished his quotability. His anti-Hollywood tirades were part of the director's mythmaking, even as they became part of his undoing.

Altman bragged about kicking Barbra Streisand out of his

office at Lion's Gate after a screening of *Nashville* because she was a "rude bitch" who was self-absorbed. He said Oscar-winner George C. Scott was a "lousy actor" and "a caricature of himself." He complained about Malibu neighbor Steve McQueen's salary demands and said McQueen was not worth the money. He criticized Marlon Brando and Robert Redford and Gene Hackman and others—he seemed to be incontinent on the subject of big American stars—and though he often scored points with interviewers, in the end it was at his own expense. These people have friends, and their friends have friends.

Throughout the Seventies, Altman had migrated from studio to studio. Now, he could count up credits at five of the major seven—excluding venerable/vengeful Universal and G-rated Disney—that were available to him. Paramount, Twentieth Century-Fox, Metro-Goldwyn-Mayer/ United Artists, Warner's, Columbia—each, in turn, had supported Altman and his filmmaking. The director had not been shy about mentioning in the press the names of those he felt had betrayed him by screwing up his films in the marketplace—James Aubrey at MGM, Gordon Stulberg at Twentieth Century-Fox, John Daley at Hemdale, and so on. The Twentieth Century-Fox relationship had lasted the longest, and now Altman was openly feuding with the distribution wing at that studio, whose executives held *Health* hostage.

The Academy of Motion Picture Arts and Sciences had bypassed his accomplishments for ten years. In an interview the director said the Academy was comprised of "widows of guys who have been dead for thirty-three years." That pretty much ensured that the Academy would bypass his films for the next ten years.

The Hollywood unions had it in for Altman. Altman had circumvented and publicly flogged them all along; some of this was necessity—how else could he direct so many flea-budgeted films?—some of it was just petty. The unions were opposed to his runaway (filmed outside the U.S. and union jurisdiction) productions and inflamed by his disparaging comments in interviews.*

Robert Aldrich, a political progressive who was president of the Directors Guild for a spell in the Seventies, spoke off the record to one reporter, heavily excoriating Altman. That was the off- or on-the-record viewpoint in Hollywood union after union. It didn't matter that Altman was an artistic director whom someone like the idiosyncratic Aldrich ought to admire.

The Screen Extras Guild routinely picketed Altman's Lion's Gate productions. The Writers Guild knew Altman to be fractious with scriptwriters. There were not too many other important directors who could have claimed, in the late Seventies, to have terminally antagonized so many big stars, big studio executives, big film organizations, and big Hollywood unions.

Altman's refuge had long been the film critics, only now, with his films more open-ended and downright peculiar, they, too, began to lambast or ignore him (while those in the smaller cities had trouble seeing the films in order to be in a position, even, to take a position). The critics had discovered Altman honestly and boosted him. He had courted them in return. Only now, the intimacy of some of those relationships began to backfire.

No single notice was more integral to the Altman mystique than Pauline Kael's preview of *Nashville*, and she and the director enjoyed a brief, torrid mutual admiration. But when Kael came to Hollywood in the mid-Seventies, for what was a disastrous attempt to go to work on the production side at Paramount, Kael and Altman came to a parting of the ways.

The director offended the preeminent film critic over dinner in Westwood after a screening of *Buffalo Bill and the Indians*, which Kael had to admit she did not like. Altman,

---

*Altman had again gone public with union problems during the filming of *Health*, claiming that in Florida he had had to pay "outrageous salaries" to members of the local Teamsters for union certification. Although such complaints were commonplace, the accepted routine in Hollywood was to grin and bear it.

for his part, had had a few too many drinks, and embarrassed her before his retinue. She left Los Angeles shortly thereafter to return to her reviewing post at *The New Yorker*, and her criticism thereafter is relatively restrained in its mention of Altman, once adjudged by her to be *the* cutting-edge American director.

(A "ripple effect" of this incident was seeded in the minds of the hundreds of "Kaelites" across the United States—film critics who owed some allegiance either to Kael personally, or to her style of reviewing, and who could be expected to take umbrage on her behalf. The word got around.)

The new critical distaste for Altman was in part a reaction to the critical overenthusiasm in the first place, but it was also part of a growing unease not only with the films but with the cult of the man.

Never one to be politic, Altman took to singling out the critics by name, and reviewing *them* as if they were *films*, which only added fuel to the fire. Altman could be injudicious, to put it mildly. He called Stephen Farber, who wrote regularly in *The New York Times*, "a hatchet man and paid assassin." Columnist Rex Reed, Altman implied in another interview, "has a personal problem with me. I had a hotel room next to him in Cannes in 1970. And he left his door open. . . . I don't want to go into it, but anyway he's gone after me on every picture. . . ." Other film critics may or may not have aligned themselves with Farber or Reed, but they had to be looking over their shoulders.

As Altman was reveling in his anti-Hollywood poses, moreover, many of the alternative newspapers that had championed him were going under; and many youth-generation film critics were now striving to prove themselves in touch with the mainstream. At the time of *Three Women*, for example, Peter Biskind, an editor of the alternative newsmagazine *7 Days*, could write without apparent irony that, for such a "listless, pointless, and mindless assemblage of footage [as *Three Women*]," in the People's Republic of China, a director like Altman "would be sent to plant rice for twelve months before being allowed near a camera."

(Rather a bracing comment for an avowed alternative critic.)

Later, Biskind became editor of *American Film*, the magazine of the American Film Institute, and still later, he graduated to an association with *Premiere*, sponsored by Australian media magnate Rupert Murdoch. In any event, Biskind and critics like him were shuffling toward the center of cultural commentary, even as Altman was moving toward the fringe. Now, at this crossroads of Altman's career, it became truly maverick to embrace Altman; and film critics as a profession are not truly maverick; if anything, there is a herd instinct among them.

The subtext of all this reaction against Altman's films was the man himself, his lifestyle and his pronouncements. Other directors could smoke marijuana; other directors did and still do drugs. This is well known, even if people do not normally parade it. It is acceptable in Hollywood, to a limited extent.

But in interview after interview, here was Altman smoking Thai stick and downing his Cutty Sark, and going on about his ability to handle certain excesses. It made people wary, even people who might normally be compatible with that lifestyle.* *Is he stoned while directing?* people wondered. *Does Altman even care about how his films turn out. . . ?*

Altman's abuse and temper tantrums, whether stoned or straight, now filtered into print. He would invite a journalist in the door and unload the up-to-the-minute invective of his thinking. Mary Murphy of *New West* magazine was in his presence when Shelley Duvall broke her contract for *A Wedding*, at a time when Altman was being battered by poor reviews and box office for *Three Women* in the South and the Midwest. "Oh, the pain, the pain, the pain . . ." he moaned,

---

*One motion-picture star, an Oscar-winner who donated time and money to the National Organization for the Normalization of Marijuana Laws (NORML), told one reporter (off-the-record, naturally) that he would never work for a director like Altman, who was always stoned on the set! It may have been Alice-in-Wonderland logic, but that is the point—Altman had a way of making Hollywood nervous, even about its own dubious practices.

adding brightly, "I know a cure . . . I'll go off to Paris and be rich and arrogant and look down on people." That article was widely discussed in Hollywood.

No occasion was too sacrosanct. Altman's good sense was deserting him, and he seemed increasingly isolated even among his adherents. The drug bingeing was having an effect not only on the waywardness of the films, but on the vaunted family atmosphere on the set. Passing the joint sealed the "mystical bargain" of filmmaking, Altman had told Aljean Harmetz of *The New York Times* back in 1973. But now, those on the set who did not indulge in drugs or who skipped the dailies of their own accord felt the tension of Altman's Us. vs. Them delineations.

To the press, Altman still appeared in the guise of a jaunty antiestablishment filmmaking lodestar. But he was deeply unhinged by losing the Oscar—first for *M*A*S*H* and then for *Nashville*—by the dwindling box-office receipts and the unreleased films, by the prosaic misery of a chronic bad back, by the deaths of his parents and the loss of friends on the battlefield of his ambition, by his inability to summon the old common sense when combatting the studios and executives. Hollywood, where he had strived to succeed for over thirty years, was now anathema to the director, and vice versa.

Visitors to Westwood, and later to the new Lion's Gate offices in West Los Angeles, were struck by the preponderance of European plaques and by the glaring absence of American awards, as if Altman himself chose to emphasize this imbalance in his career. His love of Europe was pronounced, and he talked about Paris as if he had once lived there. In conversations with associates, he would refer to "those commercial types who took away my Oscar," and for the benefit of visitors he would point to the courtyard and say, "Doesn't it seem very European to you?"

Altman was in the high tide of seeing himself as a displaced American, as a European in Hollywood. Wistfully he would recall that the original spelling of his name was very German, with two *n*'s, and he would proclaim Vittorio Gassman to be the greatest of his current ensemble of actors because he was a Gassman—*German* really, forget the Vittorio.

Things Germanic filled his mind. Drunk and rambling, Altman would rant about international bankers and "Levantine types," those "Levantine types" who ran the studios in Hollywood. It was almost a comical thing, boiling to the surface at the end of a particularly hard day in a conversation with a producer over the phone. "Jew!" Altman would shout. Friends excused it as the director's way of rattling someone. It was a Kansas City provincialism.

A lot of Hollywood's reasons for shunning Altman were small-minded. But there was, too, the distinct impression that this director, from Middle America and a German Catholic background, was in the depths of his heart contemptuous and hateful toward them (whether they were Jewish or not). Thankfully, this aspect of Robert Altman never found voice in one of his motion pictures, yet it was always there, hovering, a constant of his dark side.

Chapter
33

"I YAM WHAT I YAM"

The unlikely ingredients for Robert Altman's fourteenth feature film since *M*A*S*H* included a debonair producer with a reputation as a lady's man, an eccentric and difficult rock composer, an Eastern urban intellectual cartoonist worried about the integrity of his screenplay, a wildly popular TV star making his calculated screen debut, and a coproducing arrangement that was a first between a Hollywood studio (Paramount) and wholesome-oriented Disney—all of this in the grip of a director many believed was on a downhill slide.

It was, in the words of Altman himself, "the weirdest possible combination."

Popeye (Robin Williams) and Olive Oyl (Shelley
Duvall) in the musical *Popeye,* Altman's Water-
loo.

Even as Altman's career was being written off by many
U.S. critics after the successive "disappointments" of *A
Wedding, Quintet,* and *A Perfect Couple*—and even as his
latest movie was rumored to be in ill-*Health* by gossip columnists—improbably, Altman was now to direct, with his
biggest budget ever, a musical about a comic-strip hero, for
family audiences.

The history of *Popeye* began with a producer who kept the
faith with Altman—Robert Evans, the one-time offbeat actor
(he plays a smirking villain in *The Friend Who Walked the
West* and a credible Irving Thalberg in *Man of a Thousand
Faces*) and then high-powered Paramount executive whose
publicized romances have sometimes overshadowed his
work as a serious producer. An old-fashioned producer in one
sense, Evans has loved making movies, whether nursing an
embarrassing flop (like *Players,* starring ex-wife Ali McGraw)
or a proud piece of work (like *The Godfather* or *Chinatown*).
On May 13, 1977—in an interview, characteristically,
Evans remembers the exact date—Evans emerged from a
Broadway theatre after seeing *Annie,* flushed with emotion.
He called Paramount on the West Coast to inaugurate bidding
on the film rights. When the price tag soared to $10 million,

Evans dropped out. Then he got a call from an executive in the Famous Music division at Paramount, who reminded him that Paramount owned the rights to the cartoon character, Popeye the Sailor. What about a live-action Popeye musical?

Evans was bowled over by the idea. He called pal Dustin Hoffman, because they were in the market for something together, and Hoffman said—*brilliant!* Richard Sylbert, then an executive producer working with Evans, suggested contacting Jules Feiffer to do the screenplay, "because Feiffer is the only guy who can make cartoon characters come alive on the screen." Evans tracked down the celebrated *Village Voice* chronicler of love, politics, and midlife angst at a dinner party in New York City, and long-distance over the phone, he offered *Popeye* to him.

The man who had scripted (originally for the stage) *Little Murders* and *Carnal Knowledge* had not written a produced screenplay since the early 1970s. The call from Evans, whom he had met socially, he regarded as a godsend, because Feiffer knew and cherished the work of E. C. Segar, Popeye's creator. Even though Feiffer viewed Evans as "the traditional type of Hollywood producer which, of course, I didn't think very highly of," he found that he "liked him and got along with him right from the start."

Feiffer told Evans he would write *Popeye* if he could emulate the amiable sensibility of Segar's original Popeye, and not the animated Popeye of the Fleischer brothers, who produced those boisterous Popeye cartoons in the late 1930s and early 1940s. "He said, 'I want you to do whatever you want to do,'" recollects Feiffer. "Now sometimes you'll hear that and it'll turn out to be bullshit. In this case, it wasn't, not because I overwhelmed him, but because Segar so clearly made sense."

Feiffer began by rereading *Popeye: The First Fifty Years* by Bud Sagendorf, a volume about Segar's career. Segar was a go-getter from Chester, Illinois, where he once held a job painting billboards on the sides of barns. After writing an illustrated column of daily occurrences for the *Chicago American*, he was offered a niche with the King Features syndicate in New York City. The Oyl family grew out of a strip he created for the Hearst syndicate, called "Thimble Theatre." Popeye made his debut as a character in 1929.

"To have this come out of the blue—to allow me to pay homage to this great talent whom practically nobody has heard of anymore, except cartoonists—was like a boon to me," says Feiffer. "What I loved about the tone of Segar's Popeye is how civil he was about the awfulness of everybody. He lived in a world in which every character was corrupt, jealous, greedy, and did terrible things to each other—all except Popeye. And somehow he was not mean-spirited. It was not the world of Al Capp where ugliness really seemed ugly. There was a genuine charm, and, a word that keeps coming back to me, a *civility* toward his view of the universe."

Feiffer borrowed lavishly from Segar for his original treatment, but created a world of his own in the make-believe town of Sweethaven. He decided to write the story around Popeye and Olive Oyl's romance, and around Popeye's search for his long-lost daddy. Sweethaven is tyrannized by the Commodore, an evil presence who turns out to be Popeye's poppa.

Evans made one stipulation: He wanted the movie to be about "affirmation and morality," an entertainment for kids as well as adults. The two agreed that the movie's theme should be Popeye's own credo: "I Yam What I Yam (And That's All That I Yam)."

"Quite frankly," says Evans, "that's what attracted me to *Popeye* more than anything else. Though it was written fifty years ago, it's so much more today than it was fifty years ago. That's what I wanted to get across in the story—that one line. People are individuals. They are what they are."

Lily Tomlin was announced as Olive Oyl. Hal Ashby signed on as director. Dustin Hoffman took tap-dancing lessons and began working with a choreographer. Everybody at Paramount agreed that Hoffman's involvement made it a very "bankable" project. Ashby, Hoffman, and Evans went out and drank vodka and ate caviar to celebrate doing the picture together.

Then something went wrong—what, nobody can put their finger on. Feiffer's early drafts were a little too "special effecty," as he himself admits, but the rewriting, emphasizing the "personal relationships," went well. When there were fifty or sixty pages of screenplay to be read, there was a series of meetings with everyone concerned. Inexplicably to Feiffer, Hoffman began to back off. When Feiffer met with his old friend Hoffman, things ended up "very messy."

Recalls Feiffer: "It ended up just very unfriendly, and I still don't remember finding out a damn thing about what he felt about the movie."

To the astonishment of practically everyone, Evans supported his screenwriter and not his "bankable" star. Evans telephoned Feiffer and was matter-of-fact about Hoffman's departure from the project, guarding Feiffer from the potential stigma in Hollywood. Hoffman and Evans did not speak to one another for almost a year.

"He couldn't believe that I stayed with Jules rather than him," says Evans, "but I believed Jules was right. I didn't want to star-fuck. Everyone told me I was wrong. With Dustin, I had a 'go' from Paramount. Without Dustin, I had nothing but a script."

Time passed, enthusiasms waned. Tomlin's status was unclear, Ashby moved on to a multipicture deal with Lorimar, Paramount got cold feet. Evans walked into a meeting of higher-ups at Paramount, and argued that the property was so strong that *anyone* could play Popeye, even someone like that guy who was on the cover of *People* magazine last week, what's-his-name.

"It was the strangest thing," Evans remembers. "I said, 'Fellas, you don't need a star for this picture, anyone can play Popeye.' Now I didn't even know who Robin Williams was, frankly, but I knew that he'd just come out in a series and was the talk of the town. I had never seen *Mork and Mindy*. I said, 'For chrissakes, we could use . . . Robin Williams.' The name just popped off my tongue. Michael Eisner said, 'Robin Williams, what an idea!' And Barry Diller said, 'Wow, that's great!' And that's how the whole thing started."

Suddenly, with Williams, an irresistibly funny improvisational actor who was TV's newest rage (and conveniently affiliated with Paramount through ABC-TV), the project was given fresh impetus. Gilda Radner, considered hot because of her visibility on *Saturday Night Live*, was regarded as the best bet for Olive Oyl. And Evans went shopping for a director.

The teaming-up of Evans and Altman, an insider and an outsider in Hollywood's terms, seemed no more preposterous to others than it did to them, at first.

"Without knowing him," admits Altman, "I thought it would be a disaster. I don't like the kind of pictures he makes, I don't like the kind of publicity he is associated with." For his part, Evans made no bones about saying he didn't like Altman's last several pictures, "but I judge a director by his best, not his worst."

Yet they had a couple of things in common—among them, a mutual friend engaged in packaging the script, and the same back doctor.

"One night," Evans recalls, "I was at Elaine's restaurant [in New York], and I saw Bob [Altman] there. He couldn't walk, he was in so much pain. He had a terrible back injury. I said, 'Bob, I have a doctor for you,' and I got him an appointment with my doctor, who practically saved my life.

"The next time I saw Bob, it was also at Elaine's. He said to me, 'Bob, I can't tell you what it means to me. I'm a new man now.' So I took the back of a check, and I sent it over to his table. I wrote on it, 'You owe me a picture,' and asked him to sign it. He crossed out 'picture' and wrote, 'I owe you my life.'"

Other directors were considered—including Arthur Penn and Mike Nichols. But Sam Cohn, the New York agent who played matchmaker behind the scenes for *Popeye*, gave Altman a copy of the script and asked the director for his opinion of it. Altman read it, decided it was "difficult but would make a helluva movie," and told Cohn that he would love to direct it "if I could get assurances that I would have the controls." Why hadn't anyone offered it to him?

So Evans met with Altman and came away impressed by his "unique vision" of the movie. Much to Paramount's chagrin, Evans did ask Altman to direct. Though Paramount had benefited from the prestige success of *Nashville*, the studio would have preferred to hold out for the insurance of a "box-office director" for *Popeye*.

"Everyone they suggested, I turned down," remembers Evans. "I just insisted on Bob. Then I had Robin back me. I just stuck to my guns. They had a very, very important and commercial director who wanted to do it. And I said, 'I won't make it with him because I know what the picture will look like before it's done.' It's got to be exciting to make it. I'd rather take a chance on falling on my ass but possibly hitting magic than just make something that's predictable. Many times I've fallen on my ass but many times I've touched magic too.

Paramount finally gave in. With the hiring of Altman came the commitment of Lion's Gate as well as Altman's vision, or "Altman's colors," as Paul Dooley puts it. Central to that vision was Altman's notion of populating and embellishing the "world" of Sweethaven with his own ensemble. With Evans heavily involved in preparations for *Urban Cowboy* in Texas, Altman and his company took over the momentum on *Popeye*—assembling the remaining cast and crew.

Altman regular Dooley was an obvious choice as Wimpy. The Broadway trouper Ray Walston was signed as Popeye's long-lost Daddy (one of the frequent directors of Walston's television triumph of the 1960s, *My Favorite Martian*, was Oscar Rudolph, Alan Rudolph's father). After consulting with Reza Badiyi, among others, Altman picked Paul L. Smith from *Midnight Express* as the cartoon heavy, Bluto.

Various composers had been under scrutiny from the beginning—Randy Newman, Leonard Cohen (again), Paul Mc-

Cartney, even John Lennon. But Altman gravitated to singer-
songwriter Harry Nilsson, the pop iconoclast whose previous
movie experience included singing the Fred Neil theme song
for *Midnight Cowboy* in 1969.

"Nobody wanted him at first except Robin," Altman recalls. "Everyone said, 'You'll get in trouble with him—he'll
get drunk, he won't do it, he's washed up.' As a matter of
fact, I said all of those things about Harry to Robin myself
one day. Then I went home and thought about it and said to
myself, 'Jesus, that's what people are saying about me!' So I
called Harry Nilsson, because I had never met him in my
life, and we got along terrifically."

With Nilsson at work cranking out representative tunes,
Altman put in a transatlantic phone call to Shelley Duvall,
who was in London for a one-year stretch shooting Stanley
Kubrick's *The Shining*. Gilda Radner was stalling on terms,
and, besides, Altman had other ideas. Altman told Duvall
that he had the role she was born to play: Olive Oyl.

"Whenever Bob offers me a movie," Duvall recalls, "I
never even think twice about it. Later, it will come about.
You see, I trust him very much."

The trouble was that Shelley Duvall "couldn't get herself
arrested [in Hollywood] except for films I used her in," in
Altman's words. Despite her critical success in *Three
Women*, and despite her audience recognition in Europe, Paramount needed some convincing about Shelley Duvall. As
soon as she returned from abroad therefore, Duvall went into
a recording studio with Nilsson for an afternoon. She heard
Olive Oyl's plaintive "He Needs Me" for the first time, and
cut a version of the song while reading the lyrics cold off the
page.

Together with Nilsson, Altman then dubbed the Duvall
tune over a clip featuring a Shelley Duvall highlight from
Thieves Like Us. Also, Altman dubbed the "Sweethaven National Anthem" over a clip from *Buffalo Bill and the Indians*, Bluto's "I'm Mean" over a Paul L. Smith trailer for a
spaghetti Western, and "Swee'pea's Lullaby" over a scene
with Keith Carradine and his dog from *Thieves*.

The director threw a little party over at Lion's Gate in West Los Angeles for Paramount muckamucks, spouses, friends, and lovers. The night's entertainment included the four movie clips. Gulf and Western Chairman of the Board Charles Bluhdorn was there. So were Paramount production chiefs Michael Eisner and Barry Diller. Nilsson's music went over big—as did Shelley Duvall. "I think it was Mrs. Bluhdorn who said, 'She looks just like Olive Oyl!'" recalls Duvall. "Thank you, Mrs. Bluhdorn," she responded.

Gilda Radner, ironically a friend of Duvall's, bowed out. Shelley Duvall was in.

Apprehension about Altman, meanwhile, was not confined to Paramount.

Feiffer had met Altman in Vancouver in 1971 while shooting *Carnal Knowledge.* Altman was just several miles away, filming *McCabe.* Indeed, the two casts partied on weekends together. (It was Feiffer, parenthetically, who made the auspicious introduction of Jack Nicholson to Warren Beatty at one of these comminglings. Nicholson, according to Feiffer, impressed by Beatty's charisma and superior height, rocked back on his heels and exclaimed, "Now, *that's* what a movie star looks like!")

So Feiffer knew Altman, and admired his work. But Feiffer was also a stickler for the protection of his writing, and he knew of the director's reputation for improvisation and script repair. His early conversations with Altman about *Popeye* were pleasant enough, but Feiffer felt "vaguely dissatisfied" and was not sure he trusted the director.

One of the things that disquieted him is that Altman seemed a lot more interested in the townfolk of Sweethaven, who were a marginal factor in Feiffer's original script, than in the principals of the story.

"He talked about them a lot more than he talked about the characters of Popeye and Olive Oyl," says Feiffer. "That's what scared me in the early conversations. Altman said, 'Well, just to shoot the script would be boring.' That bothered me because I didn't think it was boring at all. But it was his movie, and I couldn't start yelling cop until it became clear that he was destroying the script."

When Feiffer first heard Nilsson's music, he grew even more agitated, convinced that in at least one instance the composer had written lyrics out of character with the screenplay. When Feiffer complained to Altman, there were sparks.

"Bob took umbrage with me because I was questioning his ability to handle his work," remembers Feiffer. "He thought Harry [Nilsson] was doing a fine job. His feeling was basically that this is an argument not worth having because he can fix anything up when it comes to the shooting and why worry about it.

"There were long-distance conversations that boiled over, there were arguments where he would walk out of a room. And when we came to Malta, he, Harry, and I, all of us as it turns out, thought this was going to be impossible. Just the reverse became clear."

It was Altman who finally settled on the by-then popular location of the island of Malta, which is situated halfway around the world from the film capital—in the middle of the Mediterranean Sea, equidistant from Tunisia and the boot-heel of Italy.

This was a continuation of Altman's practice, since TV days in the Sixties, of avoiding a studio sound stage.* Going on location had become almost an obsession with Altman, though it made less and less sense for some of the films. In this case, being so far away from the studios helped to drive the budget up, and became part of the ordeal of making the movie. The below-the-line figure may have been tempered by hiring Maltese carpenters and artisans and a largely Italian camera crew (director of photography would be Fellini's

---

*The more money they give you, the director liked to tell associates, the more they like to stand behind you and watch. This was the most money a film company had ever given him. Indeed, there were stipulations in his contract that if Altman went over budget, he would forfeit a share of his salary. The director and Paramount ended up in litigation, later on, over this clause, each blaming the other when the Popeye costs soared to a reported $20 million-plus.

cameraman, Giuseppe Rotunno, whose U.S. work includes *Carnal Knowledge* and *All That Jazz*), but there were hidden costs in the remoteness.

A secluded bay on the northwest tip of the principal island of Malta provided the site of the storybook town created by Canadian production designer Wolf Kroeger. The special-effects tank on Malta accommodated the underwater footage. But partly because of the inclement weather the production encountered, and partly because of the director's close-in visual strategy, there was barely a glimpse in the finished film of Malta itself, the island where Saint Paul was once shipwrecked.

By now Altman's wariness extended to the press, and the remoteness of the Republic of Malta also served the function of keeping nosy journalists away. Unlike the days of *Nashville*, which were come-one, come-all, only privileged contributors to *Rolling Stone, American Film,* and a French magazine were screened and invited on the set. Requests were routinely denied from prestigious and well-circulated publications, and when a snoopy reporter from *The Los Angeles Times*, on the scent of the Altman-in-trouble angle, flew in from Israel expressly to cover the story, she was refused access to the set.

Events justified the precaution. More troubled indeed than any previous Altman production, the shooting was complicated by foul weather, a spiraling budget, special-effects snafus, near-fatal accidents and injuries on location, and real and imagined friction behind the camera.

Location planning began in October of 1979. The crew began to erect the spectacular set, a mock town nestled in a cove, consisting of shops, hotels, shanty houses, a cafe, a chapel, a sawmill, and a floating casino. The detail and ornamentation were to be painstaking. There was a complement of sheds, barges, tugboats, gangways, boardwalks, and timberchutes. The Oyl family home was replete with a garden, dining room, upstairs, parlor, and front and side porches.

On the high ground, workmen built the production complex—a plaster shop, a makeup and carpentry lab, a wardrobe unit, a rehearsal hall, a dining hall, editing quarters, a recording studio and projection room for dailies (to be flown in from Rome), and a production office. Sentries were posted in booths at the end of a dirt lane leading to the bay. Artists were putting touches on a twenty-foot statue of Oxblood Oxheart, the behemoth who wrestles Popeye in the story.

Meanwhile, Altman was sure he was not going to be able to work with Evans or Feiffer. Feiffer was sure he was not going to be able to work with Nilsson or Altman. And Nilsson was not at all sure what he was getting into.

"Then," recalls Feiffer, "when we finally got down to story sessions—which Altman hates to get into, it takes forever to get him to agree to it—we got down to some of the best script sessions I've had since Mike Nichols and I worked together [on *Carnal Knowledge*]. Very tight. Very detailed. Full of ideas while not drowning the characters. Enlivening and elucidating. So it left me euphoric, and I heard when he got back to New York he told people he was euphoric also."

The musical differences were smoothed over, and a truce reigned until January, when filming was to begin. Though mollified, Feiffer was still suspicious and progressively upset as Altman spent many days during rehearsal working with the cartooney "extras." The comedy was being taken in a physical direction. Then when Robin Williams began to improvise freely in the early days of shooting, with a stream of muttered asides and fractured oaths, Feiffer began to grumble.

He complained about Williams to Altman, who complained about Feiffer to Evans.

"Since this was Robin's first movie," recalls Feiffer, "he [Altman] simply didn't want to interfere with [Williams's] creative process. He thought it would throw him for a loop. That wasn't the way he directed, he said. That became a strong difference. I really thought we were at loggerheads.

"Nonetheless," Feiffer continues, "I saw him soon afterwards, deep in conversation with Robin. I was quite moved by that, that what seemed like a hard line was no longer a hard line. Then Altman said I should speak to Robin myself."

Subsequently, Feiffer spoke to Robin Williams "strictly alone, within the confines of what Bob had said to him. Having been involved in this before with actors, when I first got into theatre, I did not want to whipsaw an actor between the writer and a director, which never helps. My point was that after he arrived at an improvisation, he should start thinking about how to clean it up, dropping lines like 'you know' and those quirky lines that don't help and are no more than clutter."

Additionally, Feiffer was invited by Altman to join editor Tony Lombardo in the editing room on location and work on scenes that worried him, cleaning up dialogue if necessary.

It was not long before Feiffer was won over—swept away by the experience of the filming, seduced by the contagion of the dailies, ultimately swayed by Altman's "vision."

By March he was not only rewriting pages on demand overnight, but rewriting the ending of *Popeye* to correspond with the vicissitudes of the beginning (and of Altman's changes of mind).

"The way Altman shoots sometimes alters or makes unnecessary later scenes in the script," explains Feiffer.

"In the beginning, I was [in Malta] to keep an eye on things in case Altman deviated suspiciously from the script. I felt like the cop on the production. Then when I felt more and more confidence with what he was doing—and where there were changes I felt they really made a substantial contribution to the work—it became more of a job to try and coordinate the remainder of the script with the atmosphere that was developing on the film."

As for Evans, well, if the stateside rumors were to be taken at face value, the producer and Altman had each other in a stranglehold.

The opposite was the case. Occupied with postproduction for *Urban Cowboy*, Evans would fly to the island for a crucial few days or so at a whirl. The word that he had arrived, and been sighted at the island's casinos in the company of a national beauty queen, clearly buoyed the *Popeye* company, many of whom were misled by their image of him at first, only to discover that his zest was infectious.

Evans avoided the actual set ("I don't have to hang around, I have nothing to prove") but would show up at dailies, view the day's clips, and then announce afterward that *Popeye* was as "magical" as anything he had ever been associated with.

He would declare the first cut worthy of three or four hours' duration, give Altman a bear hug, and sweep blissfully out of the room.

Despite the unexpected goodwill between Feiffer, Evans, and Altman, the other problems were considerable, though the cast and crew, for the most part, were cushioned from knowledge of them.

For one thing, Tommy Thompson, Altman's lieutenant harking back to *Brewster McCloud* and before that to television days in the 1950s, quit *Popeye* and Lion's Gate just as location work was shifting into high gear.

"Egg," Thompson, and Scott Bushnell had been responsible for preproduction on the Malta location. It had developed into a showdown between the two remaining members of the "talent trust" and the woman who was ascending in power to become "the only person I talk to creatively," in Altman's words.

"Egg" and Thompson had clashed with Scott Bushnell, initially, over the Wolf Kroeger set—which Thompson felt was, under Bushnell's encouragement, evolving in a grim and foreboding, Germanic direction. Thompson felt that the director was going to have to struggle against that tone throughout the picture.* The design, argued Thompson, ought instead to be up, lightsome, antic.

---

*Thompson makes the interesting point that on the evidence of the finished film, the director did, indeed, struggle against the design pictorially, even though he himself had authorized it—and that Kroeger's lavishly detailed fishing village is, in any case, like many another Altman set, cut away from or glimpsed claustrophobically.

Altman sided with Bushnell.

Thompson was back in New York for a conference with Altman when Scott Bushnell telephoned to complain that there was not enough petty cash available for her to make a weekend shopping expedition to Rome for costumes and props. It was, Thompson felt, another chit in her campaign to gain control of the production purse strings. Thompson happened to be in the apartment with Altman when Bushnell called, and after Altman upbraided Thompson for this oversight, his longtime friend and assistant exploded. Thompson resigned and stalked out of the building. He proceeded to midtown to have a quiet lunch with his wife at the Russian Tea Room and to feel, for the first time in years, an oppressive burden lifted.

Thompson never worked for or spoke to Altman again, and Scott Bushnell moved up.

Besides this, there were unforeseen technical problems, the most peculiar of which was that the specially designed "spinach muscles" for Popeye proved unacceptable. Altman was thrown off his sequential shooting rhythm and had to film around Robin Williams for nearly four weeks while new forearms were being fitted.

The boozing and the drug-imbibing on an Altman location reached new heights in Malta, in part because of the heavy cocaine use among the musician clique. But the frequent night shooting and "island fever" also heightened the prevalence of drugs among the cast and crew. The Maltese authorities watched the airport for the smuggling of such contraband, but it was brought in in the underclothing of some girlfriends and wives.

Ironically, the night shooting and the production pressures kept Altman relatively straight, even off the set. But the mystique the director had been cultivating throughout the 1970s—the festive atmosphere on location, the tolerance of drugs and alcohol—was backfiring.

Between the pressures of his first movie role and the strained relationship with his wife, Valerie Velardi, Robin

Williams did not need the temptation of cocaine. Her career (she was a dancer) was going nowhere; his was skyrocketing. The tabloids were harping on the tensions in their marriage. While Williams was acting in front of the camera, Velardi was decompressing with the musicians. In the predawn hours after filming, Williams would show up at that night's drug scene and launch into shouting matches. The whole company was painfully aware of their unhappiness and rooting for a reconciliation; not to mention, everyone was rooting for Williams to relax finally into his characterization.

Any one of these happenings would have been enough to demoralize people under normal circumstances—but on an Altman set, the drama is diffuse, and the *Popeye* company was, for the most part, humming with satisfaction. It was to be the last full-blown Altman "family" filmmaking.

As usual, Altman had taken enormous care and pleasure in nourishing the community that surrounded him on location—the John Fordian-like circle of friends and loyalists that would inhabit the imaginary world of *Popeye*, and that would become a reservoir of fortitude during filming; resulting in, as Canadian actor Wayne Robson, an Altman regular, put it, a thoroughly enjoyable "celebration of life."

The Felliniesque (Fellini was like a spiritual godfather to the production) troupe recruited for *Popeye* included Canadian stage actors such as Robson, struggling Off-Broadway types, the Pickle Family Circus with Bill Irwin from San Francisco, jugglers and acrobats, Italian stuntmen, the a cappella Steinettes from *Health*, the British and L.A. session musicians, and numerous stock-company venerables (Robert Fortier, the drunk on the ice in *McCabe*, again playing the town drunk in *Popeye*).

Cast and crew had been encouraged to bring along family and friends. By this time, Altman's own family entourage included wife Kathryn, and sons Steve Altman and Bobby Altman, both working their way up the hierarchy of the technical crafts. Altman's daughter, Christine Altman Hurt, from Nebraska, was also along, caring for her one-year-old son, Wesley Ivan Hurt, making his debut in grandfather's

movie as Swee'pea, the baby. (Christine's manifest estrangement from her famous father added yet another dollop of tension to the proceedings.)

Whenever possible, relatives and lovers were also cast in
Popeye or put on salary as part of the crew. It was somehow
typical of Altman that he personally involved himself in
housing arrangements for the company—locating living
quarters in empty flats scattered around Malta or in the
nearby Danish vacation colony, and insisting on such family
conveniences as operating kitchens. It was also typical that,
when the *Popeye* troupe got off the plane from Rome during
the first week of January and were shuttled to the set, the
director himself was on hand to greet them in old-shoe fashion, and to escort them around the grounds as if he were
their weekend host.

"Now that's something, ordinarily, that I think would be
taken over by the assistant director or somebody," says
Feiffer. "I mean, there are all sorts of jobs that he does and
wants to do that, on other productions, other people would
be doing. But he really has to be in on everything and wants
to know everything and is virtually aware of everything."

The arrival of the company was followed by weeks of rehearsal, shooting tests, juggling and acrobatic and dance
classes. The mood was one of getting to know new friends,
"a sense of play," in Feiffer's words. "I had much more the
feeling of putting on an Off-Broadway play than of putting on
a multimillion-dollar Hollywood musical. . . . There was
very little sense of hierarchy or pecking order. There was a
kind of relaxation about it, an openness."

Came one day, Altman gathered the company together in
the rehearsal hall and announced that he did not want three-
dimensional characters for *Popeye*, he wanted "silhouettes."
Then the director spent time individually with each of the
roughly fifty actors, singers, dancers, and circus people, selecting their characteristic costume and makeup. With each
of them he developed a "pick-a-tick," a kind of distinctive
quirk.

Off-camera in Malta, Altman's "sense of community" was

cultivated by tournaments of every stripe, especially backgammon (everyone was eventually dragged into a game with
Altman). Movies—first Altman's, then Alan Rudolph's, Robert Benton's, and Robert M. Young's, then Rotunno's, then
all of the Disney cartoon classics—were flown in for weekend double features. Talent shows (with everyone pitching in
their novelty) were organized for days off. Dailies were communal get-togethers, with popcorn circulating and kids hoot-
ing in the aisles, and afterward, brisk give-and-take with
opinions from everybody.

The musicians formed a club and dubbed themselves The
Falcons. Shelley Duvall published a regular edition of *The
Falconette Gazette,* a five- or six-page mimeo of drawings,
adages, spaces for doodling, gossip ("Sam Cohn will arrive
Tuesday, sans tie"), letters from readers, crossword puzzles,
up-to-date reportage of the backgammon tourneys, items of
strange note, "this and that (mostly that)."

Birthdays were celebrated with cakes and surprise parties.
After hours, there were parties and more parties. Altman
could be expected to put in an appearance. Often he and
Kathryn were the hosts.

"You would expect Kathryn and Bob to have Robin and
Shelley and myself and Paul Smith and certain people to dinner periodically," explains Paul Dooley, "as a kind of protocol in a way, because we're principals. But they don't treat
it that way. I [would] walk by their compound on my way
home and sometimes the gate would be open and you could
see what's happening there on a given evening.

"You'd see all the Pickle Family Circus invited in. There
was an evening just with the director for the people who
didn't have particularly big parts . . . I'm sure everybody
went to Bob's house a couple of times for dinner. That
doesn't happen on most movies."

If there were such a thing as purists of the musical genre,
Altman was bound and determined to offend them with
Popeye. The music as well as the dance underwent an un-

conventional "refining process" in Malta that was typically free-form in its ultimate manifestation.

Although many dance and movement classes were logged by the cast, the dancing on camera was not slick and fancily choreographed, like some high-gloss musical, but ragged and loose. An "un-musical," was the catchword. This seems to have caught some of the company by surprise, although the director said he had it in the back of his mind all along.

How it worked in practice was, to say the least, unusual. If, for instance, Robin Williams had a few bars of spotlight music in an upcoming scene, Sharon Kinney, the ex–Twyla Tharp dancer who was one of *Popeye*'s choreographers, might map out a few steps with Williams—in a way that would allow the director plenty of leeway to get specific during the actual filming.

The gymnastic training, the tap-dancing lessons, the seven months of working out like a prizefighter—were all largely, as Robin Williams noted, only a conditioning for his reflexes, not an education in dance. There were to be no dance steps per se.

At least three of *Popeye*'s songs were written by Nilsson on the island. Songs written expressly for one character were being given by Altman to another. Late in the filming, the director was not sure what the final sequence of the tunes would be, since plans for later editing included "mixing songs up, putting two together, one song following another and immediately in the same scene, then you don't have another one for a while."

The six-track studio built on the island for Nilsson and crew was a sound engineer's miracle (or maybe *nightmare* would be the right word). Padded with egg crates for sound insulation, the studio was hardly "state-of-the-art," and recording was sometimes interrupted by mysterious echo chambers and sixteen-hour blackouts.

The small retinue of musicians gathered under Nilsson's leadership to lay down the recorded demos and playback tapes for each day's filming included such rock-world nota-

bles as banjo player Doug Dillard, bass guitarist Klaus Voorman (a Beatles session-man), percussionist Ray Cooper (Elton
John's drummer), and musical arranger Van Dyke Parks, all
of them doubling as townfolk of Sweethaven.

The "walking music" composed by Nilsson for *Popeye*
was so called because it is "music that walks along with
Popeye throughout the film." The basic tracks were laid
down in studio sessions in Malta and were supposed to be
(maybe, maybe not—the director was still deciding) overdub-
bed later on for the sound track.

Only, Altman's changeability caught the moody Nilsson
off guard, and there was a flare-up between them. A mercurial egomaniac with the alternating temperament of a
grizzly and a pussycat, Nilsson left the island in a rage only
halfway through the filming, and most of the tracks were
never rerecorded with any sheen. That is why the songs
sound a little shaggy, which was just fine with Altman. Van
Dyke Parks finished up the orchestration, much later, in
London.

Late one night, after shooting had wrapped for the day, Altman unwound in the living room of his bungalow with a
Scotch and soda in hand.

The burden of working under incessant pressure on a scale
that went against his nature showed up in the weary lines of
his face. Through the Lion's Gate clipping service, Altman
was fully aware of the hostile media climate that was chip-
ping away at his leverage with the studios, and at his own
reserve of self-confidence.*

Ironically, far from being drugged-out and spendthrift on
location, Altman was a Rock of Gibraltar in the increasingly
stormy seas.

In an interview, Altman said he felt particularly bad for
capable people who had worked with him and did excellent
work, and who were now stigmatized for being in a sup-

---

*Typical of the Altman snipes was a definition of "looped" published in *Los
Angeles* magazine, at the time, as "something Robert Altman tends to get in his
trailer."

posedly "disappointing" Altman picture. (He mentioned Paul Dooley and Marta Heflin, on his mind from the recent *A Perfect Couple*.)

"I have a couple of small pictures in mind I'd like to do that normally I'd have no trouble doing, with unknown people," Altman said, "but they're going to be hard to do now, thanks to the critics." He added, "I'm incapable of giving them what they want me to give them. I'm talking about the critics—and also the public, possibly."

Altman well knew that *Popeye* was a crucial movie for him, a commercial one ostensibly, one that would give him an opportunity to rebound from the point of view of the industry, and one that would hopefully give him momentum for other, more personal projects. A quid pro quo. The truth of that was tempting him to react perversely, to subvert if possible the logic of the system, to succeed by failing. To eff the ineffable.

During that interview Altman talked a little bit about *Popeye*, and how a cartoon sailor made sense as an Altman picture.

"The only thing we're doing in *Popeye*," he explained, "is showing a microcosm of an oppressed society. The whole key to *Popeye* is Segar's 'I Yam What I Yam.' These people are not what they are. They are what people tell them to be. They have never seen the man who is their dictator.

"That's the way most people are in dictatorships or most societies—capitalist or communist or whatever—we behave out of fear of something we don't even know is going to happen. And we all try to be something else."

When this supposed "message" of *Popeye* was later quoted to the screenwriter, Feiffer laughed heartily and said that Altman's imagination was overripe about such things.

But wait. The real message was not very complicated for anybody, critic or otherwise, who might care to ponder what a movie like *Popeye* was doing in the custody of a director like Altman. 'I Yam What I Yam.' Altman is what he is.

Indeed, *Popeye* was the opening sally in a decade-long insistence on that theme. From Popeye to Richard Nixon, from

Mona in *Come Back to the Five and Dime, Jimmy Dean, Jimmy Dean,* to (more merrily) Bruce and Prudence in *Beyond Therapy,* to, finally, Queeg in *The Caine Mutiny Court-Martial* and Presidential candidate Jack Tanner, there is defiance, and defensiveness, from Altman, as he parades increasingly pretzeled-up social misfits. 'I Yam What I Yam.' That silly little E. C. Segar maxim suited the director just fine.

The *Popeye* trials seemed to drag on and on. In March there was still another two months of shooting ahead, then a month of difficult underwater footage with Popeye battling an octopus (very anticlimactic and seemingly tacked-on in the final film). Then there were months of postproduction— while Lion's Gate sorted out Williams's muttered asides and the musical numbers. Back in the states, Altman continued to take it on the chin with Twentieth Century-Fox's limited release of *Health.*

Popeye was nay-sayed by that most elusive and suspect of Hollywood grapevines, "word of mouth." *American Film* magazine, for one, canceled its pending cover story after intercepting the negative rumors, then rescheduled the article, after editing it to neutralize the positive slant on Altman.

When the picture was finally released, for the Christmas season of 1980, the critics took one step back and scratched their heads in more puzzlement than usual. Finally, they issued a resounding "Maybe!"

It was hard not to warm up to such a truly likable film, even if it was impossible to make sense of all its weirdnesses. "Maybe!" What there is of a plot gets sidetracked by a spiritless gambling scene aboard a floating casino and by a tedious Freudian subtext of Popeye's estrangement from his Daddy: two Altman obsessions. "Maybe!" And yet . . . it is a singular film in many respects, with a madcap ambience, two luminous central performances (Williams and Duvall), and keen fantastical touches throughout.

It did not matter what the critics said anyway. This was a

children's movie, the sort of children's movie that adults could perhaps enjoy, and vice versa. In the end, *Popeye* grossed impressively at movie theatres, especially considering that so many of the ticket sales were at reduced prices to children and families. And it has had a healthy afterlife in video.

Regardless, the preconceptions, the filming troubles, the budget overruns, and the ambivalent critical reception had foredoomed *Popeye*. Altman's film never did overcome its initial taint, and despite the cumulative, worldwide $60 million-plus from moviegoers, it is still believed to have "fared poorly" (John Taylor's words in *Storming the Magic Kingdom*) at the box office. Ironically, Altman's most popular film ever, after *M*A*S*H*, *Popeye* also proved his Waterloo in Hollywood.

PART
6

"For me, the evening of my life has not yet come. But for the boy who, forty years ago, used to lie in bed in Yorba Linda, California, and dream of traveling to far-off places when he heard the train whistle in the night, I can say even now that the day has indeed been splendid."

—*Richard Nixon,*
Six Crises

Chapter
34

THE
EIGHTIES

Popeye's woeful reception forced Altman to extreme measures. In 1981, the director sold Lion's Gate and his Malibu residence, and moved his family and streamlined operations to New York City, where he began his decade-long "minimalist" period of directing literate dramatic properties on shoestring budgets for stage, home video, television, and limited theatrical release.

The darling of box office and critics, for *M*A*S*H*, had come full circle to being regarded in Hollywood as anathema to both. The official line (promulgated in the French film magazines) was that Altman was trying "the small format as a means of circumventing the traditional film distribution circuits." In reality, Altman was desperately seeking survival, and retreating to the small format as a last contingency in the downward spiral of his relations with the major studios.

He was entering a period of heightened isolation and paranoia, writer's block and writer dependency, bungled studio assignments and independent films financed out of pocket, and strangled career moves that included directing opera, beer commercials, and network television—anything that would pay.

This great American director, obsessed with himself, his enemies, and his own comedown, was entering a decade when he would no longer make movies about America and the culture of which he was once such a trenchant observer. Altman would be making narrowly focused movies primarily about himself, and about his own movies.

Come Back to the Five and Dime, Jimmy Dean, Jimmy Dean was among other things Altman's commentary on *The Delinquents* and *The James Dean Story*. *O.C. and Stiggs* was yet another kiss-off to that youth genre—and to whatever lingering hopes Hollywood might have for the director. *Secret Honor* was not just a Nixon diatribe. It was an Altman diatribe, with Altman's words erupting out of the character of the maligned President.

Streamers was *M*A*S*H* revisited, this time without any guffaws. Altman told interviewers that he could not with integrity produce a military comedy in the era of the Grenada invasion, but what did he mean?—that the era of the Vietnam War was funnier? The truth was that the director himself was rancid and disordered, and it was reflected in the strengths and weaknesses of his films during the decade of the Eighties.

It was a long, hard, troubled decade. Any other person might have buckled under. But the director not only weathered the period, he emerged with notable films, and with, if anything, a strengthened reputation.

As astonishing as it may have seemed to some, a detour into live theatre made absolute sense for Robert Altman. The director had a sentimental attachment to the stage, dating back to

The three women of *Come Back to the 5 and Dime, Jimmy Dean, Jimmy Dean*: Mona (Sandy Dennis), Sissy (Cher), and Joanne (Karen Black). This "filmed theater" presentation brought Altman back to the fore.

Kansas City, and the usual Hollywood inferiority complex toward Broadway and live performance. He had been haunting acting workshops and backstage dressing rooms for years, picking out his players. Critics did wonder that this director, so notorious for ravaging the Hollywood script, could now film plays without changing a word. But some of that notoriety was inflated. And it was a comfort to Altman, at this stage of his career and personal instability, to surrender himself to the words of Harold Pinter, Sam Shepard, and David Rabe, not to mention Marsha Norman, Ed Graczyk, and Christopher Durang.

When Altman sold Lion's Gate in 1981, it was to a consortium headed by Jonathan Taplin, the producer of the rockumentary about The Band, *The Last Waltz*, for $2 million. Only one person in the company knew about the transaction beforehand: Scott Bushnell. The rest, including Robert Eggenweiler, who was president of the postproduction center, learned about it when Altman called the staff in and gave the announcement. "Egg" left Altman, after twenty years, a disillusioned man.

The only soldier in the war by that point, anyway, was Bushnell, whose love for the legitimate theatre predated and exceeded Altman's own. Her hold over the director, as he floundered, was complete, even if it cut both ways and she was the perfect foil for all his schemes and tirades. "She existed only for him," says an insider. "She asked nothing. Not even a credit."

Her credit ought to have been: *She kept him a'goin'*. The "talent trust," after all this time, had been reduced to one person only. That, as much as anything, accounts for Altman's films in the Eighties being as preordained and circumscribed as they once, in the Seventies, were unpredictable and all over the map. The pricipal unpredictable thing about a play that has already been performed and published, after all, is the decision to film it.

Bushnell's theatre ties were extensive. Her former husband, William Bushnell, had eventually left the American Theatre Ensemble in San Francisco and established a base in Los Angeles with the Los Angeles Actors' Theatre, where he was known as an outstanding director and producer. The Bushnells' conversations with Altman about directing theatre pieces gained impetus when, after what happened to *Popeye*, two focal Altman projects collapsed.

The first, and more widely reported, was *Lone Star*, an Off-Broadway comedy by James McClure about a Vietnam War returnee. It was to star a pre-*Aliens* Sigourney Weaver and Powers Boothe. The script was prepared, and preproduction in swing, when *Lone Star* became the first domino to topple, in the spring of 1981. Norbert Auerbach, the new president of MGM, who did not like what he was reading about *Popeye*, and who had problems of his own in trying to recover from his studio's $36 million-plus fiasco, *Heaven's Gate*, said no to *Lone Star*. It remains unfilmed.

The second project, less widely reported, was more of a psychic setback. In London for postproduction finishing of *Popeye*, Altman had rendezvoused with *Cold Day* scriptwriter Gillian Freeman in order to brainstorm one of those female-oriented films that have given him sustenance in his career. This one, based on Altman's concept, was to be called *Easter Egg Hunt*. It was set in 1915 at a young ladies' finishing school in Great Britain, and dealt with sexual delirium and abortion.

Gilliam Freeman had a script ready to go before the fallout from *Popeye*. Indeed, there was a tentative cast, and Altman was in Montreal scouting locations when the financing from independent sources fell through. (It was during this trip to Montreal that Altman met Canadian Pierre Mignot, who became his cinematographer throughout the Eighties.) Gillian Freeman went ahead and published a novel of the story that Altman still hopes to film one day. But its failure to go ahead in 1981 was a blow to his self-esteem.

Altman was in Canada, in midsummer, when he was reached by *The New York Times* for comment on the sale of Lion's Gate. He was downcast. "I had no choice," he was quoted as saying, in an unguarded moment. "Nobody was answering the phone."

By then, Altman had already directed two one-acters for the Los Angeles Actors' Theatre. His appetite was whetted, and he could read the signs of the immediate future.

The one-acters came about when Leo Burmeister, who was slated for the cast of *Lone Star*, asked Altman to direct *Rattlesnake in a Cooler*, an essay on Western myths written by an actor-playwright by the name of Frank South, and intended as an actors' showcase. The Bushnells encouraged Altman to pair *Rattlesnake* with another monological one-acter by Frank South, *Precious Blood*, about conflicting memories of family and a rape.

The double bill played in June of 1981, and Hollywood was properly flummoxed. This director who ought to be on his ass from the shellacking of *Popeye* was acting as if he had more important things on his mind, like directing elite theatre for small audiences. Quite accustomed to New York stage directors panting for a foot in the door of motion pictures, Hollywood people were not really sure what to make of the opposite scenario. Los Angeles theatre critics, who theoretically had the advantage of having no previously published bias about Altman and his films, reviewed these one-acters generously—even ecstatically. It added up to the antithesis of a career move—certainly it was not going to do anything for Altman's career in Hollywood—yet it accrued to his favor.

When *Easter Egg* went by the boards, Altman found himself at one of those periodic professional nadirs that he was all too familiar with—only this was the worst one since the early Sixties when the director had been dismissed from *Kraft*. It was *Two by South*, whose genesis was owed to the Bushnells, that catalyzed Altman's very necessary flight to New York City. In the press Altman liked to characterize it as voluntary and strategic, but in every sense it was an escape from nowhere.

Two by South was restaged at the St. Clement's Theatre in Manhattan in the fall of 1981, and then taped there for a Hearst-ABC cultural cable presentation. The stage notices were triumphant. Walter Kerr of *The New York Times* wrote, "Mr. Altman can manage the medium." (After seeing Altman's staging of *Jimmy Dean, Jimmy Dean* a year later, Kerr wrote, "Scratch that.")

Though it links up with his fascination with macho Western Americana and his predilection for Tennessee Williams-style floridity, *Two by South* remains an oddity among his credits, important only insofar as it led to Altman's decision to direct other filmed plays.

Come Back to the Five and Dime, Jimmy Dean, Jimmy Dean was yet another soul-barer "in the Inge-Williams vein," in the words of the playwright Ed Graczyk, a director of a Columbus, Ohio, little theatre, whose two previous stage plays had been performed only in regional settings. Altman learned about the play through the Bushnells, and announced plans to present it on Broadway.

The text of the play was somewhat half-baked; but the director would probably have been titillated by *Jimmy Dean,*

Jimmy Dean (with its female nerve-rattling, its anti-James Deanism, its sex-reversal climax) even if he had not just then been hopelessly in search of something to occupy his time.

Set inside a rundown Woolworth's in a small Texas town called McCarthy (nice touch, that), it follows a reunion of James Dean disciples commemorating the twentieth anniversary of the film star's death. "Memory shifts" transport the characters between 1975 and 1955—and the flashbacks record the frenzied fan reaction to Dean's arrival in a nearby town to film his last movie, *Giant.*

Especially in his trio of principal characters, Altman marshaled what is truly one of his inspired casts.

Sandy Dennis was the high-strung asthmatic clerk who had worked in the dimestore for twenty years, and who carried a torch (and possibly the legacy of an illegitimate son) from her brief contact with Dean. The pop singer Cher, at a low point in her musical career, had come to New York to study acting with Lee Strasberg; she was plucked by Altman to portray an earthy, wisecracking waitress with artificial breasts who is another of the Dean diehards. And the mystery guest who shows up to even old scores is Karen Black, who in the course of the charged drama reveals herself to have undergone a transexual operation.

The backers dropped off at the last minute, and Altman had to pour some $200,000 of his own money into the production. When most of the reviews were unfavorable, the play had to close after only a short run. At that point, Altman was determined to recoup his costs, and to prove the critics wrong by filming the damn thing masterfully.

The producer of the film version of *Jimmy Dean, Jimmy Dean*—who became Altman's friend and adjunct for several years—was a former sports reporter and documentarist by

---

*The play was roundly panned by, among others, the hard-to-please John Simon (long an Altman detractor) and the ranking critic of *The New York Times,* Frank Rich. Altman made a faux pas when he appeared on ABC's *20/20* and made the stipulation that Frank Rich's review not be mentioned. That was bait to the producer, who went ahead and cited it anyway, on camera, leaving the director frothing at the mouth and having to be restrained while the camera recorded his rage. This made for good television, even if it made for bad imagemaking.

the name of Peter Newman, whom Altman liked to introduce to people as "the Jew with the money."

Newman worshiped Altman, which made him a likely re-
cruit. At the time, Mark Goodson, the game show host, was
staking Newman to some production coin to produce low-
budget cable programs. When Newman discovered that
Jimmy Dean, Jimmy Dean was opening three blocks from
his Times Square office, he hustled over and met the director. They put together a deal for the cable filming. Though,
Newman says, Altman never let on that he had it in mind to
release *Jimmy Dean, Jimmy Dean* theatrically, that was the
director's hidden agenda all along.

Budgeted at $850,000, it became a feature of perverse radi-
ance, beautifully photographed by Pierre Mignot in super-16.
Altman performed interesting maneuvers with mirrors and
an exquisitely detailed set, yet the flashbacks were not in the
least intrusive, and in general it was a controlled stunt of
filmmaking that compared with Altman's best of the past.*

Immediately, the director was reestablished with sympathetic film critics, who pointed out among its other merits
bedazzling performances from the three leading actresses.
(Indeed, *Jimmy Dean, Jimmy Dean* was to catapult Cher into
one of the surprise career makeovers of the Eighties—one of
the few times Altman's quirky starmaking has crossed over
to the broader public.) A roundtable of *Los Angeles Times*
film critics, later in the decade, found *Jimmy Dean, Jimmy
Dean* tentatively included on the in-house Ten Best list of
films of the Eighties.

But Altman's frame of mind was short of triumphal. The
critics had ceased to have any real meaning. The director was
still scrambling, wretched, vindictive.

---

*It was such taut filmmaking, says producer Newman, in part because Altman had
the advantage of having rehearsed for thirty performances Off-Broadway and then
for another fifty performances on Broadway—so that, for the first time in his
career, the director had the equivalent of a totally rehearsed vehicle that had
already been polished during some eighty dry runs.

Jimmy Dean, Jimmy Dean did as well as it did (its modest earnings helped establish a small distribution company, Cinecom) partly because Altman carted it around the world to film festivals where the director was on the program to be feted. Altman would have the film cans of *Jimmy Dean, Jimmy Dean* under one arm, *Health* under the other. He was sometimes cash-poor and there were embarrassing situations where his credit card was called into question. On the long plane flights there would be drunken recriminations, the rehashing of grudges against old enemies, tears shed over the falling-away of former friends, and a recital of his steadfast, and surprisingly fresh, bottom-line resentment that he had not been allowed to break through as a director with *M*A*S*H* until he was past the age of forty. Newman would be there to listen, and drink along.

Altman would go anywhere if the ticket was paid for. It was kind of a joke between him and Newman, often his traveling companion.

Once, there was a gap between film festival bookings in Toronto and Venice and Deauville, and the director sandwiched in an invitation to a small retrospective in Knokke, Belgium. Altman and Newman stayed up all night on the plane, tossing down drinks.

"The fella who ran the Knokke Film Festival was there to greet us," recalls Newman. He was eighteen years old and had a cape on. We were carrying each other off the plane. The guy looked at Bob—you could tell Bob was his idol— and said, 'Mr. Altman, Mr. Altman, there is only one question I must ask you . . .'

"We were really gone. It was obvious the question was going to be something like 'Why did the woman die at the end of *Nashville*?' Bob looked at him and said, 'Yes, what is your question?' The guy said, 'Why would you come to our film festival?' We realized it was a pretty absurd thing."

Altman would wax nostalgic. He would reminisce about the days when he was sitting in one of those glass-enclosed cafés near Bloomingdale's, numb on Percodan because of his bad back, and observing the people standing in line waiting to see *Nashville*. How much it meant to him that people were fighting to get into a Robert Altman film!

He would recall the time he was introduced at the New York Film Festival, at the premiere of *A Wedding*, as "the greatest living American director." Well, Altman was *still living!*—but the critics were fickle, and they no longer recognized him for what he was.

Altman would forecast the same pitiful death for himself as Erich von Stroheim, who as an actor specialized in playing autocratic Huns, and who as a perfectionist director was a Hollywood outcast in tragic quest of films that never materialized. Riddled with cancer, at least von Stroheim had the good sense (said Altman) to die in France.

It was unwise to mention old acquaintances who were enjoying momentary success. Alan Rudolph called Altman up when he was in New York to promote his MGM movie about mysterious cattle mutilations, *Endangered Species*. Over dinner at a fancy New York eatery, Altman was heard to scream at producer Carolyn Pfeiffer and writer-director Rudolph, this latter the loyalest of the loyal, accusing them of going over to the enemy camp.

"How could you possibly make this movie for a studio? Don't you know they are the *enemies*? Don't you know what I've taught you? I'm embarrassed by you. . . ." (Within a year Altman would be angling to direct his own MGM project.)

It was not safe to mention another director in his presence. Mentioning Woody Allen could mean trouble. Altman would profess to abhor Woody Allen—primarily because Allen was flourishing with audiences and with the critics, while Altman was stagnating. At Elaine's Restaurant in New York, Altman always made a point of sitting with his back to Woody Allen.

Ann Arbor, Michigan, was a port in the storm. In the early 1980s, Altman accepted a visiting lectureship at the University of Michigan there, and enjoyed his responsibilities. As project after project fell through for him—a play about a brain-damaged boy and a preacher, the filming of a Thomas

Berger novel about feuding families in the Thirties, a Broadway musical comedy about the life of nineteenth-century New Orleans-born composer Louis Moreau Gottschalk, etc., etc.—Altman was surrounded by devout, unquestioning, youthful film students who were also conscripted as gofers for his more off-the-cuff productions. It was good for them, and it was good for him.

Aunt Pauline had been an opera singer. Now, Altman, who admitted he could not read music, became the director of a college production of Igor Stravinsky's *Rake's Progress*. Altman spent ten thousand dollars of his own money, bringing in professionals like set designer Wolf Kroeger. Altman expanded the play to 140 characters, mostly all on stage all the time, and changed the setting to a hellish insane asylum. He says he "half-dreamed" the notion while lying in bed on a Saturday morning. "I liked the morality and cynicism of the play," he told *The Kansas City Star*, which had dispatched a reporter to the scene of the hometown artist's latest adventure.

His production of *Rake's Progress* earned him a complimentary review in *Newsweek*. The experience was tonic for Altman—at the same time as it was just killing time.

Streamers was a play Altman had been waiting around to film since 1976, when Mike Nichols directed it for the stage. But the vital production money had not materialized. When the money did appear to come through, Altman went to Texas, where preproduction began at the Las Colinas studios outside Dallas. When the money evaporated at the eleventh hour, again Altman had to bankroll the project.

David Rabe's title comes from the mordant ditty (sung to the melody of Stephen Foster's "Beautiful Dreamer") about parachutes that fail to open. It is sung in the play by two dipsomaniacal career soldiers:

> Beautiful streamer,
> Open for me,
> The sky is above me,
> But no canopy.

The setting is an army barracks during the early days of the Vietnam War. Three young soldiers are waiting to be shipped out. As they reveal their interweaving destinies, a fourth soldier joins them, a pathological jive-ass who incites their fear and prejudices. In the end, there is an impromptu stabbing.

Though the script was the same one that won the New York Drama Critics Award as Best American Play in 1976, it expressed some familiar Altman concerns: the free-fall of reality, the homophobia that is the flip side of macho posturing, the inhumanity of the military machine. The film was more excruciating than the most angst-ridden *Combat* and, some said, more upsetting than the play. It was Altman taking a walk on the "dark" side, and as much as anything else it reflected the director's need to come to terms with himself.

Precision acting, probing camerawork, richly hued design: *Streamers* must be regarded as Altman's one unqualified success of the Eighties. The superb ensemble of actors (Mitchell Lichenstein, Matthew Modine, David Alan Grier, Michael Wright, Guy Boyd, George Dzundra) shared the Golden Lion Best Acting Award at the Venice Film Festival in 1982, and the film cropped up on many critics' year-end best lists.

Meanwhile, Peter Newman, ambitious to produce his own motion pictures, was seeding money toward a screenplay based on a *National Lampoon* article by Tod Carroll and Ted Mann called "The Ugly, Monstrous, Mind-Roasting Summer of O.C. and Stiggs." Altman was aware of the script in development, and he acted as if he was happy for Newman; but he regarded *O.C. and Stiggs* (as it came to be called) as the kid's pipe dream, and not his sort of thing anyway.

When the script by Mann and Donald Cantrell was finished, the reaction from Hollywood was swift. Studios bid against each other for the rights, and several noted directors said they wanted to film it. This farcical story of two savagely delinquent teenagers who destroy the peace and harmony of a family bloated with all-American pretense seemed very much in synch with the "youth" trend in films that was all the rage at that moment.

At that point, Altman came to Newman and expressed chagrin that he had not been asked to direct *O.C. and Stiggs.* So Newman, because he still believed in Altman and because he hoped this could be the director's entree back into Hollywood, asked Altman to be his director.

The two of them flew to Los Angeles to meet with Freddie Fields and Frank Yablans, the reigning duo at Metro-Goldwyn-Mayer. Fields, who had been the director's agent once, had given Altman a tentative okay, and ran preliminary interference with Yablans, reputed to be one of the toughminded producers in town. Newman and Altman had their pitch down. They were selling *O.C. and Stiggs* as a combination of *M*A*S*H* and *Nashville*—they were calling it *M*A*S*Hville.* It would be set in a Southwestern city—with its two lead characters (reminiscent of Hawkeye and Trapper John) stuck in a place where they do not want to be, and so reacting with social anarchy.

Never mind that Altman himself had railed in interviews against the wave of insipid teen movies that had seemed in recent years to dominate the film industry's output. In the meeting with Fields and Yablans, he was talking out of both sides of his mouth for the opportunity to direct just such a picture.

"Now Bob," said Yablans, "I'm going to let you make this movie. You've got a go. But there are a couple of things you've got to promise me. Number one is, you've got to shoot the script."

Altman promised to shoot the script.

"Number two is," continued Yablans, "I don't want to read in any papers that MGM is an asshole or that we are the bad guys if this movie doesn't work out. We're going at this together. You've got to give me your word as a man that we don't bad-mouth each other later on."

Altman gave his word.

Then Fields, a bouncy agent type of guy, piped up. "And listen Bob," he contributed, "you know how, uh, in some of your movies, you hear the rain here and the guys there?" Fields spread his arms for emphasis. "Can't we have the guys here and the rain there?"

Here was the president of the studio trying to explain with his hands where he wanted the sound and where he wanted the image, and to warn Altman off making some type of European-type art picture.

Altman said, "Sure, Freddie."

They signed a contract with a $7 million "go," and only six weeks later Altman and crowd were in Phoenix for filming.

"The second he would get a go," says Newman, "he would rush into it, because he had been disappointed too many times. There would be forty people on the payroll the next morning, because he knew well enough that regimes could change. . . .

"One reason people have taken risks on Bob and will continue to take risks," continues Newman, "is because everyone thinks they can tame the wild beast. It's a form of conceit. They are the ones who are going to bring this guy back. Bob doesn't need bringing back. Bob just needs understanding."

The wild and perhaps not woolly enough cast was thrown together quickly: Daniel Jenkins (regional stage experience) and Neill Barry (television, Off-Broadway, and minor films) as O.C. and Stiggs, respectively; Paul Dooley; *Saturday Night Live* alumna Jane Curtin; Jon Cryer and Laura Urstein as members of the Schwab family; Dennis Hopper, in one of those special-billed roles that marked his Eighties comeback, as a loony Viet vet; and Donald May *(Roaring Twenties)*, Louis Nye, Tina Louise *(Gilligan's Island)*, ex-Litto client Melvin Van Peebles, Ray Walston, Martin Mull, Bob Uecker, Cynthia Nixon, and Carla Borelli.

Down in Phoenix, Altman set about breaking his word, rewriting the script and bad-rapping MGM. Newman says Altman probably never wanted to direct O.C. *and Stiggs* in the first place—that he decided to direct it only when it appeared as if he was not going to be asked to direct it.

The rarely photographed Scott Bushnell (at right) watching O.C. (Neill Barry), Altman, and Stiggs (Daniel H. Jenkins) confer on the set of the *National Lampoon*-based comedy *O.C. and Stiggs*. The singularly unfunny film sat on the studio shelf for three years before being released to a dismal critical reception. (MGM)

Altman closeted himself in a room for several days and tore up the script, this script that everyone had pronounced sublime. The novice screenwriters were not informed or consulted. Indeed, they were advised not to come to location, to back off on any complaints, and to be happy that their baby was in the hands of a superb director like Altman.

One of the things Altman did in the rewrite was to turn the focus of the script around so that it was much more about the two delinquents than it was about the family they had a vendetta against. In the original script, the Schwabs represented straight America, and hence there was more of a motivation for the vendetta. Now, with his self-absorption, Altman made the film coldly, narrowly, and unsympathetically about O.C. and Stiggs. It was a kind of a laying waste of his own upper-middle-class boyhood.

His only real confidante was Bushnell, who was a twenty-four-hour extension of the director's personality, no matter that her credit would vary from film to film. There were others, such as cameraman Pierre Mignot, who were essential to whatever film Altman was working on—but they were a category apart from Bushnell, and there was little group give-and-take.

The temperature in Phoenix soared at times to a blistering 100+ degrees. Altman reveled in the perversity of it, as he had in the cold of *Quintet*. A little suffering made it more of a martyrdom. Altman put some effort into reviving the by-gone fun-for-all atmosphere, but the extreme weather—and the fact that people in the cast and crew were divided into camps based on their relative immersion in the "family"— gave an edge to it.

"He still forces—forces might be a little bit too strong a word—but whenever he goes on location—he forces you to watch all of his movies," says Newman. "We had to watch *Quintet* four times. I think he still believes that he was given unfair treatment in the press about that movie.

"From what I hear of the old days, it's been a long time since the old family feeling. It's funny. Some of the elements still remain. The democracy's still there. Everyone's invited to dailies. There are parties all the time—things like that that other filmmakers wouldn't conceive of. Yet there was a lot of . . . it went beyond tension."

A lot of the tension was self-imposed. It was not enough to eviscerate the script. Altman seemed intent on sabotaging his relationship with the studio that had given him money and trust. He would not return phone calls from MGM. He would not even let Newman return phone calls.

"At least let me talk to them and be a diplomat," Newman would plead. "I don't want any diplomacy," Altman would scornfully reply. "They are the enemy. You've got to understand that these folks are the enemy. Nothing good can come out of trying to mediate with them."

Even at that, no one had any idea that the movie was going to turn out to be so awful. Most of the cast and crew was protected from the behind-the-scenes fracases. There was steady laughter at the dailies. Moreover, Altman had invited many of the old gang down to Arizona to try to resurrect the spirit of Altman past. That added an aura of togetherness that was not borne out in reality. Robert Fortier, Nina van Pallandt, Thomas Hal Phillips, etc.—they walk through *O.C. and Stiggs* punning about other Altman movies as if trying to liven up a dead party.

Even Louis Lombardo was on the scene, entreated by Altman to help out on the editing.

"A lot of people thought while we were making the movie that this thing was going to be really good," says Newman. "It's impossible when you're on location with one of Bob's movies to know what is really happening. I contend that part of his style of shooting is not only because it's his style—an unorthodox way of editing and everything—but part of it is as a device of self-protection. Because no studio executive could ever take over one of his movies and tell what it is he's shooting. The sound is all over the place. There's no continuity. It's very hard to tell what you have or don't have. We thought we had something. We really did."

At a certain point in the editing process, the director began to edit behind Louis Lombardo's back, changing nuances and slants. Altman had never done anything like that before, says Lombardo.

Altman seemed hostile, short-fused. They would be working until two or three in the morning. The director would charge in and without warning start shouting at all the editors. Lombardo would stop the Moviola and say, "Bob, what the fuck are you screaming so much about?" Altman would mumble, "I don't know, I don't know. . . . And boom, out the door he goes," says Lombardo. "He didn't know himself.

"He was not the Bob Altman I knew," continues Lombardo. "He was totally different—a different man. More paranoid and real angry. [Before], it was so much *fun* to be with this guy."

Lombardo came to believe that Bushnell, whom he had never liked and vice versa, was painting lewd pictures for

Altman of duplicity in the cutting room. It was the familiar treason: Lombardo was siding with producer Newman, who was siding with MGM, which wanted to pander to the audience. Lombardo left the picture. It was not the first time Lombardo left Altman, but he says it will be the last. Like others before him, the editor of *Brewster McCloud, McCabe and Mrs. Miller, The Long Goodbye, California Split,* and *Thieves Like Us* believes he was being targeted by Bushnell.

"I was the last one," he shrugs, "and she finally got me, too."

In the end, Altman's version of *O.C. and Stiggs* had one of the worst audience previews in MGM history. Fields and Yablans practically went down on their knees to convince Altman to recut it. He refused. The picture went on the shelf. The studio did not write it off for taxes, but successive regimes came and went, and no one, not even Alan Ladd Jr. when he took control of MGM in the mid-Seventies, felt this particular Altman film was releaseable.

While *O.C. and Stiggs* was receiving a year's worth of postproduction glaze in New York City, Altman was putting a lot more energy into the 16mm one-man film that a second team was editing across the street in Bushnell's apartment.

Secret Honor had begun as a play at the Los Angeles Actors' Theatre under the sponsorship of William Bushnell. Donald Freed, the political activist who had researched and written about the Kennedy assassination *(Executive Action)* and the crimes of the CIA, had now cowritten, with an ex-government attorney named Arnold M. Stone, a rather astounding one-person show about Richard M. Nixon, starring an actor by the name of Philip Baker Hall. In their imagined drama, the President, during one long, hand-wringing night, rants and raves in the Oval Office, en route to a bizarre, self-serving conspiracy-oriented explanation of Watergate and his life. The unusual play offered a ruthless and at the same time compassionate portrayal of Nixon's character. Altman saw it, adored it, and organized its move to Off-Broadway in New York. There, *Secret Honor* attracted positive reviews (Alt-

Philip Baker Hall as Richard Nixon in *Secret Honor*. Altman's bravura filming of the one-man play had prismatic personal and political relevance. (Demetrios Demetropoulos/Los Angeles Actors' Theatre)

man had nothing to do with the staging) but scant audiences, which made Altman all the more resolved to film it.

Nixon's hold on Altman had deepened over the course of time. Like a lot of Americans, Altman, a lifelong political progressive, found that the Reagan Era made him practically sentimental for the old dodger. The director enjoyed showing off a letter Nixon had written to him, saying his daughter Julie's favorite movie happened to be *Nashville*, and did Altman have a copy of it that he might send to her? Altman sent a courteous reply, and in return received an autographed copy of Nixon's autobiography.

In Los Angeles, Freed had given actor Philip Baker Hall and stage director Robert Harders a free hand to shave and embroider the script. After which, *Secret Honor* always remained substantially the same—the night-long harangue by a wronged Nixon. Altman never had to add or change a word.

What was Altman's greatest contribution? "Just the courage of filming it," says Freed.

Altman proposed to film the play in Ann Arbor with a coalition of student personnel and some of his long-timers. The major difference between the play and the film was the new, cluttered set, created by Stephen Altman, and the battery of video screens, which Altman zeroed in on thematically and visually to lend variety.

Harders came along to Ann Arbor as a kind of Thirties-style dialogue director. Altman, still and always diffident about rehearsals, was more concerned with technical matters and the crew. Harders rehearsed Philip Baker Hall by night. Altman filmed him by day. Hall, on camera every minute for a grueling performance, worked so hard during the shooting that his tie was perpetually drenched with sweat to the tip.

It was a singular performance, and a film unlike anything Altman had done: the panoply of characters pared to one, the common-denominator technology, the seeming defense of Nixon. Though arduous to watch, it rewards patience. Released in 1983, *Secret Honor* was hailed as a rigorous masterwork by many U.S. critics, made annual best lists, and achieved renown overseas particularly.

Altman's zeal for the subject ought not to have surprised anyone familiar with his current frame of mind. In a strange way, the director had begun to see himself as Hollywood's Nixon. Nixon's tapes, Altman's movies. Nixon's Watergate, Altman's *Popeye*. Nixon the mutant, Altman the action painter. The script, the film, Philip Baker Hall's performance, the director's own career, seemed to build logically to the point in the climax where Nixon utters words that could have been formulated in Altman's mouth:

> They said they wouldn't buy a used car from me, but they gave me the biggest vote in American history. Then they flushed me down the toilet. And they wanted me to stay down. They wanted me to kill myself. Well, I won't do it. If they want me dead, they'll have to do it.

Fuck 'em! Fuck 'em! Fuck 'em! Fuck 'em! Fuck 'em! Fuck 'em! Fuck 'em! Fuck 'em! Fuck 'em! . . .
[repeatedly, against a chorus of "Four more years!"]

While Altman was in Ann Arbor, he also tarried to shoot test footage for Chiat Day, an agency handling beer commercials. Though his films were once again wowing some critics, Altman was ravenous for work and for money. The director lost the contract he was seeking when the brewing company decided to switch agency representatives.

Altman could be maddening about money. Now there was friction about it in the small circle that gathered for each successive film. The director took his usual large fees while asking the cast and crew to work for scale. The morality of the democracy had broken down. Altman would be discussing the pay scale with a newcomer and poor-mouthing his resources, while in the adjacent office his accountant could be heard on the phone finalizing the purchase of a new Mercedes for one of his sons. And the issue of money always became twisted into a test of loyalty.

"I didn't ask for anything," says one of the people in Altman's group during part of the Eighties. "I was afraid to.

"I realize that a certain process goes on. When you hook up with Bob or rather when he hooks you in, you're brought into a family situation. You have lunches together—home-style, Scotty cooking—you're brought in, and you feel you belong.

"Bob, of course, is the father. One feels you will be taken care of in the family, and that it would be out of place to ask Dad. Along with this is a kind of Jungian sense of betrayal toward anyone who dares to assert his individuality. That kind of betrayal is the worst thing that can happen within the family and is unforgivable."

Money became a surrogate for ego, the raison d'être for choosing which film to make. In the past, Altman had been offered an opportunity to direct Sam Shepard's play *Fool for Love*. But Scott Bushnell had seen it in San Francisco and

Bewildered May (Kim Basinger) in Altman's version of Sam Shepard's play *Fool for Love*.

pronounced it "too weird." Shepard, who had admired
Jimmy Dean, Jimmy Dean, called to say that Altman could
have the rights to any one of his rarely filmed plays. It was
not until Cannon came up with the money that Altman
evinced the slightest interest. That was the impetus: money.

"When he came to New York, he started doing projects not
because he wanted to," says Newman, "but because they
could get done. It's at the stage now where I think nearly
anyone can go to Bob and say I got a project, it's financed,
and I'd like you to direct it—and he's probably going to do it.
He used to say he would never work with Cannon. Well, he
did a movie with Cannon. I'm sure he never would have
worked for New World [before]. Well, he did a movie with
New World. . . .

"He just wanted to keep working," says Newman. "He
would do things if they would go. His feeling was, maybe it

isn't the project I want to do, but I'll shape it the way I want to."

Fool for Love was a phantasmagorical play about a rodeo drifter tormented with love for his half-sister. Their drunken, stormy free-for-all, in a tacky motel room, is observed by a ghostly father figure from the past.

Altman inveigled Shepard into joining a cast that included Kim Basinger, Harry Dean Stanton, and (as the gentleman caller) Randy Quaid. Cannon wanted the film to be amply budgeted, at $6 million, so Altman had to justify the high ceiling in part by opening the play up into an exterior neon-and-adobe motel and gas station set, created by Stephen Altman—which was authentic if somewhat irrelevant (weren't there a hundred others like it in and around Santa Fe, where they were filming?). It was the first of the director's filmed plays to venture outside the established set, and critics who compared the play to the film said it was a decision that resulted in a certain flaccidity. Altman countered that he had never read the stage directions, which stipulated that the pacing of Shepard's battle royal of lust and romantic culpability ought to be "relentless."

You might think that Altman would be talking all this over with his star, who also happened to be his playwright, while together on location. You would be wrong. Professing nothing but respect for each other, the cowboy playwright and the cowboy-hatted director barely spoke to each other—about Shepard's role, the film, or presumably, even the weather. The result was a film that, while earnest, was studied and humorless.

More than one critic hailed *Fool for Love* as a stunning collaboration. "Altman displays his genius for turning a play into a true film, exploding its tight theatrical form into gorgeous, haunting images, and a dance of devious and direct rhythms," said *Newsweek*, which had the film on the cover in 1986 as part of an overall paean to Shepard. Others felt obliged to detest Altman's latest filmed play.

It was completely logical material for someone weaned on

Tennessee Williams and William Inge, on years of bus stops and one-night stands, on country music and Western hero hype. *Fool for Love* also had a smoldering subtext that allowed Altman to stir the embers of his own family life: for the lead character has a tempestuous relationship with his father; and in the storyline there are deep, dark intimations of brother-sister incest.

EPILOGUE:
PARIS, FRANCE

In 1985, the year Orson Welles died of a massive heart attack in Los Angeles, Robert Altman moved his offices to Paris, the obscure object of his desire.

The director installed a fireplace and hung a huge *Buffalo Bill* poster in his offices in a modernized stable in the Latin Quarter.

Altman loved Paris. He drank it all in. He was an "expatriate" now (although he shied away from that word in interviews), just like his good friend Irwin Shaw, and Preston Sturges and Erich von Stroheim and Orson Welles, and others rejected and unappreciated by America. The French had enthusiasm for Jerry Lewis and even Richard Nixon; the former President was installed in the prestigious Academy of Fine Arts in Paris, alongside such members as the Spanish painter Salvador Dali and the Italian film director Federico Fellini.

Yet Altman had a childlike inability to adapt to Paris. He tried to learn French, but it still came out Missouri twang, and he could never remember more than a couple of key phrases. Kathryn, or Scott Bushnell, always had to help out. Altman preferred the restaurants where he was recognized and where the waiters knew what he favored on the menu. It embarrassed him when the maitre d' did not recognize him.

He was like Jacques Tati in one of those comedies where poor Monsieur Hulot cannot quite seem to conform to modernity. Altman had a brand-new Mercedes with leather seats that he was inordinately proud of even though it was always proving too big for Paris streets and parking places. Altman insisted on driving himself to work every day. He had a reserved parking spot in an underground lot, to which access was via a steep ramp whose gate was timed to close in blackness after a certain interval. Altman's parking space was unfortunately rather far from the gate. Altman had to pull in a space three inches too small for the Mercedes, squeeze out of the car, and race to get out of the parking lot before the lights went out and the gate closed. It was a daily drama. It always made his associates laugh, affectionately, to see this world-class director, a sixty-year-old man, racing to get out in time.

Altman moved all of his postproduction work to Paris. For television, he filmed—in Paris—*The Laundromat* (an early play by Marsha Norman, in which two female strangers meet and unravel in a twenty-four-hour laundromat in a small Kentucky town) and later, *Beyond Therapy*. Never mind that they were supposed to be taking place in the United States. He talked about other projects with genuine Parisian settings, including one about the annual "ready-to-wear" Paris fashion revels that Susannah York was working up into a screenplay. But these other movies never got made, and the Altman films made in Paris had almost nothing of Paris in them.

Pierre Mignot was still responsible for the cinematography of most of Altman's films, and Allan Nicholls usually showed up in the credits in some capacity. But most of these long-timers did not live in Paris, or they lived there, for a

Altman, his wife Kathryn, and two Altman sons, Bobby and Stephen, at the Cannes Film Festival for the screening of *Fool for Love*. (Wide World Photos)

specific project, for only a short time. They did not feel the same way about Paris as Altman did, and they were not as nomadic with their families and their lives.

The nucleus of the films was just Altman, his family (Stephen Altman was increasingly central to the filmmaking process), and Bushnell. Kathryn had one ear, and Bushnell the other. Kathryn was Mrs. Robert Altman, but Bushnell was figuratively the Olympian deity Hera, married to Zeus and ferociously jealous of her possible rivals. It was the role Bushnell chose to play, mothering the films.

The dislike between Kathryn and Bushnell was an open secret. Kathryn believed Bushnell to be a deleterious influence on Altman's career, and in a strange, unspoken way, they were rivals for his attention. Altman knew it, and seemed to enjoy playing them off against each other. Neither of them would ever leave him.

"It has come down to *her* and *her*," says a former member of the "talent trust."

"Scotty is so loyal to Bob," says another insider. "She would literally take off her shoes and run over burning coals for him. She loves him so completely. It's almost tragic, something very moving."

One person who noticed that Altman's films in recent years had become exceedingly Pinteresque, with their unexplained circumstances and auras of menace, was the British playwright himself, Harold Pinter.

Pinter proclaimed *Secret Honor* to be a stupendous achievement, and he, Donald Freed, and Altman got together in London, became great pals, and planned projects together. Two of Pinter's plays from the late Fifties, *The Dumb Waiter* and *The Room*, were subsequently filmed by Altman for ABC television. The former starred John Travolta, adopting an unlikely British accent, and English actor Tom Conti, as two hired hit men waiting for their mysterious target. *The Room* had Linda Hunt, Donald Pleasance, and pop stylist Annie Lennox of the Eurythmics in an existential struggle for identity in an apartment dwelling. If Sidney Lumet had directed these "mini-films," he would be acclaimed for his artistic courage. Altman filmed them with little publicity. They had rich, subdued style as well as enviable casting. No doubt, in the future, *The Dumb Waiter* and *The Room* are destined to become fodder for some college course on theatrical arcana.

Television, once the bane of Altman's existence, was now the director's salvation. Altman could keep busy dishing up classy fare to the major networks and the cable suppliers. It kept him occupied while all the more personal and ambitious projects bobbed out of range.

As always, there was a spate of those other possibilities— properties optioned and development deals; and Altman needed writers to move things along. It always seemed as if one property was just about to steam ahead even as the script of another had to be shaped up over the weekend. The writing was always under pressure, even though the films never seemed to materialize.

Robert Harders was the newest in a long line of closet writers for Altman. Altman brought Harders to New York from Los Angeles to meet with the director about a script called *Biarritz*, which was set in a European hotel for wealthy vacationers. Jon Voight had been discussed as the star of an international cast. Altman free-associated some ideas, and Harders went back to California to work on writing, sending pages to Altman via Federal Express every couple of days, and taking notes by phone.

Although *Biarritz* never got off the ground, Harders received a desperate call from Bushnell one day. Altman had been hired to adapt Ernest Hemingway's *Across the River and Into the Trees* by the man to whom the rights had acceded. Altman had written about fifty pages of script and reached an impasse. The script was due by the end of the week! Could Harders come right away?

Harders flew to Santa Fe, where Altman was then directing *Fool for Love*. He read the novel on the plane and was excited. He met with Altman and Bushnell, and was briefed. The leads were supposed to be Roy Scheider and Julie Christie. In one blind, feverish, uninterrupted stint of writing, Harders did the job. He thought the script was pretty good. Then *Across the River and Into the Trees* fell through too.

Then, there was *Heat*, with Burt Reynolds in the lead. That was another Hollywood disaster. Altman's associates could not believe he had agreed to direct the film. Altman had forsworn the producer, Elliott Kastner, possibly the worst of all his enemies, long, long ago. But Carol Burnett was always after Altman to work with Burt Reynolds, Altman liked Reynolds, and Reynold's career was in the doldrums too. It was a chance to show up Hollywood. It was money, and it was work. Altman said yes—and called in Harders.

Altman detested the commerciality of the William Goldman script. (Goldman was the astute screenwriter of *Butch Cassidy and the Sundance Kid, All the President's Men,* among many others.) Harders flew to Las Vegas, where they were beginning preproduction, and began to rehash the script. Altman flew East to meet with Goldman and to let him know the script was inadequate. To Altman's surprise, he found Goldman to be a nice man. He ended up liking him. Walking with the director, his hands in one of those deep-pocket sweaters, Goldman told Altman it was a "kick-ass" script, and Altman realized he could not face the writer down.

Chagrined, the director went back to Las Vegas. Altman used a technicality to escape from his contract—Pierre Mignot could not obtain the necessary U.S. working papers in order to serve as Altman's cinematographer. He was out. Actor Elliott Gould called Altman to cheer him up and recited to him inspirational baseball poetry by Edmund Vance Cooke.

It was a good thing, though. *Heat* was a mess in the filming. Burt Reynolds punched the director in the face, and the film had to be finished by someone else, who adopted a pseudonym. When released, the film pleased neither audiences nor critics. Still, the incident showed that, again, Altman was unable to negotiate the Hollywood hurdles.

The most magical, the most elusive project of all was *Nashville 12,* or the characters of *Nashville* twelve years later. Producer Jerry Weintraub, through Paramount, which owned the rights, asked Altman to consider doing a sequel. Such a project would be fraught with risk. *Nashville* was one of the director's greatest films. Would Altman irreparably harm his reputation by failing? Did he any longer have the breadth for the subject?

All of the major cast members expressed interest, and Altman had Joan Tewkesbury over for dinner. They began to have elliptical conversations about the storyline. Altman wanted to go down some murky trails with the characters undergoing rapes and breakdowns, and Tewkesbury was becoming uncomfortable with it. "Bob," she argued, "you can't do this, you have to give these characters some *hope. . . ."*

From Paris, Altman summoned Harders. Would he like to write *Nashville 12?* Harders was stunned and flattered. Harders admired the screenplay of *Nashville* as much as that of any movie he had ever seen, and he declared he would be proud to give it a try.

Harders spent several months, first in Paris and later in Santa Monica, working on *Nashville 12.* When Altman returned to Los Angeles, he read and approved Harders's script, and it was handed in to producer Weintraub, who requested some revisions. Harders flew to Montreal (where Altman was filming one of the Pinter plays) and worked side by side with Altman trying to give the script the necessary rewrite. Back in Los Angeles, Weintraub continued to have objections, especially to Altman's rather pessimistic ending, and Harders was designated to work out the changes.

By the time a year had elapsed, everyone was weary of the script compromises, and the title of *Nashville 12* had to be changed to *Nashville 13,* and finally to *Nashville, Nashville.* No one could predict how long it would be, if ever, before the script would be filmed.

Altman never did speak to Tewkesbury about it again. When the director returned to Los Angeles promoting one of his films, she learned through the grapevine that the script was being written by someone else, someone she had never met or talked to, Robert Harders.

"I guess he [Altman] just figured I was going to be a pain in the ass," she says.

In 1987, the first Altman comedy of the decade was released. *Beyond Therapy,* an adaptation of the Christopher Durang play about the foibles of friendship, love, and modern psychiatry, starred Jeff Goldblum, Julie Hagerty, Glenda Jackson, Tom Conti, Christopher Guest, and Genevieve Paige. It had many pixillated moments. But the critics found it shallow and forced, compared to more stellar comedies in Altman's resume.

It happened to be released the same year as *O.C. and*

Stiggs, which was finally dribbled to a couple of theatres by MGM in order to clear rights for home video. Both films were mentioned on many critics' "worst" lists at the end of the year, the first time such a thing had happened in Robert Altman's career.

The critics might have been forgiven for predicting that the director had reached the end of his creative tether. But the critics, as 1988 was to prove, were wrong.

Nineteen eighty-eight was the year Robert Altman directed the "Les Boréades" segment from the opera anthology film *Aria,* the network television special *The Caine Mutiny Court-Martial,* and the Home Box Office series presentation *Tanner '88.*

Aria had contributions from such noted directors as Australian Bruce Beresford, Britishers Nicolas Roeg and Ken Russell, and Frenchman Jean-Luc Godard. Altman chose as his selection the "Aria: Suite des Ventes" ("Continuous Winds"), "Lieu Désolé" ("Desolate Place"), and "Jouissons, Jouissons" ("Rejoice, Rejoice!") from Jean-Philippe Rameau's "Les Boréades." He set his "mini-film" in the eighteenth century, when it was written, and at the Renelagh Theatre, where it was performed. He chose to turn his camera, not on the stage, but on the audience, which was filled—as was the charitable gesture in those days—with inmates from lunatic asylums.

The critics did not necessarily appreciate Altman's piece, which was as Godardian as Godard's. His writhing, gesticulating, sexed-up audience of garishly costumed gargoyles seemed, on the surface, to have no point. But it was more than a bold visual stroke. It added up to the director's most barbarous assault ever on the haute bourgeoisie, and another Altman ode to the transcendent, healing qualities of art.

The Caine Mutiny Court-Martial was adapted from Herman Wouk's Pulitzer Prize-winning novel, which was the basis for the 1954 motion picture starring Humphrey Bogart. Here was Altman back on familiar ground, probing principles of leadership, and skewering military rationale. The persuasive cast included Brad Davis as Captain Queeg, Jeff

Cartoonist (and scriptwriter) Garry Trudeau, Altman long-timer Michael Murphy, and the director, between scenes of *Tanner '88*. (Darkhorse Productions)

Daniels as the accused mutineer, Eric Bogosian as his reluctant defender, and Michael Murphy as the ranking officer of the tribunal.

The television critics heaped praise on Altman's pinpoint direction of the actors and of the drama. Some of them commented on the superfluousness of the tagged-on "victory" celebration at the end—a trademark scene for Altman. But, among other things, that was a chance for the director to view himself through a gauze as the Bogosian character, an obstreperous Jew, a drunken time-bomb, ranting belligerently about personal and political responsibility.

Then came *Tanner '88*—a Home Box Office series for which Altman did multiple episodes. In cartoon panelist Garry ("Doonesbury") Trudeau, Altman found the perfect writer to lampoon presidential campaign politics. In longtime cohort Michael Murphy, Altman had an actor who could roll with the punches and deliver some very nice ones of his own. The guest stars—from E. G. Marshall and Rebecca De Mornay, to losing candidates Bruce Babbitt and Robert Dole, to country-and-westerner Waylon Jennings and newspaper columnist Mary McGrory—livened up the disconnected scenes.

Trudeau's stone-skipping approach to comedy permitted the director to be superficial, after which any depth was a bonus. The series wavered in every category, except novelty. Television critics, no doubt jaded by their customary network fixes, were thrilled by an intelligent video series about the presidential race that was broadcast concurrently with the 1988 campaign. It was one of the fringe benefits of the director's forced exile from motion pictures that—even as Altman was being rejected by one whole school of critics— he was being hailed by another.

June 1989. Robert Altman gets up in the morning and looks in the mirror. He might be in Malibu or in New York or in Montreal or in Paris.

In twenty years he has made over twenty films, at least one a year, more if you count the telefilms and the producer credits. No other American director can claim to have done as much over that period of time. And Altman has often done it on his own, in his own way, in spite of the studios and the financiers.

He could quit this morning and his legend would not be diminished. He will always be regarded as one of the greatest film directors (if not the greatest) of the contemporary era. He wins points on body of work, on specific films that will never be considered less than seminal, on his stylistic influences on a generation of moviemakers, and on his technological prowess.

When Sight and Sound, *the magazine of the British Film Institute, polled international film critics as to the finest films of the Seventies, only one director had more than one film on the Top Ten list—Altman—with* McCabe and Mrs Miller, *and* Nashville. Petulia *ranked number one in the* poll, incidentally, which, since Altman developed the film in embryo, might be considered to make it three out of ten.

When the Royal Film Archive of Belgium polled some two hundred international film critics as to the most important and misappreciated films since the beginning of the cinema, only twenty-five American directors cleared one hundred votes. Altman was the only active, living American director among them. Nine of his films received votes, with McCabe and Nashville leading the pack.

When James Monaco polled twenty-one distinguished critics for the best U.S. films of the decade of the Seventies in his 1984 book American Film Now, Nashville turned up as Number Two (twelve votes), close behind The Godfather (fourteen votes). But Altman led among active directors with twenty-one votes for six films, including Nashville, McCabe and Mrs. Miller, Three Women, M*A*S*H, Thieves Like Us, and The Long Goodbye.

Robert Altman wakes up in the morning and thinks about making a movie today. Some of his former friends think he should quit before he disgraces himself with weaker and weaker vehicles. Some people who know him wish he would make a warmhearted movie, a fun and entertaining movie, a commercial movie, because he could, if he truly wanted to, maybe.

But Altman cannot quit. Film is in his blood. And he still has something to prove. If he has six dollars, or $6 million, you can bet he will direct a movie today. And even if you are putting up the money for it, Altman is going to make whatever movie he wants to.

The director looks in the mirror, and his attention is distracted by something in the back of his mind. Altman does not think much about Kansas City these days, but occasionally he flashes on growing up there, on B.C. and the Altman building, the Catholics and Calvin. Altman thinks about being a flyer, long ago, and about being in Hollywood during the 1940s. Altman thinks about all those years in television and doing every kind of rotten job that came along before he was already forty. Suddenly, along came M*A*S*H, and *then he was such a hero, a big hero—only Altman knew it all the time, because he is an Altman.*

The director thinks about all those people, those names, the old names and the new names, on the "enemies" list. They are enemies still, no matter how much time has passed. Altman remembers. He will not forget nor forgive. He will show them. Emotion flickers across his face, and the eyes harden.

"Bob is like a general always on the verge of some external defeat," says Elliott Gould.

"Bob likes his own turbulence," says John Considine. "I think that's where he finds his peace. He's like a rapids guide who, if he can chart his own white-water trip, even though it is dangerous, he feels good. That's where he feels at one."

"He'll come out of it," says Louis Lombardo. "I know he will. Because he's one talented man."

"Bob is like a huge furnace that will burn forever," says Alan Rudolph.

Robert Altman keeps-a-goin'.

NOTES AND CREDITS

CALVIN INDUSTRIES, SHORT SUBJECTS, AND TELEVISION

The Calvin Industrials

Out of some sixty films, it might be foolhardy to attempt to highlight the best of Robert Altman's Calvin industrials—especially when most are lost and forgotten and will probably never be viewed in public again. But some won awards, some are warmly recollected by the people who toiled on them, and some have an affinity with his later Hollywood features:

• *The Magic Bond.* This one had a fairly steep budget for a production of interviews, staged scenes, and newsreel explicating the Veterans of Foreign Wars history and credo. Location footage includes scenes of the National Home of the VFW in Jackson, Michigan, of a national VFW convention, and of a veterans' parade in Boston. Cameraman Arthur Goodell remembers Altman setting up for the elaborate parade coverage around Boston Commons, and then instructing him to "dry-run" the cameras all day, just to make the parade officials feel good. Then Altman did his "usual disappearing act" into the nightclubs and bars of Boston's infamous "Combat Zone," while the Calvin crew pointed the camera at marching bands and memorial units.

Altman (back to camera) directing a highway
safety film.

Much of the film is jingoistic, laying out time-worn VFW riffs
that assail citizen apathy, juvenile delinquency, neglect of veterans, and shifty Reds both foreign and domestic. Journalist Bob
Considine narrates a script extolling "the magic of comradeship"
and "team spirit." Richard Sarafian is among the actors.

What startles is the five-minute opening segment, tagged on by
Altman to the sanctioned VFW script. It is like a scene from another movie: a hellish window on a situation of war. A squadron is
trapped; booze and cigarettes circulate among the doomed soldiers;
crumbling plaster and exploding bombs punctuate a monologue
about circumstance and death. It is a *Combat* segment in embryo.

● *The Perfect Crime.* Sponsored by Caterpillar and the National
Safety Council. Here, Altman created another nightmarish prelude
before settling down to the agreed-upon spiel.

The film opens brutally with the murder of a mother and child during a nighttime robbery of a neighborhood grocery store. The killer is apprehended after appropriate public outcry. What does all this have to do with safe-driving precepts? Virtually nothing—except that a more truly "perfect crime" occurs, in the next sequence of harrowing subjective photography, when a reckless driver causes a crash that kills his own wife and his child. The narrator admonishes: "Yet there is no public indignation, so killer gets away scot-free . . ."

The message, of all things, is that if taxpayers invested in better roads built by sturdy Caterpillar heavy equipment, then this roadway misfortune might be avoided. This Altman-directed short won one of the eighteen "little Oscars" awarded by the association of industrial filmmakers in 1955.

● *The Last Mile.* A twenty-minute highway cautionary film that begins with an atmospheric takeoff of the final scene in *Angels With Dirty Faces.* Down "the last mile" to the electric chair walks a condemned killer accompanied by a prayerful cleric and a pensive warden. Altman's effective camerawork cuts between close-ups of the final footsteps of the convict and the spectacular car crash-ups that were the meat and potatoes of these safety films.

The message: Every day more people travel "the last mile" on the highway than are executed for capital crimes in the nation's prisons. With good roads built by safety-conscious Cat crews, fewer road victims will meet their fates. This film, too, won national safety awards in 1953.

● *The Sound of Bells.* This sales film is cited by both cameraman Charley Paddock and producer Frank Barhydt as exemplary of Altman and one of the finest of all the Calvin films.

It is a lonely Christmas Eve at a gas station. Santa Claus drives in for a fill-up in a car stuffed with packages and toys. The jolly one is low on cash, so in return for a tank of gas he promises the incredulous station owner a flood of new customers over the coming new year. Each of these Santa-sent customers will be made known to the attendant by "the sound of bells."

Well . . . the new customers do start arriving and buying tires in droves. Sandwiched in with the poker-faced humor is a lot of practical information, tips about politeness with customers, threading and cross-switching tires, and other dealer concerns.

A year later, it is Christmas Eve again, and the station owner is waiting, with a special gift of his own, to see if Santa Claus will return. The station owner is played by Keith Painton, a local radio announcer who appears again and again in Altman's Calvin films. The only sound track here is the mysterious and recurring jingle of bells.

● Every year there was at least one high-school rules-of-sports film—alternating football, basketball, and baseball. Partly because Altman was a sports buff, and partly because he liked to abscond to far locations, Altman usually directed it. Critics who believe Altman is incapable of telling a straightforward tale, or following a script, should be condemned to see these twenty-six-minute bon-bons of info-packed setups and drive-ahead exposition. They are all rules and tips, chalkboard diagrams, slow-motion live-action, inter-spersed with advertising plugs for Wheaties and Wilson Sporting Goods (the erstwhile sponsors).

Altman spiced these films up with "moments" that probably looked exceedingly resourceful at the time: a dream sequence in *Modern Football* (1951); a story-within-the-story "frame" in *King Basketball* (1952), in which Altman, impersonating a nattily dressed Hollywood director, comments satirically on cinema sports clichés; cameo appearances, as in *Modern Baseball* (1953), from the likes of such baseball greats as Ford Frick, Casey Stengel, Connie Mack, Lou Boudreau, Smokey Burgess, and Roy Campanella; and vaudeville-type gags in *Better Football* (1954), with William Frawley providing comedy relief as a pigskin coach who cannot resist the one-liner.

With the higher budget and the distance from Calvin overseers, Altman could be more ambitious. The sports-rules films were often shot in the Southwest, in conjunction with one of the par-ticipating high schools. There would be unusual (for Calvin) crane and dolly expenses. In the middle of a silly expository item like *Better Football*, one is openmouthed when all of a sudden the cam-era swoops down on the field into the middle of a huddle, a dra-matic and expensive visual exclamation mark.

Other less orthodox expenses could also be rationalized. One time, Richard Peabody, then a Calvin assistant director, accom-panied Altman to Mesa, Arizona. They arrived in the dead of winter to discover that a rare frost had turned the grass on the local football field into an ugly shade of brown. Altman pulled out the Yellow Pages and called local painter after painter, until he found one who was willing to daub the football field a shamrock green. It cost several hundred dollars, recalls Peabody. And it may not have been a strictly artistic decision. After all, it would take at least three days to dry, and in the meantime the two Calvin employees could run up their per diems and have quite the swinging time.

● Other significant Calvin titles directed by Altman include: *The Builders* (Southern Pine Association), *The Dirty Look* (spon-sored by Gulf Oil, written by Frank Barhydt, and starring William Frawley as a prattling barber), and *Honeymoon for Harriet* (for International Harvester, and starring Jim Lantz and Altman's second wife, Lotus Corelli).

Independent Projects

Short commercial films directed by Altman during the Kansas City years, independent of the Calvin company, include *Fashion Faire* (Nellie Don), *The Model's Handbook* (Eileen and Gerald Ford), and *Grand Stand Rookie* (Kansas City Athletics/Holsum Bread).

Serial Television

Pulse of the City (1953–1954)

Altman was coproducer (with Robert Woodburn) and director of this fifteen-minute dramatic anthology series syndicated on the Dumont network. The series was filmed in Kansas City and starred local thespians and Calvin talent, some of whom materialized in Hollywood later on.

Alfred Hitchcock Presents (1957–1958)

Two episodes only of this illustrious progenitor of the "twist ending" type of suspense series, hosted (and creatively supervised) by the famous director with the roly-poly profile, Alfred Hitchcock. "The Young One," with Carol Lynley, Jeanette Nolan, and Vince Edwards, was broadcast late in 1957, and "Together," with Joseph Cotten and Christine White, was aired early in 1958. See *Alfred Hitchcock Presents* by John McCarty and Brian Kelleher (St. Martin's Press, 1985) for extensive detail and background on the individual segments.

The Whirlybirds (1957–1958)

Half-hour adventure series with unique (for the 1950s) premise, pilots operating a for-hire helicopter service that specialized in law enforcement and daredevil rescues. Syndicated for two seasons by Desilu. Altman did some writing and directed more than a dozen episodes, including "The Midnight Show," "A Matter of Trust," "Guilty of Old Age," "Christmas in June," "Til Death Do Us Part," "Time Limit," "Experiment X-74," "The Big Lie," "The Perfect Crime," "The Unknown Soldier," "Two of a Kind," "In Ways Mysterious," "The Black Maria," and "The Sitting."

U.S. Marshall (a.k.a. Sheriff of Cochise) (1957–1958)

Also produced by Desilu for syndication. John Bromfield as contemporary law enforcement officer Frank Morgan of Cochise County, Arizona, Stan Jones as Deputy Olson. Altman directed multiple episodes of the half-hour series, including "Tapes for Murder," "Special Delivery," "Paper Bullets," "Backfire" (with Charles Aidman and Susan Davis in the cast), "The Third Miracle" (with Charles Aidman and Bert Remsen), and "Tarnished Star." The last-named, above par, featured Henry Hull as an over-the-hill deputy who foils a couple of hardened prison escapees by leading them around in circles in the desert.

Oh! Susannah (a.k.a. The Gale Storm Show) (1959)

Half-hour situation comedy starring Gale Storm as a shipboard social director. In prime time (CBS) and reruns (ABC), between 1956 and 1959. Altman checked in for at least one episode of this undistinguished series in its final season when it was being filmed at Desilu.

The Millionaire (1958–1959)

Altman came on as director in the fourth year of the five-year run of this half-hour series. His spurt of activity included "The Dan Howell Story," "Millionaire Frank Butler," "Millionaire Angela Temple," "Millionaire Karl Miller" (starring John Carradine), "Millionaire Maureen Reynolds," "Millionaire Sergeant Matthew

John Bromfield in the syndicated *U.S. Marshall*, a.k.a. *Sheriff of Cochise*. (British Film Institute)

Brogan," "Millionaire Jackson Greene" (starring Joanna Moore), and "Millionaire Timothy MacKail." John T. Kelley wrote one Altman-directed segment, "Millionaire Doctor Joseph Frye." Kelley and Altman collaborated on the script for another, "Millionaire Alicia Osante," a story with a beauty pageant milieu, which for some reason was not directed by Altman. And Altman is credited with the adaptation of "Millionaire Andrew C. Cooley," which he also directed.

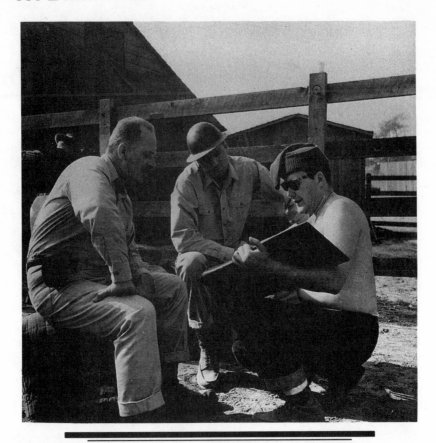

Keenan Wynn, Bob Mathias, and Altman confer on the *Troubleshooters* set. (Wisconsin Center for Film and Theatre Research)

The Troubleshooters (1959)

Half-hour dramatic series produced on the Desilu lot, by Frederick Ziv and United Artists, for syndication. Altman directed half of the twenty-six episodes of the single season of production. Cast included Keenan Wynn (as the honcho of a globe-trotting Caterpillar crew), former Olympic star Bob Mathias, stuntman-dancer Robert Fortier, and the director's ex-brother-in-law, Chet Allen. Altman's episodes included "Liquid Death," "The Law and the Profits" (a.k.a. "Disaster"), "Trouble at Elbow Bend," "The Lower Depths," "Tiger Culhane," "Moment of Terror," "Gino," "Swing Shift" (a.k.a. "Trouble at the Orphanage"), "Harry Maru," "The Town That Wouldn't Die," "Señorita," "Fire in the Hole," "No Stone Unturned," and "The Carnival" (a.k.a. "The Cat-Skinner"). John T. Kelley was credited with scriptwork on "Moment of Terror," "No Stone Unturned," and "The Carnival." Altman cowrote "Gino" and "The Cat-Skinner," his only script credits on the program.

Highlights of the Altman episodes:

● "Gino" was his tip of the hat to Vittorio De Sica's *The Bicycle Thief*, which is paid explicit homage in the dialogue. In this episode, a ragamuffin Italian kid steals Kodiak's (Wynn) cherished motorcycle, and is drafted into the Cat crew as part of a moral rehabilitation effort. Not much else happens in the low-key drama, but you can recognize the wheels turning.

● "The Cat-Skinner" spotlights Fortier, who performs mime in a tall tale about a crippled adolescent whose medical expenses are offset by funds raised from an impromptu circus staged by the Cat-men. The combination of shtick and heart-sleeve sentiment was not uncharacteristic of some of Altman's better television episodes.

● Most intriguing of all is "No Stone Unturned," written by Altman confidant John T. Kelley. It is one of Altman's most political television shows, albeit coming from a relatively undidactic filmmaker.

The setting this time was a fictional land in Asia. By their presence in the region, the troubleshooters have upset the age-old relationship between a village chieftain and his villagers, and endangered the annual sweet-potato crop. The crisis ends when Kodiak sacrifices his scheduling to make amends and assist with the harvest. The moral of the story is supplied by the area chieftain, who warns Kodiak in no uncertain terms about meddling in foreign cultures. Not particularly hard-hitting or eloquent, the episode nevertheless stood, in 1959, as the director's (and Kelley's) parable about brotherhood against the backdrop of the expanding Vietnam War.

The Detectives (1959–1962)

Robert Taylor starred as the captain of a squad of metropolitan plainclothes cops who take turns solving crimes in the half-hour episodes. (The series went to one hour when it shifted networks, from ABC to NBC, in 1961.) Altman directed one or more episodes.

Lawman (1959)

Altman directed one or more episodes, including "The Robbery," written by Dean Riesner, with Robert Ridgeley among the cast. Not the most original of the Warner's Westerns, this half-hour series nonetheless had star chemistry in its two leads—John Russell as Marshal Dan Troop of Laramie, Wyoming, and Peter Brown as his deputy.

Sugarfoot/Bronco Hour (1959–1960)

Several episodes of these alternating Western series were directed by Altman. *Sugarfoot* starred Will Hutchins as a tinhorn Easterner roaming the West while studying law by correspondence, while *Bronco* had Ty Hardin as a post-Civil War drifter ranging the Texas plains. Altman's *Bronco*'s included "The Mustangers," which featured Kenneth Tobey and Robert Ridgeley in the story about a murder investigation impeded by the spit-and-polish of a young Army lieutenant; while among his *Sugarfoot*'s is "Apollo With a

Will Hutchins (center) in "The Highbinder" episode of *Sugarfoot*. (Warner Brothers)

Roger Moore (left) and Tim Graham in "Bolt Out of the Blue" segment of *Maverick*. (Warner Brothers)

Gun," a picaresque romance set in Virginia City on the Fourth of July, and "The Highbinder," with Tom Brewster (a.k.a. Sugarfoot) in the middle of a vicious tong war in San Francisco.

Hawaiian Eye (1959)

Dubbed "77 Sunset Strip played in Hawaii," this one-hour Warner's series featured a swinging detective agency headquartered in a

Honolulu hotel. Bob Conrad and Anthony Eisley alternated as leads, while Connie Stevens played a perky singer-photographer named Cricket, and Poncie Ponce was memorable as a nutsy island cabbie. Altman's single episode was "Three Tickets to Lani," about a trio of scam artists duping elderly gentlemen—taut, action-filled, clichéd.

Maverick (1960)

Altman directed only one episode of this classic TV Western— about two wisecracking brothers, lady's men and dapper card-sharks, who rotated adventures in the Wild West. James Garner (later in Altman's *Health*) and Jack Kelly played the brothers Maverick, while Roger Moore came on in the 1960–1961 season as their cousin Beauregard. Kansas Citian Diane Brewster had a repeating role. Altman's episode, "Bolt Out of the Blue," was written and directed by him, starred Moore, and was up to the highest sardonic standards of the series. Harold E. "Hal" Stine, photographer of *M*A*S*H*, was behind the camera.

The Roaring Twenties (1960–1961)

Hour-long *Untouchables*-style dramatic series about the Prohibition Era, set in New York, centered around a newspaper city room and the Charleston Club. Regulars included Dorothy Provine as singer Pinky Pinkham, Donald May (who crops up in Altman films thereafter) as reporter Pat Garrison, Rex Reason as reporter Scott Norris, John Dehner as reporter Duke Williams, Mike Road as Lieutenant Joe Switoski, Gary Vinson as copyboy Chris Higby, and James Flavin as Howard. Altman directed numerous episodes, including "The Prairie Flower," "Brother's Keeper," "The White Carnation," "Dance Marathon," "Two a Day," "Right Off the Boat [Parts I and II]," "Royal Tour," and "Standing Room Only" (the latter, starring Keenan Wynn, and Altman's only script credit for the series).

Highlight of the Altman segments was "The Prairie Flower," another early indication of the director's fascination with the crosscurrents of femininity, creativity, and sexual psychosis. Pat Crowley plays a starstruck Midwesterner who connives her way into the part of stand-in for a Broadway headliner (Patrice Wymore). In Robert J. Shaw's script, the tone is mordant, the plotting faceted, the backstage elements crisp and knowing. The violence of

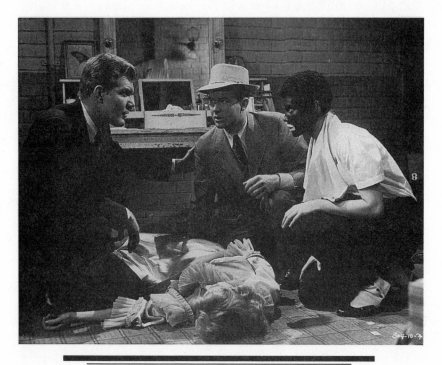

Donald May (left) in the "Two a Day" episode of
The Roaring Twenties. (Warner Brothers)

the climactic bathtub murder is all the more shocking and uncompromising for the fact that both the murderer and (nude) victim are
female!

Surfside Six (1960–1961)

The precursor of *Miami Vice,* the prehip, *Hawaiian Eye*-derivative
Surfside Six featured a trio of private detectives stationed in a
houseboat adjacent to a Miami Beach hotel. Troy Donahue, Van
Williams, Lee Patterson, Diane McBain, and Margarita Sierra were
regulars. Altman directed (and touched up the script of) at least one
episode, "Thieves Among Honor," a.k.a. "A Touch of Larceny."

Bonanza (1960–1961)

The Mount Rushmore of television Westerns, *Bonanza* featured four manly characters, three disparate sons and their proud papa, the Cartwright family, reigning over the Ponderosa spread near Virginia City.

Lorne Greene, Dan Blocker, Michael Landon, and Pernell Roberts (who left after the 1965 season) were the virile quartet who launched fourteen seasons of the one-hour program that still has international syndication. Altman came on in the second season and directed multiple episodes, including "Silent Thunder," "Bank Run," "The Duke," "The Rival," "The Dream Riders," "The Many Faces of Gideon Finch," "The Secret," and "Sam Hill."

Notable episodes among those Altman directed:

• "Silent Thunder," with Stella Stevens, was an "absolute masterpiece," recalls producer David Dortort, about "an abused creature who out of the care and understanding and tenderness of the scenario was salvaged into a wonderful, beautiful person." This story of a deaf-and-dumb frontierswoman brought to healing dovetails with an Altman subtext that is mulled differently in films such as *Three Women* and *A Perfect Couple:* that of the emotional or physical cripple, the ugly duckling, the societal reject, brought to flower by empathy and love.

Altman's camerawork on *Bonanza* episodes like this one was always very simple. You can sense the director concentrating on the performances and the emotional directness—unlike, say, *Combat,* where there was always such virtuosic imagery.

• "The Dream Riders" episode might be considered an obvious forerunner of the freedom-of-flight soliloquys of *Countdown,* *Brewster McCloud,* and *Streamers.* When a renegade Army major (an old pal of Ben Cartwright's) arrives at the Ponderosa to launch his dream fleet of airships, Hoss, Altman's alter ego, discovers "adventure in his soul" and falls in love with flying. At the elaborate finale, after a bank robbery, a double-cross, and much cross-purpose, the major (who turns out to be a "fake") is gunned down. His dream airship soars aloft without him.

• In "The Many Faces of Gideon Finch," the torch of romance and revenge is passed between Little Joe and Hoss with such dizzying comic twists and turns that at the end, two old codgers remark that compared to events at the Alamo it's been a plumb tuckering day in Virginia City. In the story, addled ingenue Sue Anne Langdon is being wooed simultaneously by the rivalrous Cartwright brothers—while an intertwining subplot threatens death to the chosen one. Yet another allegory about being loved for the inner

Claude Akins (left) in "Sam Hill" segment of
Bonanza. (Republic Pictures)

self, this episode is effortlessly lightweight, showing the director in
a relaxed vein.

● "The Rival" is about a blood feud, lynching fever, and another
of Hoss's stumblebum courtships. It so happens that Hoss can
identify a member of a lynch mob (Charles Aidman) whom he
knows to be a lifelong Cartwright family friend—and not so coincidentally the rival for affections of his latest sweetheart (Peggy
Ann Garner). The lynching premise devolves into something even
more poisonous when it turns out that there is another shadowy
"rival"—a brother of the accused, locked out of his mother's love,
whose monomaniacal grudge has triggered the plot.

The conviction of the actors makes it worthwhile, even when the pat superficialities pile up. But in an episode like this one, you can sense Altman's impatience with television and the artificial tidiness of the medium. In the end, when his camera pulls back high overhead, pondering these foibled mortals—it may be (as the camera ascends) that the director is commenting wittily on the limitations of filmmaking on the sound stage.

M Squad (1961)

Altman directed one episode ("Lovers' Lane Killing") of this half-hour crime show with Lee Marvin as a Chicago plainclothesman attached to a homicide unit.

Route 66 (1961)

As created by writer Stirling Silliphant, Route 66 offered the quintessential misadventures of two cross-country drifters, Tod Stiles (Martin Milner) and Buzz Murdock (George Maharis). (Maharis was eventually replaced by Glenn Corbett.) Altman's single episode, "Some of the People, Some of the Time," starred Keenan Wynn in an offbeat, seriocomic yarn about a con artist who sponsors a small-town talent revue with a trip to Hollywood as the prize.

Peter Gunn (1961)

Altman checked in for one episode ("The Murder Bond") of this private-eye series produced by writer-director Blake Edwards, and starring Mark Stevens. An incisive analysis of same is volunteered by television/film buff/scholar Howard Prouty:

"It's probably best not to make too much out of the general weirdness of this particular episode. From what I've seen of the series (several dozen episodes), such elements as the 'offbeat' character (who usually helps move the plot along by providing an important lead for Gunn) and the general 'video noir' look (Phil Lathrop was the series' most notable cinematographer) are par for the course.

"This particular episode, I think, is sort of ultra-typical; it's right in the mainstream (the writers Tony Barrett and Lewis Reed being far and away the series' most frequent contributors), yet it seems exceptionally 'dense' and fully-packed—several offbeat characters instead of the usual one, for instance.

"In terms of genre-related issues, it's hard to avoid the feeling that there is some spiritual kinship with [Altman's] *The Long Goodbye*. Beneath the surface of both Stevens/Gunn's ultra-coolness and Gould/Marlowe's shambling nonchalance lurks a moral code that is, I think, strikingly similar. While it's a little difficult to visualize Stevens and Gould switching roles, I have no such trouble imagining Peter Gunn pumping a fair amount of lead into Terry Lennox (although, obviously, not within the confines of a late-50s/early-60s TV show)."

Bus Stop (1961)

Quality anthology hour, based loosely on the William Inge play, revolving around a small town on the interstate bus route in Rocky Mountain territory. Regulars included diner-owner Marilyn Maxwell, waitress Joan Freeman, sheriff Rex Reason, and district attorney Richard Anderson. Robert Blees served as producer under Roy Huggins for Twentieth Century-Fox. Altman directed several episodes during its first and only season, including "The Covering Darkness" (with Robert Redford and Barbara Baxley), "County General" (with Donald May and Dianne Foster), "And the Pursuit of Evil" (with Keenan Wynn and James MacArthur), "Summer Lightning" (with Steve Forrest), and "Door Without a Key" (with Howard Duff and Pippa Scott). Altman is credited with the story contribution for the Howard Duff episode.

The director's most unnerving segment ("A Lion Walks Among Us") starred pop idol Fabian as a demented killer. Its broadcast caused public outcry and denunciation from a Congressional committee, contributing to the series's demise.

But also notable are "County General" and "Door Without a Key." The former is a compelling indictment of child abuse, while the latter has some eroticism between stars Duff and Scott. They (Duff and Scott) play two reluctant child kidnappers who—in an unlikely plot twist typical of this period for Altman, when he was still struggling with his Catholicism—surrender themselves to the police at the end, professing their guilt. You can see vestiges of this hang-up (criminals confessing and asking forgiveness) throughout the arc of Altman's television career—from the "Black Maria" episode of *The Whirlybirds* through "The Long, Lost Life of Edward Smalley" of the *Kraft* series.

Vic Morrow and Rick Jason of *Combat*. (National Film Archive/London)

The Gallant Men (1962)

Altman directed only the two-hour pilot episode ("Battle Zone") of this World War II saga of the American campaign in Italy, as witnessed and reported by a war correspondent (Robert McQueeney).

Combat (1962–1963)

The archetypal television war series, depicting the travail and exploits of a U.S. platoon in the European theater during World War

II. The two leads were Rick Jason (as Lt. Gil Hanley) and Vic Morrow (Sgt. Chip Saunders), but the rest of the believable ensemble were Pierre Jalbert (Caje), Jack Hogan (Kirby), Richard Peabody (Littlejohn), Steven Rogers (Doc Walton), and nightclub comedian Shecky Greene (Pvt. Braddock). Robert Blees produced, Robert B. Hauser was director of photography, Leonard Rosenman composed the score. Altman directed roughly half the episodes of the first season, including "Forgotten Front" (with Albert Paulsen), "Rear Echelon Commandos" (with John Considine among the cast), "Any Second Now" (with Alex Davion and Donald May), "Escape to Nowhere" (with Albert Paulsen), "Cat and Mouse" (starring Albert Salmi), "I Swear by Apollo" (with Swedish director Gunnar Hellstrom and John Considine among the cast), "The Prisoner" (with Keenan Wynn), "The Volunteer," "Off Limits," "Survival" (with Michael Murphy among the cast).

A rundown of the first season's high points would have to include:

● "Forgotten Front," the first episode, based on a story by noted science-fiction writer Richard (*Duel*) Matheson. It starred Albert Paulsen as a German POW captured by the *Combat* squad behind enemy lines; a hindrance to their progress, the squad debates whether to kill him off. According to producer Blees, Altman actually filmed the execution of the Paulsen character. This was thought to be too much to stomach, so the televised ending finesses the issue.

● "The Volunteer," about a young French boy who idolizes the American troops. As adroitly scripted by Gene Levitt, it is a tale with virtually no dialogue. In the filming Altman transmitted great feeling for the boy (played by Sergei Prieur), the atmosphere, and the deeper emotions of the storyline. When Levitt (who eventually took over as producer of the *Combat* series) saw the episode for the first time, he admits to being flabbergasted. "As a matter of fact, it was an eye-opener for me," says Levitt, "because writers always think that they did it. Until you see what a fine director's hand can do and then you think, 'Jesus, I wrote that?'"

● "Off Limits" (written by George W. George's frequent screenplay collaborator, George Slavin) gave Altman an opportunity to deal with marital infidelity within the context of a wartime hospital zone. Jeremy Slate (a GI wounded on patrol), Peggy Ann Garner (as his wife, a nurse), and William Windom (as the staff doctor who is having an affair with Peggy Ann Garner, and who, in the end, must perform lifesaving surgery on his rival) costar.

This was a subject with personal ramifications for the director. As was sometimes typical of *Combat*, Vic Morrow, the nominal star of the episode, is reduced to being a bystander in the story, a witness—except at the end, when the Peggy Ann Garner character begs forgiveness from Sgt. Saunders (Morrow), who has observed her improprieties. Sgt. Saunders refuses, saying he has no right to judge, and is only the shepherd of one flock—his own squad of men.

● Altman's own writing at this stage of his career had dramatic clarity. One of the best of the early *Combat* episodes was (his script) "Cat and Mouse," with Sgt. Saunders temporarily assigned to duty under hard-ass military lifer Albert Salmi (who in real life was married to Peggy Ann Garner). Salmi is a gung ho officer who drives his men deeper and deeper into jeopardy, with Sgt. Saunders (Morrow), the voice of experience and dread, doing his best to undermine his authority.

At last, the two infantrymen are pinned inside a windmill together. They hide in the nooks and crannies of the busily churning structure, which is occupied by German reconnaissance. They are cut off from escape and in mounting danger.

In the storyline, they disagree on a plan of action. Sgt. Saunders wants to use the radio to signal for help. Salmi's character is afraid the Germans will pick up the frequency of any radio signal, yet he covers for his cowardice by excoriating Saunders and the "shoe-clerk volunteers" who have diluted the bravery of the U.S. military. It emerges that Salmi has a dark secret—previously, he was judged unfit to be an officer and stripped of his rank. Though this is a standard dramatic device, it is a pattern in Altman's films— the blemish on the past of a main character, which comments somehow on his manhood.

Inevitably, the Salmi character winds up sacrificing himself to effect Morrow's escape. When Sgt. Saunders returns, he is told that his report no longer has any strategic value. A thoroughly battered Morrow then remarks on the folly of war, and in essence, on the imperfection of all human relationships. "I never had an easier time hating a man," he says of the Salmi character, "and I'll never have a harder time forgetting one."

The episode is filmed as if by Josef von Sternberg through all manner of visual impedimenta—through holes in the ceiling and cracks in the floorboard, from behind a spinning waterwheel. It is a tour de force of tight-fit photography, with the command post observed from the point of view of a floor vent and a prowling stray cat, fussed over by the Germans. And with the architecture of the windmill, of course there is ample excuse for the director's crucifix imagery.

Robert Vaughan and Dianne Foster in the "Death of a Dream" episode of *Kraft*, directed by Altman. (Copyright © by Universal City Studios Inc. Courtesy of MCA Publishing Rights, a Division of MCA Inc.)

Kraft Mystery Theatre (1962–1963)

As distinct from *Kraft Suspense Theatre*, this one-hour dramatic anthology series utilized mystery-suspense dramas filmed in England, as well as some originals, and some programs already seen on CBS's *Westinghouse Desilu Playhouse*, filmed at Desilu Studios in Hollywood. This series was more pro forma than its namesake successor, also sponsored by Kraft.

Mickey Rooney in "The Hunt" for *Kraft*, from
Altman's co-story. (Copyright © by Universal
City Studios Inc. Courtesy of MCA Publishing
Rights, a Division of MCA Inc.)

Altman's "Death of a Dream," for example, was a histrionic, improbable suspenser that featured Robert Vaughn as a negligent husband and father who—because he is transfixed by the potential
payoff of the American Dream—gets snarled up in a killing and a
double-cross. (Altman regular Dianne Foster plays his wife.)
Though technically well-made, it is the least personal of Altman's
telefilms during this period.

Altman's other episodes included "The Sound of Murder" (with
Alex Davion) and "The Image Merchants" (script by John T. Kel-
ley, with a cast that included Melvyn Douglas, MacDonald Carey,
Geraldine Brooks, and Dianne Foster).

Kraft Suspense Theatre (1963–1964)

Hour-long anthology series, produced for Kraft at Universal by Roy Huggins. Altman lasted as writer-director-producer for only a handful of episodes, but they stand with his finest work in television.

"The Hunt," which derived from Altman's costory but was not directed by him, featured Bruce Dern, James Caan, and Mickey Rooney in a white-knuckled suspense tale about a stranger in a small town, the sadistic local sheriff, and a bloodthirsty posse of yokels and dogs. "The Long, Lost Life of Edward Smalley," from Altman's story, was an expressionistic descent into guilt, wartime memories, and the vagaries of law. "Nightmare in Chicago," about a killer on the prowl in the Midwest, was so effective that, after airing it on television, Universal released it to movie theatres in some U.S. markets, Canada, and Europe.

Parenthetically, "Nightmare in Chicago" writer Donald Moessinger (and his brother David) worked with Altman more than once during the television years, but Moessinger did not appreciate the director's penchant for rewriting his scripts. Altman could not figure out why Moessinger would get so upset. Screenwriter Brian McKay says he and Altman were walking on the Universal lot one day when they espied Moessinger up ahead; but as Moessinger saw them approaching, he was seen to duck down an alley to avoid Altman. "What's wrong with him?" McKay quotes the exasperated director. "Sure, I changed one of his scripts, but I shot the other one practically *as is*, just to make up for it!"

The Long Hot Summer (1965)

Altman directed the pilot episode of this hour-long, prime-time serial based on the film of the same name, which was in turn derived from William Faulkner's *The Hamlet*. Set in the fictional Southern town of Frenchman's Bend, principal characters were played by Edmond O'Brien, Roy Thinnes, Dan O'Herlihy, and Nancy Malone.

Chicago, Chicago (a.k.a. Night Watch) (1966)

Two-hour pilot episode for a weekly series that was dropped from the final schedule of the network, and which was written by Brian McKay and Robert Eggenweiler, directed by Altman, and produced by Ray Wagner, with most of the Westwood "talent trust" represented among the craft credits. Cast of this "harbor *Dragnet*" set in

Chicago included Carroll O'Connor and Andrew Duggan. The pilot was aired several times as a telefilm.

Miscellany

Including *Rat Patrol; East Side, West Side; Mr. Novak;* and *Gunsmoke.* Altman may or may not have directed one episode or more of these series, respectively. They are sometimes claimed in Altman listings or interviews, but the poor state of television archivism makes individual segment credits difficult to pinpoint. At this point, they must be considered subjects for further research.

Short Subjects

Altman's short subjects from the 1960s includes four ColorSonics, produced for video-jukebox distribution, and a number of "home movies."

The ColorSonics include *The Party,* a Bobby Troupe number, and two vignettes featuring exotic stripper Lili St. Cyr.

The "home movies" of the period include:

● The nine-minute *Pot au Feu* (1966), a witty essay on marijuana and philosophy of life with French pretensions and subtitles. It was financed out-of-pocket by Altman, agent George Litto, and Donald Factor, the cosmetics heir. "It's very special to me because my mother and father, who are both dead, appear in it," Altman has said.

● An eleven-minute comedy called *The Life of Kathryn Reed,* photographed in black-and-white, and full of private jokes and innuendo. It sketches the life and career of Altman's third wife. Altman has referred to it as "the best film I ever made. It was her birthday, and things hadn't been going well with the company. . . ."

The Life of Kathryn Reed was filmed and edited in two days. Ted Knight serves as narrator, Carroll O'Connor's wife plays Altman's mother-in-law, the music is composed by John Williams. "I was in trouble," Altman has said, "and this was my gift to my wife."

Leo Burmeister in *Rattlesnake in a Cooler*.
(Richard S. Bailey/Los Angeles Actors' Theatre)

Network and Cable Specials

Two by South (Alpha Repertory Television Service, 1982)

Including: *Rattlesnake in a Cooler* and *Precious Blood*.
Producer and director, Altman; writer, Frank South.
Cast: Leo Burmester, Guy Boyd, and Alfre Woodard.

Altman, directing Carol Burnett and Amy
Madigan in the made-for-cable *The Laundromat.*

The Laundromat (A Byck/Lancaster Production of a Sandcastle 5 Film, 1985)

Producers, Dann Byck and David Lancaster; executive producer,
Scott Bushnell; director, Altman; written by Marsha Norman; director of photography, Pierre Mignot; production designer, David Gropman; editor, Luce Grunenwaldt; associate producer, Jean-Francois
Casamayou; production manager, Daniel Wuhrmann, assistant director, Allan Nicholls; production administrator, Doug Cole; art
director, Serge Douy; costume designer, John Hay; property master,
Stephen Altman; camera operator, Jean Lepine; camera assistant,
Philippe Ros; sound mixer, Daniel Brisseau; re-recording, Neil Walwer; script supervisor, Dominique Piat; gaffer, Pierre Abraham; key
grip, Charlie Frees; sound editor, Catherine D'Hoir; production as-

John Travolta and Tom Conti in Harold Pinter's
The Dumb Waiter. (Capital Cities/ABC)

sistant, Veronique Aubouy; songs performed by Alberta Hunter, courtesy of CBS Records; songs written and performed by Danny Darst, courtesy of Al Gallico Music Corp., including "Common Folk," "Somebody's Daddy" and "Can't Make a Livin' on the Road"; special thanks to Frog Films, Paris, France, Radio Station WLCU of Louisville, Kentucky, and Guy Laine Post Productions.
Songs include: "Downhearted Blues," "Some Sweet Day," "I'm Having a Good Time," "Black Man," "The Love I Have for You," "My Castle's Rockin'," by Alberta Hunter; "I Cried for You," by G. Armheim, A. Freed, and A. Lyman; and "My Handy Man Ain't Handy No More," by A. Reed and E. Blake.
Cast: Carol Burnett (Alberta Johnson); Amy Madigan (Deedee Johnson); Michael Wright (Shooter Stevens).

The Dumb Waiter (Secret Castle Productions, ABC, 1987)

Producer and director, Altman; executive producer, Scott Bushnell; written by Harold Pinter; director of photography, Pierre Mignot; designed by Violette Daneau; music by Judith Gruber-Stitzer; set decorator, Frances Calder; camera operator, Jean Lepine.
Cast: John Travolta (Ben) and Tom Conti (Gus).

The Room (Secret Castle Productions Inc., ABC, 1987)

Producer and director, Altman; executive producer, Scott Bushnell; written by Harold Pinter; director of photography, Pierre Mignot; designed by Violette Daneau; music by Judith Gruber-Stitzer; edited by Jennifer Auge; set decorator, Frances Calder; camera operator, Jean Lepine.
Cast: Linda Hunt (Rose Hudd); Annie Lennox (Mrs. Sands); Julian Sands (Toddy Sands); David Hemblen (Mr. Hudd); Abbott Anderson (Riley); Donald Pleasance (Mr. Kidd).

The Caine Mutiny Court-Martial
(The Maltese Companies Inc./Wouk/Ware
Productions/Sandcastle 5 Productions/Columbia Pictures
Television, 1988)

Producers, Altman and John Flaxman; director, Altman; writer, Herman Wouk; director of photography, Jacek Laskus; editor, Dorian Harris; production designer, Stephen Altman; executive producers, Ray Volpe and Joseph Wouk; supervising producer, Scott Bushnell; coexecutive producer, Ed Griles; production manager/first assistant director, Allan Nicholls; second assistant director, Rob Corn; associate producers, Matthew Seig, Valerie Ross; script supervisor, Arthur Masella; wardrobe, Kristine Flones; set decorator, Tony Maccario; property master, James Monroe; music editor, Dan Edelstein; sound editor, Bernard Hajdenberg/Sound Dimensions; rerecording mixer, Reilly Steele/Sound One Corporation; camera operator, Jean Lepine; sound mixer, Mark Ulano; gaffer, Jonathan Lumlet; key grip, John Savka; titles by Kevin Duggan; laboratory, Alpha Cine; color by TVC; cameras by Moviecam; shot on location at Port Townsend in Washington State.
Cast: Eric Bogosian (Lt. Barney Greenwald); Jeff Daniels (Lt. Stephen Maryk); Brad Davis (Lt. Comm. Phillip Francis Queeg); Peter Gallagher (Lt. Comm. John Challee); Michael Murphy (Capt.

The cast of *The Caine Mutiny Court-Martial.*

Blakley); Kevin J. O'Connor (Lt. Thomas Keefer); Daniel Jenkins (Lt., Jr. Grade, Willis Seward Keith); Danny Darst (Capt. Randolph Southward); Ken Michels (Dr. Bird); David Miller (Stenographer); Matt Malloy, David Barnett, Ken Jones (Legal Assistants); Brian Haley, Matt Smith, L. W. Wyman (Party Guests).

Tanner '88 (Zenith and Darkhorse Productions/Home Box Office, 1988)

Director, Altman; written by Garry B. Trudeau; director of photography, Jean Lepine; individual segments edited by Alison Ellwood, Judith Sobol, Ruth Foster, Dorian Harris, Sean-Michael Connor; assistant editors, Regis Kimble, Rob Kobrin; associate director/stage manager, Allan Nicholls; line producer, Mark Jaffee; location manager, Jack Kney; production coordinators, Valerie Ross, Mary Fran Loftus; second-unit camera, Wally Pfister; production auditor, Michael McCormick; script supervisors, Christine Guarnaccia, Wendy Lee Roberts; art director, Stephen Altman; prop master, Jerry Fleming; property assistant, Jacqui Arnot; wardrobe/makeup, Kristine Flones; camera assistant, Tom McGrath; video technician, Al Vazquez; utility, Anthony De Fonzo, Jonathan Flaks; gaffer, Don Muchow; grips, Denis Hann, Nick Grande, John McElwain, Mike Gulbin, Tom Grunke, Roger Kimpton; best boy, Glenn Miller; sound mixer, Steve Ning; boom operators, George Leong, Laura Derrick, Phil Spradlin; art department assistant, Howard Solomon; production assistants, Matthew Altman, Anne Kaplan; equipment by Telstar Video; on-line editors, R.T. Burden, Douglas Tishman, National Video Industries, Mark Fish, and Telstar Editing; audio postproduction, John Albeas, Howard Schwartz Recording; production assistant, Robert Hilferty; publicist, Cathy Keller; research consultant, Frank Baryhdt; political consultant, Sydney Blumenthal; associate producer, Matthew Seig; produced by Scott Bushnell; executive producers, Altman and Garry B. Trudeau.
Episodes include: "The Dark Horse" (60 minutes) and (all other segments are 30 minutes) "For Real," "The Night of the Twinkies," "Bagels With Bruce," "Child's Play," "The Great Escape," "Something Borrowed, Something New" (a.k.a. "The Girlfriend Factor"), "The Boiler Room," and "The Reality Check."
Regulars include: Michael Murphy, Pamela Reed, Cynthia Nixon, Kevin J. O'Connor, Daniel Jenkins, Jim Fyfe, Matt Malloy, Ilana Levine, Veronica Cartwright, Wendy Crewson, Greg Procaccino, Sandra Bowie, Frank Baryhdt.
Guest stars include: Waylon Jennings, Cleavon Little, E.G. Marshall, John Considine, Harry Anderson.
As Themselves: G. David Hughes, Sen. Robert Dole, Rev. Pat Robertson, Mary McGrory, Sidney Blumenthal, Hodding Carter, James Davidson, Patt Derian, Peter Edelman, Aviel Ginzburg, Pamela Ginzburg, Rep. Mickey Leland, Rep. Ed Markey, Chris Mathews, Kirk O'Donnell, Bob Squier, Danny Darst and the Danny Darst Band, The New Grass Revival, The Fisk Jubilee Singers, Gov.

Michael Murphy, star of *Tanner '88.*

Bruce Babbitt, Joan Cushing, Rebecca De Mornay, Dorothy Sarnoff, Kim Cranston, Sandra J. Burud, Harlow, Linda Ellerbee, Ralph Nader, Gloria Steinem, Art Buchwald, Rep. Lee Hamilton, Studs Terkel, QTMC, Lynn Russell, and Kitty Dukakis.

FILMOGRAPHY

Christmas Eve (UA, 1947), 90 minutes

Producer, Benedict Bogeaus; director, Edwin L. Marin; story, Laurence Stallings, Richard H. Landau [Altman, uncredited contribution]; screenplay, Stallings; art director, Ernst Fegte; set decorator,

A family tableaux from *Christmas Eve.*(Wisconsin Center for Film and Theatre Research)

Eugene Redd; music, Heinz Roemheld; music director, David Chudnow; assistant director, Joseph Depew; sound, William Lynch; camera, Gordon Avil; editor, James Smith.
Cast: George Raft (Mario Torio); George Brent (Michael Brooks); Randolph Scott (Jonathan); Joan Blondell (Ann Nelson); Virginia Field (Claire); Dolores Moran (Jean); Ann Harding (Matilda Reid); Reginald Denny (Phillip Hastings); Carl Harbord (Dr. Doremus); Clarence Kolb (Judge Alston); John Litel (F.B.I. Agent); Joe Sawyer (Gimlet); Douglass Dumbrille (Dr. Bunyan); Dennis Hoey (Williams); Molly Lamont (Harriett); Walter Sande (Hood); Konstantin Shayne (Reichman); Marie Blake (Girl Reporter); Soledad Jimenez (Rosita); Holly Bane (Mike Regan, Page Boy).

Priscilla Lane and Lawrence Tierney in *Body-guard*.

Bodyguard (RKO, 1948), 62 minutes

Producer, Sid Rogell; director, Richard Fleischer; screenplay, Fred Niblo, Jr. and Harry Essex, based on a story by George W. George and Robert Altman; cinematographer, Robert de Grasse; music, Paul Sawtell; musical director, C. Bakaleinikoff; editor, Elmo Williams; art directors, Albert S. D'Agostino and Field Gray; sound, Earl A. Wolcott and Terry Kellum; sets, Darrel Silvera and James Altwies; special effects, Russell A. Cully.
Cast: Lawrence Tierney (Mike Carter); Priscilla Lane (Doris Brewster); Philip Reed (Freddie Dysen); June Clayworth (Connie); Elisabeth Risdon (Gene Dysen); Steve Brodie (Fenton); Frank Fenton (Lieutenant Borden); Charles Cane (Captain Wayne).

Corn's-A-Poppin' (Crest, 1951), 62 minutes

Director, Robert Woodburn; screenplay, Robert Altman and Robert Woodburn; musical director, John J. Thompson Jr.; director of photography, Robert Woodburn; lead cameraman, William Veerkamp;

Jerry Wallace and Little Cora Weiss in *Corn's-A-Poppin'*. (Eddie Brandts' Saturday Matinee)

assistant cameraman, Tommy Stockwell; sound director, Eldredge W. White; art director, Chet Allen; office interiors, John A. Marshall Co.; wardrobe, Ann Robbins.

Cast: Jerry Wallace (Johnny Wilson); Pat McReynolds (Sheila Burns); James Lantz (Waldo Crummit); Keith Painton (Thaddeus Pinwhistle); Noralee Benedict (Lillian Gravelguard); Dora Walls (Agatha Quake); Little Cora Weiss (Susie Wilson); and featuring Hobie Shepp and the Cowtown Wranglers.

Songs: "On Our Way to Mars" (Leon and Rafael René); "Running after Love," by arrangement with Skinner Music Company; "Patches on My Heart" (Jimmy Carlyle); "Mamma, Wanna Balloon" (Eve Monroy and Jean Andes); "Achin' Heart" (Hobie Shepp).

Tom Laughlin (far right) and others in a scene from *The Delinquents*.(Eddie Brandt's Saturday Matinee)

The Delinquents (UA, 1957), 75 minutes.

Producer, Altman; writer and director, Altman; cinematographer, Charles Paddock; music, Bill Nolan Quintet Minus Two; song, "The Dirty Rock Boogie," by Bill Nolan and Ronnie Norman, sung by Julia Lee; editor, Helene Turner; art director, Chet Allen; assistant director, Reza Badiyi; sound, Bob Post; sound effects, Fred Brown; camera operator, Harry Birch; production manager, Joan Altman.
Cast: Tom Laughlin (Scotty); Peter Miller (Cholly); Richard Bakalyan (Eddy); Rosemary Howard (Janice); Helene Hawley (Mrs. White); Leonard Belove (Mr. White); Lotus Corelli (Mrs. Wilson); James Lantz (Mr. Wilson); Christine Altman (Sissy); George Kuhn (Jay); Pat Stedman (Meg); Norman Zands (Chizzy); James Leria (Steve); Jet Pinkston (Molly); Kermit Echols (Bartender); Joe Adelman (Station Attendant).

A scene from *The James Dean Story.* (Wisconsin Center for Film and Theatre Research)

The James Dean Story (Warner Brothers, 1957), 82 minutes

Producers, directors, and editors, George W. George and Altman; screenplay, Stewart Stern; music, Leith Stevens; production designer, Louis Clyde Stoumen; titles designed by Maurice Binder; title illustrations, David Stone Martin; sound, Cathey Burrow; sound designers, Bert Schoenfeld, James Nelson, and Jack Kirschner; still sequences designed by Camera Eye Pictures, Inc.; theme song, "Let Me Be Loved," by Jay Livingston and Ray Evans, sung by Tommy Sands; assistant to the producers, Louis Lombardo; narration, Martin Gabel.

Contributing photographers: Dennis Stock, Roy Schatt, Frank Worth, Weegee, Edward Martin, Dick Miller, Peter Basch, Carlyle Blackwell Jr., Tom Caffrey, Jack Delano, Murray Garrett, Paul Gilliam, Globe Photos, Inc., Fred Jordan, Impact Photos, Inc., Louis Lombardo, Magnum Photos, Inc., Russ Meyer, Don Ornitz, Paul Popesil, Charles Robinson, Jack Stager, Phil Stern, Louis Clyde Stoumen, William Veerkamp, Wide World Photos, Inc., UCLA Theatre Arts, California Highway Patrol.

Nightmare in Chicago, a.k.a. *Once Upon a Savage Night* (Roncom/Universal, 1964), 81 minutes

Producer, Altman; director, Altman; screenplay, Donald Moessinger, based on William P. McGivern's novel *Death on the Turnpike;* cinematographer, Bud Thackery; music, Johnny Williams; associate producer, Robert Eggenweiler; film editors, Danford B. Greene and Larry D. Lester; sound, Ed Somers; costume supervisor, Vincent Dee; assistant to the producer, Reza Badiyi; assistant director, James M. Walters, Jr.; musical supervisor, Stanley Wilson; makeup, Fred Sottlle and Walter Schwartz; hair stylist, Larry Germain.

Cast: Charles McGraw (Harry Brockman); Robert Ridgeley (Dan McVea); Ted Knight (Commissioner Lombardo); Philip Abbott (Myron Ellis); Barbara Turner (Bernadette Wells); Charlene Lee (Wynnette); Douglas A. Alleman (Ralph); Arlene Kieta (The Blonde); John Alonzo (Officer Miller); Robert C. Harris (Officer Newman).

Ted Knight (at left), Robert Duvall, and James
Caan in *Countdown*.

Countdown (Warner Brothers, 1968), 101 minutes

Executive producer, William Conrad; director, Altman; assistant
director, Victor Vallejo; screenplay, Loring Mandel, based on Hank
Searls's novel *The Pilgrim Project*; cinematographer, William W.
Spencer; art director, Jack Poplin; set decoration, Ralph S. Hurst;
music, Leonard Rosenman; sound, Everett A. Hughes; editor, Gene
Milford.
Cast: James Caan (Lee Stegler); Robert Duvall (Chiz); Joanna
Moore (Mickey); Barbara Baxley (Jean); Charles Aidman (Gus);
Steve Ihnat (Ross); Michael Murphy (Rick); Ted Knight (Larson);
Stephen Coit (Ehrman); John Rayner (Dunc); Charles Irving
(Seidel); Bobby Riha Jr. (Stevie).

That Cold Day in the Park (Commonwealth, 1969), 110 minutes

Producers, Donald Factor and Leon Mirell; director, Altman;
screenplay, Gillian Freeman, based on the novel by Richard Miles;

Sandy Dennis in *That Cold Day in the Park.*

cinematographer, Laszlo Kovacs; music, Johnny Mandel; editor, Danford B. Greene; art director, Leon Ericksen; associate producer, Robert Eggenweiler; assistant director, Harold Schneider; second assistant director, Graeme Clifford; sound, John Gusselle; production manager, James Margellos.

Cast: Sandy Dennis (Frances Austen); Michael Burns (The Boy); Suzanne Benton (Nina); John Garfield Jr. (Nick); Luana Anders (Sylvia); Michael Murphy (The Rounder); Edward Greenhalgh (Dr. Stevenson); Doris Buckingham (Mrs. Ebury); Frank Wade (Mr. Ebury); Alicia Ammon (Mrs. Pitt); Lloyd Berry (Mr. Pitt); Linda Sorensen (The Prostitute); Rae Brown (Mrs. Parnell).

*M*A*S*H* (Twentieth Century-Fox, 1969), 116 minutes

Producer, Ingo Preminger; director, Altman; screenplay, Ring Lardner Jr., based on the novel by Richard Hooker; cinematographer, Harold E. Stine; music, Johnny Mandel; song, "Sui-

Donald Sutherland and Elliott Gould in
M*A*S*H.

cide Is Painless," lyrics by Mike Altman, music by Johnny Mandel;
editor, Danford B. Greene; art directors, Jack Martin Smith and
Arthur Lonergan; associate producer, Leon Ericksen; assistant director, Ray Taylor Jr.; assistant to the producer, Y. Ross Levy;
sound, Bernard Freericks and John Stack; orchestration, Herbert
Spencer; title theme performed by Ahman Jamal; makeup supervisor, Dan Striepeke; makeup artist, Lester Berns; hair stylist,
Edith Lindon; medical advisor, Dr. David Sachs; unit production
manager, Norman A. Cook; title design, Pacific Title and Art Studio; set decoration, Walter M. Scott and Stuart A. Reiss; special
effects, L. B. Abbott and Art Cruickshank; processes, Color by Deluxe, Panavision.
Cast: Donald Sutherland (Capt. "Hawkeye" Pierce); Elliott Gould
(Capt. "Trapper" John McIntyre); Tom Skerritt (Capt. "Duke" Forrest); Sally Kellerman (Major Margaret "Hot Lips" Houlihan); Robert Duvall (Major Frank Burns); Jo Ann Pflug (Lt. Dish); Father
"Dago Red" Mulcahy (René Auberjonois); Roger Bowen (Col.

Henry Blake); Gary Burghoff (Cpl. Radar O'Reilly); David Arkin
(Sgt. Major Vollmer); Fred Williamson (Capt. Oliver Wendell
"Spearchucker" Jones); Michael Murphy (Capt. "Me Lay" Mar-
ston); Kim Atwood (Ho-Jon); Tim Brown (Cpl. Judson); Indus
Arthur (Lt. Leslie); John Schuck (Capt. Walt Waldowski, the
"Painless Pole"); Ken Prymus (Pfc. Seidman); Dawne Damon
(Capt. Scorch); Carl Gottlieb (Ugly John); Tamara Horrocks (Capt.
"Knocko" McCarthy); G. Wood (Gen. Hammond); Bobby Troup
(Sgt. Gorman); Bud Cort (Pvt. Warren Boone); Danny Goldman
(Capt. Murrhardt); Corey Fischer (Capt. Bandini); J. B. Douglas
(Col. Wallace C. Merrill); Yoko Young (Japanese Servant); and foot-
ball players, Ben Davidson, Fran Tarkenton, Howard Williams,
Jack Concannon, John Myers, Tom Woodeschick, Tommy Brown,
Buck Buchanan, Nolan Smith.

Brewster McCloud (Metro-Goldwyn-Mayer, 1970), 104 minutes

Producer, Lou Adler; director, Altman; screenplay, Doran William
Cannon; assistant to the producer, Ross Levy; cinematographers,
Jordan Cronenweth and Lamar Boren; music, Gene Page; editor
and second-unit director, Louis Lombardo; wings designed by Leon
Ericksen; art directors, George W. Davis and Preston Ames; associ-
ate producers, Robert Eggenweiler and James Margellos; assistant
director, Tommy Thompson; sound, Harry W. Tetrick and William
McCaughey; makeup, Edwin Butterworth; hair stylist, Dorothy
White; casting, Gary Wayne Chason; processes, Metrocolor, Pan-
avision.
Cast: Bud Cort (Brewster McCloud); Sally Kellerman (Louise); Mi-
chael Murphy (Shaft); William Windom (Weeks); Shelley Duvall
(Suzanne); René Aubjerjonois (The Lecturer); Stacy Keach (Abra-
ham Wright); John Schuck (Johnson); Margaret Hamilton (Daphne
Heap); Jennifer Salt (Hope); Corey Fischer (Hines); G. Wood (Cran-
dall); Bert Remsen (Douglas Breen); William Baldwin (Bernard);
William Henry Bennet (Conductor); Gary Wayne Chason (Camera
Store Clerk); Ellis Gilbert (Butler); Verdie Henshaw (Manager,
Feathered Nest Sanitorium); Robert Warner (Assistant Manager,
Camera Store); Keith V. Erickson (Professor Aggnout); Thomas
Danko (Color Lab Man); W. E. Terry Jr. (Police Chaplain); Ronnie
Cammack (Wendel); Dixie M. Taylor (Manager, Tanninger's Nurs-
ing Home); Pearl Coffey Chason (Nursing Home Attendant); Ame-
lia Parker (Nursing Home Manageress).
Songs: "Last of the Unnatural Acts" and "The First and Last Thing

The cast finale of *Brewster McCloud*. (Museum
of Modern Art)

You Do" written and sung by John Phillips, "White Feather
Wings," written by John Phillips and sung by Merry Clayton, "I
Promise Not to Tell," composed by Rosamund Johnson and sung
by John Phillips, "Lift Every Voice and Sing," composed by James
Weldon Johnson and sung by Merry Clayton.

McCabe and Mrs. Miller (Warner Brothers, 1970), 121 minutes

Producers, David Foster and Mitchell Brower; director, Altman;
screenplay, Robert Altman and Brian McKay, based on the novel
McCabe by Edmund Naughton; cinematographer, Vilmos Zsigmond; songs, Leonard Cohen; fiddler, Brantley F. Kearns; editor
and second-unit director, Louis Lombardo; production designer,
Leon Ericksen; art directors, Philip Thomas and Al Locatelli; asso-

The two stars of *McCabe and Mrs. Miller.*
(Academy of Motion Picture Arts and Sciences)

ciate producer, Robert Eggenweiler; assistant director, Tommy
Thompson; second assistant director, Irby Smith; sound, John V.
Gusselle and William A. Thompson; continuity, Joan Maguire;
makeup, Robert Jiras, Ed Butterworth, and Phyllis Newman; hair
stylist, Barry Richardson; wardrobe, Ilse Richter; unit production
manager, James Margellos; second-unit photography, Rod Park-
hurst; casting, Graeme Clifford; sound mixer, Barry P. Jones; property master, Syd Greenwood; title design, Anthony Goldschmidt;
special effects, Marcel Vercoutere; processes, Technicolor, Panavision.

Cast: Warren Beatty (John Q. McCabe); Julie Christie (Mrs. Miller [Constance]); René Auberjonois (Patrick Sheehan); Hugh Millais (Dog Butler); Shelley Duvall (Ida Coyl); Michael Murphy (Eugene Sears); John Schuck (Smalley); Corey Rischer (Mr. Elliott, the Preacher); William Devane (Clement Samuels, the Lawyer); Anthony Holland (Ernie Hollander); Bert Remsen (Bart Coyl); Keith Carradine (Cowboy); Jace Vander Veen (Breed); Manfred Schulz (Kid); Jackie Crossland (Lily); Elizabeth Murphy (Kate); Linda Sorenson (Blanche); Elizabeth Knight (Birdie); Maysie Hoy (Maysie); Linda Kupecek (Ruth); Janet Wright (Eunice); Carey Lee McKenzie (Alma); Tom Hill (Archer); Jeremy Newsom (Jeremy Berg); Wayne Robson (Sheehan's Bartender); Jack Riley (Riley Quinn); Robert Fortier (Town Drunk); Wayne Grace (McCabe's Bartender); Wesley Taylor (Shorty Dunn); Anne Cameron (Mrs. Dunn); Graeme Campbell (Bill Cubbs); J. S. Johnson (J.J.); Joe Clarke (Joe Shortreed); Harry Trader (Andy Anderson); Edwin Collier (Gilchrist); Terence Kelly (Quigley); Brantley F. Kearns (Fiddler); Don Francks (Buffalo); Rodney Gage (Sumner Washington); Lili Francks (Mrs. Washington); Joan McGuire, Harvey Lowe, Eric Schneider, Milos Zalovic, Claudine Melgrave, Derek Deurvorst, Alexander Diakun, Gordon Robertson.

Images (Columbia Pictures/A Lion's Gate-Hemdale Group Production, 1972), 101 minutes

Producer, Tommy Thompson; director, Altman; screenplay, Altman (with passages from *In Search of Unicorns* by Susannah York); cinematographer, Vilmos Zsigmond; music, John Williams; editor, Graeme Clifford; production designer, Leon Ericksen; assistant to the producer, Jean D'Oncieu; assistant director, Seamus Byrne; sound recordist, Liam Saurin; sounds, Stomu Yamash'ta; dubbing mixer, Doug Turner; boom operator, Noel Quinn; gaffer, Jack Conroy; continuity, Joan Bennett; makeup, Toni Delaney; hair stylist, Barry Richardson; wardrobe, Jack Gallagher; Miss York's clothes, Raymond Ray; grip, Paddy Keogh; production manager, Sheila Collins; camera assistants, Earl Clark and Nico Vermuelin; assistant editors, Michael Kelliher, David Spiers, and Robin Buick; sound editor, Rodney Holland.
Cast: Susannah York (Cathryn); René Auberjonois (Hugh); Marcel Bozzuffi (Rene); Hugh Millais (Marcel); Cathryn Harrison (Susannah); John Morley (Neighbor).

Susannah York as the haunted heroine of *Images.*

The Long Goodbye (United Artists, 1973), 112 minutes

Producer, Jerry Bick; director, Altman; screenplay, Leigh Brackett, based on the novel by Raymond Chandler; executive producer, Elliott Kastner; cinematographer, Vilmos Zsigmond; music, John Williams; title song, Johnny Mercer and John Williams, played by the Dave Grusin Trio; editor, Lou Lombardo; associate producer, Robert Eggenweiler; assistant director, Tommy Thompson; sound, John V. Speak; gaffer, Randy Glass; script supervisor, Adele Bravos; makeup, Bill Miller; hair stylist, Lynda Gurasich; wardrobe (male) Kent James and (female) Marjorie Wahl; key grip, Ken Adams; processes, Technicolor, Panavision.

Cast: Elliott Gould (Philip Marlowe); Nina van Pallandt (Eileen Wade); Sterling Hayden (Roger Wade); Mark Rydell (Marty Augustine); Henry Gibson (Dr. Verringer); David Arkin (Harry); Jim Bouton (Terry Lennox); Warren Berlinger (Morgan); Jo Ann Brody (Jo Ann Eggenweiler); Jack Knight (Hood); Pepe Callahan (Pepe); Vince Palmieri (Hood); Arnold Strong (Hood); Arnold Schwarzeneg-

From left: Sterling Hayden, Elliott Gould, Nina van Pallandt, and Henry Gibson in *The Long Goodbye.*

ger (Muscle Man); Rutanya Alda (Marlowe's Neighbor); Tammy Shaw (Marlowe's Neighbor); Jack Riley (Piano Player); Ken Sansom (Colony Guard); Danny Goldman (Bartender); Sybil Scotford (Real Estate Lady); Steve Coit (Detective Farmer); Tracy Harris (Detective); Jerry Jones (Detective Green); Rodney Moss (Clerk); Kate Murtagh (Nurse).

Thieves Like Us (United Artists, 1974), 123 minutes

Director, Altman; screenplay, Calder Willingham, Joan Tewkesbury, and Robert Altman, based on Edward Anderson's novel; executive producer, George Litto; cinematographer, Jean Boffety; editor, Lou Lombardo; visual consultant, Jack DeGovia; assistant visual consultant, Scott Bushnell; associate producers, Robert Eggenweiler and Thomas Hal Phillips; assistant director, Tommy

Keith Carradine (at wheel) and escapees in
Thieves Like Us.

Thompson; second assistant director, Mike Kusley; sound mixer,
Don Matthews; camera crew, George Bouillet, James Blandford,
and Harry Walsh III; property master, Marty Wunderlich; cars, Paul
Neanover and Jean D'Oncieu; grips, Eddie Lara, Dennis Kuneff, and
Billy Record; Cinemobile Systems; assistant editors, Tony Lom-
bardo and Dennis Hill; dubbing mixer, Richard Voriseck; radio re-
search, John Dunning; research historian, Carol Gister; process,
DeLuxe Color.
Cast: Keith Carradine (Bowie); Shelley Duvall (Keechie Mobley);
John Schuck (Elmo [Chicamaw] Mobley); Bert Remsen (T-Dub
Masefield); Louise Fletcher (Mattie); Ann Latham (Lula); Tom
Skerritt (Dee Mobley); Al Scott (Captain Stammers); John Roper
(Jasbo); Mary Waits (Noel Joy); Rodney Lee Jr. (James Mattingly);
William Watters (Alvin); Joan Tewkesbury (Lady in Train Station);
Dr. Edward Fisher (Bank Hostage); Josephine Bennett (Bank Hos-
tage); Howard Warner (Bank Hostage); Eleanor Mathews (Woman
in Accident); Pam Warner (Coca-Cola Girl); Walter Cooper (Sher-
iff); Lloyd Jones (Sheriff).

Elliott Gould, Ann Prentiss, and George Segal in
California Split.

California Split (Columbia, 1974), 111 minutes

Producers, Altman and Joseph Walsh; director, Altman; screenplay,
Joseph Walsh; executive producers, Aaron Spelling and Leonard
Goldberg; cinematographer, Paul Lohmann; music played and sung
by Phyllis Shotwell; editor, Lou Lombardo; art director, Leon
Ericksen; associate producer, Robert Eggenweiler; assistant director, Tommy Thompson; second assistant director, Alan Rudolph;
sound mixer, Jim Webb; dubbing mixer, Richard Fortman; camera
operator, Edward Koons; assistants, Richard Colean and Ron Fran-
tzvog; gaffer, Randy Glass; sound crew, Chris McLaughlin and
George Wycoff; script supervisor, Carole Gister; production coordinator, Kelly Marshall; makeup, Joe di Bella; wardrobe, Hugh
McFarland; grips, Harry Rez, Tom Doherty, and Eddie Lara; casting, Scott Bushnell; assistant editors, Tony Lombardo and Dennis
Hill; sound editor, Kay Rose (Lion's Gate 8-Track Sound Services);
assistant, Randy Kelley; set decorator, Sam Jones; property master,
Jerry Graham; editorial assistants, Marion Segal and Stephen W.

Altman; assistant to the producers, Jac Cashin; title design, Dan Perri; title editor, O. Nicholas Brown; processes, Color, Panavision. **Cast:** George Segal (Bill Denny); Elliott Gould (Charlie Waters); Ann Prentiss (Barbara Miller); Gwen Welles (Susan Peters); Edward Walsh (Lew); Joseph Walsh (Sparkie); Bert Remsen (Helen Brown); Barbara London (Lady on the Bus); Barbara Ruick (Reno Barmaid); Jay Fletcher (Robber); Jeff Goldblum (Lloyd Harris); Barbara Colby (Receptionist); Vince Palmieri (First Bartender); Alyce Passman (Go-Go Girl); Joanne Strauss (Mother); Jack Riley (Second Bartender); Sierra Bandit (Woman at Bar); John Considine (Man at Bar); Eugene Troobnick (Harvey); Richard Kennedy (Used Car Salesman); John Winston (Tenor); Bill Duffy (Kenny); Mike Greene (Reno Dealer); Tom Signorelli (Nugie); Sharon Compton (Nugie's Wife); California Club poker players, Arnold Herzstein, Marc Cavell, Alvin Weissman, Mickey Fox, and Carol Lohmann; Reno poker players, "Amarillo Slim" Preston, Winston Lee, Harry Drackett, Thomas Hal Phillips, Ted Say, and A. J. Hood; most of the other players, from Synanon.

Nashville (Paramount, 1975), 159 minutes

Producer, Altman; director, Altman; screenplay, Joan Tewkesbury; executive producers, Martin Starger and Jerry Weintraub; cinematographer, Paul Lohmann; music arranged and supervised by Richard Baskin; editors, Sidney Levin and Dennis Hill; associate producers, Robert Eggenweiler and Scott Bushnell; assistant directors, Tommy Thompson and Alan Rudolph; sound, Jim Webb and Chris McLaughlin; camera operator, Edward Koons; gaffers, Randy Glass and Mike Marlett; script supervisor, Joyce King; makeup, Tommy Thompson; hair stylist, Ann Wadlington; wardrobe, Jules Melillo; grips, Harry Pez and Eddie Lara; casting (local), Joann Doster; assistant editors, Tony Lombardo and Tom Walls; sound editor, William A. Sawyer; assistant, Randy Kelley; property master, Bob Anderson; political campaign, Thomas Hal Phillips; production coordinator, Kelly Marshall; assistant to the producer, Jac Cashin; sound system, Lion's Gate 8-Track Sound; rerecording mixer, Richard Portman; music recorded by Gene Eichelberger and Johnny Rosen; production assistants, Angel Dominguez, Ron Hecht, Steve Altman, Mark Eggenweiler, Maysie Hoy, Allan Highfill, Roger Frappier; title design, Dan Perri; production secretary, Elaine Bradish.

Henry Gibson sings "200 Years" in *Nashville*.

Cast: David Arkin (Norman); Barbara Baxley (Lady Pearl); Ned Beatty (Delbert Reese); Karen Black (Connie White); Ronee Blakley (Barbara Jean); Timothy Brown (Tommy Brown); Keith Carradine (Tom Frank); Geraldine Chaplin (Opal); Robert Doqui (Wade); Shelley Duvall (L.A. Joan); Allen Garfield (Barnett); Henry Gibson (Haven Hamilton); Scott Glenn (Pfc. Glenn Kelly); Jeff Goldblum (Tricycle Man); Barbara Harris (Albuquerque); David Hayward (Kenny Fraiser); Michael Murphy (John Triplette); Allan Nicholls (Bill); Dave Peel (Bud Hamilton); Christina Raines (Mary); Bert Remsen (Star); Lily Tomlin (Linnea Reese); Gwen Welles (Sueleen Gay); Keenan Wynn (Mr. Green).
Featuring: James Dan Calvert (Jimmy Reese); Donna Denton (Donna Reese); Merle Kilgore (Trout); Carol McGinnis (Jewel); Sheila Bailey (Smokey Mountain Laurel); Richard Baskin (Frog); Jonnie Barnett, Vassar Clements, Misty Mountain Boys, Sue Barton, Patti Bryant, Elliott Gould, Julie Christie (Themselves).
Songs: "200 Years," lyrics by Henry Gibson, music by Richard Baskin; "Yes, I Do," lyrics and music by Richard Baskin and Lily Tomlin; "Down to the River," lyrics and music by Ronee Blakley; "Let Me Be the One," lyrics and music by Richard Baskin; "Sing a Song," lyrics and music by Joe Raposo; "The Heart of a Gentle Woman," lyrics and music by Dave Peel; "Bluebird," lyrics and

music by Ronee Blakley; "The Day I Looked Jesus in the Eye," lyrics and music by Richard Baskin and Robert Altman; "Memphis," lyrics and music by Karen Black; "I Don't Know If I Found It in You," lyrics and music by Karen Black; "For the Sake of the Children," lyrics and music by Richard Baskin and Richard Reicheg; "Keep a Goin'," lyrics by Henry Gibson, music by Richard Baskin and Henry Gibson; "Swing Low, Sweet Chariot," arrangements by Millie Clements; "Rolling Stone," lyrics and music by Karen Black; "Honey," lyrics and music by Keith Carradine; "Tapedeck in His Tractor (The Cowboy Song)," lyrics and music by Ronee Blakley; "Dues," lyrics and music by Ronee Blakley; "I Never Get Enough," lyrics and music by Richard Baskin and Ben Raleigh; "Rose's Cafe," lyrics and music by Allan Nicholls; "Old Man Mississippi," lyrics and music by Juan Grizzle; "My Baby's Cookin' in Another Man's Pan," lyrics and music by Jonnie Barnett; "One, I Love You," lyrics and music by Richard Baskin; "I'm Easy," lyrics and music by Keith Carradine; "It Don't Worry Me," lyrics and music by Keith Carradine; "Since You've Gone," lyrics and music by Gary Busey; "Trouble in the U.S.A.," lyrics and music by Arlene Barnett; "My Idaho Home," lyrics and music by Ronee Blakley.

Buffalo Bill and The Indians, or, Sitting Bull's History Lesson (United Artists, 1976), 123 minutes

Producer, Altman; director, Altman; screenplay, Alan Rudolph and Robert Altman, based on the play *Indians* by Arthur Kopit; executive producer, David Susskind; production executive, Tommy Thompson; cinematographer, Paul Lohmann; production designer, Tony Masters; music, Richard Baskin; editors, Peter Appleton and Dennis Hill; art director, Jack Maxsted; associate producers, Robert Eggenweiler, Scott Bushnell, and Jac Cashin; assistant director, Tommy Thompson; second assistant director, Rob Lockwood; sound, Jim Webb and Chris McLaughlin; sound system, Lion's Gate 8-Track Sound; camera operators, Eddie Koons and Jack Richards; gaffer, J. Michael Marlett; titan boom, Norman Walke; script supervisor, John Binder; unit manager, Les Kimber; makeup, Monty Westmore; scenic artist, Rusty Cox; costume designer, Anthony Powell; wardrobe, Jules Melillo; costume assistant, Allen Highfill; grip, Art Brooker; assistant editors, Tony Lombardo, Tom Walls, and Mark Eggenweiler; apprentice editor, Steve Altman; set decorator and property master, Denny Parrish; assistant, Graham Sumner; sound editor, Richard Oswald; rerecording mixer, Richard

Paul Newman in *Buffalo Bill and the Indians.*
(Wisconsin Center for Film and Theatre Research)

Portman; special effects, Joe Zomar, Logan Frazee, Bill Zomar,
Terry Frazee, and John Thomas; head wrangler, John Scott; steam
engines and other units on loan from Reynolds museum, Wet-
askiwin, Alberta, Canada; location, Stoney Indian Reserve, Alberta,
Canada; presented by Dino De Laurentiis; processes, Color, Pan-
avision.
Cast: Paul Newman (The Star, William F. Cody, "Buffalo Bill");
Joel Grey (The Producer, Nate Salsbury); Kevin McCarthy (The
Publicist, Major Arizona John Burke); Harvey Keitel (The Relative,

Ed Goodman); Allan Nicholls (The Journalist, Colonel Prentiss Ingraham); Geraldine Chaplin (The Sure Shot, Annie Oakley); John Considine (The Sure Shot's Manager); Robert Doqui (The Wrangler, Osborne Dart); Mike Kaplan (The Treasurer, Jules Keen); Bert Remsen (The Bartender, Crutch); Bonnie Leaders (The Mezzo-Contralto, Margaret); Noelle Rogers (The Lyric-Coloratura, Lucille Du Charmes); Evelyn Lear (The Lyric-Soprano, Nina Cavalini); Denver Pyle (The Indian Agent, McLaughlin); Frank Kaquitts (The Indian, Chief Sitting Bull); Will Sampson (The Interpreter, William Halsey); Ken Krossa (The Arenic Director, Johnny Baker); Fred N. Larsen (The King of the Cowboys, Buck Taylor); Jerry and Joy Duce (The Cowboy Trick Riders); Alex Green and Gary MacKenzie (The Mexican Whip and Fast Draw Act); Humphrey Gratz (The Old Soldier); Pat McCormick (The President of the United States, Grover Cleveland); Shelley Duvall (The First Lady, Frances Folsom Cleveland); E. L. Doctorow (The Speech Writer, O. W. Fizician); Burt Lancaster (The Legend Maker, Ned Buntline); Pluto Calcedona, loaned by Raflyn Farms, Snohomish, Washington (The Horse, Brigham); brave cowboys and fierce Indians played by fierce Indians and brave cowboys from the Stoney Indian Reserve and the Calgary Stampede.

Three Women (Lion's Gate Films/Twentieth Century-Fox, 1977), 124 minutes

Producer, Altman; screenplay, Altman; production executive, Tommy Thompson; cinematographer, Chuck Rosher; music, Gerald Busby; editor, Dennis Hill; visual consultant, J. Allen Highfill; titles, Dan Perri; art director, James D. Vance; associate producers, Robert Eggenweiler and Scott Bushnell; second assistant director, Carol Himes; sound, Jim Webb and Chris McLaughlin; rerecording mixer, Richard Portman; camera operator, John Bailey; camera assistants, Robert E. Dawes Jr. and Glenn Shimada; postproduction supervisor, Bill Sawyer; sound editors, David M. Horton, Bill Phillips; gaffer, Tim Evans; postproduction, Westwood Editorial; music editor, Tom Walls; makeup, Monty Westmore; hair stylist, Kaye Downall; wardrobe, Jules Melillo; props, Richard Salesko; property assistant, Michael Ayers; best boy, John Garcia; grip, Harry Rez; best boy grip, Jacque L. Wallace; murals, Bodhi Wind; dolly grip, Robert L. Bennett; assistant editors, Tony Lombardo, Mark Eggenweiler, and Maisie Hoy; sound editors, David M. Horton and Bill Phillips; sets, Patricia Resnick; processes, DeLuxe, Panavision.

Robert Fortier and Sissy Spacek in *Three Women*.

Cast: Shelley Duvall (Millie Lammoreaux); Sissy Spacek (Pinky Rose); Janice Rule (Willie Hart); Robert Fortier (Edgar Hart); Ruth Nelson (Mrs. Rose); John Cromwell (Mr. Rose); Sierra Pecheur (Mrs. Bunweill); Craig Richard Nelson (Dr. Maas); Maysie Hoy (Doris); Belita Moreno (Alcira); Leslie Ann Hudson (Polly); Patricia Ann Hudson (Peggy); Beverly Ross (Deidre); John Davey (Dr. Norton).

A Wedding (Lion's Gate Films/Twentieth Century-Fox, 1978), 124 minutes

Producer, Altman; director, Altman; screenplay, John Considine, Patricia Resnick, Allan Nicholls, and Altman, based on a story by Altman and Considine; cinematographer, Charles Rosher; camera operators, Jack Richards, Steve Poster; camera assistants, Jim Blanford, Ed Nielsen, Gerrit Dangremond; title design, Pat Ryan; titles

Lillian Gish and Geraldine Chaplin in *A Wedding*.

and opticals, Pacific Title; music supervisor, Tom Walls; "Bird on a Wire," composed and sung by Leonard Cohen; fanfare music composer, John Hotchkis; music editor, Ted Whitfield; location music recorded by Jim Bourgeois and Jim Stuebe; sound, Jim Webb, Chris McLaughlin, Jim Bourgeois, Jim Stuebe; sound rerecording, Richard Portman; sound editors, Sam Gemette, Hal Sanders; postproduction, Westwood Editorial; postproduction supervisor, Bill Sawyer; costumes, J. Allen Highfill; editor, Tony Lombardo; assistant editors, John Carr, Michael Altman; assistant director, Tommy Thompson; second assistant directors, Peter Bergquist, Bob Dahlin; makeup, Monty Westmore; hairdresser, Jerry Turnage; props, Dennis J. Parrish; props assistants, Steve Altman, Jeff Renfrow; production coordinator, Victoria Barney; production assistant, Carole Keagy; associate producers, Robert Eggenweiler, Scott Bushnell; executive producer, Tommy Thompson; gaffers, Tim Evans, Jim Miller; painting of "Bride for the People" by Sally Benton; choir, The Choir of St. Luke's Episcopal Church, Evanston,

Illinois, conducted by Richard Webster; The Chicago Brass Ensemble, Robert Rushford, Betty Di Sorei; church organist, Ruth Peliz. **Cast:** Lillian Gish (Nettie Sloan); Ruth Nelson (Beatrice Sloan Cory); Ann Ryerson (Victoria Cory); Desi Arnaz Jr. (Dino Corelli); Belita Moreno (Daphne Corelli); Vittorio Gassman (Louis Corelli); Nina van Pallandt (Regina Corelli); Virginia Vestoff (Clarice Sloan); Dina Merrill (Antoinette Sloan Goddard); Pat McCormick (Mackenzie Goddard); Luigi Proietti (Little Dino); Carol Burnett (Tulip Brenner); Paul Dooley (Snooks Brenner); Amy Stryker (Muffin Brenner); Mia Farrow (Buffy Brenner); Dennis Christopher (Hughie Brenner); Mary Seibel (Marge Spar); Margaret Ladd (Ruby Spar); Gerald Busby (David Ruteledge); Peggy Ann Garner (Candice Ruteledge); Mark R. Deming (Matthew Ruteledge); David Brand, Chris Brand, Amy Brand, Jenny Brand, Jeffrey Jones, Jay D. Jones, Courtney MacArthur, Paul D. Keller III (the Ruteledge children); Cedric Scott (Randolph); Robert Fortier (Jim Harbor); Maureen Steindler (Libby Clinton); Geraldine Chaplin (Rita Billingsley); Mona Abboud (Melba Lear); Viveca Lindfors (Ingrid Hellstrom); Lauren Hutton (Flo Farmer); Allan Nicholls (Jake Jacobs); Maysie Hoy (Casey); John Considine (Jeff Kuykendal); Patricia Resnick (Redford); Margery Bond (Lombardo); Dennis Franz (Koons); Harold C. Johnson (Oscar Edwards); Alexander Sopenar (Victor); Howard Duff (Dr. Jules Meecham); John Cromwell (Monsignor Martin); Bert Remsen (William Williamson); Pamela Dawber (Tracy Farrell); Gavan O'Herlihy (Wilson Briggs); Craig Richard Nelson (Captain Reedley Roots); Jeffrey S. Perry (Bunky LeMay); Lesley Rogers (Rosie Bean); Timothy Thomerson (Russel Bean); Beverly Ross (Janet Schulman); David Fitzgerald (Kevin Clinton); Susan Kendall Newman (Chris Clinton); Ellie Albers (violinist); Tony Llorens (pianist); Chuck Bank's Big Band with Chris La Kome.

Quintet (Lion's Gate/Twentieth Century-Fox, 1979), 110 minutes

Producer, Altman; director, Altman; screenplay, Frank Barhydt, Robert Altman, and Patricia Resnick, based on a story by Altman, Lionel Chetwynd, and Patricia Resnick; photography, Jean Boffety; camera operator, Paul Van der Linden; camera assistants, Al Smith, Andy Chmura, Robert Guertin; special effects, Tom Fisher, John Thomas; title design, Patrice Ryan; titles and opticals, Pacific Title; art director, Wolf Kroeger; production designer, Leon Ericksen; music composed and conducted by Tom Pierson; music editor, Tom Whitfield; music performed by The London Symphony Or-

Altman directs a scene for *Quintet.*

chestra; sound, Robert Gravenor; sound editors, Sam Gemette, Hal Sanders; sound rerecording, Richard Portman; postproduction, Westwood Editorial; special sound effects designer, David Horton; sound system, Lion's Gate 8-Track Sound; costume designer, Scott Bushnell; costumer, J. Allen Highfill; wardrobe, John Hay; editor, Dennis M. Hill; assistant editors, William Hoy, Raja R. Gosnell; assistant director, Tommy Thompson; second assistant director, Charles Braive; assistants to producer, Elaine di Bello Bradish, David Fitzgerald; assistant to art director, Stephane Reichel.

Cast: Paul Newman (Essex); Vittorio Gassman (St. Christopher); Fernando Rey (Grigor); Bibi Andersson (Ambrosia); Brigitte Fossey (Vivia); Nina van Pallandt (Deuca); David Langton (Goldstar); Tom Hill (Francha); Monique Mercure (Redstone's Companion); Craig Richard Nelson (Redstone); Maruska Stankova (Jaspera); Anne Gerety (Aeon); Michael Maillot (Obelus); Max Fleck (Marchand de Bois); François Berd (Hospice Woman).

A Perfect Couple (Lion's Gate/Twentieth Century-Fox, 1979), 111 minutes

Producer, Altman; director, Altman; screenplay, Altman and Allan Nicholls; photography, Edmond L. Koons; camera operator, Jan Keisser; camera assistant, Cal Roberts; special effects, Tom Fisher; title design, Patrice Ryan; titles and opticals, Pacific Title; color timer, Bob Hagans; negative editor, Jack Hooper; music produced by Allan Nicholls; sound, Robert Gravenor, Don Merritt; sound system, Lion's Gate 8-Track Sound; sound editors, David Horton, Sam Gemette; assistants to sound editors, Raja R. Gosnell, Eric Whitfield; sound rerecording, Richard Portman; music recorded by Dave Palmer; music editor, Ted Whitfield; costumes, Beth Alexander; editor, Tony Lombardo; assistant director, Tommy Thompson; second assistant director, Bill Cosentino; associate producers, Robert Eggenweiler and Scott Bushnell; assistant to producer, Elaine di Bello Bradish; makeup, Tom Tuttle; hairdresser, Jerry Turnage; script supervisor, Luca Kouimelis; props, Steven Altman; project coordinator, Victoria Barney; project auditor, Dick Dubuque; executive producer, Tommy Thompson; gaffer, Randy Glass; key grip, Tom Prophet Jr.; "Keepin' 'Em Off the Streets" Stage Show, Leon Ericksen; set designer, Leon Ericksen; costumes, Anna Vilms; lighting, Charlie Anderson; road manager, Greg Mulgrew; roadie, Jim Kunellis; processes, DeLuxe Color, Panavision.
Cast: Paul Dooley (Alex Theodopoulos); Marta Heflin (Sheila Shea); Titos Vandis (Panos); Belita Moreno (Eleousa); Henry Gibson (Fred Bott); Dimitra Arliss (Athena); Allan Nicholls (Dana 115); Ann Ryerson (Skye 147); Poppy Lagos (Melpomeni Bott); Dennis Franz (Costa); Margery Bond (Wilma); Mona Golabek (Mona); Terry Wills (Ben); Susan Blakeman (Penelope Bott); Melanie Bishop (Star); Fred Bier, Jette Seear (The Imperfect Couple); Ted Neeley (Teddy); Heather MacRae (Mary); Tomi-Lee Bradley (Sydney-Ray); Steven Sharp (Bobbi); "Keepin' 'Em Off the Streets" members: Tony Berg (Lead Guitar and Musical Director of the Band); Craig Doerge (Keyboards); Jeff Eyrich (Bass Guitar); David Luell (Saxophone); Butch Sandford (Guitar); Art Wood (Drums); special guest appearance by Ren Woods; Mona Golabek (Piano Soloist); The Los Angeles Philharmonic Orchestra, conducted by Tom Pierson.
Songs: "Somp'ins Got a Hold on Me," lyrics and music by Tony Berg and Ted Neeley, performed by Tomi-Lee Bradley and Steven Sharp; "Hurricane," lyrics and music by Tony Berg, Ted Neeley, and Allan Nicholls, performed by Ted Neeley and the Group; "Week-End Holiday," lyrics and music by Allan Nicholls, B. G. Gibson and Tony Berg, performed by Ted Neeley; "Won't Some-

The Greek family of *A Perfect Couple*.

body Care?," lyrics and music by Tony Berg and Allan Nicholls, performed by Marta Heflin and Steven Sharp; "Love Is All There Is," lyrics and music by Allan Nicholls, Tony Berg, and Ted Neeley, performed by Heather MacRae; "Searchin' for the Light," lyrics and music by Tomi-Lee Bradley, Tony Berg, Allan Nicholls, and Ted Neeley, performed by Tomi-Lee Bradley; "Lonely Millionaire," lyrics and music by Cliff DeYoung and Tony Berg, performed by Steven Sharp and Marta Heflin; "Fantasy," lyrics and music by Allan Nicholls, performed by Heather MacRae and the Group; "Don't Take Forever," lyrics and music by Allan Nicholls, B.G. Gibson, and Tony Berg, performed by Tomi-Lee Bradley and the Group; "Let the Music Play," lyrics and music by Allan Nicholls and Oatis Stephens, performed by the Group; "Goodbye Friends," lyrics and music by Allan Nicholls, performed by the Group (including Ren Woods); "Adieu Mes Amis" (Romance Concerto), performed by the Los Angeles Philharmonic, conducted by Tom Pierson with Mona Golabek, Piano Soloist, music by Tom Pierson and Allan Nicholls.

From left: Lauren Bacall, Dick Cavett, Carol Burnett, and Glenda Jackson in *Health*.

Health (Lion's Gate/Twentieth Century-Fox, 1980), 96 minutes

Producer, Altman; director, Altman; screenplay, Frank Barhydt, Altman, and Paul Dooley; photography, Edmond Koons; art director, Jacqueline S. Price; music, Joseph Byrd; songs, Allan Nicholls and the Steinettes; sound, Robert Gravenor, Don Merritt; editors, Tony Lombardo, Dennis M. Hill, Tom Benko; assistant editor, Bill Hoy; makeup, Monty Westmore; hairdressers, Jerry Turnage; associate producers, Robert Eggenweiler, Scott Bushnell; executive producer, Tommy Thompson; processes, DeLuxe Color, Panavision. **Cast:** Glenda Jackson (Isabella Garnell); Carol Burnett (Gloria Burbank); James Garner (Harry Wolff); Lauren Bacall (Esther Brill); Dick Cavett (Himself); Paul Dooley (Harold Gainey); Donald Moffatt (Colonel Cody); Henry Gibson (Bobby Hammer); Diane Stilwell (Willow Wertz); MacIntyre Dixon (Fred Munson); Alfre Woodard (Sally Benbow); Ann Ryerson (Dr. Ruth Ann Jackle); Allan Nicholls (Jake Jacobs); Margery Bond (Daisy Bell); Georgann Johnson (Lily Bell); Mina Kolb (Iris Bell); Bob Fortier (Henderson); Nancy Foster (Gilda); Julie Janney, Diane Shaffer, Nathalie Blossom, Patty Katz (The Steinettes).

Popeye (Paramount/Walt Disney, 1980), 114 minutes

Producer, Robert Evans; director, Altman; screenplay, Jules Feiffer; photography, Giuseppe Rotunno, A.S.C.; camera operators, Giovanni Fiore, Gianfranco Trasunto; assistant operators, Luigi Bernardini, Mauro Merchetti, Gian Maria Majorana; underwater camera operator, Lorenzo Battaglia; camera assistants, Robert Reed Altman, Maurizio Zampagni; title design, Patrice Ryan; production designer, Wolf Kroeger; assistant art directors, Reg Bream, Stephane Reichel; set decorator, Jack Stephens; music, Harry Nilsson; additional score, Tom Pierson; supervising music editor, Ted Whitfield; music editor, Richard Whitfield; assistant music editor, Leslie A. Whitfield; sound, Robert Gravenor; supervising sound editor, Sam Gemette; sound editors, Sam Shaw, John Larson, Larry Singer, Bill Phillips, Michael Ford, Hal Sanders; supervising re-recording mixer, Michael Minkler, C.A.S.; scoring and music re-recording mixer, Don Wallin; rerecording engineer, Steve Brimmer; sound effects editors, Teresa Eckton, Andy Patterson; sound effects consultant, Rodney Holland; postproduction coordinator, Suzanne Hines; postproduction sound and editorial facilities, Lion's Gate Sound; boom man, Don Merritt; recorder, Doug Shulman; location engineer, Randy Honaker; costume designer, Scott Bushnell; costume supervisor, John Hay; costume construction, Kate McDermott; costume mistress, Yvonne Zarb Cousin; supervising editor, Tony Lombardo; editors, John W. Holmes, A.C.E., David Simmons; additional editing, Raja R. Gosnell; assistant editors, Paul Rubell, Stephen Tucker, Eric Whitfield, Bob Lederman; first assistant directors, Bob Dahlin, Victor Tourjansky; makeup supervisor, Giancarlo Del Brocco; makeup artist, Alfredo Tiberi; makeup assistants, Gilberto Provenghi, Alvaro Rossi; chief hairdresser, Maria Teresa Corridoni; hairdressers, Aldo Signoretti, Gabriella Borzelli; hairdresser assistant, Rita Innocenzi; publicist, Bridget Terry; publicity assistants, Rita Galea, Cathy Keller; unit photographer, Paul Ronald; script supervisor, Luca Kouimelis; property master, Stephen Altman; property man, John Bucklin; unit manager, Paulo Lucidi; unit coordinators, David Levy, Peter Bray; associate producer, Scott Bushnell; executive producer, C. O. Erickson; choreographers, Sharon Kinney, Hovey Burgess; Robin Williams's dance numbers staged by Lou Wills; special effects coordinator, Allen Hall; special effects assistant, Robert Willard; technical advisors, R. J. Hohman, Steve Foster; stunt coordinator, Roberto Messina; construction coordinator, Stephane Reichel; construction manager, Alvaro Belsole; gaffer, Rudolfo Bramucci; key grips, Miro Salvatore, Alberto Emidi; talent coordinator, Rick Sparks; executive assistant

Ray Walston and Robin Williams in *Popeye.*

to Robert Evans, Barbara Kalish; assistants to Robert Evans, Cathy
Chazan, Stephanie Aranas; assistant to Robin Williams, Mark Rut-
tenberg; auditor, Richard Dubuque; assistant accountant, Luciano
Tartaglia; controller, Tim Engel; master carpenters, Gaetano Mi-
ranti, Bert Bowers; master painter, Gugliemo Modestini; sculptors,
Angelo Marta, Angelo Zaccaria, Michael Stroud; draftsmen, Lester
Smith, Stephen Bream; animated artifacts created by Cos-
mekinetics, Ellis Burman, Bob Williams; opticals by Cinema Re-
search; physical therapist, James A. Rumsey; European production
manager, Frederick Muller; transportation captain, Bill Turner;
process, Technovision.
Cast: Robin Williams (Popeye); Shelley Duvall (Olive Oyl); Ray
Walston (Poopdeck Pappy); Paul Dooley (Wimpy); Paul L. Smith
(Bluto); Richard Libertini (Geezil); Donald Moffatt (Taxman); Mac-
Intyre Dixon (Cole Oyl); Roberta Maxwell (Nana Oyl); Donovan
Scott (Castor Oyl); Allan Nicholls (Rough House); Wesley Ivan
Hurt (Swee'pea); Bill Irwin (Ham Gravy, The Old Boyfriend); Rob-
ert Fortier (Bill Barnacle, The Town Drunk); David McCharen

(Harry Hotcash, The Gambler); Sharon Kinney (Cherry, His Moll); Peter Bray (Oxblood Oxheart); Linda Hunt (Mrs. Oxheart, His Mom); Geoff Hoyle (Scoop, The Reporter); Wayne Robson (Chizzelflint, The Pawnbroker); Larry Pisoni (Chico, The Dishwasher); Carlo Pellegrini (Swifty, The Cook); Susan Kingsley (La Verne, The Waitress); Michael Christensen (Splatz, The Janitor); Ray Cooper (The Preacher); Noel Parenti (Slick, The Milkman); Karen McCormick (Rosie, The Milkmaid); John Bristol (Bear, The Hermit); Julie Janney (Mena Walfleur); Patty Katz (Mina Walfleur); Diane Shaffer (Mona Walfleur); Nathalie Blossom (Blossom Walfleur); Dennis Franz (Spike); Carlos Brown (Slug); Ned Dowd (Butch); Hovey Burgess (Mort); Roberto Messina (Gozo); Pietro Torrisi (Bolo); Margery Bond (Daisy); Judy Burgess (Petunia); Saundra MacDonald (Violet); Eve Knoller (Min); Peggy Pisoni (Pickelina); Barbara Zegler (Daphne); Paul Zegler (Mayor Stonefeller); Pamela Burrell (Mrs. Stonefeller); David Arkin (The Mailman/Policeman); Klaus Voorman (Von Schnitzel, The Conductor); Doug Dillard (Clem, The Banjo Player); Van Dyke Parks (Hoagy, The Piano Player); Stan Wilson (Oscar, The Barber); Roberto Dell'Aqua (Chimneysweep); Valerie Velardi (Cindy, The Drudge).
Songs: "Everything Is Food," "Everybody's Got to Eat," "He's Large," "He Needs Me," "Swee'pea's Lullaby," "Din' We," "Sweethaven," "Blow Me Down," "Sailin'," "It's Not Easy Being Me," "I'm Mean," and "Kids," music and lyrics by Harry Nilsson; "I'm Popeye the Sailor Man," by Sammy Lerner.

Come Back to the Five and Dime, Jimmy Dean, Jimmy Dean (Sandcastle 5 Productions/Mark Goodson Presentation/Viacom Enterprises/Cinecom International Films, 1982), 102 minutes

Producer, Scott Bushnell; executive producer, Giraud Chester; director, Altman; assistant director, Sonja Webster; screenplay, Ed Graczyk, based on his play; cinematographer, Pierre Mignot; production design, David Cropman; production executive, Peter Newman; production manager, Sonja Webster; production coordinator, Doug Cole; costumes, Scott Bushnell; music, Allan Nicholls; editor, Jason Rosenfield; sound design, Richard Fitzgerald; lighting design, Paul Gallo; originally produced on Broadway by Dan Fisher, Joseph Clapsaddle, Joel Brykman, and Jack Lawrence.
Cast: Sandy Dennis (Mona); Cher (Sissy); Karen Black (Joanne); Sudie Bond (Juanita); Marta Heflin (Edna Louise); Kathy Bates (Stella Mae); Mark Patton (Joe).

Altman directing the "filmed play" of *Come Back to the 5 and Dime, Jimmy Dean, Jimmy Dean.*

Streamers (Mileti Productions/United Artists Classics, 1983), 118 minutes

Producers, Altman and Nick J. Mileti; executive producers, Robert Michael Geiser and John Roberdeau; director, Altman; associate producer, Scott Bushnell; assistant director, Allan Nicholls; screenplay, David Rabe, from his play; cinematographer, Pierre Mignot; art director, Steve Altman; set decoration, Robert Brown; set design, Wolf Kroeger; costumes, Scott Bushnell; editor, Norman C. Smith.

Cast: Mitchell Lichenstein (Richie); Matthew Modine (Billy); David Alan Grier (Roger); Michael Wright (Carlyle); Guy Boyd (Rooney); George Dzundza (Cokes); Albert Macklin (Martin).

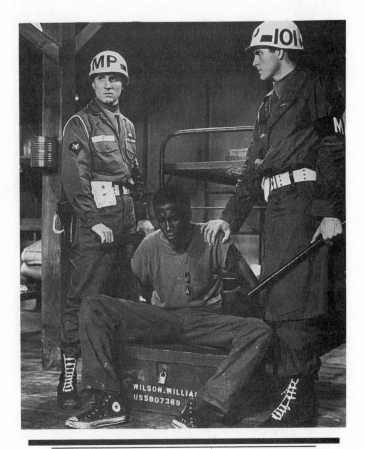

Michael Wright (center) at the climax of
Streamers.

Secret Honor (Sandcastle 5 Productions, Inc., in cooperation with University of Michigan and the Los Angeles Actors' Theatre, 1983), 85 minutes

Producer, Altman; director, Altman; written by Donald Freed and Arnold M. Stone; executive producer, Scott Bushnell; associate director, Robert Harders; director of photography, Pierre Mignot; editor, Juliet Weber; art director, Stephen Altman; musical score, George Burt; associate producer, Doug Cole; assistant director, Allan Nicholls; stage manager, John Brigleb; camera operator, Jean Lepine; sound mixer, Andy Aaron; assistant editor, Mickey Ka-

Philip Baker Hall as President Nixon in *Secret Honor*.

czorowski; sound editor, Bernard Hajdenberg; rerecording, Paul Coombe, Sound One, Inc.; gaffer, Jonathan Lumley; electrician, Joey Forsyth; key grip, Tom Grunke; music performed by Contemporary Directions Ensemble, University of Michigan, School of Music, conducted by Carl St. Clair; postproduction coordinator, Matthew Seig; special thanks to the following University of Michigan students: Amy Alkon, Cynthia Baka, Sarah Bassett, Michael Coleman, John Cooper, Paul Devlin, Mark Ferguson, Charles Frank, Michael Frierson, Diane Grad, Bob Hercules, Robert Hersh, Randy Howe, Jim King, Chris Laxton, Deborah Lewis, Bruce Lixey,

Peter Mercurio, Ellen Paglinauan, Kevin Pearson, Garry Perrine, Toni Perrine, Larry Shapiro, Jonathan Twyman, Lelahni Wessinger, Peter Kaiser; the world premiere of *Secret Honor* was produced by Diane White and Adam Leipzig at the Los Angeles Actors' Theatre, Los Angeles, California, Bill Bushnell, artistic producing director; filmed at the University of Michigan, Martha Cooke Building, Rosalee Moore, director; color and blowup by Movielab; titles and opticals by The Optical House, New York.

Cast: Philip Baker Hall (President Richard M. Nixon).

Fool for Love (The Cannon Group, 1986), 107 minutes

Producer, Menahem Golan and Yoram Globus; director, Altman; screenplay by Sam Shepard; director of photography, Pierre Mignot; edited by Luce Grunenwaldt and Steve Dunn; production design, Stephen Altman; music by George Burt; associate producers, Scott Bushnell, Mati Raz; executive in charge of production, Jeffrey Silver; unit production manager, Allan Nicholls; first assistant director, Ned Dowd; second assistant director, Steve Dunn; camera operator, Jean Lepine; first assistant cameraman, René Daigle; second assistant cameramen, Robert Reed Altman, Murray Van Dyke; assistant editors, Nathalie LeGuay, Katya Furse Chelli, Michael Altman; sound editor, Catherine D'Hoir; assistant sound editor, Pascal Marzin; rerecording mixers, Neil Walmer, Jacques Thomas Gerard; rerecorded at Paris-Studios-Billancourt; sound mixer, Daniel Brisseau; boom operator, Eric DeVulder; sound assistant, Jean-Marie Blondel; makeup/hairdresser, David Forrest; wardrobe, Kristine Flones-Czeski; set decorator, John Hay; property master, Anthony Maccario; location accountant, Kathi Hibbs; script supervisor, Luca Kouimelis; gaffer, Jonathan Lumely; best boy, Janet Saetta; dolly grip, Tom Grunke; key grip, Bruce Hamme; best boy, Arley Thomsen; assistant to art director, Robin Laughlin; sketch artist, Al Eylar; painter, John Beauvais; construction coordinator, Ben Zeller; construction foreman, Jamie Archer; production secretary, Joan Patchen; production assistants, Kevin St. John, Laurel Hargarten; livestock furnished by Bar YL Services Limited; livestock coordinator, Steve Meador; music recording, Studio de la Grande Armée; assistant to the composer, Joseph Makholm; conductor, Michel Ganot; songs "Let's Ride," "It Comes and Goes," "Go Rosa," "You Lied Your Way," "First and Last Real Cowboy," "Call Me Up," and "Love Shy," written and performed by Sandy Rogers; "Why Wyoming," written and performed by Sandy Rogers and Louise Kirchen; "Honky Tonk Hero" and "Black Rose," writ-

Sam Shepard, playwright and star of *Fool for Love*.

ten by Billy Joe Shaver and performed by Waylon Jennings (courtesy of RCA); production equipment and facilities, Keylite PSI: cameras by Joe Dunton Cameras; color by Rank Laboratories.
Cast: Sam Shepard (Eddie); Kim Basinger (May); Harry Dean Stanton (Old Man); Randy Quaid (Martin); Martha Crawford (May's Mother); Louise Egolf (Eddie's Mother); Sura Cox (Teenage May); Jonathan Skinner (Teenage Eddie); April Russell (Young May); Deborah McNaughton (The Countess); Lon Hill (Mr. Valdez).

The pixillated cast members of *Beyond Therapy*.

Beyond Therapy (A Sandcastle 5 Film/New World Pictures/A Roger Berlind Production, 1987), 93 minutes

Producer, Steven M. Haft; executive producer, Roger Berlind; director, Altman; screenplay, Christopher Durang and Altman, based on the play by Durang; director of photography, Pierre Mignot; music, Gabriel Yared; supervising editor, Steve Dunn; production design, Stephen Altman; associate producer, Scott Bushnell; New World production executive, Paul Almond; Sandcastle 5 production executive, Matthew Seig; production manager, Daniel Wuhrmann; first assistant director, Yann Gilbert; second assistant director, Patrick Cartoux; costume designer, John Hay; art director, Annie Sénéchal; assistant art director, Arnaud de Moléron; property master,

Roland Jacob; costumer, Claudia Périno; wardrobe assistant, Brigitte Le Brigand; makeup, Ronaldo Ribeiro de Abreu, Dominique de Vorges; hair, Alain Bernard; camera operator, Jean Lepine; first assistant, Nicolas Brunet; second assistant, Natalie Mauger; still photographer, R. Reed Altman; sound mixers, Philippe Lioret, Daniel Belanger; boom operator, Frédéric Pardon; script supervisor, Kathleen Fonmarty; location manager, Christine Raspillère; production controller, Danielle Foatelli; production coordinator, Agnès Berméjo; casting assistant, Guylène Péan; production assistant, Xavier Legris; assistant director trainee, François Goizé; key grip, Charles Freess; grips, Jean-Yves Freess, Jacques Stricanne; gaffer, Pierre Abraham; electricians, Michel Gonckel, Pierre Darmon, Serge-Antoine Croisy; foley, Jean-Pierre LeLong; foley assistant, Mario Melchiorri; editor, Jennifer Augé; sound editor, Françoise Coispeau; assistant editors, Pascal Marzin, Serge Rinaldi; apprentice editor, Karen Logan; sound assistant, Yves Lainé; rerecording mixer, Neil Walwer; rerecording studio, G.L.P.P.; computer overdubbing, Studio A.D.S.R., Georges Rodi; music recording engineer, Bruno Lambert, Studios de la Grande Armée; piano, Maurice Vander; bass, Pierre Michelot; drums, Daniel Humair; saxophone, Jean-Louis Chautemps; lighting equipment, Transpalux; cameras, Samuelson Alga Cinema; laboratory, Eclair; titles, Euro-Titres; "Someone to Watch Over Me," special performance by Yves Montand; "Someone to Watch Over Me," words and music by George and Ira Gershwin, also performed by Linda Ronstadt and by Lena Horne; special thanks to restaurant "Les Bouchons," Novotel–Paris Les Halles, Manuel Canovas, BOA, JAPA, SCAPA, Librairie Internationale Offilib.

Cast: Julie Hagerty (Prudence); Jeff Goldblum (Bruce); Glenda Jackson (Charlotte); Tom Conti (Stuart); Christopher Guest (Bob); Geneviève Page (Ziai); Cris Campion (Andrew); Sandrine Dumas (Cindy); Bertrand Bonvoisin (Le Gérant); Nicole Evans (The Cashier); Louis-Marie Taillefer (Le Chef); Matthew Lesniak (Mr. Bean); Laure Killing (Charlie); Gilbert Blin, Vincent Longuemare (Waiters); Françoise Armel, Sylvie Lenoir, Annie Monnier, Jeanne Cellard, Hélène Constantine, Yvette Prayer, Joan Tyrell (Zizi's Friends).

The harassed Schwab family of *O.C. and Stiggs*.

O.C. and Stiggs (Metro-Goldwyn-Mayer [filmed in 1983], 1987), 109 minutes

Producer, Altman and Peter Newman; director, Altman; screenplay by Donald Cantrell and Ted Mann, based on a story by Tod Carroll and Ted Mann; director of photography, Pierre Mignot; production designer/associate producer, Scott Bushnell; art director, David Gropman; editor, Elizabeth Kling; special music by King Sunny Ade and his African Beats; executive producer, Lewis Allen. **Cast:** Daniel H. Jenkins (O.C.); Neill Barry (Stiggs); Paul Dooley (Randall Schwab); Jane Curtin (Elinore Schwab); Martin Mull (Pat Coletti); Dennis Hopper (Sponson); Ray Walston (Gramps); Louis Nye (Garth Sloan); Melvin Van Peebles (Wino Bob); Tina Louise (Florence Beaugereaux); Cynthia Nixon (Michelle); Laura Urstein (Lenora Schwab); Jon Cryer (Randall Schwab Jr.); Donald May (Jack Stiggs); Clara Borelli (Stella Stiggs); James Gilsenan (Barney); Victor Ho (Frank Tang); and Bob Uecker (himself).

Altman's "Les Boréades" segment from *Aria*.

Aria (Lightyear Entertainment/Virgin Vision/Miramax Films, 1988), 90 minutes

Producer, Don Boyd; multiple directors include: Nicolas Roeg, Charles Sturridge, Jean-Luc Godard, Julien Temple, Bruce Beresford, Franc Roddam, Ken Russell, Derek Jarman, Bill Bryden, and Altman. Altman's segment, "Les Boréades," features music by Jean-Philippe Rameau, the "Suite des Ventes," "Lieu Désolé," and "Jouissons, Jouissons," as sung by Jennifer Smith, Anne Marie Radde, and Phillip Langridge.

AS PRODUCER ONLY

(Lion's Gate Films)

Welcome to L.A. (1977), 106 minutes

Director: Alan Rudolph. Cast includes: Keith Carradine, Sally Kellerman, Geraldine Chaplin, Harvey Keitel, Lauren Hutton, Viveca Lindfors, Sissy Spacek, Denver Pyle, John Considine, and Richard Baskin.

The Late Show (1977), 94 minutes

Director: Robert Benton. Cast includes: Art Carney, Lily Tomlin, Bill Macy, Eugene Roche, Joanna Cassidy, John Considine, and Howard Duff.

Remember My Name (1978), 96 minutes

Director: Alan Rudolph. Cast includes: Geraldine Chaplin, Anthony Perkins, Moses Gunn, Berry Berenson, Jeff Goldblum, and Timothy Thomerson

Rich Kids (1979), 101 minutes

Director: Robert M. Young. Cast includes: Trini Alvarado, Jeremy Levy, John Lithgow, Kathryn Walker, Terry Kiser, and Paul Dooley.

Altman and his Eighties cinematographer Pierre
Mignot on the job filming *O.C. and Stiggs*. (MGM)

BIBLIOGRAPHY

Essential books that I have thumbed and plumbed (and occasionally quoted from):

Altman, Robert, and Rudolph, Alan, *Buffalo Bill and the Indians, or, Sitting Bull's History Lesson.* Bantam, New York, 1976.

AuWerter, Russell, "Robert Altman," from *Directors in Action,* edited by Bob Thomas. (Bobbs Merrill, Indianapolis and New York, 1973).

Bourget, Jean-Loup, *Robert Altman.* Edilig, France, 1981.

Feineman, Neil, *Persistence of Vision: The Films of Robert Altman.* Arno Press (University of Florida), 1976.

Fink, Guido, *I Film di Robert Altman.* Gremese Editore, Italy, 1982.

Jacobs, Diane, *Hollywood Renaissance.* A. S. Barnes/Tantivy Press, New Jersey/London, England, 1977.

Kagan, Norman, *American Skeptic: Robert Altman's Genre-Commentary Films.* Pierian Press, Ann Arbor, 1982.

Karp, Alan, *The Films of Robert Altman.* Scarecrow Press, Metuchen, New Jersey, 1981.

Kass, Judith M., *Robert Altman, American Innovator.* Popular Library, New York, 1978.

Kolker, Robert Phillip, *A Cinema of Loneliness: Penn, Kubrick, Scorsese, Spielberg, Altman.* Oxford University Press, New York, 1988.

Magrelli, Enrico, *Robert Altman.* La Nuova Italia, Italy, 1977.

McClelland, C. Kirk, *On Making a Movie: Brewster McCloud.* New American Library, New York, 1971.

Plecki, Gerard, *Robert Altman*. Twayne Publishers, Boston, 1985.

Terry, Bridget, *The Popeye Story*. Dell, New York, 1980.

Tewkesbury, Joan, *Nashville*. Bantam, New York, 1976.

Waxman, Virginia Wright, and Bisplinghoft, Gretchen, *Robert Altman: A Guide to References and Resources*. G. K. Hall, Boston, 1984.

Wilson, David, "Robert Altman," from *Close-Up: The Contemporary Director*, edited by Jon Iuska. Scarecrow Press, Inc., Metuchen, New Jersey, 1981.

Indispensable interviews and magazine articles:

Altman, Robert, "Dialogue on Film," *American Film*, February 1975.

Byrne, Connie, and Lopez, William O., "Nashville," *Film Quarterly*, Winter 1975–76.

Cook, Bruce, "Bob and Pauline: A Fickle Affair," *American Film*, December–January 1978.

Cutts, John, "M*A*S*H, McCloud, and McCabe," *Films and Filming*, November 1971.

Harmetz, Aljean, "The Fifteenth Man Who Was Asked to Direct 'M*A*S*H' (And Did) Makes a Peculiar Western," *The New York Times Magazine*, June 20, 1971.

Hodenfield, Chris, "Zoom Lens Voyeur: A Few Moments with *Nashville*'s Bob Altman," *Rolling Stone*, July 17, 1975.

Kasindorf, Jeanie, "Inside Hollywood," *New West*, March 26, 1979.

Macklin, F. Anthony, "The Artist and the Multitude Are Natural Enemies," *Film Heritage*, Winter 1976–77.

Murphy, Mary, "Crisis of a Cult Figure," *New West*, May 23, 1977.

Nash, Alanna, "Joan Tewkesbury," *Films in Review*, Fall 1976.

Tewkesbury, Joan, "Dialogue on Film," *American Film*, March 1979.

Williamson, Bruce, "Playboy Interview: Robert Altman," *Playboy*, August 1976.

INDEX

Page numbers in *italics* refer to illustrations.

629